P9-APS-378

THE IDG BOOKS STRATEGIES ADVANTAGE

We at IDG Books Worldwide created the second edition of *Client/Server Strategies* to meet your growing need for access to the most complete and accurate computer information available. Our books work the way you do: They focus on accomplishing specific goals — not learning random functions. Our books are not long-winded manuals or dry reference tomes. In each book, expert authors help you understand new technology and teach you how to evaluate its usefulness for your needs. Easy-to-follow, comprehensive coverage and clear language and design — it's all here.

The authors of IDG books are uniquely qualified to give you expert advice as well as to provide insightful tips and techniques not found anywhere else. Our authors maintain close contact with end users through feedback from articles, training sessions, e-mail exchanges, user group participation, and consulting work. Because our authors know the realities of daily computer use and are directly tied to the reader, our books have a strategic advantage.

Our authors have the experience to approach a topic in the most efficient manner, and we know that you, the reader, will benefit from a "one-on-one" relationship with the author. Our research shows that readers make computer book purchases because they want expert advice. Because readers want to benefit from the author's experience, the author's voice is always present in an IDG book.

You will find what you need in this book whether you read it from cover to cover, section by section, or simply one topic at a time. As a computer user, you deserve a comprehensive resource of answers. We at IDG Books Worldwide are proud to deliver that resource with *Client/Server Strategies,* Second Edition.

CLIENT/SERVER STRATEGIES

2ND EDITION

A SURVIVAL GUIDE FOR CORPORATE REENGINEERS

David Vaskevitch

IDG Books Worldwide, Inc.
An International Data Group Company

Foster City, CA ◆ Chicago, IL ◆ Indianapolis, IN ◆ Braintree, MA ◆ Dallas, TX

Client/Server Strategies: A Survival Guide for Corporate Reengineers, Second Edition

Published by
IDG Books Worldwide, Inc.
An International Data Group Company
919 E. Hillsdale Blvd.
Suite 400
Foster City, CA 94404

Text and art copyright © 1995 by David Vaskevitch. All rights reserved. No part of this book, including interior design, cover design, and icons, may be reproduced or transmitted in any form, by any means (electronic, photocopying, recording, or otherwise) without the prior written permission of the publisher.

Images © 1995 PhotoDics, Inc.

Library of Congress Catalog Card No.: 95-77665

ISBN: 1-56884-455-7

Printed in the United States of America

10 9 8 7 6 5 4 3 2 1

2B/ST/RQ/ZV

Distributed in the United States by IDG Books Worldwide, Inc.

Distributed by Macmillan Canada for Canada; by Computer and Technical Books for the Caribbean Basin; by Contemporanea de Ediciones for Venezuela; by Distribuidora Cuspide for Argentina; by CITEC for Brazil; by Ediciones ZETA S.C.R. Ltda. for Peru; by Editorial Limusa SA for Mexico; by Transworld Publishers Limited in the United Kingdom and Europe; by Al-Maiman Publishers & Distributors for Saudi Arabia; by Simron Pty. Ltd. for South Africa; by IDG Communications (HK) Ltd. for Hong Kong; by Toppan Company Ltd. for Japan; by Addison Wesley Publishing Company for Korea; by Longman Singapore Publishers Ltd. for Singapore, Malaysia, Thailand, and Indonesia; by Unalis Corporation for Taiwan; by WS Computer Publishing Company, Inc. for the Philippines; by WoodsLane Pty. Ltd. for Australia; by WoodsLane Enterprises Ltd. for New Zealand.

For general information on IDG Books Worldwide's books in the U.S., please call our Consumer Customer Service department at 800-762-2974. For reseller information, including discounts and premium sales, please call our Reseller Customer Service department at 800-434-3422.

For information on where to purchase IDG Books Worldwide's books outside the U.S., contact IDG Books Worldwide at 415-655-3021 or fax 415-655-3295.

For information on translations, contact Marc Jeffrey Mikulich, Director, Foreign & Subsidiary Rights, at IDG Books Worldwide, 415-655-3018 or fax 415-655-3295.

For sales inquiries and special prices for bulk quantities, write to the address above or call IDG Books Worldwide at 415-655-3200.

For information on using IDG Books Worldwide's books in the classroom, or ordering examination copies, contact Jim Kelly at 800-434-2086.

For authorization to photocopy items for corporate, personal, or educational use, please contact Copyright Clearance Center, 222 Rosewood Drive, Danvers, MA 01923, or fax 508-750-4470.

Limit of Liability/Disclaimer of Warranty: The author and publisher have used their best efforts in preparing this book. IDG Books Worldwide, Inc., and the authors make no representation or warranties with respect to the accuracy or completeness of the contents of this book and specifically disclaim any implied warranties of merchantability or fitness for any particular purpose and shall in no event be liable for any loss of profit or any other commercial damage, including but not limited to special, incidental, consequential, or other damages.

Trademarks: All brand names and product names used in this book are trademarks, registered trademarks, or trade names of their respective holders. IDG Books Worldwide is not associated with any product or vendor mentioned in this book.

is a trademark under exclusive license to IDG Books Worldwide, Inc., from International Data Group, Inc.

About the Author

David Vaskevitch has been working with computers since 1966. In the early '70s he built one of the first electronic mail systems, linking dozens of users across Canada. For the last 12 years he has been directly involved in the personal computer and client/server revolution, first at 3Com, and today at Microsoft Corporation. He has a rare ability to explain complex technical subjects in understandable terms and to bring together technical, personal, and cultural forces acting on a problem into new perspectives for readers of all types.

ABOUT IDG BOOKS WORLDWIDE

Welcome to the world of IDG Books Worldwide.

IDG Books Worldwide, Inc., is a subsidiary of International Data Group, the world's largest publisher of computer-related information and the leading global provider of information services on information technology. IDG was founded more than 25 years ago and now employs more than 7,500 people worldwide. IDG publishes more than 235 computer publications in 67 countries (see listing below). More than 70 million people read one or more IDG publications each month.

Launched in 1990, IDG Books Worldwide is today the #1 publisher of best-selling computer books in the United States. We are proud to have received 8 awards from the Computer Press Association in recognition of editorial excellence, and our best-selling ...For Dummies® series has more than 19 million copies in print with translations in 28 languages. IDG Books Worldwide, through a recent joint venture with IDG's Hi-Tech Beijing, became the first U.S. publisher to publish a computer book in the People's Republic of China. In record time, IDG Books Worldwide has become the first choice for millions of readers around the world who want to learn how to better manage their businesses.

Our mission is simple: Every one of our books is designed to bring extra value and skill-building instructions to the reader. Our books are written by experts who understand and care about our readers. The knowledge base of our editorial staff comes from years of experience in publishing, education, and journalism — experience which we use to produce books for the '90s. In short, we care about books, so we attract the best people. We devote special attention to details such as audience, interior design, use of icons, and illustrations. And because we use an efficient process of authoring, editing, and desktop publishing our books electronically, we can spend more time ensuring superior content and spend less time on the technicalities of making books.

You can count on our commitment to deliver high-quality books at competitive prices on topics consumers want to read about. At IDG Books Worldwide, we value quality, and we have been delivering quality for more than 25 years. You'll find no better book on a subject than an IDG book.

John Kilcullen
President and CEO
IDG Books Worldwide, Inc.

WINNER
Eighth Annual
Computer Press
Awards ≥ 1992

WINNER
Ninth Annual
Computer Press
Awards ≥ 1993

IDG
BOOKS
WORLDWIDE

IDG Books Worldwide, Inc., is a subsidiary of International Data Group, the world's largest publisher of computer-related information and the leading global provider of information services on information technology. International Data Group publishes over 235 computer publications in 67 countries. More than seventy million people read one or more International Data Group publications each month. The officers are Patrick J. McGovern, Founder and Board Chairman; Kelly Conlin, President; Jim Casella, Chief Operating Officer. International Data Group's publications include: **ARGENTINA'S** Computerworld Argentina, Infoworld Argentina; **AUSTRALIA'S** Computerworld Australia, Computer Living, Australian PC World, Australian Macworld, Network World, Mobile Business Australia, Publish!, Reseller, IDG Sources; **AUSTRIA'S** Computerwelt Oesterreich, PC Test; **BELGIUM'S** Data News (CW); **BOLIVIA'S** Computerworld; **BRAZIL'S** Computerworld, Connections, Game Power, Mundo Unix, PC World, Publish, Super Game; **BULGARIA'S** Computerworld Bulgaria, PC & Mac World Bulgaria, Network World Bulgaria; **CANADA'S** CIO Canada, Computerworld Canada, InfoCanada, Network World Canada, Reseller; **CHILE'S** Computerworld Chile, Informatica; **COLOMBIA'S** Computerworld Colombia, PC World; **COSTA RICA'S** PC World; **CZECH REPUBLIC'S** Computerworld, Elektronika, PC World; **DENMARK'S** Communications World, Computerworld Denmark, Computerworld Focus, Macintosh Produktkatalog, Macworld Danmark, PC World Danmark, PC Produktguide, Tech World, Windows World; **ECUADOR'S** PC World Ecuador; **EGYPT'S** Computerworld (CW) Middle East, PC World Middle East; **FINLAND'S** MikroPC, Tietoviikko, Tietoverkko; **FRANCE'S** Distributique, GOLDEN MAC, Le Guide du Monde Informatique, Le Monde Informatique, Telecoms & Reseaux; **GERMANY'S** Computerwoche, Computerwoche Focus, Computerwoche Extra, Electronic Entertainment, Gamepro, Information Management, Macwelt, Netzwelt, PC Welt, Publish, Publish; **GREECE'S** Publish & Macworld; **HONG KONG'S** Computerworld Hong Kong, PC World Hong Kong; **HUNGARY'S** Computerworld SZT, PC World; **INDIA'S** Computers & Communications; **INDONESIA'S** Info Komputer; **IRELAND'S** ComputerScope; **ISRAEL'S** Beyond Windows, Computerworld Israel, Multimedia, PC World Israel; **ITALY'S** Computerworld Italia, Lotus Magazine, Macworld Italia, Networking Italia, PC Shopping Italy, PC World Italia; **JAPAN'S** Computerworld Today, Information Systems World, Macworld Japan, Nikkei Personal Computing, SunWorld Japan, Windows World; **KENYA'S** East African Computer News; **KOREA'S** Computerworld Korea, Macworld Korea, PC World Korea; **LATIN AMERICA'S** GamePro; **MALAYSIA'S** Computerworld Malaysia, PC World Malaysia; **MEXICO'S** Compu Edicion, Compu Manufactura, Computacion/Punto de Venta, Computerworld Mexico, MacWorld, Mundo Unix, PC World, Windows; **THE NETHERLANDS'** Computer! Totaal, Computable (CW), LAN Magazine, Lotus Magazine, MacWorld; **NEW ZEALAND'S** Computer Buyer, Computerworld New Zealand, Network World, New Zealand PC World; **NIGERIA'S** PC World Africa; **NORWAY'S** Computerworld Norge, Lotusworld Norge, Macworld Norge, Maxi Data, Networld, PC World Ekspress, PC World Nettverk, PC World Norge, PC World's Produktguide, Publish& Multimedia World, Student Data, Unix World, Windowsworld; **PAKISTAN'S** PC World Pakistan; **PANAMA'S** PC World Panama; **PERU'S** Computerworld Peru, PC World; **PEOPLE'S REPUBLIC OF CHINA'S** China Computerworld, China Infoworld, China PC Info Magazine, Computer Fan, PC World China, Electronics International, Electronics Today/Multimedia World, Electronic Product World, China Network World, Software World Magazine, Telecom Product World; **PHILIPPINES'** Computerworld Philippines, PC Digest (PCW); **POLAND'S** Computerworld Poland, Computerworld Special Report, Networld, PC World/Komputer, Sunworld; **PORTUGAL'S** Cerebro/PC World, Correio Informatico/Computerworld, MacIn; **ROMANIA'S** Computerworld, PC World, Telecom Romania; **RUSSIA'S** Computerworld-Moscow, Mir - PK (PCW), Sety (Networks); **SINGAPORE'S** Computerworld Southeast Asia, PC World Singapore; **SLOVENIA'S** Monitor Magazine; **SOUTH AFRICA'S** Computer Mail (CIO), Computing S.A., Network World S.A., Software World; **SPAIN'S** Advanced Systems, Amiga World, Computerworld Espana, Communicaciones World, Macworld Espana, NeXTWORLD, Super Juegos (GamePro), PC World Espana, Publish; **SWEDEN'S** Attack, ComputerSweden, Corporate Computing, Macworld, Mikrodatorn, Natverk & Kommunikation, PC World, CAP & Design, Datalngenjoren, Maxi Data,Windows World; **SWITZERLAND'S** Computerworld Schweiz, Macworld Schweiz, PC Tip; **TAIWAN'S** Computerworld Taiwan, PC World Taiwan; **THAILAND'S** Thai Computerworld; **TURKEY'S** Computerworld Monitor, Macworld Turkiye, PC World Turkiye; **UKRAINE'S** Computerworld, Computers+Software Magazine; **UNITED KINGDOM'S** Computing/Computerworld, Connexion/Network World, Lotus Magazine, Macworld, Open Computing/Sunworld; **UNITED STATES'** Advanced Systems, AmigaWorld, Cable in the Classroom, CD Review, CIO, Computerworld, Computerworld Client/Server Journal, Digital Video, DOS World, Electronic Entertainment Magazine (E2), Federal Computer Week, Game Hits, GamePro, IDG Books Worldwide, Infoworld, Laser Event, Macworld, Maximize, Multimedia World, Network World, PC Letter, PC World, Publish, SWATPro, Video Event; **URUGUAY'S** PC World Uruguay; **VENEZUELA'S** Computerworld Venezuela, PC World; **VIETNAM'S** PC World Vietnam. 08/30/95

DEDICATION

To my father, the first Theodore
and
To Arlene, Theodore, Rachel, and Helen

Never be afraid to remind me about what's important.

ACKNOWLEDGMENTS

For helping make this book happen: David Solomon, Erik Dafforn, Kevin Strehlo, Patty Stonesifer, Claudette Moore, Anne Owen, and Ron Nutter.

For helping me be the person I am: Peter Meincke, Bob Metcalfe, Scott Oki, Mike Maples, Adam Bosworth, and Tom Barton.

For putting up with me and making life worthwhile: Shulamit Vaskevitch, Ruth Morgenthau, Arlene, Theodore, Rachel, and Helen Vaskevitch.

(The Publisher would like to give special thanks to Patrick J. McGovern, without whom this book would not have been possible.)

CREDITS

Publisher
Karen Bluestein

Acquisitions Manager
Gregory Croy

Acquisitions Editor
Ellen C. Camm

Brand Manager
Melisa M. Duffy

Editorial Director
Andy Cummings

Editorial Assistant
Nate Holdread

Production Director
Beth Jenkins

Supervisor of Project Coordination
Cindy L. Phipps

Supervisor of Page Layout
Kathie S. Schnorr

Pre-Press Coordination
Steve Peake
Tony Augsburger
Patricia R. Reynolds
Theresa Sánchez-Baker
Elizabeth Cárdenas-Nelson

Media/Archive Coordination
Leslie Popplewell

Graphic Coordination
Shelley Lea
Gina Scott
Carla Radzikinas

Project Editor
Erik Dafforn

Editor
Anne Owen

Technical Reviewer
Ron Nutter

Associate Project Coordinator
J. Tyler Connor

Production Page Layout
Linda M. Boyer
Maridee V. Ennis
Todd Klemme
Anna Rohrer

Proofreaders
Henry Lazarek
Phil Worthington
Gwenette Gaddis
Dwight Ramsey
Robert Springer

Indexer
David Heiret

Book Design
IDG Production Staff

CONTENTS AT A GLANCE

TABLE OF CONTENTS

CHAPTER 3: BUSINESS REVOLUTION, TECHNICAL REVOLUTION — THE CLIENT/SERVER OFFICE OF THE FUTURE 49

PART II: THE TECHNOLOGY: DEMYSTIFYING COMPUTERS AND NETWORKS 67

CHAPTER 4: GUI, UI — CAN COMPUTERS BE USABLE? 69

PART III: DESIGNING AND BUILDING CLIENT/SERVER SYSTEMS 309

CHAPTER 11: A CONCEPTUAL FRAMEWORK FOR THE FUTURE 311

CHAPTER 12: APPLICATION ARCHITECTURE: A BETTER WAY OF DESIGNING APPLICATIONS 331

CHAPTER 15: TOOLS: IMPLEMENTS FOR BUILDING SYSTEMS 413

FOREWORD

Client/server is not just a buzzword. It's two buzzwords. It's two buzzwords that you cannot afford to ignore if you seek any future in computing. Yeah, you can say *client* is a fancy word for *personal computer* and that a *server* is where shared files are kept — calling a spade a shovel — but that's where client/server technology has been, not where it's going. David Vaskevitch knows where client/server is going and he tells it all — *all* — right in this book.

David Vaskevitch and I worked together during the mid-1980s at 3Com Corporation, where we struggled to turn personal computer local-area networks (PC LANs) into mainframes and minicomputers, only cheaper, faster, and better than had been done before. We didn't exactly succeed at what we set out to do, but we were right there in the thick of it, making all sorts of unanticipated and important differences in the way that people used networked PCs. If IBM and DEC had been listening to us then, it would have saved them a lot of trouble. Or they would have gotten it over with sooner.

I think the term *client/server* was coined in the 1970s at the Xerox Palo Alto Research Center. We were building some of the earliest personal computers there and were trying to figure out how to organize the software that ran on them, especially when they were tied together in networks. The software organization that seemed to bear the most fruit had portions of computer applications spread out among cooperating machines, and those portions cooperated in a stylized way. Each cooperation (and there were more than one per application) was driven by software acting as the client, making requests and getting service from the other. It seemed best for the server side of such cooperations to remain passive, speaking only when spoken to. We began to call this style of software cooperation *client/server computing*.

The earliest client/server application (most people don't think of it this way) was laser printing. We built the mother of all laser printers in 1974 and found ourselves trying to figure out how to feed it a 500-dot-per-inch page each second. Do the arithmetic and you'll see we had a networking problem — hence the need for LANs — but we also had a massive computing problem. The solution, of course, was a division of labor, with document formatting on our desktop client machines and implied font and scanning functions on the printer server.

The second client/server application was terminal switching over LANs. The idea was to connect dumb terminals to mainframes and minicomputers. We put some of the microcomputers in front of banks of terminals and others in front of each mainframe and minicomputer. These terminal server boxes connected over a LAN cooperated to perform protocol translations, speed matching, and host switching for attached terminals. Any terminal server could be either a client or a server for each of its communication ports, depending on whether a terminal or host was attached.

The third client/server application was file service. Applications running on desktop microcomputers would make occasional file accesses and these would be redirected through the LAN to microcomputers attached to large disks. The file servers managed shared access to the disks while the desktop clients performed the file data processing particular to each client.

Today the term *client/server* refers mostly to database servers and the user interface and application processing machines that share them. The language usually employed to connect the clients to their database servers is the standard SQL. This is the client/server that is gradually transforming — if not quickly eliminating — mainframes and minicomputers and causing major disruptions in the structure of the computer industry. This is also the client/server that is enabling much of business process reengineering. And it is from here that David Vaskevitch's *Client/Server Strategies* takes off.

David is never at a loss for words. In fact, it is virtually impossible to have less than a half-hour conversation with him on any subject. On the subject of client/server, I've always suspected he had a great book in him. I was right. Here it is.

Bob Metcalfe
Ethernet inventor and 3Com founder
now Executive Correspondent, *InfoWorld*

INTRODUCTION

Will personal computers replace mainframes? If so, why hasn't it already happened? Where do clients, servers, and networks fit into the picture? What does it all mean? Is it just technology, or is there a more fundamental change afoot?

HOW PERSONAL COMPUTER TECHNOLOGY WILL CHANGE BUSINESSES IN THE '90S

There is a personal computer revolution in progress, and it's all about downsizing. Million-dollar mainframes are being replaced by personal computer networks costing only thousands. This is *computer downsizing*. Companies implementing *Business Process Reengineering* are downsizing organizationally too — trimming layers of middle management and pushing decision making closer to the front line. Doing more work with fewer people, organizations are being forced to take empowerment seriously. What is the number one tool that can be used to directly empower individuals and teams? A computer system that the individual and the team can control directly. So, rather than replacing the mainframe with a smaller, but still centrally controlled, less expensive computer, the downsizing revolution calls for replacing the mainframe with hundreds of smaller systems, all talking to each other, and each serving the needs of local teams and individuals. This is *cultural downsizing*: shifting the control of the organization's central, computer-based nervous system out to local offices and self-managed teams. The result is distributed computer systems that support decentralized decision making and are driven by empowered employees who focus on product quality and responsiveness to customers' needs. This is the client/server revolution of the '90s.

HOW BIG IS THE CHANGE, AND HOW DO YOU DEAL WITH IT?

Computers — particularly personal computers — are hot. After 40 years of constant technical change, glowing predictions, and neverending complexity, computers are finally being used by millions of people world-wide every day. *In spite of this, the computer revolution is only now about to begin.* Consider the way computers are *really* used. First, most people don't use them at all. That's right; even though the computer industry now ships over 20 million computers per year, only about one-third of the desks in U.S. offices have computers of any kind on them; in other countries, the invasion has even less of a beachhead. Over 100 million homes in the U.S. have color televisions; most homes don't have even a single computer, except of course for those built into VCRs, microwaves, and Nintendos. In fact, Nintendos are far more widespread than *real* computers. Ignoring the numbers, for a moment, how about the effect computers have had on our cultures and organizations?

In the '60s, forecasters made a variety of predictions, including the eventual existence of computers that could understand speech, read handwriting, facilitate meetings, and replace assistants. On a larger scale, predictions claimed that offices would become first paperless, then disappear entirely as more and more workers used networks to work from their homes. Companies would communicate with each other globally, taking advantage of sophisticated conferencing and electronic mail systems to replace travel, face-to-face meetings, letters, and even telephone calls. Factories would become totally automated, allowing the world's material needs to be met without human labor and producing goods exactly when needed, requiring no intervening bureaucracy to make it all work. Finally, the computer would facilitate major cultural changes at both an organizational and personal level. Computer-supported communication would eliminate complex hierarchical organizational structures, which would promote rapid and democratic decision making based on empowered teams and employees and constant, instantaneous information flow across all levels of the organization. At a personal level, jobs were to be enriched, and the world itself by now was to be a global village, with friendships being formed electronically and information available globally. Homes, connected into the worldwide network, were to be the gateway into the future.

Exciting to contemplate, but today all of this has the ring of science fiction. HAL, the intelligent computer of *2001: A Space Odyssey,* appears no more likely today than he did a decade ago. At a more mundane level, after four decades of extensive and expensive computerization, most organizations still operate quite similarly to the way they did in the '50s, and although computers have simplified and sped up many processes, they have hardly revolutionized the way most businesses run. In the '90s, however, that is changing. It is hard to say whether by the turn of the century computers will play grand master chess, understand and speak English (or any other language) as well as a person, or be able to play the role of a human friend or assistant. It is clear, though, that amazing things are finally taking place — in a way that is becoming visible to normal human beings. Notebook computers, unimaginable only 10 years ago, are now used routinely by students, homemakers, and office workers. Children play computer games with incredible graphics on home machines more powerful than the mainframes of the '60s.

In the next 10 years, computers will finally change the fundamental way people organize and run businesses of all sizes. This book is about that change, and as such has to deal with business, people, culture, and technology. Before even starting the discussion of these changes and how they will happen, the topic raises key questions about causes and effects.

For over 20 years, managers and technologists have argued about the relationship between computers and the organizations that use them. Can technology *cause* organizational change? Or do organizational requirements really drive the development of new technologies? Going a step further, which comes first today, and which *should* come first?

The answer is *both* come first. To understand the computer revolution that is now underway, you must understand both the cultural changes happening in organizations, *and* the technical changes that support — and are caused by — those cultural changes.

Yes, this is a business book. And yes, this book is also a fundamentally technical book about computers. Most of all, this book discusses how computers will both force and permit people to change fundamental concepts about how they run their organizations and themselves. The changes are not necessarily caused by the technology itself, but this very technology will facilitate other fundamental trends such as personal empowerment, Business Process Reengineering, and self-managed teams. The fundamental business and personal trends will change organizations and companies, but those trends will not happen without the computer technology to make it all possible.

Client/Server Strategies, 2nd Edition, is aimed at both technical and nontechnical readers. People approaching the book without a background in computers will find, for the first time, an approachable explanation of personal computers, networks, software, mainframes, GUIs, clients, and servers, and how to use a combination of these elements to run organizations more effectively. Technical readers, on the other hand, will find that this book stretches them to think about computers in new ways, particularly in linking technical and cultural concepts. Finally, executives and senior managers, challenged by downsizing in all its forms, will find this book a prescription for the future that brings business and technical considerations together in a meaningful and pragmatic way.

Broadly speaking, this book is organized into four major sections:

I. *Crisis and Revolution:* The first section of the book lays the computer revolution out, complete, at a very high level. The chapters in this part discuss the current midlife crisis of the computer industry and its relationship to the computer-business revolution of the '90s. The final chapter in this section explores the client/server office of the future.

II. *The Technology: Demystifying Computers and Networks:* The second and biggest section of the book explains how the technical parts of the client/server future actually work. Aimed at both nontechnical and technical readers, this section does more than just explain technology; it teases out the fundamental philosophical principles behind mainframes, networks, personal computers, and all the other boxes you hear about every day.

III. *Designing and Building Client/Server Systems:* The third section of the book talks about the computer and organizational systems of the '90s — what they will look like, how they will affect workers every day in the office, and most importantly, how they will be designed. Approaching the topic of information system design from the same perspective as the second section, Part III explains the core philosophical issues that drive the development of current and next-generation business systems.

IV. *Conclusion: The Global Village:* The final section looks beyond the office and into the next century to see how the same technological and cultural shifts that will affect our organizations so dramatically will also reach into our home and personal lives.

IS THIS BOOK REALLY WORTH READING?

No question about it, this book has quite a few pages. Why bother reading it? The answer is simple. The world is changing around us. Business Process Reengineering and global competition are forcing companies to work in new ways. That much is clear from reading the papers and watching what happens in our culture every day. What may not be so clear is the central role that computers are playing in making it all happen.

With the arrival of the personal computer, the computer revolution is finally under way in a fashion that will affect every man, woman, and child, in *at least* the Western world, over the next decade. What is perhaps less clear is that those personal computers and the mainframes and minicomputers they will talk to (and eventually replace) will affect not only individuals, but companies and organizations as well. Understanding those changes is a requirement for being in control — personally and professionally — during the years ahead. What this book uniquely provides is the business background, and just as importantly, the technical framework to understand the revolution as it unfolds.

DEMYSTIFYING: CAN COMPUTERS BE UNDERSTOOD?

Although the downsizing revolution of the '90s is profoundly business and technical, the technical part definitely requires the most understanding by the affected population. What I'm trying to say, subtly, is that *the time has come to understand what computers are all about.* The question is, *can it be done?* Of course many people — programmers, systems analysts, and circuit design engineers, for example — do understand computers very well. Others — including most people who work with them — don't understand computers and their potential at all. The type of understanding I call for requires work by every reader of this book. But the understanding you need, in many ways deeper than the purely technical view that many "computer people" have, is one that any literate adult should be able to acquire by reading what follows.

Only about half of the people trained on personal computers have the foggiest concept of what a mainframe is, how it works, and why it is fundamentally different from a personal computer. The other half of that population, many of whom literally helped invent the computer as people know it today, have trouble believing that the personal computer is really more than a toy, or at best, a powerful appliance. To those people, mainframes and databases are the only real computer. While two halves may make a whole, in this case that whole is far less than the whole world; most of the real world understands neither mainframes nor personal computers. Then there are the networks, both wide-area and local-area: does anybody really understand *them?* So what remains is as Winston Churchill once said, a riddle wrapped in a mystery inside an enigma.

A fundamental goal of this book is to demystify computers. If they are a mystery when you start this book, by the time you finish, those same computers should play a clear role in your mind as tools for personal, social, cultural, and organizational change. This raises an interesting and perhaps scary question: what requirements will be made of you, the reader? Not *too* many.

✦ First, you should have had a significant amount of experience using at least one computer. *Use* can mean using a word processor to write, a spreadsheet to prepare budgets, even computer-based games, as long as they are reasonably sophisticated.

✦ Second, you do *not* need a technical background. You do, however, need to stretch your thinking. Demystification doesn't mean talking about circuits, electrons, equations, or programming statements. It does mean thinking about familiar terms such as *information, communication, coordination,* and *cooperation* in new ways. Occasionally, I will ask you to keep a few simple numbers in your head as I discuss some of the implications of size or speed regarding the way things happen.

✦ Third, if you do have a technical background, you need to be even more prepared than other readers to suspend disbelief, a chapter at a time, and think in new ways about what you *thought* you knew. Most of all, if you are a technical person, the hardest part will be thinking about computers in a broader context than you're probably accustomed to.

✦ Finally, and most importantly, if this book is to achieve its purpose, you must be *willing to learn* and *prepared to believe* that it's possible to sort this all out. Computers may be mysterious but they are far from magical. Understanding all the aspects of how a car, an airplane, or a television work is beyond the reach of most users of these machines. Understanding what they *do*, how they are *used*, and most of all, their impact on our lives, however, is straightforward.

If it's that simple, you might ask why everyone doesn't already understand computers, yet somehow can perceive their long-term impact on organizations. The answer, in a word, is *time*. In 10 years, computers will have changed society. They haven't yet, but they will. If your goal is to understand these changes both *before* and *as* they are happening, this book is for you.

Why should you bother? Computers, once understood, are fascinating. The kinds of changes society is in the midst of, for all the fascination of the technology itself, are even more interesting and compelling. From the prespective of understanding and mental stimulation alone, there's ample reason to invest the effort. More importantly, the changes I'm talking about will create incredible opportunities for improvement, advancement, and gaining competitive advantage — both personally and professionally. Most of all, read this book to be in control of these changes as they happen. And have fun.

PART I

CRISIS AND REVOLUTION

The three chapters in Part I lay the foundation for the rest of the book. The first chapter describes the current crisis state of the computer industry. At one time that industry was the shining beacon for the industrial world, and certainly for the United States. Led by IBM, the most admired company in the world, dozens of other companies including DEC, Wang, Apple, CDC, and Univac were proof positive that in at least one segment, American companies could innovate and lead. Companies in many different countries began to view the computer industry as a stable foundation on which they could build a strong employment base. Today much of that is changed, and many people wonder where the industry is going.

The turmoil in the industry has profound implications not only for the companies that build computers, but also for the many organizations that use them. Betrayed by the loss of a single, consistent, unwavering vision portrayed by a true blue unimpeachable industry leader, many organizations wonder where that sense of technological direction will come from in the years ahead. Chapter 1 provides the background for understanding how this crisis of substance and confidence came to be.

While the computer crisis has been building, a business revolution of at least equal scope has been developing as well. Originally based on the Total Quality Management movement of the last three decades, Business Process Reengineering is today's tool for determining how managers should structure their organizations. The basic philosophical precepts of both Business Process Reengineering and Total Quality Management call for a fundamentally different way of working — and thinking — at individual, departmental, and corporate levels. This new way of working creates a very real need for a new kind of information system based on providing support for distributed, self-managed teams. That's what Chapter 2 is about.

Chapter 3 brings the first two chapters together. It defines the new computer industry that will develop out of today's crisis. That new industry will provide the technology, and eventually the systems, required to support Business Process Reengineering's organizational structures. By the end of Chapter 3 you will have a clear, conceptual picture of the new computer world order that will exist in the years ahead.

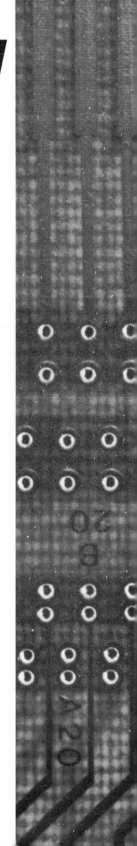

CHAPTER 1

Midlife Crisis for an Industry

Since the 1950s, the computer industry has moved through birth, adolescence, maturity — and into a profound midlife crisis. IBM, once the very model of a successful twentieth-century business, is viewed by many as obsolete, yet nobody knows where to look for a new industry leader. Users and vendors of computers are asking themselves profound questions that challenge fundamental beliefs about the computer industry:

✦ *Are mainframes obsolete?* Mainframes are supposed to be obsolete or on the verge of being obsolete. However, none of the replacement technologies are mature enough to truly replace the mainframes. True or false? If true, how do we manage the increasingly expensive, hard-to-maintain mainframe software base?

✦ *Can personal computers run the entire business?* Personal computers can do more than word processing and spreadsheets, right? So why is it so hard to actually build personal computer applications that perform broader functions in the organization? How can a company justify the increasing cost of maintaining personal computers, their networks, their servers, and their burgeoning support staffs?

✦ *Are new software tools always better than the old ones?* New software development tools are supposedly hundreds of times faster than traditional, COBOL-based techniques. Yet, whenever it comes time to develop or enhance the big, enterprise-wide applications that really run the business, COBOL, the COBOL-literate programmers, and all the tools that go with them win the day. Will it be possible to develop applications faster? And how do you satisfy the users who are growing spoiled by the friendly applications they see developed so quickly in the PC world (even if those applications are small in scope)?

✦ *How do the PC software developers and the mainframe software developers talk to each other?* Whom do you believe when one camp talks about disciplined development, operational considerations, and the real world, while the other camp shows us faster development, friendlier interfaces, and lower costs? Is there a way to get the best of both? And do you have to eliminate one set of positions to get there?

DEFINING MEANING, VALUES, AND IDENTITY FOR COMPUTERS AND THEIR USERS

Until recently, the computer's role in the world was easy to understand. Mainframes provided business solutions. Perhaps they were too expensive for some applications and organizations. However, once the economies of scale were present, IBM or DEC had the system, the strategy, and the solution. Along with the hardware and the software, these companies clearly defined the organizational structures, the professional staff, and even the consultants to use. On the other side of the computer coin, personal computers offered word processing, budgeting, and desktop publishing just as televisions and stereos offered personal entertainment. Both mainframes and PCs were computers, but other than that, they were unrelated. The leaders of the personal computer industry were IBM and Apple — and the path was simple and unambiguous. During the '60s, '70s, and '80s, computers became cheaper, better, and easier to use every year. To a large extent, along with death and taxes, one of the few constants of the last few decades was the constant progress in the computer world.

Suddenly in the 1990s, computers became confusing: roles have become confused, and progress no longer seems quite as certain. Not just IBM, but DEC, Apple, Compaq, and all the other leaders are being forced to redefine their businesses in almost every way; the alternative is extinction. The boundaries between business computers and personal computers are becoming blurred. All of the beliefs that business people and computer people have about computers are being challenged, too.

This book provides a new framework for understanding how computers will be used in the future. First, this chapter explores the computer crisis of the '90s in more depth so that you can understand the full magnitude of the challenge lying ahead. Because that challenge is so heavily grounded in the history of the computer industry, that's what this chapter is about: the history of computer usage in organizations. Later in the book, I'll look at some of the technical underpinnings of the computer world.

This chapter looks at computers from management, user, and business perspectives. After all, computer technology has become one of the largest costs in organizations.

Also, as Business Process Reengineering reshapes the way companies work, organizations must invest in yet *more* information technology. So it's important to understand how the people doing all the investing — the managers and users — have come to feel about their work and computers. The result of this analysis will be a view of the computer crisis of the '90s, a crisis that is more profound than most people realize.

1900–1949: ELECTRONIC CALCULATORS

During the first half of this century, computers were scientific curiosities used only for complex scientific and engineering calculations. Although they were powerful compared to mechanical calculators, computers of the time were built for specific purposes and were very limited in functionality.

1950S: ELECTRONIC BRAIN

In the 1950s, *stored program* computers were invented. By loading instructions into memory, stored program computers could carry out tasks as varied as the imaginations of the users. The modern computer age was born. At the beginning of the '50s, computers were physically enormous, expensive, and very difficult to program and use. Memory was limited to a few thousand bytes, and communication with the machine took place through paper tapes, punched cards, or even handset toggle switches. Programming languages had not been invented, so even simple applications took extensive time to develop. During the entire decade of the 1950s, only a few dozen machines were sold, each costing hundreds of thousands of dollars.

Decade	Theme	Technology
1950s	Electronic brain	Programming languages

The single biggest computer achievement of the 1950s was the invention of *programming languages*. Before that invention occurred, programmers worked strictly with the ones and zeros used by the computer itself. A programming language is a notation — sometimes similar to English, sometimes mathematical in appearance — designed to be understandable by humans rather than computers. The whole point of programming languages is to allow people to think in their own terms when working with computers rather than have to constantly deal with the bits and bytes built into the machine. By introducing languages as a high-level tool for programming computers, the '50s made application development truly approachable for the first time. Even 40 years later, COBOL and FORTRAN (introduced in the '50s) are still two of the most heavily used programming languages in the world.

However, even with stored program capability and programming languages, computers in the '50s were still very limited in function. Permanent storage — disks and tapes — had not been invented, so databases were not possible. The primary function of computers in the '50s was still computation. Yet computers made it possible to build large models involving millions of calculations. Those models allowed users to forecast budgets, plan factory schedules, forecast the weather, and even predict elections.

As television was taking off, a computer was used (for the first time in this role) to predict the outcome of the Eisenhower election based on early poll returns. In retrospect, extrapolating early returns involves no wizardry at all. In fact, high-speed communications — telephones and telegraphs — played a much larger role in the whole affair than the computer did. Nonetheless, the idea of an electronic brain somehow seeing into the future captured the imagination of millions. Computers, previously mysterious, suddenly appeared understandable. By the end of the 1950s, computers fascinated the public.

1960s: BUSINESS MACHINE

In the '60s, a decade of unbounded hope, computers really learned to walk. People began to view computers as artificial intelligences that might well one day replace people in all kinds of tasks. By the middle of the '60s, computer companies had realized that the potential marketplace was huge — much larger than the few dozen computers that IBM predicted as the market size in the '50s. With the introduction of permanent storage, particularly magnetic disks, databases became possible.

Decade	Theme	Technology
1950s	Electronic brain	Programming languages
1960s	Business machine	Operating systems

The database, in turn, promoted a vision of a "databased" organization, in which the computer could act as a central coordinator for company-wide activities. In this vision, the database became a key corporate resource. For the first time, people were viewing computers not just as arcane predictive devices. Instead, they saw computers as a true competitive advantage. The idea of information systems for business took shape. In other words, computers became important business machines.

1960s DREAMS

Early in the 1960s, President John F. Kennedy committed the United States to putting a man on the moon by the end of the decade. Technology had moved to center stage. Naturally, computer scientists and others were able to dream just as boldly as anybody else. Driving a great deal of this optimism was a new view of computers. Unlike the devices of the '50s, computers were now able to work with far more than numbers and graphs. In the future, people thought computers might be able to process letters, words, concepts, and potentially even emotions. Words, concepts, and emotions provide a pretty broad palette — even for computer visionaries. As part of a decade of unbounded hope, the computer contributed its fair share of fond dreams.

When you can conceive of the computer as the first machine that amplifies the brain, why not take a step further? Imagine that same computer eventually *replacing* the human brain. In fact, why not think of the brain as itself being just a form of chemical computer? Consider some of the ambitious goals that people had set for computers during the '60s:

+ Computers would be able to read handwriting, recognize spoken sentences, translate the results into digital form, and, most ambitious of all, *understand* what they were receiving.

+ Computers would be able to translate from any human language (like English, German, or French) to any other language, taking into account idioms and ambiguities, and produce better translations than even gifted human translators.

+ Computers would be able to play grand master level chess and world-class Go.

+ Computers would be able to exhibit learning behavior and carry out most mental tasks that humans do today.

1960S DISILLUSIONMENT: COMPUTERS CAN'T LEARN (YET)

Most of the predictions listed previously seem just as far away today as they did 30 years ago. Even if programmers can make computers play chess better today, they still don't know how to teach a computer to learn very well. That most basic of human attributes — the ability to learn — is still reserved for people, not computers. So the '60s also marked the first big period of disillusionment with computers; they were not electronic brains or replacements for humans, per se.

1960S ACCOMPLISHMENTS: COMPUTERS FOR BUSINESS

Today the computer is the tool par excellence of the (large) organization. Early in the 1960s, people still thought of computers as large calculating machines. Occasionally, advanced thinkers started to think about them as potential artificial intelligences. However, by the end of the decade, a new role was clear: the computer was a superb tool for automating complex business processes.

Computer technology itself played a major role in elevating computers into this humdrum and yet invaluable role inside organizations. All through the '50s and early '60s, computers ran just one application at a time. Ironically, the electronic brains of the '50s were just as personal as today's PCs; it's just that their use was restricted to a few dozen privileged computer scientists worldwide. During the '50s, programming was done sitting at the computer's console, and programs were run during personally reserved time slots; virtually a personal computer in many ways.

The '60s also saw the development of modern operating systems. In fact, three of the four leading big computer operating systems of the '90s, OS/360 (the predecessor of MVS), UNIX, and DOS/360 (unrelated to MS-DOS), all were developed in the '60s. These operating systems allowed the computer to be a shared, constantly available resource. Suddenly, computers became big business: both in the sense of being a big market and in the sense of making big businesses more efficient.

Much of this book describes the ways that computers are now *changing* the way large organizations operate. In the '60s, rather than *changing* organizations, computers *preserved* them. Large organizations that were previously drowning in paperwork suddenly found that computer technology allowed them to preserve their existing structures efficiently. Rather than change existing processes, computers made them faster. In fact, one of the adages of the computer industry, still viewed by some as wisdom today, is that a business process should never be automated until it basically works; don't *change* the process — just make it *faster*.

Although computers in the '60s did not fundamentally *change* business organizations, they played a major role in *keeping* those organizations functional as they grew. The 1960s was a decade of multinational corporations, worldwide airline reservations systems, global banking, and worldwide credit cards. Conglomeration and acquisition became a normal route to corporate growth. At the center of all this *bigness* was the computer. The computer made complex, centrally controlled bureaucracies possible. It mattered little that these bureaucracies simply automated many of the inflexibilities and overheads of the past. Growth for its own sake was the song of the period.

By the end of the 1960s, computers had become truly indispensable for any large organization. Along with big computers and big computer systems, organizations invested massively in computer departments, programmers, professional and support staff, and custom applications software. By 1970, most large organizations were *amazed* at the amount of money they were spending on *information technology (IT)*. Companies were suddenly spending millions of dollars on what was previously a non-existent budget category. At first, IT line items were classified simply as accounting expenditures, buried somewhere. However, as costs continued to escalate and staffs continued to grow, soon the amounts became too large to be buried. Suddenly, management was spending anywhere from $1/2$ percent to 10 percent of its total budget on this newfangled computer stuff.

To put this in perspective, realize that in 1950 no business budget anywhere made any provision for IT expenditures at all; it wasn't possible. Even as recently as 1960, IT expenditures were typically limited to a handful of big companies with specialized needs. Also, in 1960, chances were good that any particularly large IT budget was directly associated with either scientific research or engineering design; the cost could be directly justified in connection with development of new products. By 1970, though, every large company was spending a significant part of its budget on computers. And, at last, by 1970, it appeared that most companies had built most of the applications that made sense. Expensive, probably worth it, and finally containable in cost — what a relief.

1970s: The Databased Corporation

After finally reaching an apparent plateau, the entire computer world changed between 1968 and 1972. Databases, terminals, networks, and permanent storage (disks) all became practical at about the same time. The result of this new technology was to cause almost all existing applications to become obsolete and to create a need for a whole class of new applications. These applications would collectively dwarf everything that had come before in terms of cost and complexity.

Decade	Theme	Technology
1950s	Electronic brain	Programming languages
1960s	Business machine	Operating systems
1970s	Databased corporation	Databases, terminals, and networks

Until the database revolution that ushered in the 1970s, many senior managers had a hard time fully understanding the potential of computers. At first they viewed computers just as part of the administrative accounting systems. Later, when IT costs continued to grow, management felt uncomfortable, but many decided to ignore it. Databases, terminals, and networks changed all that.

In every large organization, isolation is a fundamental fear. The bread and butter of every business school and business magazine are stories about senior management teams that lose touch with their markets and customers because they can't get access to accurate information in a timely fashion. All of a sudden, the computer promised to fix that isolation problem.

In the early '70s, the concepts associated with *on-line databases* — databases connected to and fed by networked terminals — suddenly were being described in the *Harvard Business Review*, not just in technical magazines read only by computer professionals, but in business magazines normally read *only* by executives. Management could arrange to eliminate *all* isolation by

✦ Viewing information as a key corporate resource

✦ Building a totally consistent, company-wide, integrated database

✦ Ensuring that information was entered into and updated in that database as soon as that information entered the company

Sales information, customer complaints, up-to-date costs, inventory, and cash levels — you could view all of these at the touch of a keyboard in accurate and consistent form. Just build an on-line database, create a company-wide communications network, and put terminals everywhere, and the dream becomes reality. After all, compared to putting a man on the moon or making computers play chess as well as grand masters, how hard can building the total corporate database be?

The '70s were a remarkable decade from a management and expenditure perspective. In just 20 years, from 1950 to 1970, companies that didn't even have budget categories for IT built entire IT organizations and budgets that were on the verge of being unsupportable. Yet, by the beginning of the '70s, virtually all of those same companies, after reading the *Harvard Business Review* and similar publications, committed themselves to computer expenditures yet again, many times higher than before. That's what it takes to build a totally wired, database-centered organization.

How much should an organization spend on information technology? In 1970, very few people asked this question; by 1980, everybody wanted to know. As the computer industry developed into a major industrial, economic sector in its own right, a legion of consultants and academics analyzed spending patterns to answer the question. By the late '70s, a rough rule of thumb had emerged: organizations should target spending around 1 percent of their expense budgets on IT.

Keep this 1 percent number in the right context. The number is averaged across a hugely diverse range of companies. Therefore, like all averages, the 1 percent rule applied loosely to everyone and strictly to no one. For example, manufacturing companies really should have been spending around 1 percent of their budgets on computer expenditures if industry averages were any indication at all. However, banks, investment brokers, and insurance companies should have been spending around 10 percent of their (noninterest expense) budgets on information technology. Information is their *product*. At the other extreme, retail organizations had razor-thin margins and needed to keep IT costs closer to $1/2$ percent of budgets.

The '70s were marked by two key trends in management's understanding of computers:

1. **The executive team learned how computer and on-line databases could make their enterprises more competitive.** In particular, senior managers saw computer-based information systems as tools for keeping the top of the company in touch with customers and daily trends, and eliminating the dreaded isolation from reality.

2. **Management realized that building a modern on-line organization was hugely expensive.** Yet by about 1980, management believed that they had rules of thumb for appropriate expenditure levels and a broad base of experience on how to build modern information systems in a controlled fashion.

Most of all, the 1970s produced a *vision* for the future: information is instantly available, is always up-to-date, is organized in a consistent database that allows a company to operate faster, and enables everybody in the organization to stay in touch with the real world. A fine vision to keep in front of us.

1980S: THE BEGINNING OF THE END AND THE END OF THE BEGINNING

The '80s were a profoundly schizophrenic period for both the computer industry and its customers. On one hand, mainframe-based systems and the approaches to building them were finally becoming mature and predictable. Many organizations could begin to think of a future in which most of the applications required to run the business would be in place around a coherent, shared database. So in the safe, comfortable mainframe world, management in the '80s felt that the beginning of the end, in terms of meeting users' needs, was in sight. On the other hand, that was the same decade in which the personal computer turned the entire computing world on its ear. By the end of the 1980s, personal computers had totally changed users' expectations and created a demand for a completely new class of applications and computer systems. In the personal computer world, the decade was not the beginning of the end, but the end of the beginning. The end of the beginning? Yes. By 1989, even mainframers had to admit that personal computers were here to stay, and at the same time, personal computer bigots realized that those same personal computers needed to grow up and play a role in running the business. Making users more productive was not enough; the PCs had to produce a bottom-line return. The next two sections of this chapter examine these two opposing views of the '80s in more detail and show how they eventually came together to create the situation driving the computer industry in the '90s.

1980s, TAKE ONE: AN ADULT INDUSTRY — SOFTWARE ENGINEERING FOR MAINFRAMES

The 1980s were a period of profound contradiction. First, the personal computer industry was working through its infancy; I'll get to that in the next section. Second, the conventional, run-the-business mainframe industry was dealing with a serious midlife crisis at the same time that technology itself was largely standing still.

Decade	Theme	Technology
1950s	Electronic brain	Programming languages
1960s	Business machine	Operating systems
1970s	Databased corporation	Databases, terminals, and networks
1980s	Software engineering	CASE, methodology

Standing still? What about minicomputers, packet switching, computer-aided software engineering (CASE), and so on? Yes, there was continuing ferment and change in the big computer industry. Computers continued to get better at a pace truly frightening to anyone charged with managing them. At the same time, large computer technology at the end of the 1980s was very similar to the technology at the beginning of the same decade: faster, cheaper, more widely available, with lots of new features, but basically unchanged qualitatively. For example, a mainframe application built in 1980 looked virtually identical to one built in 1990; unchanged in all ways that matter to users. By 1990, terminals had become commodities costing a few hundred dollars. The relational database model had become dominant. Software development tools had changed enough to be almost completely different than they were ten years ago. Still, if you were to take the largest applications run by most organizations and compare both the applications and the infrastructure supporting them over the ten-year period, you would find surprisingly little change. Even the acronyms hardly changed: MVS, IMS, CICS, VMS, COBOL, DB2, SNA, DECnet, MPE, Guardian, JES, IDMS, and on and on. So what changed?

In 1970, business had big dreams: on-line corporations, wired desktops, totally consistent databases. By 1980, the reality had set in: the vision was far harder to implement than anyone had imagined. However, rather than back off, the industry hunkered down and developed the necessary tools, disciplines, and methodologies required to make possible the big systems required by the dream. Not just possible, but *predictably* possible. Management was willing to accept big budgets and long delivery schedules, but only if the promised applications would actually arrive on schedule and in good working order.

By 1980, the computer industry was beginning to *mature*. In March 1979, the *Harvard Business Review* published a milestone article by Richard Nolan. That article (following the work of an earlier *HBR* article written in 1974 by Nolan and a colleague, Cyrus Gibson) documented the stages most organizations go through to build increasingly sophisticated computer systems company-wide. In a sense, Nolan, discussing stages of growth and maturation, was like the Dr. Spock of computer development. Just as a generation of American parents learned about the stages of child development from Spock, a generation of business and computer managers learned to recognize computer organizational maturation from Richard Nolan.

Technically, the industry was *not* really standing still. True, big computers, their databases, and related development tools had reached a plateau with little qualitative change. However, the focus and energy of the big-computer industry shifted from the computers and databases to the process of *designing and building applications*. Computers were here to stay. Management was even excited about them. But the new question was, *how do you build applications for those computers in some kind of disciplined fashion?*

In many ways, the changes taking place during the early '80s in the mainframe world were very similar to the changes taking place now in the personal computer and client/server world. First, technology revolving around databases, networks, and terminals offered substantial business benefits. Second, knowing how to predictably and reliably build large applications to take advantage of this technology was a problem. Third, system development professionals gradually learned how to make this technology work in a trustworthy fashion.

So the 1980s were a period when business focused on converting application development from an art to an engineering discipline. This conversion process yielded two highly visible outcomes: *methodology* and *CASE*.

METHODOLOGY

A *methodology* is a formal prescription, a road map describing how software should be built. *Methodologies* range from loose frameworks that describe basic design approaches to 60-book encyclopedias that define every step, every hour and minute, and every organizational function required to build an application. As you would expect, an industry desperate for predictability and cost control grabbed at methodology as a saving grace, and the result was partly a huge religious fad. However, at the core of each methodology was a fundamental insight: *software design* is a formal process, one that can be studied and improved. Much of this book is devoted to laying out a framework for the next generation of *design methodology*, one that supports development of distributed applications.

COMPUTER-AIDED SOFTWARE ENGINEERING

Along with the development of methodologies (and there were many of them) came the software tools to support both the methodologies and the design process: *CASE (computer-aided software engineering)*. Why not use computers to help write programs? If software design is to become an engineering discipline, why not have computer-aided software engineering tools? And thus was born a billion-dollar industry.

Consulting firms developed, taught, and marketed methodologies all over the world. CASE vendors offered tools to automate both design and the associated methodologies. And, finally, system integrators offered the ultimate in predictability: they would guarantee to build applications within a budget, transferring any risk of overrun from user to integrator. So by 1990, CASE became a billion dollar industry segment devoted to building better applications more predictably.

Methodologies, CASE tools, and system integrators do not represent absolute guarantees of perfect systems always finished on time; nonetheless, the big-computer industry reached maturity at the end of the 1980s. MIS organizations *do* know how to build big systems. Methodologies *do* prescribe ways to build high-quality systems. CASE tools *do* support analysts, designers, and developers in building bigger systems better. And for those projects that warrant it, system integrators *do* offer reliable application delivery within fixed budgets. MIS, vendors, and the industry as a whole had every reason to feel proud of the state of the art by 1990. However, while the industry was growing up, the world around them was changing completely. To see this, revisit the '80s from the second perspective, that of the personal computer.

1980s, TAKE TWO: PERSONAL COMPUTERS — ARE THEY TOYS OR APPLIANCES?

The 1980s marked the decade of the personal computer. By 1990, there were 30 thousand mainframes in the world — the largest population of mainframes you're ever likely to see. In that same year, there were over 30 *million* personal computers.

Decade	Theme	Technology
1950s	Electronic brain	Programming languages
1960s	Business machine	Operating systems
1970s	Databased corporation	Databases, terminals, and networks
1980s	Software engineering	CASE, methodology
	Personal computing	Personal computers, graphical interfaces, and local-area networks

In the '80s, the personal computer industry went through the same kind of birth process that mainframes went through in the 1950s. For the first half of the decade, management and MIS were convinced that personal computers were just a passing fad. After all, calculators were a big deal in the 1970s, and although they didn't disappear, they hardly had a profound effect on any company either fiscally or organizationally. So why should the next electronic wave be any different? In fact, why not think of personal computers as just bigger, better calculators? Wait long enough and PCs would also become cheap, dispensable, and not worth thinking about anymore.

However, by 1985 it had become clear that personal computers were here to stay, and in a way different from calculators. Rather than personal computers becoming cheaper, users were making them more expensive with their insatiable need for more power, more storage, and more display resolution. Even peripherals were evolving. As dot-matrix printers became inexpensive, users discovered laser printers. As fast as disk price per byte dropped, users developed a need for many more bytes. So not only were personal computers here to stay, but costs were going up, not down. Even in the face of rapidly improving PC technology, users' appetites for ever more power was generating such a healthy demand that personal computer expenditures continued to increase faster than computer prices were falling. Still, even in 1985, nobody imagined that personal computer expenditures would ever catch up with — let alone exceed — mainframe costs. However, it was clear that personal computers were changing users' expectations.

Until the second half of the '80s, most individuals had only limited access to computers. Even if they had a terminal on their desk, that terminal was typically used only to run applications developed and maintained by the central IT organization. True, some engineers and scientists had regular access to timesharing systems with new tools like word processors and other personal tools — but they were a tiny minority. And although dedicated word processing systems from Wang, NBI, and others were starting to show a new way of using computers, those word processors really weren't computers. They were just expensive appliances, like copiers — so they, too, were ignored.

By 1985, all that comfortable smugness was starting to change. Several million users had been exposed to Multimate, VisiCalc, 1-2-3, dBASE, and WordStar. While addressing special needs, these applications were also dramatically easier to learn and use than mainframe applications. In particular, VisiCalc, 1-2-3, and dBASE were starting to make users think in new ways — those tools could be used to build custom applications:

✦ Why wait for MIS to develop a sales forecasting system when your local hacker can build the same system in three days at his desk?

✦ Why wait, particularly when the system developed in three days will be easier to use, more flexible, and will run on cheaper hardware?

✦ And, most of all, why wait when the MIS system will take two years, cost tens of thousands of dollars, and then be too expensive to run anyway?

Of course, the applications that could be developed with 1-2-3 and dBASE were highly limited in nature: they never dealt with shared information and were not capable of handling large amounts of data. So the threat to MIS, while starting to be visible, was still clearly very limited in scope.

Still, around 1985 computer professionals started taking PCs seriously for the first time — and when they did, they didn't like what they saw. The first dislike stems from a basic cultural division between MIS staffs and PC users that still exists today. This division is responsible for many of the problems that must be solved in the '90s as users move to the next plateau of computing. Simply put, MIS concluded that all those millions of personal computers were fancy toys or sophisticated appliances. Remember that the MIS community was wrestling with all the issues of building serious applications in a predictable fashion. From that perspective, PCs lacked all of the infrastructure so painfully built up in the mainframe and minicomputer world over a 20-year period. For example, PCs lacked all of the sophisticated timesharing and transactionally-oriented operating systems, all of the industrial-strength databases, all of the batch-scheduling facilities, and all of the CASE tools and modern programming languages.

So the MIS community woke up around 1985, poked and sniffed at the personal computer revolution, decided it was irrelevant to everything they were doing, and went back to sleep. And the worst of it is that *they were right*. Personal computers in 1985 could not be used to build run-the-business applications, no way, no how. And because those large business applications still needed to be built and run, it's hard to see how the big computer community could have reacted much differently. There just aren't enough hours in the day to live twice.

The result of that disregard is the cultural split we all live with today. Because the MIS computer professionals found early personal computers inadequate, a new breed of computer professional grew up during the '80s. Yesterday's teenage hackers, dBASE, 1-2-3, BASIC, and C programmers have become today's client/server gurus. Yesterday's basement developers have become today's personal computer system integrators. And yesterday's computer club president has become today's network computer manager. A completely separate *personal* computer profession has grown up to parallel the *MIS* computer profession. And integrating those two professions — with different value systems, different technical backgrounds, and different beliefs — is one of the challenges of the '90s.

1990s: Client/Server and Distributed Computing

The technical results of personal computer technology are clear and obvious: graphical user interfaces that are easy to use, virtually unlimited access to computer power on individual desks, and a new way of thinking about computers and the applications that run on them. What's not so obvious are the business implications of PCs. The question management thought had been answered in 1980 came back with renewed force in the 1990s: *How much is the right amount to spend on information technology?* This time the question is far more serious. To see why, consider both the personal computer revolution *and* mainframe costs while all those personal computers were being bought.

Decade	Theme	Technology
1950s	Electronic brain	Programming languages
1960s	Business machine	Operating systems
1970s	Databased corporation	Databases, terminals, and networks
1980s	Software engineering	CASE, methodology
	Personal Computing	Personal computers, graphical minterfaces, and local-area networks
1990s	Client/server	Distributed computing

Office Automation

At least today, personal computers are *office machines*. The personal computer industry is based on concepts of *office automation* first made popular in the '70s. At that time, American management was just starting to be concerned about global competition. *Investment* was a much-discussed topic: how much should organizations be investing in the future? Along with investment, another concern was *overhead*, particularly in the form of bureaucracy. At the time, one popular theory was that office workers, the ones who populate that bureaucracy, didn't have enough support. Why not *invest in the office* just like *investing in the factory*? According to this theory, a factory is a plant for processing physical goods, and an office is a plant for processing information. Given this model, why not invest in equipment to help office workers, now called *information workers*, to process that information more efficiently? Hence, the concept of *office automation* was born.

Today, office automation is usually associated with dreams of *paperless offices*: administrative systems in which all forms, reports, and other paper have been replaced by magical computer screens. Although this is in fact a goal of office automation, it is much more important to remember the other and original goals:

✦ Increase the efficiency of the office worker.

✦ Make administrative processes cheaper and faster.

✦ Reduce overhead cost tremendously.

In many ways, personal computers both helped and hurt office automation. They helped office automation because they made easy-to-use computers truly inexpensive, landing the machines on many more desks more quickly than even the most ambitious office automation prophets ever predicted. Yet personal computers hurt office automation because they demonstrated that the goal of eliminating paper, simplifying administrative processes, and changing the office takes far more than just technology. Today's office has more paper than ever. Laser printers, desktop publishing, spreadsheets, and electronic mail systems generate more paper faster than ever. Thus in the early '80s, the first international *Office Automation Conference* took place, and by the mid-'80s, the last one ever marked the end of the office automation dream in its late-'70s, technology-driven form.

What was happening to mainframe computer costs while personal computers were creeping onto desks all over the world? First, classical IT costs continued to increase. That average cost of 1 percent had increased to 1.5 percent of corporate budgets by 1990. Information-intensive companies — the banks and insurance companies — were spending around 15 percent of their budgets on computers. Worse, this 50 percent budgetary increase, because it's expressed as a fraction of the total budget, is automatically adjusted for inflation (see Figure 1-1). So the cost of growing the mainframe or minicomputer system that ran the business grew by well over 50 percent through the 1980s. Bad enough.

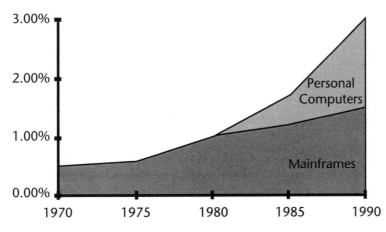

Figure 1-1: Classical IT costs and PC costs as a percentage of organization budgets.

At the same time, expenditures on personal computers had grown to be fully equal to expenditures on MIS by the end of the 1980s. So while the average company was spending about 1.5 percent of its budget on mainframe applications, the same company was spending another 1.5 percent of its budget on personal computers. Therefore, the total IT budget, including classical IT and personal computers, had increased from around 1 percent to around 3 percent. Even worse, banks and insurance companies were spending about 25 percent to 35 percent of their noninterest budgets on computers — the largest single noninterest cost in the entire company. So IT expenditures by the end of the '80s had tripled. Most companies had reached the point where they were simply spending more than they could afford on computers.

DRAWING THE LINE

The 1990s can best be characterized as the decade in which management finally decided that they couldn't take the mounting IT costs anymore. Something had to give. The simplest way to understand the dilemma is to consider mainframes and personal computers in their worst light:

+ Mainframe systems run the business. However, they are hugely expensive, hard to use, inflexible, and time-consuming to develop. Still, the systems definitely pay their own way; after all, they run the business. Every transaction, every piece of work done on a mainframe can be, and is, justified on an ROI (*return on investment*, the classical management measure of investment justification) basis; new mainframe applications don't get built unless there's a solid business reason for doing so.

+ Personal computers make individuals more productive. They're easy to use, and application development is relatively quick and flexible. The problem is that personal computers can't be used to run the business. Although individual personal computers are inexpensive, in the aggregate they cost as much as mainframes. They require support, network connections and servers, and a variety of other infrastructures. Worst of all, the costs are virtually impossible to justify on an ROI basis because personal computers meet the needs of the individual, not the organization.

In a sense, it is precisely the failure of the office automation dream that has created this dilemma. Originally, personal computers *were* supposed to run parts of the business. By eliminating paper and making procedures more efficient, they were *supposed* to pay for themselves. The problem is that it just didn't turn out that way. Personal computers yielded personal benefits, but not in ways that generate a measurable payback.

In the early 1990s, the Bureau of Labor Statistics studied office worker capital investment and any associated productivity increase. The startling result of the study was that through the '80s, American companies *did* steadily build a significant level of capital investment in the office (see Figure 1-2). Management put serious money into building the information factory of the future. Personal computers were a large part of that investment. During that same period of time, office worker productivity remained virtually unchanged. How could that be?

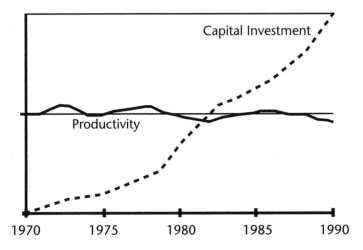

Capital Investment

Productivity

1970   1975   1980   1985   1990

Figure 1-2: Office worker capital investment and productivity from 1970 to 1990.

A PAINFUL QUESTION

Personal computers are *supposed* to make individuals more productive; *personal productivity* is what computers are all about, right? Think about all the people you know who use desktop machines for various projects. Writing with a word processor is certainly *better* than writing with a pen or typewriter, and preparing a budget or sales forecast is infinitely easier with a spreadsheet than with a calculator. But is the user of that word processor or spreadsheet actually *more productive*? Does he or she get more work done in less time? Consider the lowly office memo. I used to dash off a quick note by hand or dictation machine. For short notes, I just sent the handwritten version along; for more elaborate communications, a typewritten version was prepared and distributed. Because the process was so painful, memos were kept short and simple. Similarly, budgets and forecasts, limited by the awkwardness of hand calculation, were always reduced to minimal state, too.

With personal computers, simplicity with work went out the door. In theory, you could produce the same simple typewritten memo, using a word processor, and send it out in less time. Instead, the memo grew in length, graduated to multicolumn format, and gained multiple fonts, embedded graphics, and elegant formatting. Budgets became even more sophisticated. Spreadsheets made it possible for even the most elementary business proposition to be dressed up to illustrate multiple scenarios, complex alternatives, and masses of detail. Forecasts with dozens of formulas became the exception, not the rule. So instead of doing the same work in less time, or more work in the same amount of time, so-called information workers found themselves doing *more work in more time*. And worst of all, work on personal computers fell into categories not directly related to bottom-line return on investment.

A PAINFUL ANSWER

Does a somewhat better justification for a project make a business more competitive? How about a slightly more elaborate sales forecast or a dressed-up progress report? The problem with most of the work done on personal computers is that much of this work is only *indirectly* related to the line functions that keep the business going. In effect, the personal computers acquired during the '80s packed a double whammy at the organization and the IT budget. In the first place, those computers made their users only marginally more productive. And even where PCs have led to more productivity, the gains are applied in ways that yield only indirect return on investment — ways that don't show up on the bottom line.

Finally, while apparently not contributing to the bottom line, personal computers did spoil users. Personal computer users, now accustomed to windows-based, mouse-driven graphical applications, find mainframe applications painfully hard to learn and use. As users run those mainframe applications on the personal computer screen using terminal-emulation software, the discrepancy becomes particularly painful. The user gets to see the clunky order-entry form right there on the very same screen sitting next to the neat, attractive, powerful spreadsheet. Here is perhaps the ultimate irony: not only have personal computers not provided a return on capital investment, but worse, they make their users not want to use the other computers that *do* provide a return.

During the 1990s, organizations must adopt a completely new perspective on the use of computers. In the aggregate, computer costs are out of control. The mainframes and their databases run the business, and that function must be carried forward. However, you can't afford to keep paying for those mainframes while also paying for a completely parallel infrastructure centered around personal computers. The personal computers are too expensive, as well. PCs now cost as much as the mainframes, but serve personal needs only. As things stand today, senior management can't get rid of either mainframes *or* personal computers. The mainframes run the business, and the personal computers have come to be viewed as entitlements (and you know how hard it is to take entitlements away) by users everywhere. There's the dilemma. What we need is a breakthrough. The first impulse is to look on the technical front. However, the answer isn't there; it's on the business front. The next section tells why.

TUNING, DOWNSIZING, RIGHTSIZING, DOWNSIZING AFTER ALL

What is the best way to understand the technical and business revolution of the '90s? The tables in the following four sections frame this question by placing technology in the vertical axis and business practices in the horizontal axis.

TUNING

Faced with rapid changes in both technology and business organization, most companies start out by doing as little as possible (see Table 1-1). In other words, they tune the existing systems. This is not enough.

Table 1-1   **Tuning Existing Systems**

	Same Business Model	New Business Model
New Technology		
Same Technology	Tuning	

DOWNSIZING

Downsizing is another approach. If mainframes *and* personal computers are too expensive, why not get rid of one? After all, it's common knowledge that PCs are becoming as powerful as mainframes were just a few years ago. Why not just replace all of the mainframes with a few networked personal computers? In simple terms, this is the core idea behind the computer *downsizing* movement of the early '90s (see Table 1-2).

Table 1-2   **Downsizing Systems**

	Same Business Model	New Business Model
New Technology	Downsizing	
Same Technology	Tuning	

The problem is that *downsizing* carried out in a simple-minded way just doesn't work. Mainframe applications are generally very complex and depend a great deal on the sophisticated operating systems and databases that are part of the mainframe environment. To make downsizing really work, you must find some way to *convert* those applications to run on personal computers that may or may not be networked. The process better be a *conversion* instead of a *rewrite* — because rewriting those applications will typically cost as much as any savings generated by the move. Besides, rewriting applications takes a long time, but organizations don't stand still that long. Nobody can afford to wait through an entire rewrite for potential cost savings. So to make *simple downsizing* work, you would need a conversion — and a fast one at that.

Unfortunately, large, sophisticated, mainframe-based applications *cannot* be converted to run on personal computers. There are many technical reasons for this: dependence on databases, TP monitors, terminal orientation, and so on. Mainframe and network/PC system architectures are *very* different. An application originally written for one system needs to be fundamentally rewritten to run well in the other environment. All of this means that there is no simple way to eliminate the cost of both mainframe and personal computer infrastructures.

RIGHTSIZING

Many industry pundits decided that if large-scale downsizing doesn't work, some variation of downsizing must still be practical. Instead of downsizing, simply *rightsize* (see Table 1-3). Aside from any technical and business merits of the approach, the term *rightsizing* has a certain emotional appeal. *Downsizing*, after all, carries with it connotations of shrinking companies, smaller workforces, and large-scale layoffs. Rightsizing, on the other hand, starts out with none of this negative emotional baggage.

Table 1-3   **Rightsizing Systems**

	Same Business Model	*New Business Model*
New Technology	Rightsizing	
Same Technology	Tuning	

So what is *rightsizing*? *Rightsizing* is a euphemism for the phrase *personal computers are really toys*. The reasoning behind the term *rightsizing* goes something like this:

✦ Everybody knows that straightforward conversion of big, mainframe-based applications isn't practical.

✦ Everybody (whoever "everybody" is) knows that those big applications that run the business can't be made to run on PC systems. The fact that the real applications can't be converted is just a symptom of a larger problem: PCs don't have the performance, the operating systems, or the overall throughput to run the big, serious applications.

✦ There has to be some way to gain some more return on investment from PCs.

✦ PCs should be reserved for smaller applications. After all, those smaller applications just clutter up the mainframe anyway: they're a nuisance to write, a bother to keep running, their users generate pesky demands, and now there's a nice smaller home they can live in.

In effect, *rightsizing* is a euphemism for *moving toy applications to toy machines and leaving the real machines to run the real applications*. The strategy also won't work. It won't work because having the mainframes and PCs is too expensive, and because PC systems are much more powerful than is being recognized. But most of all, a *business revolution* is in the works that calls for a new approach to building systems... period. The new approach *does* provide the justification for rewriting the applications that run the business. If converting is too complex, don't convert. If the cost of a rewrite is too frightening, just wait. Soon the reasons and financial justifications for that rewrite will present themselves.

DOWNSIZING AFTER ALL

After playing through all the variations on downsizing and rightsizing computer systems, some organizations settle on yet another choice: ignore the technology and the computer systems altogether (see Table 1-4). After all, if those computer systems are so stubbornly hard to downsize and if rightsizing doesn't yield enough benefits, maybe the solution is to ignore those pesky computers. Focus on the business. Reengineer the processes. And, somehow, when the business runs more effectively, either the computer problems will magically go away or profitability will increase so much that you can ignore the computer problems anyway. Sounds fine, but also doesn't work.

Table 1-4   Business Process Reengineering without Computer System Downsizing

	Same Business Model	*New Business Model*
New Technology	Downsizing	
Same Technology	Tuning	BPR

As you'll see in the next chapter, *Business Process Reengineering (BPR)* actually depends heavily on new information technology. In fact, the whole point of reengineering is to use computers to redesign the organization. A reengineered corporation provides the justification required for rewriting all those existing mainframe applications. Besides, rewriting those mainframe applications will help the organization meet the new requirements that reengineering calls for anyway. Ultimately, reengineering will yield a *distributed computer system* that combines the strengths of mainframes and personal computers. The new distributed system will bolster the reengineered processes, strengthen self-managed teams, and empower employees, as I discuss in the next chapter.

As the final form of the matrix shows, downsizing is driven by Business Process Reengineering (see Table 1-5). Conversion *isn't* possible. Mainframe applications *won't* run largely unchanged on PCs, networked or not. But properly rewritten, the applications required to run even very large organizations *can* run on networked personal computers.

**Table 1-5   Business Process Reengineering with
                 Computer System Downsizing**

	Same Business Model	*New Business Model*
New Technology	Downsizing	Breakthrough
Same Technology	Tuning	BPR

The resulting systems *will* have all the performance, throughput, and sophistication required in a real business environment. True, the applications will be written in a completely new way. But once written, they exhibit flexibility, scalability, and friendliness unheard of in today's big application world. The key is realizing that technical forces will not make all this happen. Instead, new *business forces* will make those costs incredibly affordable. The next chapter looks at the business forces that can drive this change.

CHAPTER 2

THE BUSINESS REVOLUTION OF THE '90S

After World War II, Japan found its economy completely destroyed. Much of its physical and industrial infrastructure was ruined. The country began to search for ways to rebuild the economy and decided to view the future as an opportunity to build better plants and factories than anyone had ever built before. The goal was simple: to build manufactured goods that could compete world-wide based on high quality at low cost. A simple goal, but how to do it? The answer lay in *Total Quality Management.*

Today *quality* and *Total Quality Management (TQM)* have become an accepted part of management culture. Beyond being a fad, TQM is now so accepted that some might consider it passé. As a result of TQM, Japanese companies developed a reputation for building some of the best products in the world. This accomplishment is particularly amazing considering how much change was required to get there. In the late '50s, as some companies began to introduce big computers, very few people outside of Asia recognized Japanese products. In the '60s, while Japanese transistor radios started making their way abroad, their reputation was simple: cheap junk. In the early '70s, Japanese cars started penetrating the United States, but their reputation was similar to that of the electronics: inexpensive, cheaply assembled cars, competing primarily on the basis of price. My, how things have changed.

Today, in almost every segment in which Japanese companies compete, their products are considered to be some of the best designed, best built, longest lasting, and best looking. Even in the luxury car market, long the last bastion of German and American domination, the Lexus, Infiniti, and Acura have made incredible strides in gaining equal standing with the likes of Mercedes, BMW, Cadillac, and Lincoln. In other industries, such as home entertainment, the Japanese virtually own the market. By focusing on TQM, Japanese companies compete even when their products cost more than the competition. That's quite a change for an entire country to pull off in just 30 years.

Some people might consider TQM to be passé; nonetheless, most people have only the vaguest idea what it's about. Fortunately, although TQM is no longer talked about in the religious fashion of the '80s, *Business Process Reengineering (BPR)* is a direct extension of TQM. BPR is at least as much of a fad today as TQM was several years ago. So in a way, TQM lives on. This is fortunate because the fundamental principles underlying both TQM and BPR are critical to restructuring American and European businesses — both in the factory *and* in the office — to make them competitive in the future.

What *are* TQM and BPR about? *Processes.* In a nutshell, organizations and their management teams are working through a fundamental conceptual shift — a paradigm shift — that involves thinking about work in terms of *processes* instead of *tasks.* To see why this concept is so fundamental, I'm going to look at the roots of TQM and the process improvement model behind it.

PHYSICAL FACTORIES, INFORMATION FACTORIES

Suppose that you have a factory and you need to make it better. What does *better* mean? More products built in less time? Higher-quality products with fewer defects? Lower manufacturing costs? Less parts inventory? More product produced per unit time and more product produced per worker? Happier workers? Happier customers? Happier managers? All of these are aspects of a better factory.

I'm talking about factories that produce physical goods, like cars, televisions, and airplanes, of course. But can *better* apply to *information factories,* as well? An information factory is any group of workers that processes information. A front office environment that processes orders, schedules shipments, responds to customer complaints, issues bills, accepts payments, orders inventory, and keeps all the books straight is an information factory. The products it produces are shipments, bills, customer records, account files, and so on. Sales and marketing organizations can be thought of as factories, too. Those departments produce sales calls, promotions, advertisements, brochures, orders, and (hopefully) satisfied customers.

Computer organizations like to think of themselves as information factories. A couple of years ago, a brief spate of articles and papers documented experiments that originated in Japan. These experiments modeled software development directly after a factory, including reusable parts and an inventory. In addition, the experimenters converted the concept of code development into one of parts assembly. That particular concept proved to be less than totally practical; however, the idea of viewing the MIS organization as an information factory that produces systems is still very appealing to computer managers who are eager to find ways to develop better, faster, and less expensive software.

It is so attractive to think of these office organizations as factories because of the tremendous changes that have occurred in factory organizations — particularly in Japan — over the past 30 years. If cars, televisions, and airplanes can be produced so much better, why can't the rest of the organization be made to improve just as much? TQM results in better car factories, but could it result in better information factories, too? Great idea, but what exactly *is* TQM?

To understand TQM, go back to the list of things that make a factory better, such as more product, fewer defects, and less production time. How does that happen? The answer is to think of the entire factory as a *system*. A system is a collection of inter-connected parts, all tied together by a describable *process*. The *process* is the key. TQM teaches that the key to better production is improvement of the process, and the key to improvement of the process is understanding and measurement.

ASSEMBLY LINES AND BUREAUCRACIES

Until recently, the processes behind most manufacturing plants were poorly under-stood at best. Management over the last century has focused on tasks, often to the exclusion of processes. The bureaucracies so common to most large organizations are a direct consequence of the task orientation that originally drove the growth of the modern corporation. Task orientation is a natural outgrowth of mass production and assembly lines. Assembly lines revolve around the idea of dividing complex processes into simple steps that can be carried out repetitively by workers with little training. This assembly line model of process simplification, applied in both the manufacturing plant and in the office, led directly to today's big, slow, top-heavy organizations. Un-derstanding the route from mass production to top-heavy bureaucracy is critical to understanding the process-oriented alternative; this section looks at that route in more detail.

Assembly lines are built around specialization of a function. Take a product that has to be manufactured, divide the work over and over into smaller and smaller tasks, and when the tasks are small enough, you have an assembly line. At the turn of the cen-tury this concept — applied to automobile production — facilitated building cars by the millions. Unfortunately, after a large assembly line is put into place, there is no straightforward way for it to become more and more effective over time.

The classical task-oriented production system is based on two fundamental assumptions:

✦ In a large organization, individual production workers cannot be trusted to make basic decisions involving company policies and rules. Front-line workers should not be asked to think.

✦ Information collection and the associated rule enforcement can be done only after the fact by channeling information manually to specialists in the middle of the organization's managerial structure. Bureaucracies are intrinsically necessary in larger organizations.

Although these two assumptions may seem somewhat removed from TQM, the connection is surprisingly intimate.

Consider the large organization. At the top is an executive team that develops strategic plans, visions, long-range goals, and tactical plans to make the strategies real. At the bottom are (tens of) thousands of workers in offices and factories that build products, take orders, send out bills, accept payments, and generally make the business run. Any large organization has three fundamental problems that stem directly from size:

+ *Planning:* Translating long-range strategies into shorter-range action plans that produce the results in the vision.

+ *Coordination:* Coordinating scarce resources throughout the company so that the organization runs at maximum capacity without running out of cash, credit, inventory, manufacturing capacity, and so on.

+ *Policy enforcement:* Enforcing rules and policies consistently throughout the organization.

In a small organization, all three of these problems are handled straightforwardly because communication lines are short, information is available everywhere immediately, and workers can refer decisions to appropriate parts of the company quickly and easily. In a big organization, however, these three issues are fundamental deterrents to growth if not addressed properly. The result is the uncontrollable bureaucracy.

Suppose that a customer places a large order. Usually, either a salesperson or an order-entry clerk accepts that order. After the order is written up, it's sent to the credit department to ensure that the customer has sufficient credit available. At this point, two things happen. First, a credit-authorization clerk interprets company rules in a consistent way by ensuring that customers who become overextended may no longer place orders. Although simple to describe, the typical rules controlling when customers are considered delinquent, when exceptions can be made, what special approvals may be required, and so on, are generally quite complex. Having a functional specialist ensures that these rules are interpreted both consistently and correctly. Second, the credit department can ensure that the company does not become overextended. Depending on a variety of external factors, orders that might normally be processed immediately may be delayed to preserve scarce cash resources.

Next, the order moves to the scheduling department, which checks inventory, plans production, and decides when and in what sequence orders are filled. Again, functional specialists interpret policy consistently (which customers come first, when special production runs can be planned, and so on) and coordinate scarce resources (such as inventory and production capacity). When the scheduling department determines the order fulfillment date, the shipping department schedules delivery, again enforcing policy and coordinating scarce resources. The process continues through the generation of bills, recording of payment, and so on. In many companies, dozens of functional specialists may handle a typical order by the time the order is fulfilled.

To gain some perspective, picture the typical organization as a large pyramid with the executive team occupying the small peak and the front line employees living at the broad base. All the steps in the process of handling the order occur in the middle of this pyramid; this is the so-called middle management layer. Now, however, the function of that middle management layer is very well defined — middle management is the place where the company stores its business rules. Of the three functions requiring multiple layers of management — successive refinement of plans, coordination of scarce resources, and consistent interpretation of policy — all but the first can be defined as *implementation of business rules.* The idea that *consistent interpretation of policy* is an implementation of business rules is clear. Coordination of scarce resources — scheduling manufacturing, allocating credit dollars, managing limited inventory — is an important expression of the organization's business rules, also. These rules determine when extra production shifts can be scheduled, how long customers should wait for limited products, how much inventory should be on hand, when the company may use third-party shippers to make up for internal delivery limitations, and so on. The way that a large organization arranges for all these business rules to be implemented in a way that can be trusted is by creating a large and sophisticated middle management layer.

Middle management plays two key roles, each of which corresponds to the last two functions: coordination of scarce resources and consistent interpretation of policy. Both functions relate directly to the amount of trust that can be placed in front-line workers. First, middle management interprets policy consistently. An important rule of accounting with a great deal of history behind it says that every important transaction should require two persons for completion. This rule neatly expresses a central dilemma of big companies: how to ensure that rules are really enforced. If salespeople can make credit decisions, won't they be too generous to their customers? If customer-service personnel are allowed to decide about product returns and emergency shipments, won't it be too easy for them to appease the customer too frequently (that is, to the detriment of cost-efficiency)? The obvious answer, suggested by both accountants and common sense, is to split the transaction. The salesperson takes the order, but the credit department decides whether to honor it. The customer service clerk receives the complaint, but only the service manager can authorize a return. In this way, complex rules can be enforced correctly, rule changes can be accommodated relatively quickly, and most important of all, front-line staff never face a conflict of interest.

In the coordination of scarce resources, the case for centralized functional specialists is even more clear. How can manufacturing be scheduled effectively except by a person who can juggle all the outstanding orders at one time? How can inventory of scarce parts be managed unless one person controls all movement in and out of storage? How does the company manage scarce credit dollars effectively unless that company processes all requests at a single location?

All of this effectively explains how the management structure evolved in most large organizations throughout the world. Without sophisticated computer systems — and a new way of thinking about organizational effectiveness — this style of hierarchical structure is the only way to run a large organization.

MAKING PROCESSES BETTER

Somewhere in the 1980s, around the time that foreign cars were redefining the automobile marketplace, American companies awoke to the issue of global competition. As one industry after another found itself under attack from within and without, management started asking questions. From those questions came the idea of taking the *benchmarking* concept and applying it to business. In the engineering world, a *benchmark* is a comparison test, run at a standardized workbench, to establish meaningful numeric comparison between two competitive designs. Applying the benchmarking concept to a business allows processes inside two companies to be directly compared, on the basis of some numeric measure, to gauge one company's performance against another. The results of benchmarking can be startling, to say the least.

In some instances, foreign competitors could build products with as little as one quarter the cost accepted as normal elsewhere. In one case reported by Michael Hammer in the *Harvard Business Review,* Ford Motor Company discovered a competitor running its accounts payable department with less than 10 percent of the staff required to process the same volume of work at Ford. At the same time, as customers were making clear, the quality of products coming out of the competitor's inexpensive but efficient process was substantially higher than anything seen in the past.

By the late '80s the cars, televisions, and other appliances produced in new business environments became synonymous with quality itself. How did that happen, and how could quality — usually associated with increased cost — actually lead to lower cost and increased efficiency?

THE QUALITY GOES IN (JUST) BEFORE THE NAME GOES ON

Historically, quality has been a property determined after the fact. Products get built, on an assembly line, by workers who have virtually no control over the process they are part of. At the end of the assembly line, products are inspected for quality, and, as the Zenith jingle says, the quality goes in before the name goes on. Unfortunately, by the time the inspection takes place, it's far too late to have an impact on quality.

Modern products have many parts; at its best, inspection can test such products only in a superficial fashion. Turning a television on, taking a car for a short drive, and running a computer through a quick diagnostic test really stress very little of the overall system. The classical answer to this question is statistical: take a small number of the final products and take them completely apart to gain a picture of how deep the quality really goes. However, this overall approach to building complex products is fundamentally flawed when it comes to quality.

Suppose that in building a particular part, one of many making up a larger product, the error rate is about 1 per 100,000 or 1:100,000. In other words, for every 100,000 parts built, only one is fundamentally flawed. Sounds like a minuscule error rate, right? Wrong. In a product as complex as a car, even an error rate as low as 1 per 100,000 per part will result in every car built having at least one part with an error. How can this be?

Suppose that you roll a pair of dice, and any time you roll a five, that represents an error. With one die, errors occur one-sixth of the time; a result with no error occurs 83 percent of the time. With two dice, errors occur in 11 out of 36 rolls; the correct result comes up 69 percent of the time. With 10 dice, a roll with no errors (that is, no fives) occurs only 16 percent of the time. By the time you get to 100 dice, rolls with no errors almost never occur (.00000012 percent of the time). Of course, an error rate of 1:100,000 is much smaller than 1:6, but cars, televisions, and computers have far more than ten or a hundred parts in them. If even an error rate as low as 1:100,000 is too high, how on earth can a company build products in the real world? That's the question the TQM movement forces businesses to look at.

The answer to building better parts and better products has two parts:

✦ Don't wait until the end.

✦ Focus on the *process* instead of on the *task*.

Consider how one bad part was built into the finished product in the first place. This happened because the product process is an assembly line. The person building that part has no intrinsic way of knowing that the part is bad because he or she is producing that part in isolation from the bigger job being carried out by the assembly line as a whole. To see how this works, and how it might work differently, imagine a mechanical device, perhaps a farm tractor with 1,000 parts, and two different ways of manufacturing such a vehicle.

The assembly-line technique calls for each of the 1,000 parts to be built individually; at the end, all 1,000 parts are assembled and the tractor is inspected on the way out of the factory. Statistically, even if each part is out of whack one time out of 100,000, this factory will almost never produce a completely correct tractor. After all, with 1,000 parts, one of them is bound to have a problem.

Now imagine a different factory that builds tractors in a very modular fashion. Each tractor has ten major assemblies, each with ten subassemblies, each in turn with ten parts. Altogether, this second factory still produces tractors with 1,000 parts; the difference is the steps they take to get there. Each subassembly is produced by an individual; as part of the production process, the individual calibrates his or her subassembly carefully, weeding out defective parts in the process and producing subassemblies that perform perfectly each time. In turn, each assembly is assembled by a trained individual who calibrates that assembly. Occasionally, an assembly is rejected and the subassemblies are sent back to the appropriate part of the factory; but when an assembly is done, it works and works well. Finally, the complete tractor is put together by someone working with only ten assemblies, each already properly calibrated. The chances that the worker won't be able to deal with the variations introduced by only ten assemblies are pretty minimal, so the final assembly step almost always goes completely smoothly. Best of all, because each tractor is finished and calibrated by someone who can ensure that it works just right, there is no inspection process on the way out.

In the first factory, quality goes in right at the end; tractors are inspected after they are built. Indeed, quality can't go in any earlier because until the end, each tractor is just a box of parts. In the second factory, quality goes in at every step. Each subassembly, each assembly, and finally each tractor is built and calibrated to ensure perfect operation. That the entire process in the second factory is built to ensure quality is an intrinsic part of the entire production line.

PROCESS UNDERSTANDING, PROCESS IMPROVEMENT

At the center of the Total Quality Management movement is the idea that *errors don't happen at the end of a production line.* The assembly-line approach starts with the assumption that a product is built step by step, but only at the end can you tell what you've got. This idea in turn is based on the two fundamental principles at the heart of the assembly line:

✦ In a large organization, individual production workers cannot be trusted to make basic decisions involving company policies and rules. Front-line workers shouldn't be asked to think.

✦ Information collection and the associated rule enforcement can be done only after the fact by channeling information manually to specialists located in the middle of the organization. Bureaucracies are intrinsically necessary in larger organizations.

The first rule says that assembly-line workers are robots, and the second rule says that you can tell how well the robots have done only by measuring their work and analyzing the collected information after the fact. TQM says that both these rules are wrong.

Why are robots such a problem? Well, remember that if even one part in 100,000 is wrong, almost every finished product going out the door will have some problem somewhere. The problem is that robots can't be asked to build parts that never have problems. Robots can build parts that rarely have problems, but that's not good enough. We need parts that never have problems, and robots can't do that.

Robots? Come on, isn't that an exaggeration? In *Modern Times,* Charlie Chaplin worked on an assembly line so repetitively that by the end of the day, his arms repeated the same motion even though the work shift had ended. That's a robot — the same type of robot that can put a Coke can in a drive shaft and create the legends that buying a car built on a Monday or Friday is a recipe for disaster. Assembly-line work may draw on the body, but it puts little emphasis on the associated brain. Factories can be exciting places to work, and they can also be spiritless machines in which people become cogs. The people are not the problem; the system is. And what TQM is about is altering that system so that factories build on the abilities of the people in them.

SELF-REGULATING PROCESSES: TURNING THE WORLD INSIDE OUT

TQM takes the assembly-line system's two rules and turns them inside out. Rather than measure quality after products are built, TQM says to just make them perfect to begin with. Rather than accept the idea that some parts will be wrong, establish processes that ensure that only perfect parts are ever built. How can that be? Instead of having unthinking robots, disconnected from any information about the parts they're building, have the producers of the parts become responsible for ensuring that those parts are perfect before they ever get built into the product.

The assembly-line philosophy says that *the manufacturing process is very complex; simplify it by slicing it up into simple tasks.* Because each task is simple, there is no way for the output of that task to be perfect. Simplicity means exactly slicing and dicing the overall manufacturing process up so fine that the tasks involve no thinking. Without thinking, there can be no quality.

What does *quality* mean? Quality means *consistency of results.* Cars that always work. Televisions that always have exactly the right colors. Not only does the car work, but also every part of the car *works exactly as it's supposed to.* Where does consistency come from?

In theory, it should be possible to design machines and processes that always produce the same results. In practice, there is too much variation in the real world for this to be possible. There is, however, an alternative: *machines and processes that regulate themselves.*

A home heating system is a good example of a self-regulating system. In the face of all the changes in the outside world, getting a furnace to maintain a completely stable temperature is a hopeless task. But with the help of a thermostat telling the furnace when to turn on and off, stable temperatures are the norm. After the thermostat is set, the heating system regulates itself.

In the same way, the tractor factory that builds tractors out of assemblies and subassemblies can produce consistently high-quality tractors. This is because the production of each of the assemblies and subassemblies is a *self-regulating process.* In the example, two factors made production of the tractor modules self-regulating:

◆ Each production worker was responsible for building and calibrating the tractor, assembly, or subassembly. Rather than having just a task to do, each worker ran his or her own process.

✦ Each worker was provided with the tests, instruments, and other equipment to complete the calibration of the module. Rather than collect information to send on to other parts of the organization, that worker was provided with enough data to know for himself or herself how well each assembly was built.

More than just tuning existing production techniques, the result of TQM is to turn the conventional factory inside out. Instead of focusing on the manufacturing process just long enough to slice it into tasks, TQM demands that companies combine those tasks back into processes. Moreover, the subprocesses have to be self-regulating, so all of a sudden the picture of the typical production worker needs to be reexamined, too. Information becomes a valuable part of the manufacturing process itself rather than a by-product that can be used to determine how well the process worked after the fact. Information derived as part of the manufacturing process is now fed right back into the process — *at the time it is derived* — to keep the process self-regulating.

SELF-MANAGED PROCESSES, SELF-MANAGED TEAMS

The biggest change caused by TQM is the change to the role of the classical production worker. As the focus of the factory changes from small, self-contained tasks to larger, self-regulating processes, the role of the worker changes from unthinking robot to constantly thinking member of a self-regulating team. What is a *self-regulating team*?

During that period of time in the '80s when it briefly appeared that American car manufacturers might even be driven out of business by foreign imports, General Motors set about to build a completely new division. The Saturn division was charged with the mission of building a new kind of car company based on the best principles that could be discovered world-wide for building better cars. After careful study, one of the central principles the division identified was the need to eliminate the distinction between managers and workers.

In a classical factory, workers build products while managers measure how they're doing. When improvements are required, the managers divide up the unthinking tasks in new ways, tell the workers their new assignments, and hope for the best — all after the fact. As I've discussed, the problem is that this schizophrenic process, with management and workers divided, just doesn't produce products that are good enough — even at its best. "Nearly" perfect parts make a product that is far from perfect. Perfect parts — always perfect, not just mostly perfect — lead to perfect products, but robot workers and disconnected managers never produce always perfect parts.

In the process of creating itself, the Saturn division followed the example set by the Japanese and eliminated the distinction between managers and workers. Why not build a complete factory where every process is self-regulating? Why not build a factory, even in the United States, where every part is built to be perfect? A factory that produces cars that can compete with Japanese and German cars on their own terms? Are such factories possible?

The '80s, the same period during which the need for a Saturn division became evident, saw a real revolution in thinking about quality. That revolution eventually became most evident in the eyes of customers. Historically, even as recently as the '60s, industrial products in general were viewed as throwaway. A television set, for example, could be expected to work for several years, start needing repairs, and eventually require complete replacement. Automobiles, toasters, lawn mowers, and other industrial consumer products were simply assumed to be intrinsically imperfect with relatively short lifetimes. Repairs and downtime were an accepted fact of life.

By the end of the '80s, consumers were accustomed to a new class of industrial appliance that worked perfectly, lasted for a very long time, and virtually never broke. Television sets that last for 10 or 15 years with no adjustments, automobiles that don't require any service for 100,000 miles (and keep running even through missed oil changes), and microwave ovens that have never seen a repair are now routine. Most personal computer users, for example, wouldn't even know how to find a repair facility to start with because equipment today practically never breaks. Perhaps some of this new reliability is due to simple advances in technology, including the replacement of vacuum tubes by transistors. Perhaps, but what is the explanation for the deserved reputation of Japanese cars for working perfectly forever, or the fact that Maytag advertises the lonely existence of its repair team? Twenty years ago new cars always had at least one part that didn't work right; today we just assume perfection. Here are three explanations for that change:

✦ Factories and organizations built up entirely around self-regulating processes

✦ Processes that ensure that every part is perfect before it ever gets into the product

✦ Factories that build products so well that after-the-fact inspection is irrelevant

The profound change in both actual product quality and the perception of that quality by customers revolves completely around these self-regulating processes. Self-regulating processes require a completely new style of organization. And getting there requires a complete reexamination of all the processes inside a company — not just the physical manufacturing processes.

The first question to ask about self-regulating processes is *who is the self that is doing the regulating?* The answer, obvious only after the fact, is *the workers or team responsible for implementing that process.* Robots, at least unthinking ones, cannot be self-regulating. Self-regulation means that the process implementors are able to modify the process while it is running. Modification of the process requires thinking.

To have self-regulating processes, the two rules at the core of the assembly-line philosophy have to be rewritten:

✦ In every organization, large or small, production workers must be responsible for all the basic decisions involving the work they do. Their jobs must be constructed in such a way that by making appropriate decisions dynamically, the workers can control their environment enough to ensure the production of perfect work products all the time.

✦ All the information that a production worker needs to produce perfect products should be available to that worker all the time. If necessary, information generated in other parts of the organization should be channeled to that worker in real-time in order to allow the worker to make the decisions required to produce only perfect parts and products. Wherever possible, all decisions related to work product quality should be made by the people doing the work at the time the work is being done.

Compared to the philosophy underlying assembly lines, these two rules place a great deal of responsibility on the shoulders of production and front-line workers of all kinds. Putting these rules into place requires two fundamental changes in organization — one mechanical and the other philosophical.

The mechanical change involves rethinking the structure of the organization itself. Assembly lines, with their focus on narrowly defined tasks, make self-regulating processes virtually impossible; the specific tasks are too limited in scope to allow production workers to have enough control to guarantee perfect products. Consequently, the first step required to implement the new TQM-driven ground rules is the redesign of the fundamental production process and all the jobs in it. The scope of that redesign is all-encompassing and reaches farther than this book can deal with in detail. If you're in the mood to stimulate your thinking about this topic, however, a good book is *The Goal*, by Eleyahu Goldratt and Jeff Cox.

One example illustrates the fundamental nature of the shift. In an assembly-line world, manufacturers and their suppliers are locked into an adversarial relationship. The manufacturer buys parts at the lowest possible price, and the suppliers compete with each other for the manufacturer's business. The market is a jungle, and the fittest survive. *Do whatever is required to win the business; do whatever is required to get the lowest possible price from your suppliers.* That's the world most managers, marketers, and salespeople know. If the entire production process is to be self-regulating and if every part must be perfect, then clearly external suppliers are an intrinsic part of that picture. If suppliers are to be self-regulating, they need access to a great deal of information about product requirements, performance of the parts they supply, and so on. In fact, those suppliers are part of the team that incorporates their parts into the actual product. If they're part of the team, how can there be an adversarial relationship? And if they're not part of the team, how can the process they're part of be self-regulating? There it is: the revolution in progress. Suddenly suppliers, historically almost enemies, are not just friends but integral parts of the bigger family that builds the product. They're not just *not* enemies, not just friends — they're members of the family.

This example illustrates how far the organizational redesign required by TQM really extends. It also illustrates another fundamental aspect of that redesign: a focus on larger processes instead of smaller tasks. A basic consequence of that shift is a focus on teams instead of individual workers. Many times the task performed by an individual production worker can be enlarged enough so that that worker can be responsible for a self-regulating process. Instead of tightening a single hinge all day, a worker assembles complete doors and tests them to ensure perfection. Other times, in order to enlarge that task to become a self-regulating process, a team has to be assembled. Instead of installing just a spark plug, the worker becomes part of a team that assembles and tests complete engines.

All of this leads to the second fundamental organizational shift associated with TQM: a philosophical shift more profound than the mechanical shift I just described. The philosophical shift involves converting workers who historically have been unthinking assembly-line robots into *thinking owners of self-regulating processes*. Redesigning jobs and organizations is an intellectual process. Perhaps that process is demanding and intricate, but given smart enough people with enough experience, that intellectual process is quite straightforward. Converting unthinking robots into owners of self-regulating processes, on the other hand, is a cultural shift. That cultural shift is now the primary challenge confronting TQM, BPR, and as it turns out, client/server.

What was the biggest challenge facing the Saturn project? Not redesigning the factory, not developing engineering plans for a new type of car, and not deciding where to build the physical plant. The biggest challenge was empowering the employees so that they could participate in self-managed teams. If every engine, every transmission, every dashboard had to be perfect every time, the teams producing those engines, transmissions, and dashboards needed to have a new attitude. The mindset that *I'm here from 9 to 5, and management can worry about it if defect rates get too high or the process isn't quite right* had been proven not to work. Instead, every worker on every team had to believe that he or she was responsible for ensuring that every item built is perfect and that nobody else will fix problems if he or she doesn't. This set of values and beliefs is very different from what is normal in most manufacturing plants. What's being described is no less than a cultural revolution.

Instituting this kind of cultural turn requires a great deal of work, significant investment, and plenty of time. At Saturn and at other companies around the world, workers, managers, and supervisors found themselves participating in Outward Bound courses — walking tightropes and jumping from high poles. More than just trying new things together, supervisors, managers, and workers had to start learning to know each other *as people,* understanding each other's needs, and supporting each other as part of the same team. Tough stuff, but the alternative, not responding to global competition, is tougher.

THE OFFICE AS FACTORY — BUSINESS PROCESSES VERSUS BUSINESS TASKS

If an organization is to consist entirely of self-regulating processes, those processes have to reach far beyond the factory floor. Here are some important reasons why:

✦ The cost of the nonfactory segment of every organization (accounting, human resources, and so on) is a significant part of the total cost of every product.

✦ A mistake in processing an order, handling a complaint, or processing a payment can leave a customer just as unhappy as a defective product can.

✦ The self-regulating processes found on a factory floor end up grinding to a halt unless they are supported by equally self-regulating processes in the rest of the organization.

Products can't be built on time with inventory that doesn't exist. Incorrect specifications can cause just as many wrong parts as teams that don't build parts right. So it's not surprising that, after TQM had started revolutionizing the manufacturing environment itself, the next step was for the same philosophy to start finding its way into the rest of the organization.

TQM encourages us to think about broad processes instead of individual tasks. When the same thinking is applied to information and office processes, the results are surprising. Quality is often thought of in terms of defects and product performance. Productivity, however, should not be overlooked. Productivity means not only processing orders correctly, but also focusing on the amount of time it takes to process orders.

In fact, the classical complaint about information-based procedures generally deals with time, not accuracy. *My order took three weeks! The company took nine weeks to handle my complaint! How can a loan application take 17 days?* Why are bureaucracies so slow and inflexible? That's what everybody wants to know. The answer revolves around tasks.

Office procedures, much like manufacturing processes, historically have been designed around the philosophy of the assembly line. Complex processes are reduced to very small tasks that can be carried out by unskilled, unthinking workers. All important decisions are funneled to the middle of the organization where the business rules are stored. This organizational structure has two basic consequences.

First, step-by-step, task-oriented information processes are incredibly slow. Each task is always associated with a queue. As an order, a complaint, or an application travels through the organization, it spends more time in queues than it does being processed.

Task-oriented information processes are also inflexible. The biggest complaint about bureaucracies is that they are both slow *and* inflexible. How often have you been frustrated because a so-called customer service representative says he or she can't change the rules? On the flip side, how do service-oriented organizations create a reputation for outstanding service? By empowering their front-line employees to make decisions. Nordstrom, the clothing retailer, has built a world-wide reputation for service and the customer loyalty that goes with it by empowering its sales staff to make the decisions required to meet the customer's needs. In one mythical story, a customer service representative allowed a customer to return a pair of snow tires, even though Nordstrom sells nothing to do with cars. The value in terms of reputation gained from employees and teams empowered to ensure customer satisfaction far outweighs the costs associated with potentially suboptimal decisions.

Another example, cited by Michael Hammer and James Champy in *Reengineering the Corporation* (Harper Business Books, 1993), illustrates the change in philosophy and practice behind reengineering business processes. Recall the three problems associated with size; the problems solved by the classical bureaucracy: planning, coordination, and policy enforcement. IBM Credit Corporation historically processed credit applications in a little over seven days. Each application was handled by five different specialists, each in a different department, to ensure that policies were enforced consistently and that the scarce credit resource was coordinated effectively. By establishing a single team to handle each request and empowering it with the authority and responsibility for rule enforcement, loan application time was trimmed from seven days to four hours. Trimmed? Seven days to four hours? By moving responsibility for business rules out to the front line, the credit approval process was more than trimmed; it was radically redefined.

Business Process Reengineering involves applying the same critical eye that works in the factory to the procedures and processes found in the office environment. As in the factory, the shift is fundamental and simultaneously mechanical and philosophical. The mechanical shift involves rethinking all the processes found in an organization to make them all self-regulating. Along the way, business rule enforcement and coordination decisions get moved out to the front line. The philosophical shift involves convincing office workers (who were previously unthinking and had no responsibility for their results) to start thinking and taking total responsibility for their results.

Take a look at one last example of the impact that reengineering can have and then look at its impact on the classical bureaucratic model. Then, Chapter 3 lays out the technical requirements of TQM, BPR, and process orientation.

THE VIRTUAL SALES OFFICE

A large manufacturing organization, once first in its market segment, had lost market share steadily over a 20-year period of time, finally occupying the number three spot in most customer surveys while barely holding on to the number one spot in actual share points. After months of agonizing self-examination, management arrived at a fundamental strategic conclusion with two resulting decisions:

✦ The company decided that the only way to regain the hearts and minds of its customers was through customer service as projected through the sales force. For a variety of reasons, the alternative of building the most innovative products or the products with the lowest price was not possible. Customers had said, however, that good products with great service would do the trick.

✦ Building the sales force and providing them with the tools to provide excellent customer service was the path to survival and success.

✦ In addition, despite the imperatives associated with the two decisions, sales costs had to be reduced.

Contradictory objectives? Yes, but the paradigm shifts so often beloved by planners and consultants alike are often derived directly from such contradictory requirements. After more investigation, the management team developed a picture of sales costs that revealed that one of the largest components of the cost picture was the physical sales offices — the bricks and mortar with desks inside. Studying the function of the sales offices and customers' feelings about the sales force, management saw a surprising picture.

Beyond their social function, the sales offices in this company had the primary function of data communication. Salespeople visited sales offices to enter orders at terminals and to print territory reports about their customers at printers located at the sales offices. How did customers feel about all those orders entered at the terminals?

Mad as heck. When asked what they wanted most in the way of improved customer service, most customers responded with a simple request: process my orders faster. A prototypical story tells the rest. A small customer ordered some products from his salesman specifying next-day delivery; the customer needed the product for an installation scheduled for the day after that. The salesman promised to meet the request and drove specially to his office to enter the order. Like always, the order was processed through four different departments. In spite of being marked "urgent" and requiring next-day delivery, the order made it through only two departments the first day. On arriving at the third department, the shipping scheduler interpreted company policy narrowly and decided the order wasn't big enough to warrant expedited delivery. The fourth department, responsible for (among other things) customer satisfaction, realized that the terms of the order had been altered, but because of the small size of the order, elected to notify the customer by regular mail. The result? Three days after placing the order, the customer was notified by mail that his order would arrive the following week as part of a regular shipment. One set of rules interpreted consistently led to one less customer to worry about in the future.

Today the company has shut down almost all of its physical sales offices. Each salesperson has been provided with a notebook computer equipped with a cellular modem. The savings associated with shutting down the sales offices allowed the company to grow the sales force by 5 percent while still reducing net sales cost by 3 percent. Best of all, each notebook computer contains an order processing application that understands all the company's key business rules. That notebook communicates with regional servers that manage inventory, schedule shipments, and can commit to *guaranteed delivery dates*.

Each salesperson has both a sales target and a profitability target for his or her territory and customer base. Each decision to expedite a shipment, each decision to honor an unusual return request, and each potential exception to the default rules can be evaluated *on the spot* in terms of its impact on profitability. Of course, the salesperson can make his or her own subjective judgment about the impact on future sales. Best of all, though, when the salesperson promises next-day delivery, the promise has value and meaning.

The new result? The customers are amazed. The products they buy are still solid in terms of price and features, but for the need they fill, that middle-of-the-road positioning is fine. More important, the big, old company suddenly offers better service, and best of all, promises customers can count on. Not only that, but as the same customers say in unsolicited letters, they get previously unimaginable flexibility. As those letters say, the salespeople truly represent their company now; they don't just receive orders that are processed elsewhere; instead, they *are* the company for their customers.

BUREAUCRACY: A NEW MODEL

Applied to both the factory and the office, TQM and BPR represent a new model for thinking about companies and the people who work for them. Much more than just a clever technique for improving efficiency, these two approaches call for a fundamental cultural shift that promises to enrich jobs, produce better products at lower costs, and finally make bureaucracies flexible after all. So why do we even need bureaucracies?

Recall again the three fundamental roles of the bureaucracy: planning, coordination, and policy enforcement. Based on these three roles, what is the smallest bureaucracy really needed? There is an answer.

Elliott Jaques has studied organizations for over 40 years. Writing in the *Harvard Business Review* in 1990, he asserts that the fundamental defining characteristic of organizational size, other than number of employees, is hierarchy. In a hierarchical organization, there is a leader at the top of the hierarchy. In each successive layer of the hierarchy, managers have other employees reporting to them. First invented by the military, hierarchical command and control is a fine structure for organizing large numbers of people around a common purpose.

Jaques reminds us of the importance of the third function of a hierarchy — planning — which is the first role of a bureaucracy. That function deals with the development of long-range plans and the translation of those plans into tactical action plans, one year at a time. Based on his research, Professor Jaques even tells how many layers of hierarchy are required — at a minimum — to deal with this planning and translation of vision into function. The model developed by Jaques deals with time frames.

How far ahead is a worker at each level of the hierarchy required to plan in doing his or her normal job? More controversially, what is a fair level of pay (in 1990 dollars) for a worker with the responsibility for looking ahead a certain distance into the future? The answers appear in Table 2-1. Smaller organizations, those with no requirement or ability to plan more than two years into the future, can make do with four levels of hierarchy. Of course, a really small company, working from day to day, doesn't need even that much. However, even the very biggest company, planning 20 years into the future, should be able to function very effectively with only seven layers of hierarchy. How can that be? Don't typical big companies have dozens of levels?

Yes, companies typically have many more layers of hierarchy and bureaucracy than this model suggests. These companies also have cultural models that suggest that no manager can have more than 7 to 10 direct reports — the classical span of control. And finally, these organizations operate in climates with low levels of trust and minimal empowerment, which creates a need for complex, top-heavy bureaucracies to implement all the business rules that keep the company running.

Table 2-1   A Model for Bureaucratic Hierarchy

Level	Typical Title	Time Span	Fair Pay
1	Worker	1 Day	$20,000
2	Supervisor	3 Months	$38,000
3	Manager	1 Year	$68,000
4	General Manager	2 Years	$130,000
5	President	5 Years	$260,000
6	EVP	10 Years	$520,000
7	CEO	20 Years	$1,040,000

Recently, advocates and advanced practitioners of BPR, TQM, employee empowerment, and self-managed teams have begun suggesting that the classical span of control may be too limited. In an organization with self-regulating processes and truly empowered employees, a manager may potentially be capable of handling larger numbers of employees reporting to him or her. The same movement also suggests that the central bureaucracy responsible for enforcing business rules and coordinating resources not only is not required, but actually is a cause of poor performance.

A new model for the future is emerging. Hierarchical organizations are not disappearing. What may be disappearing is the bureaucracy normally associated with both size and hierarchy. To put this in perspective, consider the *American Heritage Dictionary*'s definition of the term *bureaucracy*:

1. a. Administration of a government chiefly through bureaus staffed with nonelective officials. b. The departments and their officials as a group.

2. Government marked by diffusion of authority among numerous offices and adherence to inflexible rules of operation.

3. An administrative system in which the need to follow complex procedures impedes effective action.

Clearly, if organizations that no longer impede effective action can be built, that is a desirable outcome and a strong base for business revolution. That's what this book is about.

CHAPTER 3

BUSINESS REVOLUTION, TECHNICAL REVOLUTION — THE CLIENT/SERVER OFFICE OF THE FUTURE

While the computer industry faces a crisis, the organizations that use computers are changing both operationally and culturally. At the heart of the changes is a new framework for understanding and using computers. The current changes will result in a resolution of the computer industry crisis first explored in Chapter 1. That resolution will be based on the TQM and BPR principles described in the last chapter. This chapter synthesizes material from the two previous chapters and describes what the computer revolution of the 1990s is *really* about. Based on the organizational and cultural changes that TQM and BPR have forced, this chapter describes the office of the future, an office based on distributed computer systems specifically designed to meet the needs of self-managed teams.

The computer industry crisis, and the industry leadership vacuum that goes with it, is a sign of revolution. The rapid advances in technology (resulting in children's toys containing microprocessors more powerful than the mainframes of the 1960s) are another clear sign of revolution. Most of all, this revolution has developed as millions of personal computer users, now exposed to graphical interfaces, expect and, in some cases, demand changes. I have described some catalysts of the revolution, but what exactly is this revolution all about?

Are the changes in the computer industry coming from business or technology? The technology has certainly been changing rapidly enough that it is easy to believe that technology itself may be driving the changes all around us. One cannot deny, however, that business has also been changing at least as rapidly as technology. Perhaps the business and technological changes are somehow related? After all, many other technological inventions, including the telephone, the airplane, and the elevator, have fundamentally altered organizations through an intimately linked set of technical and organizational changes. To further explore the relationship between business and technological change, I pose two questions:

✦ Where is the computer revolution today? In other words, how are computers being used to run organizations now, and what changes are coming?

✦ What is the state of business organizations today? Is there a way of understanding the evolving business culture to trace relationships to the technical revolution?

Although these questions seem rather broad, I feel that they can be adequately answered. As it turns out, there are *two* revolutions sweeping through the business world that are directly dependent on each other:

1. The personal computer client/server revolution is changing the very definition of computers. Computers are defined by the ways in which they are used, and client/server is opening up a world of new uses for computers. In a short time, users worldwide will view computers in a completely different light. Effective use of client/server technology requires a new organizational style — that is, a new way of doing business.

2. Business Process Reengineering is redefining the way organizations run. More than just replacing laborious and slow processes with smooth and fast ones, it is redefining jobs, responsibilities, missions, and broad corporate cultures. Business Process Reengineering requires vastly different information technology. Without question, BPR isn't possible without new computer systems, and those new systems have to be built in different ways from all past computer systems.

So there you have it: a technical change that requires new ways of doing business and a business change that requires new technology. Which comes first? Which is more fundamental? Is there a way to know where to start? That's what this chapter and the rest of the book are all about.

FREEDOM: THE NEED FOR SELF-CONTROL

In Chapter 1, I used the matrix in Table 3-1 to talk about the problems with downsizing, rightsizing, and focusing on technology alone. For the most part, the focus in that chapter was on the unbearable cost pressures introduced by the need to maintain both mainframe and personal computer infrastructures. With computer budgets triple those of 20 years ago, these cost pressures have created a legitimate crisis, but there's another, more human dimension to the crisis that I only briefly alluded to in Chapter 1.

Table 3-1   Business/Technology Combinations and Their Results

	Same Business Model	*New Business Model*
New Technology	Downsizing	Breakthrough
Same Technology	Tuning	BPR

Personal computers are much easier to use than mainframes. Running an order-entry application in a window on a personal computer screen makes this discrepancy painfully clear. An order-entry form doesn't have the mouse-driven interface, pull-down menus, dialog boxes, or any of the other usability features that characterize the modern graphical spreadsheet or word processor. This aspect of the human crisis came up in Chapter 1. But there's more.

In the mid-1980s, several hundred ordinary office workers were surveyed to determine their personal views of computers and technology. When asked about the term *personal computers*, these office workers without exception instantly thought of two words. The first word, not surprisingly, was *friendliness*. They did not view personal computers as threatening even though many of the same respondents did admit to concerns about learning to use these friendly machines. The second word explains why friendliness transcended any potential fear. That second word was *freedom*. In the minds of the surveyed population, personal computers provide users with the freedom to control their lives and the freedom to use that computer power in the way that they feel is best.

PEOPLE (AND DOGS) NEED TO BE IN CONTROL

Martin Seligman is a professor and psychologist who has studied the causes and treatment of depression for several decades. In *Learned Optimism* (Knopf, 1990), he describes a series of experiments, carried out in the 1960s, that first gave him a clue to the importance of feeling *in control*. To help you understand the importance of this feeling of being in control, it's worth describing one of those early experiments that lead Seligman to his breakthrough discoveries.

The experiment has two parts: one in which training takes place and the other during which results are measured. During the training phase, dogs are split into three groups. One group is placed into cages where light shocks are administered. The dogs can avoid the shocks by pressing a button with their noses whenever they hear a sound that comes just before the shocks. This group of dogs typically learns very quickly to avoid being shocked. The second group of dogs receives shocks at the same time as the first group but has no way of avoiding or turning off the shocks. The third group of dogs receives no shocks at all during this first phase of the experiment.

In the second part of the experiment, all three groups of dogs are placed into cages divided into two parts by a low barrier. The experimenters administer shocks preceded by the ringing of a bell. The dogs can avoid the shocks simply by jumping over the barrier. As you'd expect, the first and third groups of dogs learn quickly to jump over the barrier when the bell rings. The second group of dogs, the ones who were unavoidably shocked, lie down in their cage, whimper, and simply accept the shocks they receive without trying any of the behaviors that would prevent the shocks.

Can dogs really get depressed? Who knows? What Seligman does go on to show in his published works is that learned helplessness in people is directly linked to depression. In addition, he shows that optimism, which can be learned, is fundamental to both happiness (or at least lack of depression) and mental health.

Throughout history, revolutions have been fought in the quest for personal freedom. In the workplace, the entire point of the movement toward empowerment and self-management is that individuals who control their own lives feel better and produce better results.

COMPUTERS AND PERSONAL FREEDOM

The personal computer is the first computer that individuals own and control. Once exposed to VisiCalc, many managers knew immediately that they would never do a budget by hand again. Even if it meant sneaking in the acquisition of an Apple II, Osborne, or IBM PC as some form of office appliance or furniture, those managers knew that they would find a way to get that computer into the office. And once in the office, that personal computer was *theirs*. Nobody told those managers how to use their computers, what software to run on it, or anything else about the use of those personal computers. Those managers, by using their personal computers, were in control of their own lives.

The tripling of computer budgets in companies large and small was not a matter of choice. Certainly every expenditure on the mainframe side of the house was carefully considered and controlled. The acquisition of all those personal computers, the software, and even the networks that eventually grew up around them occurred whether upper management liked it or not. Because computers gave users increased control over their lives, users did whatever they had to do to acquire those machines.

To really understand the power of this phenomenon, consider the success, or lack thereof, of attempts to standardize on software in large organizations. As users acquired spreadsheets, word processors, databases, and project managers, support started becoming a real issue. In addition, the cost of the software itself eventually grew to the point at which central purchasing, control, and vendor negotiation made too much sense to ignore. The natural reaction of most large organizations was to try standardizing on as small a set of hardware and software products as possible. Given a standard list of products, support could be simplified, better prices could be negotiated, and perhaps the whole messy situation could be brought under control.

In general, most computer purchases are *centrally funded.* Mainframes are always bought by companies in some central way; few individuals have enough money either personally or in their departmental budgets to buy a mainframe. In the mid-1980s, even though standardization was starting to become popular, most personal computer software was *individually funded.* Most personal computer software was bought by individuals either personally or out of an individual departmental budget. Even today, thousands of copies of spreadsheets are bought on personal credit cards and then later charged to expense reports. Other copies are bought by mail order and paid for with miscellaneous expense checks. If the process of charging the company gets too complicated, most office workers will buy a $300 (street price) tool themselves if the gain appears high enough.

The phrase "central purchasing" immediately brings to mind pictures of products being delivered by the truckload to immense central shipping docks. Surprisingly, the dealers who specialize in selling to Fortune 500 companies (dealers such as Corporate Software, 800 Software, and Software Spectrum) report that their average order size is only four units. Big companies may buy millions of dollars of software per year, but even these big companies buy that software three or four units at a time. Those three or four unit orders are all based on personal decisions made by individuals who need particular products at particular times.

As a result, even in big organizations, standardization doesn't work when it comes to software. Some degree of standardization is possible, but only after the fact. Rather than carefully studying the available software products and then analytically picking the best tool or the best vendor, an organization really has to wait until the users vote with their pocketbooks. When the users have picked the products they want to use, the organization can then standardize on those products as the ones that will get the most and best support.

It is because of the very power of the personal computer freedom movement that computers like the Macintosh became successful. When Apple introduced the Macintosh in the early 1980s, the IBM PC had already dominated the corporate computer world so completely that most observers gave Apple no chance of success with the Mac. After all, the IBM PC was a good computer with a wealth of software to go with it, and IBM was the choice everybody felt safe with. Companies large and small were quick to endorse the IBM PC as the safe standard — the one they would support and the only one users should buy.

Nonetheless, because computer purchases are *individually directed* and in spite of active opposition from most large organizations, the Mac succeeded beyond anybody's expectations on a completely grass-roots basis. As users tested the Mac's features and produced visibly better results, other users exercised their personal freedom to select computer tools, and the Mac took off.

Again and again, this personal freedom has allowed products like WordPerfect, NetWare, and Paradox to appeal to individual tastes, build a following, and take off. On a larger scale, the expression of personal freedom through the choice of personal computer tools has made the growth of the personal computer budget completely inevitable for organizations of all sizes.

IS THE REVOLUTION ABOUT THE CLIENT?

If the spread of personal computers sitting on desktops is such a powerful movement, then perhaps the computer revolution of the 1990s is about those personal computers? In the client/server world, those personal computers are called *clients*. A client is a kind of customer, a customer who uses *services*. Stores have customers who buy physical products. Lawyers, architects, designers, and accountants have clients who buy services rather than tangible products. A desktop or notebook personal computer is a client for the services provided by mainframes, servers, minicomputers, and other shared computers. In client/server technospeak, it's obvious that the computer revolution of the 1990s is about the client.

The client is certainly a major driver in today's computer revolution. It is the box that is bringing the revolution in front of the faces of tens of millions of previously uninterested individuals. The client is not only in their faces, it is also showing them a future that is dramatically different than the computer world of the past: an environment that promotes personal choice, personal freedom, and applications that are increasingly easy to understand. Most of all, the future promises a world in which users are in control. That world of clients, however, is *not* what the computer revolution of the 1990s is about.

Spreadsheets and word processors may make individuals more productive, but they don't pay for themselves. More importantly, personal productivity tools do not, have not, and will not by themselves change the way organizations work. They may enrich individual jobs and even make life a little more fun, but by themselves, neither personal computers nor their applications truly empower people. If personal computers by themselves were going to significantly accelerate the shift to self-managed teams, surely that shift would already be visible. Read any book about the business revolution, empowered individuals, and self-managed teams, and you'll find that personal computers are not even mentioned.

But what about all the radical changes that the increased use of personal computers introduced? What about all the dissatisfaction people feel when they compare the order-entry application of the past with the personal computer application of today? What about the unbearably high costs of supporting both personal and corporate computers? Don't all of those factors involve personal computers and clients?

YOU CAN'T FOOL ALL THE PEOPLE ALL THE TIME

It is true that most users are dissatisfied with the user interface of mainframe based, terminal-oriented applications. As a result, it is easy to conclude that replacing the user interface will make users happier and more productive. Aside from eliminating complaints, there is a major motivation driving this approach. Most large organizations are run by and around mainframes. Over the past 30 years, billions of dollars have been invested in writing the applications that run on those big computers. The cost of those applications and the cost of potentially converting them dwarfs both the cost of the mainframes themselves *and* any potential cost savings from simply replacing mainframes with personal computers. If there is a way, though, to move all those mainframe applications into the future by providing them with modern, graphical front ends, then the investment in application code can be preserved, the organization can keep running without disruption, and users will be happy.

Technically, putting a friendly-looking, graphical front end on mainframe applications is both feasible and relatively easy to do. A variety of tools, evocatively named *screen scrapers,* have been developed to make this job quick, easy, and painless.

A terminal-based application functions by displaying forms, one by one, on the screen of a terminal. The personal computer is capable of fooling the mainframe and acting like a terminal so that the mainframe application can't even tell that it is talking to a personal computer. A screen scraper is a piece of software sitting inside the personal computer that intercepts the forms intended to be shown to the user and makes them available for conversion. Conceptually, the screen scraper scrapes the form off the screen just as a person might scrape wallpaper off a wall.

After the form is scraped, these screen-scraping tools can actually manipulate it in very sophisticated ways with very little work. A field that calls for a product code can be converted into a scrolling list that allows the user to see all the potential product codes, choose the correct one with a mouse, and send the entry back to the mainframe. Features like pull-down menus, mouse support, radio buttons, color, and multiple windows can be added to a 25-year-old application in just a few hours work per form. Best of all, after everything is converted, the mainframe can't tell the difference.

At first glance, an application properly redesigned with a screen scraper looks totally different. The application is often referred to as having a *graphical veneer.* As a piece of particle board can be made to look like solid oak by gluing a veneer onto it, a programmer can make a mainframe application look like it uses a completely modern graphical interface. There are problems with this approach, though. To really understand them, an example is required.

A large midwestern organization decided to rewrite a 20-year-old application, moving completely to a client/server approach. The application, based around two mainframes with several thousand terminals, processed millions of transactions per day.

Not surprisingly, the job of rewriting the application was projected to take several years. As a first step, the MIS department decided to put a graphical front end on the existing application. With this improvement, the users and customer service representatives around the country could gain some immediate benefits.

After four months of work, the first step in building the graphical veneer was complete. The programmers altered the order-entry application, an application that previously consisted of 93 forms designed to be displayed on the screen one at a time. They converted the 93 forms into 81 graphical displays designed to run in a color, mouse-driven environment based on Microsoft Windows. Management brought in a representative group of users to see and test the new user interface.

At first, the users were very excited. The new interface looked very nice; many functions were simpler to understand; less memorization was required; and the whole thing just plain looked better. After this initial reaction, the group of users went away for two days to really test out the new system. After less than a day, they returned not looking very happy.

The first thing the users discovered was that the new system was not really new, which was true because none of the code on the mainframe had been changed at all. Although a few steps had been streamlined and some functions were more self-explanatory, the fundamental flow and operation of the original was unchanged.

Even though the basic operation of the system wasn't different, the external appearance was *totally changed*. The application, used by several thousand customer service representatives around the country, depended heavily on an extensive training program, carefully developed documentation, and a sophisticated multilevel help center. All of these supports kept thousands of service reps productive all the time, even in the face of employee turnover, policy changes, and unexpected problems. By changing the external appearance of the system so completely, the MIS department made obsolete their documentation, training programs, help protocols, and problem determination procedures so painfully built up over the years. The cost of rebuilding all that surrounding infrastructure made the cost of building the graphical veneer appear insignificant in comparison.

Even worse, all the really big problems in the system — missing functionality and built-in inflexibility — were still present. "Make it better" is what the users said. "We did" was the response of the team that built the veneer. "Did not." "Did too." You get the picture.

Graphical veneers are designed to fool users. They make old applications *appear* new. In the process, they do bring some benefits in terms of simplification and ease of use. But as Abraham Lincoln said, "You may fool all the people some of the time; you can even fool some of the people all the time; but you can't fool all of the people all the time." Screen scrapers are a fine first step, but that's all they are. Really significant change requires more. The reason is simple: the client is a major catalyst for change, but the real revolution is not about the client.

INFORMATION AT YOUR FINGERTIPS

Bill Gates, the founder of Microsoft and one of the true visionaries of the computer industry, is blessed with an ability to predict future technological trends. For most of the 1980s, he believed that the quest for graphical applications with increased power and ease of use was the chief challenge confronting the industry. In the early 1990s, he forecast that the new challenge will be *putting information at people's fingertips*. Today, the phrase *information at your fingertips* (*IAYF* for short) has become Microsoft's slogan of the decade, but what does it entail?

In the early days of computers, users were excited to be able to build small spreadsheets and write better memos with their word processors. If developing a budget or forecast meant reentering information generated by another, often bigger computer, users didn't care. The net result was still far faster than doing the same work by hand. As time passed, spreadsheets got bigger as people packed more and more information into them, and consequently, user requirements began to change.

Today, users still want to use spreadsheets, project managers, and desktop databases to analyze information, but they no longer want to enter all that information by hand. Why can't that information be sucked directly out of the mainframe, resulting in analysis based on up-to-date data? Once generated, why can't a forecast be immediately shared with other organization-wide users so that they can refine and build on the data without having to reenter any information? People want the computers on their desks to be gateways to information located all over the world; they want to combine data from many sources quickly and easily. That's what I mean by information at your fingertips. Getting it is a problem.

WHY ACCESS (AND PARADOX AND dBASE) HAS NO ACCESS

Since about 1987, marketing surveys of users have revealed that access to corporate data is at the top of everybody's list of desired features. Sure, spreadsheets and graphics packages should continue to get better, but for most users, they're already good enough. Most users have no problem manipulating or presenting information effectively. They simply want better access to information.

I've illustrated the problem in Figure 3-1. In most organizations, all the data sits in either the center ring or the outer ring. The center represents all the painstakingly collected and carefully guarded data sitting in corporate databases. Ordinary users are allowed to access that data through specially written query programs — programs that allow for no flexibility at all. The outer ring consists of all the data sitting on users' desktops. In many companies, there is now as much data sitting here as in the central databases. The data on the desktop is generally entered by hand, completely unshared, and usually out-of-date as soon as it's entered. What's missing is any data in the middle ring. That middle ring consists of data that is the property of the workgroup, team, or department. Many users can share and update such data, but in most companies, that middle ring just doesn't exist.

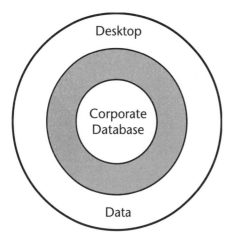

Figure 3-1: Finding the data in an organization.

In fact, there is no easy way to create workgroup-level data, so the middle ring actually represents a kind of barrier, an impermeable wall separating the users and their desktop computers from the consistent, up-to-date data sitting in the corporate mainframe. Why does this barrier exist?

The computer industry is certainly aware that users have a need to access data in corporate databases. A variety of desktop databases such as Access, Paradox, dBASE IV, and Approach have been built specifically to facilitate such access. These desktop products in turn connect to a variety of *gateway* products that typically run on servers to provide the connectivity required to talk to the mainframes and their database software. Paradox, Access, and the other products speak *SQL (structured query language)* for their users. They pipe this language through to the mainframe and then accept the returned result, hiding the entire complex process from the individuals who initiated the original information request. The software *now available* allows users to access information, but this very access leads to another completely different problem.

Historically, when talking to audiences that include the operational staff responsible for mainframe databases, I've frequently asked them how they feel about users generating ad hoc queries that run against the databases in their care. The usual response is either an uncomfortable silence or sometimes a strained giggle. Why? Because these audiences find the very idea beyond belief that users might be allowed, let alone encouraged, to run queries generated on the fly against production databases.

Most queries of any interest contain aggregates of one form or another. An aggregate is a sum, an average, a count, or any function that requires the application of an arithmetic operation against *every record* in the database. Who's the biggest customer? How many red widgets did the company sell last year? What are the average sales by salesperson by territory? All of these questions and more require the computation of aggregates against either entire databases or major portions of those databases. The problem is that production databases are shared by hundreds or thousands of users all working on the same mainframe. Ad hoc queries bring mainframes to their knees because they often require access to large parts of the database. When the mainframe comes to its knees, the business literally stops running. Worst of all, if users are creating their own queries, then nobody can predict the load on the computer. As a result, not only will the mainframe grind to a halt, but it won't even be possible to predict or schedule that halt. That's obviously not an acceptable situation in a production environment. So in practice, dBASE, Access, and Paradox users are just not allowed to access the real data.

YOU'RE RESPONSIBLE — JUST DON'T ASK ANY QUESTIONS

Picture this conversation: you're encouraging a group of customer service representatives to become empowered. These people are the same ones who were so unhappy with the graphical veneer. "You are responsible for customer satisfaction," you tell them. "Make decisions, make exceptions, do what it takes, and don't depend on anybody else to solve the customer's problems." A hand goes up. "Can we have access to customer histories? Can we access the information required to understand why a customer order has been refused by the credit department? Can we tell customers why their shipment is late or why they're on shipment hold?" You uncomfortably acknowledge the problem and promise to check with MIS. The MIS department starts talking about application backlogs, overloaded mainframes, and the complexity of handling changes to applications written 20 years ago. So you're in a bind. You want to empower the service reps, but it seems impossible to provide them with the information required to solve customer problems. You can offer only responsibility without the ability to get needed information — responsibility without authority. That's hardly empowering.

Even unlimited ad hoc access to data is not enough for true empowerment. A large oil company sells approximately a billion dollars of product annually through a group of independent sales agents who represent separate companies with no direct connection to the oil company. Each time an agent makes a sale to one of his or her customers, the price for the sale is set by the company so that the hourly fluctuations in spot oil prices can be adequately accommodated. This form of pricing requires that the sales agents send all orders to the oil company for processing. Customers receive their invoices from the oil company, not from the sales agents. Over time, the process of entering and reentering the orders led to an increasingly high error rate. Customers who received bills with serious mistakes sent them back, and they became annoyed at the perceived poor service. Every year, the agents asked the company for two changes in their overall operation. First, they asked for the ability to generate bills themselves. And second, they asked for the ability to customize the billing program to meet the unique needs of their particular marketplaces. After all, each agent represented a different class of customer, and that was the reason for selling through independent agents in the first place. But the agents were all being forced to carry out business in a uniform fashion. Each year, right after the agents asked for custom billing and more control, the oil company carefully explained to them why no central system could accommodate the huge number of variations required to meet the needs of the wide variety of market segments the agents covered. Stalemate. And certainly not empowerment. The catch here is that the agents were asking not just for ad hoc *access* to data, but also for customized programs for *changing* the data. If MIS staffs have trouble believing in the possibility of ad hoc access to data, they can't even begin to comprehend the concept of customized changes. The programs that change the information in mainframe databases are the most carefully tested, most jealously guarded, innermost of inner circles in the MIS temple.

INTO THE MIDDLE RING

What is the solution to the challenge of filling that middle ring? How can desktop users be provided with ad hoc data access without killing the mainframe? And unimaginable as it may be, isn't there some way that agents, workgroups, and self-managed teams can customize the programs that update the data without breaking the entire database infrastructure built up by MIS? The answer to both questions depends on a new element: the server.

Why can't users run ad hoc queries and ask any question of the database they want? Because it will kill the mainframe. How about if there were more mainframes? Obviously, if there were enough mainframes, users could ask any questions they want. Of course, mainframes are expensive, so this might all be easier said than done. Just adding one or two mainframes still isn't enough. For example, it's easy to imagine having a mainframe for production use and another mainframe just to handle ad hoc queries. Easy to imagine but still far from adequate. Any single user running complex queries could steal the new mainframe away from all the other users. So adding two or three or four new mainframes may not be enough.

Personal computers really have become almost as powerful as mainframes. A shared personal computer with a copy of the mainframe database can answer complex ad hoc queries as easily as a mainframe. Because that personal computer is shared by only a small number of users, it may well answer those questions faster than a mainframe. Also, a personal computer may cost only $5,000, $10,000, or $20,000. Clearly, inexpensive computers can be purchased by the dozens or even the hundreds. Every workgroup can have its own server; large teams can even have several servers. Servers provide access to shared data to several desktop computers, all connected together over a network.

A server can solve the first part of the problem — providing ad hoc access. Remember the case of the customer service representatives with the 20-year-old mainframe application and the new graphical veneer? After careful self-examination, the MIS department decided to rewrite part of the order-entry system even before the larger rewrite of the entire mainframe application was close to complete. For the second rewrite of the user interface to the order-entry application, MIS made some effective changes. Even though the core order-entry software on the mainframe was to remain unchanged, a great deal of the data about customers, products, and orders was downloaded to regional servers located in the field. The servers contained copies of the data; all the master updates were still centralized on the mainframe. The use of servers provided a way of making the system better.

The application interface, originally consisting of 93 forms and then converted to 81 window displays, underwent another rewrite. This time, instead of a forms-oriented approach, MIS split the application into two parts. The actual order-entry forms, consisting of only six screens, were left unchanged. The other 75 screens — designed to allow service reps to answer questions about products and orders — were completely redesigned. Instead of providing specific screens to answer particular preselected questions, the designers provided the service reps with a series of general purpose query tools for poking around through the entire database of customers, products, and orders. The more general query tool was more powerful, and it involved far fewer screens. In fact, this third version of the application consisted of only 27 screens. Of course, these screens were far more interactive than were the previous 81 or 93 forms. They made extensive use of pop-up windows, drop-down lists, and the like.

When first exposed to the again-rewritten system, the service reps were shocked and discouraged. The new screens, with their dynamic interaction and fluid screen layouts, looked complex and forbidding. Still, they agreed to go away and give the new software a real trial. This time, after two days, the users came back grinning from ear to ear.

The representatives reported that the new screens were not nearly as complex as they first appeared. Each screen packed in a great deal of information and represented an entire world of query-based exploration, but the options available at any given point in time were relatively self-explanatory. In addition, the reps had discovered a new idea. The query tools lent themselves to experimentation. In the old system of fixed forms, experimentation was an alien concept. Either a specific form existed to answer a particular question or the question could not be handled. The new system actually encouraged experimentation. The users felt that the new system might even be fun! After several hours, they concluded that the new system was at least as easy to use as the old one.

Then something really interesting happened. The service reps had elected to try their new system in parallel to the old one. Sitting next to service reps entering orders with the old system at terminals, other reps entered the same orders into the new system at personal computers. At first, the new system was painful to use. It wasn't even possible to keep up with the old system as the reps learned the new software. After a while, the two systems seemed comparable. Then the breakthrough occurred. A customer's order was rejected by the old system. The customer insisted that someone had made a mistake, but the old system provided no way of finding out the reason for the refusal. As the rep handling this customer was about to hang up, his parallel buddy signaled him to hold on. Using the new system and its general query tools, the two reps quickly determined that the customer was on hold because of a late payment. The customer, who had systematically paid all bills on time for over 20 years, was over his credit limit by only $42. The reps made an on-the-spot exception, the order was processed, and the customer was thrilled. Guess what these prospective users spent the next two days doing? They looked for problems and solved them with their new-found access to data. Even without a direct connection to the real system, the new system of servers, by allowing its users to ask questions, empowered them to solve customer problems.

Obviously, the new system depends totally on having plenty of cheap servers. The alternative, dozens of mainframes, would never have been cost effective. But that's the point. On a small scale, by redesigning the business process to allow service reps unlimited access to data along with the authority to make exceptions to company rules, a self-regulating process is created. That process could not exist without PC-based server technology. The new process coupled with the new technology creates a breakthrough in customer satisfaction (see Table 3-2).

**Table 3-2   Business/Technology Combinations
and Their Results**

	Same Business Model	*New Business Model*
New Technology	Downsizing	Breakthrough
Same Technology	Tuning	BPR

CLIENT/SERVER: IT'S ABOUT THE SERVER

What about the case in which the users need to not only access the data in unique ways, but also change it on a custom basis? Why can't users and teams be allowed to customize applications that change the data? Programming is hard, so most users might never be able to build the programs that make such customization possible. But that's not the reason. In fact, desktop databases that make accessing data easy — for example, Approach, Paradox, and Access — also make it easy to write programs to change that data. Writing those kinds of programs may still require some technical talent, but the task is now simple enough that thousands of consultants and departmental power users are more than up to the task. So the issue is neither complexity nor lack of tools.

In Chapter 2, I associated bureaucracy with three fundamental organizational needs: planning, coordination, and policy enforcement. Two of those, coordination of scarce resources and consistent policy enforcement, essentially amounted to the implementation of business rules. A large part of the mainframe's job is enforcing those rules. In fact, why don't users get to write programs that change data in the corporate database? Because the programs they write can't be guaranteed to obey the company's business rules. Because users don't have the detailed training to know what all those business rules are, their programs that change data are *guaranteed* to break company rules. The corporate database represents information that has been carefully collected in a way that ensures that no rules have been broken and all data is consistent. So allowing users to change data on their own may render the entire database useless. Pretty horrifying.

The server changes that entire picture. Servers don't sit on desktops. They don't belong to any particular user. In fact, servers can be locked up in a computer room, secured in a wiring closet, or even if they're in the office, protected from users by lock and key. The server is the first computer that can be the property of *both* the workgroup and the corporation as a whole. MIS can program the server to enforce business rules. That enforcement can be built in so that when teams write their own applications, any database changes that break the rules are rejected. Teams can write their own applications by studying the elaborate documentation describing all the company's rules; or they can, like most users, write their applications pretending that no rules exist. Either way, if their application breaks rules, the application won't run. When the application is fixed so that it doesn't break any rules, then it will run.

Taking advantage of this approach, the oil company in the earlier example wrote a server-based application that allowed agents to enter orders directly. Pricing was still done centrally through a communication link with the central mainframe. The servers, however, produced the actual invoices. Because the servers eliminated the need for the manual reentry of orders, errors virtually disappeared, a fact that both the customers and the agents immediately appreciated. The savings associated with the elimination of the reentry paid for most of the system in less than a year. Best of all, within six months of the installation of the system, over half of the agents developed both customized billing programs and customized data-driven marketing programs. Costs went down, market share went up, and everybody was happy. The server allowed the oil company to retain centralized control over pricing and some other aspects of billing while still allowing the individual sales agents to access data and even modify that data in a customized fashion.

What is client/server about? Client/server is primarily about the server:

1. Distribution of processing

2. Distribution of data

3. Graphical user interface

The server allows data to be distributed across many computers and other servers so that self-managed teams and empowered employees can ask questions often and in complex ways. The server also allows processing to be distributed out to the teams so that they can customize applications to meet their particular needs while still safeguarding company business rules. Without the server, both those forms of distribution are impossible.

Of course, client/server is about the client, too. It's third on the list. Having a graphical user interface is important. Without it, applications are too hard to learn and use. If, however, one element had to be dropped off the list, graphical clients, for all their visible appeal, would disappear before distribution of data or distribution of processing. Mainframes with graphical veneers fool people for a short period of time, but in the long term, they don't lead to any business or organizational revolutions. Providing teams and individuals with unlimited access to data and the ability to customize business procedures to meet their local needs does lead to revolution. BPR and TQM call for these changes. For the best possible revolution, though, try to meet the needs of both the client and the server.

BUSINESS REVOLUTION, TECHNICAL REVOLUTION

In the book *Reengineering the Corporation*, Michael Hammer and James Champy devote a single chapter to the role of information technology. Every example of reengineering in the book revolves around some critical change in the use of that technology. Ford redesigned its accounts payable department, eliminating the need for vendors to invoice the company for products it purchases. After a product is ordered, a computer database keeps track of the orders so that incoming shipments can be inspected and accepted at the time of arrival. When they're accepted, payment is initiated automatically. Now 125 people do the work that previously required 500. In another example, at IBM credit, a computer system collects the information and business rules required to process a loan application so that a single individual could process the entire application with no outside assistance. In the Ford system, the computer helps manage data. In the IBM system, the computer helps to manage all the rules applying to each loan situation. The results are equally dramatic: loan processing time was slashed from seven days to four hours. These examples illustrate the role of computer technology in making BPR possible. What is not so obvious is that in order to really succeed, BPR requires a change in technology.

The change is a direct consequence of the shift to self-regulating processes and self-managed teams. Self-managed teams are generally not very large — typically 5 to 12 people in size. The point is to replace task-oriented jobs with slightly larger, self-regulating processes. If the processes and their teams get too big, then they either can't be truly self-regulating or they just have to be divided up again. Self-managed teams, in turn, need access to data and the ability to customize business procedures. Both require access to more flexible computer resources than are possible in a centralized environment.

An insurance company faced with escalating costs in its health care program decided to focus on converting its physicians into self-managed teams. As part of his or her practice, each physician was given more control over the treatments prescribed to patients. No longer would anyone force these practitioners to ask for permission each time a procedure or treatment seemed advisable. At the same time, the company provided the doctors with profitability targets along with incentives to make those targets happen. The problem was that the doctors needed the ability to access historical data on the fly as they made treatment decisions. They also wanted the ability to customize their office procedures to streamline common operations. Although the doctors' requirements could have been accommodated on the existing mainframe-based systems, the result would have been a need for one mainframe per 20 doctors. The insurance company decided to go with easily affordable, distributed servers that provide the same service. The results included lower costs, better health care, more productive doctors, and a more profitable insurance company.

This example is very similar to the others I discuss in this chapter. Companies need to provide individual teams and departments with the ability to access corporate data while allowing them to change some of that data to meet their local needs. Banks, insurance companies, retail chains, distributors, travel agencies, hotels, and many other businesses all face the same problems. Self-managed teams need self-managed databases and applications. Servers with distributed databases are the key to making this happen.

The new organization calls for new technology; the new technology requires new organizational structures to pay for the change. Put the two together, and a breakthrough will happen.

A Different World

Today, there are about 30,000 mainframes spread around the world — probably as many mainframes as there will ever be. In addition, there are approximately 300,000 super mini-computers, such as the AS 400 and the larger VAXes, that run smaller companies and departments of larger companies. Altogether, the larger companies of the world are run by about 350,000 large computers of various kinds. In thinking about the computer revolution of the 1990s, most prognosticators assume that clients and servers will replace those big computers. Being generous, that assumption would imply replacing or augmenting 350,000 big computers with perhaps one or two million servers.

Each of the big computers is sold through a direct sales force. Because each big computer represents a highly specialized technology, each requires extensive installation and support. For example, CICS, one of the major components of the IBM operating system, can be installed only by either IBM personnel or highly trained customer-employed gurus whose only job is to keep it running. Changes to big systems won't be simple.

The United States Congress recently passed a law providing family leave under special circumstances to all employees working for companies with more than 50 workers. In reporting on this statute, the August 15, 1993, issue of the *New York Times* drew on census and Bureau of Labor data and found that only 4 percent of American companies had over 50 employees. Of course, this 4 percent of the corporate sector represents 34 percent of the workers in the United States. Putting this another way, 66 percent of working Americans work for companies with fewer than 50 employees.

These companies obviously don't have mainframes or super minicomputers, but many have computer systems or will have them by the end of the decade. So how many servers will there be in the near future?

In the United States alone, there are over 11 million business establishments. A business establishment is a location that at least one worker reports to on a full-time basis. By the turn of the century or shortly thereafter, every business establishment in the country and most of the business establishments in the rest of the world will have at least one computer. Each establishment is likely to have a server, too. In small locations, the server and the desktop computer may be the same. In larger establishments, the server will be separate and dedicated, and in the largest establishments, there may be many servers.

These servers will process orders, manage inventory, schedule shipments, balance accounts, reserve seats, issue paychecks, and carry out all of the hundreds of other tasks required to keep an organization running. Servers will run around the clock at most establishments, doing work even when no employee is present to initiate new requests. The servers of the world will be the brains and nervous systems of the organizations around them. Servants of their local self-managed teams, these servers will help create a world of self-regulating processes and empowered employees.

In such a world, information at your fingertips will be reality, but the computer industry that helped make it real will be quite different from what it is today. If there are currently 11 million business establishments in the United States and probably 30 million worldwide, then the world of the future is likely to have from 50 million to 100 million servers.

A direct sales force cannot sell 50 million servers, and all of them can't be installed and maintained by a few carefully trained gurus. Servers and the software that makes them run will become the next major packaged-product boom driving change and growth in the computer industry. To get there, though, servers have to become more like everyday appliances.

The business process revolution combined with the client/server revolution will cause major changes. The road to change is a little hard to predict, but the final result, at least today, seems relatively clear.

The rest of this book describes the underlying technology that will make all the changes possible. First, I will describe and explain the technical elements of the client/server world. After presenting that information, I describe the ways in which the client/server applications of the future will be designed.

PART II

THE TECHNOLOGY: DEMYSTIFYING COMPUTERS AND NETWORKS

Seven big chapters: this is by far the most ambitious part of the book. Should you read it? For both technical and nontechnical readers the answer is an absolute yes. For the same reasons and for different reasons. The common reason is that gaining an understanding of the technology *and the reasons for that technology* will provide the means for truly participating in the coming revolution.

FOR THE NONTECHNICAL READER

One reason you might decide to not read Part II is because you're afraid it's too hard to understand. Technology, however, can be explained at many different levels. Some of these levels are too abstract to be useful; some are too detailed to be understandable. The trick is striking the right balance.

That's what Part II is about for non-technical readers: taking important computer concepts, picking the ones that matter, and explaining each of them in a few minutes based on common sense. Why does it take seven chapters? Because the computer industry has developed some amazing and amazingly useful concepts in 40 years. Simply put, there are seven chapters of explanation because there are seven chapters of material *worth* explaining.

FOR THE TECHNICAL READER

Never trust anyone over thirty. That was the motto of the generation growing up in the '60s. And that is the motto of many personal computer-based developers who just don't know what to think about mainframes, databases, and all the professionals who work with them.

Never trust anyone under thirty. That's what many of those mainframe-based professionals think about the undisciplined, inexperienced youngsters producing all those flashy (but shallow) applications running little toy PCs.

One reason for technical people to read Part II is because it builds some bridges between these two camps. You can't afford to choose between the large application-centered, database-oriented world of the mainframe, and the personally focused, graphical world of the PC. You need them both, and bridges are required to make that fusion happen.

The *American Heritage Dictionary* defines *philosophy* as "the critique and analysis of fundamental beliefs as they come to be conceptualized and formulated." Many of the fundamental beliefs driving the computer industry need that kind of critique and analysis much more frequently than is normally the case today. Can PCs replace mainframes? That question can't be answered rationally until some other questions are asked. What makes a mainframe different? Is it just a bigger PC, or is a PC just a smaller mainframe? What about LANs — where do they fit into this picture?

The same dictionary also talks about *philosophy* in terms of investigating the causes and laws underlying reality. That's what the next seven chapters are about.

CHAPTER 4

GUI, UI — CAN COMPUTERS BE USABLE?

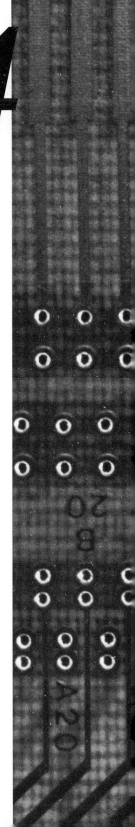

Computers are hard to use. Learning to use them in the first place is hard, but even after months of experience, many users still have trouble with common tasks that should be easy to accomplish. VCRs are hard to use, too. Cars are not. Yet a car — particularly its entertainment system, power windows, and seven-way seats — is at least as complex as a VCR, and most computer applications should be approachable by any adult who can drive. Consider the following three challenges:

✦ Flying to a foreign country with a different language, renting a car, and getting to a new destination at night.

✦ Buying a new VCR and immediately programming it to record a show running the following night.

✦ Buying a computer application (a project-management package, for example) and using it to plan a short vacation trip.

In theory, the first task ought to be the most difficult, and the third task should be the easiest. After all, the computer application involves no new hardware, talks to you in English, and is designed to actively help its users. Yet, without a doubt, most adults would be guaranteed to succeed at the first task, would have concerns about the second, and would be highly skeptical about their probability of successfully using the new software product.

THE INTIMIDATING INTERFACE

Why would noncomputer tasks be so much less threatening? Why does the little challenge in the last paragraph strike a resonant chord with so many people? Because cars, electronic appliances, and most other technical products that people use every day have much more mature packaging than computers. To be more precise, although you don't normally think of a car as having a *user interface*, it does. And the user interface of a car, after 90 years of development, is far more mature than the user interface of most computer applications. The car's user interface, and the user interface of the highways — street signs, traffic lights, and so on — have become so refined that even driving in a foreign country has become possible with no advance training. The challenge is to make computers as nonthreatening and easy to use as any other appliance, and the way to get there is to focus on the user interface, or the *UI*.

Computers have become dramatically simpler to use in the last decade. Mainframe systems were once so forbidding that only systems professionals and highly trained end users could be trusted to work with them. Yet today, children teach themselves to use Macintoshes and Windows-based PCs every day. Something has changed, and yet, as the three previous tasks show, more change is required before computers become as easy to use as they should be. Some of that change, both in the past and in the future, revolves around the computers themselves — the hardware — and much more around the programmers who build the software that runs on those computers.

Computers have become much simpler to use over the past ten years, yet many people still find them forbiddingly incomprehensible. "Intuitive" interfaces turn out to be anything but intuitive when put to the acid test of the real world. Does this mean that computers can never be made *really* approachable? Or are personal computers as easy to use as they're ever going to be — which makes the problem cultural?

IT'S NOT YOUR FAULT

Don't blame yourself just yet. Computers still have a long way to go. I make this statement on the basis of simply watching trained computer professionals struggle with supposedly state-of-the-art interfaces and applications. Computer software — personal computer software, in particular — is much easier to use today than ever before. At the same time, however, even sophisticated software reviewers, application developers, and other experienced experts often struggle for hours the first time they use any particular package, trying to figure out how to initiate supposedly easy operations. So if normal humans have trouble using computers at times, it's not surprising; there is still a long way to go. Does this mean that computers can never be easy to use? Perhaps. At the same time, in watching children play computer games, administrative assistants produce complex multicolumn newsletters, and managers handle their diaries totally electronically, it's clear that personal computers have become usable in a way that was never the case until very recently.

What makes a personal computer different from a terminal? Why can't a mainframe be as easy to use as a personal computer, *ever?* What is it about the personal computer that virtually necessitates having a computer on every user's desk? The answer to all three questions is the *graphical user interface,* often called the *GUI* (pronounced *gooey*). Understanding GUIs, ironically, is a particular problem for terminal-oriented developers with years of *user interface* (UI) experience. First-time personal computer users, even children, often have a better understanding of what GUIs are about than the systems professionals charged with developing the next generation of graphical applications.

Any discussion of *graphical user interfaces* has to start by considering the reason for making the interface graphical in the first place: providing a powerful and evocative mechanism for computers and users to talk to each other. Broadly, then, the GUIs are a particularly powerful class of *user interfaces* (UIs). The *American Heritage Dictionary* defines an interface as: "1. A surface forming a common boundary between adjacent regions. 2. a. A point at which independent systems or diverse groups interact. b. The device or system by which interaction at an interface is effected." By following this definition, the *user interface* is the boundary between the computer and a person working with or through the computer to carry out some set of tasks. Sometimes the person is telling the computer what to do, and sometimes it's the other way around. Drawing a little further on the definition, the user interface is also a device or system. Specifically, in a personal computer environment, the user interface consists of the screen, the mouse, and the keyboard. In a more advanced system, the user interface might also include speakers, a microphone, and even specialized devices such as pens, eye-movement trackers, and touch-sensitive areas.

Literally speaking, the user interface consists of hardware. However, the hardware is generally the smallest part of the story. *Making computers usable is very hard!* Most of the elements people think of as built-in parts of their personal computers have actually been around for many years, long before personal computers even existed. For example, the color screens, windows, menus, and graphics users stare at so intently have been common since the early '70s. The mouse, too, as a pointing device, was invented in the '60s. Yet word processing packages, until recently, have taken only limited advantage of these hardware elements. Put this problem into perspective by considering the gap between what users can easily conceptualize and what their software tools enable them to do.

GREAT EXPECTATIONS

Every computer user reads books, magazines, newspapers, and newsletters every day. These publications routinely use multiple columns, pictures, and fonts to simplify the presentation of information. Ideally, then, that same user would expect to be able to use an expensive computer and word processor to produce printed material looking like what he or she reads every day. Either by using an example or by saying the words, describing the format of that material is easy: a three-column newsletter, with a picture of the author in the center of the page, with text flowing around it. Ten years ago, such a newsletter could not have been produced with a personal computer. Five years ago, it would have required a combination of specialized software products and considerable training. Finally, in the last two years, word processing software reached the point where most users could build such a newsletter on a normal personal computer with no external training or advice. Yet the appearance of the hardware — the keyboard, the screen, the mouse — has hardly changed during that ten years. Yes, the computers have gotten faster, but that speed has been only an indirect factor. Two other changes *have* occurred that have revolutionized the perception of computers and what they can do:

✦ Standard graphical user interfaces have provided an environment in which new ways of interacting with computers are now possible.

✦ The programmers who build applications have developed an understanding of how those GUI elements can be used to develop a new breed of software that talks to users in ways different from ways of the past.

Most programmers think of GUIs in terms of a small number of immediately recognizable elements: mouse support, pull-down menus, overlapping windows, and pop-up dialog boxes to display errors. Throw in some color and a modicum of pictorial or graphic display, and that must be the whole thing! Applications with this set of features can be built around both terminal-based systems and very low-powered PCs. For example, products for first-time users, such as First Choice and the early versions of Microsoft Works, offered pull-down menus, windows, mouse support, and dialog boxes, all on 8088-based monochrome PCs with 256K of memory or less. At the same time, nobody thought of these applications as graphical. Something must be missing from the definition. Not only that, but the missing elements must somehow require a great deal of computer power because one thing everybody agrees on is that GUIs work well on only fast machines.

A graphical user interface is based on the following four features:

✦ Common user interface

✦ High-resolution, bitmapped, color display

✦ What you see is what you get (WYSIWYG)

✦ Direct manipulation

In turn, moving into a GUI world requires three things:

✦ Hardware that makes these four features possible

✦ System software that makes it easy for application developers to build graphical applications

✦ The broad availability of applications written this way

Today, GUI is the accepted standard in at least three environments: the PC with Windows and with OS/2, the Mac with its own operating system, and on UNIX workstations with several operating systems. The following sections take a look at the characteristics of a GUI, one at a time.

COMMON USER INTERFACES

In the early '80s, it was common for every new application to have its own completely unique user interface defining the basic commands available while using that particular application. The Macintosh was the first mass-market computer to introduce the concept of a common user interface to a wide audience. After several years, market researchers discovered an interesting pattern: Mac users worked with an average of over four different applications each, and PC users tended to limit themselves to an average of only two different applications each. In retrospect, the reasons for this pattern are obvious.

Consider the situation confronting a pre-GUI PC user with a basketful of tools. Perhaps the user starts each day with 1-2-3; the leading non-GUI spreadsheet has a command structure based on a hierarchical menu at the top of the screen. Next, as the user moves to WordPerfect, the screen starts off blank to leave plenty of room for text. WordPerfect then calls for extensive use of function keys, coupled with a menu at the bottom of the screen. dBASE, in turn, uses dot commands and a scrolling style of interaction, and so on.

Each new application requires that the user learn how to control the computer completely from scratch. All the little habits and shortcuts, acquired so painfully over time, are useless when moving to the next application, even if it comes from the same vendor (Paradox, SideKick, and Quattro Pro, for example). Worse, even if the user has the time and patience to struggle through several complete learning curves, imagine how complex it is to keep all the separate interaction modes in context if the user now wants to use the tools in an integrated fashion. Little wonder that, until recently, PC users gave up after learning their first or second application.

The common user interface of a GUI defines a standard way of commanding the computer to do things. The use of pull-down menus, coupled with a help system, enables the user to explore the application, literally discovering commands often without having to read any documentation. Furthermore, because all applications use the same broad structure, after learning how to use that first application, the user has, in many ways, learned to use them all. All of this becomes particularly crucial when you picture several applications, each in its own window, running on the same screen at the same time. Having a common user interface in the multitasking world of the '90s is not only convenient, it's essential.

Making life easy for users through common interfaces requires more than just a standard way of building pull-down menus, displaying windows, and so on. At one level, much of the infrastructure required to have cross-application commonality comes from the underlying operating system: Windows, the Mac, and so on. At this level, the emergence of a small number of standard GUI operating systems has been a huge boon for both users and developers of applications. At another level, building easy-to-understand applications with a high degree of commonality and cross-application integration, requires a high degree of sophistication on the part of both individual developers and the organizations for whom they work.

Standard UIs that are easy to understand across many applications require sophisticated standards. Some of these standards come from industry leaders such as IBM, Microsoft, and Apple. Many others, though, are specific to the needs of each organization as it builds and buys applications. Standards can be specified and enforced at two levels. The ideal is to have all standards supported and enforced by tools that also make designers and developers more productive. At the same time, many critical standards — relating to naming, broad style, and so on — can be expressed only on paper. Either way, to get the most out of GUIs, building on the huge head start already provided by today's windowing systems, every large organization involved in significant development should be thinking carefully about its UI standards.

Common interfaces are important, but they're far from enough; a good GUI is also powerful and intuitive in ways that no terminal-based interface can equal.

GRAPHICAL SUPPORT: VIRTUAL REALITY

Watching a travel agent work with an airline reservation system offers an excellent window into user interfaces of 20 years ago. Computers, at that time, were thought of as working with words and numbers. Naturally, then, the screen attached to the millions of terminals found all over the world was a place where users could display these words and numbers. All the information in such a system appears in the form of characters — either letters or numbers; for this reason, this style of interface has come to be known as *character-based*.

Imagine a passenger reserving a seat on a particular airplane, asking for an aisle seat, just behind the wing, preferably an exit row, and wanting to be as far as possible from the smoking section of the plane. In the world of characters and numbers, the agent sees a seat number — perhaps 23B — and then has to determine in some other way whether that seat is appropriate. With luck, the agent may just know whether B is an aisle seat on this type of aircraft, but what about the other criteria? Perhaps the airline provides each agent with a set of diagrams showing the seat layout in every type of plane. Or the agent can ask the computer a series of questions about the seat. Either way, helping the passenger is a lot of work; but what's the alternative?

BEING THERE

In a graphical world, the screen displays more than characters; it displays pictures, too. When the passenger asks to pick a seat, the agent calls a seat-layout diagram directly onto the screen; it is immediately obvious whether the seat is on an aisle, where it is in relationship to the wing, how far it is from the smoking section, and whether it is an exit row. Rather than give the agent a faster way of asking about the seat, it's now unnecessary to ask at all; the information is visible immediately.

Graphical displays even make it easier to deal with words and numbers. One of the problems with designing a newsletter, for example, is that it is often hard to tell how the page will really look after all the text and pictures are put together. Historically, page-layout software allowed the user to specify the layout, but the result could be seen only after sending the result to the printer. Running back and forth from the printer to the screen quickly becomes tiring and tedious. Moreover, because printing takes a long time, the overall process was expensive in terms of time and materials.

In a graphical world, the computer displays the layout of the printed page directly on the screen. Multiple columns, pictures, and fonts all appear on the screen exactly as they will look when printed. Now, the only reason to send output to the printer is when you're really done with your work.

Being able to display pictorial information directly on the screen makes existing applications dramatically simpler, but it also opens up new classes of applications. For example, a customer service rep can display a map showing a customer's home and the closest service centers or stores to give driving directions over the phone. Such an application might work in a character world, but it would be unimaginably harder to use. Similarly, an architect can display a floor plan and allow clients to directly see the result of moving a wall, a door, or a piece of furniture. More prosaically, 35mm slides can be constructed on the screen, enabling nontechnical managers to build their own graphics, knowing that what they see on the screen is exactly what they will be projecting when their slides are produced.

THE COMPUTERIZED COCKPIT

Underlying all of these examples is a single common principle: virtual reality. Most people have heard of fighter pilots learning to fly in advanced simulators based on the same concept. Wearing a special helmet, the pilot sees two tiny screens, one in front of each eye, projecting lifelike images indistinguishable from those he or she would see sitting in a real cockpit. The pilot's chair, mounted on a special hydraulic system, simulates the acceleration, deceleration, rocking, and twisting the pilot would experience in real flight. Special headphones provide the sounds. Put it all together, and normal civilians get motion sickness in seconds without ever leaving the ground. By providing the pilot with all the sensory inputs he or she would experience in the real world, the simulation creates a *virtually real world.* By simulating reality, pilots can learn to fly while on the ground. Displaying an equivalent set of letters and numbers specifying the status of the airplane at all times would not even come close to being the same. The graphical environment (and, in this case, the physical hydraulic system, too) makes the application work.

The airline-reservation system, the word processor, the customer service system, the architectural program, and the aircraft simulator all have models of the real world in their memory; the computer represents the world in its *head,* so to speak. Virtual reality involves projecting that model of the real world directly for the user. Instead of converting the model of the world into words and numbers, the computer attempts to portray that real world as it is.

In a limited sense, GUIs are a special case of virtual reality at work. By projecting the interior of the plane directly, the computer shows directly where the seats are. By displaying the page as the printer will print it, the computer eliminates all the questions and guesswork associated with getting the final appearance to be right. The map of stores and service locations instantly shows the combination of right and left turns that gets the customer to his or her destination, and so on.

In the computer world, GUI as virtual reality is often referred to as *WYSIWYG*, short for *What You See Is What You Get*. Typically, this term is used when talking about word processors: the words, fonts, columns, and other appearances you see on the screen are, ideally, exactly what you get when you print. For several years, WYSIWYG (pronounced *wizzy wig*) was the key selling feature for leading word processors for the simple reason that the amount of time saved by not having to run from printer to computer and back again was enough, at that time, to cause users to switch to a new word processor.

WYSIWYG and virtual reality are two sides of the same coin, both important in allowing computers to interact more naturally with humans. Essentially, the key is to eliminate translation so that the interaction can be as direct as possible. However, displaying the world is not enough to make applications natural, easy to use, and to make interaction immediate; users must be able to manipulate that displayed world directly.

DIRECT MANIPULATION: LIVING IN THE VIRTUAL WORLD

Not only did the original airline-reservation systems use words and numbers to display information, those same words and numbers formed the command vocabulary that drove the system. Travel agents used verbal commands — abbreviated words and phrases — to ask for information and to make reservations. The computer responded with equally abbreviated words and phrases. The system, while fast and powerful, required prolonged training — initiation into its rites — and was completely opaque to outsiders.

Early word processors and spreadsheets were based on the same central concept: that computers and humans would interact with each other by using commands, words, and phrases. Abbreviation was the trick to make this interaction quick and continuous. Thus WordStar, the first popular word processor, used arcane codes to represent common editing operations; beyond that, text formatting, such as bolding and centering, was accomplished by embedding equally arcane codes directly into the text of the document. 1-2-3's basic command structure, in the same way, consisted of carefully chosen command words combined into phrases; users would then pick particular commands by entering the first letter of each word. Changing the width of a column, for instance, meant first choosing to work with *Workspace,* then specifying the *Column* set of commands, and finally picking *Width.* After abbreviating, the user would type */WCW;* it was fast, but hardly intuitively meaningful.

Going back to the virtual reality model, how should the user control the application? In a virtual world, users wear bodysuits and gloves; special sensors enable the computer to know whenever the user turns his or her head or moves his or her eyes. Every movement of a finger, every step, causes the virtual body to move correspondingly. When the user looks to the left, the computer displays the precise sights (and sounds) the user would see in reality. Even if today's virtual reality simulations can't do exactly what I've just described, the concept is immediately appealing and clearly intuitive and natural; but what relationship does it have to mundane applications like word processing and airline reservations?

SOMETHING FOR EVERYONE

The core concept behind interaction in virtual reality is *direct manipulation:* the idea that users manipulate parts of the virtual world *directly,* as projected, instead of through the intermediary of word-based commands. The same concept can be applied directly to most applications with startling results in both ease of use and power of interaction:

✦ A travel agent can reserve a seat by pointing to it with a mouse and clicking on the seat directly. If the passenger wants to move to a different seat, the mouse can be used to *drag* the passenger from the old seat to the new one.

✦ A picture embedded in a newsletter page can be moved from one place to another by dragging it. The user doesn't think about, let alone enter, coordinates like *twips, pixels, picas, or inches;* instead, as the picture is dragged, the computer automatically adjusts the surrounding text to flow around the picture wherever it ends up.

✦ A column in the newsletter can be made wider or narrower by dragging its right or left margin in one direction or another. Similarly, an embedded picture can be shrunken or enlarged by dragging its boundaries. The user is directly manipulating elements of the real world that the computer is already so kindly displaying.

✦ An architect can move walls, furniture, doors, and windows by literally dragging them around. Each time the user significantly changes the structure, the drawing application adjusts the light coming into the room to show how the new arrangement will really look, complete with shading and shadows.

DRAG AND DROP

These examples all illustrate one particular direct manipulation technique called *drag and drop,* which involves selecting a displayed object, dragging it to a new location with the mouse, and then dropping it where it is supposed to be. Beyond the obvious uses of drag and drop, mostly revolving around geometrical placement in space, there are many less obvious uses that are still immediately recognizable when they are implemented. For instance, dragging a chair onto a garbage can quickly becomes a familiar way for an architect to eliminate furniture from a room. Similarly, having a *palette* of furniture enables the architect to drag new items (furniture, walls, doors, appliances) into rooms, essentially creating something out of nothing. Clicking on a spray can, selecting a color by clicking, and then dragging the spray can over parts of a picture to color them in, once seen, can be learned in seconds by even a four-year-old.

In general, drag and drop provides hundreds of opportunities to control the computer world in a direct, intuitive, and, best of all, efficient fashion. The best thing about drag and drop is that small adjustments are made directly by just moving the hand back and forth. Comparing this to the paradigm of only a few years ago — setting values, looking at printouts, and going back and forth painfully for hours — shows how much UI concepts have advanced in a relatively short period of time.

Drag and drop is particularly appealing because it is so directly analogous to what people do in the real world. However, there are also other direct manipulation approaches that, although less similar to the real world, are still very powerful in continuing to eliminate the need for commands, typing, and interpretation by users.

Although the computer may be simulating the real world, the virtual reality it projects still is based on the software running underneath it. As a result, the virtual world, although never quite as tangible as the real thing, can also be in many ways more intelligent and aware than the real world. Extending direct manipulation depends on taking advantage of the idea that technology can make virtual objects become *self aware.*

In Wonderland, Alice found that apparently everyday objects had magical properties: they exhibited awareness, could answer questions, and often could even talk back in unexpected ways. Objects in virtual worlds can be made to have the same properties, although in slightly less magical ways. Today, there are several standard ways of interacting with objects in the virtual world of GUIs. Drag and drop is one approach; the two other standard approaches are *double-click* and *property inspection.*

DOUBLE-CLICK AND PROPERTY INSPECTION

Both *double–click* and *property inspection* implement the same concept: drilling down into an object to look at its underlying properties. In the real world, objects have properties: color, size, weight, name, cost, and so on. (The word *object* is often used in many technical contexts in which it can be given complex and even mystical meanings. Here, I mean the word in the normal English — subject, verb, object — sense.) In just the same way, objects in the virtual world have properties, too: seat number, picture size, column width, chair color, store address, and so on. Many of these properties are visible if you display the object properly in its world setting — that's what graphical display is all about. And in the same way, many of these properties can be manipulated directly by moving the object in its world — that's drag and drop. No matter how creative people are, there will probably always be properties that should be represented indirectly. That's where *drilling* comes in.

Increasingly, today's software writers are providing standard ways of inspecting the properties of an object that can't be manipulated by dragging. Two such approaches used in many applications are clicking the left mouse button twice (double-clicking) while pointing at the object and clicking the mouse's right button (left button for lefties). This action, called *property inspection*, enables the user to immediately inspect and set key properties of the selected object.

Ugly? Less direct than drag and drop? Yes, but property inspection is still much more direct and efficient than its alternative, command-based interaction. To understand this, consider the alternative. Every application has a command interface, even in a direct manipulation world. In most GUIs, these commands are accessed through pulldown menus, each of which provides access to a list of 10 to 20 commands. Setting the color of a line in a graph means knowing which command in which menu to use, moving the mouse to the top of the screen, pulling down the menu, and getting to the right command. Alternatively, by double-clicking on the line, you can immediately see and change the line's color with no guessing and little mouse movement.

Microsoft Excel incorporates both *drag and drop* and *drilling down* in its graphing module. A user can change the underlying values associated with the points on a graph by dragging those points up and down — making the data value in the accompanying spreadsheet bigger and smaller. By double-clicking on the graph, the user also can change the color and thickness of its line, the shapes of the markers denoting points, and even the type of graph.

To consider a more complex example, imagine a town-planning application that displays a street map as its starting point. The user can add structures from a palette on the side of the screen or rearrange existing structures by dragging them around. Double-clicking on a building shows its floor plan and a text table describing the building's use, inhabitants, square footage, and so on. Similarly, double-clicking on a street brings up a table indicating its width, construction, and traffic capacity. This example shows that even virtual worlds can exist at many levels. Just as Alice was able to shrink and discover a whole new part of Wonderland, computer users can drill down from one virtual world to another by double-clicking.

Direct manipulation (whether it takes the form of drag and drop or double-clicking, and whether the result is as exciting as another complete reality projection or as mundane as a property table) has one important aspect: the user explores and controls the graphical world without having to find or invoke commands. The commands are still there (both for more complex operations and for verbally oriented users), but the combination of rich graphical display and direct manipulation enables the user to explore and control a visual world without expressing actions in words or phrases.

ONE PERSON, ONE COMPUTER

What does it take to actually build the kind of GUIs just discussed? In short, a computer on every desktop, dedicated to the needs of a single user. To understand why this is so, consider the requirements imposed by the need to first project the virtually real, WYSIWYG world, and then look at how it's possible for the user to manipulate it directly. In doing so, the following sections discuss *event-driven applications, mouse control, fonts, bitmapped displays,* and *windowing software.* When you've finished reading this chapter, these terms will seem quite approachable — really.

EVENT-DRIVEN APPLICATIONS

The one-person, one-computer story really starts long before the days of graphical user interfaces; the core is *event-driven applications.* Consider what happens when a user works the keyboard while using a spreadsheet. Each time the user enters a new number in a cell, the entire spreadsheet may be recalculated. The computer is then forced to redraw all the numbers on the screen to keep the display current. Conceptually, the entry of the new number can be thought of as an event in the life of the spreadsheet. The occurrence of the event launches the recalculation and redisplay of the spreadsheet. Fortunately, even the fastest user can't enter new numbers very quickly.

Now imagine what happens when the user holds down a cursor key causing the spreadsheet to scroll left. When the cursor key is held down, it *repeats* at the rate of about 15 times per second. This means that 900 times per minute, the spreadsheet program is receiving a keystroke telling it to scroll the spreadsheet to the left. And each time the spreadsheet moves, the underlying program has to redraw the entire screen. This is a new model for two things: how a computer program receives its instructions and how much work is required each time one of those instructions is received.

Classical applications, such as the airline-reservation model, operate on a conversational principle: people talk to the computer, which in turn talks back. The whole cycle is called a conversation. The travel agent enters a phrase asking the computer about the availability of certain flights, and the computer responds with the requested information. Other times, the computer asks the agent for certain information, perhaps about the passenger, and the agent is the one responsible for responding. Overall, the conversations between the computer and the user are structured in predetermined sequences called *dialogues.* For example, the sequence of ten questions and answers required to report a piece of lost baggage is always the same: when the agent triggers that dialogue, the computer always asks the same questions, and the interaction continues in a fixed sequence until the questions have all been answered.

A spreadsheet, by contrast, lives a much less ordered life. Sitting in front of the personal computer, the user has a wide range of choices at all times. He or she can enter new numbers, change existing ones, alter the width of a column, scroll the spreadsheet in any direction, split the screen into two parts, print part of the sheet, and so on. Furthermore, unlike the reservation system, where commands consist of words and phrases, many of the user's actions are triggered by single keystrokes.

Digging deeper, every user keystroke turns out to be an event that the spreadsheet must respond to! Every time the user does anything — presses any key — the personal computer program must respond. For example, when the user enters a number, the spreadsheet decides whether it is part of a formula, whether the formula is complete, and whether the digit is at the right margin and the entire number (five digits long) has to be wrapped to the next line. This is what is meant by *event-driven programming*.

INPUT FROM ALL OVER

In a character-oriented world, events are always keystrokes because the keyboard is the only input device. However, in a GUI world, the mouse (and perhaps a pen or a touch-sensitive screen) can also create events. In the character world, as well, only one program at a time is running, so interpreting the events is relatively straightforward. In the GUI world, however, consecutive events can be directed at a spreadsheet, a word processor, a drawing package, and an electronic mail program, depending on where the user moves the mouse. As a result, an event-driven program creates a world of tremendous variety — a world in which the application program is interpreting actions and doing meaningful work frequently, often many times per second.

The first consequence of the event-driven paradigm is that just keeping up with all the user's actions requires quite a bit of computer horsepower. However, when you consider the amount of work each action translates into, the need for computer power escalates even more rapidly. Even in the character world, keeping a spreadsheet display up to date means being prepared to redraw the entire computer screen, sometimes many times per second. Spreadsheets lose a lot of their appeal when recalculation takes a second or when scrolling is less than instantaneous. This is the reason that the spreadsheet — originally VisiCalc and then 1-2-3 — was the first application that virtually demanded a dedicated personal computer.

As it turns out, though, however demanding event-driven interaction is in the character world, it is infinitely worse (from the perspective of computer power needed) in the GUI world. Talking about running many programs at once gave a hint, but this is only a small part of the GUI story in terms of creating a need for super-high-powered personal computers.

To see how complex the GUI concept gets, watch the computer at work as you move your mouse around. A corresponding *pointer* moves around on the screen, apparently moving smoothly and continuously as you move your hand. As the mouse moves from one part of the screen to another, the shape of the pointer changes: sometimes it's an arrow, sometimes an hourglass, at other times a double-headed arrow, enabling you to resize windows, and some of the time an *I-beam* marking a text-insertion point. What causes that pointer to move and change shape? Hundreds of times per second, the personal computer checks to see whether the mouse has moved. Each time the mouse moves, the computer repaints the mouse pointer on the screen, first erasing the old mouse pointer and then drawing a new one. Before repainting the pointer, the mouse software checks where the pointer is on the screen and then makes an appropriate decision about the shape of the pointer. The amount of computer processing required just to track the mouse would be enough to occupy a significant fraction of the computing capacity of an early 1960s mainframe. In addition, all of that processing is *background* work just to enable you to have the illusion of a smoothly tracking pointer to correspond to your mouse (hand) movements. After doing the background work, the computer still has to have enough processing power left for the real work of the application.

Graphical mouse support gives a new meaning to event-driven programming in at least three ways. First, events now occur hundreds of times per second. A modern mouse has a resolution of about 400 points per inch; each time the mouse moves $1/400$ of an inch in any direction, the computer generates a new event. Second, supporting all the mouse shapes and superimposing the mouse cursor over the other information increases the amount of work done each time an event occurs. As the cursor moves around the screen, the computer must erase the old cursor, replace it with the information previously displayed there on the screen, and redraw the cursor, possibly with a different shape, in a new location. It's enough to make you tired even thinking about it. Finally, to make things worse, the mouse gives the user new freedom to move around the screen. In a windowed environment, successive mouse clicks can activate completely different applications, forcing the computer to do a tremendous amount of work to keep up with the user. Yet all of this only hints at the real implications of GUI, which become evident only by looking at the information displayed on the screen.

The airline-reservation terminal that defined the character-oriented world described earlier displayed a screen full of letters and numbers (characters) at fixed positions on the screen. On a terminal, each row of the screen holds exactly 80 characters, and the screen displays exactly 24 of these rows altogether. When the computer sends a stream of characters to the terminal, the screen's job is quite easy; it displays the characters in sequence. In this world, the terminal is a relatively dumb device; the central computer has all the smarts.

Now suppose that you want to start varying the appearance of some of the letters displayed on the screen. Character size is often measured in *points,* a term used by typesetters and printers. Twelve points are equal to $1/6$ inch. Typically, books use 12-point characters, and terminals display their letters and numbers in 10-point type. For the sake of example, suppose that you are displaying a flight itinerary: the title is in 24-point type, the section headings for each leg of the trip are 14-point, the flight numbers are 10-point, and the detailed flight information (departure time, airport name, and so on) are in rather small 8-point characters so you can pack a lot of information into a small space. Although this may sound like quite a variety, examining any page of a newspaper or newsletter shows at least this much variation in character font usage. So what does this have to do with GUI, personal computers, and the death of terminals?

So Many Choices, So Little Time

First, think about how much work is involved in displaying the flight itinerary on the screen. Originally, the central computer simply sent characters to the terminal, which displayed them on the screen. If, for example, that computer wanted to display *Flight 84: Rome to Milan Departs Da Vinci Airport 9:30 a.m., Arrives Lenata Airport 10:35 a.m.*, it just sent that line to the computer. (The line of characters would be represented as a sequence of *bytes*. Essentially, a byte is a number, ranging from 0 to 255. The 256 possible bytes correspond to a numeric code that assigns a number to every letter and digit as well as all the possible punctuation, symbols, and other characters used on the screen.) In the graphical world, however, a lot of thought is required to determine how to display that line. Consider a few of the details.

Every different character can be drawn in an almost infinite number of ways:

✦ Font sizes range from 6 to 72 points (and sometimes even beyond 72 points).

✦ Character styles include bold, italic, underlined, shadowed, and hollow.

✦ The font can be chosen from among hundreds, some looking dramatically different from others.

✦ A variety of color effects can be used, with different colors changing literally from letter to letter.

✦ The position of the letters on the screen is no longer fixed. For instance, if the itinerary title is in 24-point type, each letter takes up three times as much horizontal space (rows) as the 8-point type used for itinerary details. To further complicate matters, in a graphical environment, letters are proportionally spaced: an *i* takes much less space on each line than a *w*. As a result, even after computing how to draw characters, a considerable amount of computer power is required to decide where exactly to then put those characters on the screen. And, as a kind of final kicker, each time any changes are made on the screen, the positions of *all* the subsequent letters and numbers must be recomputed. If this sounds like a huge amount of work, it is!

All of this means that considerable computer power is required to decide how to draw each letter on the screen. The description of a single letter, which previously consisted of a single byte representing a number from 1 to 256, now requires dozens of bytes to describe the font, size, style, color, and so on. Also, a significant amount of computer power has become necessary to decide how to actually draw that letter, often requiring as much processing power as the entire original application required.

BITMAPS, CHARACTER MAPS, PICTURES, AND BANDWIDTH

This might sound scary, both in terms of how much work the computer is doing and in terms of you, the reader, understanding how it all fits into the larger, conceptual model of how personal computers work in the GUI world. It's time to step back and put the GUI world into an overall framework that helps you size up the work being done.

Think of a terminal as a very simple computer. It has a keyboard, a screen, a small amount of memory (used to store the information displayed on the screen), and a small computer, which translates the information in the memory into characters on the screen. Typically, a terminal with a 24 × 80 screen (24 rows of 80 characters each) has a character buffer (the memory used to hold the characters) of 1,920 bytes.

On a terminal, the characters in the buffer are displayed on the screen by converting them into dots, or *pixels,* in a matrix. If you've ever looked at a newspaper through a magnifying glass, this process should seem familiar: the apparently smooth lines defining the words on the page are, in fact, made up of many individual dots, each too small to be seen by the human eye. Computer screens work the same way: a screen has thousands of dots that can be turned on and off to display letters, numbers, graphs, and even pictures. This may seem like a crude way to display information, but even high-resolution photographs manage to represent subtle artistic images by using dots in exactly the same way; the primary difference is the number of dots per inch.

Think about some numbers for just a few minutes; really, it won't be painful, and it won't take long. Generally, a terminal displays characters by using a 7 × 5 matrix — each letter or digit is represented by a little rectangle of dots 7 rows high with 5 dots in each row. That's 35 dots, or pixels, per character; 1,920 rectangles on the screen; 67,200 pixels, or *bits,* all together. (A *bit* is an acronym for *binary digit,* the computer's basic unit of memory storage. A *byte* is composed of eight bits.)

Although some people may think of terminals as being passive, dumb devices, most terminals manufactured in the last 15 years have been built around a microprocessor; it's just that the computer inside the terminal is dedicated to the job of acting in a particular way. Therefore, what you have is a computer with a keyboard, a screen, and a memory. The memory has three components:

✦ The character buffer I've already described, holding 1,920 characters

✦ Enough memory to run the program, which makes the computer into a terminal

✦ Another 67,200 bits, or 8,400 bytes, of *display* memory to represent the individual positions on the screen

The computer converts characters in the display buffer into pixel representations in the display memory; specialized electronics then display this directly on the screen.

Having struggled this far, the first number to keep in mind is the size of the display memory: 67,200 bits or 8,400 bytes of information the computer must manage on a regular basis to keep a coherent image on the screen.

Early personal computers, such as the Apple II and the first IBM PCs, were built around character-oriented displays, just like terminals. Even with these early devices, you can start to see the difference between character and graphical horse-power requirements.

The *display adapter* card that plugged into a slot and drove the screen contained a display memory with, yes, 67,200 bits of information (in fact, sometimes the display memory could be twice as big if each pixel on the screen could be shown with two levels of brightness).

Start, then, with a simple comparison. An airline reservation system deals with words and sentences. Asking about a flight results in a few hundred characters of information, at the most, being put on the screen. Not much change to manage.

A character-oriented spreadsheet, right off the bat, has to be able to change the entire screen each time the user presses any key on the keyboard. Each time the screen is updated, the computer managing the screen has to be able to manipulate 1,920 characters of data, perhaps 10 or 15 times per second. Now, instead of displaying 200 to 300 characters, the computer managing the display has to move more than 15,000 characters per second to keep up with the user's requirements for recalculation and scrolling. Each time a character is moved from one place to another on the screen, it's the computer that's doing the moving — so all of a sudden, with the introduction of spreadsheets, the computer is doing almost 100 times as much work, just to keep the screen up to date for the user.

But watch what happens in the world of bitmaps! Now the computer has to do more than just move characters from one place to another on the screen; it has to decide exactly how to draw those characters in the right font and size. As a result, it has to recompute exactly where each character goes on the screen. To get a handle on the relative amount of work involved, think back to the discussion of pixels. A small VGA color screen is 480 pixels wide and 640 pixels high: that's 307,200 pixels. In order to handle 256 colors, each pixel is stored in a byte of memory; that means the display adapter in the GUI computer has more memory (over 300K) than most IBM PC XTs of only 10 years ago. Many users have 15-inch or 17-inch monitors, allowing more windows and more work to appear on the screen at one time. This means more pixels, typically 1,024 rows with 780 pixels each. In this case, the display adapter needs 800K of memory to represent the screen; almost one megabyte on the display adapter card alone!

Okay, now to the bottom line. Each time the mouse moves, each time a window grows or shrinks, each time the spreadsheet scrolls or recalculates, the contents of the entire screen may need to be rearranged. True, some changes affect only part of the screen, but the system still must appear instantaneous not just in the best case, but in the worst case, too. So the user needs to have enough processing power to allow the entire screen to be rearranged several times per second and always have that rearrangement appear natural and smooth — instantaneous. That means being able to move around up to 800K of information, several times per second, including all the calculations required to compute mouse shape, character drawing, proportional spacing, and so on.

Although it was possible to manage 1,920 characters from a distance, managing close to a million bytes of screen information in the same way just doesn't work. In a nutshell, a GUI interface involves managing 500 times as much information, processing that information more frequently in more complex ways, and making the whole thing appear instantaneous all the time. No wonder the only way to make GUI work is to supply every user with a computer. In fact, when you get right down to it, many of today's personal computers really consist of several computers, all in one box, including one specially adapted just to the needs of the GUI. The next section explores that idea a little further.

GUI 2000: SOUND AND FURY

It's safe to say that graphical interfaces have already changed the face of computing, literally creating the need for individual users to have dedicated computers on their desks and, in the process, making software usable by normal human beings. Yet, the need to build humanly usable interfaces will lead to even more dramatic changes in the years ahead.

Several years ago, Kodak started shipping its *Photo CD* technology: you now can move snapshots and photographs from cardboard boxes in your cupboards onto digital compact disks that you can carry around in your shirt pocket. Each CD can hold several hundred photographs. The advantages are obvious: savings in space, the ability to search through picture libraries based on key words, and best of all, photographs that can now be edited, combined, and printed. Editing in particular means being able to remove that telephone pole sticking out of Aunt Millie's head, being able to correct for the effects of overexposure, or as a joke, being able to put Uncle Fred's mustache on your fifth-grade art teacher. This all raises an interesting question: are GUIs good enough to really do justice to photographs?

To equal a photograph or magazine page, personal computer GUIs would have to improve in four areas: *speed, resolution, size,* and *form factor*. Resolution is the simplest; computers need to display denser information, primarily in the form of more colors. Early computers capable of displaying 8 or 16 colors would transform pictures into "Romper Room"-like cartoons. Graphic artists and psychologists have determined that depicting pictures realistically requires the use of approximately 16 million distinct colors. It is true that most people can name only 10 to 20 colors. It is also true that in side-by-side comparisons, nobody can tell the difference between adjacent colors in a spectrum of 256 colors ranging from red to blue. Nonetheless, to handle all the subtle effects implicit in shadows, shading, and reflections, 16 million color variations are required. And as a result, normal people can quickly tell the difference between limited representations of images with only 256 colors and photo-realistic renderings using the richer complete color spectrum.

SPEED

The need for graphics will continue to create an insatiable hunger for ever faster computers. Even today, the one complaint about GUIs is that they just are not fast enough. On most computers, opening a complex window takes time. After a while, most users get tired of watching the computer paint the elements of the window one at a time. This has led to the recent introduction of *graphics accelerators,* display adapters with special computers (and large amounts of memory) built right in. The display adapter can now draw lines, move windows around on the screen, and paint characters in various shapes and sizes. Because the computer on the display adapter is specially designed only to complete these common graphics operations optimally, it can update the screen very quickly. And best of all, the display adapter is now offloading the main computer, leaving it free to do other work for the user. So one result of the continuing drive for ever-faster graphics is the fact that many users already have not one computer on their desk, but two: the general personal computer doing most of the work and the specialized display adapter computer helping it. The result? GUIs that are about three times as fast. Windows now *snap* open; pictures appear to *pop* onto the screen; the act of flipping from one page of text to another no longer involves a perceptible delay. Users love it! But that's just the beginning.

Today's fast 486 computers are barely fast enough to make today's GUIs run fast enough. With the advent of Pentiums, Power PCs, and graphics accelerators, windows finally snap open, and pages scroll instantly. Yet the graphics systems described earlier require the computer to handle eight times as much information. All of a sudden, graphics won't be fast enough — *again!* It's true: cost aside, even today's fastest personal computers are not fast enough to handle full-sized, photorealistic graphics. What this means is simple: the need for computers to keep getting faster won't go away, and as faster computers are introduced, users will continue upgrading their old systems as they realize the necessity of putting mustaches on fifth-grade teachers.

RESOLUTION

Compare the quality and quantity of information displayed on an average magazine page, and it quickly becomes clear that there is a huge gap between computer displays and the needs of real-life graphic imaging. Even a $1,024 \times 768$ screen running in 256-color mode is still far from being as good as the average picture coming out of a home camera. Even the lowest-quality magazine page does a much better job of conveying complex information quickly than personal computers can do at their best. And because everyone is used to photograph- and magazine-quality pictures every day, why not expect the same from supposedly fancy and sophisticated computers? So how much improvement does that mean?

Talking numbers, catching up with the real world requires personal computers to start dealing with 16 million colors, which means representing every pixel on the screen in 24-bit form — three times as much information as manufacturers provide today with 256-color displays.

SIZE

Next, displays have to be bigger; at least big enough to comfortably display an $8^1/_2 \times 11$-inch page. Ideally, the display should show two pages on the screen at one time; that's what a magazine or a book offers. And, as an option, why not have a tabletop or an entire wall capable of displaying information? That way, instead of whiteboards, you could just draw on computer screens and then print, save, or send the information when you were done. Again, converting this into numbers, I'm talking about a minimum of $1,280 \times 1,024$ pixels to display a page and, ideally, 1,280 rows with 2,048 pixels each to show two pages side by side.

Suppose that you could buy a computer today with a $1,280 \times 2,048$ (two-page) pixel display capable of displaying 16 million colors; how much display memory would that require? Eight megabytes of display memory! Most personal computers today have from 4MB to 8MB of main memory; only a year ago, 2MB was the norm. Servers often have 16MB to 32MB of main memory to serve multiple users efficiently. Yet, now I'm talking about the display memory alone, contained on the display adapter card, having 8MB of memory. This has two fundamental implications: high cost and the need for a very fast microprocessor. The cost factor says that even if you could build a screen cheaply enough, just the cost of memory today would be a significant obstacle to widespread adoption of large high-resolution displays; the display memory alone would cost about $400. However, as memory continues to decrease in price, this will become a nonissue.

FORM

Today, computer displays are based on television technology. As screens get bigger, the television tubes they require get deeper and heavier, too. A 15-inch screen weighs about 35 pounds; at 17 inches, the weight goes to 60 pounds; a 21-inch display not only weighs 75 pounds, but also fills an entire desk. Beyond big and heavy, as displays get bigger, they also get expensive — sometimes prohibitively expensive. Yet to display two pages side by side requires a display that is at least 30 inches in size. The answer to this problem is *flat display technology* — just now becoming available on notebook and laptop computers. Only two years ago, color notebooks were expensive, slow, and unreliable. Today, they are affordable, fast, and easier on the eyes than many full-size screens.

So just extrapolating today's computers and applications forward presents the following picture: Personal computers in several years will be at least eight times as fast with displays capable of displaying two side-by-side magazine pages in photorealistic color on a flat screen that will hang on a wall or be embedded on a desk. Advanced versions of the same computers will drive wall-sized displays and will have correspondingly more power and memory to keep up with the huge amount of information being displayed and managed at one time. Your 8MB Pentium SuperVGA machine will look like a toy in comparison; the user of 1998 will wonder how anybody tolerated the crudely limited, slow graphical environment you're just getting used to today.

To consider the rest of the future, look at two other change vectors: animation and portability. At one level, animation is easy to think about: everyone takes televisions, VCRs, and movies for granted. It's easy to shrug off the potential for animation by saying that it's hard to imagine how static applications could be improved through movement. In the same vein, early moviemakers had trouble seeing the potential for speech, and at first, both color television and color movies were viewed as just fads. At the same time, it is true today that very few people have a clear idea of how computer applications will evolve in a world of interactive video instead of the photographic still-image application world of today. Two things, though, are certain:

✦ When they arrive, the changes to how people use personal computers will be even more dramatic than what GUI has already brought in the last ten years. It is likely that the next user interface revolution after GUI will in some way revolve around sound and motion.

✦ The computer horsepower requirements associated with true support for sound and motion are so far beyond current technology, in affordable form, that that revolution is *at least* five years away from even starting. If displaying relatively static real-life images is still five years away from broad-scale affordability, then displaying those same images in motion is five years beyond that.

Real-life static graphics defines the horizon in terms of the visual quality, but what is the horizon in terms of *where* and *how* users will work with the information they see?

GUI TO GO

About 1980, Alan Kay, a researcher at Xerox's Palo Alto Research Center, coined the term *Dynabook* to describe a personal computer that could be powerful enough, small enough, and easy enough to use and take everywhere as a replacement for pads, binders, notebooks, and writing paper. Kay not only described the computer, but also the test that would signal its arrival. A computer qualifies as a Dynabook when it is so convenient in every way that you not only use it to record grocery lists routinely, but you also take it to the store every time. In 1990, that goal was still a dream. Today, notebook and subnotebook (or *handbook*) computers represent substantial progress toward the dream; in five years, it should be reality. Three basic issues must be resolved to make the dream completely real: power, interaction mechanisms, and software.

POWER

The goal is to pack sufficient computer power into a box that is small and light enough to be convenient. Until recently, display technology was a real issue. Today's flat color displays, however, are on the verge of being good enough to be used all day, every day. And within a short time, flat displays will be the rival of conventional displays. At the same time, as microcomputers continue to get smaller, faster, and cheaper, it is only a matter of several years before power and size will no longer be the factors stopping all people from having Dynabooks.

It might appear that battery technology is a gating factor. After all, a Dynabook that lasts only two hours isn't much of a notebook replacement. However, batteries are improving rapidly. In the future, improved microprocessors and displays will require much less power than they do today. As a result, tomorrow's computer notebooks will run for many hours on normal alkaline batteries; when the batteries run out, buy a new set at the drugstore and do a quick swap. And if ecological concerns mount, stores will recycle old batteries, recharging them and passing them on to the next customer. Or everyone will carry two sets of batteries and have a third set in the charger at home, ready to rotate each night.

INTERACTION TECHNOLOGY

For all of its simplicity and efficiency on a desktop, a mouse doesn't work in a portable environment. Finding room to roll the mouse around on an airplane tray is a marginal proposition; when it comes to taking notes sitting on the grass, the mouse becomes completely useless. The keyboard presents a different set of issues. Like the mouse, the keyboard takes space, making it harder to carry the Dynabook everywhere. The smaller the keyboard gets, the harder it is to make the keys big enough to support touch typing. Finally, in many meetings, even though the computer is being used on a table where keyboarding works mechanically, the sound and action associated with typing are often just intrusive enough to make the keyboard unwelcome.

At the beginning of this decade, pen technology was a popular candidate for replacing keyboards. In many ways, the pen is just an even more natural form of direct manipulation. Quite often, the computer screen is simulating a page of information; acting like electronic paper. The invention of the pen is just an attempt to take one step closer to making electronic paper more like real paper. (Ironically, in trying to make computers more naturally approachable, the industry came full circle, back to pen and paper, only in electronic form.) The only problem is that pen technology is still quite far from being mature. As we'll see, in just a few paragraphs, replacing keyboards by pens turned out to be much harder to do than anyone had guessed. But the thought of using a pen still helps you appreciate what users really need.

In a way, thinking about a computer without a keyboard or mouse makes you step back and ask what the user interface is really about, underneath it all. The answer is *talking to the computer*. Talking? Forgetting about computers then, if I'm talking about talking, how is it normally done? How do you talk to other people? The answer is either *talk* or *write*. This brings the discussion to the dream computer interface, and with it, the dream personal computer.

SOFTWARE

Mouse-driven, graphical applications are easier to use than the old command-driven systems of the past, but as you've already observed, they're still far from being actually *easy* to use. Imagine, though, if you could literally *tell* computers what to do! For instance, instead of typing words into a word processor, why not speak into the microphone and have the computer convert speech into writing? And, at a meeting, why not be able to literally take notes with an electronic pen, including sentences, abbreviations, pictures, and diagrams? The computer could recognize scribbling and convert it into neat, readable, printed words and pictures!

Attractive and simple, but is it efficient? The average person writes with a pen at about 20 words per minute, types anywhere from 50 to 100 words per minute, and speaks at 200 words per minute. Sounds fast to me! In addition, drawing pictures directly on the screen with a pen has to be faster and more direct than trying to manipulate points and lines with a mouse. So the new dream computer wins on every count — except one. It can't be built today.

In 1991, industry pundits were predicting that by 1993 pens would have made keyboards and mice obsolete. By 1993, many of the same prophets were ready to forget that pens had ever existed. What happened? First, building usable pen systems turned out to be harder than expected. Battery life is an issue, pens are hard to work with in situations when the screen is at an angle (your arm gets tired), and early pen-based systems were too heavy and too expensive. As a result, mechanical issues alone relegated pen computing to specialized niche markets. All of these superficial issues, though, duck the real point. Pens *should* be useful; why aren't they more common?

In 1993, several true commodity, pen-based machines were introduced. Compaq, in particular, spent a great deal of money advertising and promoting the *Concerto*, a well-designed portable notebook computer that could be used either with its pen or with its detachable keyboard. NCR, Grid, Toshiba, and IBM all introduced competitors to the Concerto in the same year. Finally, consumers had mass market, relatively inexpensive pen-based computers that could be bought off the shelf. Yet now, just two years later, virtually all these machines have disappeared. Towards the end of the same year, with a huge amount of fanfare, Apple introduced the *Newton*, a shirt pocket-sized computer that depended on a pen as its primary input device. Priced at under $1,000, marketed extensively, and broadly available within a year, the Newton, too, had been relegated to the pigeonhole reserved for interesting historical footnotes. What happened? Why did the Concerto, the pen-based IBM Thinkpad, and the Newton all fail? Was it the pen, or something else? The answer is simple: the software just wasn't good enough. However, the pen worked, and people immediately took to it. In demonstrations, users were also instantly compelled to try the pen, and most of the time they found it easy to use right away. The problem though was simple. People want to write with pens, and computers are not yet even close to being able to recognize writing. Without writing recognition, pens are just cute alternatives to mice. Cute but expensive and saddled with troubling mechanical limitations. The limitations would be irrelevant if writing were possible; but take away writing, relegate the pen to being merely a pointing device, and the pen suddenly becomes a liability rather than a convenience.

In a way, IBM, Compaq, and Apple did us all a huge favor by building such good pen-based machines, refining them, and then marketing them so well. We all got to participate in an important experiment. At the time that the first edition of this book was written, the experiment was incomplete, and it was impossible to really say how useful pen-based computing, sans writing recognition, would be. Now the experiment has been run, the votes are in, and the results are clear. People want pens, but only if writing recognition goes with them. And without computers that can read writing, pens are useful, at best, in specific, limited, niche markets.

For now (and for the foreseeable future) computers cannot recognize talking or writing. Yes, some computer systems can deal with spoken input in very limited situations. Your car phone can be trained to *phone home,* and your television can just as easily *go to channel seven.* However, computer systems in general cannot recognize spoken input even as well as a three-year-old child. In the same way, computers can be trained to recognize printed characters, entered into fixed gridlike locations on a form, with reasonable accuracy. The same computers, however, can no more recognize free-form written sentences than they can write books.

Recognizing speech, whether spoken or written, is hard. To put this in perspective, let me recall a personal situation. Several years ago, I worked for a manager who traveled frequently. On his trips he read memos and wrote notes in the margins, and on his return he passed the memos on to me. About three-fourths of the time, I could not read his notes. Half of that time, when I showed the notes to him, he couldn't read them either. In a similar vein, think about all the dialects and accents associated with English and then imagine a person (let alone a computer) being able to recognize them all. Speech recognition is hard, even for people, and is beyond the capabilities of today's computers.

Schoolchildren start by learning to write printed characters. Then, in about the third grade, they learn to write *cursive* characters — letters connected to each other instead of written out separately. Put another way, these children learn about writing versus printing. Because it is so much faster to write connected letters, most people routinely use cursive to take notes. Trained stenographers take cursive a step further and use shorthand, a highly efficient form of cursive writing.

Today's best computer writing-recognition programs are just starting to learn to tell reliably where one letter ends and the next begins when dealing with cursive writing! Even when dealing with printed input, accuracy rates often are well under 50 percent; the computer would literally convert to garbage over half of the letters you entered.

And when it comes to spoken input, the situation is even worse.

To really understand this situation, consider *Optical Character Recognition (OCR)*. OCR systems read printed pages and convert them into computer form. In other words, OCR typically reads text generated by computer printers and converts that text back into a form the computer can deal with directly. Printed text is highly regular and easily readable by all humans and has none of the interpretation problems associated with handwriting. Every human can read printed text with virtually 100 percent accuracy; computers can't. Only recently has OCR reached the point where it is faster to *scan in* documents than it is to completely retype the text by hand.

So if computers have trouble reading printed text, how long will it be before they can read handwriting and recognize spoken words? In the early '60s, many prognosticators confidently predicted that speaking typewriters would be common by the '70s. A speaking typewriter, of course, doesn't speak so much as it listens and understands. The idea, of course, is exactly what I described before: a word processor you can speak to. And yet, 30 years later, the market isn't close to achieving that easily described goal.

I can predict three things:

✦ Computers *will* one day recognize speech.

✦ Although it is still likely to occur in most of our lifetimes, this event is far enough away that nobody can accurately predict when it will happen.

✦ Like everything else associated with great user interfaces, speech recognition, whether written or oral, will require huge amounts of cheap computer power, creating further impetus for making unbelievably powerful personal computers.

PERSONAL COMPUTER, PERSONAL ASSISTANT; ELECTRONIC DESK, ELECTRONIC AGENT

We began this chapter by considering the issue of why computers are so hard to use. Focusing on the user interface led quickly to the concept of virtual reality, graphical environments, and direct manipulation. By providing people with a direct portrayal of a variety of artificially real universes, the computer can enable people to work directly with electronic houses, pages, streets, and airplanes. The GUI enables users to see these electronic objects as they will finally exist after those users have finished working with them inside the computer. Then, through direct manipulation, the GUI facilitates manipulation of these objects without requiring knowledge of a new command language.

The virtually real GUI world is so compelling that it has redefined (or perhaps defined in the first place) the concept of making computer software usable. In this process, though, it has created a need for huge amounts of computer power. The only way to provide GUIs is to provide each user with a computer. In moving from the terminal-based systems of the past to today's graphical applications, suddenly the GUI alone requires the equivalent of yesterday's mainframe sitting on each user's desk.

Although today's personal computers are hundreds of times faster than those of just 15 years ago, PCs have just recently become fast enough to run GUIs with adequate performance. Even more than the applications running behind the UIs, the user interface itself has driven the explosive need for ever faster personal computers. Word processors today are not necessarily more powerful than those found on mainframes 20 years ago. The difference is that today's word processors are *usable* — the power is accessible by millions. The GUI has made this possible, and the need for the horsepower to drive those GUIs has created the personal computer industry. The GUIs made software usable, and the usability of the software made computers desirable.

The first major conclusion of this chapter is that the computer systems of the future will depend on having a *powerful* computer on every user's desk; the design of the UI that appears on that computer will make or break the applications of tomorrow.

Second, even today's personal computers and user interfaces are far from adequate. As technology moves toward photorealistic images, full-page displays, sound, and animation, the desktop computer of the year 2000 will make today's machines look like crude, slow toys. And in the same year, the computer everyone carries in his or her pocket will have a processor equivalent to *today's* mainframe. In addition, it will support the software that enables speech recognition in at least written (and possibly spoken) form.

In wrapping up the consideration of the personal computer of the future, pause for a moment and think about what becomes possible when all citizens have constant access, at their desk, in their home, and in their pocket, to unimaginable amounts of processing power and memory. I examine the implications of this later in the book. As a hint, though, the adventure you and I will share is the invention of the personal assistant of the future. Whether you think of the computer as an electronic desk or a personal assistant, either way it becomes a personal agent. Making software easy is half the story. The other half of the story is tapping the power of this tireless servant to actively help people all day long.

CHAPTER 5

THE SERVER — CLIENT/SERVER THE FIRST TIME AROUND

Most people intuitively know what a personal computer is, but what in the world is a server? The term *server* has two general connotations:

✦ A piece of hardware that provides shared services in a networked environment

✦ A software component that provides a generalized functional service to other software components

The first connotation is relatively easy to deal with — it's the subject of this chapter. The second use of the term is much more abstract, and I talk about it later in the book when I discuss the whole *client/server* issue in more general terms. So for now, *server* means a piece of hardware — a computer playing the role of a server.

The beauty of personal computers is that they are *personal* — dedicated to the needs of an individual — and not shared. At the same time, most people need to share things all the time; that's where the server comes in. The role of a server is to facilitate sharing; it is a broker of shared information and services.

Since this book uses the terms *server* and *service* quite frequently, let's see how the *American Heritage Dictionary* defines *service:*

"1. The occupation or duties of a servant. 2. Employment in duties or work for another. 3. Work or duties performed for a superior. 4. Work done for others as an occupation or business: provides full catering service. 5. A facility providing the public with the use of something, such as water or transportation. 6. An act of assistance or benefit to another or others; favor."

SHARING RESOURCES

Looking at all these definitions, one ends up with the idea that a server does work for others. That's exactly right: the purpose of a server is to do work for all the personal computers that depend on it. Why can't they just do the work themselves? Generally, because most of the server's work involves managing *shared resources* — resources that are used by many people, by either one person at a time or several people simultaneously. Because personal computers are not shared, they have no way of easily coordinating with other computers when it comes to these shared resources. That's why servers are needed.

If servers provide services, for whom do they provide them? Personal computers used by individuals, of course. Because both the servers and the machines they provide services for are computers, there should be a term to describe the computers that receive the services. You guessed it — *client*. So the first definition of *client/server* revolves around shared computers called *servers* that manage shared resources and provide access to those shared resources as a service to their *clients*. As I discuss later, this is only the simplest and least exciting form of client/server, but it provides a simple and solid foundation to begin exploring the topic; the following section explains more about what servers really do and how they came to do it.

THE BIRTH OF THE NETWORK: PRINTER SHARING

In the late '70s, personal computers had become cheap enough to sit on desks, but printers and disks were still expensive. Because most people don't print all day long, the obvious solution was to share the printer. Later, as storage became more of an issue, sharing expensive disks became a useful solution, as well.

As long as all the PCs sharing a printer are near each other, sharing can be accomplished by moving the printer and switching cables. After a while, though, particularly when many PCs are involved, cable switching becomes tedious. Another alternative, often referred to as *sneakernet,* is to carry floppy disks back and forth. This way, the printer remains connected to one computer, perhaps at the desk of an administrative assistant; users carry their files on a floppy disk to get them printed. Of course, this introduces other inconveniences. And, in both cases, people end up physically waiting in line to print.

Before long, switch boxes became common; these allowed a printer to be shared by several personal computers without requiring physical movement. Some sophisticated switches even detect incoming printing and switch the printer to the correct computer automatically. At this point, two problems are left: users still have to wait in line to the get to the printer during busy periods, and even the best switches can handle only small numbers of computers.

Finally, around 1982, as *local-area networks (LANs)* were becoming practical, the idea of having a computer manage the printer started becoming popular. On a LAN, every computer is connected to every other computer. So if one of the computers is dedicated to *managing* a printer, that computer and the printer attached to it are available to all other users. At the expense of now having a general-purpose computer replace the switch box, users gain the advantage of all computers on the network having access to the printers managed by that computer. That computer managing the printer is called a *server*. It is serving the other computers by providing them with *print services* — services based on the availability of a printer.

SERVER SERVICES

Beyond increased access (broader switching capabilities), how can the server help? First, it can *spool* printing. Whenever a personal computer on the network is ready to print, the server can accept its printed output *immediately*. If the printer is currently busy printing something else, the server can save the output to disk until the printer is free; this is called *spooling*. Even if the printer is free, the server can still help by speeding up the process. Normally, a computer can generate output much faster than even the fastest printer can print it. After initiating the printing, however, the server can spool all of the output for the requesting computer so that while the server manages the completion of the printing process, the requesting computer can become free to do other work very quickly.

Looking deeper into the intricacies of printing, a server can provide a rich menu of services around this apparently simple function:

✦ The server can manage several printers, automatically sending printing to the first free printer. The user gets the benefit of load balancing across several printers.

✦ The server can keep track of special paper and ensure that a print job is held in its *queue* (the queue is the waiting line that print jobs are kept in until it is their turn to be printed; the server may have several such queues or lines) until at least one printer has the right kind of paper loaded.

✦ Print jobs can be scheduled to run at regular intervals; because the server is turned on all the time, it can run the jobs even if the original requester's machine is not even connected at the time.

✦ If a print job fails, perhaps due to a paper jam or power failure, the server can restart the job from its spool file without asking the user to re-enter the print request.

✦ Access to printers can be both extended and restricted. After expensive devices, such as color printers, are attached to a server, they become broadly available on the network. At the same time, the server can be programmed to accept jobs only from specified users or to look for a password before accepting printing, thus protecting expensive printers from being abused.

✦ The server can keep track of the workload, print usage reports, and identify potential bottlenecks that may suggest adding printers, sending work to other servers, and so on.

Generically, these services are a function of the fact that the server is both specialized and shared. Because it is shared, it can balance work across many printers and provide broad accessibility. Because it is dedicated to this service, the print server can be left on all the time, and users can count on it doing its assigned job. Best of all, no matter how loaded (or overloaded) the server gets, nobody's personal machine is directly affected.

Before leaving the print server and moving on to disks, the next section discusses how the server actually works. In particular, how is printing sent to the server instead of to a local printer?

FOOLING THE COMPUTER

Before the introduction of the server, when a user wanted to print, that printer was always directly attached to his or her computer. Generally, computers are built with a fixed number of printer *ports*. A port is a plug or socket that an external device, such as a printer or modem, can plug into. Typically, these ports are called LPT1, LPT2, and LPT3. In addition, most personal computers have up to four communications ports (COM1–COM4) that also can be used for printing. The computer's operating system has built-in facilities to handle printing, directly tied to the ports just described, and the application software uses those facilities to generate printed output. So given all of that, how does output get sent to the server without the application knowing?

Here's the problem. Even in 1982, when print servers were starting to be available, there was already a lot of application software written — WordStar, dBASE, 1-2-3, VisiCalc, and thousands of other packages. All of these packages already *knew* how to print, and any "solution" that made that software no longer work would be unacceptable. The application software thought it knew exactly how to print, and, even worse, this knowledge was used by the application in other ways, too — beyond pure output. For example, the application used the names of the printer ports to ask the user which printer to use. So the question was, is there a way to give the user, the application software, and the local operating system access to networked printers, while still somehow making those printers look local? That's exactly what the network software running in each workstation does with the help of the network server; it makes a remote printer appear to be a physically attached local printer. All of this is accomplished through a sleight of hand called *redirection:* the application thinks it is sending output to a local printer, but the network redirects that output invisibly to the server.

Even in today's networking software, an essential function of the network is to fool the user's personal computer into thinking that it has access to some nonexistent local facilities. More correctly, the facilities that appear to be local do exist, but they are attached to another computer called a server that resides in some completely different network location. When the LAN software is installed in your personal computer, it includes a *redirector* that intercepts printed output (and as is discussed later, disk requests) and sends that output across the network to the server.

LOGICAL DEVICES

Conceptually, the network and server are providing the user's computer with a *logical printer*. In other words, the user's computer thinks that it is physically connected to a printer. To the application software, the virtual, or logical, printer acts in every way like a real printer. More importantly, the printer is shared by many users, but this too is completely hidden. So the user's computer acts as if it has a local, dedicated printer, and the print server ensures that this illusion remains intact.

SHARING HARD DISK SPACE

The first IBM PC offered either a floppy disk or a cassette tape interface. Unfortunately, both floppies and cassettes are too slow and small to store large amounts of information. Further, hard disks were so expensive that users couldn't afford to have their own. As a result, disk drives were the second major resource usually attached to servers.

In the early 1980s, many users shared the hard disk in a server, but only in a very limited sense. Borrowing from the successful printer sharing model, early network software gave each user the illusion of a dedicated, personal, local disk drive. In fact, the early documentation for these systems described these shared disks as *logical floppies*. Typically, a personal computer at that time had one or two floppy disk drives used to store all information. The server provided the illusion of having extra floppy drives. If the first two drives were drives A: and B:, the server magically added drive C:, and maybe even drive D:, as well. To the user, the logical floppies were like local floppies in every way but one: the disks couldn't be taken out of the computer.

Looking at it from the server perspective, you can see how limited this sharing model really is. The server starts out with a reasonably large hard disk drive. This drive is then divided into pieces of a fixed size that correspond to the logical floppy disks. As each user connects to the server, the user is, in turn, connected to their personal logical drive. This model, no longer very common, is referred to as *disk sharing* or *disk service*. Yes, the server was sharing its expensive hard disk among many users, but none of those users could share any information with other users. Short of sending physical floppies back and forth, no facilities were provided for the users to exchange data (technically, primitive facilities for true sharing existed, but practically no one made use of them).

BENEFITS OF DISK SERVICE

With all of these limitations, was having the server around much of a plus? Not by today's standards, of course, but the disk service model did offer significant benefits to users:

✦ Expensive disks could be shared by many users who otherwise could not afford permanent storage.

✦ Even running across the network, the fast server disk often gave better performance than the slower disk of a personal computer. Even today, servers often have disks that are faster than the disks found in local workstations. In addition, the server generally has large amounts of main memory cache dedicated to making its disks appear really fast. All of this gives users the luxury of both shared resources and better performance.

✦ By spreading many users across a larger disk, space was used more efficiently; individual users were less likely to run out of space.

✦ By assigning an administrator to take care of the server, backup could be automated. Users never back up their own computers, even today. However, if the server was backed up, many users could be saved the grief of losing data.

In fact, what you see here is the beginning of a trend, which only now is being reversed, in which servers are more popular for sharing printers than for sharing disk-based information. The problem is that in a world where the unit of sharing is the logical disk, attaching printers to a server has many more benefits than attaching disks. As a result, after the introduction of the XT, personal hard disks became increasingly common in spite of the benefits of shared disks. Printers, however, were another story. Early printers, based on dot-matrix technology, fell rapidly in price. On the other hand, as prices fell, newer technologies became more attractive, and users continued to want more expensive printers. For instance, after being exposed to the speed and quality of early laser printers, most users quickly became committed to them. Later, as these printers fell in price, the technology of newer PostScript-based printers continued to keep prices high. More recently, as advances in color, speed, resolution, and paper handling become more common, users continue to find that the printer they really want is the one they can't afford. The ultimate answer, therefore, has remained constant: use a server, share the printer.

Logically, the first generation of servers introduced the concept of logical devices: the network offered the user access to a variety of shared facilities attached to servers. The server managed these facilities, providing them to many individual personal computers all at the same time; each user, however, would act as if the logical device were all his own, physically attached to his computer. As far as sharing printers goes, this model was great at the time it was invented and continues to be a winner today. For unlocking the true potential of servers as information-sharing engines, though, there needs to be some model for sharing information stored on disks that goes way beyond the notion of a logical floppy. As a first step in that direction, consider how a disk can act like a file cabinet, providing a way of organizing large amounts of information so that they can be stored and retrieved quickly and reliably.

ORGANIZING FILES ELECTRONICALLY

Imagine a small law office with lawyers and other staff members all serving a common set of clients (*serving* and *clients* are meant here in the traditional sense — professionals have always had clients to whom they provide services). How does the law office organize its information on paper, and how would the same information be organized in a computer?

Typically, an office organizes its clients and cases in file folders, which sit in file cabinets. Ultimately, though, after finding the right cabinet, opening the right drawer, and finding the right file, you end up with a document in your hand. The point of most filing systems, in the real world, is to organize documents.

SAME SYSTEM, MORE SPACE

In the computer world, as in the real world, the document is the basic unit of information; however, in the computer world, the information is stored on a disk instead of in a file folder. A document can be a spreadsheet, a memo generated by a word processor, a project plan, a slide presentation, or even a database. Later, when I come back to the topic of databases, you'll see that databases also can be more complex, intrinsically shared structures. For most users, though, a database is first thought of as a simple, personally owned form of document that holds collections of records. For example, a secretary preparing for a conference may have an agenda, a budget, a project plan, and an invitation list. To the secretary, all four items are just different classes of documents, worked on with a variety of tools and all supporting the common goal of having a successful conference.

Computer documents are stored in *files*. Again, the term *file* can have many meanings, but for most users, a file is the place on the computer's disk where documents are stored. Typically, at the time the document is stored, the file in which it is placed is given a name, and that name becomes the handle for retrieving the document in the future.

Before 1983, most personal computers assumed that every user would deal with a relatively small set of files, all of which could be kept in one place. In an office environment, this is the equivalent of keeping all your work in a single file drawer, with no hanging file folders to provide a second level of organization. Even for an individual, a simple single stack of file folders quickly becomes too limited a structure to handle large amounts of information.

The list of the names of all the files on a disk is called a *directory*. The directory simply can be thought of as the file folder: it is the place where the documents are kept together. Every disk has at least one directory; it's the place you store and find files. For instance, when you receive a floppy disk from someone else, the first thing you probably do is look at its directory, which tells you the names of all the files on that disk. Early personal computers insisted that all the files on a disk, no matter how large, had to be kept in a single list in a single directory.

HIERARCHICAL DIRECTORY STRUCTURES

In 1983, personal computers began copying the concept of hierarchical directory structures from large computers. Oddly, this relatively simple concept is one of the most difficult for most personal computer users to understand. Going back to the office scenario, filing cabinets are always organized hierarchically. What is this *hierarchy* concept? The trusty *American Heritage Dictionary* defines hierarchy as follows:

"1. a. A body of persons organized or classified according to rank or authority. b. A body of entities arranged in a graded series. 2. A body of clergy organized into successive ranks or grades with each level subordinate to the one above."

This definition might be considered a hint, but knowing how to apply it to a computer system is a bit mysterious. Go back to the hypothetical office and look at its filing system. The law firm's file cabinets are classified by type of client. In each cabinet, specific drawers are dedicated to particular clients (although smaller clients may share a drawer). Inside the drawers, hanging file folders provide another level of organization — the specific case. Within each hanging folder, individual file folders are labeled by project or document. And finally, within each folder, clips, staples, and so on are used to provide an additional level of organization.

Because this concept is so crucial and comes up so often in computer-based storage systems, Table 5-1 shows what I've just described.

Table 5-1   A Typical Hierarchical Filing System

Level	Subject	Physical Location
1	Type of client	File cabinet
2	Client	Drawer
3	Case/major project	Hanging folder
4	Project/document	File folder
5	Related papers	Staple, paper clip

If you compare this way of structuring the filing system to a classical organization diagram for a company, you can see where the term *hierarchy* came from. The diagram looks exactly like a reporting hierarchy five levels deep. The top level is "type of client"; beneath it is "specific client," and so on. Here's the trick to quickly and easily understanding what this all means: keep thinking back to the physical filing cabinet. It's immediately obvious how drawers relate to cabinets, how hanging folders relate to drawers, and so on. In fact, a file cabinet represents a set of *filing systems within filing systems*. A hanging folder is just a slightly bigger file folder that holds other file folders. Similarly, a drawer is a kind of mechanical, metal folder that, in turn, holds more folders. In general, each level in the filing cabinet groups sets of folders into yet a bigger folder. The concept related to hierarchies that makes this come together is *nesting*.

A hierarchical structure is another word for a *nested* structure. Nesting means that objects are tucked inside each other, just like nesting dolls. Russian babushka dolls are a standard offering at crafts fairs everywhere. Opening the outer doll reveals a smaller one inside. Opening the second one reveals another, and so on, until you get to a doll almost too small to hold. A hierarchical structure works the same way. An organization starts with the president, to whom one or more vice presidents report. Each vice president represents an entire organization, just like a smaller babushka. Going down a level, each vice president has people reporting to him or her, and each of those people represents a smaller organization, and so on, until you get to the bottom of the organization.

Computer disks are organized in the same way. Each computer disk has a hierarchical directory structure. Each level of the hierarchy can be thought of as a file folder that literally holds computer files. In addition, though, each level of the directory hierarchy can hold more directories in turn, making the whole thing hierarchical, or nested.

Who decides what the file system hierarchy looks like? The user does. The beauty of a computer file hierarchy is that it can be organized and rearranged with no manual labor. And, best of all, when the hierarchy is rearranged, the computer automatically rearranges all the files in the directories (folders) with no manual shuffling required.

To complete the example, Table 5-2 shows the kind of directory structure this mythical legal firm might set up.

Table 5-2   A Typical Hierarchical Computer Filing System

Level	Topic
1	East Coast Clients
2	Rhubarb Steel Company
3	Incorporation Matters
4	Articles of Incorporation
1	West Coast Clients
2	Pacific Chemicals Corporation
3	Environmental Legislation
4	Toxic Waste Act Requirements

Before the computer, East Coast Clients might have been a filing cabinet; now it's just the top level of the directory. Similarly, Articles of Incorporation could have been a rather bulky hanging folder; electronically, it's just a directory, with plenty of room for either documents or more levels of filing hierarchy below it. Babushkas nested forever!

So how does all of this relate to the server?

FILE SHARING: THE SERVER AS ELECTRONIC FILING CABINET

Perhaps one lawyer is working on a purchase agreement, and another staff member wants to check the articles of incorporation for the same client. Can a server facilitate this kind of sharing? To see how, consider how the same scenario would work in a pre-computer world. In most small companies, staff members retrieve contracts, correspondence, and other material from filing cabinets at will. To eliminate confusion, some simple checkout system probably is set up. If a lawyer is working on a contract making changes, the lawyer fills out a slip, thereby checking it out, and leaves the checkout slip in the filing cabinet to let everybody know what's going on. A little later, a paralegal can still retrieve the articles of incorporation from the same client file, also filling out a checkout slip.

In the logical device world, the server plays no role in expediting this process; in fact, it makes the process more complicated. Staff members can save documents on their logical disks at the server, but after they do, nobody else can access any of those documents. If a particular lawyer works on the purchase agreement one day and the articles of incorporation the next, both would likely end up on the lawyer's personal logical disk, making it impossible for anybody else to access those documents. As a result, given this model, the server ends up being used purely for temporary storage; staff members keep copies of the document on the server as long as the documents are checked out, and they erase the server copies when the documents are checked back into the filing system.

Given this approach, as the law firm comes to depend on its word processing software more and more, floppy disks become the primary filing medium. Copies of the floppies are stored in the file cabinet folders, or a completely parallel filing system is set up, consisting of floppy disks arranged by client, subject, and document name. Of course, because these documents are on floppy disks, they are not significantly easier to share or organize than paper documents, and the need for two parallel systems — one for paper and one for floppies — is a definite nuisance. Worst of all, in this environment, electronic information travels at the speed of legs; documents are carried from one place to another by hand. Sneakernet lives. Even today, in organizations with large, sophisticated networks, this is often the standard mechanism for document sharing.

SHARING THE FILE, NOT THE DISK

In 1983, Novell introduced the concept of *file sharing* as an alternative to the *disk sharing* model just discussed. The idea is to no longer split the server's hard disk into separate, discrete, logical floppy disks. Instead, keep the hard disk as one disk and let everybody work on the same disk at the same time. The server then becomes an electronic filing cabinet. The following paragraphs discuss the model one step at a time.

First, remember that the disk no longer gets divided up into many smaller logical disks. Instead, every user sees the same, single large disk. At first glance, it's hard to tell if this is a convenience or a nuisance. Without hierarchical directories, a single large disk, shared by all users, is unworkable. As users add documents to the shared disk, the list of names quickly becomes long. Everybody has trouble finding specific documents. Soon, people start forgetting the names of their documents, and searching through a long list becomes tedious very quickly.

Worse, people sometimes make mistakes and delete the wrong document because it's too hard to keep filenames straight. As a result, the workers make life tough not only for themselves, but also for others. In addition, finding all the documents related to a particular subject or project is just plain impossible in this environment. So without some way of organizing all the documents on a disk in some meaningful way, sharing the disk makes no sense.

With a hierarchical directory structure, users can treat the big shared disk like an electronic filing cabinet. In fact, the disk becomes equivalent to *many* electronic filing cabinets because it can hold a great deal of information and because its hierarchical directory structure is much richer and more flexible than any cabinet could ever be. With this structure in place, it becomes very practical for all users to share a single disk. By organizing documents into nested folders, information can be organized into containers that enable many users to work on the same disk without running into each other.

Looking at it another way, the single directory model is the same as having all documents in a single file drawer — everybody would be butting heads all the time trying to share that drawer. With the hierarchical structure, enough drawers become available that people generally stay out of each other's way. Still, how does the sharing itself work?

THE FILE SHARING ENVIRONMENT

In a nutshell, the file service model introduced by Novell in 1983 implements the same *checkout* scheme for computer documents that the mythical law firm used with paper documents. In a file sharing environment, the unit of sharing is the *document* or *file.* Any number of users can all be working in the same disk on the same server all at once. As long as they are all working with different documents, no conflict arises. If one lawyer edits a purchase agreement with the word processor while another works on an associated project schedule, there's no problem because they are working on different documents. In the meantime, whenever a user is working with a document, it is checked out to him or her exclusively. If another user then tries to work with the *same document at the same time,* the server reports that the document is in use. It's simple, effective, and all implemented without any manual checkout slips.

With this one step forward, the primary use of the server shifted from printer sharing — still an important use today — to electronic filing and document sharing. Like the printer, the server adds many benefits:

✦ All documents are now accessible from anywhere on the network without physical movement — no more sneakernet.

✦ Coordination of access to documents is implemented automatically so that only one person at a time modifies a file. The electronic coordination process eliminates the delay inherent in the manual system. Documents no longer spend time in transit, checked out the whole time; instead, checkout and checkin occur instantaneously at the time the document is opened and closed over the network.

✦ Automatic backup procedures provide many levels of protection against disaster, including the possibility of keeping copies of critical information off-site. Furthermore, if backup is done regularly, previous versions of documents quickly can be retrieved from the backups if questions arise regarding the document's history.

✦ Users can create very sophisticated filing structures. Having folders within folders within folders is possible and easy; folders can no longer be too full, and moving information from one folder to another requires only a few keystrokes. Best of all, with good backup procedures, mistakes are easy to rectify.

✦ The server can enforce arbitrarily strict security procedures. Users can implement passwords and create authorization lists to directly control who can see what. Unlike the manual world, all of this can be accomplished without restricting overall access to the server and the information it contains; now the user can access all information instantly, limited only by security clearance.

✦ Best of all, as I discuss later, the computer can tirelessly implement sophisticated search procedures, including keyword and phrase retrieval, so that if a document isn't where you expected it, there's still hope of finding it.

ELECTRONIC FILING: ONE SMALL STEP FOR HUMANKIND

Before considering the next stage in the evolution of the server, I'd like to spend a moment on the implications of even the simplest kind of file sharing just described. Most companies spend huge amounts of money filing, storing, managing, and retrieving documents. This expenditure happens at every level of the organization. Individuals maintain file cabinets in their offices, workgroups have shared files, departments have file rooms, and all large companies have sophisticated central filing systems.

Many of those same companies could make their filing systems vastly more efficient by just implementing some of the technology just described. True, a simple server file sharing model is not enough to handle all the filing requirements of departments and companies. But it is enough to handle many of those needs. Ironically, many of these companies already have installed the servers needed to simplify their filing, but they are unaware that with some simple reorganization, these same servers could be used in new ways — with no additional investment required in hardware, software, or installation.

As an example, consider the following informal study. Several years ago I gave a speech to a group of lawyers at an American Bar Association meeting. I described a document-sharing scenario in which, sitting at my workstation, I could retrieve contracts instantly, work on those agreements, and have the network automatically manage the checkout and checkin processes. As I was describing this technology, which at the time was already ten years old, the audience became quite agitated. So to understand the reaction, I asked a series of questions. The answers illustrate the point:

✦ Every lawyer in the room considered the document-sharing scenario I described as highly desirable, worth spending money for, and a feature that would immediately contribute to increased productivity.

✦ Of the hundred or so lawyers in the room, representing some of the largest and most advanced law firms in the country, only about five had implemented anything like the filing system described.

✦ About 90 of the lawyers had computers on either their desks or the desk of their assistant.

✦ About 80 of the lawyers (90 percent of those with PCs) had networks already installed and running that offered file sharing as a feature.

What this example illustrates is how progress so greatly depends on education and cultural change. It is exciting to think about the client/server revolution and about the link between corporate downsizing, personal empowerment, computer downsizing, and completely new ways to use computer technology. In the process of thinking about these topics, you will discover many things that can be done today to make progress and many pieces that are still missing. Most of the time, however, the biggest impediment to making more effective use of computers is not missing technology; it's personal and organizational inertia.

FROM PASSIVE TO ACTIVE: THE SERVER AS DATABASE MANAGER

Database is both a business and technical term. Because the database is so central to the overall client/server shift, I devote Chapters 9 and 10 to the topic. However, no section on servers would be complete without at least introducing the topic.

THREE TYPES OF DATABASE

Database products come in three flavors. Products such as Paradox, dBASE, and Access enable users primarily to work at their desks with collections of records. All three products contain powerful facilities for sorting, reporting, expressing queries, and so on. At this level, databases enable users to work with *private* databases, similar to simple collections of index cards or Rolodex cards, all stored in a single file. Just as with a text document or a spreadsheet, the user opens the database, has exclusive access to it until done, and then closes it. In fact, Paradox, dBASE, and Access also contain the second flavor of product in the same box: they enable many users, all of whom can be working with the same data at the same time, to share a database. Each of these products includes not only the facilities to enable users to manipulate data, but also the underlying features that facilitate database sharing. Finally, specialized, high-performance products such as Oracle, SQLserver, and DB2 — the third flavor of products — are built for the sole purpose of facilitating database sharing, with the added twist of providing this service for very large populations of users, all of whom can use the same data at the same time.

In these last two types of databases, the common thread is the idea of an increased degree of sharing compared even to the file sharing model. In the *logical device* environment, users were able to share entire logical disks. If one user was working with a logical disk, no other user was able to access any of the information on that disk. With the introduction of *directory service,* users could share at the document level. Many users could all work in the same directory structure, but only one user at a time could work with a particular document. Finally, the database model enables many users to even work on the same file at the same time; the unit of sharing becomes the database record.

Look more closely at some of the terms, particularly *database* and *record.* A *database* is a special kind of file that can be shared by many users at the same time. In the case of most files, representing documents, it just doesn't make sense for more than one person at a time to be making changes. For instance, suppose that several people were all working on the same memo at the same time: how do they keep from getting in each other's way? In a database, this problem is solved by organizing the information in the file into records and then arranging for each record to be changed by only one person at a time. Consider the following example.

Imagine a time-tracking system for a legal office. Each time a staff member does some work for a client, the staff member fills out a form, which causes the time to automatically be recorded in a database. At the end of each month, the computer prints neatly summarized bills from these records. In addition, at any time in the month, a client can call up and be told his or her running total to date. In this case, the database stores project time sheets, each of which is stored in a single record.

Clearly, even though several people may be doing work for the same client at any given moment, only one of them can be allowed to update the particular timesheet at a time. (This assumes, of course, that time is recorded on the basis of a *one timesheet per client* project. The system could also have been arranged to have a timesheet for each staff member.) The database provides this protection by *locking the record;* the first user to read the record gets to add his or her time in and when the user is done, the next one in line adds his or her time, and so on.

INFORMATION SHARING MODELS

The concepts of sharing and locking are concepts you've seen before. Acting as an electronic file cabinet, a server enables users to share directories, folders, and documents. If two users try to access the same document at the same time, the second one in line is told that the document is already in use: it's locked, and he has to wait until the first user is done before he can make changes. The differences between the two models are the amount of information that gets locked at any time, and the behavior the user sees when he tries to access a locked record. In fact, backing up a level in the world view, you can now compare three models of sharing, as shown in Table 5-3. The disk server shares at the unit of entire logical disks, the file server shares documents, and the database server shares records. The new idea that the database introduces is a new locking behavior.

Table 5-3   Information Sharing Models
                        and Their Units

Model	Unit of Sharing
Logical device	Entire disk
Directory service	Single file
Database	Record

Trying to check out a document currently in use by someone else results in a message telling you that the document is not available. Some modern word processors will even report who is working on the document you want. After you receive that report, your only recourse is to either wait and try again or somehow contact the other person working on the document. Logically, this locking behavior is based on the idea that documents are pretty big; people work on them for long periods of time, so it doesn't make sense to keep you waiting until the document becomes free; it could take hours or even days.

Databases can be set up to act like a document manager; they can simply refuse to allow you to work on records while anybody else is working on them. Typically, however, databases introduce another option, a *queue*. In most databases, if you try to change a record that somebody else is currently changing, the database makes you wait in line. As with documents, only one person at a time gets to change the record, but now nobody ever gets told that the record is unavailable.

This waiting behavior makes sense because the unit of sharing is now so small. A typical database record may relate to the description of a single part, inventory for a particular product, a timesheet for an individual, or single phone message from a list of hundreds. Think back to the idea of sets of Rolodex cards. An ideal database facilitates sharing at the level of an individual card. Because the record is so granular, representing such a small amount of information, whoever is working with it typically finishes quickly; waiting becomes a reasonable strategy. To really understand why record sharing, locks, and this new locking model are so important, you need to think about why databases are important in the first place.

DATABASES: WHO NEEDS THEM?

The term *database* has a variety of meanings with subtle gradations. Definitions range from "the central concept that defines why many companies use computers to run their business in the first place" to "a simple tool for keeping track of invitation lists, spare parts, telephone numbers, and other small collections of records I use personally." In Chapters 9 and 10, I explore the topic of databases in more detail from both a business and a technical perspective. For now, though, consider databases that are somewhere in the middle — between the big systems used to run entire organizations and the simple personal record managers each person could carry around in a shirt pocket. The central distinction is sharing in a team environment.

SHARING WITH THE TEAM

Consider a sales office that wants to share leads, simplify tracking of phone messages, and keep common files on outstanding orders. Perhaps five to ten salespeople and their support staff are involved — less than 20 people in all. A server, the company's electronic filing cabinet, provides a very convenient way of making all the proposals, letters, and proposal requests available to the team without extensive manual filing. Because the server can be accessed through phone lines, salespeople can file and retrieve documents while on the road. Still, document sharing provides only very limited team coordination. That's where the database comes in.

By keeping contact reports, phone messages, telephone numbers, and proposal specifications in a database, everybody can be working with the same information at the same time. Suppose that phone numbers were once stored in documents. All phone numbers probably would have been collected in a customer list; as soon as anyone accessed a phone number, everyone else was locked out. By making the unit of sharing finer, the database has immediately reduced the possibility of a lock even being encountered: although it is quite likely that two people are likely to need access to the phone list at one time, it is pretty uncommon for two people to need to look up the same phone number at the same time.

COMMUNICATION AND CONTROL

Coordination has two faces: communication and control. Communication means that the members of a team have a way of letting each other know what's going on. By having a common, shared phone list, everybody gets to know automatically when a phone number changes. And, best of all, it happens without having to go around to tell people. Sometimes, however, communication is not enough. When a phone number changes, it isn't critical that everybody knows immediately. Using the old phone number leads to either a recording with the new number or a failed phone call; either way, the caller knows what to do next. At times, the impact of having the wrong information is more serious; that's when control as well as communication is required.

Suppose that a price quotation for a customer changes and a salesperson doesn't find out. If the salesperson then tells the customer the wrong price, all sorts of problems arise. The solution is to have everybody look in a single place whenever he or she wants to check on price quotations. Ideally, the place where people look always reflects all changes to the quotation and is therefore always up to date. That's the point of a database. And having a computer act as the controller of the shared information makes it possible for teams to function much more effectively than has been possible in the past.

ALTERNATIVES AND EXCUSES

Suppose that there was no computer to act as an information controller. Then in the case of quotations, someone would have to appoint a single person as the information controller. Perhaps a salesperson servicing the account is appointed as the account owner. Then everyone would agree that that person is the only one who can approve a price quotation and that everyone should ask that salesperson before quoting a price to a customer. Similarly, in the case of inventory, to avoid allocating parts more than once, someone would appoint a person as an inventory controller and agree to always ask that person before committing inventory for orders. Of course, the problem with this system is that when the person acting as controller is busy, unavailable, or even getting a drink of water, everything grinds to a halt. This results in the infamous symptom associated with this strategy: *I can't commit to the price until I check with the manager.*

Alternatively, the company could implement some paper-based system where price quotations, inventory levels, delivery dates, and so on, are always recorded in a single, agreed-upon place — perhaps a control board or a special binder. In this case, a different set of problems arises. A worker can quote a price, reserve a part, or schedule a delivery in *only* two situations: if the worker is where the control board or binder is or if the worker is talking on the phone to somebody who has access to the control information. This type of system is recognizable immediately when sales and service people tell their customers this: *I'll let you know the price and delivery after I check back at the office.*

The beauty of a database is that because it runs on a shared server, the database is never busy and never away on vacation, and the database can be accessed from any computer connected to it through the network or through telephone lines. All of a sudden, teams can start sharing information and, better yet, *controlling* the information so that everybody is always guaranteed to see the most up-to-date version of the information, even though many people are using and changing that information concurrently. The very idea of a database, even in the small team environment, revolves around two assumptions:

✦ All information is available all the time; nobody is ever told that some information is unavailable.

✦ Any given piece of information is controlled by the database so that only one person at a time can change it. If several people want to change exactly the same piece of information, the database ensures that they are queued so that they change the information one at a time, and each one sees the results of all the changes made before them.

To see how these two rules interact, consider an inventory situation. A sales office is sponsoring a seminar with limited seating; the group can accommodate only 25 attendees. Because invitations will be extended and RSVPs processed by the whole team, a database is set up to control attendance. The database tracks invitations, RSVPs, and the total number of accepted invitations. Each time an RSVP indicates that a different person will attend, the record showing the total count is increased by one. When that count reaches 25, no more attendees are accepted. The question is, with RSVPs being processed by the entire team, how can they be sure that a sudden rush of replies near the end doesn't result in 30 people coming when the seminar room seats only 25? On the other hand, how can the sales team, as it talks to customers, act responsive by letting them know immediately, without asking anybody else, whether there is still room left at the seminar?

ADVANTAGES TO THE DATABASE

Using the shared database to control the attendance count answers both questions. As salespeople talk to customers, they can check with the database to see how many people are registered for the seminar. Any number of salespeople can check the invitation count at a given moment, without requiring the help of any central human coordinator. Each salesperson can add a guest to the invitation list, knowing that, even if another salesperson is trying to do the same thing, each will add his or her guest to the count one at a time. And when the 25-person limit is reached, the database makes sure that everybody knows immediately.

The same database can do the following things:

✦ Keep customers' addresses up to date, ensuring that if someone changes a client's address while someone else is trying to change the phone number, neither change will be lost.

✦ Track supplies of sales literature so that if two people try to reserve large quantities at the same time, the first one gets the requested amount, and the other finds out how much is remaining, if not the requested amount.

✦ Record phone messages, allowing them to be picked up from home or on the road, even though they were recorded just seconds ago at the office.

✦ Maintain a running tally of sales wins, impartially recording who reached key targets first in the race to be first.

All of these examples illustrate two facts: why databases play such a unique and crucial role in supporting workgroups, and why it is the ability to share records, guaranteeing constant (but controlled) access, that makes databases able to play this key role.

SERVER/SERVANT

Now you can understand the server in perspective and appreciate the first, albeit simple, meaning of *client/server*. Clients and servers are just computers. In fact, the beauty of the whole approach is that the exact same boxes, designed to be inexpensive and easy-to-install personal computers, can function as both client and server. The personal computer sitting on a desktop, dedicated to meeting the needs of a single individual, is hugely attractive; as a result, competitive pressures have resulted in making this technology a valuable but routine commodity.

At the same time, even in a world of unbelievably powerful and completely personal computers, there is a strong need for sharing information and resources. Historically, in the computer world, expensive mainframes and minicomputers have provided this kind of sharing. Databases, for instance, have been common on mainframes for over two decades. The personal computer server, on the other hand, was born with a much simpler destiny in mind. Originally, personal computer servers provided a mechanism for sharing expensive hardware. I've talked about printer and disk sharing; in fact, personal computer servers enable individuals to share many other kinds of expensive hardware, as well. For example, servers on a network can facilitate sharing of modems, communication lines, connections to mainframes, faxes, image scanners, color plotters, and so on.

In the beginning, even though personal computers had started to act as servers, there was still a clear distinction between big and small computers: big computers controlled shared information; small computers, even when acting as servers, operated only with individual information. By providing print spooling and other hardware-oriented sharing, servers took a small step in the direction of the big computers, while still leaving this major distinction intact.

With the introduction of file sharing and then of databases, even small servers became information-sharing devices. As I explore later, the mere sharing of information is quite far from being enough to replace mainframes and minicomputers. At the same time, by providing a mechanism for sharing and controlling the sharing of information, servers became in many ways the equivalent of mainframes for small workgroups. The local sales office that could never have had a customized client-tracking system written on the mainframe can now build the system itself by using a database running on a small server.

A server coordinating and controlling the sharing of information for a group of people in this way has made a critical functional transition from being a passive sharing device to being an active servant. Printer sharing, disk sharing, and modem sharing all can take place via fancy switching devices. Conceptually, the switcher provides the illusion that each user has sole access to the shared hardware, in much the same way that a shared telephone switching system provides the illusion that every pair of users has a dedicated telephone line connecting them. In fact, many modern phone systems (PBXs, for example) provide this kind of device sharing for personal computers connected to corporate telephone networks. Even so, this kind of sharing is basically passive in nature, acting as a silent extension of the personal computers themselves. Put simply, sharing a printer, modem, or disk saves money; users can do the same thing less expensively than if they had no server, but they can't do anything new.

File sharing, and even more so database sharing, provides fundamentally new capabilities to users — capabilities that are intrinsically dependent on the fact that the server is a computer and not just a fancy switching device. Even at the document-sharing level, it is the server, using its computer-based intelligence, that is able to keep track of who is using documents and to tell waiting users who has the document checked out. At this level, the computer is acting like a library clerk, actively understanding the names and characteristics of the documents it is managing. When it comes to sharing records, the computer, as server, is playing an even more active role, keeping track of records, helping users find those records, and ensuring that users line up in an orderly fashion when it comes time to make changes to shared information. In this role, the computer is acting as inventory controller, seminar registration coordinator, central filing clerk, and sales contest judge. Sounds pretty active to me.

In fact, the server is a kind of tireless servant — a servant who provides services to a variety of clients, each of whom is also a computer. In this environment, each user has sole control over a computer that acts as his or her aide. That personal computer, acting as a kind of electronic desk, amplifies the individual user's capabilities, providing tools for doing individual activities more quickly or more easily. The server, in the same environment, is an electronic office. It is both master and servant, controlling access to information but following the directions of the workgroup as a whole. What really makes this system powerful, though, is the way the personal computers and the servers all work together. And the facility that enables that cooperation is the network — the technical component I look at next.

CHAPTER 6

THE LOCAL-AREA NETWORK — A NEW TYPE OF COMPUTER

What is a network, and what is *not* a network? The term *LAN* stands for *local-area network*. A LAN is a high-speed network that interconnects terminals and computers over very short distances; the equipment usually is contained within a single building. Because of the short distances over which it operates, the LAN is able to transmit information *very* quickly. And precisely because of the LAN's speed, it really *is not* a network.

LANs originally connected large populations of terminals to computers that were located close by. By using special heavy-duty wiring similar to the coaxial wiring used in cable television systems, computers were able to communicate with the terminals so fast that information could always be displayed on the screen almost instantly. For applications that involved the display of large amounts of information, this was an obvious advantage. Used in this way, a LAN is just what its name states: a network that operates in a local environment.

To understand how a LAN can be used in a way that makes it no longer a LAN, it is necessary to look at some of the underlying numbers that define the operating characteristics of this important technology. It may sound like this is getting pretty technical, but as the dentist says, "It won't take very long, and it won't hurt that bad."

NETWORKS INSIDE NETWORKS INSIDE NETWORKS

What is a network? A network (sometimes called a *net*) is a mechanism for connecting computing devices. Where are networks found? Certainly connecting big computers and terminals, but they are also found in surprising places. Inside every computer is a network. Every computer consists of a collection of computer components: disks, printers, memory, the computing unit, status displays, and so on. A specialized, high-speed network connects all these components. Sometimes this net is called a *backplane,* sometimes a *channel,* and sometimes a *bus.* In this discussion, I use the term *bus* most often. In a mainframe, there are two levels of network inside the computer. Inside the box containing the main computer is a network of particularly high speed. Outside the box is a slower but still very high-speed network running out to all the disks. In between these two networks is a bus structure called the *channel.* The channel is significant because information can flow only from the computer, to its disks, and back at channel speeds. The channel in most mainframes built in the 1980s operated at about two million bytes per second.

To put these speeds in perspective, consider a modern high-speed modem: a transmission rate of 14.4 kilobits per second (Kbps) is considered pretty nice. A speed of 14.4 Kbps translates into about 1,800 bytes per second. In comparison, at two million bytes per second, the mainframe channel operates over *1,000 times faster* than the high-speed modem. Little wonder that channels and buses can't be thought of as even remotely comparable to modem-based networks.

Like a mainframe, a personal computer has inside it a bus network that connects the memory, the central computer, the disks, the option slots, and so on. The option slots, which sit on this bus, are particularly significant because in a personal computer, most of the internal components are connected by plugging them into option slots. So in many ways, the speed of a personal computer is defined by the speed at which information can flow through those option slots. In most personal computers, that speed is about two million bytes per second, about the same speed as the 1980s mainframes.

Mainframes, minicomputers, and personal computers are built around interconnection structures that literally are networks, but nobody thinks about those computers in this way. For example, you would probably never go through the following thought sequence:

✦ I need to add a hard disk to my personal computer.

✦ I want the entire computing system to be fast, so I'll make sure I get a fast hard disk.

✦ To install it, I'll plug the new disk (or the new controller card) into an option slot.

✦ The option slot is really part of a network, and networks are slow. I'll have to figure out a way to connect the disk directly to my computer's central computer.

One reason you might not take that last logical step is because you are probably not aware of the network inside your computer. Another reason is that there is no performance disadvantage to the option slot approach. Both reasons together produce the point: for all practical purposes, your computer is a *computer,* not a *network.* In a real sense, the bus/slot structure *is* a network, but in another very real sense, it is *not* a network. The purpose of a network is to connect multiple computers and terminals, generally over long distances. The purpose of the bus structure inside a computer is to tie together discrete computers to create a functioning computer system. Thinking of an internal bus as a network is missing the whole point.

How fast is a LAN? An Ethernet runs at close to two million bytes per second, the same speed as the bus inside a mainframe and the option slot bus in most PCs! Aside from being an interesting numeric comparison, what does this mean? Suppose that you set up a server with a particularly fast disk. Often, a personal computer can consistently retrieve data from that server disk *faster* than it can retrieve the same data from its own local hard disk! The network is functioning as an extension of the personal computer's internal bus structure. Users can access components attached to the LAN as fast or faster than they can access components attached to the bus structure inside the personal computer itself. In a sense, the LAN is an extension of the personal computer. Or perhaps the personal computer has become an extension of the server attached to the LAN? Or both?

ELIMINATING THE CEILING, SMOOTHING THE STEPS, AND SAVING YOUR JOB

To understand the initial attraction of LAN-based computer architectures, it is necessary to hark back to the days of big computers and the budgetary perils associated with them. And, lest you forget, these times of fear are still very real for any Vice President of Computer Systems with a large mainframe or minicomputer in his or her budget.

Mainframes and minicomputers are very expensive. To put their prices into perspective, they cost as much as some good-sized buildings. Any capital acquisition costing millions of dollars requires careful justification, and gaining approval for big computers has always been an important part of the job of any senior computer person. Compared to most capital equipment, however, computers have an unusual characteristic: it is very hard to accurately predict how long they will be useful. The usefulness of a computer is based on three factors:

✦ How long it takes to wear out

✦ The rate at which it becomes obsolete

✦ When users will eat through its capacity

Obviously, the first factor is a joke when it comes to computers; they don't wear out. Obsolescence, however, can be a legitimate risk with computers because technology changes so quickly. Companies have occasionally been trapped by buying systems just before major new functionality or features became available in the next generation. Generally, though, vendors go out of their way to protect their customers. So obsolescence, scary as it sounds, is not a huge factor in limiting the useful life of a computer. The third factor, capacity, is the issue. Because computers typically run out of capacity so quickly, the other two factors never come into play.

When justifying the acquisition of a major new mainframe, the main task is forecasting how long the computer will last before a major upgrade or a complete new system is needed. Unfortunately, no matter how carefully the forecast is done, users' appetites for computer power are insatiable. Adding more capacity — whether in the form of disk space, faster computers, or more RAM — is just the tip of the iceberg. With the added capacity, response time is better than expected, more applications can be run, and away you (and your department) go.

In an age of personal computers costing under $5,000, saturating the server is hardly an issue; when the server runs out of storage or can't produce answers fast enough, buying one is fast and cheap. If that server were a $5 million mainframe, however, saturation could bring sweat to the brow. Picture the situation: management in your company has barely gotten over the cost of the last computer system, the schedule slips in getting the software running, and the complaints start coming in from users about apparently missing features or hard-to-use functions. Finally, the Management Information Systems department (MIS) comes back and reports that without a $2 million upgrade, the next round of functional improvements will have to be postponed. Angry to begin with, management asks how long the upgrade will last — ten years would be fine. Instead, after considerable explanation, MIS admits that the upgrade is only an interim step; in 18 months the entire system will have to be replaced with its big sister at an incremental cost of over $3 million. To make matters worse, a long-delayed operating system conversion will tie up the entire development staff for six months at the time of that upgrade. Without the conversion, the upgrade won't work, and response time will grind to a halt.

As this process is unfolding, the company's chief information officer (CIO) is without a doubt polishing his or her résumé just in case management runs out of patience or understanding — commodities that are never in great supply when it comes to expensive computers.

Perhaps this story sounds exaggerated, but for many who lived or are living through the travails of large computer liability, it's close to home. Mainframes are large and expensive, and capacity comes in chunks that also are large and expensive. Buying a mainframe in the first place is a huge commitment for a business. Often, that big computer has *too much* capacity at first, and companies often consider selling their excess computer horsepower. Later, as more and more applications come on-line, capacity becomes more and more scarce. Because an upgrade is so expensive, businesses try to avoid it as long as possible, which results in poor service to users. With a mainframe, it's either feast or famine, and it's almost impossible to predict the cycle.

Mainframes are not unique in this respect; many other large capital acquisitions work the same way. Office buildings are often either largely vacant or so full that hiring must completely stop. Airports may have excess capacity for years, but new construction almost never begins until congestion has become unbearable. The problem is not that mainframes are somehow bad, they're just so expensive.

Is there an alternative? (Never ask the reader a question unless you know the answer.) Of course. The answer is not cheaper computer power, although that is always desirable, so much as it's computer power that can be acquired in bite-size pieces. To elaborate on the last paragraph, the *precise* problem with mainframes is not that they're so expensive, but that they come in *such big chunks*.

Think of mainframe costs as a staircase. The first step — around $5 million — is a killer; small companies can't climb even that one. The next step is also pretty big, again in the millions. The remaining steps — every time more memory, more disks, or a faster computer is needed — are also huge, until finally (and worst of all) you run completely out of steps.

Take that staircase and flatten it out. Make each of the steps smaller, but provide many more stairs so that you can still climb just as high. That's what minicomputers did: provided smaller steps, but more of them. The steps involved both smaller and less expensive computers. The lower expense made the entry cost more palatable. And by promising that many small computers could do the same job as a single big one, the minicomputer companies found a way to keep the stairs small.

In reality, the minicomputer staircase runs into a ceiling sooner than the mainframe. Eventually, even a large number of minicomputers runs out of capacity. But the combination of the expensive mainframe and a host of smaller minicomputers surrounding it offered a more attractive (that is, less scary) set of steps into the future for many corporations. This concept accounts for much of the success of Digital Equipment Corporation (DEC) and its competitors, but even this path contains some pretty big steps.

The attraction of LAN-based architecture is twofold: the steps go away, and the ceiling disappears. The steps go away because PC-based servers are so inexpensive. Adding servers one at a time as demand grows leads to a cost curve that is virtually flat — a ramp instead of stairs. The ceiling goes away because the LAN-based architecture offers the potential of almost unlimited computer power, just by having enough PCs and servers. For shell-shocked MIS personnel, the attraction is that they might keep their jobs. After all, a $5,000 computer addition is much easier to think about than one that costs a thousand times that amount.

THE NETWORK IS THE COMPUTER; THE BUILDING IS THE BOX

In the mid-1970s, Bob Metcalfe of Xerox's Palo Alto Research Center (PARC) invented local-area networks as mechanisms for connecting personal workstations, servers, and printers. At the time, PARC was creating a variety of components and systems that foreshadowed much of today's office-oriented client/server revolution. However, the focus at PARC was personal. Systems facilitated individuals working alone, working in teams, and interacting with other individuals and teams. Ethernet, the first working LAN, was not seen as a tool for potentially replacing all the bigger computers and terminals used to run businesses. Instead, LANs were seen as a complement to the mainframes and minicomputers of the time.

As papers and articles began to focus on LANs, Datapoint Corporation, a Texas computer vendor, decided that the LAN concept, which was so compelling at the personal level, could be even more compelling in the world of big computers. In the late '70s, Datapoint introduced the *Attached Resource Computer* built around the *ARCNET*, a proprietary LAN technology. For the first time, MIS had a commercial alternative to the big-step staircase of mainframe capital.

ARCNET systems were built around two types of computers, which would be called *clients* and *servers* today. In addition, ARCNET systems provided two new ideas about this new style of computing:

✦ Both clients and servers were relatively inexpensive.

✦ Because ARCNET was so fast, the entire system — the combination of clients, servers, and the network — could be thought of as one large computer.

The second idea thoroughly changes the very conception of what a computer is.

SEEING THE LAN AS A COMPUTER

In a Datapoint system, the local net is so fast that it really should *not* be thought of as a network. Instead, compare the entire Datapoint system to a classical computer system. A large Datapoint installation with hundreds of workstations and dozens of servers would service a large building with high-speed LAN cable running throughout the entire building.

If a mainframe provided the same services, the mainframe's computer would be in a special room, and the system would use a network (in the traditional sense) to bring the terminals to the computer. As I've already discussed, however, that computer would consist of a special network — the computer itself — but that internal network is so fast that it should not be considered a network. So in the classical environment, the computer is located inside a series of boxes: the largest box is the computer room, and inside it is a series of smaller boxes containing disks, memory, and the main system cabinet, in which the central computer lives. Finally, snaking through this set of nesting boxes is a set of wires and buses that, again, is really too fast to be called a network.

Here's the new thought: all of a sudden, the Datapoint system allows the entire office building that everybody works in to be the box that contains the computer system.

Fancy rooms are no longer needed, nor is a low-speed network needed to bring the terminals to the computer. The computer and the office building are now intertwined, just like the nervous system of any living being. This might sound neat, but is it *revolutionary?* The answer is yes, but the full impact of this method of building computers is being seen only now, over a decade since Datapoint introduced the concept and over 20 years since the invention of Ethernet.

The short-term impact of attached resource computing was important but less than revolutionary. It offered MIS that first glimpse of a nonthreatening and adaptive architecture for buying and growing computer systems. The beauty of ARCNET was that each time a server or work-station was installed, the *central computer itself* was being expanded. With terminal-based computer systems, adding a terminal adds workload to the central computer without adding any computing capacity. How could a new terminal add capacity? After all, the terminal is a passive device, a kind of conduit through which the user approaches the computer itself. And as I discussed earlier, the central computer could be grown only in large chunks that cost a great deal of money.

In the LAN environment, *there is no central computer.* Instead, there's a *distributed computer system.* In fact, you can't point to a single box — or even a single room — and say, "There's the computer. I wonder how it's doing." Even if all the servers are kept in a computer room, you still can't equate that room with the computer or understand how much capacity is available by looking at that room because the clients — the users' individual workstations — are an integral part of the overall computer system. In a real client/server system, the workstations are more than just intelligent terminals. A major part of the overall work of the system is done *in* the workstation. This style of computing is sometimes called *cooperative processing.* For now, just remember that *the network is a computer.* The computer is the combination of all the servers, all the workstations, and all the high-speed cables connecting them. The network is the computer in exactly the same sense that a mainframe — which consists of computing components connected by a bus — is a computer.

The first conceptual impact of the client/server LAN-based revolution was the introduction of a smoothly growing, adaptive computer system. Starting with a single workstation, an organization could grow an integrated computer system, adding servers and workstations at any rate that made sense. That computer system would smoothly adapt its capacity to the number of users connected to it. If you add a user, you add a workstation and the associated computing capacity required to service that user. As a result, the entire configuration gets bigger and faster, not overloaded and more attenuated. Add servers periodically, but put them close to the users. The servers aren't very expensive, so don't worry too much about the decision. Add a server to meet the needs of a workgroup or department, and take the cost out of that workgroup's or department's own budget, without having to revise the capital budget for the entire organization. Build a system, grow that system, and respond to user's needs. You no longer have to worry about making a single capital decision so big that a miscalculation could leave thousands of users with inadequate service and put your career at risk along the way. Perhaps this new idea is not revolutionary from an overall organizational or societal perspective, but it's not hard to see why it would be compelling for MIS workers.

SEEING THE BUILDING AS A BOX

Although ARCNET itself is not widely used today, the Datapoint architecture established an important precedent. It demonstrated not only that the network could be the computer, but also that the building could be the box. When I described the classical computer system in terms of a set of nesting boxes, I said that the biggest box (which enclosed the overall system) was the computer room. In the LAN environment, the biggest box is the entire building. Aside from the important cost implications I just talked about, the LAN approach also made people think about computers in a different way — a way that in the long-term had even more impact than the reduction of cost-based fears. Putting the computer in a central location also implies putting all the associated peripheral facilities (printers, disks, and so on) in the same central location. In the classical system, computers printed reports, but that happened centrally. The reports were distributed through interoffice mail. Databases were maintained on computers and accessible through terminals, but the databases were centrally controlled and were maintained for the convenience of the organization, not to be truly responsive to the needs of individuals.

The second major impact of the ARC system was to make people understand that business computers, like personal computers, could be responsive to the needs of single users. On an ARC system, for instance, a printer could be located anywhere. Furthermore, if a user wanted a custom report, it might take a long time for his or her own workstation or departmental server to produce that report, but producing the report did not drag down the single computer servicing the entire company. And because the printer could be located conveniently down the hall, producing that custom report on demand might save the user time because he or she could request it whenever necessary.

Today, of course, this sounds routine; personal computers provide this functionality constantly. Yet, even in 1995, although personal computers are now on most desks, they are still not used to run the business. Most large organizations still depend on the central mainframe or minicomputer for that need. The case is worse for many small businesses. Big central computers are too expensive, and the personal computers can't handle shared data well enough; therefore, data is still processed by hand. While the hardware reality that Datapoint introduced in the early '80s is definitely here, the business reality — the opportunity to really capitalize on that hardware — is still ahead of us. The key point is to finally build on the fact that not only can you make the network *be* the computer and have the building be the box, but you also can apply that style of computing to running the business. So if the potential has been there to realize this new vision for so long, why hasn't it happened?

PARC, followed by Datapoint, created this conceptual legacy for businesses to capitalize on. But Datapoint's development of the vision still missed some elements that were required to enable a true revolution in the way organizations run. Although the actual computing resources of an ARC system were distributed around entire buildings, the style of applications being built on those computing resources was virtually identical to the style of mainframe applications. In theory, the workstations were capable of changing the way people interacted with computers, but in practice, they still looked like terminals. The servers were *capable* of providing business applications customized to the needs of individual workgroups, but in practice, the servers provided standard, inflexible applications exactly like those running on mainframes. The cost and capacity adaptability of the system represented a breakthrough, but the ways in which the system was used fell short of fueling a revolution. What was wrong with the equation?

For a revolution to occur, the equation had to include the lessons learned from the fact that millions of personal computers were being sold at the very same time that Datapoint was installing ARCNETs.

THESIS, ANTITHESIS, SYNTHESIS

George Hegel, one of the more opaque philosophers of the modern era, proposed that great breakthroughs in thinking happen in three stages:

1. *Thesis:* First, an idea is proposed.

2. *Antithesis:* Second, the opposite idea, the *antithesis,* is considered. This is often frustrating because both the thesis and the antithesis have merit, but they are apparently irreconcilable.

3. *Synthesis:* Finally (typically in a dramatic breakthrough), a completely new idea arises, based on a combination of the two old ideas. The new idea brings the two old ideas together — *synthesizing* the thesis and its antithesis.

The first step to finding such a synthetic breakthrough is to clearly articulate what the key idea and its opposite are. This enables you to see what the apparently impossible reconciliation needs to accomplish. The opposites in the case of client/server, once stated, come into sharp focus quickly.

Historically, the mainframe and its sibling minicomputer have stood for things shared. As boxes too expensive to devote to individual goals, the big computers had the job of providing shared access to information, coordinating use of scarce resources, and being a constantly available enforcer of corporate policies. By definition, the big computer is an organizational asset whose very purpose in life is to meet the needs of the many and follow the lead of the hierarchy that runs the company.

By comparison, the personal computer is (as its name states) *personal.* It sits on a person's desk, holds his or her information only, probably has no way of allowing that information to be shared, and coordinates nothing. Instead of enforcing policies, the PC provides the user with the very means for adapting those policies and frameworks to his or her needs. The personal computer is an individual asset whose reason for being is to meet the needs of one user and do exactly what that user tells it to do.

This dramatic contrast shows the problem: there's nothing in the middle. Having a personal computer is great, but what about when you need to share information with others or have an agent to coordinate resources? Using that big mainframe to keep everything coordinated is fine, too, but what about the needs of the individual? The differences appear irreconcilable (exactly the hint needed to seek a breakthrough). More important, these opposing needs deal with more than computers. I'm talking about finding a way to reconcile the needs of the individual with those of the organization, a theme that echoed through organizational halls long before computers were around. Can the two be related? Is it possible to suggest, with a straight face, that the client/server revolution might have something to do with terms such as democracy, empowerment, and finding a balance between the needs of the big organization and those of the tiny individual? That is precisely the point I am inching toward, but first I'll try for a slightly more modest synthesis. The journey toward changing society, or at least organizations, begins by showing what happens when the personal computer finally learns how to cohabitate with the mainframe.

BAMBI MEETS GODZILLA: USABILITY VERSUS CONTROL

In other chapters of this book, I explore the client, the server, and the network in some detail. Compared to terminal-based interaction, the client provides the user with a completely new way of working with computers based on the idea of the graphical user interface, or GUI (which in turn is based on precepts of virtual reality). The promise (or consequence) of the GUI is that terminal-based interaction will never be acceptable again. By tapping into the enormous amount of computer horsepower and memory that can now be put onto people's desks (and even under their arms to carry around), you can take the world of data and convert it into a virtual world of live information — a world that the user literally can walk around in. Pages spring into existence, houses appear on the screen, and by moving the mouse or pointing at the screen, you can drive around on streets. All this happens with almost no physical movement. Completing the picture, direct manipulation enables the user to reach into (or out of) the virtual world and control its parts naturally, instead of forcing that user to remember a set of arcane commands.

There are two prices to pay for this awesome creation of virtual new worlds, only one of which I fully explored in the preceding chapter. The first price is that all users must have their own computer, under their own control, sitting on their desks, under their arms, or on the grass in front of them as they explore and control those virtual worlds. That world might be as mundane as a printed page or as exciting as an aircraft simulation that includes photorealistic scenery from around the world. Regardless, all the power, realism, and intimately interactive control over those virtual worlds are made possible only by the dedicated devotion of huge amounts of processing power and memory to the single user. The first price is committing to personal computers: each person needs at least one computer. A second price, however, didn't appear until the client/server concept appeared.

CLOTHING THE VIRTUAL WORLD

Virtual worlds of all kinds are built on huge amounts of data. The term *scenery from around the world* initiates three questions:

✦ Where does the scenery come from?

✦ Where are the pictures stored?

✦ How did those pictures get into the computer?

The second question — *Where are the pictures stored?* — is the easiest to answer by itself, and the answer helps elaborate on the other two questions. There is only one place those pictures can be stored: *in a very personal computer that projects the virtual world.* When I discussed the huge amount of processing a personal computer does just to display a spreadsheet on the screen, I pointed out that a great deal of that processing revolved around that actual process of display. *One of the key tasks of a personal computer is providing visualizations of virtual worlds.* Visualizations require huge amounts of data, and all that data must be processed at incredible speeds so that the user can move around in his or her own world, without apparent delay, hesitation, or degradation in image quality.

What can virtual worlds possibly have to do with computers, organizations, and business? Aircraft designers, architects, and maybe even page-layout artists might want to live in business-oriented virtual worlds, but what about normal, everyday people who don't know what a *bodysuit* is (it's the apparatus that researchers wear while exploring virtual worlds)? A marketing manager exploring pricing alternatives is living in a virtual world. The manager's ideal discussion certainly revolves around *what ifs, alternative scenarios,* and *best case/worst case models* — all of which describe alternative universes. Planning production schedules for a factory requires the creation of a small virtual world. Explaining driving directions to the closest service center works better if you can drive around the streets on your screen. Even placing an order or recording a complaint is easier if you can see a virtual image of the product while talking to the customer on the phone.

The scale may be smaller for some business applications, but the very point of the GUI — its capability to simplify, streamline, and facilitate interaction with the computer — revolves around the creation of some form of virtual world. Virtual worlds are created by displaying high-quality pictures (and perhaps sounds). Even if the pictures portray only numbers and words, the presentation is better when the pictorial representation is richer. Graphical spreadsheets work better precisely because they are *graphical;* in other words, they display numbers and graphs richly in many fonts and colors, and they can combine many different kinds of information on the screen at one time. Better pictures mean better virtual worlds, which mean better applications.

Creating virtual worlds requires instant access to huge amounts of data. The data has to be stored in the personal computer. About a page ago, I asked three questions: Where does the scenery come from, where are the pictures stored, and how did they get there? I've answered the second question, but what about the other two? Where do the pictures and the information to create the pictures come from? There's the rub.

MAKING *HERE* MEET *NOW*

Most of the information you work with in your personal-computer-generated virtual worlds comes from somewhere else. True, computer games can be self-contained. With the advent of CD-ROMs, which can store and transport huge amounts of information on very small, inexpensive disks, an aircraft simulator could have scenery for dozens of airports and cities all on a single CD. In organizations, however, the situation is more challenging. First, organizations revolve around huge amounts of data, more than could be put on any reasonable number of CD-ROMs. Worse, that information is constantly changing. Insisting that all the information you work with must be stored inside only your own personal computer is like claiming that the same aircraft simulator now enables you to fly real airplanes, as well. Imagine controlling an airplane, taking off, flying somewhere, and landing, all the while being blindfolded. To make it better, instead of being blindfolded, you get to look at a screen that shows the scenery for the route you're taking, but the images you see are the ones photographed several years ago. You're watching five-year-old images, but you're landing a real airplane today! What about all the other airplanes, the dog running across the runway, or the sudden patch of wind? Of course, the whole thing is preposterous. But what if the alternative is flying the same plane, having access to the real information, but the information is fed to you on a computer screen in the form of words and numbers? Not much better, right?

Client/server combines the virtual worlds made possible by personal computers with the real and realtime information contained only in the organizational computers. Now there is an answer to the question of where the scenery comes from. It comes from the organizational computer — the server or the mainframe. By itself, this is the correct answer, the only answer, but also an answer that doesn't work. The reason it doesn't work revolves around the third question: *How did those pictures get into the computer?*

For virtual worlds to be useful, they must be part of a shared, realtime universe. Orders must be placed around actual inventory. Appointments at service centers must reflect commitments for time slots that will be honored. Price scenarios must be built on real, recent sales data. Factory production runs must be planned only around actual customer demand, real parts availability, and the true availability schedules for equipment and people. So all these virtual worlds require access to data that can come from only one place: the organizational computer. Not only does the data have to come from that shared computer, but as the data changes, the new data has to be put back into the organizational computer immediately. After all, after a product unit is sold, it can't be sold again. After an appointment is given out, that time is gone. And so on.

The need to work with realtime, up-to-date information implies that computer users must have direct access to the data in the central organizational computer. After all, as I said in the discussion of the server database, the whole point of the shared computer is that it coordinates access to information for the many so that the individual can access that information directly without human help. That's how Bambi meets Godzilla.

THE LOVABLE FAWN

In the infamous short filmstrip *Bambi Meets Godzilla*, lovable little Bambi, the fawn, meets Godzilla, the huge monster, who immediately steps on Bambi, crushing him. Who's Bambi and who's Godzilla? Bambi, of course, is the cute little personal computer. The very name implies a connection, often emotional, to its owner. People — no, *individuals* — buy personal computers precisely because they are *personal*. Personal means friendliness, power, and most of all, control. Any teenager's parent appreciates just how much having control over one's life means. A personal computer brings direct, no-questions-asked control over a personal information appliance. A PC is a tireless servant who does whatever you tell it to.

Godzilla? The mainframe. Mainframes are the opposite of personal: central, unapproachable, and full of forbidding interfaces. In addition, mainframes are controlled by a central bureaucracy. Worst of all, individuals do not control the mainframe; the mainframe controls *them*. In the classical central application I discussed earlier, every task processed through the mainframe is controlled by the mainframe. The user may initiate the task, but the central computer lays out the steps, one by one. In many big companies, the mainframe lays out not only the small steps, but the big ones, too: each day it lays out the production schedule, the delivery schedule, and the list of orders to be processed for approval. Orwellian, perhaps, but Godzilla? The mainframe may be the ultimate control freak, but isn't it a bit unfair to portray it as somehow crushing the personal, adorable, desktop computer?

The opportunity for Godzilla to break loose comes from that first question: *Where does the scenery come from?* Suppose that a product manager has developed a sophisticated model for analyzing prospective price changes — a small virtual world. To run the model quickly, producing complex three-dimensional graphs that portray various tradeoffs (production costs versus market demand versus competitor response), the marketer needs access to a large amount of data *in his or her own computer*. As long as that data doesn't have to be up-to-date, no problem. Unfortunately, this product manager's pricing model becomes very successful. Unfortunately?

As the company depends more and more on the pricing model, the company decides to use it in several highly competitive, high-volume, and volatile markets. The product manager is being considered for a promotion, and a challenge arises. How can the company alter the model to deal with rapidly changing data in an environment where many people are involved in each pricing decision? Obviously, the data can't be stored in each user's personal computer anymore. For one thing, the prices are changing too rapidly to justify continuous updating of the individual PCs. Worse, be-cause several people are involved in each pricing decision, their models all must be working from the same data, looking at the same what-if scenarios, and considering the same changes. The only way to facilitate that kind of data sharing is to store the data somewhere else.

How about the mainframe?

THERE GOES BAMBI

Here's the catch. As soon as the data and the GUI are no longer in the same com-puter, the virtual world stops working. The entire basis for the construction of the graphical interface — the portrayal of virtual realities and the ability to directly ma-nipulate parts of that real world — was that the user's own computer could access and manipulate huge amounts of information constantly and instantly. Virtual worlds are possible only when the information driving the application is in the same computer as the application.

From the user's perspective, as the application becomes too successful, the data driv-ing the application is moved to a minicomputer or mainframe, the graphical interface becomes unworkable, and the ability to work in a powerful virtual world suddenly disappears. Somehow the mainframe reached out, co-opted the personal computer, and turned it into a slightly better terminal. Godzilla has crushed Bambi.

Overstatement? Do personal computers really become terminals when connected to mainframes? Can you take advantage of that personal computer's power even when connected to the mainframe, to bring some GUI to the world of sharing? Isn't there some way to have both — graphical worlds *and* sharing? No. Yes. Yes and No. And finally, Yes! Consider these questions one at a time.

VENEERS: TRANSFORMING LEAD INTO GOLD

Millions of people have personal computers that talk to mainframe- and minicom-puter-based applications. Most of the time, the PC becomes a terminal while talking to the bigger computer. These PCs display exactly the same information a terminal would display, but they display it on their computer screen. In a multitasking environ-ment, you can add a touch of sophistication by confining the terminal screen to a window while running personal tools (such as word processors, spreadsheets, and mail) in other windows. This configuration allows these personal tools to assist you in dealing with the mainframe. Seeing these windows side-by-side on the screen, how-ever, makes it painfully obvious how primitive and limited the terminal interface is compared to everything else on the screen.

Many technical designers reached an obvious conclusion: there *must* be a way to take the terminal interface and make it simpler and more powerful by making it more graphical. Designers created a variety of tools they hoped would *transform* a terminal screen into a graphical window-based form. In the end, that hope turned out to be just that: a hope. Although the tools described in the next few paragraphs work, making mainframe applications easy to use requires more than a simple transformation of the screens the user sees.

Normally, a mainframe sends sets of data, or *forms,* to terminals that display the data on the screen. Replacing the terminal with a personal computer introduces a new layer of intelligence into the equation. You can program the personal computer to be somewhat *self-aware.* When the mainframe sends a form to the personal computer, the PC is capable of doing something other than just painting it on the screen. A class of tools called *screen scrapers* or *graphical veneers* traps the form and, instead of displaying the original form, dresses it up to look prettier. Products such as Easel, Viewpoint, and Rhumba all fall into the category of screen scrapers.

THE ALCHEMIST'S TOOLS

The veneer concept is possible because the screen scraper can intercept the form (which otherwise would go straight to the screen) and keep the form in its memory. Then the screen scraper analyzes that form. The instructions that normally tell the terminal what to do with the data become the basis for the screen scraper's analysis. Instead of displaying the form on its screen, the personal computer stores the form in its memory. The PC then takes the parts of the form one at a time and converts them into more understandable elements of an equivalent graphical form.

Where the old form insisted on entry of a part number, the new form displays a list of part names enabling the user to pick the right one. Where the old form used cryptic codes to indicate mode of shipment, the new form provides a list of *radio buttons* (Express, Overnight, or Normal delivery) to pick from. Cryptic error messages become help boxes with varying levels of detail selected by the user. By the time the scraper is done, the final form looks nothing like the original. Each element of the form is more attractive and easier to understand. In many cases, entire forms disappear as multiple repetitive sequences are folded into smaller, more powerful, more intuitive graphical forms. The screen scraper appears to offer the user a new, more graphical world — a world where the mainframe can't even tell anything has happened. Magical? Maybe, maybe not.

The magic is accomplished by a combination of the new powerful screen-scraping graphical veneer tools and programmers in whose hands the screen transformation takes place. Graphical transformation of applications is a very attractive concept. The transformation process is relatively rapid and painless, the users *do* end up with improved applications, and no changes are required to the mainframe resident code. So what's the catch? How do you get from magical transformations to Godzilla crushing Bambi? First, you have to know what's really happening when the tools scrape the screen.

BEHIND THE SMOKE

Unfortunately, not much at all is happening. Just as gluing a veneer of fine wood onto a particle board base does not convert a table into solid oak, scraping off the terminal-oriented screen and replacing it with a graphical veneer does not convert the mainframe resident code into a graphical application. In addition, most users see through a graphical veneer in a matter of days. Graphical veneers really don't transform mainframe-based applications after all. The problem, though, is worse than that.

In an ironic sense, mainframe applications are *supposed* to be hard to use when centrally directed. They're not designed to make individual users more powerful. So the fact that a screen scraper doesn't change the mainframe's ease of use, while perhaps disappointing, is hardly surprising. Personal computers, on the other hand, are easy to use and do make individual users more powerful, but they work only with personal data. Whenever the user needs to work with up-to-date or shared data, the data has to come from the mainframe. As I said earlier, even if the mainframe has a screen scraper, lead does not become gold. In addition, the powerful, graphical application the user *already had* reverts back to the terminal world. In a real sense, not only has lead *not* turned into gold, but by connecting the PC to the mainframe, *gold turns into lead.*

But let's be honest. Nobody expects mainframe-based applications to get better just because users access those applications through a PC. And everybody is excited about the newfound power the personal computer gives users to work with data in new ways. The catch comes when the applications built on the personal computer grow up. Soon, data requirements become sophisticated, and applications grow. To enable those same applications — that were not originally written for the mainframe — to work with realtime, shared data, the applications must move to the mainframe. That's when Godzilla crushes Bambi — when gold turns into lead.

Yes, personal computers really become terminals when connected to mainframes. And yes, users can take advantage of the power of that personal computer, even when the PC is connected to the mainframe, to bring *some* GUI to the world of sharing. There is some way to have both graphical worlds *and* sharing, but neither personal computers nor mainframes alone are enough. A new kind of computer must accomplish this trick — a computer that combines the characteristics of both personal computers *and* mainframes: the LAN.

THE GREAT CONTRADICTION

The design of this new type of computer revolves around the three questions at the center of every virtual world: where does the scenery come from, where are the pictures stored, and how did they get there? You know almost the whole answer.

The pictures come from a single computer acting as a shared computer, an organizational computer, and a database computer. The point of the last section is that although a virtual world may start out revolving around personal information, sitting on a single person's desktop in an organizational environment, the virtual world quickly has to be shared. The information from which the virtual world is constructed has to be totally up-to-the-minute, and changes made by you have to be visible by everybody else as soon as you make those changes. The information at the center of virtual worlds comes from another computer, not from the personal computer.

At the same time, that information *must* be stored in the same computer you work with; otherwise, you can't generate a realistic virtual world. Whether the virtual world is a simple three-dimensional pricing model or a complex geographical map, in all cases the personal computer has to work with basic information *stored in its own memory*. The only way to create virtual, graphical worlds is to have the application, the information, and the graphical display in the same computer.

That is the great contradiction: how did the data get there? If the data is in the personal computer, the result is great applications, virtual worlds, and irrelevant data. You can fly your plane, but the runway you're seeing, the planes you're avoiding, and the dogs on the runway are based on three-year-old data. You might as well be flying with your eyes closed. If the data, pictures, and numbers are in the mainframe — the shared computer — you can't access them fast enough from your personal computer to have graphical displays. You fly the plane, but instead of looking out the window, your only source of information (although realtime) is based on words slowly being printed on a single screen. Now you get to fly the plane in realtime, but by the time the teletype tells you about the dog on the runway, you've already hit it.

The whole problem revolves around the data location contradiction. Put the data in the personal computer, and virtual worlds come into existence. However, those worlds are static, not shared, and based on history only. Put the data in the shared computer, and the world becomes dynamic, shared, and up-to-date. However, the virtual worlds disappear, and the real-time world is flat, one-dimensional, hard to work with, and limiting. Not an appealing choice.

THE FINAL SYNTHESIS

From this contradiction arises not just an opportunity, but also a driving need to view the LAN as a new kind of computer, not a network. In this new perception of the system, the personal computers, the network, and the servers are all viewed as one large computer system. The network *is* the computer; the computer is the network.

Where are the data, the pictures, and the numbers? In the computer. But now, the computer has both personally dedicated and organizationally shared elements. Accessing data from the disk drive inside your personal computer is fast, but accessing data from a server on the LAN is *faster*. The data needs to be in your computer, and the LAN *is* your computer. One part of the LAN — the personal computer on your desk — is dedicated to you; another part is dedicated to sharing. Through the LAN, they're all one big computer — a single integrated system.

Where do the pictures and the data come from? They come from the shared computer so that you have an up-to-date virtual world and your changes are immediately shared. How did those pictures, numbers, and data *get* there? On a LAN, the question loses its meaning. Your computer and the organizational computer are the same. It's one big computer system.

Precisely because a LAN is not a network — precisely because it is so fast that information can be accessed as quickly across the LAN as across the internal bus structure of my personal computer — there is a new synthesis. The result combines the virtues of Bambi (personal computing, graphics, and virtual worlds) with its antithesis, Godzilla (shared computing, databases, and coordinated control), to deliver a new synthesis: shared virtual worlds. If the personal computer is the electronic desk, then the LAN is the electronic office.

THE ELECTRONIC OFFICE

At this point, you should have a basic understanding of the truly new foundation element in the computing systems of the '90s. Personal computers play an important role, providing the engine for generating graphical worlds. Servers are the sharing engines, coordinating access to a variety of shared resources ranging from printers to databases. The LAN links personal computers and servers, forming a completely new type of computer system in which personal data and shared data are the same. This system provides a base on which shared virtual worlds can be built where we all share the same information and where changes I make are seen by you instantly. The beauty of the LAN is that it facilitates this shared world while leaving each user the power and autonomy offered by his or her own personal computer. At the beginning of this chapter, I introduced the LAN as the network that's not a network. What do you do if you really need a network after all, for example, to connect offices all around the world? That's what the next chapter is about.

CHAPTER 7

WIDE-AREA NETWORKS — CONNECTING THE WORLD

When I wrote the first edition of this book, networks were hardly a hot topic. Few nontechnical people had any concept of what networks even were. Yet, in a short period of time, the Information Highway has become sufficiently popular to even figure in national politics. In the '90s, the Internet and the World Wide Web are achieving much of the same notoriety that personal computers achieved during the '80s. As a result, while few people understand what networks are really about, suddenly wide-area networks (WANs), providing the glue that ties computers together all over the world, are hot topics of conversation. Just as it took over a decade for personal computers to mature to the point where they truly were widely usable, global networks, while interesting to talk about, are still far from being ready for serious prime time. This chapter is about those WANs, where they come from, what they are truly useful for today, and where they are going in the future.

By interconnecting computers and local-area networks (LANs) wherever they may be located, WANs will convert the entire world into a global village, make telecommuting possible, change the meaning of the word *office*, and put information at your fingertips on a scale that today is literally unheard of. In the last chapter, you learned about LANs — networks that are not really networks. This chapter is about *real* networks, the WANs.

To understand these real networks, you need to consider them from three perspectives. First, you'll look at the underlying network technology itself, both in terms of how networks evolved and in terms of how they work today. Second, you'll learn about *electronic mail*, the major application that has already caused a great deal of true cultural change. Third, you'll look at networks through the World Wide Web, bulletin boards, and internal applications like Lotus Notes. These networks are providing a form of community memory that builds on electronic mail to make the global village, at least at a corporate level, complete.

Finally, as you consider how all the various elements of the worldwide network fit together, you'll find cooperating components coming into the picture. Chapter 3 discussed the surprising places that cooperating components would show up; this chapter is the first of those places.

To begin with, consider the role of the classical network. The trusty *American Heritage Dictionary* defines a *network* like this:

1. An openwork fabric or structure in which rope, thread, or wires cross at regular intervals.

2. Something resembling a net in consisting of a number of parts, passages, lines, or routes that cross, branch out, or interconnect: an espionage network; a network of railways.

3. A chain of interconnected radio or television broadcasting stations, usually sharing a large proportion of their programs.

4. A group or system of electric components and connecting circuitry designed to function in a specific manner.

As the definition points out, networks existed long before computers. For example, a "network of highways" would have made immediate sense to a listener in the '50s — before computer networks had been invented. Similarly, many people commonly understand the phrase "television network" than understand any computer-related network terms. Drawing again on the definition, the common elements in these usages of the word relate to the concepts of structure, connections and interconnections, and components, and tying them together into a larger whole. Computer networks are based precisely on this set of concepts; the term, of course, is based on the networks that existed in other forms at the time computer networks were invented.

The central concept behind a computer network is *connectivity*. The network facilitates the interconnection of computers, terminals, printers, and other computers — without having to worry about the mechanics of how the connection is made. Achieving worry-free, thought-free, any-to-any connectivity is critical to the eventual long-term success of client/server systems — if they are to fulfill their potential.

WIDE-AREA NETWORKS: FOOLING THE PHONE SYSTEM

In the beginning, to borrow a biblical phrase, networks were invented to connect terminals to computers. In the late '60s, as terminals became common, it became very attractive to start locating terminals wherever a company did business. For big companies, this meant spreading terminals out all over the world. As terminals became ubiquitous, and as computer applications that could talk to terminals became common, there was a need to give terminals the capability to talk to more than one computer system. For example, a company originally might have installed a terminal to facilitate order entry, perhaps to enter the orders for a particular product family. However, once the terminal was placed on a desk, the user started wondering why the same terminal couldn't be used to check on the status of orders, schedule deliveries, enter customer complaints, record payments, and so on.

This is why. In that same beginning, each terminal was connected to a single, specific computer by a dedicated, special-purpose communications line. If the terminal was in the same building as the computer, the connection was a physical cable — a set of wires that literally connected the computer to the terminal. Later, as terminals spread to remote locations, special dedicated phone lines were used for the same purpose. During these early years, these remote terminals operated, literally, by fooling the phone system. Telephone companies in those days provided dedicated telephone lines as a way of facilitating voice communications for large companies; a special leased line enabled branch offices to be connected to head offices. This bypassed the complexity of the long-distance network, and it saved the company some money along the way. So whether they were local or remote, early terminals were once connected to their computers through a dedicated connection.

Naturally, when users began to ask about talking to more than one computer, this raised some eyebrows, and at first no straightforward answer was apparent. As hard as this might be to believe (or picture), the initial answer was simple: put another terminal on the desk. And in fact, through the '70s, and even into the early '80s, many desktops ended up with two, three, four, or as many as seven or eight screens and keyboards on them. This cozy situation was not limited to clerical or entry-level positions, either. Some of the most demanding consumers of information are market traders — individuals who make and lose millions every day trading stocks, bonds, commodities, and currencies. These traders are totally dependent on incoming information: the more sources of information they can receive, the more ways they can analyze that information, and in turn, the more money they can make (and lose) every minute. As a result, until recently, the most cluttered desks — the ones with the largest numbers of screens and keyboards — were those of highly paid and highly skilled brokers. Finally, in case you are thinking that such complex conglomerations of equipment are never seen by ordinary humans, think back to your visions of airplane cockpits, rocket launches, and the control centers of nuclear plants — all seen regularly by millions on television sets around the world. All of these environments involve highly skilled people, working with many screens at one time, drawing information from a large number of separate computer systems, to do their jobs. So the need to exchange information with many different sources is at least moderately common.

HOW MANY (COMPUTER) SCREENS SHOULD A USER HAVE?

Obviously, while the operator of a nuclear submarine may need (and even want) to view many screens at one time, the average person is happy with (or will tolerate) one at most. Consequently, some mechanism is required to enable the user's terminal to talk to many computers. One way to solve this problem is with a simple switch located at the user's desk (this is similar in concept to the switch used for a shared printer, discussed in the preceding chapter). The switch would allow a single terminal to talk to many computers by shifting back and forth across the still-separate dedicated lines running to the remote (and local) machines.

Having all these dedicated lines is a problem, too. In the first place, having individual lines connecting terminals to computers is an expensive proposition. Each line in a building requires wires running throughout much of the office structure. As terminals are added, and as each terminal talks to more and more computers, pretty soon there aren't enough wires to go around. Long-distance connections are even more of a problem because of their expense. Having permanent, dedicated long-distance circuits between every terminal and all the computers it might use becomes prohibitively expensive almost instantly. Finally, all those connections are a physical problem for both the computer and the terminal. At the computer end, supporting thousands of connections, many of which are not in use at any particular time, quickly becomes too expensive to be affordable. And at the terminal end, having lots of wires, while feasible, is hardly practical, let alone neat or compact.

When this problem first presented itself, a straightforward solution quickly appeared based on an older technology: the telephone system. By the '70s, the telephone system had already reached the point where any telephone in the Western world could connect itself to any other telephone in the Western world by simply punching in a series of digits. The connections were usually fast and for the most part transparent, at least for voice conversation. Why not find a way to send data over the same network? If this could be done, giving every computer a phone number and giving every terminal a phone would enable any terminal to connect to any computer. No sooner said than done.

As it turns out, with the invention of the modem, computers and terminals could talk to each other over normal phone lines, and the telephone system couldn't even tell that it was data moving back and forth, not voices. This concept of fooling the phone system was critical because it meant that, without having to invent and build a complete alternative worldwide interconnection network — an undertaking that would take years — widespread and highly flexible computer-to-terminal connectivity became possible almost instantly.

Many of today's simple networks are still based on this simple technology. In fact, the same technology enables any personal computer owner, by dedicating a PC and investing in several extra phone lines, to create a public bulletin board. Think about the power of this technology. A teenager, with no outside assistance and by spending less than $5,000, can establish a database and communications environment that strangers all over the world can tap into and use. Connectivity to the max. Yet, for all of its power, this approach still had some fundamental limitations.

The voice-based telephone system was never designed to handle high volumes of data in an environment where dropping a connection or losing a bit could have catastrophic consequences for the terminal or computer participating in the conversation. Furthermore, even ignoring the issues of reliability and integrity just raised, the voice system is completely inadequate for allowing even terminals to talk to computers very quickly, let alone the even higher speed requirements imposed by computers talking to computers. After this problem became clear, entrepreneurs rushed forward to start inventing, building, and selling new technologies to facilitate data communication.

WITHSTANDING NUCLEAR ATTACK

During the '70s, network design focused on two primary problems: 1) providing inexpensive conduits for transporting large amounts of data quickly and 2) ensuring that the data would be transported reliably and accurately. To understand the first challenge, consider the needs of a terminal user. As I covered in the section about GUIs and UIs, a terminal screen holds about 2,000 characters of information. In the early '70s, the typical voice-grade phone line could carry about 120 characters (bytes) per second. As a result, sending an entire screen of information from the computer to the terminal could take 15 to 20 seconds — an eon for the human waiting at the other end. With special equipment and carefully conditioned phone lines, this screen transmittal time could be reduced to under a second, but most customers couldn't afford to pay for such expensive facilities between all their terminals and computers.

To understand the second problem — reliability — recall again the design goals of the original phone system: transmission of voices. The resulting analog (as opposed to digital) system was never built to provide a noise-free environment; most people don't care and can't even tell if their phone conversation is accompanied by constant or intermittent background noise. In fact, people are particularly good at understanding spoken conversation even in the presence of surrounding noises of all kinds; computers, on the other hand, are prone to just not work in this kind of environment.

The solution to both problems relies on a single observation: even though computers and terminals send large amounts of information in very short periods of time, there are also long periods where no information is being exchanged. The reason this observation is so critical is that all the solutions to the problems of capacity and reliability involve the use of very expensive communications lines and equipment. However, if computer traffic is in fact bursty — information is sent back and forth in relatively short but intense bursts with long periods of silence in between — then these expensive facilities can be shared by many users. In that case, these otherwise too expensive facilities become affordable.

What's required to facilitate this kind of sharing? A dedicated computer that can allow many terminals and computers to all share a common communication line. You've seen this before; it's a *server*. The specialized network switching computers of the late '70s, sometimes called *network nodes*, were in fact the earliest form of specialized servers. Sharing alone solves half the network problem: it allows several computers and terminals to share a communication line, making it affordable to have a much more expensive and capacious link than would otherwise have been possible. How about reliability, though?

Reliability has three aspects: availability, accuracy, and resilience. Availability is simply a measure of how often the network is there when you need it: 99.7 percent availability, for example, would mean that, averaged over some long period, a network was available 23.928 hours (all but 4 minutes and 19 seconds) of every 24-hour day. Accuracy, of course, measures what percent of the information transmitted through the network arrives at its destination unchanged; typically, a network drops as few as one bit in many billions. Resilience — how well the network can withstand failures of individual components — is the final aspect of availability. For example, if a single modem or telephone line goes down, can the network somehow patch information so that it flows around the failed components?

Just as terminals were becoming really popular, the armed forces began to realize the tremendous advantages of using terminals tied to computers to coordinate and control military units spread around the world. For the first time, it was possible to imagine having all parts of a distributed military operation constantly being coordinated with each other; headquarters command and control could be located anywhere and still stay up to date all the time. Unfortunately, when such a system is introduced, the organization quickly reaches the point of total dependency — where it can no longer function when the communications network goes down. This is a case where the issues of availability, accuracy, and resiliency are taken to their limits. For this reason, in 1975, the Defense Advanced Research Projects Agency (DARPA) funded research into the construction of highly reliable networks. In fact, the goal of the research was the design of a computer communications network that could continue to function even in the face of nuclear attack — a network that could tolerate the complete destruction of multiple major components and still work smoothly.

PACKET SWITCHING: SOME ASSEMBLY REQUIRED

The result of this research, still at the center of most network designs today, is the concept of *packet switching*. Consider a message that needs to be sent from a terminal to a computer or from one computer to another. Now imagine chopping that message into equal-sized packets. Each packet can be thought of as a little envelope containing a small part of the message. Having divided the message up into chunks, the network now transmits those chunks one at a time. After sending each packet, the network node (the communications server) waits to find out whether the packet was received correctly at the other end; if not, the packet is retransmitted until it is received correctly.

Without going any further, such a network is already vastly more accurate and tolerant of failure than before. For example, if a lightning storm causes a phone line to be temporarily noisy, the network simply retransmits packets until the noise dies down. Furthermore, because the packets being sent over and over are relatively small, even a small lull in the storm allows packets to get through so that progress is made, even if a little at a time. This eliminates the situation in which a long message had to be retransmitted over and over for a very long time just because a single bit error somewhere in the message caused it to be rejected each time.

Today, even in very noisy environments, error-correcting modems built on these principles provide virtually error-free transmission by implementing packet transmission and error detection and retransmission, as just described. This approach even has an unexpected benefit. At first, it might seem that doing all this work would slow things down: transmissions have to be cut up into packets, each packet has to be checked for accuracy on receipt, some packets have to be retransmitted, and finally, at the other end, the packets have to be reassembled. But as it turns out, this approach leads to more throughput, not less.

The accuracy of a communications line depends on the rate at which information is pumped through it. The faster you shove data through the line, the closer to its limits you will push it, and the more errors you will see. A line that looks totally error free at 100 characters per second may introduce errors into 1 to 5 percent of the characters at 1,000 characters per second. Normally, this would force you to drive the line at the slower speed. However, with error-correcting modems, you can safely run the line at a substantially higher speed, knowing that the occasional error will be detected and corrected. One reason that modems today commonly run at 14,400 or even 28,800 bits per second — over ten times the speeds common only five years ago — is that those modems now contain tiny computers that implement packet-based error-tolerance techniques. In fact, having these computers built right into the modems makes them much faster in not just one but two ways. While the computer is busy splitting the data up into packets, checking for errors and retransmitting when necessary, they are also compressing the data at the same time. That is, when the computer sees repeating characters or patterns, it automatically sends the repeated data only once. So packets, when supported by intelligent (computer-based) modems, are actually faster because the phone line can be driven faster and because compression allows more data to be transmitted in less time.

What has been described so far is *packet-based transmission*; where does the *switching* come into play? The use of packets enables users to tolerate noisy lines, but what if the line goes away altogether? That's where *packet switching* comes into play.

The network described until now consists of three components: terminals, computers, and network nodes. The nodes are specialized servers that convert messages into packets, handle error detection and retransmission, and so on. How are the nodes connected to each other? Earlier I discussed the use of the phone system to replace direct connections between terminals and computers. This facilitated a shift from a scenario where every terminal was connected to all computers it talked to by a direct connection, to a scenario where the connection was initiated by placing a phone call. With the arrival of packet switching, direct connections come back into play. But now, I'm talking about direct connections between network nodes instead of between terminals and computers or between computers and computers.

To understand this transition, go back to the very idea of a network — conceptually, a web of connections that allows components attached to the network to talk to each other. In the very early days, the network consisted entirely of direct connections: fast, but very expensive and inflexible. Every time a new connection was required, a direct link was established between the terminal and the new computer it wanted to access. Soon, the country would have been covered with wires. By using the phone system and placing telephone calls to computers, this direct connection network was replaced with the phone network itself. This new approach was highly flexible, but very limited in throughput; dial-up phone lines simply can't handle large volumes of information. That puts you between a rock and hard place: high throughput with unacceptably high cost and rigidity or low-cost flexible networking with very limited throughput.

What makes the telephone network so flexible? Its switching capability. By entering a telephone number, you enable the telephone exchange to build a connection "on the fly" that can take you to any other phone in the world within seconds. If telephone exchanges can switch calls from any phone to any other, why can't computer-based network nodes do the same thing? They can, of course — that's the *switching* in *packet switching*.

MAY I HAVE YOUR PHONE NUMBER PLEASE?

To finish explaining packet switching, I need one more conceptual building block: *addressing*. How does a terminal get to ask for a connection to a particular computer? In the dedicated-line world, the answer was simple: you didn't get to ask. Going through the telephone network too, the answer is easy: dial a telephone number. The telephone number functions as an address; it specifies the destination you want to be connected to. The word *address* means, in fact, just what you think it does. Just as every person has a street address, allowing mail delivery, every telephone subscriber has a telephone address that allows the delivery of phone calls. The street address consists of words and numbers; the telephone address, of course, is just a number. The point is that addressing schemes are not new ideas; they solve a big problem in communications. If new types of networks are going to exist, new types of addressing will have to exist along with them.

So an important part of a packet-switched network (and other computer networks, too) is the addressing scheme. Conceptually, this is pretty simple. A terminal is connected to a network node. The terminal may be either directly connected or it may access the network node through a local phone call. Initially, the terminal may communicate with that node, but until some instructions are given, any information goes to the node and no farther.

The first thing the terminal does is specify a network address, asking the node to establish a connection to a computer connected to that address. What do addresses look like? They can be names, numbers, or any other construct that can be programmed into a computer; the network node, after all, is just a computer. How does the network node know what connections are available? It stores a directory in its memory; again, it's a computer. Now to the key question.

How are nodes connected to each other? Recall the very first discussion about networks and the cost and rigidity associated with having too many direct connections. The existence of network nodes between the terminals and the computers doesn't make having too many direct connections suddenly affordable. Network nodes do, however, introduce a new possibility: *store and forward.*

Suppose that you want to connect a terminal in San Francisco to a computer in New York. And suppose that you have a link from San Francisco to Denver, and another from Denver to New York. Wouldn't it be nice if you could somehow join those links together into one big link? That's precisely what a packet-switching network makes possible in this scenario:

1. The user requests a connection to a computer in New York.

2. The San Francisco network node knows that there's no direct link to New York but that there is a route through an intermediate node in Denver, and it permits the connection to be established.

3. Each time information flows back and forth, it moves first from San Francisco to Denver and then on to New York, or vice versa.

What happens when the link from Denver to New York gets very busy? If a packet arrives from San Francisco and the line to New York is too busy to accept it, the Denver node stores the packet, queues it, and when its turn comes, forwards the packet to the New York computer. That's why this is called *store and forward.* Okay, okay, how does all of this relate to reliability, resiliency, and nuclear attack?

Suppose that the simple network has grown. Now there are connections from San Francisco to Los Angeles, Portland, Seattle, Denver, Chicago, and Dallas. Each of these in turn is connected to New York. Now if the node in Denver goes down, the San Francisco node can still get through by using one of these other intermediate cities.

All of this is pretty simplistic; to appreciate the true resiliency of packet switching, consider what a real network might look like. Imagine building a network of nodes connecting offices across the country. Pictorially, such a network looks like a flight diagram; in many fundamental ways, all large networks are similar. Now look at resiliency in action at two levels: dealing with complete failures and dealing with softer failures, such as busy or exceptionally noisy links.

NO RESERVATIONS — WE'LL JUST PLAY IT BY EAR

First, pick through all the routes a packet can use to get from San Francisco to New York. For example: San Francisco, Portland, Seattle, Chicago, Minneapolis, Cincinnati, New York is a perfectly fine route, and if enough intermediate nodes or communications links go down, it might be the only route. This theoretical network is not complex compared to many real-world nets, but it offers literally dozens of routes between almost any two points on the network. Even if quite a few nodes and links go down, many connection paths are still open.

Alternative routing is very useful, even when nodes and links haven't gone down. Suppose that one worker is sending a huge report from New York to Denver, just as someone else asks for a screen of information from New York at the San Francisco-based terminal. The New York network node, noticing that transmissions to Denver are taking a long time, picks another route; the user can't tell which route — all the user sees is continuing immediate response.

The best thing about packet switching is that it is adaptive and dynamic. This means that the network picks the best route for information over and over each time information has to be sent. Moreover, the computer can replan the route continuously, packet by packet, and node by node, as information moves through the network. For instance, if a packet reaches Denver but has trouble getting directly to San Francisco, it can go instead through Portland or perhaps Seattle. Different packets can take different routes as the network continuously adapts itself to the conditions around it.

A packet-switching network practically defines availability and resiliency. Information routes are changed on the fly, even in the middle of messages, adapting not only to failures, but also to heavy traffic and noise on the line. And when conditions improve, links are repaired, traffic dies down, and noise goes away, the network, without human intervention, adapts to the new circumstances, too.

To fully appreciate this self-adaptive behavior, I recall a sales demonstration that manufacturers of network nodes used to present to their prospective customers. The sales representative set up two network nodes with several lines interconnecting them. A high-speed printer was attached to one node and a computer to the other, with a report being sent to the printer. At the beginning of the demonstration, the printer plowed through the pages quickly. The sales rep then began unplugging wires interconnecting the two nodes. As this disconnection progressed, the printer slowed down, printing less and less quickly, until eventually, when the last wire was unplugged, printing ground to a halt. Later, as the representative plugged the wires back in, printing began, moving faster and faster, until, with all the wires finally reconnected, the printer again produced pages at full speed. For all of its naive simplicity, this simple demonstration explains adaptive behavior better than many long explanations do.

NETWORKING THE WORLD — THE CORPORATE GLOBAL VILLAGE

Packet-switched networks are so strategically important in the client/server world because of the degree of shared infrastructure they facilitate. Because many people can share the nodes in a switched network, it becomes economical to interconnect these nodes with very high-speed links. Understandably, high-speed links become more expensive as they get longer. For example, trans-oceanic communications lines are particularly expensive, as are lines running across continents. However, the switching behavior of packet networks allows a small number of super-high-speed long-haul lines to service many more network nodes spread across the country. Conceptually, this structure is just like the feeder networks used by airlines to bring passengers in from secondary cities to the gateways they use for long-haul routes. By using switching in a store-and-forward environment, users at nodes in even very small locations can still access super-high-speed links reaching around the world. And the resiliency of the network against failures and bottlenecks makes the construction of large networks both feasible and attractive.

Originally, packet-switched networks were used primarily by the government and very large companies. By the late '70s, however, several public packet-switched networks had become widely available. As a result, any computer or terminal anywhere in the (Western) world could access a local packet-switched network node and reach out through a relatively high-speed and totally noise-free connection to any computer — no matter where it was located — as long as that computer had a connection to the network.

These public networks had a fundamental cultural impact as well as a technical one. This impact is based on three factors: distance-independent pricing, the development of electronic mail, and the development of community memory systems. The overall effect of these three factors was to convert the world into a "corporate global village." With the original invention of the telephone and the airplane, the world became a much smaller place, both for organizations and for individuals. The true impact of the wide-area network, while not complete, will magnify this shrinking of the world, eliminating the effect of geographical distance. Given the availability of packet-switched networks, electronic mail, and community memory, teams located in any number of locations can operate almost as efficiently and effectively as teams located all in the same office. Effectively, the world shrinks to feel like a village where all locations feel as though they are within arm's reach. This chapter explores how today's technology is on the verge of making this true for organizations. The end of the book takes the same trend a step further into the home and the personal global village.

In the *Wizard of Oz*, Dorothy discovers that by clicking her heels three times she can be transported home instantly; even contemplating a form of magic that makes distance disappear fills us all with wonder. In a way, the fundamental transformation that a wide-area network introduces is the idea that distance no longer matters. Long-distance telephone call pricing, for example, is generally based on the distance the call travels. In a packet-switched network, though, distance has very little to do with the true cost of building and maintaining the network. Rather, in a computer network environment, almost all the costs are related to the volume of information being transmitted. So, from the beginning, the cost of using a computer network has been based only on the quantity of information being transmitted and sometimes on the speed at which it is being sent, but not on how far it is going.

Two fundamental applications have developed to take advantage of the distance-eliminating effect of the network: electronic mail and community memory. Each has enormous cultural impact on organizations and users, changing the way people work in fundamental ways. Because mail is the older and more mature technology, it will be examined first.

ELECTRONIC MAIL: CHANGING THE WORLD

Early users of computer networks quickly noticed that they could use the computer as a convenient drop-off point to deliver messages to other users in a variety of locations. Why not develop software specifically designed to facilitate message exchange? What I'm talking about, of course, is the birth of *electronic mail.*

Electronic mail is very simple to understand. A sender types a message, such as a memo or letter, from the keyboard and then specifies a list of recipients for the message or mail. When finished, the sender presses a send key, enters a send command, or in some other way lets the computer know that the message is ready to go. The computer (in a moment I discuss which computer I'm talking about) takes the message (or *e-mail*, as it's often called) and stores it in a special *e-mail database*, sometimes called a *mail store.* Later, when a recipient checks for e-mail, the computer tells the recipient about the new message, along with any other messages that may have come in, and the recipient can read the mail at any time.

The power and beauty of e-mail stem from a sort of contradiction: it is instantaneous, yet it doesn't operate in realtime; it is this exact conundrum that makes it wonderful. E-mail is instantaneous because when a piece of mail is sent, it is *immediately available* worldwide. In other words, the moment I hit the send key, you can immediately read my mail even if you are in another country or continent. At the same time, because mail is stored for later retrieval, if you are not available at the time I send my mail, it doesn't matter; after I hit the send key, I can forget about the mail, knowing that it will be delivered to you the next time you connect to the e-mail database. To understand electronic mail in context, compare it to the two standard alternative communication mechanisms: telephones and memos.

Telephones are instantaneous, but they also work in realtime. If I call you and you pick up the phone, we are connected immediately; however, if you're not there, we start playing phone tag, sometimes forever. The phone tag is based on the realtime nature of the telephone system; if you're not there, telephone conversation simply doesn't happen because the system can operate only in realtime.

Memos are not instantaneous but have the advantage of operating in extended time. The term *extended time* means simply that a communication happens whether you're available immediately or at some later time without the communicator being responsible for extending the communication through time; the extended time mechanism gets the message through. Memos work this way automatically, of course. If I send you a memo, it sits in your In box until you get to it. I don't have to worry about trying to send the memo to you over and over (as I would using the phone); I put it in the interoffice mail and depend on your In box to store it until you are ready to read it. The problem with memos, of course, is that they are far too slow.

Electronic mail falls right in the middle. It's instantaneous, arriving almost before it's sent, but it's queued as well, so that after it's sent, e-mail waits patiently forever with no extra action required. Electronic mail also is constantly accessible. At any time, from any location, a user can always pick up his or her e-mail. So it is instantaneous, like a phone, but constantly available, like a memo. The one thing e-mail lacks is true interactivity — the capability to hold a literal two-way conversation. However, by providing instant delivery, constant access and availability, and automatic queuing, e-mail changes organizations. E-mail, as it turns out, is a cultural change agent. When it's widely adopted in an organization, it radically changes the way people work.

ELECTRONIC MAIL AS AN AGENT OF CULTURAL CHANGE

To begin with, e-mail usually makes the phone stop ringing. The telephone is generally useful for immediate conversation — questions and requests that can't wait. At the same time, telephone tag is so common that most people find the phone as much of a nuisance as it is a convenience. In addition, for the receiver of a phone call, the telephone is a prime interruption agent. Historically, however, the only alternatives to the telephone were face-to-face discussion, which requires physical travel, or memos, which take a long time to produce and distribute.

Because e-mail arrives as soon as it is sent, often literally, it has the most important spontaneity characteristics of the telephone. It stays queued until the receiver reads it, thus eliminating phone tag. To make the picture complete, an e-mail message can just as easily be sent to 50 people as it can to one person, so it eliminates the need to make multiple phone calls. In this respect, e-mail is better than a memo too, because unlike paper documents, a message sent to 50 people can be sent to all 50 with a single keystroke, with no duplication or distribution required. So sending e-mail brings peace of mind; after it's sent, I know that it will be delivered immediately and read as soon as the recipient gets to his or her mail.

THE THREE FACES OF E-MAIL

For receivers, e-mail provides fast access to communications while still providing control over interruptions. The beauty of e-mail is that you get to decide how often and when in the day you go through your mail. Most systems provide three levels of control:

1. *Alert:* A flashing mailbox, special envelope icon, or text message can appear on your screen whenever new mail arrives in your In box. That way, you can work on a spreadsheet while expecting a critical piece of mail, without having to continually check your In box.

2. *Title:* Typically, mail systems display all the titles of (read and unread) mail in your In box. People are very good at scanning this type of display very rapidly, looking at the name of the sender, the time it was sent, and the title of the message itself, which indicates the topic. In addition, some systems provide special flags — color coding or special icons like the exclamation mark — to call out urgent mail. The advantage of the title display is that, once alerted or on a periodic check of the In box, you can tell whether any special mail is present and go to those messages immediately, while leaving other, less important mail until a more convenient time.

3. *Individual messages:* Finally, of course, every mail system provides a mechanism for reading mail, replying to messages, and creating new mail to send out. Even at this point, although the user is finally reduced to reading through messages one by one, the mail system provides significant advantages over both the telephone and conventional paper-based memos. First of all, people can read text at speeds ranging from 200 words per minute all the way up to 1,500 words per minute. Slower readers can achieve speeds near the top of the range when they are skimming, and some gifted readers can read continuously at these high speeds. However, even the lowest speed — 200 words per minute — is still significantly higher than the average speaking and hearing speed, a marked improvement over both phone conversation and voice mail. The net result (no pun intended) is that even when it comes to dealing with the full messages themselves, sorting through an electronic In box is faster than the manual equivalent and certainly faster than dealing with voice mail.

To see how these three levels fit together, picture a typical scenario. Each time you enter your office — in the morning, after lunch, and so on — you scan through your In box to see what new messages are there, who they're from, and what they're about. Unlike voice mail, for instance, the scanning process takes just a few seconds as your eyes flip through the titles. Occasionally, you see an e-mail message that seems important; you quickly open it, scan through the contents, again at warp speed, and decide whether to spend more time on it. At times of peak activity, you may have to flip through several messages in this way; these messages become your initial notification of something at work, followed by responses from all the other people involved with the particular issue.

Even reading through ten messages in sequence often can be done in just ten keystrokes; you read the first couple of paragraphs of each and then move on to the next message. Through the rest of the day, as you work first on a memo and then on your sales forecast, the mail system periodically alerts you to the presence of new incoming mail; sometimes you care, and sometimes you don't, but either way the alert, although immediate, is also unobtrusive (unlike a telephone). Finally, once a day, at a time of personal choice, you spend half an hour going through your In box, methodically dealing with all the information, requests, and questions that have come in that last day.

AROUND THE CORNER OR AROUND THE WORLD

Does this description of a day centered around e-mail seem quite innocuous — hardly a major change in working lifestyle? Consider that the electronic messages I described could have originated in countries all over the world. Also, consider the impact of sending an alert on an issue to people all over a building — and all over the world — immediately, without having to pick up the phone many times, without waiting for a memo to arrive, and without having to schedule a teleconference. The ability to include many people on a distribution list makes it easy to broaden the scope of a discussion, and in turn, each of those people can easily forward the entire message when he or she receives it. Because the mail always arrives immediately, all those involved are able to participate in several rounds of discussion with the circle of participants steadily broadening. Each new participant, as he or she receives forwarded mail, is able to review the entire context of the discussion without anybody having to take the time to repeat oral descriptions (let alone suffering the information loss implicit in orally passing information around a circle). Finally, all the players are able to interact fluidly without either having to wait for memos or suffer from constant telephone interruptions. For the international participants, e-mail makes it possible to be directly involved in the issue, in realtime, despite time-zone differences.

The cultural impact of electronic mail is best described and summarized by one extensive, carefully instrumented military experiment. In this experiment, an electronic mail system was successful in the following ways:

✦ Decreasing the volume of memos and telephone calls by more than four times.

✦ Facilitating faster decision-making and reporting newly made decisions to more people sooner.

✦ Changing patterns of communication. Before the implementation of e-mail, almost all conversation was vertical — between adjacent levels in the chain of command. In the electronic mail environment, organizational members were free to send mail to anyone else on the system, including high-ranking officers and people in completely different parts of the organization. This mail was not only condoned organization wide, it was also encouraged.

Reaching beyond efficiency, any communications technology that eliminates phone calls and memos, accelerates decision making, results in increased consensus, and significantly democratizes the pattern of communication itself can truly be described as a cultural change agent.

All of this aside, probably the most telling measure of the importance of electronic mail is its popularity. For many users, e-mail — not word processing, spreadsheet, or database — is the application they run most every day. E-mail is the first application they turn on at the beginning of the day, the first tool they turn to on returning to the office, and the software they spend the largest number of hours interacting with most days. Speaking of mission critical, in most companies, electronic mail, even ahead of the network itself, is the component whose absence is noticed the soonest and whose failure will result in the largest number of complaints, the most quickly, when problems occur.

NETWORKING: THE SECOND GENERATION

When networks were first invented, the original goal was to connect terminals to computers. Similarly, when electronic mail first became popular, the communications path always involved a terminal talking to a computer through a network. Thus, first generation networks provided terminal to computer communication. With the growth of packet switching, users could quickly and easily access their home computer from any location in the world, and any given computer could service users no matter where they were located. What happens, though, when users on separate electronic mail systems want to start communicating with each other?

The original answer to this question was, "Each person should use several electronic mail systems." Just as originally users had several terminals on their desks, the e-mail equivalent is having accounts on multiple e-mail systems. This is in fact a very modern problem. It has become routine for me to receive business cards that include a CompuServe, MCImail, and perhaps an Internet e-mail address all on the same card.

While having several e-mail accounts may be modern, it is hardly convenient and quickly becomes unworkable. Imagine, for example, a research scientist who routinely communicates with other scientists at 15 or 20 universities and corporate research labs. Each lab has its own e-mail system; does this mean that the scientist has to have 20 e-mail accounts and, to stay current, has to check each account regularly to receive mail? Even if this were somehow workable, how does the scientist send a given piece of mail to colleagues on these foreign e-mail systems? By copying mail 15 or 20 times? Doesn't this negate many of the original benefits that e-mail was supposed to provide in the first place?

The problem of connecting multiple e-mail systems is very similar to the problem that phone companies faced in the 1920s. By then, individual telephone exchanges had become relatively common, but no mechanism existed for connecting exchanges to each other. Once that problem was solved, telephones became vastly more interesting because suddenly, communication became possible across the country instead of just within a single community. The second generation of networking had a similar impact on the computer community.

While the first generation of networks connected terminals to computers, the second generation connected computers to computers. Once computers could talk to each other across high-speed communications links, three major applications became possible: computers could share information with each other, electronic mail systems could be interconnected, and distributed databases became possible. The first application is discussed later in this chapter; distributed databases are covered in other chapters. It is the impact on e-mail that needs to be considered now.

The original implementations of electronic mail all ran on large computers: mainframes and minicomputers. So the original impetus for using networks to interconnect e-mail systems was focused on connecting these large computers to each other. However, these large computers were (and are) relatively few in number. So while interconnecting them offers strong benefits, it is also true that users might have been willing to live with separated e-mail systems on big computers for some considerable period of time. The fact that so many business cards have multiple e-mail addresses on them even today is silent witness to this fact. However, as e-mail grew in popularity, an entire second e-mail community began growing rapidly, one which made e-mail interconnection a virtual requirement.

Even before servers and LANs became available, the trend towards running e-mail systems on smaller and smaller computers had already begun. Digital Equipment Corporation (DEC) is one company that took advantage of the growing popularity of electronic mail in this way. DEC used the popularity of e-mail to sell its VAX minicomputers, which ran corporate mail systems more cost-effectively than mainframes could. A key selling point for DEC was that smaller departments and remote divisions of a company could expect better and more reliable e-mail service from their own minicomputer than they could from the central shared mainframe. For small workgroups and little companies, however, even minicomputer-based electronic mail was far too expensive. The development of LANs and personal-computer-based servers in the mid '80s gave even the smallest company or workgroup the benefits of e-mail. Consequently, today's largest electronic mail community runs on local-area networks, often tying into central mainframe-based systems that link all the LANs in a large company to form a single organization-wide mail system.

Having e-mail accounts on a small number of large e-mail systems is inconvenient but perhaps barely tolerable. What happens when there are literally thousands of e-mail systems, most running off servers connected to LANs? Nobody could possibly have or keep up with accounts on dozens or hundreds of separate systems. All of a sudden, having a way of connecting all these e-mail systems together into one big e-mail system becomes not only convenient but essential — and that requires networks that support computer to computer communication; that's what second generation networking is about.

THE ARPANET

Just as DARPA had funded the original research that led to packet-switched networks in the first place, it also funded the subsequent research which resulted in second generation networks connecting computers to each other. What DARPA found was that while packet switching was useful for failsafe missile command and control systems (the original goal), it was even more useful for general purpose communications on a daily basis. The question was, "What would happen if a large community of computers, used by researchers and military organizations, was connected together by a high-speed network on a permanent basis?"

To answer this question, DARPA agreed to fund the installation of a nationwide packet-switched network, called *ARPAnet*, the foundation from which the modern Internet grew. DARPA installed high-speed leased lines connecting about a dozen large research labs in the United States. At first, ARPAnet was used only by its developers, the software engineers working on the packet-switching technology and underlying network node engines. Soon after, however, ARPAnet's limited audience grew.

About the time that DARPA put ARPAnet into place, e-mail systems were gaining popularity at many of the same research locations being selected to be on the network. In retrospect, the result was predictable. E-mail developers and network developers discovered that combined, the two technologies were much more powerful than either one alone. To understand the resulting explosion, picture the situation existing just before. Researchers, whether in universities, corporations, or government labs, tend to work in closely related areas, even though they are widely distributed geographically. Before the advent of e-mail, these researchers had very limited means for working together, unless they were at the same institution. Publication of papers is too slow, and so is writing letters, for that matter. Telephone suffers all the disadvantages I've already discussed plus even more in an international environment. In fact, the very existence of conferences is based on the idea of providing researchers with a convenient forum to exchange notes and collaborate, but conferences don't occur frequently enough to enable people to work together. E-mail suddenly changed the whole picture.

As scientists, programmers, and researchers of all kinds quickly discovered, e-mail made collaboration across the continent almost as convenient as collaboration across the hall. Ideas could be sent to any number of people with instant delivery guaranteed. Recipients of those ideas could forward the ideas to others, and responses could return the same day. Because an e-mail message can easily include digital *attachments*, such as spreadsheets, word processing documents, and even small databases, researchers could send lab results, diagrams, and pieces of code along with their messages. The recipients received everything — the mail and all the attachments — with little additional work required by the sender.

Like the convenience of instant communication, the cost structure of e-mail and WANs also played a major role in fueling the e-mail revolution. Unlike the phone system's costs, packet-switched network costs have always been largely distance-independent. Instead, charges are based on the *amount* of information sent. As a result, for the first time, people all over the United States, and later the world, could communicate freely with each other without having to think about how far away their communications partners might be. Adding a name in France to an e-mail address list or forwarding a message to a colleague in Canada became a mere afterthought, freely entertained and put into action.

The immediate result of the creation of the ARPAnet was twofold:

+ E-mail became such a compelling application that the ARPAnet quickly grew in size and scope.

+ Several *startup organizations* grew out of DARPA's electronic mail research.

WHERE HAVE ALL THE POST OFFICES GONE?

By 1980, several parallel startups were all hard at work building toward their respective dreams for a changed world, and they were backed up by a growing set of international standards. In the United States, Telenet and Tymnet embarked on ambitious plans to build worldwide packet-switched networks. In the beginning, the goal of these networks was to connect users all over the earth to both public and private databases: the global library concept. As Telenet and Tymnet built their systems and signed up customers, governments in the rest of the world decided that this opportunity must not pass them by. As a result, phone companies in countries around the world built domestic packet-switched networks at whatever rate seemed appropriate to them. Canada, for instance, was an early leader in this technology and today has a packet-based environment that is second to none in terms of geographic coverage.

Picture the situation that existed in the late '70s. In the United States, two major network vendors (Telenet and Tymnet) along with other less prevalent competitors had developed public packet-switched networks. Abroad, where communications was more tightly controlled by the government, each major country had its own public packet-switched network: Datapac in Canada, BTnet in the United Kingdom, and so on. Subscribers to any one of these networks could talk to other subscribers on the same network. As soon as a customer on one network wanted to talk to a user of a different network, however, the whole system broke down. Each network used its own private language — its own *protocol*, as networking people say — and none of the protocols used on any one network could connect with the protocols found on any other network.

As these networks grew, connectivity became a major issue. Given access to Telenet, how do I connect to a database attached to Canada's Datapac? Or, while traveling in the UK, even if I have the local BTnet phone number, how do I get from BTnet to my server at home, which is attached to Tymnet? Finally, in the early '80s an organization called CCITT (Consultative Committee for International Telephony and Telegraphy) came to the rescue. The CCITT is a quasigovernmental organization that functions as the United Nations of telephone companies. For several decades, this organization has facilitated the development of common protocols that allow telephone and telegraph systems built by competing vendors and installed in many countries worldwide to talk to each other. These protocols, called *standards*, make the world a connected place. The CCITT publishes standards that allow worldwide telephone systems to *interoperate*, hopefully *transparently*. *Transparent interoperation* enables a telephone subscriber in Australia to dial a series of digits and immediately talk to his or her relative in Switzerland, even if the call goes through intermediate phone systems in seven other countries.

Working with networking vendors around the world, CCITT applied that same expertise and coordination to computer networking and developed a standard protocol for packet-switched networks called *X.25* (pronounced *x dot twenty-five*). X.25 prescribes how network nodes can talk to each other in a fashion that provides universal understanding at the packet-switching level. Just as telephone networks all interconnect on the basis of CCITT standards, X.25 allows all packet-switched networks to interconnect transparently.

The X.25 standard (along with some associated standards with equally riveting names such as X.3, X.75, and so on) prescribes the mechanisms with which computers talk to networks, terminals talk to networks, and networks talk to each other. As companies and network vendors worldwide adopted X.25 over a ten-year period, it became possible to count on worldwide access to computers through networks. As it turned out, however, access was not enough.

By the early '80s, Telenet and Tymnet were attracting more and more users, X.25 networks were sprouting up in other countries around the world and were becoming the industry standard, and in the public sector, dozens of universities and government sites were using ARPAnet. Everyone assumed that these networks would be used primarily for database access. In this same time frame, a number of other startups began peddling their databases, believing that the widespread availability of distance-insensitive networks would spark a demand for accessible information. The problem was (and is) that although compelling, the concept of a global library is still a distant vision.

The developers of ARPAnet had discovered a surprise hit with electronic mail, and the builders of the other networks soon made the same discovery. Their first reaction was to turn electronic mail into a product. The results were electronic mail offerings such as TeleMail, OnTyme, BTGold, Envoy, and a host of other services.

E-MAIL VIA EINSTEIN

Electronic mail requires *critical mass* in order to be successful. *Critical mass* is a concept from nuclear engineering. An atomic explosion requires a critical mass, or amount, of uranium. If less than the critical mass is present, no explosion occurs, no matter what. With the critical mass and the right engineering, an entirely different outcome results. In the same way, given a group of people who routinely communicate, electronic mail becomes effective only when the majority of the people in the group use the system. Access to mail is not enough; the majority have to use the mail system routinely. And like the bomb, the situation is very bimodal: below the critical mass, electronic mail is just a nuisance, and above critical mass, it suddenly becomes the only way to work. To see why e-mail is so use-sensitive, compare the two cases.

Below critical mass, sending e-mail is an exercise in frustration. Even after you send the message, you can't assume that everyone has read it, so you have to follow up in some other way. Similarly, reading electronic mail, while not as frustrating, still isn't very productive because important communications still arrive on paper and the telephone still rings. E-mail is just one more place to look for information, one more potential interruption cropping up through the day.

When critical mass is achieved, however, it becomes a social requirement to use e-mail all the time. All your co-workers are starting to luxuriate in immediate delivery to distribution lists without the constant annoyance of that ringing phone. If you missed a meeting or didn't participate in a discussion, they (and you) are rightly annoyed that you're not going with the flow. E-mail has suddenly become the norm! And when this happens, the cultural forces acting on individuals to stay on top of their e-mail are automatic, insidious, and totally effective. When the right level of participation is reached, e-mail becomes a self-fulfilling prophecy, but only if critical mass can be achieved.

The number of regular users required to achieve critical mass depends on the population of the group. In a small company of about 15 employees, critical mass might be 10 people. Having just those 10 using the system all the time makes it totally worthwhile. In a company of 600 employees, the same critical mass easily could be 400 people. In society at large, critical mass requires not only that millions of people use electronic mail all the time, but also that those people use the same electronic mail system all the time. After all, what's the point of sending mail to somebody on another electronic mail system when that person won't receive your message? This is the problem that network and electronic mail providers have been struggling with for over ten years.

THE VISION SPREADS

By 1985, Telenet, Tymnet, and all the other network providers realized e-mail's critical role in making networks attractive. ARPAnet had spread to Europe, Canada, and dozens of institutions in the United States. Thousands of individuals depended on

ARPAnet for routine daily communication on multitudes of interwoven issues. In fact, electronic mail had become so important that new classes of startups and standards appeared, with plans to capitalize on the opportunity.

This "opportunity" is nothing less than the replacement of *mail*, as it is known today, by *e-mail*, as it will be known tomorrow. Think about what the term *mail* means. Every day, mail carriers in every country deliver hundreds of millions of pieces of mail — love letters, contracts, bills, and all the other documents that define so much of our lives. By addressing an envelope and putting a few cents' worth of postage on it, your mail is virtually guaranteed to be delivered anywhere on earth in a matter of days (at most, weeks). Mail is so integral to society that it is one of the few services provided by almost every modern government in the world. And now I'm talking about replacing it?

For all of its advantages and conveniences, electronic mail is even more convenient and powerful than conventional mail. Why be limited to receiving mail once a day? Why not on Sundays? Why wait for weeks to hear from Africa? Is it really necessary to make ten copies of a letter, address ten envelopes, and pay for postage ten times, just to include all the right people in a conversation? And when they receive it, why should they have to copy the mail again to forward it? If mail takes three days to arrive, and a letter is forwarded three times, the last recipient is 12 days out of date! The list of potential reasons to use electronic mail instead of real mail goes on and on. Most compelling of all, because the real mail is increasingly likely to have been generated on a computer in the first place, why not then just use that computer to send the mail instantly when you're done?

That's the vision that TeleMail, MCI Mail, CompuServe, and a host of other competing services were built to serve. The market as pictured in 1985 was more than huge: the corporate market alone was indeed immense, but extrapolating forward to a day when every home, first in the U.S. and then in the Western hemisphere, and then every-where, would send and receive mail every day, the potential clearly goes far beyond huge! But is society any closer to realizing that ideal today than it was ten years ago?

Led by the CCITT, the standards community realized that X.25 and pure networking for connecting computers and terminals was just the beginning. So, actually beginning in 1982, the CCITT chartered a working group to develop a standard for interconnect-ing electronic mail systems. The result, called *X.400*, prescribes mechanisms whereby two or more e-mail systems can exchange mail, as well as other mechanisms to allow personal computers to talk to e-mail providers in a fashion that takes advantage of the intelligence of those PCs. By 1984, when the X.400 standard was finally published, many prognosticators were excitedly predicting that every mail vendor in the world would be X.400 compliant in two years. As a result, several efforts were initiated in 1985, many of which continue to this day, to start making the e-mail-linked global village a reality.

While the CCITT was laying the groundwork for all mail systems to speak the same language, startups and established companies were busy building the competing mail systems that the CCITT was planning to connect. For example, in 1985 MCI had just established the first domestic rival to AT&T for long distance services. MCI looked at electronic mail, deduced that it threatened not only postal mail but also telephone long distance, and decided that e-mail protected and complemented its core business. Similarly, around the same time General Electric, which operated one of the largest public networks and computer service bureaus in the world, saw e-mail's potential and launched an effort to establish a worldwide e-mail system.

In the mid '80s, just as public e-mail was starting to take off, two different kinds of *private* e-mail were starting to become popular, as well. One kind was based on mainframes and minicomputers installed in large corporations. IBM's Profs and DEC's All-In-One systems each built worldwide communities with several million users each. The other kind, which is even more popular today, is LAN-based electronic mail systems such as Lotus cc:Mail, Novell Groupwise, and Microsoft Mail. While these private mail systems became quite successful in their own right, the availability of public networks to extend their reach worldwide provided the final link to large scale acceptance. With the widespread popularity of public and private mail systems interconnected by global packet-switched networks, surely it should be possible for any PC or terminal user to send mail to any other PC or terminal user. And because electronic mail is always so much more popular than regular mail (when it reaches critical mass), why hasn't the postal service disappeared? Given that so many organizations are so committed to the use of mail internally, why are normal letters still the routine norm for intercompany communication? If e-mail is so great, why are postal carriers still walking their rounds?

BUILDING THE TOWER OF BABEL: THE IMPOSSIBLE TAKES A LITTLE LONGER

Postal carriers still walk the rounds for three reasons:

✦ Cultural change is a slow process, even (some would say *particularly*) in corporate environments.

✦ Interconnecting mail systems has proven stubbornly difficult to do.

✦ Beyond just connecting the networks and mail systems, providing directory services is the problem of the moment, standing in the way of the electronic mail dream. In theory, if you are using MCI Mail and I'm using CompuServe, nothing should be easier than exchanging mail. In reality, unless one of us knows the other's mail identifiers, the task may be impossible. The lack of a universal directory service — analogous to the white pages taken for granted in the telephone environment — makes what should be simple often impossible in e-mail land.

So, will electronic mail really become ubiquitous, potentially replacing the post office, or not? The answer is that that ubiquity is much closer than most people imagine. The Army Corps of Engineers has a saying: "The difficult we do immediately; the impossible takes a little longer." The "difficult" has been achieved; now society is living through the slow process of making what was once thought to be "impossible" come true.

To begin with, many large organizations routinely depend on electronic mail. It is the single most popular application for users in those organizations, and as I pointed out earlier, those users notice and complain immediately when their electronic mail becomes unavailable. It has taken a long time for this reaction to be normal, however, and e-mail is still far from ubiquitous even in the corporate environment. It has taken so long precisely because it is a social and cultural shift.

Of course, the organization that is making the shift can be less than a whole company. It would be impossible for e-mail to take hold if entire Fortune 500 companies had to adopt it all at once. Nonetheless, because mail is only moderately interesting in small groups, it requires commitment from large divisions, departments, or workgroups to really take root. The result is a paradox of the most bittersweet kind. The good news is that when e-mail catches on, it catches on quickly and on a large scale. The bad news is that for it to catch on, it must catch on quickly and on a large scale.

Fortunately, the positive experience of the ARPAnet-centered research community provided some early examples of the huge gains offered by e-mail. Because of the military nature of DARPA, these gains were quickly noticed by the army, which in turn decided to experiment very deliberately with e-mail. Being centrally controlled, military organizations are in a position to achieve critical mass literally overnight, if they decide they want to. The result was the documentation of the experimental gains noted a few pages earlier. Catching the eye of the business community, e-mail quickly gained a strong following with an impressive roster of companies worldwide.

After corporate customers caught on to the productivity benefits of electronic mail, hardware vendors such as DEC and IBM realized that a potentially enormous software opportunity lay in front of them. Not long after the big vendors, dozens of other companies followed with mail products for machines of all sizes. Today, All-In-One, PROFS, cc:Mail, Microsoft Mail, and many public systems like America Online, CompuServe, and MCI provide regular service to millions of everyday users. E-mail is on the verge of becoming pervasive in the business world. Yet somehow, even with its widespread usage, e-mail is still far from replacing real mail. How can this be?

Although there are many mail systems, each with large numbers of users, these mail systems cannot talk to each other. As in the biblical parable, the resulting tower of Babel — mail systems with incompatible protocols — cannot be combined into a larger compatible whole. The solution to this problem is far from complete but is beginning to take shape in the form of the Internet.

Today, it is safe to say that electronic mail is here to stay and is well on its way to eventually becoming at least as popular and dominant as the regular postal system. Even the problems associated with the tower of Babel are beginning to find solutions.

For example, at work I can routinely send mail messages to users on CompuServe, America Online, and any number of private e-mail systems, all in the same message; I can depend on the fact that my mail will be delivered transparently and quickly. As it turns out, though, even e-mail represents just the beginning of the cultural revolution that networks really represent. In fact, e-mail is the first step towards a broader phenomenon that I call community memory. And the Internet, the third generation network, is the enabling technology that really takes you beyond e-mail and into the world of community memory.

THE INTERNET: THIRD GENERATION NETWORKING

By the late '80s ARPAnet had outgrown DARPA's interest as well as DARPA's desire and ability to fund it. By then, however, ARPAnet's underlying protocols had been implemented so widely that ARPAnet was ready and able to become the *Internet*. The very idea of the Internet represents a step forward in thinking about wide-area networks, or WANs. First generation networks connected terminals to computers; in the second generation, computers were connected to each other. The third generation of WANs, connect networks to other networks. In fact, *internets*, as these nets are called, are a step up from second generation networks — they still connect computers to each other, but they also glue networks together.

Internets are important because they build on the idea that, in the world of LANs, the network is the computer. If personal computers tied to a LAN are to be a dominant form of computing in the '90s, then WANs need to explicitly support this style of computing. So, in a world where big computers were at the center of most large organizations, computer to computer communication was key. In a world where LANs are central, LAN to LAN communication becomes the key. Best of all, since a big computer can be just as easily connected to a LAN as can a personal computer, internets can serve the needs of both second and third generation networking users.

In the internetworked world, everybody either has a local computer or talks to a local computer. That local computer may be a large computer, such as a minicomputer or mainframe, or it may be a small computer, such as a server. In either case, the local computer provides the user with all of his or her immediate computing needs. The WAN now serves another purpose altogether: it moves electronic mail and other forms of data flexibly between computers. The computers interconnected by the WAN may be individual computers, perhaps even mainframes or minicomputers. The interconnected computers may also be the client/server computing clusters created by a LAN. As a result, WANs can connect computers with local networks of computers, and they also can connect local networks with other local networks. As LANs become more common, the interconnection of these local networks is the norm rather than the exception. Thus the WAN is often a network between networks, or an *inter*network. *Internetting* is a generic term used when networks connect networks (and computers); the *Internet* is the granddaddy of large internetworks.

The Internet is important to e-mail systems because it was the first successful attempt at interconnecting a wide variety of geographically distributed mail systems on a large scale. Starting from the original ARPAnet hub, the Internet has spread to include thousands of private- and public-sector organizations. Each of these organizations has its own e-mail systems. Often there are different types of systems within the organization. The Internet itself has *no* e-mail system; it has something much more important. The Internet gives subscribers access to any of the e-mail systems connected to it so that the subscribers can send mail to any other subscribers *no matter which e-mail systems they are connected to*. As a result, to many of the organizations connected to it, the Internet is second in importance only to the telephone network (sometimes more important).

If internetworking can work so well, why isn't it more common? Until the beginning of this decade, the primary obstacle to widespread e-mail was cultural. Today, although cultural barriers still exist (particularly in small businesses and homes), the major block is e-mail interconnection. The Internet proves the concept, but it leaves many important details to be worked out.

Even though its scale is already awe-inspiring, the Internet works particularly well because by global standards, it is still small. Moreover, the Internet is still used most heavily by research organizations, where competitive concerns are less of an issue than they are in the business world. Competition prevents internetting — particularly in the e-mail context — from catching on more widely in the commercial arena.

Particularly in this decade, e-mail has found a surprisingly broad base of users. Forums such as CompuServe, Prodigy, and MCImail are attractive to hackers, hobbyists, and small business users. Having captured these customers, the e-mail providers see them as potential lifetime customers. Looking beyond e-mail and bulletin board services, every one of these providers dreams of eventually selling all kinds of products and services in an electronic shopping world of the future. So when I talk about the dream of connecting all the mail systems together, the nightmare that immediately counters the dream for all e-mail vendors is one of previously captive consumers, now free to roam across competitive servers at will.

"INFORMATION: WHAT CITY, PLEASE?"

Superficially connecting mail systems is a straightforward and simple process. A variety of standards, including the famous X.400, already exist for connecting such systems. The Internet works because most of the computers on the Internet use the UNIX operating system, and most of the UNIX mail systems in turn have adopted a standard similar in concept to X.400. This demonstrates that as with X.25, it is possible to get all the mail systems of the world to talk together. The question is, if they did talk together, how would you look up another subscriber's e-mail address?

Well, how do you look up phone numbers? In the white pages, of course! What if you need a phone number in another city or country? Everybody knows that you call 555-1212 domestically, and the operator abroad! So simple, yet it works because provision of phone service is a regulated monopoly in every country. Even after the breakup of AT&T, local phone service (including allocation of phone numbers) is still a regulated monopoly, now with six providers, one in each region, instead of one for the whole country. And in every other country in the world, phone service is a monopoly, as well. So phone books are readily available, 555-1212 works like a charm, and even abroad the operator is always available to help.

Provision of e-mail services is the opposite of a monopoly. It's a highly competitive market with huge stakes. Some countries initially tried to regulate e-mail service provision, but it's so easy to start up an e-mail service (set up a server and publish some numbers) that practically nobody tries anymore. E-mail is not competitive only in the public arena. Competition exists at many levels, with corporate systems existing side by side with public systems, all of which compete with private specialized systems.

Competitively, this comes to a head in the directory services arena. White pages are a form of directory service, and so are the yellow pages; so is directory assistance (555-1212). In fact, even in the closely regulated phone industry, directory services is a huge industry. So where do you get directory services for e-mail? Can the directory services be made to talk to each other?

As you might expect, the industry's answer is that it's time for another standard. And, of course, the CCITT has one: *X.500*, which is X.400's sibling. X.500, first discussed in 1986, prescribes a standard for directory services to exchange information with each other and also for computers to ask questions of those directory services. Why computers? Because e-mail is driven by computers, so if you type a name into e-mail, you want your computer to be able to look up the address for that name automatically.

The problem with X.500 is that it implies giving out customer lists. Imagine approaching your biggest corporate competitor and asking for his or her entire customer list, complete with up-to-date addresses. A problem? You bet.

Perhaps this sounds like an impossible situation. If you keep in mind how far this industry has come, though, there's every reason to be hopeful. E-mail is now a major cultural component. Stories about couples meeting and even becoming engaged strictly via e-mail are now commonplace in myth, if less so in reality. E-mail *is* on its way to becoming commonplace, *and* huge barriers still need to be knocked down before mail carriers stop knocking on doors. Keeping a sense of perspective, however, it is now quite likely that by the end of the decade, e-mail, like the telephone, will have become a standard mechanism for personal and organizational communication over distance and time.

Cultural education is still required, particularly among individuals and smaller businesses. The FAX revolution is helping in that effort. It is only a small step from FAX to e-mail: the step from transmission of printed output to transmission of the underlying information itself in a form that can still be edited. E-mail systems need to become better connected, but as the ubiquity of e-mail increases, the pressure for interconnection will make this inevitable. Users will get to the point where they just won't tolerate not being able to communicate with other users anymore. Finally, as mail systems become increasingly interconnected, competition (even though it blocks directory services today) will ensure that e-mail providers confront the directory issue themselves; otherwise, external providers will do the job for them, leaving them with even less of the customer control they are so carefully trying to safeguard.

BEYOND E-MAIL: COMMUNITY MEMORY

In many ways, it is ironic that electronic mail was the first application that virtually defined what networks are about. How is that ironic? Because although networks are about communication, at the time they were being invented, technologists were convinced they would be used for everything *but* communication. Yet, as it turns out, the one application that has propelled the growth of large networks more than any other has been e-mail, which is not *primarily* about communication, it is *only* about communication. Yet for networks to achieve their true potential, you must move beyond communication — and that means creating the first electronic *community memory*.

Community memory involves the merger of two technologies: servers and electronic mail. Servers provide the means to share information so that users located anywhere can access the most recent version, while electronic mail allows those users to communicate with each other essentially instantly. What does it mean to merge these two technologies into one? Consider what happens when e-mail becomes too popular.

HOW MANY FILE CLERKS DOES MICROSOFT HAVE?

Microsoft is one company where e-mail is ubiquitous, and as a result, most employees have become file clerks. In fact, Microsoft, if thought of this way, has over ten thousand file clerks.

Suppose I send an e-mail to several other people within Microsoft. Before sending it, I think carefully about the contents, write the mail, and file it away for later retrieval. Then, each person who receives it reads it, perhaps forwards it to others, and files it away for himself or herself. Now suppose a colleague, at a later date, wants to come up to speed on the issue being addressed by the e-mail; is there any easy way for the colleague to do that? Only with the help of somebody who received that mail in the first place, and only if that original recipient took the time to file the e-mail. Electronic mail has a fundamental deficiency; it doesn't provide any form of shared memory.

REPLACE HUMANS, OR AUGMENT THEM?

Memory, whether shared or individual, is one of the most fundamental aspects of human thinking. In fact, the idea of literally improving the way people think by improving the way they remember things dates back to 1945. Writing in the *Atlantic Monthly*, Vannevar Bush in "As We May Think" set forth the basic revolution driving not only the Internet as we know it today, but most of the personal computer revolution, too.

Vannevar Bush was the individual responsible for directing the applied research efforts for all of the United States government during World War II, including such critical efforts as the Manhattan Project. With the war behind him, in the *Atlantic* article Bush reflected on the type of automated aides he imagined helping someone like him — a knowledge worker — in the not too distant future. The article, still in many ways fresh and relevant today, is particularly amazing because it predates the availability of modern computers. Nonetheless, it describes a device, called the Memex, that sounds like the kind of computer most of us would call a personal computer, but with facilities most of us would still like to have and can't. Particularly, Bush focuses on the ability to have the Memex store every piece of information — printed, heard, communicated — for subsequent retrieval on command.

Bush's paper is particularly significant because of the research and development that it subsequently spawned. Most important of all, from the perspective of community memory was the work of Doug Engelbart, and his Augmentation Research Center (ARC).

Starting in the early '60s, Engelbart began thinking about how a Memex could really be built, and how it could support teams as well as individuals in being more productive. It is hard to overestimate the impact that Engelbart had on the entire history of computers, even though his name is hardly ever mentioned any more today. At the time that Engelbart began his work, most of the facilities that we take for granted — computer screens, keyboards, personal computers, networks, mice, and more — had yet to be invented. Even Xerox's PARC (Palo Alto Research Center), often thought to be the source of these ideas, was still more than a decade away from being created. (In fact, Xerox itself was just taking off.)

In a period of about ten years, then, Engelbart and his team literally invented many of the ideas and technologies that drive our entire computer world. The mouse? Invented at the ARC (yes, invented from scratch). Windows, bulletin boards, hypertext — all invented by Engelbart and his team. Overall, the entire effort was driven by two common elements.

The first element was the idea that computers should augment humans, not replace them. Recall that this work was taking place at a time when many still believed that as computers became "artificially intelligent," they would eventually replace people. On the contrary, Engelbart believed, computers would augment and not replace people by providing community memory.

The second element was that Engelbart's team created the first successful form of community memory, which is discussed next.

COMMUNITY MEMORY

Community memory is the shared records of all the thoughts, concepts, conversations, and decisions that drive an organization. A community memory system can be thought of as a form of database, but really it isn't. Colloquially, any set of shared data is a database; in that sense, so is a community memory system. The term *database* has practically come to take on a very specialized meaning, which will be explored in more detail later in this book. Therefore, community memory is not a database in the normal sense of the word.

In many ways, in fact, a community memory is actually the exact opposite of a database system. Databases are typically highly structured, centrally located, and devoted to a single application. Community memory systems, on the other hand, are purposely structured only very loosely, highly distributed, and cross a wide variety of applications. Technically, the underpinnings of the community memory systems of the future is a technology called Hypertext, which is also the underpinnings of the World Wide Web. To understand what this all means, go back to the problem of the file clerks and see how Engelbart's system solved that problem.

Electronic mail is based on the metaphor of "sending a message." By definition, that implies that once sent, the message is carried from the sender to the receiver. Community memory changes that fundamental metaphor from "sending a message" to "pointing to a shared item."

Suppose that I am about to write an e-mail to you about a marketing experiment. This e-mail is just the most recent of a long series of messages about a marketing problem, various proposed solutions, and this one particular experimental approach to solving the problem. Now suppose that instead of sending that e-mail, I store it as a note in a shared folder on a server you can access, and then somehow bring your attention to the new item in that shared folder.

In this new world, quite a few things are different from a conventional e-mail system:

✦ There is no reason for you to file the note; it's already filed in the right folder. It arrived "prefiled."

✦ As soon as you look at this note, you have access to all the other notes in the folder, providing you with a constant context.

✦ Any new colleague entering the conversation has access to the same folder and can immediately bring himself or herself up to date without asking anyone else for help.

If all of this sounds very similar to the servers discussed in the last chapter, it is because the similarity is very real. In fact, the whole point of community memory is to combine the concept of the server as a shared filing system with the concept of the network as a communication medium. So what's missing to make the solution complete? Just convenience.

THE BIRTH OF THE BULLETIN BOARD

Most servers are designed to support users working with relatively large documents. Word processors are great for writing memos, reports, and books; a server acting as a file cabinet is designed to organize large documents of this type. A database works well with individual and smaller records, but as already mentioned, it is optimized for highly structured applications in which all the records are similar. What about e-mail? How would the server have to be designed to do a good job organizing e-mail?

Mail messages are typically quite short. The whole point of the In box is that it allows hundreds of these short messages to be scanned quickly and frequently. E-mail messages are meant to be read in context. A memo or other large document is generally written to be understandable by itself; usually considerable space is taken up at the beginning of many documents laying out background material so the reader can use the document in isolation. E-mail messages, on the other hand, are often not understandable by themselves. The operating assumption is that the reader is part of a longer conversation. In fact, there's even a name for that conversation: a *thread*. The whole point is that once an e-mail discussion is started, it often travels in several different directions, each of which becomes a thread in its own right. The entire discussion can then be thought of as a kind of tapestry built up out of many interwoven but separate threads.

What Doug Engelbart invented back in the '60s was the world's first *bulletin board*, called NLS (oNLine System). As you'll see later in this chapter, the system was really much more than just a bulletin board; but for now, even considering the bulletin board aspect of NLS gives you a valuable view of the community memory concept. So what is a bulletin board, and why is it such a compelling alternative to electronic mail?

What NLS provides is a structured environment for carrying out threaded conversations among large communities of users. The central organizing concept is the idea of the outline. Most people were first introduced to outlines in high school. Later in college, many people started using outlines as more than just a form of organizing information; instead, outlines became a great way to record all the information about a topic when taking notes or writing a paper.

NLS revolves around outlines, all of which are shared among all users of the system. Suppose that I want to start a conversation about marketing problems. I type in a few notes, perhaps as a single level at the top of a new outline. At this level, the NLS system looks a lot like a word processor of today operating in outline mode. However, there's a novel twist.

My note about marketing problems is actually part of a larger NLS conversational forum about marketing in general. This forum is shared by many users. In fact, like a conversation at a party, interested observers can add and remove themselves from the conversational forum at will. Every interested participant in a conversation is told about new conversational entries automatically. In this way, the NLS system functions just like an e-mail system. The e-mail system tells readers about new arriving messages; the NLS system tells conversationalists about new forum entries. There is one crucial difference, though.

In the e-mail system, each reader is working with his or her own private copy of the mail message; the mail system's job is to transmit copies of the message to all recipients. In the bulletin board system, on the other hand, each reader is working with a shared copy of each conversational item; the bulletin board's job is to make readers aware of new shared items without ever making copies of those items. In a very real sense, the bulletin board functions as a form of community memory.

In the NLS system, the file clerks are gone. Each reader sees new items, but they are always seen in the conversational forum where they were originally filed. Only the originator needs to decide which conversational thread an item belongs in; filing is done only once. Whenever a new participant joins a conversation, the entire contents of the bulletin board is available to him or her to catch up on history and become fully aware of the overall context.

If NLS was so great, why haven't more people heard about it; why aren't bulletin boards in general more successful? The surprising answer is that while NLS itself never became a large commercial success, it's successors — Lotus Notes, CompuServe, and America Online — have indeed become very popular. Looking further, bulletin boards have become a fundamental staple of underground communications worldwide.

LOTUS NOTES: THE CORPORATE COMMUNITY MEMORY

While NLS, later called Augment and marketed by Tymshare, never really took off, Engelbart's original vision finally found popularity in the form of a system called Lotus Notes. Today, Notes is the first commercially successful form of corporate community memory. And because community memory is still such a new concept, people, even today, have a great deal of trouble understanding what Notes is really about.

Lotus Notes was first introduced in the early '90s, about the same time that Windows and LANs were first becoming really popular. At the time, tools for building graphical applications in the Windows environments had not become commonly available. Large organizations, in particular, were looking for tools to build graphical, multi-user database applications quickly and easily. Superficially, Lotus Notes looks like a tool that meets this need. Moving beyond NLS, it makes it easy for developers to design forms that can be used to participate in conversations. To support these conversations, it provides conversational forums, called *databases*. As early users quickly discovered, Notes is not well suited at all to building true database applications. The kinds of tools that support building this type of application are discussed in Chapter 15. Instead, what Notes represented was a quick and easy way of building friendly community memory applications.

Why does Notes succeed where NLS failed? NLS was built on large, shared, time-sharing systems that could be accessed only from terminals connected to high-speed lines. While NLS could be used over low-speed, dial-up lines, it lost most of its friendly graphical appeal. So NLS could be used only at locations where terminals and high-speed access were available. Furthermore, since NLS depended on both expensive networks and expensive central machines, it in turn was expensive to use. Notes solved all these problems.

Notes was one of the first true distributed client/server applications. Notes databases (recall, these are really conversational forums) run on servers based on ordinary personal computers. Users in turn access Notes using ordinary personal computers running Windows. Finally, to make access really universal and convenient, Notes pioneered a technology called *replication*.

Sales and service organizations are the heaviest users of community applications like Notes because of their need to track customer contacts in a shared fashion. Suppose that a sales rep is about to call on a customer after several weeks away from the office. The first thing the rep wants to know is what interactions other people throughout the company have had with the customer. Logging into Notes, the rep enters the customer conversational forum, finds the topic for that customer, and looks for unread posted items. Notes flags these items for the rep's attention and by reading them, the rep is immediately updated about all outstanding contacts, all problems, and all proposed resolutions.

Watching the system in operation, the resemblance to NLS is easy to spot. The entire Notes system is organized around the concept of outlines. Each conversational area is one large outline. Drilling into outline topics reveals a hierarchy that can dive as far as the participants in the conversation care to go. By tracking multiple conversational areas, and multiple outline items, readers can participate in any number of conversational threads at one time. However, the real difference between NLS and Notes stems from the replication.

Even with WANs becoming widespread, nobody can be connected to the net all the time. Even when connected, quite often the connection is either slow or noisy, particularly while on the road. Replication solves all these problems by allowing users to keep copies of all the data they access most often on their personal machines. The trick is that the replication service keeps this data synchronized with the other copies, no matter where they might be. Consider an example.

After visiting the customer discussed in the previous scenario, the sales rep adds three notes to his Notes system. One note is a little trip report, one is a request for some new marketing material, and one is a note about a problem with a current promotional campaign. The notes, added to three different Notes forums, are entered offline while the rep is sitting on an airplane. On arriving back at the office, the rep connects his notebook computer to the corporate network. Immediately, his local copy of Notes contacts the copy of Notes in the local server, and the two copies exchange their respective updates. But the process does not stop there. That local server is only one of dozens, and each of those servers, in turn, supports many other individual users, each with his or her own notebooks and personal computers. Notes replication takes changes and ensures that they percolate all through the entire network, eventually reaching every server and every Notes machine organization wide. It is this pervasiveness that really makes Notes so useful. Now a user can have the advantages of the bulletin board's community memory and still retain the mobility associated with operating on his or her own personal machine.

What Lotus Notes has proven beyond a doubt is that community memory, in the form of a rich, customizable bulletin board system, particularly with high quality replication, is an effective next step beyond e-mail for large organizations. Notes works well within the boundaries of a single company. With its sophisticated security model and simple facilities for building custom forms, an organization can quickly and easily adapt Notes to specialized requirements. It's important to also recognize Notes' limitations.

First, it's not currently a complete replacement for electronic mail. For one thing, the population of Notes users is still relatively small, while the population of mail users is huge; therefore, the cost of cutting yourself off from the rest of the world by living only in Notes is just too high. Furthermore, Notes is best suited for facilitating somewhat structured conversations within the boundaries of a known organization, leaving e-mail still a better tool for the many random, unstructured, communications required in daily life. The fact that Notes is not a flat-out replacement for e-mail is really a non-issue because Notes and e-mail can very easily work together.

The second and more important limitation of Notes is that it is neither a database nor a tool for developing applications that drive core business processes. This observation often comes as a surprise to many Notes fans, at least initially. On the surface, one of the attractions of Notes is that it does such a good job of making shared information available throughout an organization. It's replication facilities are particularly appealing in this context because they make remote offices and laptop users first class citizens for the first time. At the same time, Notes also makes it pretty simple to develop graphical forms based applications that use this shared data. In fact, when Notes was introduced, it was one of the very few, perhaps even the only, widely available system that provided all of this in a Windows based, client/server environment. Little wonder then that eager developers saw Notes as their complete path into the client/server future.

Saying that Notes is not an appropriate tool for developing true database centered applications takes very little away from it. Notes is still a trend-setting, high-quality product with important benefits. However, when it comes to developing serious applications to run core business processes, it is not the right tool. Why? At its center, Notes it not a database. It has no concept of records. Transactions, record locking, and other key facilities required in the world of business processes are just not there. Notes was never designed to be a database in the first place, so this limitation is not surprising; yet it is still sometimes a surprise to users just becoming familiar with it. What this all means is simple. Notes is just one more part of a complete, client/server information system. It supplies bulletin board facilities, something databases don't do, and it does that job very well. No, it is not all things to all people, but then no tool ever is.

While Notes is a very strong community memory system for supporting individual organizations, what about bulletin boards for people at home, bulletin boards that cross companies, and generally, bulletin boards for the world at large? Do these make sense?

BULLETIN BOARDS FOR THE MASSES

At the same time that Notes was starting to take off in popularity, an entirely different class of bulletin board systems was finding broad spread acceptance, as well. These bulletin boards take two similar but different flavors: one institutional and one homegrown.

On the institutional front, CompuServe, America Online, Prodigy, and several other providers have successfully built services reaching several million people all over the world. At first glance, it is a little hard knowing exactly how to classify these services. Each of them offers at least four core facilities to subscribers:

✦ Electronic Mail

✦ Bulletin Boards

✦ Public Databases

✦ Electronic Shopping

Reading an America Online ad clearly leaves the impression that all four of these facilities are equally real and equally attractive. Not so. First and foremost, in terms of both utility and utilization, is electronic mail. We've already talked about it quite a lot, but suffice it to say that for many subscribers, electronic mail is the main, and often the only, service they use — and worth it, by far.

The bulletin board services offered by public systems like CompuServe represent a type of truly global community memory. While Notes allows individual organizations to pool thoughts, these public bulletin boards provide the same service literally to the world. A public bulletin board, like Notes, is organized around conversational forums and threaded conversations. However, unlike Notes, the range of topics is truly global. At one level, public bulletin boards often provide the best single place to go for technical advice of all kinds. By posting a question about even the most obscure technical problem, a user gains the advice of literally thousands of potential helpers worldwide. Furthermore, before even posting the question, the reader is more than likely to find the solution to his or her problem lurking somewhere in the thousands of notes and messages posted under most interesting topics on the board. But technical discussion is just the beginning.

Bulletin boards today have forums dealing with the weather, travel, entertainment, cars, sex, education — in short, the world. It is precisely the broad nature of the boards, and the worldwide community that inhabits them, that can make them so addictive. Addictive, like a drug in many ways. Often users find themselves starting a bulletin board session early in the evening and terminating it only to find half the night gone by. So while e-mail may be the most heavily used service overall, bulletin boards are certainly the most addictive; and with the wide range of topics covered, bulletin boards are the most controversial.

What about public databases and electronic shopping? In theory, these services should be highly attractive. It is actually hard to imagine that electronic shopping, banking, and so on, will not one day be commonplace and heavily used (this concept is explored further in the last chapter in the book). Today, though, both electronic shopping and all forms of personal electronic commerce are talked about a lot and used very little. Public databases are used slightly more. Accessing information about stock prices, airline flights, and so on, is useful, and some users use such services routinely. In fact, specialized "public" databases catering to stock brokers, travel agents, and so on, are highly successful businesses, but they serve niche markets. When it comes to serving the general public, though, public databases are used little more than electronic shopping.

So for all the discussion about public services, electronic shopping, and millions of users, what we have is a much simpler picture today, but with a twist. CompuServe, America Online, Prodigy, and their competitors do have several million users altogether. This is but a small fraction of the total personal computer user population, let alone the world population. Some people believe that the introduction of the Microsoft Network, with its close connection to Windows 95, will be the catalyst that finally brings public networks to the masses. Perhaps — but before leaping to conclusions, it is important to remember that today the two primary uses of these systems revolves around electronic mail and bulletin boards. The question then is, are these two services compelling enough today to really appeal to a wide population, or is more evolution required before the leap really happens?

No discussion of bulletin boards would be complete without touching on all the private bulletin boards located in homes and offices all over the world. As hackers came into contact with bulletin boards, many of them became addicted. It was only a matter of time until the first hacker wrote private bulletin board software. Today, by dedicating a single personal computer and a phone line to the task, any individual can set up a bulletin board in his or her house in just a few hours. These bulletin boards have become a true staple of the underground culture.

In its most innocuous form, teenagers in every city of any size use bulletin boards to exchange notes about their favorite music, chat casually, and meet other teenagers of both sexes. Bulletin board operators sponsor "GTs" or "Get Togethers," at which subscribers get to meet their conversational partners physically for the first time. All of this represents a new culture often unknown, and almost always totally alien to parents, even if those parents are computer literate products of the '70s or '80s. But bulletin boards go farther.

Of course, specialized groups — private clubs or special interest groups — can use bulletin boards to exchange information widely, but so can subversives and terrorists. What better way to exchange notes and disseminate information about targets and techniques. Of course, this is a two-edged sword. In times of repression, a single PC can quickly and easily be set up in hours to be a secret middleman keeping information flowing. Yet the same tool can just as easily be used by those whose cause is not as easily justified.

Starting with electronic mail as a cultural change agent, this discussion moved on to bulletin boards and community memory, in many ways an even larger change agent. Mail changes the work patterns of individuals, while bulletin boards affect groups of people. As you continue to consider the impact of networks, there is one more step that has potentially even larger effects. That step involves thinking even more deeply about how people communicate and about the fundamental nature of the words they use to do it. The result is the creation of a form of memory that is not just group or community oriented, but actually global in nature.

FROM TEXT TO HYPERTEXT: GLOBAL MEMORY

Looking back at Engelbart's original NLS, you discover that he thought about text and information in two fundamentally different (but related) ways. Most of the time, he believed that users wanted to think about information in a hierarchical, outline oriented fashion. Outlines provide convenient viewing frameworks, make choices obvious, and provide simple ways to expand and contract the conceptual scope of the information being worked with. At the core, though, hierarchical views of information depend on the fact that the information is basically linear in nature.

Books, music, movies, television programs, and conversations are all linear in nature. One thought follows another, and there is only one way to progress through the sequence. Our thinking, however, is far from linear. And it is from that observation that the concept of hypertext springs. A *hypertext* is collection of information that attempts to capture all (or many) of the complex possible connections that can exist between pieces of information.

Imagine an author researching a book. Over time, the author collects hundreds of three-by-five index cards representing bits of data, thoughts about content, references, and so on. Eventually, carefully filtering and sorting all the time, the author arranges the cards into a single linear sequence that becomes the basis for the book. But suppose that the author didn't have to pick a single sequence?

Think of the book as put together out of thousands of little chunks or passages of text, each representing a single thought or concept. Now also think of threads running from each such chunk or passage to all the potentially related other chunks. To make the picture complete, imagine that the reader has a mechanism that allows him or her to decide, while reading each passage, which related passage to read next.

Encountering a book on programming, a beginner takes one path through the book, and an advanced reader takes another. Putting together a dinner menu, 25 different users of a recipe book may each have a completely different path through the exact same book. But hypertext doesn't stop with single books.

Suppose that you are reading a book about building design, and you encounter a reference about architecture. Following the link, you are now reading a completely different book which, in turn, points to an article about engineering stress calculation; that link takes you to a journal. The journal article briefly mentions a famous engineer and artist; you follow the link, and you are now reading an encyclopedia article. Following a few links in the encyclopedia, each of which instantly takes you to the relevant article (no pulling books off the shelf and no finding the page), you land on a reference about color design, which takes you to an obscure set of lecture notes located on a university server. . . .

This is hypertext in action. There are many ways of thinking about hypertext, but the concept is indeed revolutionary enough to warrant having the many approaches for reaching it. Narrowly, hypertext presents a way of organizing information in a book or manual so that users can quickly follow references. Most modern help systems today use this approach to provide quick ways of jumping from topic to topic. The same system makes multimedia encyclopedias like Encarta flexible and fun, too. Looked at from another narrow perspective, hypertext presents a way of organizing mail systems, filing systems, and bulletin boards more effectively. A pure hierarchical approach forces all items to be placed in only one folder. However, most memos and messages can easily relate to several topics. By providing facilities for placing these items in several folders, and for creating links between items, hypertext makes the whole system more flexible. However, Hypertext is broader than either of these two approaches.

TED NELSON AND THE XANADU PALACE

Samuel Taylor Coleridge, a famous poet of the last century, dreamed of a fabulous pleasure palace called Xanadu. Upon awakening, he began writing down the verses describing this palace but was interrupted before he could finish. Later, he was never able to fully recapture either the vision or the words to describe it. Laboring through the '60s, '70s, and the '80s, Ted Nelson, an early hypertext visionary, had a similar experience.

Around the same time that Engelbart was building NLS, Ted Nelson was developing early text editing systems based on many of the same concepts. While Engelbart built a broader and more complete system, Nelson took the specific idea of hypertext much further.

Internal bulletin board systems create perceptions and memories that span organizations. Public bulletin board systems allow people from a wide variety of backgrounds and organizations to participate in discussions across wide distances. Still both private and public bulletin board systems tend to deal with conversations and topics that are somewhat limited in nature. This limitation stems for the hierarchical nature of the medium.

By definition, an outline deals with a single broad topic. Granted, the topic is divided and subdivided in turn, which allows for many twists and turns; still overall, the parts of the outline tend to be related to the broader outline topic area. Introducing a single new element, hypertext, changes the focus of the conversation tremendously. That new element is the *pointer*.

A pointer allows any conversational item or passage to be linked to virtually any other conversational item or passage. Creating links in this way allows arbitrarily sudden leaps of thought or obscure references to be created. More importantly, particular passages can now be included in any number of conversations. And that is what got Ted Nelson so excited.

Like many evangelists before him, Nelson wanted to solve problems on a truly global scale. In his case, Nelson's goal was nothing less than world understanding leading to world peace. How can this possibly be related to hypertext?

Nelson was fascinated with the problem of how ideas develop, spread, and become popular. The written and spoken word is part of this process. One problem with all the normal ways of transmitting information over time is the loss of attribution (attribution is the action of giving credit to the original author or the original source from which a piece of information is derived).

Say that I have an original idea that I publish in a paper or article. Somebody else sees this paper, borrows the idea, but fails or forgets to give me credit. At the center, this is the problem that Nelson's Xanadu system was designed to solve.

Xanadu was intended to be a worldwide hypertext system. It would be capable of being used by every living person on the planet, and would be able to store every written and spoken word, with all this information interlinked in the rich ways that only hypertext makes possible.

The thing that would really set Xanadu apart, though, aside from its sheer scale, was the implementation of transclusion. *Transclusion* is best thought of as a special or fancy kind of inclusion. The idea was to completely eliminate the need to ever copy text. Any time that anybody wanted to include a phrase, sentence, or paragraph from an original cite, transclusion would allow that inclusion to take place without copying. Using hypertext links instead, the included text would consist of an invisible pointer to the original. So if you wanted to use my idea, instead of copying the appropriate text from my paper, you would simply *transclude* it, incorporating it by reference. Now comes the special part.

Links of all kinds, including transclusive links, can always be viewed, followed, and traced. Thus a reader, starting with an idea, can always trace it back, farther and farther, to find the roots from which it stemmed. Thus Xanadu would provide a mechanism to support seeing where all ideas came from, and how all ideas are related to all other ideas.

Practically speaking, it's hard to even know how to think about Xanadu. Of course the system was never built; even today nobody knows how to even think about building such an all-encompassing system. The concept is obviously attractive. The idea of having all the information in the world stored in a single place; a place where every idea is linked to every related idea, with simple facilities to trace these links quickly and easily. Like the original Xanadu, this is all a dream, hard to even describe let alone build. As a real system, Xanadu today is just an interesting footnote in the history of computer science. As a concept, Ted Nelson and his Xanadu project had an impact that continues to this very day. That impact excited hundreds of key developers about hypertext and led directly to the World Wide Web and other related technologies that have very real life today and in the future.

HYPERTEXT MADE REAL: THE WORLD WIDE WEB

Hypertext has seen several real implementations in the last 25 years. The first was found in the NLS system. While Engelbart's system focused primarily on outlines, NLS also contained rich facilities for creating pointers that reached across outlines. A particularly interesting aspect of these pointers, not replicated again until the World Wide Web, was the capability to point from one computer system to another completely different computer system, although both had to be running NLS.

In the '70s and '80s, a number of experimental systems at universities, particularly Brown University, explored the medium of hypertext in some depth. One of the interesting outcomes of this work was the realization that after a while, a new link between two concepts could actually have as much value as a new piece of content. The idea that a relationship could be as valuable as primary content itself takes some getting used to. In one example of this concept at work, students in a course were assigned the project of working with a large body of hypertext-based content with the goal of finding and creating a single creative and meaningful new hypertext link.

The first widespread commercial implementation of hypertext was the Macintosh's HyperCard system. Along with event-based visual programming, HyperCard pioneered the idea of allowing even users to create links between any two parts of a stack of cards. The mechanism used was simple. First the user would select a sequence of characters (usually a word or phrase) to be the beginning of the link. After highlighting that text, the user would activate the Create Link command. HyperCard would ask the user to then navigate to the links destination point and click on a completion button. At that point, the link was complete. A reader encountering this card later would see the link text highlighted, as a kind of hot spot. Moving the mouse pointer over the hot spot changes its shape to a hand or some other evocative icon; clicking the mouse takes the reader to the destination. The primary limitation of HyperCard was that these simple links were confined to single stacks of cards.

After HyperCard, thousands of other software systems used the same basic technology to build hypertext-based help, hypertext-based encyclopedias, movie guides, and so on. In a short period of time, the idea of having pervasive and ubiquitous links all through a body of information had become commonplace. The primary limitation of all these systems was that each was self-contained, dealing with a single body of material at one time.

As hypertext was becoming common, the Internet was growing, and with it servers by the thousands were attaching themselves all over the world. Finding information within a server was often quite easy with many different types of search engines helping the user through the process. But finding a server in the first place was hard. That's where the next generation of hypertext enters the stage.

The first World Wide Web development took place at the CERN research lab in Switzerland. Programmers working there realized that the concepts of hypertext could be used to tie servers together so that users could leap from server to server with just a few keystrokes. In one fell swoop, sets of previously separate servers could now be thought of and worked with as though all those servers were part of a single, large global hypertext. Hypertext itself is often best thought of as a large web tying together otherwise disparate thoughts. This new web, unlike any before it, as it jumped from server to server, broke new ground by being world wide; hence, why not name it the *World Wide Web* (or *WWW*).

The initial WWW system was text oriented like much of the original Internet itself. The most important single invention that set the WWW apart from its predecessors was *HTML*, short for *Hypertext Markup Language*. HTML, in turn, is a specialized form of *SGML, Standard General Markup Language*. A *markup language* is a notation for describing the formatting of a document. Markup languages were first used by book and newspaper editors who would scrawl quick notations onto a story or book to indicate paragraph breaks, missing words, phrases to be printed in larger fonts, and so on. More recently, markup languages have become associated with high-end word processors and desktop publishing programs used to produce particularly complex documents. A markup language allows an editor or author to describe very powerful formatting operations to be applied to parts of a document. The author's instructions are identified by special lead-in characters to distinguish them from normal text. Once the lead-in characters are identified, the markup language can then contain arbitrarily complex sets of instructions.

In a way, the return of markup languages is somewhat ironic. The first PC-based word processors, like WordStar, used simple markup languages as their primary formatting mechanism. Millions of early PC users learned to love, or at least tolerate, these "dot" commands. One of the primary benefits of graphical word processors was the complete elimination of visible formatting commands; markup languages appeared to be gone forever. Instead, the user formatted text, the formatting was directly visible on the screen, and that was that. In fact, the word processor stored the formatting directives, in hidden form, in the document; the user could even ask to see them if desired.

HTML is a particular form of markup language designed with two purposes in mind. First, HTML provides formatting primitives particularly suited to the kinds of simple two-dimensional pages so common on the Web. Second, HTML provides navigational primitives. Essentially, these primitives allow one WWW page to point to another. All of these HTML primitives operate in design mode and in user mode. In design mode, each primitive is a visible piece of text, a sequence of characters that can be directly typed by a person. In user mode, the HTML directives all disappear. Instead, the user sees a formatted page. In place of navigational directives, the user sees highlighted text; when the user points to that text and clicks, the user jumps to the page being pointed to by the underlying HTML directive.

Why focus on an actual HTML language at all? To begin with, the HTML makes WWW pages independent of any particular workstation. Formatting directives can be interpreted one way under Windows, another way on a Macintosh, and yet another way on a character-oriented terminal. Secondly, and even more importantly, because HTML consists entirely of text strings, it can easily be generated by a computer. Thus HTML makes it quite easy to generate WWW pages programmatically.

The basic WWW, even including HTML, laid the foundation but still was not quite enough to kick the whole effort into high gear. The last kicker was the development of a graphical front end called *Mosaic*, written by Marc Andreessen, a programmer working at the supercomputer lab located at the University of Illinois. Mosaic was an application capable of running on a wide variety of workstations that made navigating the Web a point-and-click affair. Suddenly, users could traverse pages all over the world with hardly any typing. The rest, as they say, is history.

AROUND THE WORLD IN EIGHTY CLICKS

What makes the Web so different than everything that came before? The first question, of course, is what did come before? The two answers have to be bulletin board systems and the Internet.

Compared to the Web, a bulletin board system, for all its variety, is far more insular. Bulletin board systems basically run on single servers. Yes, Notes has a sophisticated replication scheme, but the point of that scheme is actually to make a network of computers all look like a single large computer. Another way of thinking about it is that Notes' replication scheme creates homogeneity: any change made anywhere is then made to appear everywhere. Bulletin board systems also tend not to be highly graphical; this is a direct consequence of the fact that they tend to run computers shared by very large numbers of people. It is also related to the fact that BBSs tend to revolve around conversational threads and topics, which in turn tend to favor text-based interaction. So the Web, beyond a limited resemblance, is not very much like a bulletin board — at least not today.

The Web fundamentally transformed the Internet by making it, for the first time, truly easy to use. The Internet, until very recently, showed a clear family resemblance to the UNIX operating systems that so many of its servers ran. And before UNIX, Tenex, Tops 10, and other hacker-oriented operating systems were dominant. As a result, the design of FTP, Gophers, and all the other utilities that made the pre-WWW Internet work favored powerful but cryptic commands that were anything but friendly. While HTML itself is anything but friendly, the Web itself, and the browsers that run on it, hide that complexity almost totally.

While the Web was different than either the Internet or BBS, it borrowed key features from each of them. The fascinating, even addictive, idea of being able to browse through a wide variety of topics just by following links from place to place came directly from the Bulletin Board. In fact, even the idea of having a simple point-and-click interface was really driven by Notes, PCs, and simple mass market systems. On the other hand, it was the Internet, with its globe-spanning connections, that made the heterogeneous and cosmopolitan nature of the WWW imaginable and possible.

The Web is unique in a way that no predecessor can really claim to copy. On any given day, a Web crawler (a person "crawling" around the Web) really has no idea at all what he or she is going to find. Leaping from server to server literally can mean hopping from country to country and continent to continent. But the variety reaches much deeper than that. Until the advent of the Web, any computer-based information system had a certain built in degree of uniformity. Even if programmers were quite creative, essentially all of them worked with the same tools, in the same system environment, and built relatively similar applications as a result. The Web, however, consists of completely separate computers, each playing the role of server, and each owned by completely different people and institutions. A developer wanting to connect to the Web has almost total freedom to decide what computer to use, which operating system to run, what tools to use, and so on. It's true that certain standard protocols — TCP/IP, HTML, GCI, and so on — are required to make the connection work; however, once those are in place, anything goes.

The variety of material found on the Web is literally, already today, beyond imagination. One server, connected to a camera, offers a view of a college dorm; another offers a picture, updated daily, of an individual's lunch bag. Stock prices, flowers for sale, personal companion ads, up-to-date news — the list goes on and on. If a developer can imagine it, and a computer can be programmed to do it, that computer can then offer its presentation over the Web. And as quickly as other users discover interesting new pages, they can add links to them, and those pages become part of the Web and are easy to find. So how do we understand this tremendous variety and what it really means — why it makes the Web so compelling, interesting, and different?

WEB SERVERS: COOPERATING COMPONENTS

In one step, the Web has brought a major new element to community memory systems: the concept of cooperating components. A bulletin board system is essentially monolithic. For all of its sophisticated replication and its capability to run across thousands of machines, Notes also is basically monolithic; the whole point is that it presents a single system image to the user. But the cost is that developers can build only what Notes lets them build. The Web is different. Every Web server can be totally different than any other Web server, yet they all communicate with each other using standard Web protocols. The result is the fascinating, distributed, heterogeneous environment seen today. As an example of the power of cooperating components, the Web is outstanding. That example is not enough yet for us to stand back and see the whole picture. What it does offer is the first example of the power of this new paradigm.

NETWORKS: BRINGING ALL THE WORLD TOGETHER

Starting with the simple idea of a network and servers, you now have several very different systems, all of which provide ways of bringing people together. How do all these different systems fit together, and what does the future hold? Begin by reviewing the systems:

✦ Electronic mail allows individuals to communicate with each other, competing with the telephone, memos, and regular mail. In its simplest form, e-mail offers one to one communication.

✦ Bulletin boards make it easy for large groups to exchange information with each other. A note posted in a conversational forum lives on indefinitely and can be read by a number of people. BBSs offer many to many communication.

✦ Finally, the Web provides a mechanism to disseminate information from a single person or group to a very large number of people. The Web is different in that the communication is entirely one way. If I create a Web page, only I can change that page. Anybody can read it, but nobody except me can write to it. So the Web essentially offers one to many communication.

What this model for electronic mail, BBSs, and the Web really shows is how different these systems are from each other. It also shows how immature networking technology still is. That maturity shows up most acutely when you start to think about how to build a system that combines the best of electronic mail, bulletin boards, and the WWW; it's not at all clear how to do that.

The true promise of wide-area networks is to eliminate the effect of distance — to make the world into a global workgroup. This change is a fundamental cultural change, one that will affect workstyles, personal relationships, and eventually even the very meaning of work. How close is all of this to happening? There are two ways to think about that question.

At a macroscopic level, it's pretty amazing to compare the claims for today's networks with the reality. By reading popular articles about the Web and the popular bulletin board services, it's easy to believe that most homes and offices are connected, shopping is about to disappear, and most commerce takes place over the net. The reality is that fewer than ten million individuals, out of a world population of billions, use the Internet on any kind of a truly regular basis. And when you consider the true usage patterns, it is electronic mail — not shopping, not banking, not even the Web itself — that is by far the dominant application. Again and again, technical pioneers report about their experiences as they start to explore the Internet. First, they quickly discover how very limited the services of the future are; shopping, banking, and commerce over the net are still safely in the future. Then they do find the Web itself to be interesting and even addictive. Finally, when time has passed and the dust has settled, the reports trickle back in, and electronic mail is it.

At a more microscopic level, why are e-mail, bulletin boards, and the Web so separated from each other? For example, why can't a bulletin board system be geographically distributed, just like the Web is? Doesn't true hypertext linking make just as much sense for bulletin board style conversations as for relatively static information? And what about e-mail? If bulletin boards are such an effective means for carrying on threaded conversations, why haven't systems like Notes merged with systems like cc:Mail and Microsoft Mail? The clear separations between all these different applications is a more detailed sign of the development and continuing change still ahead of us.

The global village is almost at hand, and the impact of the WAN on our lives is hard to over estimate. WANs will change the way people communicate and relate to each other within and across organizations. The next thing to look at is the role the computer will play in running the organizations themselves. This is the role in which the computer functions as a computing and management engine, alongside the role just explored in which it functions as a communication agent.

NETWORKS AND NON-NETWORKS

As you think about all the implications of networking, go back to the idea of cooperating components for a moment. Recall that the thing that makes the Web stand apart is that it is an early implementation of cooperating components. Yet the Web today provides functionality that is too limited to really fulfill the promise explored in Chapter 3. In fact, the Web is too limited to even compete with, let alone replace, the other dominant systems on the WANs of the world: e-mail and BBSs. Yet from a broader perspective, the beginning of a bigger answer is clear.

Imagine a Web-like environment. Users can hop from server to server quickly and easily. Now, suppose that some of those servers have grown up to the point where they are running part of the business. Suppose that sometimes when hopping from server to server, there's no person involved; it's one organization, one server, talking to another. That sounds like where you need to get, right? The question is how do you build the servers that run the business? That's where the next chapter comes in. In fact, the next chapter gets to a key question that's been looming since Chapter 1. All these distributed servers are really great, but can these systems really replace today's mainframes, and if so, why hasn't it already happened? To answer this question, you need to take a look at the mainframe itself and at what — if anything — makes it special.

CHAPTER 8

THE MAINFRAME — THE TECHNICAL SHIFT TO DISTRIBUTED SYSTEMS

I've mentioned mainframes and minicomputers previously — but I've avoided talking much about them directly. Although personal computers and LANs can do many new things, many people assume that the only computer to use for really big applications is, of course, a mainframe. Conversely, a standard assumption about LANs is that there is a strict upper limit on the size and complexity of the work they can be trusted to do. This chapter examines these two assumptions directly. I'll tackle that long-time companion, the mainframe, to see what the future might suggest, at least from a technical perspective.

Historically, building business systems was easy: start with a mainframe, plug in terminals, and grow the mainframe to keep up with the demand. With the introduction of the minicomputer, people started talking about a new breed of *distributed* systems: plug in computers at remote locations where the work was being done and distribute the workload across many smaller computers instead of funneling it all through a single monster computer. Attractive as this concept is, and in spite of many attempts over the past 20 years to make it work, most large business systems today are still highly centralized. However, new high-powered personal computers up the ante. With PCs, servers, WANs, and LANs, distributed systems become even more attractive than in the past. The question is: attractive as they are, can people build distributed systems? If so, how and when?

In this chapter, I duck the question of how to build distributed systems. Instead, I will show what a distributed system would look like *if* it were built. Then in the next part of the book, I consider the business pressures that are forcing companies to develop distributed computer systems and the somewhat surprising shifts in design approaches. These new design approaches provide a clear road map for making these distributed systems practical.

WHAT IS A MAINFRAME?

Is a mainframe intrinsically different from a personal computer? Is there special magic built into it that provides huge speed or capacity advantages? Is this special magic rare enough that it can't be reproduced in smaller and less expensive computers?

From a hardware perspective, a mainframe is not all that different from a personal computer! Heretical? Yes. But also true. In fact, what a mainframe most closely resembles is a LAN.

Any mainframe has several major components. First is the computer itself. Historically, the computer inside a mainframe was much faster than a personal computer. This speed manifested itself in two ways:

✦ The raw speed expressed in instructions per second, or cycles

✦ The amount of memory that could be addressed directly by a program

In the following sections, I discuss these two aspects of a mainframe in sequence.

BIG, BIGGER, BIGGEST: HOW MUCH IS ENOUGH?

In the chapter on LANs, I examined some of the scary implications of buying and upgrading expensive computers. One question I didn't answer is, how big *can* a computer get? And how expensive is it to make a computer big?

It is surprisingly hard to build really big computers. Mainframes cost millions of dollars, and super computers can cost many millions. However, neither of these big computers is thousands of times faster than personal computers. They cost literally thousands of times more than PCs, but they sure don't do thousands of times more work. The problem is that the price of a computer increases far faster than the power that can be built into it for the money. Another problem is worse: even with an infinite budget, there is a very real upper limit to the power of the biggest possible computer.

Airlines run into this problem every day. The central reservation system for an airline processes all of its work through a single computer. The rationale for this approach is that a passenger at any airport in the world can book flights that will take him to any other airport — all within a 24-hour period. So it makes a lot of sense to just keep all of the information about flights, seat availability, and schedules in a single place. How does the central computer keep up with the resulting volume of requests streaming in from all over the world? With great difficulty.

Many years ago, the largest airlines realized that capacity would be a huge problem for their central reservation systems. To face this challenge, they decided to write their applications in special ways that would squeeze every last ounce of computing power out of the poor, overloaded, central mainframes. So big airlines use

✦ A custom operating system called Airline Control Program (ACP)

✦ Applications written in assembler, the lowest-level programming language still around

✦ Data that is stored not in commercial databases but in special storage systems (private databases written by the airlines for themselves) optimized for fast update and retrieval

All of this proprietary, custom software has a huge cost. And all of this is still not enough.

As a result, the major airlines tend to have standing orders with the major mainframe manufacturers. When a newer, larger, faster mainframe is ready for production, the mainframe company merely provides appropriate advance notice and then just ships the computer to the airline with no questions asked. Price is not a consideration; anything that will help the airline manage capacity crunch is used as soon as it is available.

Airlines are far from unique. Many important computational problems cannot be solved simply because there is no computer fast enough to do the job. For example, weather simulation to a large extent is just as accurate at the amount of data that can be contained in the model at any one time. Keeping track of wind patterns, temperature shifts, and pressure cells over the surface of any large part of the earth quickly exceeds the capacity of even the largest super computer.

As another example, modeling the structure of a car, truck, or airplane quickly brings even the biggest computer to its knees:

✦ Tracking how it will react to various stresses

✦ Taking into account all the interactions between the parts of the structure

Additionally, designing computer chips strains computers, too. Every advance in technology makes engineers depend even more heavily on massive computers to help them interconnect millions of elements in creative new ways.

Perhaps the most compelling examples of "computer crunchers" — applications that eat big computers up and then spit them out exhausted — are the animation and visualization programs used to create videos, movies, and advertisements. Building one dinosaur motion sequence in *Jurassic Park* — lasting only seconds on the screen —

takes *hours* of computer time. Computers run smack into the brick wall imposed by the massive computational power and huge amounts of memory required to create very simple "virtually real" worlds. In the movies, the virtual worlds suddenly must be very large and quite real — at least realistic enough to fool a critical audience. Although present animation techniques produce amazing cartoons and articulated robots, those techniques are still very far from modeling the real world.

BATCH PROCESSING

Perhaps the class of applications that best characterizes mainframes are those called *batch processing* applications. Every large organization runs periodic processes that operate on large amounts of data on a daily, weekly, or monthly basis, such as the following:

+ Scheduling factories

+ Billing customers

+ Aging accounts receivable

+ Updating credit ratings

+ Computing optimum routes for fleets of delivery trucks

All of these are large, complex, heavily computational processes with two common characteristics. First, these processes manipulate large amounts of data. Second, to do the best possible job, the application often works with the entire database at one time. For example, the optimum schedule for a factory could involve juggling all the orders, sequencing delivery of parts in particular ways, and juggling the use of expensive equipment to keep that equipment constantly busy. The only way to develop that schedule is to look at the entire day's, week's, or month's production all at one time. These processes are exactly opposite to terminal-oriented applications. Instead of dealing with a relatively small amount of data, interacting constantly with a person, and doing work in small chunks, these applications process data in large batches. For that reason, this type of processing has come to be known as *batch processing*.

Originally computers did only batch processing. In the days of punched cards and printed reports (before terminals were invented), computers could only do one thing at a time. Each application ran straight through before the next application (or job, as it was called at the time) began. Batch processing was all there was.

THE FUTURE OF BATCH PROCESSING

People commonly assume that batch processing is a hangover from the past and that, over time, batch applications will disappear. Perhaps, but more likely not. The types of applications and processes just described are intrinsically batch-oriented in nature.

Some of today's batch processes will undoubtedly be redesigned as tomorrow's on-the-fly processes. But other processes will remain batch, particularly those that involve large-scale optimization across big parts of an organization.

Batch processing is important for two reasons. First, virtually every large organization has large amounts of batch processing. Second, batch processing is handled best by the mainframe.

BATCH WINDOWS

In many companies, batch runs define the size of the mainframe needed just as much as the on-line demands placed on the central database. Typically, batch processes are scheduled on a calendar. Billing happens on the first and the fifteenth of the month; receivables age on the tenth and the twentieth, bills are printed and mailed every Thursday, and so on. Each batch process is carefully timed and the average run time is determined. These run times are all overlaid on the available *batch windows*. When the run time exceeds the available window, you've got a problem. So what is this mysterious batch window?

The batch window is the period of time when the mainframe can process the intense computations of a batch job. Running batch applications during the working day would create two serious problems. First, user response time is likely to suffer. Second, many batch processes require exclusive access to the entire database. For example, scheduling a factory might assume that certain parts are in stock. When the scheduling program makes this assumption for any given part, the inventory of that part has to be locked down until the schedule is finalized. However, if the entire plant were being scheduled, then pretty soon all the inventory would get locked up and any other applications that require access to parts wouldn't run. For these two reasons, many batch jobs require a batch window to provide exclusive access to the computer and its data. And because that access must be exclusive, the batch window must be limited in size to minimize interruptions to users. In fact, the smaller the window, the better. Over time, users tend to rely more and more on constant access to their data and resent long periods of unavailability.

Unfortunately, batch processes take a long time. Furthermore, when a batch process fails, generally it must be restarted. So allowing for the possibility of failure, the individual batch jobs must occupy less than half the available window. That way, if they must be restarted, there's enough time to try over. And there's the twist.

THE GROWTH OF BATCH PROCESSES CREATES DEMAND FOR BIGGER COMPUTERS

As companies grow and their processing requirements get more sophisticated, batch processes tend to grow, too. Pretty soon, fitting the batch processes into the available windows becomes a real problem. Although many companies feel safe because they don't run global reservation systems or construct complex virtual animated worlds, they still have batch processes. Consequently, the growth of batch processing has been one of the reasons for the continuing need for mainframes.

Many companies constantly struggle with a fixed batch window, a computer that is not fast enough, and continual pressure for new applications that could add value — if only there were enough batch cycles to run them.

THE DEMAND FOR BIGGER, FASTER COMPUTERS CONTINUES

On an industrial scale, companies need very big computers — bigger than can be built — to carry out a variety of industrial-strength applications. Central database servers must be able to

◆ Track passengers and customers worldwide

◆ Constantly present up-to-date information to anybody who asks

◆ Instantly allocate scarce resources such as airplane seats and credit dollars

Complex design processes such as weather prediction and movie animation will strain even the biggest super computer. And even for companies that avoid these two classes of problems, batch processing — that mainstay of classical computing — will constantly cause people to ask for more, bigger, and faster computers.

Although big is important, it's not the whole story. Big computers are needed, but small computers are, too. To make the picture complete, all the sizes in between are needed. Here are some critical questions for '90s computing:

◆ Mainframes are great for big jobs, and personal computers work well for little tasks, but what's in between?

◆ Even if you could answer that question, isn't it complicated having to deal with two completely different kinds of computers when building applications?

◆ Last but not least, aren't mainframes really expensive and isn't there some way to do the same thing less expensively?

As I'm about to show, the answers to these questions revolve around the concept of scalability. By implementing maximum scalability, all three questions receive complete and satisfying answers.

THE SCALABILITY PROBLEM

What is *scalability*? The word is not in the dictionary. Once again the computer industry has invented a term to meet a perceived need. However, the root of scalability is scale. The *American Heritage Dictionary* defines the term *scale* as

1. A progressive classification, as of size, amount, importance, or rank.

2. To ascend in steps or stages.

Therefore, scalability is the ability to gracefully adapt to changes in size over a series of steps.

In the United States, there are over 11 million business locations or establishments: physical buildings or offices in which people work on a full-time basis. Many of these properties are owned by small businesses with only a few employees. However, many properties are owned by big companies. The mention of a big company, such as Coca-Cola, conjures images of big buildings such as skyscrapers, monster factories, and warehouses bigger than football fields. Servicing the needs of these large facilities calls for big computers. However, even the biggest companies have many locations with only a few employees: remote sales offices with two salespeople, small warehouses with a dozen staff members, regional repair centers housed in two rooms, and so on. This combination of big, medium, and small operations creates the scalability challenge. The challenge calls for not only big computers and small ones — but also all the sizes in between. The computers, the disks that attach to them, the applications that run on those computers, and the operating system software required to make it all fit together — all of these must be scalable to meet the needs of all sizes of companies, offices, and locations.

SCALING A SYSTEM TO LARGE DEMANDS

Imagine a large manufacturing company with many warehouses. In that company, the largest product distribution center may be several stories tall, cover as much land as several football fields, and operate on a completely automated basis. This warehouse may be *blacked out*; robot forklifts, automated conveyer belts, and computer-controlled picking systems handle the goods. No lights are required because no humans normally work in the facility. Obviously, such a facility would require massive computer power. Each movement in the warehouse would be tracked by the computer. In fact, were the computer to slow down, so would the warehouse. And if the computer were to break or stop, the warehouse would follow right behind. Such an environment seems made-to-measure for a huge computer such as a mainframe. However, it would be nice if the operation of the entire plant weren't tied so intimately to the health of a single machine. In a big distribution center, the obvious solution is to have two or more mainframes backing each other up. Fine. But what about smaller warehouses?

SCALING A SYSTEM TO MEDIUM DEMANDS

Suppose that the same company had regional warehouses that are still heavily automated but each contains medium amounts of inventory. Such a facility just can't justify the expense of a multimillion-dollar mainframe. Yet, if a smaller computer were used, would this mean that programmers would have to rewrite the software from the large warehouse to be useable in the medium-sized warehouse?

SCALING A SYSTEM TO SMALL DEMANDS

Finally, suppose that you are willing to write that software twice, once for a big center and once for a medium-size center with its medium-size computer. What about the small warehouse? The company may also have a network of small local centers that hold spare parts, products in heavy demand in local markets, and goods for walk-in customers. These little centers occupy a few thousand square feet and are largely not automated. Yet they still require computer systems to track inventory, orders, shipments, and so on.

INTEGRATING APPLICATIONS OF DIFFERENT SIZES AND LOCATIONS

Suppose that the computer systems at various locations must be integrated with one another so that products may be transferred back and forth without onerous and redundant paperwork. Does this mean you must maintain three completely incompatible computer systems and keep all three systems up to date with each other?

The same company could also have scalability problems in its sales organization. In major cities, the branch sales office may have hundreds of staff, handle complex orders, and require a large computer system to keep it all going. A similar office in a secondary city could have 10 to 20 salespeople and some support staff and need a moderate-size computer system. In outlying areas and new territories, the company would need a way to support solitary salespeople and offices with a staff of 5 to 10 people.

Many other parts of the organization have the same problem: accommodating extreme variations in the scale of computer power required within the same department. Recently, the desire to support mobile workers has aggravated the scalability problem.

Until recently, a company's computers were always located in its own offices and plants. However, a great deal of business activity takes place outside the company's offices and plants. Deliveries, sales calls, support activity, and site inspections all take place at the *customer's offices*. Why shouldn't the computer be there to support all the activity taking place where the customer is? Doesn't this make sense particularly in a customer-focused world? Of course, with laptop and notebook computers, the computer should be there. It makes tremendous sense for both efficiency and customer focus. With a notebook computer at a customer site, a sales representative can

✦ Book the order on the spot

✦ Confirm the price down to the last penny

✦ Eliminate any re-entry of the information

With a computer on every delivery truck, a company could

✦ Track the delivery route

✦ Confirm delivery

✦ Pick up new bills of lading electronically

Mobile computing brings the problem of scalability into acute focus. Small companies need small computers. Not surprising. Big companies need small computers just as much, though. That's more surprising. Big companies need big computers, too. The problem is that the big companies need both big computers and small ones and all the sizes in between. To make things worse, all those various sizes of computers must work with each other seamlessly. Finally, to put a sharp tip on the exclamation point, the big companies really need all these sizes of computers *to work compatibly*. Only by having all sizes of computers work compatibly does it become possible to write applications like distribution, sales support, manufacturing, service, and so on, so that just the right size of computer can be picked for each location, knowing that after the computer is picked, the application will be right there to run on it.

Isn't there some way to build a computer that can somehow be either big or small, depending on how it's put together? I'll look at those two questions one at a time. First, I'll dive down a level and see what makes a big computer big. What makes mainframes so fast? What makes them so expensive? Why do these factors imply strict upper limits on how big the mainframes can get, even if cost is no object? Then I'll consider various alternative approaches to the problem of building big computers. These other approaches will in fact lead directly to a solution to the scalability problem that builds, as you'd expect, on the technology you've come to know (and love?) in the previous chapters.

GROSCH'S LAW

Computerworld was the first major newspaper of the computer world; it's been in print for over 20 years. Herb Grosch was its original editor. For much of *Computerworld*'s life, IBM not only dominated but also virtually owned the computer marketplace — with over 80 percent market share. Herb noticed that IBM's pricing model made it very attractive for customers to buy ever bigger computers. In retrospect it's a little hard to tell whether the pricing model was driven by the cost of the underlying hardware or whether it was established by IBM as a mechanism to encourage customers to upgrade.

In any case, in the '60s and '70s, the raw speed of a computer was directly proportional to the square of its cost. In other words, spend twice as much on a computer and get four times the speed. Spend three times as much; get nine times the speed, and so on. That's Grosch's Law. Commercially, IBM's pricing model resulted in several strange artifacts. For example, companies that could not afford a really big computer got together with other companies and shared a single large computer. Sometimes one company would buy a big computer and sell a fraction of it to other companies. Other times, entrepreneurs would start up a *service bureau* and sell computer time to big companies at better rates than those companies could do on their own. And all of this based on Grosch's Law.

THE COMPUTER FAMILY CONCEPT

At any given point in time, there are a variety of technologies available for building computers. These technologies can involve radically different transistor technologies, better circuit design, techniques for making chips run faster (perhaps at the cost of higher power consumption), and so on.

To apply Grosch's Law, IBM had to accomplish two things: invest in multiple techniques to build a series of successively faster computers and design a family of compatible computers so that customers could move from one computer to another without rewriting applications.

THE IBM 360 FAMILY OF COMPUTERS

Before 1964, each new type of computer was different from all the types before it, irrespective of who built the computer. IBM and other companies constantly pushed the state of the art to develop faster and bigger computers. But moving to one of the new machines was always a traumatic experience because it required customers to rewrite all their applications. However, in 1964 IBM announced the product line that changed the computing world: the 360 *family*. The idea behind *families* is simple: design a line of computers, all built differently, but all with the same instruction set.

There are many ways of building a computer. Yet in the end, the *instruction set* defines how that computer works. An application ultimately consists of computer instructions that tell the computer what to do. So two vastly different computers will run a certain application identically as long as they both have the same instruction set. Thus, when IBM designed the 360 family of computers to all have the same instruction set, they were offering customers, for the first time, the opportunity to move applications from one computer to another without any conversion or rewriting. As time passed, IBM continued extending the 360 series, adding both bigger and smaller systems, but always maintaining instruction set compatibility. In fact, today's large IBM mainframes still have the same core instruction set as the original 360s; that 360 family continues to live on 30 years later.

THE DEC VAX FAMILY OF COMPUTERS

In the '70s, DEC used the same concept in the VAX family. Today VAX models range from desktop microcomputers all the way to million-dollar mainframe model systems, all with the same instruction set.

THE INTEL X86 FAMILY OF MICROPROCESSORS

In the '80s, Intel took a page out of history with the introduction of the X86 family of micro-processors, the central processing units (CPUs) of DOS-based personal computers. Examples of the X86 processor include the 8088, 8086, 80286, 80386, the 80486, and now the Pentium chips. This family, stretching from the original 8088 all the way to today's Pentium, has continued to add speed and functionality while still guaranteeing that every application written for the earliest processors in the family continue to run. In fact, if it weren't for Intel's strict adherence to the family concept, the IBM PC, DOS, and the whole personal computer software world would not be what it is today. By giving the X86 family a capable, powerful instruction set, Intel could plan a family of systems stretching through the '90s. Again, the family concept allows Intel to take advantage of new technology and build computers with substantially enhanced power every two to three years while promising to maintain the instruction set compatibility so crucial to stable business systems.

The concept of a computer family offers a smooth growth path in two dimensions: in price and in time. At any given point in time, a family can offer distinct computer models, often based on fundamentally different technologies while still providing instruction set compatibility. In this way, customers can buy the combination of systems that meets their needs. As time passes, the family can also be extended as new members with either lower prices or more throughput are added. Eventually, older members of the family will be dropped as they become obsolete. Now that you understand families of computers, you can understand the real application of Grosch's Law.

THE PAST ECONOMIC INCENTIVE FOR CENTRALIZATION

By the end of the 1960s, IBM and its 360 family of computers totally dominated the market. This line of computers had the price and performance that made it incredibly attractive for customers to buy the largest computer they could possibly afford. Literally, spending twice as much could easily yield four times as much computing power. Technically, IBM used different technologies through the 360 line. Thus, the fastest 360 at any given time might bear very little resemblance to the entry product in the same line. Yet because the product line all had compatible instruction sets, customers could move up the line with complete comfort.

Suppose that a company faced a choice between buying several small or medium-size 360 mainframes versus buying one much larger 360, located centrally and shared among the various locations. You guessed it: in the past, Grosch's Law guaranteed that the single larger computer would always be the better choice. The economics of Grosch's Law made the case for centralization compelling:

+ Even at the expense of extra complexity in operating the larger computer

+ Even at the loss of local control and flexibility

+ Even at the expense of being dependent on the single central site staying available (never breaking)

Also, the argument involved more than just dollars and cents. Suppose spending three times your current computing budget yields nine times as much power. You would not only save a lot of money compared to buying three computers, but also have more computer power to work with. Nine times as much power in one box is considerably more than three times as much in three boxes. Even four times in one box is a knockout compared to twice as much in two boxes. So the combination of the 360 family concept, IBM's ability to build very big boxes, and the economics inherent in Grosch's Law created the economic incentive for centralization of computer facilities in large companies.

What is all this central power that mainframes provide so well? What does it mean to say that one computer is 2 or 10 (or 100) times faster than another? Let's see what computer power is really about.

SPEED: HOW FAST CAN IT GO?

The first measure of a computer's power is simply speed: the number of instructions per second that the computer can complete. When measuring an engine or motor, people talk about the number of times the machine rotates per second: the number of cycles completed each second. Similarly in a computer, the CPU must perform a number of steps to process each instruction. The combination of such steps is called a *cycle*. Computer professionals often discuss computer speeds in *cycles per second* (one cycle per second is one hertz). However, because computers operate so quickly, computer professionals talk about millions of hertz or megahertz (MHz). Thus a 66 MHz computer completes 66 million instructions per second.

So the first measure of a computer's power is processing speed in MHz. All other things being equal, a 66 MHz computer generally finishes tasks about twice as fast as a 33 MHz computer. According to Grosch's Law, spending twice as much on a computer means you'll either be able to do four times as much work or complete most critical batch and database tasks in one-quarter of the time. As long as all other factors are the same, the faster computer will really do proportionately more work than the slower one. The problem is that all other factors *don't* stay the same.

For example, if pure speed on a single task were the only measure of performance, then personal computers would have left mainframes in the dust several years ago. Yes, in MHz, most big mainframes crank through more instructions each second than most personal computers do. But not that many more. In fact, today's personal computer grinds through as many instructions per second as the leading mainframe of only two to four years ago. If it's a race, then mainframes — at a cost thousands of times as high — have at best a four-year lead on personal computers in processing speed. Today's fast mainframe will be beaten by tomorrow's PC, and that PC will take just two to four years to do the catching up. So there must be more to power than just speed.

ADDRESS SPACE: ROOM TO GROW

The second measure of power is *address space*. Just like people, computers must keep information to work with nearby. Some of this information is kept on disk, in permanent form. But the data used most frequently in the course of running an application is kept in main memory. The term *main* distinguishes this memory, also called random-access memory (RAM), from the much slower disk memory. As the computer uses main memory, the application must refer to the various bits and pieces of information stored there. For this reason, memory is organized into fixed-sized units called *bytes*. Each byte has its own address. These addresses start at 1 and range up to the total size of the memory installed on the computer. When you buy a personal computer with 5MB of memory, you have 5 million bytes of memory, and the computer reads and writes those bytes in memory using addresses from 1 to 5 million.

ADDRESS SPACE AFFECTS COMPUTER THROUGHPUT

A computer's potential throughput is limited mainly by two factors:

✦ The amount of physical memory (RAM chips)

✦ Its address space

The computer's physical memory is determined by the number of RAM chips that can be plugged into the computer's motherboard.

However, the *address space* of a computer is defined by its instruction set. Each computer instruction consists of two parts: the instruction itself (add, multiply, and so on) and the address of the data the instruction will be applied to. In building the instruction set, the designer allocates a certain number of bits to the address. This number of bits puts a strict upper limit on the amount of memory the computer can use efficiently. Therefore, address space is the amount of memory (in bytes) that a computer's instruction set can ever use.

Early personal computers had a 16-bit address space. With a 16-bit address space, the largest amount of memory a computer can use is 64,536 bytes (64K). So programs written for the Apple II, early TRS 80s, and other machines of that time just couldn't deal with more than 64K of memory. Sixty-four thousand sounds like a big number until you start to build a reasonable-size spreadsheet. Even with early PC spreadsheet programs such as Visicalc, many users found their spreadsheets outgrowing the capacities of their machine.

Memory limitations are frustrating because often the CPU still has enough speed to keep going when it hits the address space wall. I recall overhearing several conversations in computer stores in which customers mistakenly thought that their spreadsheet could grow *if they plugged in more memory chips*. Yet the issue was not the physical memory the computer had; rather it was the fundamental capabilities of the computer instruction set itself. On a 16-bit computer, the customer's spreadsheet couldn't be made bigger, no matter what the customer did — short of moving to a completely new computer with a larger address space and a new spreadsheet that supported it.

DIFFERENCES IN ADDRESS SPACE BETWEEN MAINFRAMES AND PCS

Mainframes ran into the address space problem many years ago. Therefore, for over a decade, every serious mainframe instruction set has been based on at least a 32-bit address space: enough to reach out to over 4 billion bytes of memory. Eventually, this too may become a limitation. But at least through the early 1990s, the 32-bit address space defines the state of the art.

Is this what makes mainframes different from smaller computers? Originally, yes. Until recently, mainframes indeed had 32-bit address spaces, and most personal computers did not. The Intel 8088 and 8086 CPUs inside all the early IBM personal computers featured a somewhat extended 16-bit address space, capable of addressing just under 1MB of memory. This was (and still is) the famous 1MB DOS limitation.

The Apple II was even more limited. But Apple quickly leapfrogged Intel by selecting the Motorola 68000 as the basis for its Macintosh (the Mac). As a result, the Mac is essentially a 32-bit computer, just like mainframes. And, thanks to Apple and Motorola, Mac users have never had to face the same "RAM cram" problems as DOS users.

In 1984, Intel and IBM first broke the 1MB barrier with the introduction of the 80286 and the PC AT. The 286 offered a 24-bit address space, allowing programs to reach out to 16MB of memory at a time. Finally, in 1986, with the 386, the IBM-compatible world had a full 32-bit machine.

So originally one major difference between mainframes and personal computers was the address space. No matter how fast the CPU in a personal computer was, it simply couldn't address enough memory to handle the really big problems being run on mainframes. That era has come and gone.

USING ADDRESS SPACE EFFICIENTLY

Although personal computers now have address spaces as big as their mainframe siblings, PC applications still don't take as much advantage of those address spaces. Several factors determine how much address space an application can use. First, the computer has to have enough memory. Until recently this was a function of cost. In the 1960s, memory was so physically large and expensive that no computer had enough memory slots for even 1MB. By 1970, mainframes with over 1MB could be found, but that much memory literally cost over $1 million for the memory alone. Even in 1981, when the IBM PC was announced, memory was still so expensive that 16K machines were common, and 256K was considered a huge amount of memory. So until recently, mainframes had large amounts of memory and personal computers didn't because of cost. That's not true anymore.

Today, memory costs $30 to $50 per megabyte. Personal computers routinely arrive from the manufacturer with 4MB or even 8MB preinstalled. Bumping this figure up to 16MB or 24MB is an everyday affair even in the home. Servers with 20 to 30MB are the rule. In high throughput applications, getting up to 50MB of RAM is a $2,000 decision. So memory cost no longer creates an incentive to go with mainframes on which users can share memory. And when it comes to the technical architecture required to support truly huge amounts of memory, Digital Equipment Corporation (with its Alpha) and Silicon Graphics (with its MIPS chip) now ship personal computers with 64-bit address spaces capable of handling not just billions, but trillions of bytes of memory.

OPERATING SYSTEM SUPPORT FOR MEMORY

Last in the list of memory considerations is operating system support. Here's an area where mainframes *do* have an edge, although only a very slim one. Until 1990, personal computers really didn't make as effective use of memory as mainframes. Until that time, memory was one of the significant reasons to run big applications on mainframes. Yet even after memory became affordable and hardware instruction sets supported it, software companies still had to rewrite PC operating systems to take advantage of the newly found 32-bit address space. And that process is still underway.

Even today, one reason to favor mainframes over smaller computers for big jobs is that mainframe hardware and operating systems support large amounts of memory and large address spaces. However, in most ways that really count, both PCs and UNIX workstations have supported the memory and the address space needed by big applications for some time now. Yes, some database servers ran out of gas with only 16MB of memory, but patches allowed them to add memory up to 50 or 75MB — more than enough to meet the needs of the database. What's more, both 32-bit OS/2 and 32-bit Windows NT have been around for some time now.

So until recently, mainframes were more powerful than PCs in terms of memory, address space, and operating system support for 32-bit address space. No more; now personal computers have caught up, and as they progress over time to 64 bits, personal computers may even pass by the mainframes. In the next section, I compare permanent storage in mainframes and PCs.

PERMANENT STORAGE CAPACITY: THANKS FOR THE MEMORIES

Mainframes have very large amounts of permanent storage. In fact, much of the cost of a mainframe installation goes to the disks, tape drives, and other forms of permanent storage. Where personal computers typically have single hard disks measured in tens or hundreds of megabytes, mainframes generally have dozens of storage devices and the measurement runs from hundreds of gigabytes to many terabytes. (A *gigabyte* is 1 billion bytes. A *terabyte* is 1,000 gigabytes.)

TYPES OF MAINFRAME PERMANENT STORAGE

Mainframe storage systems are not only large but very sophisticated as well. Rather than just use a single type of disk drive, selected for either speed or capacity, a range of devices is chosen, and information is migrated automatically. Frequently accessed information is kept on special disk drives that, although expensive and relatively small, are very fast. Less frequently used data is kept on slower disk drives with more capacity. Information that is only used occasionally is kept on special, robot-driven, *mass storage systems*, or *MSSs*. An MSS looks like a large honeycombed wall with hundreds of small hexagonal cavities each holding a small roll of magnetic tape. In fact, the MSS consists of two such walls with several robot arms moving back and forth between them. As the computer asks for particular bits of information, the robot arms select the correct roll of tape, pull it out of its cave, mount it in a tape reader, and arrange to transfer the information to a disk.

BENEFITS OF AUTOMATED PERMANENT STORAGE ON MAINFRAMES

The most amazing aspect of mainframe storage systems is not the individual bits of technology, but the extent to which the whole thing works automatically. Frequently used information appears on fast disk drives as if by magic. Later, as the same information is used less frequently, the system transparently transfers the data first to slower disk drives, then later to the MSS, and perhaps eventually even to a magnetic tape stored in a cabinet — all without ever losing track of any data. While all of this is going on, the system also automatically backs up all data when it's created, whenever it changes, and whenever it moves. Therefore, in case of a catastrophe, the entire database can be re-created quickly from tapes stored at other physical locations called backup sites.

The benefits of mainframe permanent storage systems — the scale of storage, the range of storage devices, the transparent migration, and the automatic backup — are critical if a large organization is to depend on its databases as its primary information and transaction storage medium.

EVOLUTION OF PERMANENT STORAGE ON PERSONAL COMPUTERS

Until very recently, personal computers and even UNIX workstations could not come close to the size and sophistication of the mainframe permanent storage systems. Mainframe users routinely talked about storing terabytes of data. However, until five years ago, the largest disk that could be attached to a PC was under 10 gigabytes (10GB); 1,000 times smaller than a one-terabyte file. Server disks were slow, and backup generally meant either of the following:

✦ Using floppy disks ("Is this a joke?" the mainframers would ask)

✦ Transferring data very slowly to cartridge tapes capable of holding 250MB of data

Storage management and backup technology was inadequate by mainframe standards.

In the last five years, PC storage technology has changed and improved at a very rapid pace. One driving force has been disk technology. Once a 10MB disk was standard on the IBM PC XT. Today drives from 540MB to 1GB are routine. Disks not only have gotten bigger in capacity, they've gotten smaller in size, considerably faster, and very inexpensive. Notebook computers costing under $4,000 and fitting easily into a briefcase contain 500MB disk drives. Ironically, as disk drives get smaller, they get faster, too. Making disk drives fast is a mechanical issue — a struggle with the physics of moving disk heads rapidly from one track to another. However, the smaller the disk drive, the less the head weighs and the shorter the distances it travels. Presto! The same pressures that lead to more desirable smaller weights and dimensions also lead to better retrieval times.

Ultimately, advances in disk drive technology itself have made it possible for personal computer storage systems to catch up with mainframe storage systems. Furthermore, in a development that parallels the LAN revolution, database developers created a new approach to handling large amounts of data.

RAID TECHNOLOGY PROVIDES MASS PERMANENT STORAGE FOR PCS

Historically, bigger, faster databases required bigger, faster disks. The biggest, fastest disks were devices costing tens and hundreds of thousands of dollars. Until recently, these expensive disks were considered just part of the high cost of having fast mainframe databases.

In the late 1980s, *RAID* technology changed that picture permanently by providing mass permanent storage for PCs. *RAID* stands for *Redundant Arrays of Inexpensive Disks*. In a RAID system, a single large, expensive disk drive is replaced by a bunch of smaller, inexpensive disk drives. A dedicated computer built right into the RAID system box translates requests from the user's computer so that the application appears to be communicating with a single big disk. In fact, one or more of the smaller drives performs the retrieving ("read") functions and saving ("write") functions. This is good for three reasons:

✦ Expense

✦ Speed

✦ Reliability

First, a group of small drives that collectively provide a certain capacity are still substantially less expensive than a single large drive of the same capacity. So RAID saves money. In a mainframe environment, a well-built RAID system might cost one-quarter to one-half as much as an equivalent big disk. Two to four times as much storage for the same money is a pretty compelling argument all by itself.

Perhaps most surprising, RAID is often much faster than an equivalent large disk drive. The biggest performance bottleneck in a large disk drive is the delay waiting for the disk head to get to the desired track. Mainframes typically use very sophisticated software to minimize the effect of this delay. For example, by collecting incoming requests from many users, the mainframe can rearrange the requests so that the disk head moves back and forth as few times as possible. This makes for less work on the part of the disk drive. Unfortunately, user requests will have been kept waiting for this rearrangement.

The RAID system replaces the single big disk — with its single disk head — with a group of smaller disk drives, each with its own head. Even though each of these disk heads may be slower than the single bigger head, there are many of them. So the RAID system can retrieve information from many disks in parallel. RAID systems can be much faster than a single large drive.

RAID systems can be more reliable, too. In fact, they can even exhibit some degree of fail-safe operation. The *R* in RAID stands for *redundant*. Because small disks are so much less expensive than large disks, it becomes practical to build *extra* disks into every RAID system. System designers can make these extra disks redundant so that they store information that is also being stored on other disks in the same RAID system. Therefore, a RAID system can run without interruption even if a whole disk drive breaks down. No information is lost either. Because the information was stored in two places, the system is smart enough to simply get it from the disk that's still functioning when needed.

RAID has its drawbacks, too. Although RAID systems retrieve information faster in many cases, writing information back to disk in some cases can slow down appreciably because of the extra overhead associated with redundancy. And although a RAID system as a whole is very reliable, repair frequency for individual components may go up because the systems have so many more components. RAID is not perfect. Nonetheless, it represents a huge step forward. In fact, it's even safe to say that in many ways, RAID is revolutionary.

System designers can use RAID to build arbitrarily large disk storage systems by simply including enough small disks. The resulting systems will be cheaper and faster than today's mainframe storage and will contribute fail-safe operation to boot. Of course, there's no rule that says RAID can't be used in conjunction with mainframes just as easily as with PCs. That's not the point. The point is that large, high-throughput, highly reliable storage systems are now no longer limited to use only in mainframe computer rooms due to extreme costs or size.

Particularly with the introduction of RAID systems, LAN networks of personal computers began to provide users with highly tiered forms of storage. Tiered storage on a LAN is hierarchical:

1. A document on a floppy disk is copied onto the small hard drive of a notebook computer.

2. The notebook copies the document from there to the larger drive at the user's desktop docking station.

3. The docking station copies the document to the workgroup server.

4. The workgroup server passes a copy to the departmental server.

5. Finally, the departmental server forwards a copy of the document up to the corporate data center.

Tiered storage on a LAN is pretty sophisticated. The scenario just described may seem very ad hoc and unreliable compared to the carefully controlled mainframe environment. Such a personally driven system may seem happenstance and uncoordinated. However, nothing about LANs and PCs says that tiered storage on a LAN has to be that way.

Lotus Notes is one example of a system that provides automatic tiered storage by performing a function called *replication*, first described in Chapter 7. Replication is not unique to Notes and was not even invented by Lotus. However, Lotus employed replication techniques thoughtfully in designing Notes. As a result, Notes can provide a great deal of organizational information to people who can't connect frequently to central computers. Potential Notes users could be salespeople on the road, support staff in a remote office, or the entire staff of a branch located in an area with poor communications facilities.

In a replicated environment, many copies of the information must be distributed all over the network. For example, each salesperson carries around the database describing his customers, their orders, and shipments all on the notebook computer under his arm. Of course, while the salesperson may have a copy of that data, many other copies of the same data exist in the central computer, at the regional office, and on the personal computers of many other sales and support people around the company. What the Notes *Replicator* does is keep all those copies up-to-date. Perhaps this process of keeping those copies up-to-date sounds simple. In fact, it puts most mainframe storage management systems to shame in terms of sophistication.

At one time, Notes replication stood alone in the PC environment. Today, however, both replication and hierarchical storage management have become hot topics; several vendors offer products that provide these facilities. Virtually all the major database vendors are now shipping replication facilities. Most vendors, including Sybase, Informix, and Computer Associates (CA), limit updates to occurring at a single site, making the service nowhere near as interesting as Notes. Oracle, however, on the server side allows updates to occur on any database and percolates the changes automatically. On the desktop side, Microsoft's Access replicates changes across both desktops and servers in a fashion very similar to Notes.

The kind of replicated database architecture I've just talked about performs very sophisticated self-adaptive storage migration. Records are changed at individual locations, and those changes ripple out gradually to reach the rest of the network. In addition, several vendors also offer hierarchical storage management products, so the user has a complete set of choices.

The replicated database architecture represents intelligent networking at its best:

✦ Managing a storage hierarchy turns out to be meaningful in a personal and group setting, not just in a big mainframe data center. Personal computers are leapfrogging the mainframes and providing benefits never dreamed of in the days of big computers. Users can choose between hierarchical storage management and replication, using them in whatever combination best meets the needs of the business.

✦ Mass storage was previously the preserve of the mainframe. But today, mass storage has moved to PC environments as well.

PERMANENT STORAGE TECHNOLOGY FOR PCS HAS UNIQUE ADVANTAGES

Not very long ago, mainframes had much more storage, faster storage, and better-managed storage than PCs. And if you require a large, centralized database management facility, mainframes still offer benefits over PC-based storage. However, the mainframe's advantages are rapidly disappearing with the introduction of large PC servers, RAID storage, and 32-bit operating systems for PCs. What's more, if you start to consider distributed databases, PC-based storage has leaped ahead of the mainframe. Replicated databases are the state of the art for this class of application — and available only in the PC environment.

THROUGHPUT: HOW MANY ITEMS CAN YOU KEEP IN THE AIR?

The next dimension of power that comes to mind is *throughput*. More than just doing things fast, *throughput* deals with *processing as many tasks as possible in any given unit of time*. However, to maintain adequate throughput, a mainframe faces one class of problems for realtime transactions and a somewhat different class of problems for batch programs. The following sections explain further.

THROUGHPUT FOR REALTIME TRANSACTIONS

Historically, throughput has clearly distinguished mainframes from other classes of computers. Granted, supercomputers have always had bigger main memories and faster processors, and specialized database machines have boasted large arrays of disks. But when it comes to processing vast quantities of work, the mainframe stands alone even today. What is it about throughput that requires the specialized capabilities of a mainframe?

In business processes, realtime transactions are relatively small tasks that process business requests precisely when they occur. A transaction can move inventory from one location in a warehouse to another, transfer funds between bank accounts, reserve a seat on an airplane, or cause a box to be loaded onto a truck. Each of these tasks by itself involves very little computer processing. However, in a typical big organization, dozens or even hundreds of these small transactions can occur every second. Transactions are like the synapses of a business system.

Likewise, the database is the organization's central memory. In a database management system, a *transaction* is defined as a series of operations that, if completed, will always leave the database in a consistent state. That is, if you start with a consistent database and then execute a transaction, the database will again be consistent after the entry is completed. One of the primary benefits of databases is that application programmers, by structuring applications around transactions, can be assured of the database always being in a consistent state. The only caveat is that the mainframe and its software must then guarantee that every transaction will run to completion to make this all come true.

Why is it so hard to guarantee that all transactions will run to completion? Normally, computers and programs run without interruption. However, in the real world, the power can fail, software errors can occur, the computer hardware can breakdown, or an operator error can bring the system to a halt. Nonetheless, the mainframe operating system (with the help of the database) must still guarantee the successful operation of all transactions. How can it do this?

The mainframe performs its special magic by remembering:

✦ What tasks are running

✦ How far each task has progressed

✦ How each task got there

Just as a juggler can keep track of three, five, or even ten balls, the mainframe keeps track of every task being processed.

What happens after the mainframe experiences a serious problem? The mainframe knows enough about each transaction in progress to put things back the way they were before the problem occurred.

Suppose that the mainframe loses all power. Later, when the power comes back up, the mainframe will perform two general functions to recover from the system failure:

1. **Identify all tasks that started and finished.** For example, if money was taken out of a savings account *and* deposited in the appropriate checking account, the mainframe would mark the task as completed.

2. **Undo all tasks that started but did not finish.** For example, the mainframe noted that a certain pallet had been removed from an inventory location. However, the power failure prevented the mainframe from recording the truck to which the pallet had been assigned. In that case, the mainframe would reassign the pallet to the inventory location and restart the entire transaction.

If this sounds like a huge amount of work, that's because it is! And the thing that really makes the whole sleight of hand amazing is that the mainframe is juggling thousands of items in the air at one time. Unbelievable.

To understand the real magnitude of the mainframe's juggling act, consider just a few numbers. Big computer systems measure their workload in terms of *transactions per second*. For example, a really big mainframe handling credit card authorizations can receive hundreds of transactions *every second*. Yet there are 3,600 seconds in an hour. Therefore, 3,600 times per hour, the mainframe could receive a batch of 100 or more requests for spending approvals. Assume that some of these requests take over a second to make their way through the computer. In that case, the computer would have to juggle hundreds or even thousands of transactions at any given time. Remember, the mainframe has to not only keep each task moving along, but also remember everything the program has done along the way. Then, in case of a problem, the mainframe must restore the database to the pristine state that existed before the affected tasks were started.

THROUGHPUT FOR BATCH PROGRAMS

In addition to realtime transactions, a mainframe also must maintain good throughput for batch programs that are running at any given moment. In a batch program, the mainframe does not have the *realtime* constraints of transaction processing. During batch processing, the mainframe does not process hundreds of requests every second and ensure that all of them are completed in a few seconds. Instead, a batch program often takes many hours to complete. However, a batch program does share two functions with the transaction-processing program:

✦ Processing multiple tasks at one time

✦ Tracking all work so that in case of a failure, all work in progress can be undone where needed to leave the database in a consistent state

Big batch programs often work with large parts of a company's database at one time. For example, something as simple as producing a list of customers could require reading the entire customer database — perhaps many times — to convert it into sorted order. Sorting is one of those computational tasks that is easy to explain and understand, easy to request — but amazingly hard to do. In such a sorting program, the mainframe must work with the entire customer database at one time.

Ultimately, when you consider mainframe throughput in both transaction- and batch-processing environments, anything that forces the computer to retrieve large parts of its database could be a recipe for slowness. However, the miracle is that mainframes can allow large numbers of simultaneous transactions and enormous batch jobs to access major parts of a company's database — but still maintain adequate response time and database integrity (even if a system crash occurs). Quite a feat.

All of this legerdemain (sleight of hand) raises an interesting question. How did the computer industry come to develop such sophisticated mainframe software? And if mainframes are that great, why are so many people talking about doing away with these remarkable machines?

EFFECTS OF GROSCH'S LAW

As explained earlier in this chapter, Herb Grosch observed that the pricing of computers in the late '60s and early '70s made it very attractive for companies to purchase relatively few large computers and centralize the company's processing on those machines. Grosch's observation turned out to be a *law* in two ways:

✦ It represented a kind of scientific model of real-world pricing.

✦ The results of that numerical law had such a powerful effect on both computer *culture* and computer *technology* that centralized computing became the standard paradigm for the next few decades.

Think about it: there are many attractive features to a decentralized computing model revolving around small computers located where the work is done. Yet, virtually every large organization in the world runs most of its operations with large central mainframes. Grosch's Law.

TECHNICAL EFFECTS OF GROSCH'S LAW

There were several technical effects of Grosch's Law on large organizations. Three of the most important effects are:

✦ Centralization of computing to gain economics of scale

✦ Centralization of computing to simplify disaster protection

✦ Development of multiprocessor systems and networks

The following section briefly discusses the first two effects, multiprocessor systems and networks are discussed in-depth later in the chapter.

During the '60s and '70s, centralizing a company's computing resources led to tremendous economies of scale. Suppose that it's 1970 and you're responsible for planning the computer department of a large company. You have a choice between several different models of the IBM 360 mainframes (which commanded over 90 percent market share at the time). You can buy a small 360 with one unit of throughput, a medium one costing twice as much as the small 360 — but having four units of throughput — or a big 360 costing three times the price of the small 360 but having nine times the throughput.

Your 360 system includes not only a big central computer, but also lots of disk drives, tape drives for backup and mass storage, and several large, expensive printers capable of printing hundreds of lines per minute. I'm talking about boxes costing hundreds of thousands of dollars each. For example, at that time, a disk drive with a few hundred megabytes of storage could cost tens of thousands of dollars. However, a disk drive cannot be connected directly to a mainframe. Instead, the disk drive must work through an intermediate box called a *controller*. Who cares? Well, if you're doing this planning and those controllers cost lots of money, you do! Controllers can be shared between quite a few disk and tape drives — but only if those drives are located in one place to do the sharing. A pattern! Centralizing things leads to *economies of scale*. Is there more? You bet.

Even though IBM was committed to convincing its customers to centralize their computing, it was only a part of the centralization story.

Although IBM was certainly the dominant player in the '60s and '70s, the computer marketplace was still fiercely competitive, and factually speaking, every major player, every practical solution, involved technologies and cost curves that greatly favored centralization. The following section, titled "Cultural effects of Grosch's Law," talks about deeper underlying forces at work that made Grosch's observation much more of a law than was understood at the time. In addition, the factors arguing for centralization involved more than just the pure hardware.

Until recently, computers were very difficult to install and run. Even today's computers are far from simple, but at least they don't require special power, heavy-duty air conditioning, and their own special rooms. Many people are familiar with the picture of the glass-enclosed computer room with dozens of huge boxes and special white-robed staff members tending to their temple. What may not be as readily appreciated is just how special that computer room environment really was.

For example, a typical mainframe involved not only dozens of boxes, but also hundreds of thick, hard-to-maneuver, and expensive cables to connect all the parts. Running those cables around on the floor creates a mess, a safety hazard, and a huge maintenance problem. As a result, most computer rooms are built with special false floors raised about a foot off the ground. The second, higher floor is built of heavy-duty metal, supported by a special steel framework, ensuring that the weight of the computers and the people can be easily supported. After the framework is in place, the upper floor is assembled from metal tiles, coated with special nonstatic laminates, and put in place one by one. The point of having tiles is that the tiles can be lifted individually to work with the cables running between the two layers of flooring (upper and lower). And yes, building a room this way is just as expensive as it sounds.

The floor is only the beginning in a high-tech computer facility. Special fire-extinguishing equipment ensures that smoke and heat are detected quickly and the associated fire snuffed out, without using water, so that the computer and its precious data are not damaged. Sophisticated security systems ensure that only authorized people can enter the room. And last but not least, keeping all those computers, printers, tape drives, and networks running requires full-time staff, often on duty around the clock.

All of these technical factors represented a compelling argument for developing large, central computer sites. If you were a customer in the late '60s, you most likely would have been asking IBM and other vendors to develop products for bigger and bigger central computer facilities. And if you were one of those vendors, building ever larger systems satisfied both your customer's needs and the logic of the time.

CULTURAL EFFECTS OF GROSCH'S LAW

By the end of the '60s, it had become clear to most individuals involved with planning and building large computer systems that centralized systems represented both the state of the art and *the* way to build sophisticated applications. For technical people, such a vision is exciting; by definition one of the primary job-satisfaction factors for them is imagining a future and building it. Mainframe-oriented computing in the late '60s was fully as exciting to think about and work on as client/server is today. So this vision and excitement created the beginning of a major cultural movement affecting thousands of computer and business people. And the key thing to understand in looking at the second phase of the cultural movement was that those thousands of people greatly succeeded in creating centralized systems that work.

Successful cultures breed tremendous inertia, and that inertia defines the mainframe culture we live in today. Part of the inertia is simply resistance to change. In the '50s, no one even knew what a computer was. In the '60s, computers were for the most part a young person's game. Careers in the computer business were all new in those days. Today, though, entire organizations have grown up developing professional skills that all revolve around a particular style of building and running computer systems. Plans were laid, battles fought, systems built, and after 20 or 30 years, it all works. Now a major change is afoot, and people feel threatened. Part of the cultural inertia is based on resistance to change, but a larger part is based on valid reservations and concerns. The experience and expertise that those reservations and concerns represent need to be honored. To understand why that expertise is needed, look a little closer at the technical impact of Grosch's Law.

In the mid-'60s, when the mainframe as it is known today was being introduced, the systems were absolutely incapable of achieving the kind of "many balls in the air" throughput I described a few pages ago. In fact, the lack of the software to enable even simple sharing of computer facilities was a major embarrassment for IBM over a period of four years. These four years marked the amount of time required to develop OS/360, the operating system released in 1968 that first took full advantage of the capabilities introduced when the 360 family started shipping in 1964. Even OS/360 offered very limited facilities for facilitating mainframes doing many complex jobs all at the same time. As the '60s reached a close, though, it became clear to all major mainframe vendors, and IBM in particular, that throughput and ball juggling were the order of the day.

Over the next ten years a vast array of software systems were developed to allow mainframes to handle hundreds of transactions per second, run huge batch jobs with tremendous throughput, and keep massive databases running around the clock without ever losing data or processing transactions inconsistently. In many ways, the resulting products, such as MVS, CICS, IMS, HASP, and VTAM, not to mention the host of third-party software products, such as IDMS, ADABAS, and Total, truly represent some of the wonders of the Western world. To understand these products well is to be amazed and horrified at the same time.

The amazement stems from both the sophistication of the products and what they make possible. For example, it is perceived that most large companies use *relational* databases such as DB2 and Rdb to handle most of their data. That's wrong. Most large companies do *not* store most of their data in relational databases. Older databases, like IMS and IDMS and the underlying operating system's file manager (VSAM), are hard for normal people to work with, but they are *fast*. In comparison, relational databases are so slow that even today, after 15 years of ever faster computers, the performance advantages of the older databases are still so compelling that over 80 percent of the production data of large organizations remains in the data storage systems developed in the '70s. It is true that every large company has relational databases installed to help users get answers to questions. But when it comes to running the business, nothing comes close to the performance of the older systems — even if they are hard to work with.

Power and sophistication are only part of the picture. Overhead is a major factor as well, and as it turns out, complexity has a particularly ugly face that is often over-looked, too. These two factors — overhead and complexity — lead to the feeling of horror when contemplating these amazing systems. A mainframe in many ways mir-rors the large organization it serves. Today's big companies process large workloads with assurance, but the cost is a massive bureaucratic structure that is both expensive to run (overhead) and difficult to understand or change (complexity). Mainframes have exactly the same characteristics.

The nervous system of a mainframe can be monitored directly by attaching electronic probes at key points on the machine. These probes trace signals and send the infor-mation back to a separate computer that keeps track of what it sees. Analyzing the results produced by such a monitoring system can tell where a mainframe spends its time:

✦ Part of its effort goes into processing application logic: deciding whether credit is to be granted, moving inventory from one place to another, computing totals for reports. Generally speaking, this kind of directly productive work accounts for about a quarter of the capacity available in a mainframe.

✦ Another quarter goes into database-related activity: storing and retrieving information, tracking transactions so that the computer can be restored to a consistent state in the event of a disaster, and keeping the database organized on an ongoing basis so that users always see fast responses to requests. This quarter of the computer's time is, of course, directly productive, too.

Adding these two pieces together, only about half of the computer's available power is accounted for.

✦ The other half goes into the equivalent of bureaucratic overhead: operating system and utility processing. The amount eaten up by these management activities may vary from one third to one half, but in all cases it's pretty significant. By itself this figure is interesting, but not necessarily scary. It is the implication that really creates a problem. The implication is that there's a lot to manage. Pretty trite sounding, right?

Having so much to manage creates two problems in turn:

✦ First (and less important), the office is giving up a great deal of very expen-sive computer power it really can't spare. Recall that this chapter began by lamenting that even the biggest computer just isn't big enough for many problems. Now you find out those big computers are spending a major fraction of their time just keeping things sorted out — just tracking balls in the air — instead of doing the work they were purchased for. In a centralized environment, there's no choice; the direct result of funneling all the work through a single computer is a huge amount of administrative overhead to keep it all running. That's the rub.

◆ Second, most organizations find they can't keep it all running. The computer does an amazing job optimizing all the tasks, logging all the transactions, and maximizing all the throughput. However, as more and more gets piled on, the implications of a single error become magnified. If a batch run fails, is the batch window big enough to allow a rerun? As the batch job gets more complex, how many places are there in which single errors can occur? If the invoices don't get aged on schedule, are the credit limits still correct? Does that mean that if the batch runs fail, transactions can't be processed the next day?

CENTRAL PLANNING: IS IT BETTER IN THEORY OR IN PRACTICE?

Ultimately, the era of the mainframe has tested the practicality of central planning and control. In theory, by centralizing an organization's processing on either a single mainframe or a small number of mainframes, tremendous economies of scale become possible. However, just as centrally planned economies have trouble delivering on their promised economies of scale, companies have the same problems with mainframes today.

LACK OF PERSONAL FREEDOM FOR USERS

Personal computers became so popular so quickly because they promised freedom for users. Until computers became so inexpensive, nobody thought much about how restricted access to computer power was. Everybody took it for granted that a computer was a big, expensive box at the beck and call of management, but certainly not in any way a personal servant. Even if the spreadsheet had been invented first on a mainframe, it would never have taken off simply because the cost of using it would have been astronomical. Consequently, the centralized computing model automatically excludes personal computing in the way it is known today.

EXCEEDING THE CAPACITY OF MAINFRAME POWER

At root, many large organizations today have exceeded the practical limits of what their central mainframes can do. Airlines are an extreme example. An airline's largest application taxes even the largest computer. Even organizations with more modest requirements run into this limitation.

As the mainframe's limits are reached, the computer staff must scramble to improve response time for transactions, worry about how long the batch run will take, and think hard about whether a new application will require an upgrade that is too expensive.

THE DRIVE FOR MACHINE EFFICIENCY UNDERCUTS USER EFFICIENCY

As a company reaches the limits of its mainframes, the firm may begin to do things that enhance mainframe (machine) efficiency — but also undercut user efficiency.

As I've already shown, most large organizations keep their "live" information (for example, order status, shipment histories, and so on) on their central mainframes. Although part of this information may be periodically copied to servers and personal computers for marketing and management analysis, the complete database resides on the mainframe. Even though it's there on the mainframe, it's hardly accessible — because the data is not stored in relational databases. (Generally, relational databases store data in tables, allowing users to answer a wide variety of questions easily. Database models are covered extensively in Chapters 9 and 10.)

Why not keep all that data directly in a relational database? Because relational databases are too slow. However, another way to look at that problem is that mainframe power is spread too thin. Because mainframes are so expensive, you have to get a lot of work out of them, and then there isn't enough power to go around. So most companies keep most of their data in non-relational databases to which users can't posit questions flexibly.

Even the data that is in relational databases isn't really available for user questions. In many big companies, the main reason for installing relational databases is to make the programmer's life easier; the database becomes a tool to simplify application development. Fine, but what about those users?

Users also want access to data. The problem is that the questions formulated by these users often require access to major portions of the database. Any query involving a sum or an average could well cause the computer to consider every record in an entire file (a product file or a customer file, for example). This is exactly the kind of request that can bring a mainframe to its knees. Yes, the mainframe is optimized to service such requests. But even with all its vaunted throughput capability, the mainframe can service only a few such queries at one time.

In effect, queries more closely resemble batch jobs than transactions. Transactions work with only a small part of the database at one time. That's one reason thousands of them can run at one time. However, batch jobs may access the entire database. Therefore, the mainframe typically runs only a few batch jobs at once. Yet all of a sudden, users with modern query tools are asking the mainframe to process the equivalent of hundreds of batch jobs per day. A mainframe that routinely processes hundreds of transactions every second might take half an hour or more to generate the answer to a single query. And worst of all, because these queries are being formulated on the fly by users, the computer staff can't plan for or optimize around these queries. So what do they do? What any central control organization does when threatened: refuse to allow it to happen. Consequently, in most companies, even the relational databases are not really available to end users — whether or not they have the tools to ask the questions they really need to ask.

Ultimately, the mainframe continues to be a centralized beast because of its cost. And because companies insist on funneling the total workload of an entire organization through a single machine, they can't afford to allow that machine to serve the needs of the individual.

Additionally, central systems all suffer from being so complex that the central plans just don't work. For example, a large bank with hundreds of branches suffered a computer outage in the early '90s. The entire branch banking system was shut down for over four days, with all branches operating totally manually. The situation was serious enough to make the national news.

Later, senior management commissioned a task force (what else is new?) to determine how this outage could have occurred and what could be done to ensure that it would never happen again. After six months, the task force concluded that the complete cause of the shutdown could never be determined. The overall system, the interconnections between the thousands of parts and the complex sequences of activities and events happening every day, were beyond the capabilities of any single individual or even group of humans to understand.

This type of problem is neither unique nor new. When systems get too big, they get to a point where humans can no longer understand them. Yes, the systems may still operate, but not because people are able to trace the workings and understand what makes that system succeed sometimes but fail at other times.

The standard solution to this problem is to divide such large systems up into smaller parts or components. As long as the parts have well-defined ways of communicating with each other, then a larger system may result, but no single person or group of people must "operate" that larger system. Rather the larger system results from the cooperative interaction between the smaller systems. In computer terms, this type of system is a distributed system, and it is exactly cooperating components that make these distributed systems possible to build. Not only are cooperating components the key to distributed systems in general, but cooperating components are the key to making large systems manageable.

But what about cost and throughput? Don't mainframes exhibit economies of scale that make it prohibitive to do the same work with smaller computers? Aren't large computers with their sophisticated operating systems uniquely designed to process large volumes of work efficiently? Finally, isn't a centralized database stored on a single computer a fundamental requirement for controlling access to inventory, bank accounts, airplane seats, and so on? The following section discusses that question.

THE REPEAL OF GROSCH'S LAW

Even today, many large companies are continuing to consolidate data centers. Just in the last two years, one global manufacturer combined 15 medium-size data centers into four giant locations — each with a proportionately larger mainframe — and saved a great deal of money in the process. If these size-related advantages are so compelling, how can client/server systems compete? The answer lies in the successor to Grosch's Law — the experience curve.

THE EXPERIENCE CURVE

Bruce Doolin Henderson developed his most important ideas about the experience curve around the same time that Herb Grosch was formulating Grosch's Law. Before founding the Boston Consulting Group, Henderson had an illustrious career as an executive, government advisor, and consultant. In the early years of the Boston Consulting Group, Henderson discovered an interesting effect associated with products that were built in huge quantities. This effect has come to be known as the *experience curve*. Essentially, the experience curve refers to the benefits a company experiences from building a product in extremely large quantities. This section briefly describes the key benefits of the experience curve.

One benefit of the experience curve is that unit cost falls as production volume increases. Have you ever wondered how televisions could be so very inexpensive? Compared to most household appliances, all computers are far too expensive. Refrigerators, microwave ovens, stereo sound systems, VCRs, answering machines, and a host of other products — all built in the millions — cost well under $1,000.

When new technology is introduced to the consumer market, it generally starts out costing a great deal. For example, VCRs originally cost thousands of dollars. Most people refused to buy them at that price. Yet enough people did buy them for a next generation to be introduced costing less. The volume went up; more VCRs were produced; prices went down. Before long, a VCR that was easier to use and more powerful cost $250 instead of $2,500. Compact disc players went down the same curve. By now, everybody is familiar with this process, but back in the early '60s, technology was still being introduced at a relatively slow rate, and the process I've just described was not yet understood.

Another benefit of the experience curve is that experience with a product builds expertise. After working with a variety of manufacturing companies in the '50s and '60s, Bruce Henderson noticed that if a company gained an early lead in mass-producing a product, the firm would hold a major advantage over its competitors. If companies could only build enough of the products, they learned how to build the same product, perhaps even improved in quality, at a substantially lower cost than their competitors. The more these companies built, the cheaper they learned how to build the product; and thus was born the experience curve.

Building products in sufficiently high volume allows engineers to learn a lot about how the product is used, what parts of it are unreliable, which parts of the production process can be optimized, and so on. Building a product first confers an automatic advantage on the builder. On the one hand, if a new product fails, all the R&D will be a financial loss. On the other hand, if the product succeeds, the company will gain the opportunity to improve both the product and the production process — and have those improvements funded by the customers buying the product. By playing this game well, the company that mass-produces a successful product first will usually win, other things being equal.

The experience curve comes into play mainly when a product is produced in very large volumes. A volume in the millions guarantees a ride on the experience curve. However, selling just a few thousand a year, no matter what the price, really doesn't count. Volume is critical because it justifies and pays for capital investments.

To illustrate, VCRs didn't become affordable just because a few people bought them. Not at all. Instead, VCRs became inexpensive because companies sold hundreds of thousands of units — which justified the construction of large, automated factories. In turn, those factories could build VCRs in the millions, which in turn drove the price under $500. Generalized microprocessors costing $25 to $50 made VCRs unbelievably smart — without thousands of dollars of custom electronics. Those microprocessors are inexpensive because they are stamped out in huge quantities. (As with VCRs, the huge sales volume for the microprocessors justified both the engineering cost of the processor's design and the construction cost of the factories that produced them.)

However, in the computer industry, manufacturers developed many generations of mainframes, each genuinely better than the generation before. But mainframes still became more expensive. Those computer companies never got to ride the experience curve — even though they gained valuable experience building mainframes over the years. A worldwide installed base of 30,000 big computers just doesn't constitute a mass market.

Actually, the ability to build products in large volume affects much more than just manufacturing costs. Developing each new generation of computers, whether mainframes or PCs, costs tens (or hundreds) of millions of dollars. In the case of the personal computer, this cost is amortized across millions of machines. Intel, for example, ships over 40 million processors every year. The cost of R&D per processor is just a few dollars — hardly noticeable. IBM, on the other hand, ships only a few thousand mainframes each year. R&D therefore becomes a significant, sometimes huge part of the cost of those machines.

ECONOMIES OF SCALE WITH SMALL COMPUTERS

The cost of a mainframe is justified on the basis of economies of scale. Bigger computers deliver more throughput per dollar — if you can afford to buy the mainframe in the first place. However, microprocessors in small computers are based on economies of scale, too. Small computers can be much less expensive to build than mainframes — if you can just build a big enough factory to produce them in the first place. Of course, the factory has to be kept busy. Otherwise, the prices will go up again. But if production volume is high, the economies of scale favor small computers over mainframes.

This is the supreme irony. If you ignore how computers are built, mainframes are very cost-effective. Yet if you focus on computer production costs instead of computer throughput capacity, small computers become the efficiency champions — because they can be built in huge volumes inexpensively.

For example, every year a few thousand mainframes are sold, and they cost anywhere from $100,000 to millions of dollars. That same year, customers will buy approximately 300,000 engineering workstations, made by companies such as Hewlett-Packard (HP), Silicon Graphics, and Sun. The workstations are priced between $5,000 and $50,000. In absolute terms, the mainframe may be faster, but the workstation on an engineer's desk will be almost as fast — and will cost less than 10 percent of the price. In terms of how engineers use computers, these workstations are essentially mainframes packaged for individuals but built in moderately larger volumes. Workstations drive the design of the airplanes, cars, and the microprocessors discussed all through this book.

In that same year, Intel will produce about 40 million microprocessors that will go into personal computers in offices and homes. Yes, 40 *million*, and the number is still growing. Measured in unit volume, the personal computer industry is about 100 times bigger than the workstation industry — which, in turn, is about 100 times bigger than the mainframe industry. In other words, the PC market is 10,000 times larger than the mainframe market in unit volume. No wonder the experience curve triggers in one industrial segment but not the other.

PRICE COMPETITION MAKES PCS THE BUY OF THE CENTURY

Take a trip to any computer store and consider the product lines offered by any of the larger computer manufacturers: IBM, HP, Apple, Compaq, Epson, AST, and so on.

Every day, in retail locations, these vendors slug it out for the consumer's dollar. Volume sales drive competition, and competition drives prices down. This is the sharp edge at the cutting point of the experience curve. Here's why mainframes essentially can't compete on a power-for-the-dollar basis with small computers. In effect, personal computers have become the buy of the century due to the price competition caused by the consumer market, the level of capital investment that this competition and volume fosters, and the resulting experience curve in this segment of the computer market.

The forces that made PCs powerful, affordable, and available have virtually repealed (though not reversed) Grosch's Law. This repeal is still limited in some respects: if you spend more on a computer, you may get more speed — but the cost will be out of proportion to the increase in power. At one time, spending twice as much to get four times as much power represented a bargain. Today, though, spending 100 times as much merely to get ten times as much power represents a bad feeling. But is there really a choice?

Aren't mainframes really all about throughput? Even if a workstation or fast personal computer can crunch numbers as fast as a mainframe, what about processing thousands of transactions or running big batch jobs? Don't you need a single big computer to do all that in a coordinated fashion? The next section examines these questions more closely.

IS THE MAINFRAME A SINGLE BIG COMPUTER?

How does a mainframe achieve its vaunted throughput? By doing many things at one time. And how is a mainframe able to perform so many tasks so quickly? Because a mainframe is essentially a cluster of several smaller computers packaged in one box and connected together on an internal, high-speed network called a *bus*.

TASKS OF A MAINFRAME

Mainframes consist of many pieces: a computer, memory, disks, tape drives, printers, controllers, and so on. One of the things the mainframe does best is keep those pieces busy as much of the time as possible.

For example, if a transaction requires information from a disk, the mainframe doesn't simply stop working until the information comes back. Instead, the mainframe asks the disk for the data, remembers that it made that request, and performs other tasks in the meantime. A mainframe's working life consists of millions of interwoven tasks, such as the following:

✦ Starting the disk

✦ Starting the printer

✦ Starting the tape drive

✦ Getting back information from a disk

✦ Sending data to a terminal

✦ Starting another disk

✦ Starting a big batch process

Tracking all the threads keeps the computer very busy. How can one computer keep up with it all? Because the mainframe is not a single computer.

THE SMALLER COMPUTERS INSIDE A MAINFRAME

To process its formidable workload, a typical mainframe consists of several smaller computers, such as the following:

+ *Central computer:* Exercises control over all other computer components in the mainframe system. Quite often, even the "central computer" consists of still more individual computers packaged as one "unit."

+ *Channel:* A dedicated computer for talking to hard disks, tapes, and printers. Each channel has its own little programs, its own little memory, and the capability to complete tasks on its own. Most mainframes possess several channels.

+ *Disk controllers:* Computers that communicate with hard disks in the mainframe system.

+ *Network controllers:* Computers that manage the data traffic among other computers and terminals in the mainframe system.

If the mainframe is a bunch of computers acting like a single big one, why couldn't you take other kinds of smaller computers and make them act like big computers, too? In fact, why not make a bunch of personal computers do the job? (In a few paragraphs, I'll address that question.)

SIMILARITIES BETWEEN MAINFRAMES AND OTHER TYPES OF COMPUTER NETWORKS

In the '70s, some computer manufacturers noticed that mainframes were really just specialized clusters of smaller computers integrated by a custom, high-speed, internal network called a *bus.* Those vendors wondered if they could build better mainframes by really exploiting this "cluster of computers" idea.

TANDEM COMPUTERS EXPLOIT THE "CLUSTER OF COMPUTERS" CONCEPT

Tandem was the first company to really succeed with the "cluster of computers" concept. Founded by James Treybig in 1976, Tandem's original goal was to build fault-tolerant computers. Treybig observed mainframes being used increasingly in *mission-critical* applications: applications so important that a company could go under if the computer was down long enough. Why not build computers that would never fail, he wondered?

Treybig used *redundant components* to build fault tolerance into Tandem computers. In the tradition of wearing a belt *and* suspenders, a Tandem computer has at least two of every component: power supplies, computers, memories, disks, disk controllers, and so on. All components were built so that they could be removed and replaced without shutting down the system or affecting other components. There were two paths between any two components in the system.

For example, every processor could talk to every other processor in two different ways, and each disk could be reached through two different processors. As a result, if any part of the system were to malfunction, the system would keep running and notify the operator about the component failure. Then a technician could replace the failed part while the system continued to run. The users would not even be able to tell precisely when the repair had been made.

Tandem called its system *NonStop Computers* and the concept really worked. In record time, Tandem grew from nothing to sales of several hundred million dollars a year. Oddly, while nonstop operation was a major drawing card, many customers ended up buying the system for a more compelling reason than fault tolerance.

REDUNDANT PROCESSORS YIELD BIG PERFORMANCE GAINS

A Tandem system can easily consist of more than just two processors; while two make it work nonstop, you could expand the system up to 16 processors. Each Tandem processor was about equivalent to a decent-sized minicomputer of the time, far less powerful than a mainframe. However, 16 of the little processors side-by-side in the same computer was another story. And that's what drew customers.

Large corporations discovered that a fully expanded Tandem computer was an absolute powerhouse at processing transactions. In fact, a fully loaded Tandem with 16 processors and additional components could easily process three to four times the number of transactions per second that even the largest mainframe could handle. Yet even fully equipped, the Tandem was less than half the price of a mainframe. It's easy to see why hundreds of customers bought these machines:

✦ Huge additional processing capacity (many companies were exceeding the capacity of their existing mainframes)

✦ A lower price than new mainframes commanded

✦ The capacity to be expanded in easy stages without ever replacing the entire unit (no more expensive replacement upgrades to justify)

✦ The capability to run some applications in fault-tolerant mode

Later on, certain technical limitations in the system caused Tandem to stumble at a time in its history when it might have been able to eclipse other mainframe makers. As a result, Tandem today is a billion-dollar company — very successful, but still a niche player in the industry. Yet Tandem proved that a system of relatively small computers could perform as well as a mainframe at transaction processing — one of the most common mainframe tasks.

POWER GAINS THAT ARE PROPORTIONAL TO COST INCREASES

The Tandem computers represented a repeal of Grosch's Law. Essentially, in the world of Tandems and mainframes, big computers still must handle the serious work of big organizations. However, with the Tandem computers, the cost of additional computer power was now *directly proportional* to the increased cost due to additional components. You still would have to buy a big computer, but spending twice as much might yield twice as much computer power.

GROSCH'S LAW: FROM REPEAL TO FULL REVERSAL

Mainframes, Tandems, and minicomputers are simply not produced in large enough quantities to ride the experience curve. After you realize that even big computers are just clusters of smaller computers, it is only natural to keep coming back to the question of using small, high-volume computers to build those clusters. Why can't you build the equivalent of a mainframe out of the same microprocessors used to build personal computers? Why not have a machine modeled after the Tandem — but use 16 or 32 or 64 processors that cost $100 instead of $50,000 each? Why not, indeed? The change is starting to happen.

MULTIPROCESSOR SERVERS

Drawing on the experience of Tandem and other firms, computer companies in the '90s created a new generation of microprocessor-based servers. Often called *superservers*, these computers are based on a *multiprocessor design*. Multiprocessor servers offer a particularly appealing way to achieve scalability. In a multiprocessor environment, a server can literally be scaled up on the spot by plugging in extra processors. Multiprocessor servers yield several benefits, which are explained in the following paragraphs.

COST-EFFECTIVENESS DUE TO COMMODITY PARTS

Of course, multiprocessor computers aren't new. Tandem's already done it, so has IBM, and so have many other companies. What *is* new is the idea that these multiprocessor boxes are built around commodity-priced parts that are riding the experience curve and becoming more cost effective.

Even if the overall server box is relatively expensive, all of the server's component parts won't be. Suddenly, the processor you're plugging in *can* be a $100 component. Even if you insist that each new processor must come with its own memory and even if you insist on 50MB of memory per processor, you're still talking about $10,000 per processor. And what a processor! With a 100 MHz Pentium microprocessor and 50MB of memory, you'd have more than the equivalent of a mainframe in a box that can be easily parked in a cupboard.

Multiprocessor servers make PC networks incredibly scalable, as shown in the following example:

✦ *Small offices:* In small offices, you could start by giving every employee a single workstation, costing perhaps $2,000. Later, you could have one of the workstations double as a server while still acting as a workstation. Finally, you could later upgrade that server with more memory and disk space at a cost of perhaps $3,500.

✦ *Larger offices:* In larger offices, you could install dedicated servers with yet bigger disks, tape backup devices, and more memory at $5,000 a pop.

✦ *Warehouses:* In warehouses and regional offices, you could spend $10,000 to $40,000 to install small multiprocessor servers (with up to four processors) providing the throughput of a medium-size mainframe.

✦ *Major locations:* At major locations, you could install big multiprocessor servers (with 20 or 30 processors) at a cost of $50,000 to $250,000 (depending mostly on the amount of disk storage).

If a Tandem can process transactions so well, it's not hard to imagine these multiprocessor client/server systems competing with mainframes by doing it even better, although some new software may still be required to make it possible. (More on that later.) By definition, transactions are small tasks. So if there are lots of transactions, they could be easily distributed among many small computers. But what about the batch jobs? Consider a real-world experiment that answers this question.

Remember the invoice aging process? In that job, the mainframe processed unpaid bills one by one and decided whether to:

✦ Send a letter demanding payment

✦ Charge interest

✦ Reduce the customer's credit limit

One organization runs its aging application on a large mainframe, the largest available today. Processing over 500,000 invoices each month, the aging run takes 6.5 hours. This company had written the application in a way that made it easy to convert it to run on smaller computers.

In a rather casual experiment, the company set up a network with 8 database servers and 20 personal computers functioning as computational servers. The computational servers were 66 MHz, 486-class machines. Everybody involved was convinced that the client/server application would either not run at all or take a huge amount of time to complete. After all, the total network configuration cost less than 10 percent of the mainframe's cost, so it was rather farfetched to expect a lot from the client/server system.

Elapsed run time? Thirty minutes. Although the aging process took 6.5 hours on the mainframe, the same process took only half an hour on the network of little computers. The client/server application ran more than 12 times faster than the mainframe. What can we conclude from this?

Although the results of the invoice aging experiment are promising, you can't jump to conclusions about client/server system performance. Most batch applications can't be converted to client/server systems at all. Instead, most mainframe batch jobs would have to be rewritten to run in a client/server environment. The invoice aging application worked so quickly because it was *architected* to run in both environments. Remember also that some batch applications can't be split across multiple computers at all. Having expressed these caveats, client/server systems still offer remarkable potential. Let's explore what that potential is all about.

CLIENT/SERVER SYSTEMS AS "THE NEW MAINFRAMES"

Building the networks based on small, multiprocessor servers produces startling price/performance opportunities. Grosch's Law is not only repealed, it's reversed. The less you spend on your computer, the more power you get. The less you spend, the more power you get? Historically, the best way to get more power was to buy a bigger computer. Now the best way to get more power is to buy smaller computers. True, you have to buy many of those smaller computers, but in the aggregate, many smaller computers will still produce more computer power for less money. So per computer, you get more power by spending less on each computer but buying more of them. But what about throughput (doing lots of things at one time)?

Multiprocessor servers represent a way of "building a mainframe out of personal computers." Such servers are *much* less expensive than mainframes and potentially far more expandable and fault-tolerant. What's more, multiprocessor servers share certain traits in common with mainframes.

Multiprocessor servers are still expensive because they still concentrate a lot of processing in a single box — just as mainframes do. Multiprocessor servers also require complex operating systems to coordinate all the server's work. Consequently, multiprocessor servers could suffer from the same kind of operating system overhead found in mainframes.

Worse, large servers may soon be cost effective in storing lots of work from various parts of a company or location. That trend could lead to the kind of manageability problems that plagued mainframes. So you may get less expensive computing and more scalability — but you don't necessarily get qualitatively different computing with client/server systems based around multiprocessor servers.

THE NETWORK AS A MULTIPROCESSOR SERVER

The invoice aging experiment points to an even more different direction for distributed computing than multiprocessor servers. If the client/server network collectively functions as one large computer anyway, why have multiprocessor servers? Why not let the network of personal computers function as the servers? If invoice aging runs fastest on 20 computational servers talking to 8 database servers, why should you have any big computers at all? This is the true appeal of the client/server approach.

You should be clear about the pluses and minuses of this approach. Using a network of small computers to replace a single large machine may turn out to be cheaper and, in terms of throughput, faster. But is it simpler? This is a hard question to answer. On one hand, managing a single large machine is likely to be more straightforward and therefore simpler. On the other hand, the network of small machines allows the computing power to parallel the organization's structure. Putting the computers where the work is has an appealing simplicity of its own as well. So the invoice aging example raises some disturbing questions about the real need for big computers. At last, companies can consider not having mainframes after all; technically, the possibility exists. Following through, however, requires some careful thought.

COOPERATING COMPONENTS: CAN THEY REPLACE CENTRALIZED COMPUTING?

In thinking back over the entire progression of thought in this chapter, it has arrived at a very interesting place. The entire focus has been on the mainframe, generally considered to be the epitome of monolithic, centralized computing. The first thing discovered is that the mainframe itself is in fact built out of — what? — cooperating components. The only problem is that packaged in the form of a mainframe, those components are expensive and are not easy to work with, replace, or rearrange. Then, this chapter considered other big, mainframe-like machines and found that the more a system was built not just like cooperating components, but instead literally in that form, like the Tandem, the better the performance. Finally, this chapter considered a benchmark in which the large machine disappeared altogether, and throughput was accomplished entirely by commodity component, off-the-shelf boxes. So the surprising conclusion of this exploration of big systems is that by building them out of lots of small systems, operating together as cooperating components, you get more, not less, performance than ever imagined possible.

Why have big computers at all? What the invoice aging experiment shows is that even for batch processing, you get a huge savings by going from mainframes to networks of personal computers. If batch processing, not to mention transaction processing, is more effectively handled by networked personal computers, why have big computers at all?

Yes, groups of computers may still be collected at central sites. And yes, those central sites may provide shared operational facilities. But it's no longer necessary to use big computers to combine work from lots of different places. This insight fully reverses Grosch's Law. The result is simpler computing, lower costs, and greater throughput. Of course, getting to this future will take time. It won't be appropriate in all cases. And even where appropriate, the transition won't happen in one step. But the concept fits in well with experience in many other areas.

The experience of the 20th century provides a compelling argument for decentralized operations of all kinds. Although mainframes have some remarkable capabilities, networks of personal computers — cooperating components — *can* replace the big machines. Not by personal computers alone, but definitely by networks.

Are we there today? No. Originally, personal computers were missing all of the key features of mainframes: the speed, the address space, the storage management, the hardware, and the software to support high throughput transaction and batch processing.

However, today brings a different picture. Speed is no longer a problem in large PC network applications. Additionally, PC address space is in the process of being expanded rapidly.

Granted, PC storage management is a mixed picture. In some areas, PC networks are still missing critical capabilities. Yet in other areas, PC-based products with sophisticated replication facilities are actually significantly ahead of mainframes.

Ultimately, PC client/server systems are a compelling model of the network as computer. In effect, the LAN can be a better "mainframe" than the mainframe was. The LAN can also eliminate problems with complexity and scalability that plagued mainframes. Distributed systems have complexities of their own, of course, but at least the possibility exists of being able to choose one complexity over the other. The question is, how do you sort through the design and infrastructure issues to take advantage of this new computing architecture so that choice becomes possible? That's what the rest of the book is about.

CHAPTER 9

DATABASE — THE CONCEPT

This book devotes two chapters to the database. This chapter covers the basic concepts, talking about the different ways in which the very term *database* is used, explaining how databases are built, and detailing what databases are about. Chapter 10 dives in a little deeper to deal with some architectural distinctions between classes of database products.

In theory, you can read this chapter, skip the next, and still make sense of the whole book. The second database chapter (Chapter 10) deals with words like *relational*, *hierarchical*, *network*, *object-oriented*, *schema*, *entity*, *relationship*, and *design* and can be pretty abstract and complex. At the same time, I hope by now that you understand that difficult-sounding terms are generally based on commonsense concepts. With a little patience and careful reading, virtually everyone should understand both chapters.

I split the database chapters not only to make it easy to skip a chapter, but also to make it easy to read one, rest, and then read the next. If you read both, I promise that future database discussions will make sense to you.

This chapter is a watershed in your journey through the continent of client/server.

In the United States, a series of major mountain ranges running north and south marks the continental divide: on one side of the ranges, water runs east to the Atlantic, and on the other side, rivers flow west to the Pacific. For many years, these ranges marked a critical transition point for travelers. Struggling through difficult, unknown territory, pioneers knew that if they made it over the divide, they were likely to finish their journey.

In the same way, in all the preceding technically oriented chapters, I laid the ground-work for you to start building some structure that is more than foundational.

Until now, I have talked about major components that revolve largely around hard-ware. *Graphical user interfaces (GUIs)* are based on color, screens, mice, keyboards, fast display memory, and display hardware. *Networks* depend on communications lines or fast local buses. *Servers* are computers per se, dedicated to a particular task. And *mainframes* are highly specialized pieces of hardware designed and built to pro-vide massive throughput.

Databases are different, based almost entirely on software. Time after time, the most important advances in database technology are based on software innovation alone, although the new software may take advantage of newer and faster hardware.

Databases define a watershed between hardware-centered technology and a world of software-based mechanisms. You are traveling from the land of enablement to the land of applications that are enabled. Although a PC may have a great GUI, may be attached to a super local-area network (LAN), may share a high-performance server, and may communicate with other LANs and with mainframes over a wide-area net-work (WAN), it is only as useful as the applications running in the environment. All the components I have described so far simply enable applications to run. Databases, meanwhile, *are* a class of applications. True, they enable other applications, but they are also useful even in the absence of other applications. So this chapter marks a watershed: as I talk about databases, I am taking you to the land of applications en-abled by all the technology now behind us.

Neither *client*, *server*, *LAN*, *WAN*, nor *mainframe* defines how a computer can help an organization. Databases, built on those pieces, go a good way toward providing that kind of definition. Here, for the first time, you can start to come to grips directly with the core benefits that computers deliver to companies.

WHAT IS A DATABASE?

Worldwide, the database industry generates over $5 billion in revenues every year. Products such as mainframe packages, which cost hundreds of thousands of dollars per year, server-resident databases worth tens of thousands each, and PC products such as dBASE, Paradox, and FoxPro, which cost a few hundred dollars each, are all just part of the database market.

Database is not a single concept but a family of related concepts. When the time comes to build a complete database system, you need several key components to make the whole thing work. Database users tend to be familiar with the part that they use most; as a result, they think of that part as if it were the whole database.

Using the single word *database* to refer to many things makes it hard to get a handle on the concept. As the key parts take shape, however, you can see clearly a frame-work for thinking about the design of computer systems in general and client/server systems in particular.

WHAT IS A SPREADSHEET?

What is a database? A related question: What is the best-selling database in the world? The answer, surprisingly, is 1-2-3 (or soon, perhaps, Excel). That's right, a spreadsheet. How can a spreadsheet be the best-selling database when it's not even a database? Well, recall that Lotus called the program 1-2-3 because it came with three major functions — spreadsheet, graphics, and database — unlike VisiCalc, the original spreadsheet. The programmers who wrote 1-2-3 certainly intended that it could be used as a database.

Spreadsheets enable users to organize information easily in large tables. Spreadsheets are so easy to use that beginning users don't need training or manuals to do their jobs. Even if they don't ever use formulas, users can quickly fill in successive rows, scroll back and forth, and print the tables at will. The fact that they can start filling in rows with literally no training, make changes without opening manuals, and get the job done with no programming is good.

At one time, spreadsheets were limited in size; a table couldn't have more than a few hundred rows. Not today: A typical 386- or 486-class machine with 4MB of main memory can easily handle a spreadsheet with thousands of rows. Today users can reasonably build a table with up to 10,000 rows, representing 10,000 records. That's a pretty good-sized database for most people. Salespeople, for example, rarely deal with that many customers, churches usually have fewer members, and many product marketing managers are thrilled when they gather even half that many data points to massage.

When I was a marketing manager, I needed to analyze distribution patterns for several products and determine whether stores that sold and stocked popular products also carried less popular products. The theory: my company's most successful dealers were ignoring our newer lines. I wanted to get these successful retail locations to start promoting the newer products.

I needed to analyze about 4,000 rows of information, one row for each store, and about 25 columns per row, containing dealer name, geographical information (such as city, state, and ZIP code), and, of course, sales volumes for the last year for 20 products. Overall, my little project required manipulating a database with 4,000 rows and 25 columns for a grand total of 100,000 bits of information — far more than any-body could work with by hand.

Initially, I set up this database on a large minicomputer. The minicomputer database required me to use a powerful but complex command language. Simple operations often took up to a half hour. And much to my frustration, the minicomputer would periodically be unavailable or very slow because of other scheduled activities. I easily could have downloaded the information into Paradox or dBASE, the leading data-bases of the time, but I then would have had to deal with a different command lan-guage. So, instead, I downloaded into Excel running on a Mac with 4MB of memory.

Suddenly, sorts took no time at all. I could specify a sort in a few keystrokes (basically without commands) and see the result 20 seconds later. Patterns quickly became obvious.

Did certain retailers sell more of one product than another? Were there dealers who sold none of the first product? (I found these dealers at the bottom of the sort.) Had those stores sold much of the second product? What dealers sold the most of the second product? Were dealers in a particular city or state? Regional variations in general?

I drew a graph comparing sales of one product with another. I added a column showing the ratio of the sum of a basket with six older products to the sum of another basket with all new lines.

Any spreadsheet user could quickly answer these questions. The operations are simple; all can be completed in 10 to 20 seconds. In fact, 95 percent of ordinary humans, given several days with their favorite spreadsheet, already know how to do everything in my list (and more). Little wonder, then, that I made Excel my database. And little wonder that spreadsheets are by far the leading databases in the world today — and in the foreseeable future.

WHY ALL SPREADSHEETS ARE DATABASES BUT NOT ALL DATABASES ARE SPREADSHEETS

As databases, spreadsheets have several huge advantages. They have a highly intuitive graphical interface, are useful for many other tasks (they are the Swiss army knives of the computer world), fit onto laptop and notebook computers, and are nonthreatening. Yet it doesn't feel right to say that a spreadsheet is a database, period. Databases are more than just spreadsheets.

By understanding the popularity of spreadsheets as databases, though, you can get a handle on one set of things that databases do. Databases provide users (even nontechnical users) with facilities for finding, organizing, sorting, viewing, and printing simple sets of data, primarily organized as *tables*.

The importance of tables as a way of organizing data can't be overestimated. Nothing beats a table for simplicity as a paradigm for collections of records. But this simplicity is the biggest strength *and* weakness of databases organized around the table concept. As I explain later (particularly in the next chapter), widespread recognition of the table's inherent simplicity and power has led to the rise of so-called *relational databases*; limitations in the table's expressive power will lead to the replacement of the relational model in the '90s.

Spreadsheets can represent many kinds of information, not all of which are databases or parts of databases. So what makes a set of information a database?

Records and fields are one element of a database. Suppose that you and I own a collection of videotapes we want to organize and manage. We decide to build a database. First, we decide what our database should contain. Then we design a small form on which we enter information about the videotapes. Each time we fill in a form, we create a *record*, describing a videotape. The record, in turn, contains *fields*, describing the videotape's title, length, format, subject, and author, as well as where we can find it in our collection.

At the core of any database — any size, any kind — are records. Records, in turn, consist of collections of fields. But by themselves, records and fields are not necessarily a database.

For example, we may keep track of our videotapes on 3" × 5" index cards, but if we're not well organized, we may enter different information on every card. One card may list a title and duration in minutes. Another may have a title and lead actor's name. Another may have a title, duration in hours, and information about the tape's format. Superficially, some may consider a pile of such index cards a database. But the first time we try to work with this "database" as a whole, the limitations of this approach quickly become obvious. How do we sort by length, for example, when some cards list no duration, some have durations in minutes, and some are shown in hours? Most important, even if we can deal with the inconsistency, we don't have a standard way to find the information about duration on the card. Knowing how to find information in a record is a particularly tricky issue in a database environment; when we solve this problem, we convert a pile of random records into an organized database.

Beyond issues of neatness and consistency, this problem is more philosophical: How do we know what a field or record *means*? What is the meaning of our data?

Coming to our rescue, a database provides a mechanism for interpreting, or understanding, the meaning of data. In other words, the database is more than a container for data — it provides a context for interpreting that data. Okay, that sounds pretty abstract. What does this philosophical stuff really mean to users?

Regularity, structure, and schema are part of this picture. To transform our pile of 3" × 5" cards into the beginnings of a database, we impose *regularity* on the data. Every index card in our example has content and structure. The *content* varies from card to card; the content is the actual data (*Capra, John Wayne, 35 minutes, VHS*, and so on) written on each card. On the other hand, the *structure* describes kinds of data common to all the cards; the structure may call for each card to contain (in a particular order) title, duration, subject, format, and so on. The structure description, called a *schema*, goes even further, defining how to measure or locate the kinds of data; for example, the schema defines the unit of measure for the duration field (minutes or hours — but the same for all cards) and how to recognize the title field (perhaps it's labeled "title" or maybe it's always the first field — but again, the same for all cards). To define a database table, we combine regularity and structure. Simple.

Although most people think that a *database* is just a huge collection of data, a file may contain a great deal of data and not be a database. In fact, ironically, a database actually need not contain any data to be a database. A database is defined by the organization of its data (structure and schema) and the imposition of a consistent order (regularity) to that data.

STRUCTURE GIVES MEANING TO DATABASE RECORDS

You fill in forms all the time. Start a new job and you fill in employment forms. Apply for a passport or driver's license, order a product, reserve a book at the library, or pay a speeding ticket, and you fill in forms. Does a form have any meaning by itself? Many questions of this type have surprisingly tricky answers. (Does a falling tree make a sound if nobody is present to hear it fall?) Our question, however, has a simpler answer.

Suppose that you receive by mistake a form from the company where one of your friends works. Out of curiosity, you start to fill in the form (or perhaps it's already filled in and you merely peruse it). What is the employee number? Department code? Product family? Profitability range? Part type? Employee classification? Division name? Typically, the form contains many fields that are meaningful only to somebody working for the company. Even fields with meaningful labels can easily have different interpretations at different companies.

Take something as simple as *price*: does it mean dollars or francs, purchase or lease, before or after taxes, asking or selling price? A form taken out of context is literally meaningless. It cannot be interpreted until it is placed in the framework of the environment for which it was designed. The same is true for database records.

Defining databases from a user's perspective, a database is a collection of tables, or *files*. (Generally, the terms *table* and *files* are interchangeable, as are *field* and *column*. Refer to the next chapter for some of the subtle differences between these terms). Each table contains records that, in turn, contain fields. By organizing a collection of items, such as records with fields, we are providing a regular structure that allows a user to interpret those records. The database provides a way of organizing and, therefore, understanding the data.

Databases are also self-describing — they are both a tool and the information the tool works with. In a lifelong search for self-awareness, many of us struggle for ways to define and describe ourselves. Perhaps it is a reach to talk about databases as being self-aware, but unlike most other parts of a computer system, a database can describe itself. For example, a collection of records must have a regular structure described by a schema (literally each table and record is described by a schema, which is written out in a special language that in turn can be typed in or printed out.)

Normally, we don't see this schema because it is hidden from us by the graphical database software. That software allows us to define and manipulate the structure of the database graphically. However, on request the database can be asked to tell us all about each table and its structure. But why is this self-descriptiveness so important as the capstone of our database concept?

A big difference between an ad hoc pile of 3" × 5" index cards and a database is the ability to work with the data. A database helps users find particular records, sort the records, produce statistical summaries, and so on. The reason a database can do that is that the database tools — the sorter, the query manager, the reporting tool — know how to interpret all the records in the table. Tell the database that you want to sort, and the database asks which column you want to sort.

Opening a table brings with it three things:

✦ Contents of all the records

✦ Regular structure that allows the records to be interpreted

✦ Description of that structure that allows tools to understand the table even though the tools may never have seen that table before

Ultimately, a database is both a tool and the information with which the tool works.

I've described what a database means as it applies to single tables — simple databases, but databases nonetheless. Let me explain how this concept works with our original database, the spreadsheet. Then I look at a few other examples of simple databases to see the concept in full play.

Not every spreadsheet is a database and, even in spreadsheets that contain database tables, often the whole spreadsheet is still not a database. Spreadsheets are very good at handling collections of *irregular* data — not a database or database table. In fact, the whole point of a spreadsheet is that you can just type values anywhere. Moreover, another strength of a spreadsheet is that any cell can be a formula. If all spreadsheets were databases, every row would have to contain the same formulas, and we would lose a lot of the power of the spreadsheet itself. So, for all our talk about regularity, databases are not the world. Ah, but what about the parts of a spreadsheet that are databases?

The way that Excel, 1-2-3, and other spreadsheets accommodate databases is by providing the concept of a *database range*: a single spreadsheet can have any number of these ranges. Each database range is equivalent to a single database table. A database range in a spreadsheet is a set of rows, all with the same columns, and all described by names contained in the first row of the range. In other words, a database range in a spreadsheet has the key characteristics of a database as I defined it previously: uniformity, structure, and self-descriptiveness. Where else can we find database tables?

Word processors can create and maintain simple database tables. Most word processors, for example, do an excellent job with mailing lists, including powerful mail-merge capabilities. A mail merge involves two components. First, you must create a document containing the mailing list. If you look at such a document, you will find a list of records, each with a regular set of fields, and all tied together by some form of self-descriptive structure. The mailing list may contain an initial record specifying the order in which fields can be found in the following records: Surname, First Name, Title, Mail Address, and so on. Alternatively, to allow more flexibility, each record may be self-descriptive. In the latter case, every record would have special tags, such as in the form <Surname>, <City>, and so on. Either way, a mailing list in a word processing document is just another database table.

Of course, industrial-strength database tables also all have these characteristics. Full-strength databases offer a combination of power and complexity when it comes to building and maintaining tables. On one hand, creating tables in the first place requires you to learn a whole series of complex commands. As a result, building a database table in an industrial-strength database environment is a daunting challenge for the average person. On the other hand, after you have created the database tables, the database provides powerful commands for changing and improving the tables over time. Commands are provided directly for modifying the structure of the database independent of the content; the structure, when established, can be printed, queried, and manipulated. You can combine tables with other tables in powerful ways, and the system can accommodate complex queries and reports in powerful ways as well.

Is this it? Not quite. The problem is that although the databases described so far have an appealingly simple conceptual structure, they're also far too simple and limited to deal with large problems.

As we've looked at them so far, databases are single tables or files. We can have many such tables, but surely we won't be satisfied working with just one table at a time. So this section describes how database tables get pulled together into complete databases.

A database is a collection of tables, each organized as a set of records, all pulled together by a defined set of relationships between the tables. Databases are powerful because they can create complex sets of relationships between tables.

To illustrate, suppose that your videotape collection grows and you start lending tapes out. Later, in a spirit of entrepreneurial adventure, you begin renting and selling tapes, too. Now a single file with a record per videotape is not enough. You need files to do the following:

✦ Track customers

✦ Manage the vendors you buy tapes from; special orders that can't be lost; employee lists (boy, the company's growing); and the accounting and bookkeeping records

All of a sudden, your simple database is starting to sound like the kind of large, complex system we find on mainframes. What happened?

At one level, mainframe databases and spreadsheet-resident databases are not all that different. All the information in a database is simply collections of records with a regular, defined structure. However, by representing the relationships between those sets of records, you have more than just a table — you have a database. What about these *relationship* things? They must be complicated, right? Wrong.

Suppose that a customer wants to rent a videotape for the weekend. How do you put this information in a database? First, the videotape must be represented in the database file describing all videotapes. Next, the customer has to be in another database file containing a record for each customer. If the customer is a new one, you have to create a new record for him before you can let him rent movies. As you'd expect, the customer record contains her name, address, credit card number, and so on. So far, you have two files (sometimes called tables) and no relationships.

In order to record the rental, you must create another record in a database file that contains an entry for each rental. A rental record would contain the following kinds of data:

✦ The movie

✦ The customer

✦ When the tape went out

✦ When it's due back

✦ When it was returned

I would like to look at this record in slightly more detail.

In a rental record, how will you identify the videotape being lent out? You could enter the actual title, but then how do you know which copy of the tape it was? How about title and copy number? Definitely a possibility, but you'd have to store a lot of information in two places. Consider the same question for customer: how do we identify the customer borrowing the tape? Use his name? What if two customers have the same name? How about address? What if he moves? Worse, what if he changes his name *and* moves? Or what if two customers with the same name happen to live at the same address? There must be a better way. There is.

When you create the record describing the videotape, you arrange to enter a unique identifier for the tape. For instance, every time you buy a new videotape, you assign it a unique serial number. Similarly, when a customer rents a tape for the first time, you assign him a unique customer number. Pretty standard stuff. However, you also need to identify the videotape and the customer in the rental record. So our rental record starts out with a customer ID, a videotape serial number, the date the movie went out, the due date, and so on.

Hang on a second. This means our rental record depends on our customer and videotape records. Right: the three tables are linked; there is a defined relationship between the files. Rather than duplicate customer data and videotape data in the rental record, you simply link the customer table, videotape table, and rental table together. Additionally, you might link these tables to an employee table indicating who checked the movie out. The videotape record could also be linked to supplier records so that you know where the tape was bought. Finally, you could also link the videotape record to purchasing records indicating how many copies of the tape were bought, when they were bought, and how much they cost. Even a video store may easily require a database with up to a hundred files and dozens of relationships linking all those files to each other in simple and complex ways.

Relationships that convert a set of unrelated files into a *database* truly parallel and track the operation of an organization. Designed properly, a database *is* the model of an organization's information.

A table describing a collection of videotapes can be used in lots of places: a home, a store, the library of a company. Similarly, a customer file can come from many places. Your store's database, however, consists of a customer file, a videotape file, another file tracking rentals, and another file tracking stores. That database actually does a pretty complete job describing the entire operation of *your* store. You could deduce the structure of this database from an understanding of the store's business, and conversely a trained observer could figure out quite a lot from the database about how that store runs. Because the database is such a good model of businesses, database design is centrally important to both the mainframe and client/server revolutions.

DATABASE: THE COPERNICAN COMPUTER REVOLUTION

A quick message from the sponsor. Very quickly in the last page or so, I have shifted from records and 3" × 5" cards to a discussion about models of organizations, mental maps, and databases as modeling tools. Can this have any practical outcome? Absolutely. The database concept turns out to be a very powerful *thinking tool* for understanding a major aspect of how organizations operate. Now about 20 years old, this concept is one of the first foundation blocks of the client/server revolution.

In the '50s, permanent storage was essentially unknown. Computer programs were written on paper, transcribed onto paper tape or punched cards, and then read into the computer at the time the program was run. Any data the program worked on was also read while the program was running. Then the program would process and print the altered data on paper, punched cards, or tape for later reuse. A computer program and the data it worked with were all temporary creations.

DATA STORAGE ON MAGNETIC TAPE

Magnetic tape (mag tape, for short) was the first form of permanent data storage. Like audio cassettes and videotapes, computer mag tapes can be reused many times. On a mag tape, information can be read, worked on, changed, and rewritten.

However, one problem with both cassettes and videotapes is that finding selections takes a long time. Also, getting from one end of the tape to the other takes forever. Mag tapes have all the same problems. For over a decade, the computer in popular culture came to be associated with the magnetic tapes used to store customer files, billing information, and so on. Ultimately, computer mag tapes were too limited in performance to make databases imaginable or practical.

DATA STORAGE ON MAGNETIC DISK

In the mid '60s, when the IBM 360 product family was taking off, disk storage first became practical. The early disks were huge, slow, expensive devices — hard to take seriously today. The disks themselves were enormous iron platters, specially made heavy so that their momentum would ensure smooth spinning. Yet, in spite of weighing so much that a strong person could hardly lift them, these disks were lucky to store 10 million bytes of information. Nonetheless, even with all their limitations, disks provided a key breakthrough.

Unlike a tape, a disk is a *random-access device*. Information anywhere on the disk can be retrieved about as fast as information anywhere else on the disk. No more waiting forever while the tape rewinds. No more rewriting the whole tape just to make space to insert a new item near the beginning. In fact, a magnetic disk doesn't have a beginning or end: the whole disk — or selected parts of it — are always available to be read or written. This characteristic of being able to read and write data anywhere, anytime, is referred to as *random access*: the ability to access data randomly, as computer people say. The fact that magnetic disks enabled random access led to revolutionary new methods for storing data on computers.

INDEXES FOR MAGNETIC DISKS

Because there is no beginning or end to a magnetic disk, finding any one customer record is as fast or as slow as finding any other. Furthermore, because customer records don't all have to be stored in sequence, the records can grow, shrink, change arbitrarily. But how does the program find the records on a disk? After all, they can be stored all over the disk. The answer is that the software keeps an index which lists where particular records are physically located on the disk.

So, given this random-access storage, programmers started writing applications that used indexes to keep track of records stored all over the disk. If a record changed, the application would simply write the changed record back to the disk. If the record got too big to fit into its current location on disk, the program would put it in a new location and change the index to point to the new location. Everything kept working transparently. The big, new feature? Keep the data around all the time! Yes, on-line storage.

On-line means "available on the computer at all times." Magnetic disks allowed many programs to share on-line storage. On-line storage triggered a major revolution in software design. For the first time, programmers could write applications that shared the same data.

Recall how the video store's database grew complex so quickly? Think about all the places the customer table could be used. Customers rent videotapes, receive mailings, place special orders, make complaints, apply for credit, change addresses, join clubs, enter contests, become the targets of special promotions, ad infinitum.

Now think about how many times you've entered your name and affiliation since buying your own personal computer. Doesn't every piece of software you install ask you to type your full name and organization? Perhaps it even refuses to start the installation process until you do so, which is annoying. Why can't all those applications use a standard place for recording and finding your name? If necessary, the application could start out by asking you to confirm this data, but at least you wouldn't have to enter it over and over and over.

Everybody has heard the story of the company president who calls an emergency meeting because the company has a problem. Vice presidents show up, each with his computer-generated reports ready to provide an analysis of the causes and solutions. As it turns out, everybody thinks the problem is something different. When the reports are compared, all generated from the same computer system, the numbers all violently disagree with each other. How does this happen? If everybody is operating with reports generated by the same computer, how can the resulting reports disagree so much? Although the data may come from the same computer, that data is not necessarily a consistent database. Unfortunately, databases often have multiple copies of data stored over and over. Each repetition creates a new opportunity for inconsistency and irate presidents. The Copernican computer revolution focused on eliminating inconsistencies in data.

DATABASE MANAGEMENT: SEPARATING DATA FROM BUSINESS RULES

In 1543, Nicolaus Copernicus proposed that, rather than the sun revolving around the earth, the earth revolved around the sun. He turned the world view inside out. How does the computer Copernican revolution apply to database and application design? Simply, the database revolutionary manifesto asks you to design your applications by focusing first not on the application itself but instead on the data that essentially defines the operation of your organization. Instead of having files revolving around individual programs, have programs revolving around files. The database becomes the sun, and the programs become the planets.

In the '60s, the world of computers revolved around applications. Systems were built around applications. The leading professionals were programmers. The professionals built the systems by developing the programs that the computers revolved around. In building each program, programmers spent much effort managing data. When a program ran, its tapes were mounted; when it was done, the tapes were taken down. Sometimes tapes may be shared by several programs. But fundamentally, programs came first, and everything else followed their needs. The problem with this approach is that it encourages the creation of many different files containing variations on the same information.

In the late '60s, as programmers learned about permanent random-access storage on disks, they developed a new class of software: the database management system. Programmers started to wonder why they were writing the same software to manage data over and over. Along with this thought, programmers realized that perhaps the data was actually more important than the programs that worked with it! At that point, companies began to view the *database as a key corporate resource.*

In fact, programmers began to realize that by focusing on data rather than on code, they could build applications that more effectively dealt with business change. Our video store will change in the way it operates over time; that's a certainty. As the business grows, laws change, new organizational concepts become popular, and change is one of the few constants. Each time the store operations change, software probably has to be rewritten. In fact, one of the driving forces behind the client/server revolution is the need to accommodate changes in business rules not only company-wide, but on a local basis as well.

Programs change; data doesn't. One of the early propositions of the database revolution, this rule has turned out to be true far more often than it's false. A customer remains a customer, no matter how much the business changes. She has a name, customer number, street address, age, color preference, and a host of other attributes, recorded in fields, and all of which tend to stay quite constant, even as the *rules* that drive the business change over time.

DATABASE AS ORGANIZATIONAL MEMORY

At first, databases were viewed as powerful technical tools. After a short while, though, system designers realized that the structure of the database could provide a powerful vehicle for understanding how a company was fundamentally organized. Although this idea has proven to have some fundamental limitations in practical use, a database can serve as a powerful model for the company as a whole. As a result, to design better databases, software professionals created the data model, a powerful tool in its own right.

THE DATA MODEL

To understand the power of the data model, recall the company president's emergency meeting in which every vice president has inconsistent reports from the very same computer system. Fixing this problem requires that group to make three observations:

1. Information *is* a key corporate resource.

2. An information system that makes accurate, consistent information available instantly is a competitive advantage.

3. Arriving at that point requires information to be managed differently than is

possible with purely manual approaches.

This section takes a look at these observations in more detail.

Data as a competitive advantage. In a national retail chain, how long does it take to find out which new styles are selling particularly well? (Assume that each store only reports sales back monthly through divisions, which, in turn, consolidate their summaries quarterly.) What is the exact value to the company of being able to spot hot sellers in one or two days and reorder in a week? For customers of a direct sales operation, how attractive is it to know that any product they order before midnight will be delivered before 10 the next morning, no matter where they live in the U.S.? How much can we save in our chain of video stores by being able to balance inventory across stores so that titles moving quickly at one store can be backed up by tapes from another store where the title is a dud? All of these examples share a common element: having up-to-date, accurate information is literally the same as money. It is worth spending quite a bit to have that information because of the competitive advantage and profit it will generate.

How databases generate money. Recall the client/server version one? The server allows a team to share information effectively without requiring any people to act as information coordinators. I even talked about the server acting as a database. Now I'm going to reactivate that concept and talk about what is required, from a design perspective, to make it all work. I'm going to take that term *database* and put some more substance around it. And in the process, you're going to see how tables, relationships, and models play a central role in the design of client/server systems.

DEFINITIONS OF DATABASE

Part of the reason that databases are so hard to understand is that they *are* so many different things. What are the three meanings for the word database?

✦ Central repository

✦ Personal information retrieval and analysis tool

✦ Conceptual model

In the first place, a database is a *central repository* and coordinator of data for companies, departments, and teams. By placing critical shared information in the care of the database, as you saw in the server chapter, you can control inventory, seminar invitations, airplane seats, and credit dollars. Many people can access, inspect, and change this data, all at the same time, all seeing the most up-to-date version of the information, and all without running into each other. The database manages both the information and the coordinated access to it. In this context, the database is playing a very active role. (In fact, talking about databases in this way, computer professionals often talk about database engines. The database *engine* is software that manages the basic storage functions of the database.)

PERSONAL INFORMATION RETRIEVAL AND ANALYSIS TOOL

In its second persona, the database provides individuals with facilities for retrieving and analyzing information — finding, analyzing, manipulating, displaying, and printing large amounts of data. In this context, Lotus 1-2-3 is a database. Even large database systems that do a superb job in the first role still depend entirely on other retrieval and analysis tools to make data available after it's been generated. Sometimes the tool is highly personal, used by an individual to find and work with information at a workstation. At other times, the tool is part of a large application that produces reports.

Third, *database* refers to the *conceptual model* of how a company works. The success of an organization at developing a useful conceptual model for how that business operates will most of all determine the success of that organization at building a useful database.

For example, how does an investor use information to pick stocks? There are as many answers as there are investors. A variety of ratios, patterns, and indicators can be used to evaluate prospective stocks: price-to-earnings ratios, alphas, betas, liquidity measures, comparisons to other stocks, and so on. All of these techniques attempt to reduce the mass of details that describe a company's performance to a small set of metrics that will predict future behavior. In other words, investors use models to evaluate companies. Every investor develops a model of prospective investments in his head and then uses that model to evaluate stocks one by one. Over time, the investor makes his model increasingly sophisticated and, hopefully, more accurate.

In the same way, a database is a *model*, based on data, of the real organization. Understanding how to build that model appropriately is the core issue in designing effective database applications.

Understanding database design is both important and interesting, so it's time to have a go at it, starting with the video store. By the time you're done, you'll see that a small number of core principles drive the whole process. Start by thinking about customers, employees, and people.

DESIGNING GREAT DATABASES: CENTRAL PRINCIPLES FOR CHANGING BUSINESSES

In most organizations, customers are ubiquitous; most applications deal with customers in one way or another. As a result, it's easy to design software so that customer data is spread all through the system. What happens when a customer moves: how does his address get changed everywhere? In the worst case, the customer's address is duplicated in dozens of applications, each of which has its own files, its own customer-handling programs, and its own customer screen forms. In this case, each department that deals with customers has to be told about the address change and then arrange to have that address change entered separately. This expensive and error-prone process may sound awkward, but it is by far the rule, not the exception. What's the alternative?

BENEFITS OF STORING DATA IN ONE PLACE

What would happen if all information about customers were stored in only a single file, no matter how many times that information was used in different applications? This approach has three huge advantages.

It's easier to change the data. Changes to the customer's name and all other related data can be made in a single place at a single time. As soon as the changes are made, all applications would immediately see the up-to-date information.

Consistency. By storing all the customer data in a single file, you would not be able to have two different versions of the customer record in the same system at the same time. Therefore, it would not be possible for two different reports to be in conflict about customers.

Conserves disk space. Databases get very big and disk space can be very expensive. By saving customer information in only a single file, you save a lot of disk space. In addition, because so many programs would use the one database file, you can afford to work extra hard to organize that file so that retrieval is truly fast, efficient, and flexible.

All of these benefits are related to the first idealized goal of database design: *the elimination of redundant data*. When customer records are stored in more than one place, all the copies after the first can be thought of as *redundant*. After all, a customer has only one name, one address, and one identification number. So why store that information more than once?

Cutting to the core, the most important benefit is the elimination of inconsistencies. If the same data is stored in more than one location, then no matter how careful you are in building and maintaining your applications, that data will eventually create inconsistencies. These inconsistencies are the true, fundamental cause of the conflicting answers the president gets when he tries to find out how his company is doing.

CHALLENGES OF ELIMINATING DATA REDUNDANCY

Building a data model that completely eliminates these inconsistencies has many subtle challenges, which I'll consider in the pages ahead. But the basic principle is simple: *designing a database that produces consistent and meaningful answers to questions means designing a database in which each key piece of information is stored in only a single place.* (However, databases often provide special facilities for duplicating critical data to provide users with exemplary performance. For example, a database may literally *replicate* itself so that a user can keep her own personal copy on a notebook computer she carries around. As was discussed in the previous two chapters, even this type of replication is now becoming pretty standard.)

The principle of storing data in only one place can drive the design of large databases. For example, in our video store, the principle can be applied to customers, products, rental records, payments, employees, and every other aspect of the business. In fact, if a database designer refined a design until each data element was stored in a single file only, he would produce a database that probably would be consistent over time. The benefits of this approach reach far beyond single tables.

The database can be viewed as an interconnected whole. To track a videotape rental, the customer record is *related* to a rental record, which in turn, is *related* to an inventory record keeping track of that particular tape. Also, the customer record is *related* to a credit rating record, which in turn is *related* to various payment records that can be used to compute late payments.

The common element here is the concept of relationships. A *relationship* creates a link between two records so that, for the purposes of a particular application, the two records function as one big record.

In each case, the relationship serves two dual purposes:

✦ To allow information to be stored one time only, even though it is used over and over in different combinations. The customer record, the videotape description, and the like fall into this category. Simplistically, you could store each of those records over and over each time you need the information. But for all the reasons I've already explained, storing the information once and then establishing relationships among records leads to a better design.

✦ After a record is stored in a single place, it can be used by *many* applications. For example, the customer record can be related to rental records, payment records, credit ratings, direct mail lists, club memberships, and so on.

DATA MODELS HELP COMPANIES ANTICIPATE CHANGES

The idea of relating tables to each other is incredibly powerful. For the first time, relationships among tables provide us with a tool for building a model representing all the information an organization works with. This model can provide a road map for finding this information and can also serve as a basis for ensuring that the information is stored in a consistent fashion. How do we build a model, gain an understanding of what all those relationships can look like, and do it *right?* It comes back to eliminating redundancy.

Data models allowed managers and computer professionals to start thinking about how the information and organization fitted together. Developing a design for the organization's overall database turned out to mean developing a model, a road map, for the organization's information needs. The designer who could describe a coherent scheme for organizing all the data inside computers could also describe a coherent scheme for answering most questions managers would ever ask about the health of the organization.

Suddenly, database design becomes far from a technical proposition. What's one of the toughest challenges facing any senior manager? Knowing how her organization is really doing! Problems discovered long enough in advance can almost always be solved. The challenge in most organizations is usually not solving problems per se, but finding out about those problems long enough in advance to have time to solve them. And invariably, when a company runs out of time, it was because they were either asking the wrong questions or getting the wrong answers. Now databases enable companies to ask useful questions far enough in advance to solve emerging problems.

In the early '70s, large organizations reacted slowly to new situations because they had no way of processing information quickly. By definition, large companies have thousands of employees. Each of those employees deals with quite a lot of information every day. However, it was tough to collect that information in a form that can be used by others who were often separated from one another by time, space, and organizational structure.

One obvious example involves slow-moving sales information; companies don't react quickly enough when a product sells exceptionally well or exceptionally poorly. As a less obvious example, why does the customer have to build a new credit rating each time he opens an account with a different part of the same company? The company spends money tracking payment histories multiple times and the customer gets irritated. In the meantime, the company loses an opportunity to encourage the customer to build on his reputation in one part of the company by buying other products and services in another part of the company. Yet, how often have you been told "This is the sales (or service) division, and we have different systems, so you'll have to start over"?

INTEGRATED DATABASES REVERSE OLD ASSUMPTIONS

All of these problems represent two core assumptions, which databases and *networks* neatly reverse:

1. *Old assumption:* Applications are best built in a specialized way. Each department best knows its own needs. Information must be stored in specialized ways that reflect the needs of the individual departments.

2. *Old assumption:* It takes time to get information. As a specialist, each department holds its own information and makes its own decisions. When you need information owned by a department, ask them for it. Better yet, when you need a decision that involves the information, ask the department to make the decision. And wait until your request is delivered and the response is returned.

Here's what changes in the new world:

1. *New assumption:* Applications are still built in specialized ways. However, information is a corporate resource. All records are the property of the company — not any particular department. Also, company records are best stored in a single place, where changes can be instantly reflected across all applications. After records are stored in this way, they can also be shared by all applications — so that the data becomes universally accessible. Through the power of flexible databases, all these records can be related to all other records. As your business grows, new relationships will become important, but because you stored all records in one place, relating an existing record to a new record is straightforward and easy.

2. *New assumption:* Any information is universally accessible through the network. Therefore, the database can be thought of as a universal database, making all information available everywhere, always. When a record is updated by any department, the up-to-date information immediately becomes available to all other departments everywhere. Because most information is used by many departments anyway, this further reinforces the idea that information is an organizational, not a departmental, resource.

Before continuing, go back and reread the last six or so paragraphs with the following question in mind: *how much of what is being described is fundamentally technical and how much is really a new way of thinking about organizations in general?*

When I introduced the server, you saw that by having a tireless, effectively instantaneous, and constantly accessible information coordinator, you could change the fundamental operation of a workgroup or team. Suddenly, product shipments could be confirmed or seminar attendance booked, all instantly, and all without requiring a permanent human coordinator. What is now becoming obvious is that the same principle applied on a large scale can change the fundamental operation of entire organizations of any size.

How large a central staff would it take to track credit card transactions on a global scale, assuming that it could even be done at all with a totally manual system? In fact, imagine a world without telephones, telegraphs, or computers; would a modern credit card system even be possible? The entire basis of the system is that banks, which are essentially lending money each time a credit card is used, can track the exact, up-to-the-minute spending of each individual credit card holder and know immediately every time he makes a purchase and whether he is over his limit. The database, coupled to the network, is what makes this possible.

The challenge of building a database, though, goes even further than that. A credit card database, although large, is still relatively simple because it deals with essentially a single application. The dream, expressed clearly in the early '70s, went further: every organization, big or small, could organize all its data so that all data would always be up-to-date, and all data could be related to all other data when needed.

Imagine that you're starting a new division in an existing company. Perhaps our video-tape store is branching out to computer games. Historically, even though you're part of a single company, because you're starting a new division, you would start from scratch with your own computer, your own applications, your own customer list, and so on. However, your company designed its database in the way we've been talking about. As a result, the first thing you find is that the customer list is available to you, not just as a set of mailing-list labels, but in more powerful ways. In building your business plan, you combine data in interesting new ways, considering information, never used extensively before, about video customers' families and the number of children they have. This information is critical in a game-oriented business. As you start to conduct market research, learning more about those family structures, the data you collect becomes available to others as well, through the database, and as a result the marketing department starts special mailings focusing on children's movies. Later, as you build some special software to check out your games, you are still linked to the common customer tables so that when customers move, have privileges revoked, or enter complaints, your new system automatically is part of all that. After getting your new division off the ground, on looking back you find that, through the common database, application development proceeded more quickly, with fewer problems and more powerful results than any of your past experience would have predicted. A compelling picture if we can only do it.

Summarized here are the core principles of the database revolution:

1. *Information as the center:* Applications should be designed around the database, not the other way around. The data itself is a key corporate resource, common to all departments.

2. *Eliminate redundancy:* Information should always be stored in only a single place in the database. In that way, changes can be made only one time, conflicting copies of the same information are intrinsically impossible, and space is used in the most efficient fashion possible. When information of all kinds is stored in only a single place, all information can be linked or related to all other kinds of information, making the database a supremely flexible tool for supporting company-wide analysis and planning.

3. *Source data capture:* Information should be entered into the database as soon as it is generated. In that way, the information is in its single, nonredundant, correct place from the beginning, the information is immediately available organization-wide, and changes can automatically be reflected immediately in the (only) correct copy of the data. This means entering both new information and changes to information immediately at the source where the information first enters the organization. By implication, people who work with information should have a terminal or personal computer so that they can enter information into the computerized database as soon as they receive or handle that information.

The computer is the brain, the network is the nervous system, and the database is the memory of the organization. By providing everybody with a terminal, all information becomes completely up-to-date, available to all other users, and consistently organized. Easier said than done.

In an important sense, the database became a holy grail, a religious period in the development of computer systems, that is still with us today. In the early '70s, computer professionals and business people alike committed themselves to the crusade of developing complete database systems for their organizations. The dream, the vision, still swimming in front of all our eyes, is of complete information, completely available, and completely consistent corporate wide. Why should this be so hard to do?

THE IMPOSSIBLE DREAM: DREAMING IT THROUGH THE YEARS

Database as a concept continues to be important; it is one of the keys to transforming personal computers and networks from personal appliances to empowerment engines for teams and organizations. At the same time, the concept of database, as understood for the last 20 years, has turned out in many ways to be a dead end. On both the technical and conceptual level, it is important for us to understand why it's a dead end and how it fits into the new big picture that will carry us through the next 20 years.

TRAVELING IN TIME: DATABASE PAST, DATABASE PRESENT, DATABASE FUTURE

Imagine an experiment based on time travel. In this experiment, we recruit from large organizations a sample of 100 chief information officers (CIOs) who have held their jobs for the last 20 years. (As an aside, one reason we have to imagine this experiment is that the very job we're talking about — CIO — is very risky and that the average tenure of a CIO today is only about 18 months; so finding 100 such people would be tough, even if time travel weren't a problem.) Having found our 100 MIS chiefs, we interview them every 10 years. Over 20 years, this means three sets of interviews: one at the beginning, one after 10 years, and a final interview after 20 years. In our interview, we concentrate primarily on one topic: database. We ask how they feel about the concept, what they're doing to implement one, and how they feel about their progress.

Before starting the interviews, be clear about the fact that I'm talking about ideals here. In the early '70s, many companies were convinced that *database* was about *database technology*. If the company *bought* a database, an expensive proposition because the software cost a lot, then by definition they had obviously implemented *database*. Not so, the idealists would say. By definition, any company with more than one database, in fact, had no databases! The whole point, as we've already seen, is to store all information in a *single* database, with no information stored more than once, and with the help of the database *technology*, to create an environment where all information is consistent and nonredundant and can be combined with all other information. So it's that ideal that we're going to explore with our 100 CIOs.

> *1970:* Everybody is excited. *Harvard Business Review* just conceptually described the database. Finally, a computer topic that senior management can get really excited about. After 20 years of constantly increasing computer expenditures, management is starting to question how long the organization could keep spending more on hardware, software, and application development. And suddenly, because database implies competitive advantage, it becomes critical to implement a corporate database, including the network required for source data capture. Best of all, management and users are pushing for aggressive use of the technology instead of simply focusing on potential cost reductions.

Ask any CIO in 1970 or in the first half of that decade and there would have been no question that implementing a corporate database was on the very top of her priority list. Tough? Yes. But nobody would have questioned the ability to complete the task within about ten years. And after the task was done, all CIOs would have insisted, that pesky problem of the darn president getting conflicting answers from different vice presidents would finally go away. A pesky problem, but a nice litmus test too.

> *1980:* Our 100 CIOs are a little more subdued, particularly when it comes to database. Not excited, but perhaps quietly optimistic. After ten years, no large organization has a corporate database in the sense I've described. Everybody still has data stored in lots of different places. Presidents still receive conflicting answers all the time. And combining data from different parts of the company in a way that produces meaningful answers is generally still as hard as ever. Furthermore, even in the more limited ways that databases have been implemented, the raw technology has created many challenges. The software *is* expensive, and programmers *do* have trouble learning how to use it. And worst of all, data in a database is not really any easier for users to get at than all that old data that was in separate files. So why any optimism at all?

First of all, everybody — technologists, managers, users, and consultants — all agree that database, the concept and vision, is more important than ever. Ten years of increasing computerization has just demonstrated how valuable information can be when it's up-to-date and available. And the more information that's stored in the computer, the more information kept on-line, the more important organizing that information in a flexible and useable fashion becomes. So management, although less idealistic, is even more anxious, and perhaps patiently prepared to do what it takes to end up with a usable database rather than a collection of computer files. So in 1980, CIOs are contrite but determined.

Second, having spent the better part of ten years chasing this dream, a plan appears to be in sight. That decade of experience *has* generated a lot of wisdom. Database technology has matured, and newer approaches, particularly relational databases (discussed in the next chapter) seem to offer a lot of hope. Finally, the importance of database *design* — the very topic we've already spent so much time on — has been recognized. New techniques for representing the design of a database — which we'll look at next — have been developed. Software tools have even been proposed to help database designers in their difficult task — CASE (computer-aided software engineering) — so maybe the computer can even help in the very task of figuring out how to use it better. Put all these pieces together, and CIOs feel somewhat humbled by their task and quietly optimistic that the *next* decade is the one in which their corporate databases will finally be built. Good thing too, because there's really not much choice if we're to both use computers effectively and manage our organizations well. In fact, the one scary thought in all of this is what if somebody else gets there first?

> *1990:* An uncomfortable place to be — our interview room. Nobody wants to talk about database, not really. Has anybody built the corporate database we described? If you're talking about large organizations, in 1990, or even 1995, nobody has yet built a database that is completely consistent, duplicates no data, and answers all questions. Presidents still get conflicting answers every day in virtually every company of any size.

Perhaps building such a database is no longer important? Do our CIOs rank building the corporate database as one of their top ten priorities? Interesting question, but the answers are even more interesting. Nobody wants to admit that it's a top ten priority. Yet, nobody wants to say it's not! What do we get in putting together our list of top ten priorities? Nine straightforward goals and one goal that's not *not* a top ten priority. That's right, a double negative: a priority so important that none of our CIOs will leave it off the list, and yet a priority which elicits so much frustration that not one of the hundred will put it on the list. How can this be?

In most areas of computer technology, progress is constant and rapid, and, over time, almost all tricky problems seem to solve themselves if they're just left alone for long enough. Not so, apparently, in the case of database. Here's a case where we've had a common dream for over two decades and spent large amounts of time and money, with regular infusions of new religious icons to help light the way, and yet we're still just as stubbornly as far as ever from having unified, consistent, useful corporate databases. Is there an explanation?

It turns out that the answer is yes. There are three reasons that building our vision of the corporate database has proven so difficult:

◆ *Data modeling is hard:* As I discuss in the next section, building a complete data model that represents all the information used by an entire large corporation is very hard, maybe even impossible.

✦ *Performance is a real problem:* Paradoxically, the very things that are most appropriate for designing databases to be consistent, flexible, and accurate are the very things that make those same databases complex and slow to process. As a result, once MIS professionals understood the very techniques that would best lead to highly consistent database, those same professionals were forced to recommend against using those techniques because of the performance problems they create.

✦ *The basic model is wrong:* One of the main tenets of the database crusade was the creation of a *single* and therefore *central* database for the entire organization. The idea that it was a net plus to have a single *database* turns out to be exactly the problem. Both from a perspective of *design feasibility* and from a perspective of *performance feasibility*, what we want is not one database but many. And then we want a mechanism for integrating those databases, tying them together, and providing senior management with a corporate-wide view. Even more to the point though, we need something more than just the database at the center of our world to pull all the pieces together. We need a second Copernican revolution — a new concept that builds on top of databases and provides a framework for building large, distributed systems that function in an integrated fashion.

✦ *Cooperating components:* As you'll see later in the book, that second revolution revolves around the concept of *cooperating components*. Large systems need to be decomposed into smaller, manageable systems called *components*. Each of these components, or sometimes sets of components, will have databases at their center. But the system as a whole will no longer have a single, large monolithic database at the center.

✦ *Two levels of databases are needed:* If there is no single central database, how does senior management get an overall perspective on the business? It turns out that providing that corporate-wide view does not mean that every last piece of operational data has to be in the one universal repository. In the final ironic twist of fate, as we start to think about empowered employees and self-managed teams, the last thing we want is a monolithic database. Instead, what we need as a new vision is the idea of a federation of databases, each internally consistent and all tied together by yet another database part of the federation, designed to meet the needs of senior management. The federation of databases fits in perfectly with the complementary vision of designing around cooperating components. Families of components will revolve around particular databases. The components in total form the overall business system, which is built on the basis of functional specialization and cooperation. And the databases managed by those various components form the data federation that feeds the higher level database that is watching the business as a whole.

WHEN A SPARROW FALLS, DOES THE CHIEF EXECUTIVE NEED TO KNOW?

Finally, we're in a position to articulate a database vision for the '90s. In the '60s, there was no concept of database; the application was king. In the '70s and '80s, after realizing the central importance of data, building that corporate database became the central unifying vision for every organization big and small, at least when it came to computers. How did the concept of *database* become translated into the concept of *central database*?

A database serves two major purposes:

+ The database supports the operation of the company: it tracks orders, inventory, customer addresses, payments, invoices, shipments, and all the other millions of operational records that define the nervous system of the organization.

+ The database provides a model of the organization's health and functioning that supports the analysis and decision making that defines much of management.

The combination of these *two* functions creates the apparent need for a single central database.

How closely should these two functions be linked in the structure of the database? One function, what we called the operational function, can also be defined in terms of transactional applications that operate with *realtime* data. That is, when checking the status of a shipment, we want to know where that shipment is now in realtime. The other function, the one that supports analysis and decision making, is often called *decision support*. One key aspect of decision support applications is that they do *not* operate with realtime data. Suppose that you're doing a sensitivity analysis to determine whether to raise the price on a new product line. Often this type of analysis is called *what if* because the question being answered is generally of the form what if . . . . An intrinsic characteristic of what if-analysis is that the same question is asked several times, with a single factor (in this case, the price) being changed; then the results, perhaps sales volume, are compared to see if a higher price led to lower sales. Here's the catch: suppose that you used *realtime* data in your what-if analysis. The data would keep changing underneath you all the time. Obviously, this would invalidate the whole point of your decision support system. So decision support applications, as compared to operational applications, not only don't work with realtime data, they also *can't* work with realtime data.

Historically, an important part of the database dream was the idea that analytic and transactional databases should be linked and should be one and the same. The idea behind this goal is simple, even if it's wrong. Analytic databases support managers and decision makers of all types. At the top, ideally, the president, asking that infamous question of her vice presidents, receives consistent answers and then makes decisions that affect the organization for years to come. And, *of course*, if the decisions are *that* important, they should be based on the best possible information. Without strong reasons to the contrary, it's only natural to assume that the freshest, the most up-to-date, the most *realtime* information is the best. The very term *realtime* implies that anything else is *non-realtime* and who would want information based on time that is somehow not real? So from the beginning of the database crusade, an important holy grail has been the construction of decision support systems, supporting the analytic needs of senior management, built in a way where the information in those decision support systems is based on constantly refreshed, always up-to-date information. To put this in particularly sharp focus, one of the metaphors frequently used to describe the resulting system has the chief executive of an organization sitting in an office that has a *dashboard*, just like the dashboard in a car, and by picking the right set of key indicators to display on that dashboard, he's able to run the company in a completely dynamic fashion.

What an appealing vision. Really, no sarcasm intended or implied. Picture the huge manufacturing company with factories world-wide and a sales force in every country. Nonetheless, the president of the company, in considering which products to build over the next ten years, is able to keep every sale, and every complaint, and every cost in mind all the time. Every decision is based on every piece of data known company wide, right up to the very second the decision is made. To use a biblical analogy: no sparrow falls without the senior decision maker knowing and taking that fall into account in his or her planning. Neat, but is it what we want, even if it could be built? The answer is no, it's the opposite of what we want, and the answer revolves around the role of time in running an organization.

Why does it even matter whether analytic and operational databases are the same or linked? Because the primary reason for wanting to have all the organization's data in a single large database is precisely to make this linkage possible. If you believe that eventually all decisions made by the chief executive should be related to the most up-to-date possible version of every piece of data company-wide, then the only way to do this is to have a single, consistent database. Even if the database is somehow geographically distributed, from a design perspective, the only way to link the executive's dashboard control panel to totally realtime operational data is to have all the parts of the database, company-wide, linked to each other. And it is this requirement that sets up those impossible design requirements. The conceptually impossible task of rationalizing the entire company-wide information structure and the operationally impossible task of building a computer system powerful enough to link all the information at one time both stem from this single ultimate need. If it turns out that this requirement is not only inappropriate, but even more ironically, the opposite of what we want, we can revisit the whole issue of how databases are built (and perhaps create a situation where CIOs will put database back on their top ten list in 2000 and even report their first successes). So let's see how operational and analytic databases compare.

OPERATIONAL AND ANALYTIC DATABASES: TWO SIDES OF A COIN

Table 9-1 compares some of the characteristics of the two types of databases. First, a *transactional database* by definition deals with up-to-the-minute, even up-to-the-second data. Did the order ship? Is *The African Queen* still in, or did somebody rent it out? Did you receive my check? How much do we owe you? All these questions are meaningful only if the answers are based on completely up-to-date information. If you are told that *The African Queen* is still available, but it was rented out just a minute ago, what kind of a customer happiness situation does that create? Of course at some level a database can never be totally up-to-date. If a customer takes a videotape off the shelves, intending to rent it, the database can capture the rental only when the tape shows up at the checkout stand. We can't solve that problem, but we can guarantee that the instant the tape is registered, even before the customer's other tapes are entered, before he leaves the store, that tape is marked as unavailable. That way, *operational decisions* about availability, customer status, and so on, are made based on up-to-the-minute data.

Table 9-1   Comparing the Two Types of Databases

Transactional	Analytic
Up-to-the-minute	Up to period end
Constantly changing	Snapshots
Detailed	Aggregated
Specific	Summarized
Local	Global
Recent	Historical

Analytic data is never up-to-date. Up-to-date in a management context means up to the last month, the last quarter, or the last year. Sometimes in a sales management environment up-to-date may mean up to the week or even up to the day, but never up to the minute. Why? By definition, analytic data is used to analyze patterns. Patterns virtually always involve comparisons, and those comparisons are always based on periods of time — a month, a quarter, a year, a week, or even a day. Focusing on unchanging periods of time allows comparisons to be made in a consistent fashion. Who is the most productive sales rep in each region? Compare sales figures to see who sold the most that month.

Imagine if you used up-to-date data to make the comparison. The sales rep whose sales you summed up last would always have an advantage; he or she would have a chance to have just one more sale counted in the total. Or suppose that you want to predict the effect of a price increase. You increase the price in one region but not in another and then compare sales for a quarter. Fine, once the quarter is over. Suppose that you did the analysis, though, during the middle of the quarter, using the constantly changing operational data. Suppose, in the process of doing the analysis, that you compare sales for several different product lines, looking at different customer types and different channels of distribution. Each different type of analysis involves a new report run. Because you're using live data, though, each new report run includes more and different sales and customer data than the one before. Obviously, the various reports simply can't be compared with each other, unless you wait until after the quarter is over and use the data after it's stopped changing. And, of course, that's the point: analytic databases are always based on *periodic data*. Up-to-date for an analytic database means last period's data. Of course, everybody wants last month's data the day after the month is over; still, once they get it, nobody wants it to change.

All of this brings us to the next row in our comparison table. Transactional data is constantly changing. That's why customers keep calling to find out if that part has become available or if their payment was finally received. Analytic data never changes; it's based on snapshots of the database. Just like a photographic snapshot captures frozen moments of time, analytic databases capture frozen cross-sections of the organization's data that remain static after they're captured. So when we slice and dice our payments data to determine whether frequent customers pay more regularly than occasional ones, no matter how many times we crawl through the database, picking records, computing sums, and doing comparisons, the data we work with will always be the same. That way, an earlier result can be compared directly and meaningfully with a later one. In a transactional database, multiple results *should be different*; in an analytic database, multiple results *must be the same*.

When a customer has a question, it's his data he cares about, and usually at a pretty detailed level. Did a particular shipment leave; is a specific tape in stock; how much, exactly will a given repair cost? When a question arises about a bill, the customer wants to discuss the charge, one line item at a time. As a result, operational databases can often be divided up on geographical, functional, and demographic lines. A warehouse needs the inventory counts for the stock it holds, the personnel records for the local drivers, and the bills of lading for shipments delivered by only those drivers. Finally, although operational data is quite detailed and specific, it is also generally quite recent. Of course, it is completely up-to-date — that's the point — but it also doesn't go very far back in history. For instance, a warehouse may retain shipment data for

30 to 60 days, but try tracking a shipment from two years ago. Generally, once the books are closed, which happens every month in most companies, transactional data can't be changed anymore, and most operational systems don't keep that data. Operational data is detailed, specific, local, and recent.

In contrast, analytic data is based on aggregates. How much did each salesperson sell last month? Which regions are growing and which are shrinking? When asking a question like this, nobody cares, or wants to know, about specific orders or line items. The information is first aggregated by region, sales rep, product, or customer. This immediately implies that the data is at least regional and generally global in scope. The whole point of an analytic database is to facilitate comparisons and this in turn implies keeping data from major parts of the company all in one place; no geographical partitioning here. In making comparisons, time is just as important a variable as space. Analytic databases frequently keep data going back months, quarters, years, and even decades. Obviously, to make it possible to deal with such large amounts of data, aggregation is critical: average sales per sales rep, growth rate by region, and so on. An analytic database is in many ways the opposite of a transactional one; the data is general, aggregated, summarized, and global, and it stretches far back into history.

Even at this level, you can see why operational and analytic requirements lead to distinctly different kinds of databases. The ideal operational database would be locally placed, tracking data by the second and providing a constantly up-to-date picture of its local world. The analytic database, on the other hand, would be at the center of the organization, providing product managers, analysts, and executives with a global picture based on world-wide data stretching back into history, replacing the realtime details of the analytic database with the more general patterns that form the true basis for accurate decisions. All of this raises the possibility that the transactional and analytic database may be separate entities. However, looking deeper shows that they must be separate.

THE RELATIVISTIC EFFECTS OF EXTENDED TIME

What are the real differences between the transactional and analytic databases? Space and time; but is it really both? Most transactions are localized in space, but it's not hard to imagine larger orders on a national basis that could just as easily not be very localized. So space is not a real differentiator. Time, though, is a very different matter.

In 1917, Albert Einstein first proposed that at high speeds, objects would experience time differently from how they would ordinarily. As a result, modeling the universe requires a variety of corrections to handle the varying time metrics affecting objects traveling at various speeds. If time-related effects are not corrected for, then our picture of the universe and all predictions based on those pictures will be wrong. Time plays just as many tricks on organizations as it does on the physical universe. And the primary operational characteristic of an analytic database is its ability to correct for time-related effects.

Which advertising campaigns were the most effective at getting customers into our video store? Compare them all over the period of the past year, evaluating rental volumes in dollars against the amount spent on the ad. How do we account for changes in our rental prices while doing this? Starting March 1, weekend rentals increased from $2.50 to $3.00. If we ignore this event, any ad we ran at the end of February will look spectacularly effective; after all, revenues increased very quickly that first weekend of March. But the increase had nothing to do with our ad? True, but how do we account for that? One answer: keep the price constant.

Do price increases have an effect on rental volumes? Compare sales before and after each price increase. What happens when we find out that our system, to allow us to measure advertising effectively, no longer allows us to see price changes; how do we even ask this question?

Which department in the store is most profitable: adult movies, children's films, or the general category? Suppose that we reorganized the departments halfway through last year; does that mean we can't analyze profitability for more than six months because the data from before the reorganization can't be compared with the data from after? Perhaps before the reorganization we had six departments and now we have nine? How do we account for this?

How about seasonal variations? Normally, a store does up to half of its business in the six weeks before Christmas. When analyzing a new sales commission plan, we want to correct for this seasonality, essentially subtracting the magnifying effects of the Christmas season so that any sales increases we see are caused by the new commission plan, not by the season. At the same time, if we are doing a straight dollar forecast, we want to add seasonality back in; otherwise, our forecast will come up short.

As products flow through the sales channel, the same units are often sold multiple times: first to a national distributor, then to a regional distributor, then to a local store, and finally to the final consumer. Depending on the type of analysis we do, special provisions are required to ensure that we don't either miss sales or count sales more than once.

All of these questions revolve around the effects of time. When we're dealing with time, two factors critically affect the design of the analytic database:

✦ Accurately dealing with time-related effects is very expensive; therefore, we need to look for ways to build in those corrections in advance so that the corrections don't have to be applied every time a question is asked.

✦ There is no one correct way of dealing with time. Instead a good analytic database must provide a number of corrective models in advance, and the user must be provided with guidance so that he or she selects the world/time view that is correct for the type of problem being solved.

For example, seasonality, inflation, regional variations, and price histories (price changes, adjustments) are all time-related functions. A good analytic model will maintain different world views to deal with each of these effects. Correcting for inflation is relatively expensive because an accurate adjustment will vary according to both the commodity and the market segment. However, after an adjustment technique has been chosen, the aggregates stored in the analytic database can automatically be adjusted for any combination of inflation, seasonality, regional growth rates, and so on. Similarly, the database can be set up so that one world view masks price changes, allowing comparisons to be made independent of the actual price, and another world view reflects the actual prices, as they varied through time.

The reason this is so critical is that making these adjustments turns out to be hugely expensive. For example, tracking price changes is very complex indeed. For one thing, prices generally change in a very unpredictable fashion: some product lines have stable prices, and others are forced to react to market pressure frequently. Oil prices, for example, change by the minute, while electricity is regulated and therefore changes on an annual basis. Making things worse, a price change itself is hardly a discrete event. First, the change is announced in phases; big customers find out first, then resellers, and so on. Even after a price change is announced, various preexisting conditions cause it to dribble out in stages and phases. As a result, tracking the effects of price changes accurately, as larger aggregates are computed, can require that virtually every line item of every order be processed. When this factor is combined with changes in product line composition, inflation, and other factors, the cost of rebuilding an analytic database to deal with a new model for time-related effects can be huge.

Fortunately, all of this can be dealt with very effectively in the design of an analytic database. The key concepts in planning for this design are straightforward but call for careful planning and preparation:

1. *Recognize the complexity:* Plan to deal with it by designing the analytic database very carefully. Everybody knows that transactional databases require careful design; it is often assumed that the analytic or informational database somehow falls out of that original design. Not true: designing an analytic database is at least as complex, and quite different, from designing an operational database.

2. *Confront time-related questions:* Recognize extended time as a critical design issue from the beginning and start compiling a list of difficult questions to be dealt with. The issues will be more business-oriented than technical. How will price changes be represented? What about changes in product lines and organizations over time? How will product be tracked through the design, manufacturing, selling, and accounting pipelines? What about seasonality, inflation, and regionally adjusted growth rates?

3. *Recognize at least two answers to each time-related question:* Corrections must be made for price changes so that some types of analysis can be done in a price-independent fashion; at the same time, the database also has to

provide another perspective on the same data where price changes are reflected in the data and where the price is directly visible as an analytic variable. In the same way, virtually every time-related factor has to be factored in so that it is both factored out and factored in, depending on the perspective chosen.

4. *Analyze the types of problems to be solved to pick a manageable number of perspectives:* This is the real key to developing a useable analytic database: understanding how the database will really be used. In theory there are dozens of time-related variables, and users can combine those in hundreds of complex ways. In practice, a small number, often fewer than two dozen, of carefully chosen perspectives will provide users with the views they need without requiring them to even be aware of most of the time-related variables or distortions.

The correct recognition of the effect of time and the ways in which it distorts our world views as we take longer and longer perspectives on organizational histories turns out to be both a complicator and a simplifier. On the one hand, dealing with all the time-related effects forces us to design a sophisticated and elaborate analytic database to serve the needs of senior decision makers. Building such a database is very expensive. At the same time, once the need for such a database becomes clear, it also becomes quite clear that that database must be different from the operational database. The analytic database is derived from the operational data. Of course, where else would we get our raw data? At the same time the transformations done to convert that raw data into usable form are so complex and expensive that we can't afford to do them on the fly. And even if we could afford it, the effort would be useless because by definition analytic databases are based on historical snapshots anyway, so dynamic derivation adds no value.

When we recognize that having a separate analytic database, far from being a necessary evil, is, *au contraire,* actually a virtue, all of a sudden the path to having a complete and viable database strategy becomes clear.

Not Dictatorship or Anarchy, but Federation

Historically, central databases have been necessary to serve the informational needs of the organization as a whole. At the same time, users with analytic requirements have resented those central databases because they've been slow, hard to use, and inflexible. Central databases, in a real sense, are equivalent to dictatorship: a controlled environment with high consistency but no individual freedom. The introduction of personal computers and their personal database models brought with them freedom and anarchy. Product managers could suddenly build their own databases and manipulate them with total abandon, but the data they worked with was typically limited, inaccurate, and intrinsically not shareable even within their own workgroup.

The official response to this situation, since 1970, has been the database crusade. If we only get to finish our big central database, then everybody will have a consistent set of data to work with. From an operational perspective, the bigger organizations discovered pretty quickly that a single central database could not keep up with the load. And even in a small organization, a central database certainly can't keep up with the decision support needs of analysts, managers, and executives.

Until recently, nonetheless, nobody questioned the idea that the big central database was the eventual solution; it was just taking longer than anybody had thought possible. In the meantime, companies worldwide were dealing with the present by splitting their databases anyway. On the operational front, there are some compelling advantages to distributed processing; the issue right now is how to build such systems. Even more interesting, though, is the splitting that's been happening on the analytic front.

Almost from the beginning, most organizations have found that separating the analytic and operational databases was the better part of valor. Early operational databases such as IMS, IDMS, Total, and ADABAS were very fast and reliable, but were almost unuseable for sophisticated and flexible analysis. Later, relational databases such as DB/2, Oracle, Ingres, and Sybase were excellent at supporting flexible analysis, but just couldn't keep up with the workload associated with the operational environment. So the answer was simple: split the data into at first two, later three layers. First, keep the operational data in transactionally oriented databases. Even today with the incredible growth of Oracle and other relational database vendors, it is still true that over 75 percent of operational data in big companies is in the older, nonrelational databases. Second, keep an appropriately transformed copy of the data in a relational database to support the organization's analytic needs; that's how Oracle got to be a $1 billion company. And third, make it easy for individual users to tap directly into those relational databases and transform the data even more to meet their personal and team needs. Although this split has existed in fact, for all 20 years of the database era, until very recently it was viewed as a necessary evil. One day, so the story went, when either relational databases got fast enough, transactional databases became flexible enough, or something new came on the scene, we'd all reach the promised land: all data would be in a single database and all decisions would be based on totally up-to-the-minute data. All data would be consistent, all redundancy would be eliminated, and all CIOs would stop being depressed.

In the same historical saga, the main proponent of the central, dictatorial approach was IBM. In part, this is the reason that the company, their computers, and most of all, their databases have been referred to as *Big Blue*. About five years ago, though, IBM also recognized that more than a necessary evil, separation of church and state may actually be a virtue. And thus, the *Information Warehouse* was born. An *Information Warehouse* is exactly the kind of analytic database described in the previous section. The term, as usual with IBM terms, is wonderful and terrible. Wonderful because in many ways it's immediately understandable. And terrible because it makes the problem of building one sound either too trivial or too simple. Still, count small blessings:

announcement of the goodness of Information Warehouses made the concept of analytic databases official and common.

Analytic database, Information Warehouse, or whatever, the concept is important for much more than itself. It is important because it is the key to understanding how to make corporate databases real. It tells us how to eliminate the three killer problems that kept those CIOs so frustrated for so long:

✦ *Data modeling is hard:* Building a data model for a single, all-knowing, all-encompassing database, operational and analytic all at once, is hard; in fact, it's impossible for big companies. Building data models for a series of smaller databases, though, is very doable. Operational databases can now be decoupled from each other as they are distributed out in support of the self-managed team. Analytic databases pull information together from the operational databases, but as we've seen, those analytic databases need highly different data models anyway. So keep the data model separate because you have to, and you'll have a data model you can actually build.

✦ *Performance is a real problem:* Performance is a problem in a centralized environment. It isn't a problem at all in a distributed environment. Both the operational systems and the analytic systems are distributed. Replication makes it possible to have enough departmental analytic systems to give everybody snappy performance. Everybody can run as many dynamic queries as they want. And because the workstations are now supported by the shared analytic databases, users pull data off the departmental systems to start with, but then slice and dice it in their own machines. Shared common data and unlimited horsepower, both in one solution. Because the analytic data is *directly derived* from the operational database and because the analytical database is carefully designed with consistency in mind, the president actually has a chance of getting common answers to common questions, even if she allows more than one vice president to come to the meeting.

✦ *The basic model is wrong:* The answer is neither dictatorship nor anarchy, but rather federation. The local transactional systems can be modified by the self-managed teams — freedom — but only as long as common business rules are not violated — control and coordination. The individual product manager can build his own database and sort it every three minutes — freedom — but the underlying data comes from a departmental analytic database where views are carefully constructed to ensure consistency and correct handling of time-related distortions — control and coordination. In this database world of the future, we have not one database, but thousands. Even the *central* databases, which play the key coordination role, are not really central, only linked. And all that linking leads to a new concept: federated databases. Not dictatorship, not anarchy, but federation.

DATABASE: THE POSSIBLE DREAM

Database *is* what computers are all about. Not the *only* thing they're all about, but one of *the* things they are all about. A well-designed database is a model of the organization. The information contained in it allows a manager to assess the company's health, predict the future, and solve problems before they occur. If the network is the nervous system of an organization, the database is its memory. And, like any well-organized memory, a properly constructed database allows the organization to keep its promises: prompt service, minimized extra steps for customers and employees, and courtesy. It is no accident that politicians and salespeople develop trust by making a point of remembering birthdays, names, and promises. In the same way, an organization that can remember all the details of its interactions with people — insiders and outsiders — will be an organization that builds trust over time. Databases are the key then to both health and trust.

Until now all the components we've talked about — clients, servers, networks, LANs, and mainframes — have been components we buy and use. We build on them, but essentially, as components, we use them. The database is different. As a technology, we buy it. However, the real meaning of the term *database* implies something we build, not buy. Passing through this chapter means we've crossed the divide from buying components to starting to design systems that use those components. The database is one of the three central components we design to have a complete client/server system. We'll look at the other two — processes and applications — later. The point is that you are now firmly on the way to understanding what that design is all about.

The dream of a corporate-wide database has excited executives, users, and computer professionals alike for over 20 years. Until recently, that dream has been viewed as a holy crusade: essential but unattainable. The tension between the need for understandable data models and the need for a single, totally consistent global data model has been crushing. The parallel tension between the need for local tailoring and individual freedom stacked up against the need to eliminate redundancy and have central control appeared to have created a complete impasse. Neither solution turns out to be correct. By recognizing the essential distinction between operational and transactional databases, we find a way to synthesize two apparently contradictory objectives and needs. The fundamental philosophical difference between the realtime nature of the transactional system and the extended time nature of the decision support system is the key. Because analytic databases are based on frozen snapshots of historical data anyway, there's no reason to have them dynamically computed from the realtime data on demand, even if that were possible to do. And the cost of such computation makes the linkage impossible in any case. As soon as this separation is recognized as a virtue, not just a necessary evil but a sign of IT maturity and an absolute virtue, then the need for a central database goes away. In fact, the central database is then seen as leading to less, not more, consistency.

The database vision of the '90s is, then, the vision of federated databases. Consolidation and consistency, yes. Coordination and control, yes. Personal freedom and local tailoring, also yes. As Winston Churchill said, *not the end of the end, not even the beginning of the end, but the end of the beginning.* After 20 years, hopefully, we have a plan for finally building a database that works. And the reason we can hope that it works is that we have not a bigger picture of database, but for the first time, a picture of how to build that bigger picture out of smaller pictures, each of which we know we can build.

From an even broader perspective, the database vision has driven the design of large applications for the last 25 years. We are now in the beginning stages of the next revolution as big in its own way as databases were in the early '70s. The new revolution asks us to think about applications as sets of cooperating components. In a way, it shifts the focus of design back from being highly data-centered to being much more functionally centered, without actually asking us to give up the benefits of the database view of the world. The beauty of the concept of federated databases is that it allows us to take everything we've worked so hard to accomplish in terms of database-centered design and transform it directly into the world of cooperating components. Federated databases and cooperating components — two sides of the same coin.

CHAPTER 10

DATABASE — THE TECHNICAL LANDSCAPE

The preceding chapter discussed database as a technical and a business concept. I hope that in the process, you understood that the database has been one of the central philosophical forces driving the design of large (and small) information systems for the past 20 years. This concept informs the computing community's view of both why people want computer systems in the first place and how computers should be built to meet those needs. One of the sneaky little complexities surrounding the database concept is that it is not one concept at all. The database concept is actually three things:

✦ A shared engine providing a shared repository of coordinated, controlled data

✦ A tool for retrieving, analyzing, and displaying that data

✦ A broader model for representing the state of an organization in both the short and long term

The conceptual background provided in Chapter 9 is crucial. If you don't understand the three core database concepts, you won't understand why computers are critical to the future of businesses.

Beyond the core concepts, database also embodies quite a bit of technology, and that's what this chapter is all about. I'll discuss quite a few technical terms: relational databases, network databases, hierarchical databases, object-oriented tools, query languages, database design techniques, and distributed database technology. These terms — and more — come up every time the subject of databases arises. Of course, it's impossible in the course of a single chapter (or even a single book) to completely say all there is to say about databases. It is, however, possible to absorb a relatively complete technical framework for participating in database discussions without acquiring a Ph.D. and without becoming a database programmer. That's what this chapter provides.

Understanding Databases: If You Don't Have a Religion, Get One

Computers will soon change society more than they have at any other time, and databases will play a major role in that revolutionary change. Many computer professionals, however, will readily admit that they barely understand what databases are all about. This lack of knowledge is partly due to the confusion between the three meanings of the word *database*: shared engine, personal tool, and organizational model. But there's more confusion than just that. For example, if you question a computer professional about his or her views on the issue of relational versus object-oriented databases, you'll quickly discover that nobody seems to have all the answers. The numerous creators of the leading database technologies each claim to impart mystical and magical powers that can be attained only by following the one true path: their own, of course. What's more, these magical approaches are always shrouded in arcane terms that make the average user feel ignorant; that feeling of ignorance leads directly to fear and confusion.

Confusion? Fear? Mystery? Magic? Is this the right book? Surely I can't be talking about computer databases and computer professionals? After all, the computer is the stronghold of the rational, obsessively logical programmer, right? Everything is reducible to ones and zeros, so the story goes; can it be true that these nerds, propeller heads, analysts, and programmers have allowed their safe scientific domain to be invaded by irrationality?

The invasion is real, and it has created some very real problems. The simplest way to understand these problems is to compare the computer world with that other world where analysts are common: the financial world.

According to the stereotype, financial analysts are coldly logical. They live in a world of models, just like programmers. They analyze numbers, charts, and patterns; they create sophisticated financial vehicles. Ironically enough, almost no group of individuals is more susceptible to fads and religions than financial analysts. The reason is simple: accurately understanding and predicting the market is so difficult that nobody can do it, but analysts are evaluated based on their ability to perform this impossible task well. So whenever gurus emerge who appear to offer an approach that can improve predictive performance, everybody rushes to follow their advice.

The stories of financial gurus and their effects on the market are legendary. First, the master has a small following. Some articles and news stories soon follow. New investors, eager for a quick return, beg to have their money managed. Perhaps a newsletter gets published. Television talk shows and infomercials begin to spread the word. Suddenly, every move the prophet makes is magnified by the thousands of imitators and observers world-wide. People begin to wonder if this prophet really did figure out the secret to predicting the future. Finally, it happens: the first big mistake. And two years later, you can't even remember the dethroned king or queen's name, if for no other reason than that you're busy hanging on every word of the next forecaster. Prophets, inexplicable rules and frameworks, donations, mass followings: Am I talking about finances or religion? It's hard to tell the difference.

Software developers have turned out to like, even love, religious movements too. Developing software and building systems that work is difficult. Projects come in late and over budget, and often the completed system is too slow or just doesn't work. The result is unhappy users. Then one day, out of chaos and darkness, the spirit of innovation sweeps over the surface of the waters. It might be new technology or it might be a new way of thinking, but the end result is that everyone jumps on the bandwagon or gets trained to jump on the bandwagon. A new religion is born.

Religion? It's a strong word, but accurate. In 1984, artificial intelligence (AI) was really hot. Supposedly, after years of trying, computer scientists had finally taught computers to learn. By building artificial intelligence into the applications of the future, programming would be eliminated. Software would magically adapt itself to users' needs, and companies would have systems that built themselves — hardly believable today. But for the next five years, the stock market went wild over AI. Seminars on the topic sold out, and the business press had stories to write. Obscure technologies — neural nets, rule-based languages, LISP — were all promoted, and when ordinary computer professionals asked questions, they were pointed in the direction of these unproven tools for the answers. Confused because nobody could explain simply how the new approaches would solve real problems and scared because neural nets, Prolog, and LISP were all genuinely hard to understand, those professionals shrugged and waited.

Recently, the future has been forecast to belong to object-oriented tools. About two years ago, *Business Week* put a picture of a diaper-clad baby on the magazine's front cover and claimed that object-oriented tools would one day enable infants to build complex systems in days and weeks out of prefabricated components. How will this all work? The answer involves polymorphism, a little SmallTalk, and a dash of encapsulation techniques. It's magic, and if you don't already know the secrets, you obviously never will.

All of these approaches have a grain of truth surrounded by a huge dose of hype. The list of the fads is long enough to be legitimately frightening: structured programming, CASE, AI, object-oriented tools, information engineering, relational databases, object databases, and on and on. Each new fad promises to revolutionize the entire process of building applications. Each draws on some complex and supposedly powerful core technology that can't be quickly understood. In addition, the proponents of each fad state emphatically that even though the real underpinnings are too complex to understand, if you take the framework on faith, things will get better soon. Maybe.

To confirm the seemingly magical nature of every new fad, skeptics have developed a common name to describe them all: *silver bullets*. Recall that a silver bullet is the one projectile that can kill a werewolf. Also, in American culture, the Lone Ranger used silver bullets in his trusty six-shooters. A silver bullet is that single powerful technique or technology that will finally provide us with a shining path to better software sooner. Software development is all about religion, silver bullets and all, and that's the problem.

Silver bullets and religious fads represent the voodoo curse that keeps developers and users from a complete understanding of databases. As you'll see later, they also stand between you and a complete understanding of several other important enabling technologies such as design tools, languages, and development approaches in general. To defeat the voodoo curse, you need only rely on common sense.

That's the goal of the remainder of this chapter. You'll explore the technical terms of the database landscape and convert the magical concepts into equally valid commonsense requirements and solutions. By the time you're done, you will develop an understanding of where databases came from, where they are today, and where they're going tomorrow. This understanding will involve precisely the same framework and vocabulary required to deal with the design of future computer systems so that they really meet the needs described in the last chapter.

DATABASE AS ENGINE: TYPES OF DATABASES

Recall that one of the roles a database plays is to provide organization-wide shared access to information in a controlled and coordinated fashion. To take an everyday example, when everything in a system works, only one person at a time can reserve a particular videotape, and when a customer makes a reservation, the tape will truly be available. Recall that a database really becomes interesting and powerful at the point at which it starts to deal with many interrelated files all at once.

The first databases — products such as Total, IDMS, and ADABAS — were built to support the needs of large transaction-processing applications running on mainframes. A typical transaction always worked with many files at one time. For example, renting a car requires the creation of a rental record that is linked to other records involving an automobile, a rental location, a customer, and a salesperson. This one apparently simple transaction involves five interrelated files. To put this car-rental transaction in perspective, a typical transaction in a branch banking environment requires tracking data in over 20 different files.

When customers walk up to the check out desk at a car rental location, the computer will find their names in one file, the automobile's master record in another file, a credit rating in a third file, the salesperson in another, and so on. This example illustrates one of the central problems that must be solved in designing, building, and using databases: relationships.

RELATIONSHIPS: HIERARCHICAL DATABASES

To better understand relationships, you have to start by analyzing the first supposedly complex area of database technology: hierarchical and network-oriented databases. These older approaches to database design are reputedly so complex that normal humans will never understand them. Not true, as it turns out.

Hierarchically organized data is very common. For example, an office organizational chart is a way to represent a *three-level* hierarchy — in other words, one that goes three levels deep. The president is on top, followed by vice presidents (or other managers), and then everybody else. Of course, this kind of hierarchy could just as easily go 7, 10, or 100 levels deep. (Which is not to say that a hierarchical organization is necessarily as healthy with 100 levels.)

You can also display a hierarchy diagrammatically. Figure 10-1 uses lines and boxes to display the hierarchical relationship among the parts of a car. In this case, the complete hierarchy, all the way down to the individual nuts and bolts, would have many levels, perhaps several dozen. This particular type of hierarchy, called a *bill of materials*, or BOM, is famous and even infamous in database and mainframe circles because it occurs so commonly and yet is so difficult to deal with. Figure 10-1 is the top part of a bill of materials for a car.

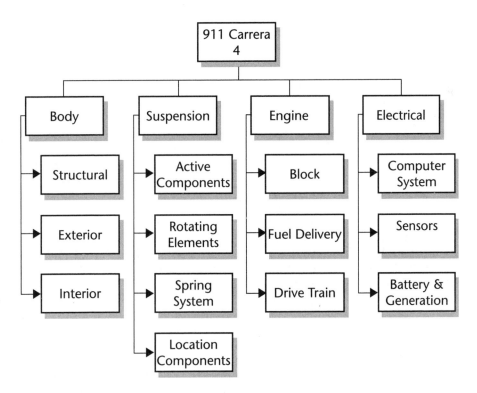

Figure 10-1: A bill of materials displays hierarchical relationships.

Organizational structures, bills of materials, tables of contents for books, project plans, subject classification in a library, agendas for meetings, and many other common collections of data can be represented hierarchically. For this reason, the earliest databases were built to represent hierarchical sets of records.

IBM's first database, IMS, still one of the most heavily used products in large organizations, is designed specifically to handle only hierarchically organized data. Similarly, one of the first products to be marketed by an independent software company was a hierarchical database called Total. Total became not only an important mainframe software product but also the major database for the HP 3000, one of the first business-oriented minicomputers.

Hierarchical databases are not hard to understand at all. They are designed to make it easy to store and retrieve records that can be organized in a strictly hierarchical relationship. A bill of materials, for example, is a snap to represent in a hierarchical database. Similarly, a simple database for customers and orders also is easy. In this case, every customer can have any number of orders, each of which can have any number of specific products, one per line item. Each line item, in turn, may have several shipment records. In the same way, each order may have several invoices and several payments associated with it.

Hierarchical databases are very simple and therefore quite easy to understand, especially if you use them to order information under headings. To understand the limitations of the hierarchical model, you need to develop some tools and concepts for talking about the databases you're building. It's time to move on to *data modeling*.

DATABASE DESIGN: DATA MODELING

Data modeling is one of those scary little terms with a very simple meaning. Just as an architect draws pictures to help clients visualize the house being designed for them, in the same way a database designer draws pictures showing the eventual organization of the information the computer will manage. The architect's pictures are a model of the house; the database designer's pictures are a model of the database. Data modeling, then, is the process of using models, typically in the form of diagrams, to develop and refine the design of an actual database.

Before moving on, I'll warn you that you are getting into an area that many consider the scariest part of the magical kingdom of database, but, as I hope you'll agree in a few pages, it's all very ordinary. I'm talking about *entities*. Entities are basic types of information stored in databases, typically in a single file or table. They are the fundamental units of data that anybody familiar with an organization would recognize when thinking about how a business works. Customers, orders, products, salespeople, and vendors are all eligible to be entities. Relationships, as you already know, are the connections between the parts (records, tables, files) of a database. Entities are the actual data, classified by type, and the relationships show how these types of data relate to each other. When you describe a database in this way, you are talking about an *entity relationship model* of that database. What does one of these ERDs, as they're called for short, look like?

The simple four-box diagram in Figure 10-2 is an entity relationship model of a database. The four entities, each in a box, are Sales Region, Salesperson, Customer, and Order. In a simple database, you might take each of these entities and make them into a database file. Your database would have one file with sales region records, one with salesperson records, and so on.

The lines with arrows in Figure 10-2 represent the relationships between the entities. Why do the lines have one-way arrowheads? The arrows are special symbols that mark *one-to-many* relationships.

✦ Each sales region has many salespeople, but each salesperson is in only a single region.

✦ Salespeople have many customers, but customers have only a single salesperson.

✦ Customers place many orders, but each order is associated with only one customer.

Figure 10-2: A relationship model of a database.

That's it: a simple but complete entity relationship model for a database. Even with this simple model, though, you can make an immediate observation: there's only one way to traverse the lines in this database. That is, given the lines and arrows, you can go from top to bottom only one step at a time, and you can't skip any steps either. Databases with this kind of a design lend themselves to hierarchical representation, and it's easy to see why: a hierarchy looks like a pyramid. Wherever you start in a hierarchy, each item leads to more items below, and when you get to the bottom of a hierarchy, there are no paths back, except for retracing your steps.

Without getting very fancy at all, Figure 10-3 adds Market Segment (for example, a bank, manufacturing company, and so on) and Products to the model. Six entities instead of four isn't much difference; it's the relationship that's really different in the new diagram. When a relationship has arrowheads at both ends, it represents a *many-to-many* relationship.

✦ Each order can have many products in it.

✦ Each product can be part of many orders.

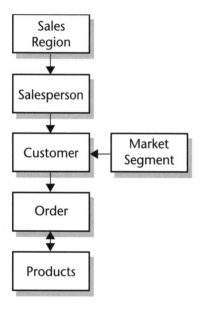

Figure 10-3: The database model with some new relationships.

The addition of Market Segment and the presence of the many-to-many relationship between Order and Products create real problems for hierarchical databases. To really see why, you need to think of hierarchical storage using a mechanical analogy — filing cabinets.

A hierarchical database can be thought of as being like an electronic file cabinet. To organize information, the first level in the hierarchy corresponds to hanging file folders, the second level to individual file folders sitting inside a hanging folder, and the third level is equivalent to individual records, documents, or forms sitting inside each folder. If the hierarchy has four levels, then the top level can be a file drawer with hanging folders in each drawer. You can even get to five levels by making entire file cabinets serve as the top level. For example, you can have a cabinet for each sales region, a drawer for each sales office, hanging folders for salespeople, individual file folders for customers, and paper forms for orders. The bottom level in a paper-based system often corresponds to lines on a single page. In this example, the fifth level represents an order form, and the sixth level represents specific line items for particular products on an order form. The beauty of a hierarchical database in a computer is that you can work with hundreds of levels if you need to.

Imagine now that you've actually stored the database in the diagram in a set of filing cabinets organized by sales region, salesperson, order, and product. Management suddenly asks for a report showing sales by region. The filing system supports the generation of this report very well. You work through the drawers, hanging folders, folders, and orders, one by one, and keep running totals as you go along. Soon you have a report. Suppose that next, management decides that it wants the same report showing sales by market segment.

Generating a report based on market segment is a nightmare given the hierarchical organization by sales region. You'd like to start with, say, sales to banks, and then look at manufacturing companies, then airlines, and so on. Banks, however, are scattered all around the world. Lots of your salespeople have banks as customers, but your files are sorted by region, not by market segment. The orders for banks are therefore scattered all through your cabinets, hanging folders, individual folders, and orders. This is a report you simply can't do any time soon. You can reorganize the filing system so that all the records are grouped by customer type in order to produce the second report, but then you won't be able to produce the first report anymore. To make matters worse, management wants both reports and a new report showing sales by product type as well. A third way of organizing the data? How can you ever do that in a hierarchical database? You can't. You need a more general form of database.

NETWORK DATABASES

About five years after the concept of databases first became popular, designers realized that many users required a more general database model that preserved the conceptual simplicity of the hierarchical approach while adding the flexibility to deal with many hierarchies at one time. The result was the development of *network databases*. The term *network* in this context has nothing to do with LANs, WANs, terminals, or any other communication technology. In fact, I'm talking about yet another meaning and use for that overused word.

One more time, here's the dictionary definition of network:

1. An openwork fabric or structure in which rope, thread, or wires cross at regular intervals

2. Something resembling a net in consisting of a number of parts, passages, lines, or routes that cross, branch out, or interconnect such as an espionage network or a network of railways

3. A chain of interconnected radio or television broadcasting stations, usually sharing a large proportion of their programs

4. A group or system of electric components and connecting circuitry designed to function in a specific manner

In this case, I want to focus on the second definition — something resembling a net in consisting of a number of parts, passages, lines, or routes that cross, branch out, or interconnect.

Figure 10-4 shows how this definition relates to the example. In the center of the figure is an order for 500 brake pads. This order of 500 brake pads is a record in the order database, which is part of the order entity in the database model. At the top of the picture, you see the Regional hierarchy. In this hierarchy, the order is related to the single salesperson who placed the order. It belongs in a single file folder in that hierarchical storage system. At the right is the Market Segment hierarchy, in which the order belongs in a completely different file folder corresponding to the type of company that placed the order. Finally, at the bottom is the Product hierarchy. In that organizational system, this same order belongs in a folder with all other orders for brake pads, which are in a bigger order for brake parts in general, which is in a drawer dealing with suspension components, and so on.

In a hierarchical database, whether manual or computerized, each record lives in only a single folder. The relationship among all of the records in the database can be drawn as a single hierarchical diagram (such as the ones in Figures 10-2 or 10-3).

A network database allows records to be in multiple folders all at the same time. The diagram for a network database shows individual records with many lines connecting those records to other records. In a hierarchical database, each record is related to a single parent record sitting above it in the hierarchy. In a network database, any record may be related to any other record.

If you were playing connect-the-dots, hierarchical databases would force you to follow very strict rules. Network databases, on the other hand, allow you to have any rules you want in terms of which dots can be connected to which.

Conceptually, a network database allows you to arrange the data into any number of hierarchical views, *all at the same time*. The sample order for 500 brake pads can be viewed in a network database as part of a regional hierarchy, part of a product hierarchy, and part of a market segment hierarchy. If the network database were a filing cabinet, it would be a filing cabinet that could magically and instantly rearrange all of its folders at the command of the user. Come at it one way and the drawers are regions; the hangers, salespeople; the folders, companies; and the forms, orders. Press a button and suddenly each drawer is a market segment with folders and forms rearranged accordingly.

Why call it a network database? Going back to the definition of network, when you draw a picture of the records and the relationships between them, the result looks like a network. The lines connecting all the records cross, branch out, and interconnect to form an openwork fabric or structure.

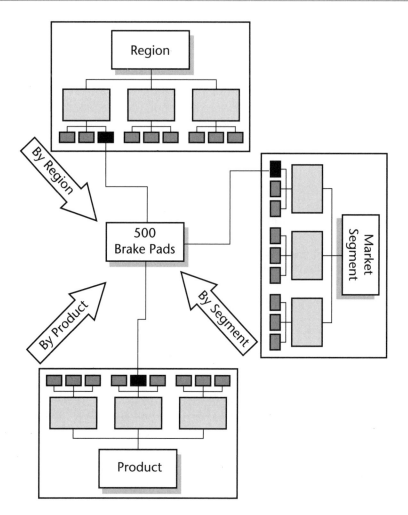

Figure 10-4: Entities interconnecting around an order.

What kinds of applications really need the flexibility of a network? A quick look at the data model (recall Figure 10-3) tells the answer: any entity with more than one arrow approaching it implies multiple hierarchies, which in turn calls for a network database representation. Both Customer and Order entities meet this requirement. Salesperson and Market Segment point to Customer, and both Products and Customer point to Order.

Each arrow tells us that the records in a file are the children of the records in the other file the arrow came from. If two arrows point to a file, each of the records in that file can have two parents. Therefore, no single hierarchy will be enough to answer all questions about a database with arrows going in more than one direction, and a network is required to allow multiple hierarchies. If this is a little hard to keep straight, go back to the example and chase it through a couple of times.

Finally, recall that when I first introduced this particular diagram as an example, I pointed out both the two arrows coming into Customer and the double-headed arrow between Order and Products (see Figure 10-3). Relationships with arrows at both ends always imply a need for network representations. Why? Because each file is the hierarchical parent of the other. For example, even if the diagram contained only Order and Products, no single hierarchy would be enough. After all, the two arrowheads indicate the ability to make the following request:

✦ Show me all orders sorted by product.

✦ Show me all products sorted by order size.

Of course, you can handle a database as simple as this one in lots of different ways. Nobody would invent network databases just to provide two different sort orders. The important point is that there are simple clues you can find in a data model that tip off the best way to think about a database and its implementation. And when databases become more complex, network representations become important, even critical. It's now time to consider a more complex database.

THE PROGRAMMER AS NAVIGATOR

Network databases are definitely more complex than hierarchical databases. In a hierarchy, there are only two directions to move from any record: up or down. In a network, there are many choices. This complexity can represent either a challenge or an opportunity. As it turns out, for the last 15 years, network structures have been viewed as a liability when in fact they are much more of an opportunity. The result has been a 15-year argument over the merits of network databases, database navigation, relational databases, and the more recent object databases and the navigational facilities they bring back from the past. To see what I'm talking about, consider a more complete and familiar example.

Even a chain of video stores requires a relatively complex data model, as shown in Figure 10-5. With a few examples just to help you start, try navigating your way through this data model.

✦ Customers rent videotapes and/or laser discs, each of which is checked out by a single salesperson. Each salesperson, of course, checks out many customers.

✦ Laser discs and videotapes, each associated with a single movie, may be acquired from several distributors and are located at several stores.

✦ Each movie may be available in laser disc or videotape format, and there may be several copies at each of several stores. Each movie is made by a single producer but may have many movie stars in it.

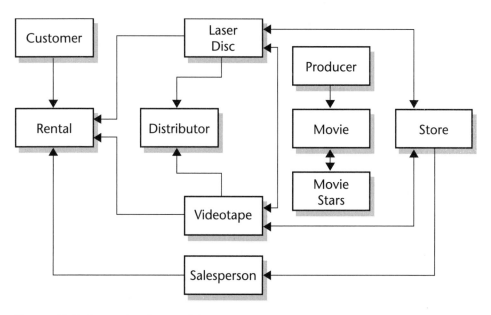

Figure 10-5: A complex data model.

To begin to understand this simple database, you'll have to steer through several boxes and lines. This exercise is sometimes referred to as *database navigation*. Navigation is only mildly interesting when just looking at the database; it becomes essential when it comes time to answer questions based on the records themselves:

✦ *Which movies are the most popular?* To answer this question, you have to look at rental records. The rental records, though, refer to particular copies of videotapes, probably by serial number. The serial number takes us to the inventory record for the copy of the videotape (or laser disc), which in turn points back to the movie title. To answer this question, you had to navigate through four sets of files (rentals, videotapes, laser discs, movies) using records in all four.

✦ *Which stars are the most popular?* You'll need to maneuver through five files this time. Besides all the files that you've already used, you also have to get back to the database file that lists the stars by movie.

✦ *Who is the most popular star in New York City?* At this point, you're using six files altogether. The problem is that the rental records don't tell you what city the customer lives in. You could go back to the customer file or, more directly, use the store file that lists the location of each store.

The process of shifting back and forth among multiple files in order to find information that will lead to answering a question is called *navigation*. Navigation can be *dynamic* or *static*.

Static navigation occurs when a programmer makes all the navigation decisions in advance and then builds the navigational path through the database into his or her application. In fact, what generally happens in the case of static navigation is that the programmer implicitly converts the network into a one-time hierarchy for the purpose of generating a report or answering a query. The three questions I just posed, for example, all involved picking a particular set of files and relationships out of the bigger database. These subsets of files and relationships are individual hierarchical databases.

Users *dynamically* navigate through a database when they are exploring data to look for patterns or to find small amounts of information. For example, consider the following, somewhat whimsical, exploratory trip:

+ I wonder why that John Wayne movie is never available when I try to rent it?

+ Start by seeing what movies John Wayne is in to be sure I have the title right. Ah, there it is.

+ Now, how many copies are available at the store I go to? Two copies. Seems strange that it would never be in. Check to see how often it gets checked out.

+ One copy was lost quite some time ago and one more recently. But I recall having trouble with other John Wayne titles. Are they somehow lost too?

+ That's strange. All the John Wayne titles seem to be gone. What about other similar movies? No, they're not lost. I wonder who checked those Wayne movies out?

+ That's it! There's a closet John Wayne movie thief at this particular store, and I've found him. This customer obviously loves Wayne movies so much that he or she borrows them and never returns them.

Tracing a path back and forth through all the files, records, and relationships to discover why a particular set of movies wasn't available would present an interesting picture. You could think of the database as an information space of interrelated data, the relationships as paths from data file to data file, and users as navigators discovering new facts as they travel through this database world.

THE PROGRAMMER AS NAVIGATOR, PART 2

In 1973, Charles Bachman, one of the pioneers of database technology, received the Turing Award, the computer industry equivalent of the Nobel prize. On the occasion of receiving the award, he presented a now famous paper entitled *The Programmer As*

Navigator. For the first time in a published paper, Bachman introduced the idea of navigating through a sea of data with exciting computer applications that allow users to explore the information resources buried in their databases. Surprisingly, 20 years later, this concept is not only misunderstood, but also often viewed as somehow either wrong or bad. And yet Bachman's concept of database use turns out to be fundamental to what users really want as they become more sophisticated.

Early databases were all built with the needs of programmers in mind. Databases and terminals became common at about the same time, and at first, nobody anticipated that users would want to query databases directly. Professional programmers wrote applications that used databases. If a user needed a question answered, the programmer built the facility to answer that question into the application program. Users with unusual or ad hoc questions simply assumed that computers had nothing to do with answering those questions.

As terminals became common, users began wondering why they couldn't get information out of the computer in some more general way without having to constantly depend on programming changes in big applications. That wonderment changed quickly into a demand on the part of users. This demand led to the development of report writer and query technology. In fact, the first software product to achieve over a million dollars in sales in its first year was a report writer produced by a company called Pansophic Systems. Its product, still aimed at programmers, allowed ad hoc reports to be produced in hours instead of in days. For the first time, programmers could be responsive to the needs of users. Pansophic advertised its product with a simple and evocative image of a skeleton sitting at a terminal, festooned with cobwebs, with the single tag line: "Tired of Waiting for Reports?" Thousands of users were tired, and Pansophic's sales took off. But in the end, even faster reports weren't enough to satisfy users.

Users want to be able to ask questions on the fly, get answers right away, and then decide what question to ask next. Sometimes the answer to the question will be a lengthy report; other times it will be just a few lines of data. Either way, all users want their data immediately, and they want to be able to ask for it without depending on technical professionals.

Hierarchical databases have fundamental problems servicing this type of need. IMS, Total, and all the other hierarchical products enforce a single hierarchical view of the data. As you've seen, even in relatively simple situations, many types of questions lead to hierarchical views that are different from the one the designer chose. Putting this another way, limiting the data representation to a single hierarchy virtually guarantees that the chosen hierarchy will be the wrong one for most users.

By the time Bachman presented his paper, though, the successor to hierarchical databases, the network database had been invented. Products like IDMS, IDS, and others allowed networked data models to be represented directly in the structure of the database. In a hierarchical database, each record has at most one parent, and that record may have many children. A network database essentially allows a record to be related to an unlimited number of other records. An order record can be related to a product record, a customer record, a shipping record, an accounting record, and so on. Network databases allow each user to take his or her own hierarchical (or even nonhierarchical) view of the data. They are called network databases precisely because the web of relationships looks like a net or network of lines.

What kinds of queries can be answered easily with a network database? All kinds. That's just the point. Because a network database can represent directly all the kinds of relationships inherent in the organization's data, that data can be navigated, explored, and queried in all kinds of interesting and powerful ways. That's why the original idea expressed by Bachman is such an exciting one. Why then did network databases gain such a bad reputation, and why were they replaced in popularity by relational technology?

Compared to hierarchical systems, network databases were a big step forward, but database technology in the early 1970s was still very immature overall. No standards existed; tools and utilities were mostly nonexistent; even experts were still figuring out what database design was all about. On the one hand, network databases quickly became quite popular among the mainframe crowd and even went on to become the basis for the first database standard, promulgated by the Conference on Data Systems Languages, or CODASYL. On the other hand, in spite of the continued advances in technology, all kinds of databases were very hard to use.

To gain a perspective on how difficult to use databases were, think about any computer technology of 10 or 20 years ago. Word processors, for example, were far harder to use than those that have spoiled us today. Most people didn't use word processors: they were too expensive, too limited, and certainly far too hard for ordinary people to use. Twenty years ago, databases and query processors were even worse.

Although network databases had the potential for facilitating flexible, powerful, and adaptable queries, the query software itself more than negated any possible advantage of the underlying database by making the whole process complex, hard to learn, and generally useless for ordinary users. In this context, network databases made things worse, not better, than simpler alternatives.

When databases were first invented, it was assumed that the only people who would use them directly would be database programmers who were highly familiar with both the database technology and the detailed design of any particular database they were working with. As a result, diagrams like the data models were considered standard working tools by all users of early databases, most of whom were programmers.

Given this background, imagine the approach the designers of the early query tools took: they assumed that their users would be just like database programmers. They therefore assumed that before users would ever ask a question, they would first have a map of the complete database and develop their own strategy for navigating through it. What's more, the picture of a real-world database is bigger and far more complex than the diagrams I've presented. Imagine the reaction of typical users, never exposed to a computer, who were asked to learn a complex query tool with a completely nongraphical interface, a tool they couldn't even use until they had understood the structure of the database completely and developed a navigational strategy to go with it! Nonstarters? You bet.

RELATIONAL DATABASES: EVERYTHING YOU'VE WANTED TO KNOW (AND WERE AFRAID TO ASK)

In the midst of this database development of the 1970s, Edgar Codd, an IBM researcher, began working on a new database model called the *relational model*. With a name like that, you might think that this model was particularly adept at dealing with relationships between files. In fact, quite the opposite. This misconception is just one of several many people have about the strengths and weaknesses of relational technology.

In mathematics, a relation is an unordered set of n-tuples. Huh? An *n-tuple* is just a set of n different values, what you would call a record. A relation is close to what you would call a file. As you may have already noticed, the discourse is getting a little muddy in a couple of significant ways.

The first, which is sneaky and slightly unfair, but not insidious, is the renaming of words. The first thing you have to quickly get used to is that in the relational world, files are *tables*, records are *rows*, and fields are *columns*. Other than forcing users to learn new vocabulary, these word shifts don't create any real problems. Codd correctly observed that although the big corporate database required complex sets of files with rich sets of permanent relationship links, most users who ask questions and explore data live in a much simpler world. In fact, most of them think not of files, records, and fields, but of tables, rows, and columns. Users are far more comfortable working with simple collections of tables than with complex sets of files and relationships. By making this observation, Codd prefigured the invention of the spreadsheet by several years.

The other problem of discourse lies in the name of the technology itself: relational databases. Paradoxically, relational systems don't handle relationships directly. Later in this chapter, I'll return to this topic to explore how a database can be called relational without representing relationships per se.

Moving away from explaining vocabulary, relational databases, unlike network and hierarchical databases, make it very easy to establish relationships between previously unrelated files on the fly. Working with a relational database, a programmer or a user can quickly and easily define a new relationship between any two tables. Relationships can even be defined between tables with no previously defined relationship. With network databases, relationships must be predefined before users can access them. Relational databases don't have this problem, and that's what makes relational systems so popular. In order to perform this little trick, relational systems introduced a new idea to the world.

From the beginning, every relational database came complete with a query language. That language, *SQL (structured query language)*, became an intrinsic part of the database. Today, it is commonplace to simply assume that SQL and databases are inseparable. In the 1970s, though, there was a sharp separation between databases and query languages. Narrowly defined, a database is simply an engine for managing shared data, and a query language is a specific tool for specifying sets of records to be retrieved from a database. Ideally, every database can be accessed through many query tools, and a query tool can work with many databases.

What do I mean by query language? For starters, a language is an agreed-on set of words, grammatical rules, and so on that allows people to communicate with each other. Computer languages, like human languages, consist of sets of words, symbols, and grammatical rules that allow humans to communicate with computers. Computer languages exist for the benefit of people, not computers. Although it is commonly assumed that computer languages — for example, COBOL, FORTRAN, Basic, and SQL — are designed for computers, they are not. In reality, they're designed to make it easy for people to tell computers what to do.

SQL: LINGUA FRANCA FOR PEOPLE OR FOR COMPUTERS?

In the 1970s, as Codd was developing his relational database theory, he concluded that one of the most basic purposes for databases was the facilitation of question asking. Codd wanted relational databases to make it easy for users to find data in them. If people are going to ask the database to find some records, he reasoned, these people need a language that will make it easy to ask for those records. And that's how SQL was born.

There is a broad perception, particularly among computer-literate professions, that SQL was the subject of careful and painstaking design. After all, the relational model with which SQL is so closely associated is believed to be one of the few parts of any computer system that is supposedly firmly grounded in a sophisticated mathematical model. People assumed that if relational databases were theoretically sound, SQL must be at least as well crafted. Not true, but don't read this paragraph the wrong way: SQL has many positive attributes. It is the most widely used database language in the world and has stood the test of time. At the same time, though, SQL in many ways shows its heritage, and that heritage is one of accidental birth. Yes, that's right: accidental birth.

In the 1970s, as Codd was starting to build prototypes of relational databases, he and his colleagues quickly discovered the need for a query language that could be used to work with the data in the engines they were building. As a pragmatic vehicle to allow their research to proceed, they designed what they originally called structured query language. As it turned out, SQL was first developed at a time when good query languages simply didn't exist. So along with the relational technology underneath it, SQL filled a vacuum, and as a result, it quickly became a standard.

Why does this matter? First, understanding the true background behind relational databases is essential to penetrating the mythology surrounding them. Second, after about ten years, a strange thing happened to both relational systems and SQL. The religious movement developing around SQL became *formal* — an unusual occurrence even for the often bizarre computer world. I'll discuss this formality later in this chapter.

So relational systems (*RDBMS* as a quick abbreviation for *Relational Database Management Systems*, or simply *RDB*) are tightly coupled to a query language called SQL. What's that got to do with network databases and ad hoc relationships? SQL makes it easy to specify ad hoc relationships between files or tables on the fly. In fact, SQL's capability to perform this task is based on an underlying *high-level operation* in the RDB — a *join*. As you'll see, however, it is not just the join that made RDBs popular. Rather, it was the fact that this powerful capability was made so accessible through the query language.

High-level operations such as joins are instructions that allow a person to tell a computer to do a whole bunch of work all in one request. A spreadsheet provides high-level operations to sort hundreds of rows, produce complex graphs, and change the formatting of an entire spreadsheet. Word processors provide high-level operations for reformatting documents, producing tables of contents, and converting documents into multicolumn formats. The key idea here is simple: provide users with tools that allow them to ask the computer to carry out high-level operations that work on large amounts of data all in one step — without any programming.

A *join* is a high-level operation that combines two previously unrelated tables into a single bigger table. For example, a table with biographical records for movie stars can be joined to another table listing movies. The joined table contains both the data for each movie (for example, title, length, producer) and the biographical data for each movie star in each movie (height, weight, birth date, current lovers, and so on).

Codd was one of the first computer pioneers to realize the importance of high-level operations. In the relational world, these are usually called *set operations* because they work with entire sets of records all in one step. The point is that high-level operations provide the user with a vocabulary for working with large amounts of information without programming. With high-level operations, the power to manipulate quantities of data is not only in the hands of programmers, but also in the hands of ordinary mortals.

So relational databases contained two breakthroughs, both of which relate to working with files and records. First, they introduced a set of high-level operations such as joins that allow users to manipulate entire databases by using a small number of powerful tools. Second, Codd and his team made these operations available directly to users through a somewhat English-like language called SQL. It is that combination that has made RDBs popular ever since.

What about SQL? Who is it for? Is it really easy to use? How does it compare to other query languages, and why is it so dominant?

What's so great about SQL? Compared to other technical languages like COBOL, C, or even Basic, SQL is relatively straightforward. To begin with, it has a far more limited objective. Unlike a conventional programming language, the mission of SQL is limited to expressing queries.

A *query* is a specification that allows a database to retrieve a specific set of records. Some examples are

✦ All movies with John Wayne in them

✦ All bills outstanding more than 30 days

✦ All Japanese cars owned by Scandinavian engineers living in California with incomes over $50,000 who have ordered from a certain catalog more than six times during the last three years

Queries may be simple, like the first two in the list, or very complex, like the last one. In addition to specifying a particular set of records, a query may also manipulate those records as a set:

✦ List all salesmen who are over 105 percent of quota and compute the average and total sales for all those salesmen by product line and by sales territory

✦ Retroactively increase salaries by 10 percent for all interior designers in Connecticut who have been with the company for more than three years

✦ Forget about (delete) all bills that have been outstanding for more than one year

The purpose of a query language is to allow all of these kinds of queries and more to be expressed so that a computer can find sets of records, make changes to them (specified in the query), and then make that changed set of records available for more queries.

SQL is a powerful language. A wide variety of sophisticated queries can be expressed effectively in the language. Query engines have been built that efficiently retrieve and manipulate sets of records based on SQL queries. So in terms of providing a powerful, high-level query language for computer professionals, SQL is an unqualified success.

SQL provides an *English-like* language for specifying queries. At the time it was designed, one of the goals was to make it possible for any computer user to learn SQL. In fact, one of the reasons for designing SQL was to allow Codd and his colleagues to learn whether a query language could be made easy to learn and use. Besides being somewhat ad hoc, SQL was also experimental. It was a considered an early experiment in ease of use. After almost two decades, the verdict is in.

SQL isn't for everyone. SQL is a powerful and dominant language, but it is too complex for most noncomputer professionals to ever learn. Contrary to the fondly proposed idea of the 1970s, not everyone will one day learn SQL. Although SQL is simpler than a language like C, it is still as far beyond the understanding of most computer users as the detailed operation of the internal combustion engine is beyond most drivers. Most drivers will never learn to adjust valve timing on their cars, and similarly, most computer users will never learn or use SQL directly. As it turns out, whether you learn it or not really doesn't matter.

Although people may never talk SQL, database tools talk it. Products such as Paradox, dBASE, Access, and dozens of others provide users with graphical mechanisms for specifying queries, viewing sets of records, and causing changes to the underlying data. These software tools speak SQL on the user's behalf. Although Codd's original intention in developing SQL was to empower end users directly, the use of SQL in applications has empowered end users even more than if the language were directly useable.

Earlier in this chapter, I asserted that database has three different meanings. SQL turns out to be a lingua franca providing a universal bridge between two sides of the database world. On the one side is the database engine. Many different software vendors have built different database engines designed to serve a variety of specialized needs. On the other side, literally hundreds of end user database tools focus on user interface, analysis, and presentation. Without SQL, there would be no easy way for all the different front-end tools to talk to the many database engines. Because SQL has become the standard, users can take it for granted that when they have chosen a personal database tool, they will then be able to use that tool to retrieve information from all the different database engines in which that data may be stored.

First you looked at hierarchical and network databases. You then started to explore the relational model, which introduced the idea of tables as a simpler way of thinking about files and records. After a side trip to learn about joins and high-level and set-oriented operations, I introduced SQL as a query language that was originally designed for people to talk to programs. As you've just seen, SQL turns out to be most useful as a language for programs to talk to other programs. Having taken you this far, I now have to dive a little deeper into databases. Specifically, you are now in a position to gain a complete understanding of tables, joins, relations, and the relational model.

RELATIONAL DATABASES: WHAT MAKES THEM RELATIONAL?

The network model is built around the idea of expressing the structure of the organization's data directly in the design of the database itself. This shows up in two ways:

1. Records have a relatively complex structure in network databases:

   • An order record contains both the header information specifying the customer's name and address and all the individual line items describing specific products, quantities, and costs.

   • An employee record contains both the employee's own personnel data and the records for each of the employee's dependents.

   • The record for a low-level part may contain both the specifications for that part and for all the subparts (components) that make it up.

2. Relationships between files are built directly into the database at the time that it's designed.

Both of these characteristics come down to the same thing: the explicit representation of relationships in a network database. Complex record structures encode detailed relationships, and interfile linkages express the higher-level relationships. Relational databases, despite the name, are based on the assumption that these relationships should not be wired into the database at all. Instead, so relational theory goes, the database and its query language should provide powerful tools, like the join operation, that allow relationships to be specified and acted upon on the fly. Going even further, the relational model calls for the structure of both the database and the records to reflect the idea of not building relationships into the database itself.

At first, this idea might sound crazy. Databases are all about relationships, so if you don't build them in, aren't you unbuilding the very thing you set out to build in the first place? Perhaps not. It's time to explore why relational proponents believe that their model is better.

The reason for not building relationships in is simple: flexibility. Also, the choice of not building relationships can lead to additional simplicity, but only sometimes. Hierarchical databases are limited because they force the choice of a single hierarchy. Network databases, no matter how many built-in relationships they have, are still limited because there will always be more relationships that users will want to create and use. The relational model solves these problems completely by allowing *any* two sets of data to be potentially linked through a relationship created on the fly.

To work its magic, a relational database depends on three principles: normalization, foreign keys, and joins. Before I explain these concepts, a word of motivation is in order. This chapter is somewhat technical. The next few sections are the most technical (but still understandable) parts of an already technical chapter. You need to know the upcoming information, though, because it come up all the time when relational databases are discussed. By spending just a small amount of time on these topics, you can learn enough to at least understand the context of RDB conversations. More important, with just three tricky concepts under your belt, you can really talk about the future of databases in a fairly complete fashion.

Normalization is the database technique for eliminating complex record structures, and foreign keys is the corresponding technique for dealing with interfile relationships. Between the two of them, these two techniques get rid of all directly expressed relationships. Joins, in turn, provide a mechanism for putting the relationships back by constructing them on the fly. Having provided that overview, I'll go into more detail.

When considered in detail, *normalization* is a complex topic, the subject of many books and papers. What I will do here is develop the concept and leave the details to computer science courses and textbooks. The simplest way to understand normalization is through an example.

A video store database has three different files dealing with people: customers, employees, and movie stars. A goal of any database is to completely eliminate redundancy so that any piece of information is stored in exactly and only one location in the database. The problem with the current structure of the video database is that information about individuals is stored in not one, but three places. An employee who is also a customer would have two records containing his or her name and address. If that employee was also a movie star (a stretch, I know), his or her name and birthdate would be in three places in the database. As you've already seen, this redundancy makes it a problem to keep data up-to-date in three locations. More important, this redundancy produces consistency errors in reports (remember the irate company president?). How does the relational model solve this problem? Through normalization.

As Figure 10-6 shows, you can normalize the people-related parts of the database by creating an additional and separate file just to store information about people. Part of normalization involves splitting out data that occurs in several files and putting it all in a common place. Besides eliminating redundancy, this technique creates a new design improvement: if you want to know about a person, there's a single starting place that will always contain the data about that person. As it turns out, this simplicity is an even bigger advantage than you might expect. To show you what I mean, consider another example of normalization.

Both the video store database and the earlier customers, orders, and products database contained a file for recording business transactions: rentals for videos and orders for products. In both cases, a non-normalized design places several product orders or rentals in a single record. Certainly this is the way it's done on paper. However, this design does create a problem when it comes to asking questions:

✦ The video database makes it easy to find all videos checked out by a single customer because that's how they're grouped. If this database were a hierarchy, the bottom level would be the rental form listing several videotapes. All forms are stuck into a customer folder, and all the folders are organized by store. What if you just want to find all the rentals of John Wayne movies? The hierarchical system forces you to read every rental record, one by one, in order to find John Wayne movie rentals.

✦ The orders database makes it easy to find orders placed by a particular customer. What if you want to find all orders for a particular product? Again, you have to read through all the order records, examine line items one by one, and pull out those items associated with the products you're interested in.

This sounds like the very flexibility problem inherent in hierarchical databases. Normalization is the final step required to make the lack of flexibility problem go away. The solution to both of these particular problems is the same: split the repetitive data — the multiple rentals and the multiple line items — out into a separate database.

In the normalized diagram (Figure 10-6), rentals of individual videotapes are collected in their own file, one record per videotape rental. In the same way, the new customers, products, and orders database (see Figure 10-7) has a separate file for line items. Conceptually, normalization is the process of taking all repetitive data that appears in more than one place and splitting it into separate files. The net effect of normalization is to eliminate all complex records from a database:

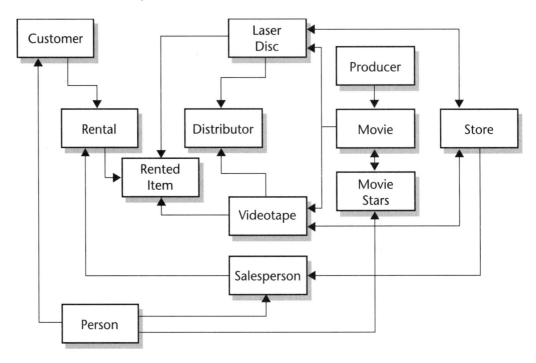

Figure 10-6: Normalizing the people-related parts of the database.

✦ Orders are stored in two simple files: the order header containing the customer's name and address and the line-item file containing individual records with a single line item each.

✦ Employees are now represented in several files. The employee's own personal data is in a single record. In addition, simple individual records are used to describe each of the employee's dependents: one record for each child, one for the spouse, and so on.

✦ Products, assemblies, parts, and components are all described in simple records. If a part is made from subparts, one record describes the main part, and each subpart is described in its own record.

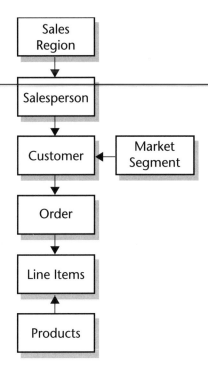

Figure 10-7: The customers, products, and orders database.

A fundamental tenet of the relational model is the use of simple tables to replace complex records. A record historically has stood for a complex structure:

✦ Records may vary in length: some employees have children; some don't.

✦ Records contain repetitive subrecords: line items, subparts, dependents.

A file composed of records can be a relatively complex structure. On the other hand, people visualize a table as a simple structure composed of rows, each with a fixed number of columns. Spreadsheets are so popular as databases because simple tabular structures are so easy to understand and work with. By definition, a relational database built around a simple (and limited) tabular structure not just encourages but also *requires* that data be normalized. Complex record structures cannot be stored directly in a relational database, so normalization is the only route through which data can be put into an RDB.

At this point, I can give you the first of three rules in the relational approach to relationships:

✦ Normalize all database designs so that redundancy and complex record structures are eliminated.

In passing, it's worth saying that normalization, although slightly tricky, is overall a very mechanical process. There are relatively straightforward rules for accomplishing the process and computer-based tools can help with the work. So normalization, even if it sounds scary, is a much easier process than you might expect. By providing a single place to find all records of a particular type, a normalized database virtually eliminates redundancy while allowing almost infinitely flexible relationship construction. How do these relationships get built if they're not built in? That's where foreign keys come in.

Records have fields; rows in tables have columns. The vocabulary's different, but the concepts are the same. The way that you generally find particular records (and rows) is by searching for particular field (column) values:

✦ All records for people over 30; records where the value of the age field is greater than 30

✦ George Washington's personnel record; the personnel record whose name field has the value George Washington

✦ The record for the part with serial number 94387A; look for the serial number field with the value 94387A

Finding records very quickly based on the value of one or two *key* fields is a common and critical operation in every database. For this reason, special facilities are built in to make these retrievals essentially instantaneous. A database will typically build and maintain an *index* on the fields that will be used for retrieval. Books have indexes that allow the reader to quickly find out what pages contain references to certain words and topics. Imagine trying to find discussions about *joins* in this book if there were no index. It would be quite difficult. A telephone book is just a huge index that allows you to find the phone numbers of people whose names you know. Finding a name if you know only the phone number is so hard that you wouldn't even try unless you have access to the phone company's *reverse index*, which lists phone numbers in numerical order along with the phone subscriber's name. Indexes make the difficult task of finding information almost trivial, and indexes are fundamental to databases.

An index provides a *key* to the data that otherwise would be locked up in the database. For this reason, indexed fields are generally called *key fields* or *key columns*. A table or file may have many key fields or no key fields (in which case records can be found only by searching through the file one record at a time). For example, a customer table may be indexed on customer name, customer number, city, and sales region. If indexes are so handy, why not just index every field? Some databases do this automatically, and most databases provide the flexibility to make indexing all fields possible. However, indexes carry with them a significant drawback. In the first place, the index takes up space on the disk. If every occurrence of every word in a book were indexed, the index would be almost as big as the book itself. Also, maintaining an index takes time. Each time a record is created, changed, or deleted, all the indexes associated with key fields have to be changed as well. Adding too many indexes makes a database run slowly. Too few indexes make retrievals slow; too many indexes make changes slow — just another trade-off designers must deal with.

Now what's a *foreign* key? It's a column added to a table that allows a relationship to be established with records in another table. Having a customer name column in an order table allows orders to be linked to the customer records they are associated with. Why is this column called a foreign key? Because the values in a foreign key column are associated with an index built on *another* table. A foreign key unlocks the link between tables. Think of the advantages of having, for example, an order record containing two foreign key fields: customer name and part number.

✦ The customer name allows you to look up the customer record in the customer table. You find that record quickly by relying on the fact that the customer name is a key field in the customer table. The customer name column in the *orders* table is a key field that is indexed in the *customer* table; hence, a foreign key.

✦ The part number in the *orders* table allows you to quickly look up part records by using the index on the *parts* table. Again, you have a field that is keyed to an index on another table.

Why are foreign keys so special? The answer is at the heart of the relational model. Network and hierarchical databases maintain relationships by using *invisible pointers*. A pointer is simply a field that points to another record, often in another file or table. For example, an order record could point to all the parts in an order. The problem with network and hierarchical databases is that you can't always see the pointers directly. This is a critical, if somewhat subtle, point that requires more explanation.

Suppose that you're looking at a printed report listing customers, their outstanding orders, and the parts associated with each order. Perhaps the report looks like this:

Acme Kennels	May 13, 1993	Dog Food	$425.13
		Cat Food	65.19
		Hamster Food	1,119.25
	May 1, 1993	Giraffe Food	$352.17
Canine Carnival	May 15, 1993	Flaming Hoops	$459.13
		Jumping Fleas	25.00

How did the database know that the customer record for Canine Carnival had any orders associated with it? The answer is that there is a pointer making the connection, but what does that mean? In a database, one way or another, every record has, or ought to have, at least one unique key associated with it, a key value that allows users to always refer to that record and only that record. This is often called the *primary* key. A customer number is a good primary key because it generally refers to one and only one customer. In fact, even manual systems have long recognized the need to create primary keys: that's where part numbers, customer numbers, general ledger account numbers, and so on, come from. The mechanism for creating primary keys has historically been a major difference between network and relational databases.

In many network databases, an application can create a record and mechanically link it to another record. That is, the programmer can create an order and say to the database: establish a link between this order record and this other customer record I'm working with at the same time. Invisibly, the network database associates an internal primary key with every record in the system. Each time someone adds an order, the database gives it an internal order number. In the same way, each customer record has an internal customer number. Users don't get to see these internal numbers, but they are there nonetheless.

Here's a simple, everyday way to think about those internal numbers. Recall all the paper forms you've ever filled out in your life (if you can bear to do that). Remember all the forms that had shaded areas to be filled in by whatever bureaucracy you happened to be dealing with. Also recall how many of those forms had specially coded serial numbers on them. Those serial numbers and shaded areas are invisible pointers. When the customs official writes your passport number on a declaration form, he or she is creating a pointer. The driver's license number on the back of a check is another pointer. The magnetically encoded account number on the front of the check is yet another.

Pointers are good, but *invisible* pointers are supposed to be bad. That's one of the tenets of relational theory. There are supposed to be two problems with invisible pointers:

✦ If relationships can be based only on invisible pointers created in advance as part of the database design, how do users get to define new relationships whenever they need to?

✦ How can a user, or even a programmer, really understand what's going on in the database when some of the data, particularly critical data like pointers, is invisible?

The last question makes a key point: pointers may be moderately obscure and somewhat subtle, but they are at the heart of what databases are all about — namely, establishing and using relationships.

It's now time for the second rule in the relational approach to databases. The first rule you already know:

✦ Normalize all database designs so that redundancy and complex record structures are eliminated.

Here is the second rule:

✦ Always use explicit and externally understandable primary and foreign keys.

What is an *explicit and externally understandable key*? Explicit means that the key can't be invisible. If, for example, an order record points to the customer record, the pointer takes the form of an explicit (that is, visible in the record, printable in a report, viewable on a screen) customer number. A passport number contained in a declaration record is an explicit foreign key.

Why call out the fact that both the foreign and primary keys must be explicit and visible? If one table is to be able to refer to another, then the *pointed to* table (the one being referred to) must have an explicit and visible (primary) key. For example, before a document or table can refer to a passport, the passport records must have the unique passport number column that becomes the basis for the explicit, visible primary key. The same goes for customer numbers, part numbers, and general ledger account numbers. Of course, when you build in the explicit, visible key in the *pointed to* table, it's a direct consequence that the table doing the pointing uses an explicit, visible foreign key as its pointer.

Why do keys have to be externally understandable? Because it makes database records more understandable. Invisible pointers and invisible primary keys are at one end of a spectrum of understandability: they are not even visible, so they have no meaning independent of the underlying database. A customer's name is at the other end of the spectrum: it is completely understandable and recognizable outside of the database it's in. A goal of relational database design is to have all keys be understandable in the same way. It's a noble objective.

In its purest form, this objective is nothing less than a crusade to eliminate all obscure, special-purpose identification numbers and codes. Few if any database designers have achieved this goal. Nobody would state the goal in as idealized a form as I have, but it is worthwhile to state the most extreme form of this noble goal so that you understand its implications.

Why have passport numbers? Nobody ever remembers them. Why not use the passport holder's name, date of birth, and address? How about driver's license numbers, Social Security numbers, or taxpayer identification numbers? Getting more picayune, why have order numbers, shipment numbers, check numbers, and so on? What happens when you call to trace a shipment and they ask for the shipment number? Perhaps you don't have the shipment number because you never received the package, and they can't trace the package until you provide a shipment number. Sound familiar? Each of these examples illustrates the fact that unique, special-purpose identification numbers, created for literally millions of individual transactions every day, are highly useful inside a computer but highly obscure to everybody outside the computer. These manufactured, unique IDs are both necessary and painfully awkward. Relational database design encourages us to eliminate them.

In practice, eliminating custom IDs is a great idea that is very difficult to fully implement. (I'll discuss this issue in the section detailing the problems of relational databases.) As it turns out, even if some or even many of the keys don't have a meaning independent of the particular database and application, you can still build a fully relational database. The important thing is to ensure that the keys are explicit and visible. If some identifiers have limited meaning away from the database, that's still acceptable. Now that you know that relational tables have explicit, visible keys, how do you use *joins* to create relationships? With just a little more explaining, all the pieces will be in place.

Table 10-1 shows fragments of four tables from the normalized video store database. The samples are fragmentary in two ways: only a very few representative rows are displayed, and only a few of the columns are listed in each row. You can quickly see key fields (like Cust #) in their *home* tables (Customers) and in their use as foreign keys (Cust # is a foreign key in the Rentals table). Tracing through the example, you should easily see how the arrangement of keys and foreign keys makes it possible to piece together complete records depicting particular rentals. That's exactly how joins work.

A *join* combines two or more tables into one bigger table based on matching up values in common columns. If you do the obvious join on the table represented in Table 10-1, you end up with Table 10-2.

And there you have a simple join. At one level, the result you see is intuitively straightforward; however, there's really quite a lot going on here. Fundamentally, though, joins do just what they say: they join several tables into one bigger table.

You'll notice in Table 10-2 that some information, such as the customer's name, is repeated quite often. That's a characteristic of joins: as you recombine previously normalized data in which repetitions are common, you naturally see repetitions again. Putting this another way, a non-normalized database stores customer names right in the rental records; the join takes normalized data and organizes it in the non-normalized fashion.

If joins are simply undoing the effects of normalization, what's the point of having done all that normalization in the first place? The trick answer is that joins are *temporary* operations used to answer a particular question. By storing the actual records in normalized form, you ensure that each data element is stored on disk at only one location. As a result, when that data is changed, the change is automatically reflected everywhere and anytime that data is used. At the same time, by using joins whenever you need to, you can allow that pieces of data to be used in a wide variety of places and in conjunction with a wide variety of other pieces of data. To the user, the reports and records (called *views*) through joins make the data available in all the places it is used in the real world, while allowing the data to be stored actually only once in the underlying database world. Now that you understand joins, you are ready for the third rule of the relational approach to relationships:

Table 10-1   Using Joins to Create Relationships

Customers

Cust #	Name	Address
9345	Babar	Celesteville
1846	Curious George	Big City

Rentals

Rental #	Cust #	Date
9345	9345	Jun 14
9346	2495	Jun 14
9347	3417	Jun 15
9348	9345	Jun 16

Tapes

Tape #	Title	Copies
19468	Babar's Adventures	12
8779	Lone Wolf	1
55611	City Nites	3
94165	Sleepy Hollow	3

Rental Items

Rental #	Item #	Tape #	Returned
9345	1	19468	Jun 16
9345	2	8779	Jun 16
9345	3	55611	Jun 17
9345	4	94165	Jun 16

Table 10-2   Joining the Data from Table 10-1

Rental Report

Name	Out	Title	Back
Babar	Jun 14	Babar's Adventures	Jun 16
Babar	Jun 14	Lone Wolf	Jun 16
Babar	Jun 14	City Nites	Jun 17
Babar	Jun 14	Sleepy Hollow	Jun 16

✦ Use joins as the mechanism for establishing and using relationships.

To summarize, using relational databases requires that you do the following:

1. Store the actual data in normalized tables with no redundant data.

2. Represent all relationships explicitly through explicit and visible foreign and primary keys.

3. Use joins (and other relational operations) to temporarily create derived tables that bring related data together whenever it's needed.

The beauty of the relational approach lies in its flexibility and lack of redundancy. In principle, any set of records can be related to almost any other set of records, and the lack of redundancy solves many of the classical consistency problems (irate president) of databases. The question now is, having built this elaborate structure, does it work?

RELATIONAL THEORY AND RELATIONSHIPS: ARE THEY RELATED?

In theory, everybody should be using only relational databases by now. All computer users should know (and maybe even speak out loud) SQL. Most large production systems built around hierarchical or network databases should be at least on the way over to relational land. Not quite.

Relational databases are very popular and the resulting industry is worth over $2 billion per year in sales. Most large, shared marketing support databases are built around some form of relational database. Most applications used to run major systems in large companies, however, are still running on top of hierarchical and network databases. Moreover, although big companies regularly experiment with the development of relationally based production systems, the truth is that most new systems started today, if they are heavily transaction-oriented, get built on top of IMS, ADABAS, IDMS, and other nonrelational systems.

Not only is this true of the present; but the future holds just as much uncertainty about relational systems. On the high-volume, personal computer front, most databases are only loosely based on the relational model, and when you consider popular systems like FoxPro and dBASE, that looseness is very loose indeed. And at the very cutting edge of database use, the next wave of database management systems, called *object-oriented databases*, is not relational at all. Many industry observers claim that OODBs are today where RDBMSs were ten years ago: look ahead another ten years, they claim, and OODB systems will displace RDBMSs just as the RDBMSs displaced the network systems before them. What's going on?

The answer to this question lies in understanding the limitations and weaknesses in the relational model from both a pragmatic and theoretical perspective. Fortunately, with the groundwork I've already laid, I can explain to you these limitations very quickly. In the process, we'll review the underlying dogma and see why the relational religion may be its own worst enemy.

As we entered relational land, one of my early observations was that RDBs didn't actually handle relationships. This limitation is at the core of the problem with RDBs as they exist today. Most people assume that the word *relational* was chosen to reflect an underlying model that expressed relationships in a powerful way. Not so. Instead, as you saw briefly, the term *relational* signifies a database model based on the mathematical theory of relations. Relations are unordered sets of tuples — tables. In a simplistic way, relations do represent relationships, but only to the extent that being a part of a table makes a record or a row related to that one table. In an everyday sense, relations have nothing to do with interfile relationships. This is not intended as a negative comment or condemnation; it is a simple statement of fact. I will now deal with one of the first dogmatic, and in my opinion, incorrect myths of the relational religion.

Is the mathematical model important? Relational databases are supposed to be particularly powerful because they are backed up by a complete mathematical model. This mathematical model is not only supposed to impart invincible powers to RDBs themselves, but it also beats competitors by pointing out that they lack the backing of an equivalently powerful mathematical model. So what about the mathematical model? What does it really do?

Almost since the invention of computer programming, idealists and others have searched for a way to either write bug-free programs based on mathematical principles or, if that isn't possible, use those same principles to prove that programs are correct after they are written. As computers and the programs that drive them have become responsible for elevators, antilock brakes, space shuttles, telephone exchanges, nuclear reactors, and other mission-critical applications, the consequences of a bug or malfunction have become increasingly serious. The problem with conventional techniques for building, testing, and supporting software-based systems is that there is no way to be sure that no bugs are present. In theory, elaborate testing, particularly when the test suites are based on years of progressive experience, should produce perfect software. In practice, there's always some last bug arising in some set of circumstances that no one could ever have foreseen and that the testing suites couldn't find. And after that last bug is eliminated, there's always another last bug, and then another. Edsgar Dijkstra, a now famous originator of the "let's-prove-it's-correct-instead-of-depending-on-testing" movement coined the phrase, "Testing can *find* bugs, but it can never prove their absence." It is in the context of never knowing when that next bug will appear that mathematical foundations appear so attractive.

Mathematics as a discipline is firmly rooted in the idea of proofs and provably correct theorems. Most sciences, including computer science, are based on experimentation. Develop a hypothesis, test it, look for a pattern, and then propose the hypothesis as a theory that explains part of the world. In most sciences, though, there's no way to prove that a theory is really, truly, and finally correct. As a result, when some new set of observations comes along that breaks the previously observed pattern, it's time to look for a new theory. For hundreds of years, astronomers (and the rest of us) believed that the sun revolved around the earth. Later, viewing the sun as the center of the universe seemed to be a better explanatory theory. Finally, the current theory views the solar system as just one more planetary system. Each theory was powerful in its time, but each was eventually replaced by another, better theory.

Mathematics, unlike physics or chemistry, is based on absolutes. Each branch of mathematics — geometry, calculus, algebra, topology — relies on an initial set of premises and definitions. When that base is in place, mathematicians are able to postulate and prove theorems that then remain absolutely true forever. It is precisely this ability to absolutely prove theorems that is so exciting about mathematics. The Newtonian theory of gravity was exciting and highly useful for hundreds of years, but Einstein's theory of relativity ultimately showed that it was wrong. The Pythagorean theorem, however, has been true for thousands of years and will continue to be true forever. *Forever* and *absolutely* are powerful adjectives, and it is the certainty that comes with that power that software developers would like to apply to the software users depend on.

Superficially, computer programs and mathematical theorems are very similar. Both are constructed entirely by humans and are based completely on words and symbols. Physics, in comparison, is focused on describing the physical universe, which is assuredly not constructed by humans and certainly based on far more than words and symbols. The fact that mathematical theorems are such verbal and abstract constructions allows people to prove theorems' validity. After all, when mathematicians prove that a theorem is true, what they are really doing is validating its derivation as a set of symbols from another set of symbols representing the premises and definitions supporting that branch of mathematics. If theorems and computer programs are both just sets of symbols derived from other sets of symbols, why can't all computer programs be proved correct?

In theory, computer programs are provable. That's right, at least in theory. It is possible to construct computer programs in such a way that along with the program itself, a programmer could also produce a mathematically sound proof asserting that the program will always do what it's supposed to. Unfortunately, turning that idea into a practical discipline has proven obstinately impossible for the entire time that programmers, computer scientists, and mathematicians have tried.

If it were provably correct that certifiably bug-free programs could be built, the payoff would be huge. For this reason, many brilliant people have expended Herculean efforts in this direction. One approach has involved building special programming languages with mathematically oriented constructs. The idea is that if each of the basic building blocks in a program is provably correct itself, it ought to be easy to build an entire program that is provably correct. Much of the appeal of the relational model revolves around this very idea. Another approach revolves around building special programs which help prove that other programs are correct or incorrect. Yet another approach involves augmenting classical programming languages with constructs that allow various assertions, claims, and premises to be inserted into otherwise normal programs to help in the process of proving them correct. In spite of all this work, when everything is said and done, provably correct programs are as much impossible today as truly artificially intelligent computers.

In a nutshell, programming is an art; it is not a science and certainly not a branch of mathematics. Yes, it would be wonderful to be able to prove that critical applications are bug free. It would be wonderful to even be able to prove that critical parts of those programs would always operate correctly. Wonderful as it might be, it can't be done today.

Before you get too discouraged about all this, try to view it in context: the glass is more than half full. At the turn of the century, mathematicians worldwide, excited about recent advances in formal symbolic logic, believed that mathematics and all of science could be converted to a mechanical footing. Bertrand Russell and Alfred North Whitehead were just completing *Principia Mathematica*, a massive set of volumes whose purpose was to lay out the foundation for all of mathematics. The idea was that with just a little more work, a complete set of definitions, premises, and axioms could be developed on which all of mathematics could be based. Given that foundation, it would then become possible to prove or disprove any theorem by using mechanical approaches alone. The complete *Principia* could by itself be the foundation for saying whether any proposed theorem was right or wrong. Even though computers and programming had not been invented, mathematicians were involved in the world's first attempt to automate the programming process.

At about the same time as Russell and Whitehead were at work, many historically difficult problems were finally being solved, and thinkers in many countries were predicting the end of science. Physics and chemistry would become complete, mathematics would shift to a complete foundation, and most future questions would become virtually self-answering.

By 1930, the mood of scientists and mathematicians had completely reversed itself based on two sets of developments. First and more well-known, a whole series of theoretical and practical discoveries demonstrated that scientific history was far from over. Relativity, quantum mechanics, advances in organic chemistry, and the discovery of radio proved that invention was still alive. The universe was infinitely more complex than nineteenth century thinkers believed. The second new input, though less well-known, was far more fundamental. That second input was a proof that proofs are limited.

In 1933, Kurt Gödel, a young mathematician, published the theorem bearing his name: Gödel's theorem. As important in its own way as the theory of relativity, this theorem proves that no matter how complete a foundation of definitions, premises, and axioms may be, there will always be questions that cannot be decided within the theoretical framework of the time. More succinctly, Gödel proved that no mathematical system can ever be complete. Every mathematical system will always lead to questions that can't be answered without extending the basic underlying system.

Depressing or exciting? For thinkers preparing for the end of history, it was depressing. Why bother laboring over some ponderous *Principia* when there's a proof that not all questions can be answered mechanically, no matter how complete the current system? For admirers of human creativity, it was exciting. People will always be required to extend mathematics and science in interesting and unexpected new ways.

Relational databases. Gödel's theorem. The search for certainty. They're all related. Bugs are uncomfortable, and not knowing that a complex computer program is bug free is an uncertainty people can easily do without. But in spite of noble efforts, valiant attempts, and Herculean labors, programming is still an art. Trivially simple computer programs can be proven correct; every computer science student learns how. To date, though, no significant or serious computer program has been proven correct, and even the best programmers don't bother spending time trying.

Even core code, that software at the center of critically important programs such as operating systems, databases, and control programs for nuclear reactors, can't be proven correct. In theory, basing a program or part of a program on a solid mathematical footing ought to have a payoff. Maybe one day it will. Today, there is no payoff. So what about the theory of relations and relational databases?

First, as I've already said, the theory of relations deals with tables (sets of tuples) and not with relationships. Even to the extent the theory is useful, it has little to say about one of the most central aspects of databases. Next, as it turns out, even having the theory has surprisingly little practical benefit. For all of the talk of RDBs being based on solid mathematical foundations, when it comes time to build, design, or use databases, nothing that happens in the real world relates back in any direct fashion to that supposedly useful theoretical infrastructure. Worst of all, the type of databases described by relational theory turn out to have some significant limitations, limitations that have caused some so-called relational databases to violate the tenets of relational theory. For example, to qualify as a relation, a database table has to be unordered. Being unordered means not sorted by customer name, not sorted by customer number, in fact not sorted by anything. In addition, being unordered means that rows don't even keep any particular order. So if you read through a table and come back to read it again, the rows may be in a different order. Even if you wanted to implement tables that are unordered, how would you do it? Would anybody want a table of that type when you were done? Ordering is fundamental to both computers and people. Reports are always printed in sorted order so that users can find things; computers maintain tables in sorted order so that programs can find things. Unordered collections are an interesting mathematical construct, but when it comes to real life, lack of order is counterproductive. Unordered tables would be hard to build (because computers like order, too), and they would be even more difficult to sell as useful tools if they could be built. Like unordered tables, relation theory as a whole is interesting in theory only. Relational databases that are truly based on mathematics are interesting in theory, but not in fact.

I can now get to the heart of the problem with relational databases: they're too simple for many real-world applications. Simplicity made relational databases popular, and that same simplicity will ultimately make them too limited for the future. Ideally, developers would like to keep that simplicity for small applications while augmenting it to handle the bigger applications.

In what way are relational databases too simple? Well, they don't handle relationships well enough. Ironic, isn't it? A database technology called relational doesn't handle relationships well enough. Relational databases do handle mathematical relations to a certain degree, but those relations are based on single tables and sometimes sets of tables, neither of which is a complete view of the kinds of relationships developers need to build real databases. How do the limitations of relational databases manifest themselves? In two ways: expressiveness and performance.

Remember the steps required to normalize a database? The elimination of redundancy is a payoff, but there is a huge cost. Normalized databases are far more complex to build and to understand than non-normalized databases. They are so complicated that ordinary users have trouble understanding them. The precise characteristics that normalization eliminates turn out to be the cornerstones of understandability. Here are some examples:

+ Families don't all have the same number of children. A table doesn't handle groups of fields, in this case representing children, that occur a variable number of times. Ordinary people expect tables of records to allow groups of fields to occur as many times as necessary. Relational databases say that this is not allowed. The result may have technical and theoretical advantages, but that same result is hard to work with.

+ Quite often, putting the line items right into the order record is the natural way to represent a record. Relational tables make this task difficult. Again, intuition, and sometimes performance, asks for one thing; relational theory dictates another.

At the level of individual records and tables, normalization takes straightforward structures and makes them both less redundant and less understandable. But does normalization have deeper drawbacks?

Normalized databases, at least big ones, are always more complex than they were before normalization happened. Individual records and files, once normalized, turn into more, sometimes many more, simple tables. The individual tables are simpler than the files they replace, but the collection of tables is generally more complex both to work with and to understand than the individual records. The sample video store database, once normalized, required four different tables to be joined to create a simple rental history report (see Tables 10-1 and 10-2).

People who don't make a living working with databases don't understand joins. Joining two tables is tough enough for most people to understand; joining four tables pushes the edge of comprehensibility. Here's the killer: many normalized databases require joins of 10, 15, 20, or even 30 tables to answer relatively simple questions. Users will never understand ten-way joins. They won't learn to do them by rote; they won't figure them out for themselves. They just can't handle joins that complex, and a ten-way join isn't particularly complex by relational standards.

The next problem with joins is that they are very slow to process. Suppose that the average customer rents 3 to 5 videotapes at a time. In a non-normalized representation, each rental record contains all the detailed rental information; that entire record is read all at one time. In a normalized design, the same retrieval requires 4 to 6 reads: one for the rental header record and 3 to 5 more for the individual normalized rental item records. In an order-entry application, orders can easily contain 35 or 40 line items each. What was a single read in a non-normalized system becomes 35 to 40 reads in the normalized database. And the problem doesn't stop with single files.

In a normalized database, every file and every record throughout the database have typically been split up into simpler tables. Departments contain subdepartments; products contain components; orders have line items; teams contain members; employees have dependents; drivers have several cars, and so on. Repetition and variability in occurrence are standard parts of the universe. Normalized databases invariably have to convert a set number of files into 3 to 10 times as many simpler tables. The tables are simpler, but the overall database isn't. And when everything is normalized, routine operations — reports, queries, transactional updates — take 3 to 4 times as many disk operations and 3 to 4 times as much computer time to process.

For small- and medium-size applications, taking 3 to 4 times as long is acceptable; for big applications, it isn't. So you can see why departmental applications and decision-support applications run on relational databases while the bigger applications that drive the business don't. But what about the idea that relational databases are simpler? Is the idea itself wrong? Where did the idea come from if it's wrong?

Back in 1973, when Bachman first pronounced the programmer as navigator, databases were hard to use — hard to use because all software was hard to use in the 1970s. Word processors (yes, they existed back then), electronic mail systems, accounting software, databases — in fact, all applications were just plain hard to use. GUIs had not been invented; mice were known by only a select few; interactive computing was just becoming popular. It's hardly surprising that as the idea of querying a database dynamically was being invented, at first it was darn hard to do.

Even as recently as 1981, word processors, spreadsheets, and most other now common applications were still so hard to use that most office workers needed extensive training just to produce simple memos with a computer. So when relational databases were being invented, databases were hard to use, not because of intrinsic limitations in the network model, but because software in general was still hard to use. The techniques and tools required to make software approachable were still to be invented.

The relational revolution did introduce several valuable ideas to the database world:

+ *Tables* are a simple way of presenting data to users. Spreadsheets later confirmed the intuitive appeal of this representation.

+ *Interactive querying:* Retrieving and manipulating data dynamically is what databases are all about for many everyday users.

+ *SQL* (pronounced *sequel*) is a very convenient standard query language for database tools and database professionals to work with data in a database-independent fashion.

+ *High-level, set-oriented operations* allow both programmers and ordinary users to find and work with large collections of records at one time without having to write programs.

+ *Joins* are a very powerful tool for linking previously unrelated records. Through the combination of the join operator and the ability of a query tool to support temporary tables that display the joined result table, users can create new sets of related records on the fly to explore and work with relationships as the need arises.

This powerful legacy helps explain part of the appeal of relational databases. The true appeal is simpler, though. IMS, IDMS, Total, ADABAS, and all the other early databases, whatever their underlying model, were designed for programmers. Even after query languages were added, they were still hard for noncomputer professionals to learn and use. Relational databases, on the other hand, were designed from the beginning to be easier to use. *Easier*, as you'll see, does not mean *easy*; just easier.

Relational databases became popular at just about the time that minicomputers and departmental systems were taking off. In the 1960s, mainframes were built to serve the needs of entire divisions or companies. By the late 1970s, departments (marketing, sales, engineering, and so on) within large organizations began purchasing relatively inexpensive minicomputers to serve the needs of white-collar professionals. The precursors to today's high-powered engineering workstations, these systems, although still too expensive for individuals, could be shared among groups of individuals. The applications running on these departmental systems — marketing analysis, simple financial forecasting, engineering analysis — were simpler than those on the mainframe. These applications were typically built by programmers, but the requirements placed on those programmers were simpler. It is for this class of applications, still programmer oriented but with simpler requirements, that the early relational databases were ideally suited.

Tables are a simple way of representing data: a programmer can explain a table to a user in a few minutes. For simple applications involving only a few tables (less than

20), a relational database allows applications, queries, and reports to be constructed quickly and easily. As DEC grew to become a $10 billion company selling departmental minicomputers, Oracle grew to become a billion-dollar software company selling relational databases to go along with DEC's VAXes. So a lot of the popularity of relational databases has to do purely with timing. As the third generation of database technology and the second generation of query programs, relational systems were the first to be even moderately easy to use. Because they were developed at just around the same time that departmental minicomputers were taking off, there was a market wave for them to catch and ride.

Two acid tests allow us to draw correct conclusions about the true success of relational databases. On the ease-of-use front, relational systems are just not particularly easy to use. Neither Oracle nor DB2 was the first to be used by housewives, school-teachers, salespeople, and millions of others. That distinction is reserved for 1-2-3, dBASE, and Paradox. Neither the underlying relational model nor SQL achieved the appropriate ease-of-use breakthrough required for true bestseller status, and the databases that did achieve this break-through ended up being nonrelational in nature. Even when it comes to handling multiple tables at one time, products like Paradox and PowerBase made this everyday task easy without using the relational model. To be clear, this does not mean that the relational model somehow failed; it is simply neither necessary nor sufficient for true ease of use.

What about the big applications? Until recently, the verdict has been out on whether the relational model would eventually turn out to be the best for running businesses. During the 1980s, normalizing databases resulted in applications that ran too slowly. However, many relational enthusiasts insisted that this problem would disappear as computers continued to get faster and as relational database vendors invented newer and more clever techniques for dealing with normalized databases. In the end, the issue has been decided on grounds that have to do with more than just raw efficiency.

BACHMAN WAS RIGHT: WE ARE NAVIGATORS OF DATA

Representing large databases in a relational form turns out to be a problem for both humans and computers. People have not become able to deal with 20 or 30 table joins, and the cost of building those large joins continues to be an issue even as computers have become faster. In one typical banking application, for example, all the queries executed by branch staff — several dozen — all turned out to involve more than 20 joins of tables. If you normalize tables, you create a need for joins.

The first thing that happens when the price for normalization is realized is that database designers start denormalizing the very database they started out by carefully normalizing in the first place. Rather than dynamically create the understandable joined tables as circumstances require, designers choose instead to build and maintain these tables as permanent parts of the database. In fact, having a catalog of such denormalized views is standard procedure in any large decision-support environment.

The benefit of maintaining these denormalized views is twofold:

1. Rather than present users with thousands of tables that they will never really figure out how to combine in complex ways, the user instead sees a small list (typically 5 to 10) of non-normalized views of the data which are immediately understandable. Along the way, the complex issues discussed in the previous chapter — dealing with extended time, multiple views of the organization, and so on — are factored out in the construction of the views.

2. Because the views are preconstructed and permanently populated, they are immediately available for access. In the Information Warehouse context, these same views can contain complex aggregations, providing another performance advantage. Even in the transactional environment, there is a significant advantage to being able to display instantly a customer's rental history in understandable form without specifying or building a 12-table view.

The implication of the decision by organizations worldwide to use these denormalized views is simple: they are going back to the network model of the 1970s. Denormalized views are nothing more nor less than complex record structures stored directly in the database. And this shift back to network structures goes much further.

A typical large relational database can easily have 50 to 100 tables. Databases with hundreds of tables are not uncommon. One complete, high-efficiency, and widely sold financial software package, built by SAP, has over 5,000 distinct tables in it. Finding your way around a database with 50, 100, or 5,000 tables is by no means easy: you need a map.

Of course, one way to build such a map is to use the type of data model shown earlier in this chapter: a network system. Why not have the database support the data model internally? In theory, every table can be related to every other one. In practice, although not every table in a database is related to every other one, keeping track of all those relationships turns out to be just as important as keeping track of the data in the first place.

With this realization, the result has been the development of the object-oriented database, or OODB. Object-oriented databases have caused as much religious hype as the relational model once did. Considered from a pure database perspective, OODBs have three unique features that distinguish them from RDBs:

✦ Complex record structures, including repeating groups of fields, can be represented directly in an object-oriented database. Employees can have multiple children; orders can contain line items directly; parts records can describe their subparts.

✦ Relationships between files can be stored directly in the database. Records can point directly to other records.

✦ Programmatic behavior can be associated directly with particular classes of records. When a customer record is deleted, the linked code can automatically delete outstanding orders.

Those first two attributes of OODBs sound suspiciously similar to a description of network databases — because they are similar. OODBs in many ways are just grown-up net-work databases. Period. The third attribute — the capability to link data to programs that get executed directly when certain events happen — is an important new idea, but that idea, called *triggers* in database-speak, has been available in relational databases since 1987 and could just as easily be added to an older network database. (*Triggers*, in fact, are exactly events that get raised by the database. These events are then associated with particular pieces of code that are executed.) In style, OODBs are more modern than network databases, but in substance, they represent a return to the network world of the past.

Does this mean that relational systems will disappear? Is the relational model somehow wrong? Not likely, and no. So what is happening?

Bachman was right: programmers are navigators on an ocean of data. Databases are about relationships between collections of records, and these relationships must be expressed directly in the database. When the database stores the relationships directly, navigating through the network of those links, both dynamically and passively, is a very important and exciting thing to do. Relationships need to be expressed at three levels:

1. Simple containment relationships are best reflected in complex record structures. Sometimes complete normalization makes sense. In other situations, it makes more sense to create more complex record structures. A database should make it easy for the database designer, not the underlying model, to decide.

2. Relationships between standard sets of records need to be represented in the database directly. Explicit keys are still great — where they make sense. In other cases, users can best express a relationship by creating a direct link directly from one record to another. True, at one level such a pointer is invisible, but in reality most large applications contain dozens of internal counters and unique fields created solely for the purpose of supporting interrecord pointers such as internal order numbers, internal line item numbers, internal serial numbers, and so on. Relational theorists would make these internal numbers externally visible. Real usage and practical common sense says that users don't want to see them, can't remember them, and depend on the computer to trace links from file to file anyway. So why not

admit the truth and build databases that support both visible and invisible interrecord links? That's what OODBs do.

3. Finally, many links between records are even more ad hoc than a data model shows. For example, a personnel record should be able to point to other records anywhere in the database. When you re-create the opportunity for interrecord pointers, the direct result is that you get the support required for such flexible linking with no extra work. Databases and information stores that support complex webs of interconnected data in this way are often called *hypertext systems.* Record-oriented databases can now be hypertext databases too.

By recognizing the importance of both the relational and the navigational models, it becomes possible to build next-generation databases that provide the best of both worlds. One can admit that Bachman was right after all without necessarily insisting that Codd (and relational systems) are wrong.

THE DATABASE FUTURE: COOPERATING COMPONENTS FROM THE INSIDE

As 1995 draws to a close, network, relational, and object databases compete with each other in somewhat different application domains. The problem is that developers (and the users they serve) are forced to choose between all the different competing models, which creates a set of essentially impossible choices. The question is this: What's the alternative? The answer revolves around understanding the one common design element true for virtually every production database design in the world today: *monolithic construction.* That's right, database systems, whether old or new, are built in a completely monolithic fashion. In some ways, this represents the supreme irony. On the one hand, the community of developers who build the database systems themselves includes some of the smartest, most highly educated and widely read developers and designers anywhere. The professionals attend conferences, keep up with modern tools, and truly represent the state of the art. Yet, when it comes to writing their own software, they build the most monolithic systems to be found anywhere. Database builders trust no one! Use the operating system's buffer manager? Never. Share a transaction manager with another software system? No way. Build it all in, make all the interfaces proprietary, and there you have a database system, whether new or old. The question now is this: What would happen if you built a database itself out of cooperating components?. To gain some perspective on this question, the following starts by recapping where the world is today.

Network and hierarchical databases still contain the vast majority of the world's production data. Only these systems can handle both the volume of data and the complex linkages between files that big applications require. Relational databases are broadly used for departmental applications. An increasing number of organizations are experimenting with the construction of distributed client/server systems with RDBs running on each server. Finally, OODBs are starting to gain a strong presence by supporting a new class of databases with moderately large collections of records with extraordinarily complex sets of interrecord relationships. For example, designing a car or airplane involves working with thousands of parts all arranged in a highly complex bill of materials. Computing the structural strength of a particular design involves chasing through all the hundreds of those parts over and over. In this environment, OODBs turn out to be over twice as fast as RDBs because they handle all the relationships so much more simply and efficiently. So there you have an overview of the leading models for serious DBMSs. Network systems are fast; relational systems offer flexible analysis; OODBs support rich data structures. Which do you want? All three? But you have to choose, and the problem doesn't end there.

While IMS and IDMS contain the majority of the production data in large organizations, the majority of the total data is contained somewhere else. In fact, it's not in databases, as we know them today, at all. Where is it? In spreadsheets, project managers, in Notes' "databases." And a great deal more data is in dBASE, Access, Paradox, Fox, and other desktop databases that, too, are never counted when figuring out where the world's data is stored. All these desktop and workgroup data stores contain over half the world's structured data.

To be very clear about what kind of data I am talking about, consider the following fact. Over 80% of spreadsheets contain no formulas other than column totals. What they do contain is tables of records. All project management packages are built up around tables containing records. Over 5 million Access users certainly are building tables containing lots of records. So when I talk about the half or more of the data not contained in classical databases — where network, hierarchical, relational, or object-oriented — it is exactly and totally database data I am talking about. It's time to start thinking about that data as part of the database world, too.

This is precisely the problem of heterogeneity that we talked about when I first introduced the concept of cooperating components. The question is, how does that concept help solve the problem? To see how this works, take a look at how the classical database is structured.

Forms
Programming Language
Query Processor
Transaction Manager
DB Store

As this list shows, a database consists, internally, of a number of components, each with a specific job to do. For instance, inside every DBMS is a record storage engine that reads from and writes records to disk, building indexes to allow rapid retrieval, and so on. Similarly, every DBMS has some form of query processor that takes a query (in SQL or some other language) and then figures out how to find the data being asked for. The problem (as you'll see) is that these components are all glued together, not interchangeable, and not even accessible to the outside world. Okay, now it's time to change that (see Figure 10-8).

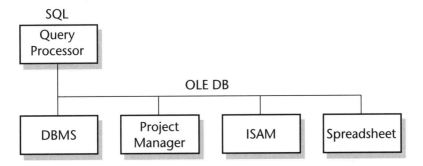

Figure 10-8: The OLE DB model.

Pick a database. It has a query processor. Now what is required for that query processor to be able to get at tables in a spreadsheet? The answer is "an interface." Or in slightly more detail, a set of predefined subroutine calls so that the query processor can do the following:

✦ Ask the spreadsheet what tables it has.

✦ For each table, ask what columns are present and what their datatypes are.

✦ Ask for the values of rows in the tables.

✦ Ask for changes to be made to those rows, for new rows to be inserted, and so on.

While such an interface clearly could exist, no one has defined it yet. At least not until very recently. I am not talking about SQL! Nor am I talking about interfaces, such as ODBC, which are designed to allow applications to talk to SQL based databases in a standard way. Why not? Well, a spreadsheet is not a database; neither is a project manager or an ISAM file package. Asking a spreadsheet to speak SQL is like asking it to become a database. If every application and tool that stored data could just become a database, then this entire discussion would be largely unnecessary. No, something different is needed.

Every database has the interface I am talking about. Every database has some form of interface that allows its query processor to talk to its underlying store. The problem is that those interfaces are *not published* and are *not standard*.

Early in 1995, Microsoft began the process of disclosing to the world of developers the details of a set of interfaces called *OLE DB*, also sometimes called *OLE Database*. This chapter will look at OLE itself more closely later, but suffice it to say that OLE, and its underlying *COM* (short for *Component Object Model*) represents Microsoft's broad framework for building objects. Within that context, OLE DB is a prescription or framework for recasting databases themselves as sets of cooperating components.

OLE DB is a relatively technical set of interfaces (specified in C and C++) that describes how any two components that work with tables and sets of records can interoperate. In OLE DB parlance, such components are called *tabular data providers* or *TDPs*.

A TDP can be a complete relational database that speaks SQL, but it doesn't have to be. A TDP, purposely, can also be a much simpler component, like a spreadsheet, word processor, or project manager that understands simple collections of records and not much more. By then adding "external" components like a query processor to the picture, it becomes possible to formulate SQL queries that retrieve data from a spreadsheet without the spreadsheet having to be a database or having to speak SQL. How does that work?

By publishing OLE DB as a potential standard interface specifically designed to sit between the previously internal components of a database, the way becomes clear to rearchitect databases themselves so that they become sets of cooperating components, too. It's now time to explore some interesting scenarios that arise from this new picture of the world:

✦ Users can store data in the container of their choice. One user can build budget forecasts in a spreadsheet, another in a project manager, and another in a true database. An OLE DB based query processor, previously an inseparable part of a monolithic database, can combine data from all these many datasources as though it was all one big database. The user of the query processor, once an SQL query has been entered, can't tell where the data came from.

✦ Many of the world's production applications run on ISAM file systems and hierarchical databases because those systems are so fast. Yet, inside every relational database is an ISAM style record store (is it struggling to get out?). By componentizing the database in this way, that underlying record store becomes directly available to developers, through the OLE DB interface. Many developers will choose to continue treating the entire system as a relational database, accessing data only through the query processor and SQL. Other developers, though, may need the additional performance, be willing to do the extra work of developing their own retrieval strategies, and use the underlying record store directly. In both cases, the data still ends up in the common database — accessible to all and consistent in nature.

✦ What happens if you replace the query processor? The first example considered the idea of being able to store data in a wide variety of storage containers, using all your favorite tools to create and edit data while still having that data accessible by way of the familiar SQL based query processor. Essentially, you have a "replaceable" storage engine. Why not be able to have a replaceable query processor, as well?

The next version of the block diagram (see Figure 10-9) shows a query processor that understand maps and geography — a geographical query processor. More than likely, it works primarily around maps projected on the screen. If it has a query language, that language is almost certainly only vaguely related to SQL.

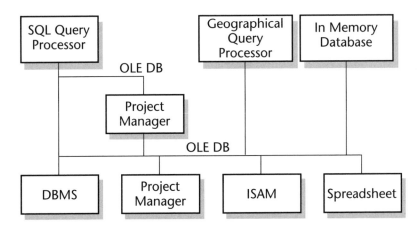

Figure 10-9: An updated version of the original block diagram.

✦ Does a query processor even have to provide a query language at all? The DBMS, the spreadsheet, the ISAM, and the other containers at the bottom of the diagram are all physical containers; they contain actual records, often entered by users. A query processor, on the other hand, is essentially a container that holds logical records — records derived from the underlying physical records in the other containers. In the database world, sets of logical records are often called *logical views*. Generally, logical views are defined in terms of SQL queries, but this is not a requirement. Given a relational database, though, it is hard to build a true logical view any other way. Consider the following problem. Suppose that I'm building an Information Warehouse, as was discussed in the last chapter. As part of the project, I write a program that performs a particularly complex form of profitability analysis. The result of this analysis is a table: profitability by product, but computed in this complex and changing fashion. Now, here's the catch. I've generated this table, but I don't want to store it anywhere because the contents of the table change according to a wide variety of external factors; if I store it, the table becomes static. Yet, at the same time, I want users to be able to work with this table just like they would work with any other table. For example, a user might want to use Access or Paradox to join this table to several other tables, physical and logical. How do I make that possible? There is an answer, and it's actually quite simple.

First, I write my computational calculator program using any programming language that makes sense. Then I build the OLE DB interfaces into my program. The profitability calculator appears to the overall database system just like any other container with tables in it. Even though all the values in my tables are calculated and derived, those values still look exactly like normal database tables to all external consumer. So a query processor, Access, or some completely different application written to talk to OLE DB directly, the tables I generate are just that — tables; the fact that values are calculated is made transparent. Now, here's an interesting twist on the whole theme. Not only can the user of my tables look at them, the user can change the table, too, if I just allow it. For example, suppose that my table contains a column with a calculated "standard cost." Depending on how I set security permissions, users (apps or people) can change the value of that standard cost, and then the profitability calculator does the right thing automatically. That right thing might be as simple as recomputing profitability for a row, or it may be as complex as modifying dozens of underlying base tables affected by the new standard cost. The beauty of the scheme is that to the consumer of the table it's just that: a table, available for examination and update.

✦ The last example, in some ways, is the most interesting because of its far-reaching implications. One of the leading database trends of the '90s is the increasing popularity of *object-oriented databases* or *OODBs*. One of the key features of such systems is their capability to take advantage of very large amounts of memory in either a workstation or a server. The rightmost box in the most recent diagram shows a component called an *In Memory Database* (*IMDB*). At one level, this is a query processor, a container holding logical records, all of which originally came from a physical container. Another way of looking at such a container is that if the container is located on a workstation, for example, it could be a staging area, or *cache*, for holding all the data a user, or the user's application, is working with, thereby taking advantage of arbitrarily large amounts of memory to improve performance. At this point, the combination of the IMDB and the underlying record store is the moral equivalent of a full OODB. OODBs do support richer data structures than classical RDBMSs; however, suppose that the underlying record store was augmented to support the same richer data structures. What would you have then? It is interesting to think about what core extensions are required to make a classical "flat" or ISAM-like record store capable of dealing with complex records. In fact, only three extensions are required. While there isn't space here for all the details, suffice it to say that by adding *GUIDs* (*Globally Unique Identifiers*), pointers (which are just GUID valued fields), and embedded tables (allowing individual columns / fields to contain complex values that are tables or structures in their own right), you end up having a complete system. Ironically, you end up with an underlying record store that looks very similar to older systems such as IMS, ADABAS, Cullinet, or Pick.

COOPERATING COMPONENTS: HAVING YOUR CAKE AND EATING IT, TOO

Putting all the examples together and building databases over again around the concept of cooperating components saves us — developers and users — from making impossible choices. Even more important, it saves databases from becoming irrelevant just as you need them most of all. Being forced to choose between flexibility, performance, and richness of data structure is an impossible choice. However, in a world of componentized databases, you can have all three. A rich variety of underlying record stores can offer the same data structures and performance that have kept large applications tied to ISAM, IMS, and IDMS for the past 30 years. Certainly, organizations will not convert their applications from these older data stores just because the performance can now be available. The rest of the cooperating component story, with its support for ubiquitous commodity computing in a highly distributed environment, is required to provide the complete motivation to make that shift happen

Once the motivation is there, however, having that performance will suddenly become critical. The performance may not be sufficient to motivate a shift, but it is certainly necessary to allow that shift to happen when the sufficient reasons are there. Componentized query processors allow you to also have the flexibility you associate with relational databases, but now that flexibility is actually amplified. Not only can you join tables created in the RDBMS in the first place, but you can also join tables created in a wide variety of other containers, as well. There's no tradeoff between flexibility and performance, per se, since it's up to the developer whether he or she writes directly to the underlying data store for performance or chooses to work completely through the relational query processor for flexibility and reduced programming effort. Finally, as record stores grow in sophistication and IMDB components become available, even OODB applications become possible — and they become possible without having to install yet another disjointed database into the environment. Data in the IMDB arrives from the same containers as used by all other applications; however, in the IMDB, large amounts of memory, optimizations to support pointers, and direct linkages to languages like C++ support applications that perform complex operations on rich data structures. Performance, flexibility, rich data structures — you can have them all; thanks to cooperating components.

Beyond the impossible choices, there is a real risk that without componentized databases, DBMSs as we know them today could be passed by, and in a very real way. Thinking about half or more of the world's structured data sitting in containers that aren't databases in the commercial sense of the word is a pretty scary thought. It is scary enough to make one wonder which is the tail, and which is the dog. However, component databases change the framework to include these data stores as first-class citizens in our database world. Databases then become mainstream in every sense of the word. The only question is can a shift as large as the shift to component database even happen?

Database technology shifts are not only possible, they're also compelling and perhaps even essential. Things will change in the database world, but the stakes this time around are far higher than ever.

Database designers made history in the 1970s when they built production applications based on network and hierarchical databases. History changed when relational databases took off, providing the foundation for departmental systems. In this decade, a new generation of complex applications has fueled the adoption of object-oriented databases. Most recently, history has seen the widespread adoption of easy-to-use, PC-based databases by millions of desktop users. Each of these shifts has been associated with relative rearrangements of the commercial landscape as corporate startups became leaders only to be eclipsed by the next generation of startups. In the end, though, relational databases did not replace network databases, and, at least until now, the PC database has not replaced either of its predecessors. Somehow there has been room for them all, but that room exists at the expense of having all of these databases run in an essentially disconnected fashion. What this history tells us is that, at least in database land, there is room for fundamental paradigm shifts. And perhaps this will be the paradigm shift that also makes all the DB pieces fit together at last.

Okay, so now you understand databases and where they are going. As promised, cooperating components play a key role in that evolution. But what about using those databases to build all those highly distributed applications? How is that done? That's what the next chapter covers.

PART III

DESIGNING AND BUILDING CLIENT/SERVER SYSTEMS

The goal of Part II was to provide a clear and perhaps even exciting picture of the client/server systems of the future. That part did not, however, provide a clear picture of how to design such systems.

Today programmers design and build large business-oriented applications using tools and methodologies developed over the last 30 years. Although many of those tools and approaches are still appropriate, clearly some new elements are required. That's what Part III is about.

When writing a section such as this one, it is tempting to immediately treat the material as a cookbook. After all, previous chapters provided lots of philosophical foundation; why not start dictating specific recipes right away? Because even with some new building blocks in place, technologists must base tomorrow's systems on a *conceptual framework* different from those in systems of the past. The first two chapters in this part develop a new *application architecture* to guide the design of a new generation of systems.

The very concept of an *application architecture* turns out to be both important and powerful. Even if you never build a distributed system, even if you continue to build only mainframe-based systems for the next 1,000 years, the application architecture developed here *will still help you design better systems* for that mainframe. *Better* means more quickly developed, easier to change, friendlier to use, and more able to work flexibly with many other systems. That's a tall order, but that's what application architecture is about.

After Chapters 11 and 12 develop the application architecture, Chapters 13-16 describe the specific methodologies, tools, and infrastructures required to build client/server systems.

Like Part II, Part III is written specifically to be useful and readable to technical and nontechnical readers alike. Rather than repeat the rationale for both types of readers, I'd rather say this: if you haven't read the introduction to Part II and are looking for motivation to read the next six chapters, go back and read that introduction now. Otherwise, welcome to this section, and as the book's introduction said, have fun.

CHAPTER 11

A CONCEPTUAL FRAMEWORK FOR THE FUTURE

How will the distributed, client/server business applications of the future get built? How does the process thinking so central to reengineering find its way into the database thinking that drives most application design? At a more mechanical level, if self-managed teams call for intrinsically distributed systems, how do you design and build those systems? This chapter sets out a broad *conceptual framework* for designing client/server applications. By itself, the framework does not answer all relevant questions. Instead, the framework lays the foundation for answering the questions in the following chapters.

In laying out this framework, I deal with both the present and the future. First, I look at the framework that has evolved for building the applications commonly running today. This framework is fundamentally inadequate; in particular it makes it hard or even impossible to build distributed, client/server applications that meet the needs of self-managed teams. Nonetheless, it is important to understand that framework to see why and how it falls short. For this reason, I spend several pages exploring the foundations underlying today's mainframe-oriented applications. Only when the existing framework is clear can you see how it can be augmented and changed to deal with the future. Perhaps it is tempting to skip to the end of the chapter and see the final answer. And perhaps it is a little frustrating to have to spend time and energy understanding what *is* just to get to what *will be*. In the end, however, the effort is worthwhile.

First, approaching tomorrow's conceptual framework in this way ensures that the mistakes of the past are not repeated. Second, it lays the groundwork for understanding not only how to build the systems of the future, but also how to make them blend smoothly with the systems of the present and past.

PHYSICAL DESIGN VERSUS LOGICAL DESIGN

Can distributed systems really be built, and how? Computer professionals have been struggling with this question for 20 years. To resolve this question, you must understand the distinction between *physical design* and *logical design*. *Physical design* talks about computers, disks, databases, communications lines, and other concrete elements of the real world. A great deal of the discussion about client/server systems deals with mechanisms for building distributed systems by jumping immediately to a discussion of what hardware should go where. Should customer data be centralized or be kept in local offices? Is it better to have a small number of big servers or a large number of small servers? *Logical design*, on the other hand, talks about the structure of the application independent of the type or location of hardware, software, and data. The central point of this chapter is that a good logical design makes client/server possible; without that logical design, distributed systems are almost impossible no matter how the boxes are arranged. So forget about distributed versus centralized for now, and focus on better application structure. After you've built better applications, you can look at how to distribute them — if it still makes sense to do so.

APPLICATION ARCHITECTURE

How do you go about designing the logical structure of an application? By using an architectural model for talking about applications — an application architecture. The nontechnical person may think that architectures are abstract, technical, and hard to understand. The analyst, programmer, or development manager may believe that most of the architectures seen recently have no real substance — that they're really *marketectures* concocted to make a particular product line appear more advanced than the competition. However, a good *application architecture* provides a framework for thinking about, designing, building, and deploying applications that fit together and work well.

People have been building computer programs for about 40 years, but they've been putting up buildings for thousands of years. Drawing from that older experience of building construction, we can distinguish three distinct phases of the process of development:

1. *Architecture.* Develop a broad plan for the overall shape of the structure, how it will look on the outside, how the floors and floor plans will be laid out to meet the needs of the inhabitants, giving the building its personality and character.

2. *Engineering.* Design the internal physical structure to support the shape and goals laid out by the architecture, taking into account strength, efficiency, and construction costs.

3. *Construction.* Build the structure using construction tools and physical materials.

In designing an application, the first and most important step is to ensure that the application really meets users' needs. Only then do engineering considerations related to strength, cost, and efficiency come in. After the engineering design is done, construction can begin. So the first task is to understand what the application is supposed to do. Based on the application's functions, you can determine which application structure will best meet those needs.

First, I want to look at the architecture of today's applications. Remember that the architecture I'm about to examine is *fundamentally inadequate* for building the distributed systems of the future. I want to look at that architecture and then discuss where and why it's wrong.

QUESTIONING MAINFRAMES

Because mainframes have been running the business for over 30 years, we must ask the following question: what does a mainframe do for the business? This is the first of four questions that drive the thinking for the next few chapters of this book:

1. What does a mainframe do?

2. How can servers replace part of a mainframe?

3. How are distributed databases designed?

4. Are distributed systems technically practical?

WHAT DOES A MAINFRAME DO FOR THE BUSINESS?

Chapter 8 explored why mainframes were more than just big, fast, expensive personal computers. However, what business function does the mainframe play? Why do companies even buy those computer systems to begin with? Superficially, the answer is to run the business. If you probe, you quickly get technical answers such as "It runs MVS, IMS, and VSAM." However, those are facilities on the mainframe that merely support business functions.

To understand what people think mainframes do, look at various proposals to replace mainframes with client/server systems. Seminars, sales presentations, and internal planning sessions yield similar views of a client/server application architecture:

✦ *Front end.* All applications have a front end, increasingly based on a graphical user interface (GUI). Today some front ends may still run on terminals, but everybody agrees that soon all front ends will run on personal computers. The role of the client is clear; it runs the front end, providing the interface to the user.

✦ *Back end.* The majority of production data resides in non-relational databases. However, there is surprisingly strong agreement that the client/server systems of the future will revolve around structured query language (SQL) and relational databases.

Table 11-1 illustrates the industry-standard application architecture.

Table 11-1   Model of the Client/Server Application Architecture

Layer	Contents
Front end	Desktop application, graphical user interface
Back end	Database, relational SQL

Essentially, here's what the table says:

✦ Simple applications, those that don't require a large shared database, can be built on the desktop alone.

✦ More complex applications require two layers: one for the desktop application and one for the database. The database can run either on the same personal computer as the desktop application or on a server. Either way, when the application gets more complex, classifying the database as a separate architectural layer becomes important.

From this architecture, some people may conclude that *the mainframe is a database.* At one level, this answer is understandable. However, at another level, this answer is actually wrong. Unfortunately, many people, including most of the computer industry, believe that mainframes are just databases.

Certainly the personal computer industry appears to view mainframes as very big databases. Listening to people in the industry, the prevailing belief maintains that "if we could just build big enough (multiprocessor) servers, robust enough operating systems, and sophisticated enough database software, those servers would finally replace the mainframe." There are many reasons to hold this belief:

✦ Many servers are either file servers or database servers. All the more sophisticated servers are sophisticated exactly because they run databases such as Sybase, Oracle, and DB2/2.

✦ The servers connect to mainframes primarily to access databases.

✦ Organizations use servers specifically to replace mainframe databases.

✦ Organizations keep applications on the mainframe usually for better database performance, database integrity, and database functionality.

It's little wonder that PC hardware and software professionals view the mainframe as merely a big database. What's more surprising is that many mainframe professionals hold this view, too. The primary argument always made by mainframe people is that — even long-term — the mainframe is at least as good a server as a PC, and perhaps even better. And because the mainframe is being portrayed as a better server than a PC server, the picture is clear. PC servers and mainframe servers compete in the *back end* layer; they're both essentially databases. The picture of the mainframe as a database may be clear, but it's also wrong; the mainframe is more than just a database.

What's wrong with this picture? On the front end, is there more than graphical desktop applications on a PC? And on the back end, are there more than databases, which are sometimes on servers and sometimes not? To answer these questions, think about a few more questions:

✦ *Where's COBOL?* Worldwide, over 2 million programmers continue to list COBOL as their primary programming language; it is the most heavily used language by those who program for a full-time living — by far. Where is COBOL in the architectural picture?

   • On the front end, are people using COBOL to develop graphical applications? Not a chance? For many developers who grew up with personal computers, BASIC is their language of choice. And certainly Microsoft, with Visual Basic and Access Basic, has provided powerful tools for building graphical applications quickly. Other GUI developers swear by SmallTalk and its relatives, such as Enfin. For highly technical work and dyed-in-the-wool hacking, there's no substitute for C and C++. And, of course, tools such as PowerBuilder and Notes either bring along their own notations or build on one of the languages I've just mentioned. COBOL is not particularly well suited for highly graphical front ends. It can be done, but why bother? So no COBOL here.

   • How about the back end, where you'd expect to find COBOL for sure? Yes, except that now we've defined the back end as the *database*, and the language we're working with is SQL. Even if you use an object-oriented database (OODB), the language will still not be COBOL; it will be SmallTalk or C++. So there's no COBOL here, either.

Unfortunately, industry seminars are presented every day with this two-layer architecture either implied or spelled right out but leaving no room for CO-BOL in the picture. COBOL isn't even *acknowledged*. It's as though the language died so long ago that everybody's forgotten it ever existed.

✦ *Where do CASE-generated programs reside?* Many leading CASE tools generate code for applications. When the CASE tool generates its COBOL or C code, *where is it used?* Not in the front end and not in the back, for the same reasons I've already discussed, so where does the CASE code go?

✦ *Where do the business rules go?* This is the core question, the one I'll use to expand the architectural model to include a third layer. Taking a few examples, where does the code go that:

- Makes credit-authorization decisions involving hundreds of rules and criteria?

- Runs a blacked-out warehouse containing millions of dollars worth of inventory, routes robot forklifts, schedules trucks, and tracks every inventory item?

- Manages seat assignments and reservations for an airline?

Each of these examples involves hundreds of thousands of lines of code that is not database code and is not front end code. This code runs business processes consisting of hundreds and thousands of business rules. The code that executes *business rules* is typically written in COBOL or generated by CASE systems with only one goal: to implement business rules. Where does all this code live?

✦ *Where's batch?* Remember all of the big programs I talked about in Chapter 8? Those big programs have no user interface components and certainly don't run on a desktop. They use a database heavily, but are not themselves either databases or database code. Rather, these batch processes also revolve around business rules and business processes.

This discussion enables me to answer that first of four questions, figuring out finally, from a business perspective, what a mainframe does. As I'll soon show, the mainframe runs business rules, providing a home for COBOL- and CASE-generated code, a place where batch programs can live happily. Understanding the true role of the mainframe answers all these tricky questions behind the bigger question of what the mainframe really does.

MAINFRAMES AND BUSINESS PROCESS AUTOMATION

Historically, the mainframe has been the central engine that runs the business by implementing all the business rules that keep the organization running. Business Process Reengineering makes the mainframe more — not less — important as the key engine that makes all the business rule-centered processes even more automatic. If you want to replace mainframes, it is that central function — the execution of business rules — that you better replace in a highly effective fashion. The central role of the client/server systems of the future will be running those business rules.

Suppose that you could keep track of every second of a mainframe's processing; what would you find out? Some of the time would go to the operating system (OS), the computer equivalent of administrative overhead. Ignore that part of the time. On most big mainframes, what's left is split about 50/50. Half goes to the database. Yet organizations don't use relational databases for high-volume applications precisely because they can't afford more than half of non-OS processing for databases. They have to reserve the other half of the computer's time — half of its *cycles*, as computer people say — to *the application*. Which brings me to the next question: *what's an application?* Generally, applications are software programs that deal closely with how an organization spends its time. To understand these applications, consider some everyday business processes.

When a customer rents a car, how long does the rental company retain a record of that rental? For the few minutes it takes to process the customer through the checkout stand? No, much longer than that. At a minimum, the car rental company retains a record of the rental until the car is returned a few days later. If the car is returned damaged, the company holds the record until all of the damages are paid. If the damage is particularly bad, the rental agency retains the record so that if this customer frequently damages rental cars, eventually the customer's status can be changed to prohibit further rentals. An apparently simple rental is a much more complex *business process*, requiring many steps and potentially lasting days, weeks, or even months.

Many business processes easily stretch into months. For example, stores order products, track their popularity, and adjust future orders to match customer demand. That process stretches over months and years.

In large companies, processing single orders can take months or even years. The order may be staged over many shipments — with products that require special manufacturing runs, complex shipping schedules, and deliveries all over the world. Even after delivery, invoices have to be cut, payments tracked, and commission payments computed. Then various accounting entries have to be made at the right times, and all entries must be reflected in monthly, quarterly, and annual reports. In other words, organizations of all sizes spend their time in *complex business* processes that consist of *many steps over a long time.*

Who keeps those processes running? For example, when a customer's bill payment is late, who decides that it's overdue? Who remembers to send out a reminder letter, schedule a phone call, and eventually change the customer's status to refuse additional orders? Who arranges for large orders to be shipped to many countries — with manuals in the right languages? Who injects parts of the orders into manufacturing runs at just the right time? And who sends out the invoices, ages them (remember the big batch process), tracks payments, calculates commissions, and posts these actions to the accounting system? The mainframe, of course, during the time reserved for running applications.

Taken separately, mainframe applications complete specific tasks. Taken together, the overall set of mainframe applications is the engine that makes business processes work. Therefore, the mainframe's true central role is *running business processes.* Maintaining the database, making data available company wide, and coordinating access *are* important — but distinctly *secondary roles.* The database, important as it is, really exists first and foremost to support the business processes. That support justifies the mainframe as the invaluable business process engine.

Is the mainframe, or its replacement, becoming *more* or *less* important as a *business process engine?* Think back to one of the primary design principles of Business Process Reengineering: the elimination of queues. To understand the role of the mainframe in making that happen, imagine that the interface to the mainframe is the smooth surface of a lake at dawn. The applications and processes running inside the machine are the fish swimming beneath the surface. Periodically, a fish jumps out of the water, causing ripples to spread over the entire surface of the lake. Those jumps correspond to processes requiring human intervention. Orders need approval; special shipments have to be scheduled manually, and so on. These human interventions disturb the system. Each time an application needs help from a person, a request is put on a queue, delay is automatic, and the process is suspended until a human completes the task. These queues, or delays, cost money and slow the system down.

Business Process Reengineering is about eliminating those queues. In the course of reengineering a process, each step, each intervention, each request for help or a decision is analyzed.

✦ Can the step be eliminated altogether? Is the analysis, approval, or decision really necessary?

✦ Can the decision be made when the process is initiated — by the person? If the decision is made early on, then the process won't be delayed by the decision later.

✦ Can the decision, analysis, or approval step be handled automatically? Can the business rules be put into a computer program so that the rules can be applied automatically without human intervention?

Ideally, then, the business processes would be *completely automatic*, with no delays and no human intervention. The surface of the water remains almost completely still with fish disturbing the calm only occasionally. Of course, like all ideals, this one will never be achieved. In fact, having organizations run completely automatically, with no human intervention, isn't even desirable. The point is not to achieve total automation, but instead to eliminate unnecessary queues, unnecessary approval, and unnecessary human intervention. The computers do their part, leaving the people with the decisions that really benefit from human input. Although even this ideal may take a long time to realize, it is at least appropriate. Achieving this ideal — eliminating all unnecessary queues — makes the role of the computer as business process agent more important than ever.

In this scenario, is the mainframe more or less important? Far more important? *The more automatic the processes become, the more critical the need for an engine to coordinate, sequence, and ensure the smooth operation of all those automatic, multistep processes.* The mainframe, or its replacement, becomes even more critically important in the reengineered future than it was in the task-focused past. Again, the true point here is not that mainframes should be eliminated per se. The point is that the function the mainframe performs, namely the automation and execution of business rules, becomes more important than ever. As you think about replacing all those mainframes, it is that central function, the automation of business rules, that you really should be thinking about most.

There is now a complete, business-oriented answer to the question, *what does a mainframe do?* A mainframe is a *business process automation engine.* It manages the execution of the business processes that keep the organization running. The mainframe is the *master of extended time.* It runs individual applications that complete particular tasks. Much more importantly, the mainframe runs the *processes that extend over time.* When a customer rents a car, no employee has to worry about remembering when the car is due back, whether the customer has damaged cars too many times in the past, and whether a specific car is available to rent. The computer handles these responsibilities. When a salesperson finally wins that big order for products to be delivered over three years, he or she doesn't have to sort out how to get products delivered in 17 countries, in six different languages, all staged over a three-year period. The mainframe arranges all shipments, ensuring that all of the right steps happen at just the right time — a month later and three years later. Commission payments? The computer triggers those at just the right time, too. Because mainframes can manage complex processes over long periods of time, business process automation is possible. By eliminating the individual schedulers, rule interpreters, and other specialists who used to run the processes one task at a time, the computer liberates workers to make those processes simpler, faster, and most automatic. The mainframe is the automatic transmission of *business process automation.* And when you eventually replace one or more mainframes, it is that automatic transmission, that business process automation function, that you will most need to replace.

BUSINESS RULES, BUSINESS SERVICES, AND BUSINESS AUTOMATION

How does the mainframe manage and implement all these business rules that keep the organization running? The answer is by running applications. The primary role of the applications running in a mainframe is to implement business rules. Business rules are all of the thousands of rules that define how the business runs.

Business processes, the same processes that Business Process Reengineering is all about, *are* business rules; in the end a process is just a collection of these business rules. Some managers and consultants may object, saying that defining processes in this way sets up a very bureaucratic view of the world. Perhaps, but computers in the end are mechanical devices, and the processes I am focusing on are the ones best suited to mechanical interpretation. Furthermore, to the extent that reengineering encourages workers to focus on the automation of processes in this way, it too is encouraging workers to focus on the mechanical element in organizational functioning. Most of all, the key to thinking of processes in terms of rules is that it allows the computer to automate the mechanical parts of the business, leaving only the truly empowering and creative part to people.

So if the applications that mainframes run are composed of sets of business rules, what do these business rules look like? How do they relate to the larger processes that reengineering focuses on? The answer is that the applications, built from business rules, implement the individual steps which define the larger business processes that keep the organization running. Here are some examples of the types of business rules I am talking about, as they relate to a company that builds, sells, and ships products. Notice that each of the examples consists of one or two rules that allow some step to happen in the bigger process of building and selling products:

+ The minimum order size accepted by the factory is $5,000. Orders that involve multiple shipments must total over $50,000, and no single shipment can be less than $2,500.

+ Commission payments are made after payment is received from the customer. Commissions are normally paid at the rate of 5 percent of the amount of the sale. However, when the customer pays his bills late, the commission is reduced by 10 percent for each 30 days the payment is late.

+ Normally, orders are filled on a first-come, first-served basis. However, when there is insufficient inventory, the customer classification number is used, with Class A customers served first, then Class B customers, and so on.

Those are examples of business rules. Superficially, it's not hard to imagine what a rule looks like. Generally, the form is *If A then B*. Sets of rules define business processes. Rules may be applied all at once or they may be applied in various sequences over long periods of times. In the preceding section, I introduced the concept of extended time; processes that happen over long periods of time are said to occur in extended time. Extended time is introduced by rules based on events that in turn occur at particular times. For example, interest is charged on invoices when they have been outstanding for over 30 days. Phrased as a program statement, the rule states that If invoice outstanding > 30 days then charge interest. The command charge interest, in turn, would trigger a set of business rules that specify the conditions for determining how much interest is due. Historically, most people have thought about computers as dealing with transactions and other events that last a short time. The essence of business process automation, however, is dealing with processes that extend over long periods of time. That's why the idea that applications can deal with business rules in this world of extended time is so important.

At last I can talk about the fundamental problem with the architecture used to build applications today — the fundamental problem that makes it so hard to even think about, let alone build, distributed applications. Today's application architecture provides no explicit home for business rules.

Where do the business rules fit into the application architecture? Simply create a layer just for them. As Table 11-2 shows, the new business rules layer lies between the top and bottom layers. These two layers have been renamed, too, to provide names that more correctly describe the functions of all of the layers.

Table 11-2   Revised Client/Server Application Architecture

Layer	Contents
Documents	Desktop applications and graphical interfaces
Business rules	Business rules and computational processes
Data management	Databases (relational and SQL)

The easiest way to explain the functioning of the new architecture is to illustrate with an example. Suppose that a customer is renting a car:

✦ The staff member working at the checkout counter is running a desktop application program in her personal computer. As part of the document layer, the desktop application presents a series of documents (forms) on the screen about available cars, customers, outstanding charges, and so on. When enough information has been entered for a complete business request, the document layer sends a request to the business rules layer.

✦ The business rules layer contains computational programs that understand the business rules associated with various task requests. One such program processes checkout requests: checking whether the customer has a reservation, whether the type of car requested is available, and determining the rental rate.

✦ As the business rules layer does its work, it periodically interacts with the database layer. The business rules layer retrieves database records for customers, cars, and rentals. When all of the checking is complete, the business rules enter transactions to record rentals, payment of charges, and vehicle status.

What is the real difference between these three layers? Particularly how are the business rule and data management layers distinguished? Table 11-3 formalizes the functions of the three layers. The paragraphs after the table describe each layer in detail.

Table 11-3 **Functions of the Layers in the Application Architecture**

Layer	Responsibility	Functions	Tools
Document	Understandable, efficient interface	Presentation, navigation, manipulation, and analysis	Graphical tools and languages
Business rules	Policy: rules and heuristics	Decision making, policy enforcement, and resource coordination	C, COBOL, rule processors, BASIC
Database	Consistent, secure data	Consistency, security, integrity, and safety	Databases, database languages

At the top is the *document* layer often also talked about and thought of as the "desktop application" layer. The *responsibility* of the document layer is to provide the *user interface* for the overall system. This layer is the most challenging to find a name for. Users think of the programs running on their desktop as applications or tools. Yet the developer of the overall system thinks of the business rules and database components as part of the application, too. In the final analysis, the basis for naming the layer revolves around what is actually presented to the user on the screen: documents. The document may be a form, a graph, a memo, or a piece of electronic mail; all of these are documents. Hence the name.

The document's responsibility is *understandability* and *efficiency*. Understandability is what GUIs are all about: presenting information in a clear format; allowing the user to control the computer without learning complex commands. Applications must also help people get the work done quickly; that's efficiency.

Understandability and efficiency are critical, but what does a document enable people to do? The function of the document layer is to provide the *user interface* to the overall system. Superficially, *user interface* refers to application windows, mice, ease of use, and other stylistic considerations. These are important, but the document layer is responsible for a great deal more:

✦ *Navigation:* The document provides a menu, form, and command structure that allow users to find what they need — whether it's a command to run or a report to print.

✦ *Presentation:* Documents displays information in various forms, including graphs, sounds, words, and numbers.

✦ *Manipulation:* The document can be used to create and change information to meet the needs of the user.

✦ *Analysis:* By combining presentation and manipulation functions, the document allows the user to perform *what if* analyses for a decision, answer, or result.

In the aggregate, the *document* layer transforms the personal computer into an *electronic desk* (see Figure 11-1). The other two layers inject information into that desk. When the document layer receives the information, it becomes the user's to work with. What makes the client/server system so empowering for users is that the document layer allows the user to work with and transform data. Unlike a terminal, which just presents data under the control of a distant computer, the document layer creates the possibility that a computer may also be present on the user's desk. That computer not only presents information and enables the user to enter data into forms, but it also enables the user to work with all the information injected into the layer by using personal productivity tools. The idea that spreadsheets, word processors, and other tools can be used to manipulate information after it enters this desktop layer creates a great deal of personal empowerment for users.

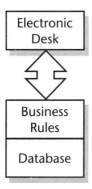

Figure 11-1: The electronic desk in the application architecture.

Finally, the software in the *document* layer is built with graphical tools, languages such as SmallTalk and Visual Basic, and high-level applications like Excel and Paradox.

The *business rules* layer is responsible for implementing the organization's policies. Policies are more than just rules. A rule is a precise statement, usually in the form of a syllogism (If... Then...). In practice, many of the decisions handled in the business rules layer are less precise than this. Instead, the software in the business rules layer is based on heuristics. A heuristic is a guideline that is often couched in probabilistic terms. For example, If the customer pays most of his bills on time, let him go over his credit limit a little. The terms most and a little prevent this statement from being a

precise rule. Nonetheless, it's easy to imagine a business rule process that implements this policy by using a combination of percentages, trend analysis, and occasional requests for human help. So the *business rule layer* is responsible for rules and
for heuristics.

Furthermore, the business rules layer implements rules and heuristics in the form of
decisions. These decisions fall into three broad categories:

✦ *Formal decisions* involve explicit requests for authorization. Is this transaction
   within the customer's credit limit? Can the order be shipped by Thursday?
   Will the company lend $7,500 to finance the purchase of this particular car?
   In these cases, a process in the business rules layer makes an explicit decision or answers a question.

✦ *Policy enforcement* decisions are implicit. Although a question may not have
   been asked, the business rules layer also enforces the implicit rules. Here are
   examples of policy-enforcement decisions:

   • Customers with outstanding orders can't be removed from the database.

   • Managers can't approve payments that exceed the manager's authorized limit.

   • No single shipment can tie up more than 10 percent of the available inventory in
     stock for critical products.

   These policies are enforced continuously — even though nobody explicitly
   asks questions that mention the rules by name.

✦ *Resource management decisions* are also implicit. Here are some examples of
   resource management decisions that the business rules layer makes:

   • Accepting orders only when inventory is in stock

   • Cutting off seminar registration when seats run out

   • Managing the scheduling of shipments to optimize delivery times

   As with other types of decisions, resource management decisions are if...then
   decisions. However, resource management decisions affect resource assignments rather than return yes/no answers to questions.

In the business rules layer, COBOL finally has a home! The software components that
define policies, business rules, and complex scheduling algorithms are most like the
large-scale COBOL applications of the last 30 years. In addition, programmers can
generate business rule components with CASE tools in rule-based systems and with
even newer classes of tools. Believe it or not, BASIC may have a role in defining many
types of business rule processes. Even spreadsheets may be solid foundations for
expressing certain formula-based rules and heuristics. Programmers could use these

and other tools to develop computational programs that implement the decisions, policies, and rules for running business processes programs over extended periods of time.

The *database management* layer is responsible for maintaining *consistent* and *secure* information. A well-designed database management layer maintains data security and data consistency while delivering good performance. The following sections provide more information about data security and data consistency.

DATA SECURITY

The main purpose of the database management layer is to ensure data security. A system must *never* accidentally lose the information it acquires. That's the point of elaborate backup procedures, expensive tape drives, and mass storage systems. Additionally, the database management layer must also make data available *only* to those who have a right to see it.

DATA CONSISTENCY

Consistency ensures that corporate presidents don't become irate, that corporate vice-presidents will get the same answers when attacking a problem, and that many files and tables can be linked together in meaningful ways. Therefore, another critical function of the database management layer is to maintain consistency in the system's data.

Put another way, *the database management layer ensures the meaning of the data it stores.* To accomplish this goal, the database management layer must make data available when needed, accept new data *only* from people allowed to enter changes, and format new data in a consistent fashion. Most important, the *design* of the database management layer must ensure consistent answers to questions now and in the future. This is the central challenge facing designers who are building client/server databases.

The main tools for building and operating the database management layer are databases, database design tools, and database languages like SQL.

ARE WE THERE YET?

The key to understanding this three-layer architecture is remembering that it is a logical architecture, not a physical one. The very same three-layer application architecture can be used to build distributed systems — but also centralized systems, too. That's the point: the three-layer application architecture is a better way of building applications — whether or not they're distributed. However, this architecture will make it easier to distribute application components, if necessary for business reasons. Therefore, the following sections describe how to use the three-layer architecture to build different types of physical systems.

PHYSICAL AND LOGICAL ARCHITECTURES

A *physical architecture* talks about the physical design of a system. Creating a physical design is the last step before either writing actual code or rushing out to buy hardware. However, a *logical architecture* is a way of thinking about the broad structure of the application while still leaving lots of choices about how it will be built physically. In designing buildings, a logical design would describe the need for a certain number of bedrooms, a living room, a family room connected to the kitchen, and so on. A physical design, on the other hand, translates the logical design into a precise floor plan complete with dimensions. The whole point of a logical architecture is to capture the broad elements of the overall design while leaving many of the particular choices purposely open.

In the computer world, physical architectures deal with choices about the types of computers installed at particular locations, the actual number of computers required to handle a particular number of users, the type of operating system running each class and type of computer, the amount of disk storage installed at various offices, and so on. The logical design, on the other hand, describes the functions the applications provide to the user, the broad division into layers within the application, and how the major functions within the application relate to each other, all without tying down all the physical options.

Many designers and programmers may look at the three-layer architecture I've just described and conclude that the architecture is physical. It is too easy to draw that conclusion because of the amount of religious controversy about the best way to build client/server systems. The specific problem is that one camp in this religious war is supposed to believe in a three-layer physical architecture. After all, this one camp argues, client/server systems are supposed to have three layers: a workstation, a server, and a mainframe. The problem is that another camp argues just as strongly that having three layers is not required for the construction of effective client/server systems.

The desktop workstation is important; everybody agrees about that. And the database has to reside somewhere; since the mainframe isn't going away, the argument goes, then it can live there. But why bother with an intermediate server? Why not have just a mainframe (as a server, if that sounds better) with lots of workstations connected to it? Of course, nobody would argue against the fact that inexpensive computers acting as servers, sitting between a mainframe and desktop personal computer, offer many advantages in terms of price, performance, and user responsiveness. The question is whether those intermediate servers are really necessary. Die-hard mainframe defenders argue that the intermediate servers, although they do have advantages, are convenient but not required. And because having more computers and more layers introduces more complexity, why not at least consider going back to just two layers? The question these defenders of the status quo will ask about the new three-layer architecture is whether it is really just another way of arguing for servers — an extra physical layer between the mainframe and the desktop computer.

The critical thing about the architecture I'm talking about is that it favors neither camp. It has nothing to with how many physical boxes and physical layers are finally used to build the running system.

This application architecture has huge advantages in terms of improved development approaches, even if all of the code runs forever on a mainframe with terminals. The architecture we are developing is a better way of designing applications — whether or not they are implemented in a distributed client/server world.

Computer professionals love to talk about physical topics: what processing should be performed on which computers, which operating system is the best, and what's the best or fastest computer. The question of *what should be done where* is particularly hot because it raises to a fever pitch all the religious issues about two-versus three-layer physical architectures. For this reason, industry consultants love to portray the *what-goes-where* controversy in diagrammatic form and, of course, attach fancy names to the alternatives. Figure 11-2 shows a typical *what-goes-where* diagram. In this figure, *M* stands for mainframe, S stands for servers, and P stands for desktop workstations and personal computers. Aside from being interesting in itself, the diagram unwittingly proves a key point: *the application architecture works well no matter how many physical layers there are.*

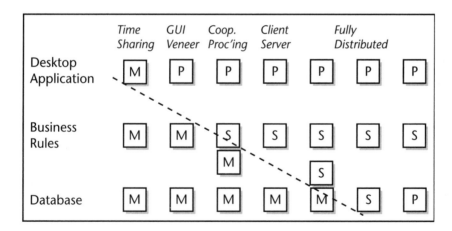

Figure 11-2: A what-goes-where diagram with mainframes, servers, and personal computers.

When you're looking at some of the columns in this diagram, consider the progression starting at the left:

✦ The standard mainframe environment implements *timesharing*; terminals all share the computer time provided by a single central computer. The three layers still make total sense. The software simply runs on a single mainframe. Of course, providing a friendly user interface on a mainframe system would be too expensive.

✦ As users become more sophisticated and demanding, it becomes tempting to implement *GUI veneers*, which make existing applications look more attractive. This satisfies users for only a very short time. Even though the desktop personal computer has now entered the picture, resulting in a two-layer physical architecture, the logical structure of the application is still best represented in three layers.

✦ To provide self-managed teams with autonomy and improved performance, an organization can move some business rule processing onto servers at local sites. In this case, the company still retains control of the database on the mainframe at a central location. IBM coined the term *cooperative processing* to describe this situation — where a local and central computer cooperate to process work. Three physical layers exist at last; the three logical layers remain constant.

✦ To achieve true *client/server* processing in a big company, a server must be able to process local transactions on its own. For example, an ATM can accept deposits and issue cash withdrawals, even if the mainframe is down.

✦ Finally, in what some MIS organizations view as the terrifying last step, *the database itself becomes distributed*, either partially or totally. The mainframe may have disappeared in these last few columns; the physical architecture may have shifted back to two layers (server and desktop); the three-layer application architecture still remains constant.

So the three-layer architecture is much more than a way of talking about distributed systems. It's also a way of talking about centralized systems, distributed systems, and everything in between. *What goes where* may be an interesting question; in fact, before a system can be built, that question must ultimately be answered. It is much more important, however, to focus first on the broad logical structure of the application alone. The beauty of the three-layer model is that it works no matter what decisions are made later about what goes where, which physical architecture is best, and how many layers of computers there will be.

Building effective distributed applications runs much deeper than just deciding where things go. Effectively designed applications can be distributed relatively easily. But ineffectively designed applications are virtually impossible to distribute. So focusing on the issue of what goes where — before you figure out how to build good applications in the first place — is a mistake of the first order:

✦ Well-designed applications, built around an appropriate application architecture, can be split any way you want and need.

✦ Poorly designed applications, without a coherent application architecture, can't be split and probably will never run well in a distributed environment.

✦ Poorly designed applications also don't run well in centralized systems.

✦ The key to effective distributed systems is effective application design.

✦ Effectively designed applications will run well in centralized configurations, distributed configurations, and everything in between.

✦ Deciding where certain layers of the application will run is a secondary decision.

✦ Using a coherent application architecture is one of the central strategies for designing effective applications and systems.

Chapter 12 takes the application architecture a step further and shows the first concrete step required to translate that architecture into better applications of all types (mainframe applications and distributed applications, for example). If you build the applications more effectively, then distribution becomes possible. However, if you start out with poorly designed applications, don't even bother trying to distribute them.

APPLICATION ARCHITECTURE: A BETTER WAY OF DESIGNING APPLICATIONS

E verybody wants better applications, but how do you produce them? In the previous chapter, I proposed a three-layer application architecture that separates the document, the business process rules, and the database management functions into separate layers of code in an application.

This chapter further describes that three-layer application architecture and shows how cooperating components play a key role in that architecture. For business and software professionals who plan carefully, the three-layer architecture built on cooperating components will provide the following benefits in future application projects:

✦ A framework for building very flexible applications that can be changed easily to meet the changing needs of the business.

✦ A high level of software reuse.

✦ Easier development of large, complex applications that can sustain high throughput levels in both decision support and transactional environments.

✦ Easier development of distributed applications that support central management and self-managed teams.

THE PROBLEM OF SCALE

If everybody wants better applications, why don't they just build them that way? After all, computer science, software engineering, and related disciplines have been around for several decades now. The problem has a lot to do with scale.

It's feasible to build high-quality small applications. Modern tools have extended the reach of small applications every year. Consequently, today a programmer can use a PC and modern software to quickly develop what would have been a large application in the '60s or '70s. This development puzzles computer professionals and amateurs. If you can build small systems quickly and painlessly with tools such as Visual Basic, PowerBuilder, and Excel, how come bigger systems are still so hard to design and build? Because large systems are qualitatively different from small ones. You must use completely different techniques to effectively design, build, and maintain large systems.

WHAT IS A BIG SYSTEM?

How can you tell the difference between a big system and a small one? At one level it's easy to tell the difference. A spreadsheet or a small application to track books in a personal library is small. The application that schedules production for an automobile factory is of course big. Along the same vein, an application to track sales prospects for a single sales office might still be small — easy to design, build, and run. By the same token, the system required to run even a single bank branch or a medium-sized furniture factory can easily turn out to be pretty big — a real challenge to get up and running no matter how good the designers and programmers are. So the first thing that becomes clear in thinking about *big* applications versus *small* ones has to do with how hard the applications are to build. Applications that are pretty easy to build using available tools can be thought of as small; it is the effort required to build them that is small. Applications that turn out to be difficult to build with available tools are the ones considered big; designing and building them requires a large effort. But how do you tell — in advance — the difference between a large and a small system?

The difference between large and small applications is surprisingly hard to define. Many readers will be inclined to say that all of their needs are simple, their team is small, and they will never need to build a large application. Yet all too many users end up painfully surprised when a "simple and small application" turns out to take forever to build; the small application turned out to be big after all and worst of all, nobody could tell in advance. So how *do* you tell the big applications from the small ones? Where's the boundary line? Is it a function of number of lines of code, connections between parts of the system, database complexity, or some other measurable factors? The answer is that there is no simple answer. The dividing line between big systems and small ones is fuzzy, at best.

However, two things are relatively clear. First, big systems are necessary in big and medium-size organizations — so you can't escape the problem of learning how to build big systems well. Second, distributed systems are intrinsically more complex than centralized systems. *Sooner* rather than later, industry movement toward client/server systems will force developers to deal with systems that are *both* bigger *and* more distributed.

Generally, big systems are complex. Therefore, big systems are also difficult to develop and hard to support. For example, big networks are hard to understand and manage. Likewise, large mainframe systems are complex and hard to keep running. Consequently, the three-layer application architecture introduced in the previous chapter is based on the following philosophy: *big is difficult — and to be manageable, big must be made small.*

DIVIDING AND CONQUERING BIG APPLICATION DEVELOPMENT PROJECTS

Divide and conquer. That's the premise behind packet-switched networks, capitalist economies, self-managed teams, distributed systems, and the three-layer application architecture. No single person can comprehend — let alone build or maintain — a very large system. Perhaps aliens on another planet can grasp every detail of systems that have thousands of parts and millions of interconnections. However, human beings on planet Earth certainly cannot.

Therefore, to design and construct better applications (let alone better *distributed* applications), we must realize that today's applications are simply too big. The software in big applications tends to be inflexible, hard to maintain, hard to distribute, and hard to reuse. But what can be done?

ABSTRACTION AND ENCAPSULATION: TWO MECHANISMS FOR TURNING BIG INTO SMALL

When you develop new systems, you must find a way to divide a big application project into a series of small ones. Of course, the overall system will still be big, but you'll reduce that big system into many small pieces, each understandable in its own right. This book proposes two mechanisms for dividing and conquering big applications: abstraction and encapsulation.

Abstraction is an analytical technique for dividing a system into multiple layers of detail. Abstraction lies at the heart of effective application architecture. (The next few paragraphs describe abstraction in greater detail.) *Encapsulation*, on the other hand, is the process of combining information and behavior into a new entity called a *component*. (Encapsulation is described more extensively in Chapter 14.)

WHAT IS AN ABSTRACTION?

An abstraction is a description that identifies the essential properties of an object while hiding its concrete details. A central principle of good system design is to develop an architecture that provides multiple levels of abstraction. When you shift upward in generality, you also move up one level in abstraction.

ABSTRACTION HIDES UNNEEDED DETAIL

By using abstraction, you can hide a mass of details that you don't need at a particular level in your application. Suppose you wanted to describe the process of walking. You could describe this process at several levels of detail, which are also called *levels of abstraction:*

+ In theory, you could describe the movements of billions of electrons, atoms, and molecules in the body of the person who's walking. However, such a description would be incomprehensible — and impossible to develop. Nobody can deal with the huge mass of intricate details in an atomic description of walking.

+ At a higher level of detail, the body is composed of millions of cells. Yet there are still way too many cells to describe walking at that level of detail.

+ At a still higher level of detail, the body consists of subsystems such as the skeleton, the muscles, the nerves, blood vessels, and so on. You *could* describe walking at this level of detail, although the resulting description would be interesting only to a doctor.

+ Finally, at the highest level of detail, the body consists of parts that every child learns: the arms, legs, feet, fingers, and so on. This level of detail is the most general, or *most abstract,* level. You could easily describe walking at this level of detail: pick up the right foot, move it forward, put it down, and so on.

Reducing the amount of detail visible at one time is a critical part of describing and designing complex systems. As the previous example shows, the primary technique for hiding detail is defining the levels of abstraction in an application.

ELEMENTS OF ABSTRACTION

A layered architecture based on abstraction has three main characteristics:

+ *Clearly defined layers:* If the architecture is truly based on abstraction, the layers should build on each other, with each layer providing a more complex and sophisticated abstraction than the layers below it. For example, cells are more complex and sophisticated than molecules; the skeletal system in turn is more complex and sophisticated than the cells that make it up, and so on. Sometimes, the term *higher level abstraction* is used to make the point about how the layers of abstractions build on each other.

◆ *Formal and explicit interfaces between the layers:* Each layer must be able to call on the services of the layer(s) below it. These interfaces define high-level operations that activate the more detailed behavior implemented by the layer below. As an analogy, your brain provides instructions for picking up your right foot and putting it down in front of your left foot. These high-level operations are translated into specific firings of neurons, activation of muscle groups, and processing of sensory feedback by the body. However, all of this detail is hidden below the high-level interface between your brain and your body. So to a large extent the interface into a layer literally defines that layer. By defining the operations that are available to the layer above it, the interface specifies exactly what aspects of the functions inside its layer are visible and available to the outside world. For example, your conscious mind does not have interface functions that allow for conscious control over the individual pulsations of the heart. As a result, control over pulse rate is not an available conscious function because it's not in the interface.

◆ *Hidden and protected details within each layer:* Hiding details is an important part of both abstraction and encapsulation. For example, your conscious mind normally thinks in terms of the high-level operations it can perform with the body: moving an arm, taking a step, and so on. At the same time, your body also literally prohibits your conscious mind from controlling the body at a more detailed level. To illustrate, when you begin to run, parts of your brain, body, and nervous system cause your heart rate to increase. After you stop, your heart will slow down again. This behavior is automatic: you couldn't control it with your conscious mind even if you wanted to.

How do layers of abstraction apply to the application architecture developed in Chapter 11? The next section explains further.

THE THREE-LAYER APPLICATION ARCHITECTURE: INCREASING LEVELS OF ABSTRACTION

In Figure 12-1, the three concentric circles represent the layers of increasing abstraction in the application architecture. The most detailed layer is the database, located at the center of the diagram. The next higher level of abstraction is the business rules layer, located outside the database management layer. Finally, the highest level of abstraction is the document layer, on the outside ring. In the figure, the outer ring is the layer that's visible to users. The inner ring is what's buried deep in the system.

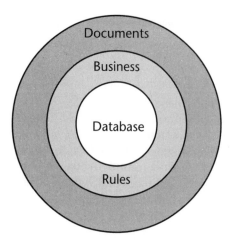

Figure 12-1: Levels of abstraction in the three-layer application architecture.

BENEFITS OF ABSTRACTION IN THE THREE-LAYER APPLICATION ARCHITECTURE

The three-layer application architecture deliberately shields each layer from the details contained in the layer below. For example, the business rules layer is shielded conceptually and mechanically from the database management layer. Generally, there are two key benefits of using abstraction to shield each layer from the details of the other layers:

✦ *Simplified application development:* Conceptually, a developer in one layer has a simpler job because he doesn't need to know or think about the details of the layer below. (The conscious mind doesn't have to worry about which neurons to fire.)

✦ *Enhanced safety and security:* Mechanically, the developer in one layer can't physically control the layer below at any level of detail. (The conscious mind isn't able to fire individual neurons, even if it wants to.) Consequently, building abstraction into your applications can enhance the safety and security of those systems.

EXAMPLES OF ABSTRACTION IN A BIG APPLICATION

Suppose that a bank teller uses a desktop application to open a new bank account for a customer. The desktop application calls on a single business rules process that opens accounts. The process that's opening the account checks with other processes to identify the following things:

✦ Other accounts the customer has open

✦ Restrictions that would prevent this type of account from being opened

✦ Special services the customer is entitled to receive

Each check involves interaction with another business rules process. All these lower-level interactions are hidden from both the teller and the desktop application that started the whole process. The developer of the desktop application does not have to worry about all the steps required to open an account. In fact, the developer is *prevented* from learning or altering the lower-level program steps.

To continue, when the business rules process is ready to open the account, it launches a series of transactions that activate the database management layer. Each transaction involves a complex set of queries and updates to specific files in the database. For example, the database management layer would do the following:

✦ Request a new account number

✦ Make sure that the account number is not in a restricted range

✦ Reserve the account number until the account is ready

✦ Record and issue the account

✦ Transfer funds from the old account

✦ Log the transfer

✦ Record the balance in the new account

Again, the designer of the business rules process doesn't have to know about these detailed steps. Instead, the database management layer performs those steps automatically when a transaction is launched in another layer of the system.

In some respects, the layers in the application architecture correspond to different levels in a bureaucracy. Keep this point in mind: by having the computer pick up the worthwhile but routine functions historically carried out by bureaucratic organizations, those functions are performed faster and more automatically, and people are freed up to be less bureaucratic themselves.

DATABASE MANAGEMENT LAYER: FILE CLERKS

The database management layer corresponds to the file clerks in an old-fashioned office. The clerks would keep track of individual ledger books, file folders, and index cards. Clerks would also follow and give instructions that are very specific — because they were moving records from one file or account to another. The clerk performing the detailed filing (database transactions) knew very little about the larger business processes causing his work. Instead, the clerk concentrated on moving the records in the proper way. For the clerks, the filing system was the whole world.

In the three-layer application architecture, the center of the application is the database management layer. As Figure 12-1 shows, everything is built on the foundation of the information in the database management layer. To a large extent, this layer is the one part of the system that could exist literally all by itself. The information has meaning and value independent of any business rules or application presentation.

BUSINESS RULE PROCESSES: MIDDLE MANAGERS

The business rules processes correspond to the functions of middle managers. As middle managers execute business rules, they generate a constant stream of detailed transactions for the clerks in the filing rooms. The clerks make the appropriate book-keeping entries and shuffle records from file to file. However, because middle managers work at a higher level of abstraction, they are unaware of the details of the filing tasks. So processing business rules in a bureaucracy requires both middle managers and file clerks — although they work at different levels of detail.

In the same way, the business rules processes rely heavily on the database management layer in the three-layer architecture. As other layers of the application generate requests for business processes, the business rules processes layer does the following:

✦ Performs the required tasks

✦ Makes decisions

✦ Launches other tasks in the business rules layer and other layers

THE DOCUMENT LAYER: SENIOR MANAGERS

The document layer can be compared to senior managers. This group enters major orders, requests product shipments, processes payments, and specifies rule changes. To perform this work, senior managers use predefined forms (applications) and request the execution of business rules processes. Each request from a senior manager triggers actions by middle managers (business rules processes) and file clerks (database transactions). However, senior managers are completely shielded from the details of those other activities.

So far I've been talking about the three-layer application architecture in informal terms. Informal descriptions are fine for providing a general understanding of a concept, but they lack the more precise detail required to actually build systems. Technically, the process of taking a concept and fleshing it out with enough detail to meet the needs of a programmer or designer is called *providing a formal description*. For example, a street address is an informal description of the location of a house, and the formal description says precisely where the house is by using the detailed language of surveyors. In the next part of this chapter, I attach more detail to the application architecture, explaining more precisely how it works. While this might sound scary or boring, it isn't. In fact, understanding this slightly more formal description is important for two reasons: first, it yields a generally better understanding of the architecture itself, and second, it is a valuable example of the process required whenever an architecture moves from initial concept to more detailed elaboration. That process of elaboration is one every organization must go through as it embraces the client/server concept. Consider the rest of the chapter both a start on that process and a dry run for the real thing.

INTERFACES: THE GLUE THAT MAKES COMPONENTS COOPERATE

Computer people frequently use the term *interface* in conversations about systems. There's the human interface, graphical interfaces, interfaces between layers in an architecture, interfaces between applications, and so on.

In the three-layer application architecture, an interface is both the surface between adjacent components in an application — *and* the device through which those components interact. To a large extent, the interface defines the external appearance of an architectural component. As an official protocol for users of a particular component, an interface performs the following functions:

✦ Tells the component what to do

✦ Inquires about the component's current state

✦ Receives the results of requested operations

In fact, in an object-oriented world, the interface becomes all-powerful. The whole point of object orientation is to encapsulate data and the programs that operate on that data into one discrete object. Consequently, the only way to work with that data will be through the interface to the corresponding object. Not only the overall layers, but even the components making up those layers become recast as objects. In that world, interfaces are the magic key to the layers and all the components within them, too.

Just as databases were at the center of the design of the applications of the '70s and '80s, components are at the center of the design of the applications of the '90s and the next century. It is *interfaces* that are at the center of the design of components that cooperate with each other effectively. *A component is defined by its interfaces.* To the extent that those interfaces are well designed, that component will be able to provide generalized services to a wide variety of other components; this is the basis for the whole idea of components that cooperate with each other. Therefore, interfaces are pretty key to making components work and work well.

TYPES OF INTERFACES IN THE THREE-LAYER APPLICATION ARCHITECTURE

The key to using the three-layer application architecture in your systems is to understand the interfaces to the three layers. The following diagram illustrates those interfaces. They include the *graphical user interface*, the *process request interface*, and the *transaction and query manager interface*.

COMMUNICATION WITHIN EACH LAYER

As shown in Figure 12-2, an interface enables a component in one layer to communicate with a component in another layer. However, an interface also enables a component to interact with another component in the *same* layer. In that same figure, communication between components in the same layer is indicated by the semicircular arrows. For example:

✦ An order-entry application on the desktop interacts with the order execution business rules process by transmitting an order-entry process request. The order execution process eventually fires off a shipment-scheduling transaction, a billing-request transaction, and a credit limit decrease transaction.

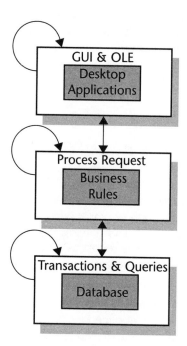

Figure 12-2: Interfaces in the three-layer application architecture.

✦ While executing the order entry process request, the order-entry application also executes a process request to the manufacturing scheduling process to build some special products. The manufacturing scheduling process then orders special parts from an inventory request process.

✦ The shipment-scheduling transaction reduces stock of a particular product below a safety limit. This shortage triggers another a process request to resolve product shortages. At a later time, removing the last item from a storage location triggers an additional transaction to mark that location as depleted of stock.

✦ Finally, the salesperson entering the order uses a spreadsheet to determine what to order. Then the salesperson embeds part of the spreadsheet into the order itself. Later, the salesperson may write a letter to the customer using a word processing file that includes the following data: part of the spreadsheet, part of the order form, and part of the shipping schedule (generated later by a shipping advice application). Every time that information from one application is embedded in, or linked to, another application, one of the interface arrows in Figure 12-2 is invoked.

What you see here, and what you'll see repeatedly, is a collection of cooperating components. The order entry component, the billing component, the shipment scheduling component, even the salesman's spreadsheet, which in this world is also just another component, all cooperate with each other. They make requests of each other, both inside and across layers; and by working together and processing these requests, wherever they may come from, the business process comes to life.

THE DESIGN OF EACH LAYER IN THE APPLICATION ARCHITECTURE

Table 12-1 provides a model for designing each layer of an application. As implied by the table, each layer is an independent entity with its own focus. To illustrate further, I'll walk through the application architecture from the lowest level of abstraction (the database management layer) to the highest level of abstraction (the document layer). As the following sections emphasize, one of the key elements that recurs throughout the architecture is the importance of keeping the three layers independent of one another.

Table 12-1	Design of Each Layer in the Three-Layer Application Architecture	
Application Layer	*Interface*	*Design Focus*
Document	GUI	Rule-independent application objects
Business rules processes	Process	User interface and data-independent decision requests
Database management	Transactions and queries	Decision-independent data

INDEPENDENCE: A TRILATERAL AGREEMENT BETWEEN THE THREE LAYERS IN THE APPLICATION ARCHITECTURE

To make documents and business rules processes independent of one another, you must avoid having business rule processes talk to users. Likewise, the database management layer must work no matter what the business rules are. Even the transactions in the database interface must not contain any business rules. (Technically, *triggers* represent linkages between the database and the business rules layer. Today, triggers are intimately tied to the database itself. However, as databases evolve to become componentized, you will be able to write triggers in the language of your choice. These triggers will be packaged as standard components. The actual trigger, in this new world, becomes a database event that is associated with a method activation on the component. The component, as just another component, can actually live and be managed in the business rule layer. Hopefully, it wont be too long until this happens.) So to keep the database management layer independent, keep business process rules strictly out of database queries and transactions.

Essentially in a well-designed application, none of the layers performs any functions that are the responsibility of the other two layers. That's where abstraction comes in. To remain independent, each layer must *hide* the details of how it operates from the other layers. Remember, the conscious mind doesn't control the firing of neurons or the heart rate. The nervous system and the detailed functioning of the heart are independent of the higher-level operations of the conscious mind. I want to show how this works in more detail, one layer at a time.

MAKING THE DATABASE MANAGEMENT LAYER INDEPENDENT

As explained previously, the database management layer is responsible for providing consistent and secure data. How does the database fulfill this heavy responsibility? By allowing access to the data only through a set of carefully defined transactions and queries.

ROLES OF TRANSACTIONS IN THE DATABASE INTERFACE

In the interface to the database management layer, transactions play three critical roles:

+ *Consistent updates:* Transactions ensure that every request is either completed as a whole or treated as though it never happened. For example, when funds are moved from one account to another, the transfer either happens completely — or not at all. Funds withdrawn from one account *must* be deposited into another account. In financial systems, this type of protection prevents funds from "disappearing." Ultimately, designing systems so that all updates are implemented solely through transactions ensures database consistency.

+ *Enforcing core business rules:* Beyond consistency, the database transactions carefully monitor and enforce core business rules. For example, any transaction that deletes a customer record will first verify that no orders, invoices, or other business actions are outstanding for that customer. Similarly, the transaction that adds an order will make sure that the customers, products, and salesperson mentioned in the order exist. If a business rule is violated, the transaction code will reject the request, undo the associated database updates, and tell the program in the business rules layer that initiated the transaction to start over.

+ *Preventing unauthorized or invalid changes to the database:* Finally, in a well-designed system, transactions are the only way to make changes to the database. So the transactional interface also functions as a gatekeeper to prevent unauthorized or invalid changes to the database.

The transactional part of the interface to the database management layer ensures that all updates are carried out in a safe, secure, and consistent fashion. Updates are not enough, however; users and programs need to be able to retrieve information from the database management layer as well as update that information. That's where queries come in.

ROLES OF QUERIES IN THE DATABASE INTERFACE

The function of the query interface into the database management layer is to provide users with an understandable and consistent way of dealing with the complex collections of records that collectively define the corporate database. In theory, users could be allowed simply to access all those records directly. However, as I've already discussed in Chapter 10, the total collection of information residing in the data management layer is hugely complicated. Typical queries can easily require records from 10, 20, or more files to be joined together. Furthermore, neither users nor application programs can be expected to understand exactly how to account for factors like currency exchange rate fluctuations, changes in product family breakdowns, or historical price changes when asking apparently simple questions. If all of these concerns are not addressed properly, then the exact situation that company presidents get so upset about arises all the time: two answers to the same question yield drastically different results. The solution to this problem is to have a formal query interface into the database management layer.

Just as the transactional interface consists of a collection of specially designed transactions that update the database correctly, the query interface consists of a specially designed set of queries that retrieves data from the database management layer correctly and consistently. Database professionals sometimes refer to these queries as *logical views*. The queries in the query interface serve three main functions:

✦ *Simplifying complex joins:* A complete database management layer for a large organization can easily have 5,000 or more individual files. Even in a small company, the databases in the database management layer can quickly grow to include dozens or hundreds of files. Users neither can nor want to understand how to combine these files in just the right way to answer simple questions. The query interface provides a world view in which these many files are reduced to a much smaller number of simpler files, each of which joins together information from many of the more elemental files containing the real data. By doing this, the query interface both simplifies the world for users and applications and ensures that the simplification is done in just the right way.

✦ *Ensuring consistency:* When you ask for the sales history of a product over the past three years, how much do you care about the effect of price changes? An answer that takes those changes into account can easily make marginal market promotions or advertising look effective. On the other hand, any analysis of profitability that ignored price changes would be wrong. The whole point of the query layer is to make sure that tricky issues such as this are handled correctly and to do so in a fashion that is relatively transparent to the application or the user asking the question. Price changes, fluctuating exchange rates, rearrangement in the composition of product families, and dozens of other variables that change with time all must be handled correctly. In addition, as products, orders, and payments move through various parts of the organization, the query interface ensures that no double counting occurs. If a customer makes a payment and later receives a refund, the query layer is responsible for ensuring that the question asked by the user or application takes account of this fact in just the correct fashion.

✦ *Security:* Appropriately constructed queries can ensure that employee salaries, customer credit limits, release dates for unannounced products, and other sensitive information are made available to only those users and applications allowed to see that information.

Overall, the query and transactional interfaces are two sides of the same coin. One allows information to be retrieved; the other allows it to be updated. Together, these two parts of the database management layer interface ensure that the information in the database management layer stays in a consistent state so that when users need the information, they can count on getting it.

MAINTAINING A CONSISTENT DATABASE

Maintaining a consistent database is the single most important function of the database management layer. The whole point of having a database in the first place — instead of just a collection of unrelated files — is having consistent data to use. A consistent database ensures that users will all end up with the same answers when they attack a certain problem. Additionally, with a consistent database, users can link many files and tables — and be confident in the results that they'll get.

CREATING A DATABASE THAT'S INDEPENDENT OF BUSINESS PROCESS RULES

Historically, programmers have mixed business rules, a user interface, and database management in the same application. In particular, business rules have been directly intermixed with database transactions. However, mixing business rules with database transactions turns out to be a major problem. The first place this problem shows up is in the lack of long-term database consistency. Long term? What's that got to do with consistency?

Maintaining long-term database consistency and managing problems associated with extended time are directly related. The design of the database — the data model — has to be independent of the business rules implemented elsewhere in the system.

Business rules express organizational policies. However, if you incorporate business policies into the design of a database, the database will become outdated when the policies change.

Suppose that you developed an application to track videotape rentals. In your application, you recorded the total cost of the rental — but omitted the rental rate and the number of days the tape was out. After all, at that time rental rates were fixed — and you could always compute how long each tape was out by simply dividing the rental fee by the daily rental cost. And because the rental cost wasn't due to change soon, you simply memorized the calculation and hardwired it into reports and programs.

However, assume that two years later management decides to increase rental rates. A little later, they also start charging more for recent releases. At the same time, they begin to promote the fact that tapes rented during the week can be kept longer. Of course by this time, your database is pretty big and you've written a lot of programs for the database in its current form. So you decide not to change it. What happens next?

After another 18 months, suppose that prices change again and management introduces even more complexities into the rental rate structure for special promotions, new classes of movies, and special membership categories. Then one day a manager asks for a report looking at checkout length and comparing it to several other variables. The manager also asks to compare rental rates against popularity. That's another report you wouldn't be able to produce. What do you say? Essentially, a frank answer would sound something like this:

> I can't answer your question because our database design included elements of the business policies themselves. When those policies changed, I became unable to produce reports involving that information. I can't compare data based on the old policies with data based on the new policies. I'm really sorry.

As you might have guessed, the solution is to make the records and fields in a database independent of current business rules and policies. For example:

✦ At first, you could compute how long a tape was checked out by simple division. The rental was $4. You charged $1 per day. Therefore, the movie was out for four days. The only information stored in the database was the net rental cost — $4.

✦ After three years, how do you do this arithmetic? Was the rate for a particular rental $1 per day because the rental took place under the old rules? Or was the rental charged under the new rules? If the rental was charged under the new rules, was it a weekend rental, a weekday rental, or a recent-release rental? How do you even know which rate was applied since none of that information is stored in the database?

Therefore, by storing rental duration and rental cost as separate fields, you would insulate the database from changes in the rental plan over time.

Making databases independent of business rules is a relative affair. Even if you take pains to insulate your database from changes in business rules, some components of your database design may change much more frequently than others. For example, storing costs in dollars is enough for domestic organizations. However, in an international organization, an application may have to handle daily changes in currency rates. Still, with enough judgment it is possible to draw the line somewhere and, based on that starting point, design a database that's independent of both the business rules and how they might change.

To build a database that's independent of business rules, follow these four guidelines:

✦ *Carefully design your database using a well-planned data model.* As difficult and expensive as it might be, there is no substitute for good database design. However, remember that designing a database doesn't have to be an all-or-nothing affair. Later, I'll explain how to build your database one component at a time.

✦ *Develop queries and transactions that provide good access to the database.* For updates, use transactions that allow access to the database but enforce basic consistency rules. Even in a post-relational world where the navigational paths are explicitly stored, many of the database structures will still be too complex for many users. Therefore, you can develop a transaction and query manager that presents a higher-level view of the data. In the case of changes, the transaction and query manager can package complex changes into larger transactions. On the retrieval side, prepackaged queries provide a simpler logical view of the more complex physical database underneath.

✦ *Allow only well-designed transactions to update the database.* Follow this guideline when you design the transaction interface to the database. Make your transactions the gatekeeper of database integrity.

✦ *Insulate the users from the details and locations of the underlying databases.* Having a formal interface in the database management layer yields an additional benefit: applications become able to deal with databases on many computers in a transparent fashion. In other words, by designing your formal transactions and queries correctly, the database interface can communicate with a variety of different databases on different computers without the user or application even knowing that this is happening.

So there you have it: a database that is independent of business rules. Building databases this way takes you back to the original vision of the database itself. Information is supposed to be a key organizational resource. It's supposed to be valuable — independent of any individual applications. And the database was supposed to make data useable even as applications changed. The old touchstone of the database believer was that *logic changes, but data doesn't.* Well, so be it. Make the database independent of the business rules.

If the database is independent of the business rules, is the converse also true? Certainly! The business rules should be completely independent of the underlying database, as the next section explains.

MAKING THE BUSINESS PROCESS RULES LAYER INDEPENDENT

The purpose of maintaining an independent business rules layer is interoperability. Aside from being an eight-syllable word, what is interoperability? In simple terms, *interoperability* is the capability to share work, share software, and do things in a consistent way throughout the company. Reusability is another term for these functions.

ELIMINATING DUPLICATION OF EFFORT

Completing a new credit application every time you deal with a new part of a big company is frustrating — not just for you, but for the company, too. The cost of maintaining several credit application procedures is wasteful. Worse, a customer can easily go over his credit limit many times just by spreading his purchases carefully among several divisions — depending on where his credit is still available. So companies have suffered from duplicated effort for a long time.

The computer equivalent of duplicated procedures is duplicated software. In the course of developing any business system, programmers generate a great deal of potentially reusable code. Here are some examples of code that might be reusable:

+ Checking customer names

+ Computing delivery routes

+ Determining inventory availability

+ Displaying product codes in the formats preferred by users

Despite the more-than-obvious benefits of reusing code, less than 5 percent of a typical project's programming is reused. So how do you get programmers to use common code? Sounds like a simple problem, right?

There are many reasons that programmers don't share code more often. But the major reason is the lack of a carefully observed separation between user interface, business rules, and database management all in the same program. In applications in which these functions and layers are intermixed, it turns out that code reuse and interoperability are very hard to achieve.

ACHIEVING INTEROPERABILITY IN THE BUSINESS PROCESS RULES

The three-layer application architecture cleanly separates business rules from documents and databases. However, this isn't the case in most existing systems. Instead, if you look at the typical application written over the past 30 years, you'll find a combination of business rules, database accesses, and user interaction code intermixed into one big program.

Suppose that you're developing the order-entry program shown in Figure 12-3. That application receives orders from a PC or terminal, processes those orders, interacts with the database, and then causes the orders to be shipped. So far, so good.

However, suppose that you decide to use a shipping application already developed in another part of the company — instead of writing your own shipping module. This software already contains the rules painfully developed over the years to facilitate accurate shipment, such as:

+ When air freight is appropriate

+ Which carriers are the best

+ How to optimize delivery routes

✦ How to calculate tariffs that apply across the country and around the world

Reusing this shipping system would yield several benefits:

✦ Reduced programming time on the order-entry system

✦ Reduced maintenance costs for the order-entry system and for all other systems that use the common shipping module

✦ Potential improvements in efficiency and customer service for the entire company — because a programmer could update one copy of the standard shipping module, and the improvements would then be automatically implemented in other applications throughout the company

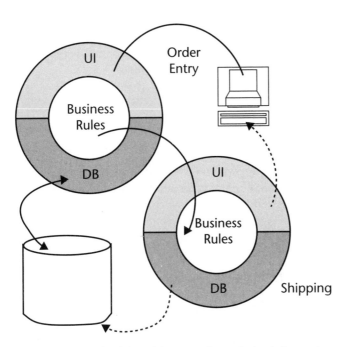

Figure 12-3: Inflexible architecture of a typical existing system.

DIFFICULTIES IN MAKING BUSINESS RULES INDEPENDENT OF OTHER LAYERS IN THE APPLICATION ARCHITECTURE

Unfortunately, most existing applications are not sufficiently general and modular to allow code reuse. Returning to the order-entry application example, suppose that the shipping module you want to reuse was originally part of a customer maintenance system. Looking back at Figure 12-3, you can see that the shipping module, like the order-entry module, has its own user interface and database functions. As a result, when the order-entry module invokes the shipping modules, guess what happens. Suddenly the user sees a strange *customer maintenance* form on the screen when requesting to ship a package. Where did this customer maintenance form come from? It certainly doesn't belong in the order-entry application.

There's more! Suppose the order entry system has its own way of recording orders and shipment dates in the database — all built into its mixed software structure. Well, guess what? The shipping module in the customer maintenance system *also* has a unique way of recording orders and shipments. So when a user asks to ship an order, the system suddenly makes strange entries in the customer maintenance database. Quite a mess, and not very usable.

Actually, this example explains two mysteries of the mainframe world:

✦ Why interoperability is so hard to achieve

✦ Why "simple" conversions of mainframe applications to take advantage of new databases and new user interfaces are not so simple

When converting big mainframe applications to new databases and new user interfaces, programmers *expect* to focus heavily on the business process rules. Unfortunately, those business rules are far from being the only functions in a big mainframe application.

Typically, over half of a mainframe application's code deals with functions *other* than business rules. For example, a typical mainframe application devotes considerable processing to updating databases and files, creating forms for terminals, showing records to users, accepting user inputs, and processing the inputs. Although Figure 12-4 depicts the components of an application as discrete layers, most existing mainframe applications mix the functions of these layers together like spaghetti.

Now suppose that you want to move from a hierarchical database system such as IMS to a relational database system such as DB2 or Oracle. In this case, you would have to laboriously restructure and test the entire application. Similarly, if you want to update the user interface from terminals to PCs — and have the PCs process most forms on the desktop — you would have to change (and possibly rewrite) the entire application.

Finally, when the team for a new development project tries to reuse the shipment module and its business rules — but *not* its customer maintenance user interaction and database updates — the result is the same: it can't be done without rewriting the whole application.

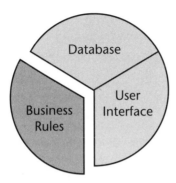

Figure 12-4: Separating the business process rules from the database and the user interface.

The solution to these problems is obvious: divide the business process rules into modular, reusable units of code. As you have probably guessed, these units of code are exactly cooperating components. In Chapter 11, I explained that by splitting out the document (displayed by the desktop application), the user can receive information, manipulate it independently (for example, with complete freedom from constraints), and send the results back into the shared system. The user and the application programmer both derive their freedom and flexibility from the same place: the architectural split into layers. For the programmer, having the business rules separated out allows those business rules to be changed, enhanced, and even rewritten without affecting the user interface. For the user, having the desktop layer independent of the business rules allows that user to manipulate the data appearing on his or her desktop, using spreadsheets, word processors, and other tools, in any way he or she likes without affecting the underlying business rules-based application code.

In the same way, separating the business rules layer and the database management layer makes the independence of the business rules layer complete. The payoff is a combination of code reusability and interoperability. Why code reusability and interoperability? Because these are the two sides of the coin called *flexibility*. Interoperability refers to taking a single piece of code that handles a task such as shipping or credit authorization and making that code perform the same function for all applications organization-wide.

Conversely, it is interoperability that makes code reuse possible. It is the company-wide use of the common module, manifesting itself in the form of interoperability across applications, that also shows up as reuse. The shipping module gets written once and then gets used over and over. To see how this is achieved by making the business rules layer independent of the other layers, reconsider how the order-entry development team could develop a shipping module in the three-layer application architecture.

Imagine that the order-entry team is ready to tackle the shipping module problem. However, in the new scenario, the customer maintenance system and its shipping module were written according to the three-layer application architecture. To focus on the software in this example, assume that the entire system will run on a mainframe with terminals just to clarify that the change I'm talking about is in the logical architecture only. Figure 12-5 illustrates the relationships between various modules in this system. This figure is an example of code reuse and interoperability in action!

Trace through some parts of the example shown in the diagram and consider these points:

✦ On the desktop, the order-entry application creates an order. This application runs in its own layer of the architecture. Consequently, the document is independent of the business rules that control order processing and certainly updates no databases.

✦ The order request is sent to the order-scheduling business rules process. This piece of code has no user interface components.

✦ The order-scheduling process sends a request to a credit authorization business rules process. The accounting department previously built the credit authorization process in another system to evaluate the creditworthiness of potential *new customers*. However, because that code was written to contain business rules only, the order-entry team can reuse the credit authorization process to evaluate a customer's creditworthiness for *new orders*. The application will not display inappropriate forms on a user's screen — or perform irrelevant database updates. So the organization can use the credit authorization code in more than one application. Interoperability: two software systems get to interoperate with each other. Again, interoperability and reuse are seen to be two sides of the same coin. On the one hand, from the programmer's perspective, credit authorization was accomplished without writing any new code; code already written as part of another application is being reused. On the other hand, the mechanism being used to achieve that reuse is interoperability: parts of two different applications interoperating with each other. What has really happened is that credit authorization has become a common process. Although originally written as part of another application, because the credit authorization business rules were split out on their own, they have become a common business rule process available to applications company-wide. As new applications need to perform credit authorization functions, they interoperate with this common process and as a result achieve code reuse.

✦ Next, the order-scheduling process requests a shipping date and commitment from the shipping business rules process (which was originally part of the customer maintenance system). Again, this new process doesn't pop up surprise screens, and it limits database activity strictly to shipping transactions. Now the order-entry team can reuse the code directly.

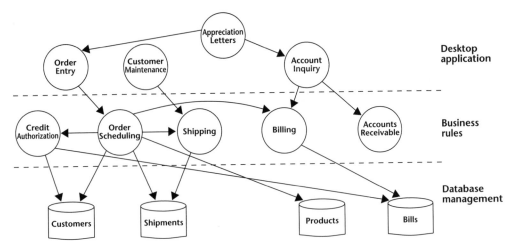

Figure 12-5: Separating the business rules layer from the database management layer to achieve interoperability in applications.

+ Finally, billing and payments are common processes in the company.

So there you have it: business rule-processes that are independent of the database and the document. What you've done is convert your monolithic application into a set of cooperating components, and these components now become the center of your entire design.

MAKING THE DOCUMENT LAYER INDEPENDENT

How would the organization benefit from making the document layer independent of the other layers? By enhancing the freedom and flexibility of users — and the organization.

FREEING USERS

A primary concern of users is adaptability. They may ask, *can I tailor the system to my needs?* Users want to view, enter, and manipulate information their *own* way. For example, one user may want to use a spreadsheet to generate part of an order. Another user may like the standard forms — but want to alter them a little. A third user may want to use a combination of a word processor and custom forms. Therefore, if the document layer is independent of the other layers, users are freed to work the way they prefer. Users will be able to make changes on the desktop — without having to worry about how those changes will affect the company's rules, policies, and procedures.

FREEING THE ORGANIZATION

Additionally, the organization will benefit from making the desktop independent. Not only is the user free from worries about the effect of his changes, so is the rest of the company.

The three-layer application architecture provides for a formal interface between the document layer and the underlying business rules processes. A desktop application sends *formal process requests* that cause the rule processes to be executed. The desktop application can do anything the user requests — both before and after sending a process request. Only the content and structure of the process request will affect the business rules process. In effect, the organization tells the user, *you're free to do things your way; our business rules are insulated from your changes to the operator interface.*

HOW RELIGIOUS SHOULD YOU BE?

If the three-layer architecture works really well, does that mean you have to be totally religious about applying it? As you probably expect, the answer is "no" for two reasons. First, for many smaller applications, a two- or even one-layer approach is often the best. Second, the three-layer approach works the best — even in the case of large applications — because those applications are transactional in nature. Whenever an application updates or changes the data, the three-layer approach provides an excellent framework for separating and encapsulating the business rules so they can be applied consistently and in a reusable fashion. How about applications that revolve (almost) entirely around retrieving and analyzing data? The best example is the so-called "information warehouse" introduced in chapters nine and ten. Such retrieval-intensive applications often lend themselves to a two-layer approach. Sometimes, even in an information warehouse, three layers still make sense — particularly when highly complex business rules are required to interpret the data. However, in many other cases, when the data (once mapped and aggregated) can be analyzed and understood quite simply, a two-layer approach is more than enough. How do you sort this all out? Use the material in these chapters to really understand the issues; then apply common sense and design sense. And for the "run the business" transactional applications, plan on three layers from the beginning.

COOPERATING COMPONENTS, THREE LAYERS: ARE THE APPLICATIONS REALLY BETTER?

Ultimately, by designing applications around cooperating components arranged in the three logical layers just described, you can improve the quality of your applications in four ways:

1. *Better databases:* By cleanly separating business rules from the underlying data, you keep the database independent of business policy changes and maintain consistent and meaningful data over long periods of time.

2. *Interoperability:* By separating business rules from the user interface and detailed database updates, you make the business rules reusable. Interoperability at the business rule-level will finally become possible.

3. *Flexibility and freedom:* By making documents truly independent of the underlying business rules, your application will better meet the needs of users. People will be able to customize the user interface without affecting the underlying business-rule processes. Conversely, you'll be able to change and enhance business rules processes without affecting the user interface.

4. *Division of labor:* Building effective client/server systems for a large organization is a big job. Developing a good client/server system requires expertise in graphical user interface design, networking, business programming, database design, database programming, distributed system design, and a host of other specific areas. Does each project team member have to know everything? No, because the application architecture provides a framework for dividing the work. As a result, you can assemble a team of computer professionals with different areas of expertise to design and build a system. In fact, as covered in a subsequent chapter, the three-layer application architecture requires exactly the kinds of skills typically available in the real world.

Even for applications destined to remain on the mainframe, the three-layer application architecture provides a very nice model for enhancing interoperability, database consistency, flexibility, and the ability to divide work in a project.

But what about facilitating distributed systems, distributed databases, and client/server systems? Yes, the application architecture lays the groundwork for those systems, too. In fact, it is also the application architecture that lays the groundwork for understanding the next major revolution following the database era: cooperating components. The architecture also leads the way to improvements in both methodologies and tools that help design and build distributed systems.

13

DESIGNING DISTRIBUTED SYSTEMS: THE COOPERATING COMPONENT REVOLUTION

After all this time, I'm ready to answer one of the hardest questions in the entire client/server world — in fact, one of the hardest questions related to development of large computer systems in general: *what are the ground rules, the model, for designing distributed applications?* How do you decide where to place the processing? How does the database get split up in some meaningful fashion? How does this relate to the standard methodologies for designing large commercial applications, methodologies built up so painfully, and finally successfully, over the years?

Because of the size and importance of the whole issue of distributed system design and the bigger issue of the design of graphical client/server applications in general, I approach the entire topic in several stages. In this chapter, then, the entire focus is on the high-level issue of distributed system design and the fundamental about-face in high-level design methodologies required to enable this kind of design. In the next chapter, this high-level approach will be folded into a more complete and general methodological framework for designing complete client/server systems. So this chapter lays out design strategy, and Chapter 14 translates that into specific methodology.

BUSINESS SERVERS: WHAT DO THEY DO?

Before hitting the big question, it's time to do a quick recap on the central elements in distributed systems: the servers. Sometime back, as the application architecture began unfolding, four basic questions were laid out, questions that would take several chapters to answer:

✦ What does a mainframe do?

✦ How can servers replace part of a mainframe?

✦ How are distributed databases designed?

✦ Are distributed systems technically practical ?

I'm now ready to answer the second question, and right after it, the third.

Recall that the primary role of the mainframe is to be a *business process automation engine,* scheduling, managing, and executing all the business rules processes that play such a prominent role in the architecture. The mainframe also plays a central role as the custodian of the corporate (and other) databases, but this role is distinctly secondary and supportive of the primary role of keeping those business processes running night and day over long periods. So what does a server do in this environment?

At one level the answer is immediately obvious: servers will run those same business rule processes that otherwise would run in the mainframe. This answer, though, carries even more weight than is apparent on the surface. *Business Process Reengineering* is about, obviously, *reengineering business processes.* The processes being reengineered are precisely the same ones that occupy that middle layer in the application architecture. As you'll see in the next chapter, this apparently trivial equation has a huge fundamental impact on the way applications are designed in the '90s as opposed to the '80s. Even before getting to that design question, though, you can tie this same equation back to the organizational revolution I talked about earlier in this book.

It is the fact that business rules are hard to change, particularly inside computers, that makes organizations rigid and makes reengineered processes hard to implement. One of the key goals in reengineering is to push decision making and judgment from the middle of the organization out. A fundamental constraint which makes that hard to do is perceived and actual inflexibility in the computer systems. *"I can't make that exception because the system won't let me do it."* That inflexibility invariably revolves around rigid implementations of business rules. It is rarely the database or the user interface that is too rigid; always it's the underlying rules. So an important step on the way to reengineered processes is putting in place an infrastructure that allows the organization's rules to be much more flexible; to lend themselves much more easily to local adaptation. At the same time, although local customization is critical, the core parts of the rules that do represent organization-wide policy must still be enforced consistently.

The problem of course is that a mainframe forces the entire organization to live with a single, centralized implementation of all those rules. Because all the rules are kept in a single place, adding exceptions for individual teams makes that single implementation too complex to manage. The answer, as you already know, is to put those rules in local servers allowing individual offices, departments, and teams to modify and extend the rules and processes of the organization to meet their local needs. Because the server is physically secure, you can trust it to enforce the unchangeable part of the rules while still allowing the other parts to be adapted. This is, naturally, the same idea I've already talked about; it's worth reviewing because it validates the application architecture and the role it assigns to servers. And as I showed near the beginning of the book, many chapters ago, I'm not just talking about a few servers, but tens of millions of always-turned-on computers dedicated to running the business rules in the middle layer of the application architecture. Quite a concept and quite an important role for all those servers to play. That brings us to that third question, the embarrassing one in the list of four questions.

HOW ARE DISTRIBUTED DATABASES (AND APPLICATIONS) DESIGNED?

Way back when, in the same chapter where the business and computer revolution came into clear focus for the first time in this book, client/server was seen to revolve around three fundamental ideas:

+ Distribution of processing

+ Distribution of data

+ Graphical user interface

The concept of having broadly distributed servers, each with its own resident database, each running business rules processes customized to the needs of the local self-managed team is certainly appealing. No question about that. The problem is that historically nobody has been able to come to grips with the challenge of designing the distributed databases implied by this model of reality.

Designing databases in the first place is already a complex challenge, as is designing big applications. Having all the data in one place provides a certain necessary simplicity to the process, which until now has been essential to making that design even possible in the first place. The concept, the dream of a distributed database environment, has been discussed extensively, both in academic and practical circles since the early '70s. With the introduction of the first minicomputers, it became clear that in many cases putting data close to the place where it is used makes a lot of sense from a reliability, performance, and cost perspective.

The problem is that the conceptual, architectural, and technical challenges associated with building these simple-to-describe systems have been overwhelming. Many technical problems have the characteristic of being trivially simple to describe and incredibly difficult to solve. Flight, long-distance communication, immortality, and holographic teleconferencing are all easy to talk about. Two of those problems are now solved, and the other two await solutions yet to be found.

Many in the technical community believe that distributed systems, or at least systems involving distributed databases, are intrinsically impossible to build on a large scale. Others believe that although distribution of data may eventually be possible, large-scale distribution of processing and decision making will just never work as well as centralized approaches. In fact, though, enough examples of working distributed systems already exist today to demonstrate both that that pessimism is unjustified and that working distributed systems are eminently possible.

Making a purchase in a large department store triggers a complex chain of events. First, the item you are buying is scanned at the cash register. The product code is sent over a local network to a store-based computer that looks up the code, determines the price, adds a descriptive label, and sends that information back to the register. After the items you are buying are totaled, the purchase amount along with credit card information read from your magnetic stripe is sent to another shared computer elsewhere in the store. That computer passes the credit validation request to a regional computer, which forwards it to the store's bank. The bank determines which home bank you deal with, asks it for authorization, debiting your available credit limit in the process. The authorization then makes its way back to the store, where the purchase is rung up and a bill printed. Finally, inventory counts are decremented, a record of the transaction is kept for later billing to your bank, and the whole process is completed. A complex, highly distributed transaction involving quite a few computers, potentially distributed across thousands of miles, is all completed in a very few seconds.

Every day at stores, supermarkets, gas stations, and banks millions of distributed transactions of this kind are completed routinely, safely, and automatically. Stores, warehouses, and central purchasing organizations each deal with their own local databases, yet the entire system functions effectively as a large, coordinated, distributed system. Financial transactions affecting consumers, stores, suppliers, and banks all complete correctly in spite of the fact that the system is distributed across not only many computers, but also many companies and even many countries. Best of all, the system scales, tolerates failures, and accommodates huge amounts of local lookup and local customization. Distribution in action.

If systems like this work so well, why is it so hard to design distributed applications in so many other business environments, where the challenges should be smaller, if anything ? The answer has to do with how applications are designed today and somewhat surprisingly with the focus (so prevalent here and elsewhere) on *tasks, transactions, and databases* instead of on *processes and components*.

A NEW HOME FOR COORDINATION: COOPERATING COMPONENTS

Consider the issue of building distributed systems in two ways. First, take a high-level view of the problem to gain a quick perspective of the solution that this book proposes. Then, drill down considerably deeper to see how to relate to the methodologies and design approaches so central to building large systems in the first place. When you're done, hopefully, the bottom-up and top-down views will come together.

Chapter 12 talked about a three-layer application architecture and the role it played in improving the design of large scale systems. You're going to revisit that topic from the perspective of distributed systems specifically. This time, the question to ask is: "*In a distributed system, where does all the coordination required to deal with distribution take place?*". You're going to get to the answer one step at a time.

First, suppose that you have a simple application best thought of in terms of a single-layer architecture. The application runs on only desktops and is built with high-productivity tools like Visual Basic or Paradox. Clearly, since your architecture has only one layer, all coordination takes place in that layer. Therefore, if your system is distributed across many desktops, the desktops just talk to each other directly. Perhaps not easy to build, but it's easy to think about. Of course, such a system doesn't scale very well. For one thing, as the number of desktops grows, having them all talk to each results in a huge amount of communication. For another thing, ensuring that all those desktops are backed up — dealing with failures when they occur, rolling out new releases of software — is just an example of why the single layer architecture lends itself only to small applications.

Most client/server applications in 1995 are built around a two-layer architecture (see Chapter 12 for more details). In this world, the decision about where coordination should take place is simple. For all the reasons just discussed and more, coordinating at the desktop level just doesn't make much sense; therefore, coordination takes place at the database level in the server. This approach is clearly better than coordinating on the desktop; the only question is whether it is good enough. Certainly, there are fewer servers than desktops, and because servers tend to be larger and more powerful, sophisticated software approaches can be used to reduce the amount of inter-server communication to manageable levels. Servers can be backed up and managed by trained staff, so that part makes sense. There's really only one question about this approach that raises big issues, and that's the question of *what's running in the server*. In our two-layer architecture, the answer is clear: *the database is running in the server*. So in our two-layer approach, it's not just the server but the database in the server that is responsible for *all coordination associated with running a distributed system*. That's the catch.

This point is considered in more detail in a few pages, but essentially, distributed databases per se *just don't work* — or at least not on any large scale. Thinking about it from the perspective of the application architecture helps make the reason clear. Distributing a system is a complex proposition. Quite a bit of knowledge is required to coordinate activities across many different sites. The database just doesn't know enough to make the decisions required for this coordination. Think about this from the perspective of the application architecture itself.

So far, this discussion has focused on the two-layer architecture. However, as you have already discovered in Chapter 12, two layers aren't enough for the bigger systems. Distributed systems are also liable to be pretty big. So for those bigger systems, you added a third layer, in the middle — a layer focused on business rules. Now you're ready to relate that layer to the challenge of distribution.

Suppose that you've built a system around a three-layer architecture: where should the coordination for distributed processing be done? Even given that it should clearly happen on a server, there are still two other possible answers: the database layer or the business process layer. Once the question is put in those terms, the answer becomes clear pretty quickly. Suppose that you have two servers at different sites talking to each other. In what layer is the communication taking place? The answer is the business process layer. You can imagine queries that combine data across several sites, but when it comes to actual business activity, that is all defined in terms of business processes anyway — cooperating components all talking to each other. And when you distribute the system, it is the cooperating components that are distributed first. So even at a high level and when given a choice, the presence of that third layer makes the choice obvious. Now here's the catch.

The business rule layer is a relatively new phenomenon. Until now, in fact since the early '70s, applications had two layers; and if distribution was required, it just seemed obvious in that two-layer world that the database should make it work. The fact that nobody could figure out how to make it happen didn't make the challenge go away. It's only with the third layer that an option even comes into view. So on one hand, this is about how the problem is conceptualized; but on the other hand, it's not unusual for that to be central to solving a problem in the first place.

So that's the high-level view of where we're headed. Distributed systems are based on coordination in the process layer. Distributed systems are built out of cooperating components. Those components are both the basis for thinking about and for building those distributed systems. And the same cooperating components become the basis for thinking about the methodology that drives the design of the whole application, distributed or not. Having said that, it's time to drill down and look at methodologies, the role they play, and how that fits into building distributed systems that work.

THE ROLE OF METHODOLOGY

It's well known that a small number of incredibly brilliant programmers sprinkled throughout the computer world are unimaginably creative *and* capable of building complex software very quickly with virtually no external framework to guide them. These programmers are responsible for many of the breakthroughs that keep the industry so exciting. Other fields have their geniuses too: their Frank Lloyd Wright, their

Marie Curie, and their Albert Einstein. Most programmers, though, the vast majority of the 6 million or so professional developers worldwide, are professional craftspeople who depend on tried-and-true techniques for building their software.

A methodology is a prescribed framework for designing and building applications. It describes a series of steps, models, and approaches that if followed carefully are most likely to lead to applications that work well. Although methodologies certainly can't guarantee that software will be great, they can promise that no major steps or elements will be overlooked due to sheer oversight.

Methodologies provide the organizational structure that allows large development teams to function in a coordinated fashion. Major business applications affect many people. They are typically built by teams of hundreds of programmers. Although the work may be divided up into smaller pieces, nonetheless some mechanism must exist for coordinating the work of all those teams. Furthermore, because perhaps thousands of users may be affected, quality is critical in terms of both avoiding problems and ensuring that requirements are truly addressed. Carefully considered methodologies help deal with all these problems of scale by providing those working on the project with common vocabulary, common approaches, and control frameworks for measuring progress.

Most of all, methodologies provide predictability and control. Andersen Consulting, for example, in 1992 had 22,000 consultants worldwide, all building applications of one kind or another for clients. Almost all of those consultants were originally hired straight out of school, often with minimal technical backgrounds. Every consultant started his or her career at Andersen by attending Andersen's private *university* in the town of St. Charles, Illinois. At St. Charles, the consultants acquire a variety of technical skills in classrooms and labs, preparing them for their initial assignments in the field. Most of all, though, every Andersen consultant is provided with a thorough grounding in Method/1, Andersen's comprehensive methodology, which governs every stage of the process of designing and building software-based business applications.

Method/1, although far from unique, provides Andersen consultants with an important edge on the job. Whether junior or very senior, a team member joining a project, in the same city or another country, can immediately tell where the project is by referring to the steps defined in the methodology. That methodology, laid out in a series of thick binders, prescribes the sequences of steps, the data to be collected at each stage, the criteria for completing milestones, the decisions to be made before choosing between alternative design approaches, the naming standards for variables, and just about every other detail that might come up while building applications. Control, predictability, and consistency; without a doubt, Method/1 plays a huge role in providing Andersen with these three valuable commodities.

To understand the true value of these three commodities, it is necessary to understand the true business of a system integrator like Andersen and its competitors. Building software is certainly an important part of the business, but in an important way, not the center of it. One of the biggest problems any MIS organization faces is the risk associated with major development projects. Software development is notorious for always being over budget and late. Andersen is in the business of risk transfer. They can't guarantee that a project won't come in late, but they *can* ensure that it never goes over budget, at least from their clients' perspective. And, of course, when they make such a guarantee — an everyday occurrence — it then becomes critical for them to know that they themselves have a basis for feeling confident in their predictions. Method/1 and the methodology it entails provide that confidence.

It's no wonder then that development organizations in general, whether internal or external, have a tendency to love methodologies. Methodologies come in a wide variety of flavors. Simple ones prescribe a few milestones, some simple rules of thumb, and perhaps some naming and coding standards. On the other hand, some complex methodologies fill bookshelves, require months of training, and prescribe every aspect of the programmer's life.

A methodology is not a silver bullet. Yet many organizations want to believe that just finding the right methodology is the answer to all development problems. The first thing to understand then is that a methodology is not a substitute for thinking, not a replacement for good design, and certainly not a silver bullet that will magically simplify development or result in transcendentally better applications.

At the core of any methodology lies first an application architecture and then a set of design strategies. This chapter focuses on the design strategies at the center of the leading present-day methodologies showing why, because they are too task-oriented, they make it almost impossible to design distributed applications. Then an alternative set of design strategies that can easily be expanded into a methodology is proposed that revolves around processes, supports BPR, and facilitates distributed designs.

INFORMATION ENGINEERING

Probably the leading methodology in widespread use today, Information engineering was originally introduced by James Martin and Clive Finklestein in the early '80s. *Information engineering* (*IE*) revolves around two core concepts:

✦ A layered, holistic approach to developing integrated applications based on a strategic information systems plan

✦ A focus on first data modeling and then functional modeling to drive the actual design process

As an organization develops a variety of applications over time, making them all fit together is a problem. Customers have only limited tolerance for providing the same information over and over as they deal with separate parts of the same organization. Sales and service people have a need to pull together information from all parts of the company to answer questions and solve problems. Programmers get tired of writing the same code over and over when the functions being provided are actually very similar. All of these examples and more point out the need for application integration.

The IE solution to these problems starts with the development of an *information system plan* (*ISP*), as shown in Figure 13-1. A high-level strategic document, the ISP covers many, perhaps even most, of the applications an organization might expect to develop over some reasonably long period of time. Focusing primarily on the design of the database, nonetheless the ISP process also deals with classical planning issues including Critical Success Factors, organizational structures, and so on. Most of all though, the ISP provides a top-level view of the overall framework tying all the organization's applications together.

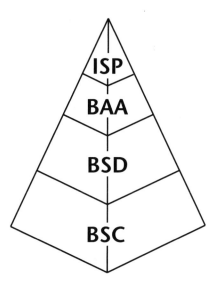

Figure 13-1: The information engineering model.

Based on the ISP, the planners then divide the company's potential application portfolio up into a number of *business areas*. The definition of the applications that make up a business area is determined in two ways. Firstly, natural organizational divisions along market segmentation and other lines are considered. In addition, though, the ISP process provides some simple tools that highlight application clustering — sets of business processes that naturally go together (have an *affinity* for each other, in IE terminology) based on common data utilization.

After prioritization, the business areas are analyzed in more detail, one by one, in a process called *business area analysis* (*BAA*) in the IE world. Each BAA provides a more detailed model of the database structures and application functions required in that particular business area.

Next, particular applications are selected for design (*business system design,* or *BSD*) and subsequent construction (*business system construction,* or *BSC*). In fact, IE then goes on to prescribe several more stages to the complete methodology-driven process including approaches to testing, release, and maintenance of applications.

Superficially then, the first major element of the IE approach is the definition of a step-by-step approach for developing integrated applications based on top-down planning. Very little, if anything, is revolutionary or even new in this approach compared to many classical planning methodologies. IE's primary contribution lay in applying these tested approaches to the planning, design, and development of computer software; a new idea at the time.

At the core of IE and other successful methodologies, though, is more than just a set of steps for planning and building from the top down. IE also prescribes a set of models and design strategies for thinking about and modeling applications. It is the models and the modeling that are really core to the issue of distributed design.

DEATH BY DATA MODELING

Current methodologies have two characteristics, both of which need to change:

✦ At an overall level, the database and the data model are viewed as being at the absolute complete center of all high-level application planning and design.

✦ When the actual computation, processing, work, and business rules are considered, as a complement to the database, they are considered from a very task-oriented perspective.

It is this pair of ground rules that has to shift.

In Figure 13-2, two labels have been added at the bottom to show the two major parts of the information engineering planning and design process. In theory, at every stage in the process, planning, design, and construction proceeds by considering two linked aspects of the application: the data model and the functional model.

In fact, though, the approach is much more unbalanced than this. The data model receives early, constant, and deep consideration, and the functional model is treated as a kind of poor relative in the entire process. There are two root reasons for this orientation, both based on solid historical considerations.

In the '60s, before databases had been invented, all design revolved around consideration of the *function* of the programs being built: the *functional model*. The database revolution (discussed almost to death in Chapters 9 and 10) changed all that. Then and now, leading thinkers about computer systems and applications proposed that applications should literally revolve around the databases providing the information required to run modern organizations. The tool used to design those databases is the data model, also discussed extensively in the same two chapters. Given that philosophy, it makes a great deal of sense to view that data model as being *the* central model driving the entire application-design process.

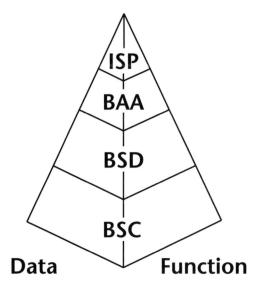

Figure 13-2: Adding the Data and Function parameters to the model.

In the early '80s, just as model-driven development, methodologies, and CASE tools were starting to really be popular, data models and database design really came into their own. The core technical design process in the Information System Planning stage of information engineering is high-level data modeling. Perhaps this sounds like a trivial or excessively technical trend to be talking about. Not so.

For two decades data modeling has been placed on a pedestal at the center of the strategic planning process. Leading gurus of both business strategic planning and effective information system planning all through the '80s firmly believed that every large organization and most small ones should develop an overall Information System Plan describing how all their applications would fit together long term. And, the gurus said, the center of that plan had to be a relatively complete, well-thought-out model of the long-term corporate database. Finally, just to make the story complete, not only was the data model critical, but also senior management was required to contribute to the development of the data model and then approve it when it was done.

This situation would be funny if it weren't so sad. And the sad results of those seeds sown ten years ago are still standing in the way of the kind of application planning and design required today. How? In three ways:

✦ First, developing a complete corporate data model is expensive and compli-cated. Many organizations set out to build these models, and after filling 30 or 40 binders over a 2 to 3 year period, they concluded that they might never finish.

✦ Senior management didn't and still doesn't understand data models. So attempts to involve them in the process are essentially doomed to failure. Senior management *does,* however, understand processes.

✦ Finally, and worst of all, a solid data model is important, but it's far from enough. No matter how good the data model, it won't lead to great applications in general, and it certainly does not provide a basis for distributed application design in particular.

How bad can this be? Most senior computer people in large organizations know stories, often many of them, about planning teams that eventually got fired for spending too long on Information System Plans. In other companies, where firing was viewed as too drastic, detailed design processes (and the CASE tools that usually went with them) came to be totally discredited. So, at worst, excessive strategic planning leads to actual career terminations, and in the best case it leads to long-term discreditation of the very design process at the heart of effective application development. And the data model had a lot to do with this overall process failure.

Ask a senior information executive if she remembers a case where a friend or colleague landed in real hot water for too much Information System Planning, wait until the reflexive wince passes, and then ask another question. Ask what that friend or colleague was doing for 6, 9, or 24 months that led into the hot water. The answer will always be the same: developing a comprehensive data model — a data model that was supposed to be the basis for that much desired integrated corporate database (in the sky). Death by data modeling. Amusing to say, but far from funny to anybody burned by this form of death in the past.

YOU CAN'T BE SERIOUS

While all this data modeling was going on, who was thinking about the other side of the application? Who was thinking about the programs, the business rules, the software itself? And while they were thinking about it, how were they doing that thinking? The first part of the answer is: they weren't thinking about it. And the second part of the answer is, that when they did think about it, they took a very task-oriented perspective.

How could they (the usual infamous *they*) not think about the applications, the rules, the part labeled *function* on the information engineering pyramid? The answer comes back to one word: *religion*. Recall that databases, particularly relational databases, became the basis for one of the first great religious movements in the computer world. CASE, methodologies, and information engineering became the basis for another great religion. And in this case, one religious movement built on the shoulders of another, resulting in a virtually unstoppable crusade.

At the center of this unstoppable movement was the idea that a data model alone was enough for the complete design of applications. Starting in 1970, the database revolution picked up a little momentum every year. With the discovery of data modeling, databases became not just a way to think about applications, but a way to design them too. Finally, by the mid '80s, some leading methodologists honestly believed that not only was the data model central, it might well be the only model required to describe a complete application. Such a belief, if taken to its logical conclusion, would imply that complete large applications could be designed *based on data models alone.* This fits in with the view, still widely held, that client/server applications consist of only a front end and a back end, and that mainframes are, after all, just databases.

Of course, just a little thought about the relative role of data and functional models leads to the almost instant reaction: *you can't be serious.* And, truth be told, nobody (except some well-paid gurus) believed that large applications could be designed by completing the design of the database and data model alone. The problem is that all this one-sided focus on the data model and its development led to a rich framework for database design while the corresponding framework for functional design virtually stood still in its development. Simply put, the functional model that existed until recently was so poorly suited to supporting high-level design as to be almost useless. The result was that, absent another model, the data model was the only one available to support the high-level planning and design process.

TASK ORIENTATION STRIKES AGAIN: THE WORLD IS CONNECTED AFTER ALL

All of this discussion should be starting to sound familiar in a scary kind of way. Recall that the basis for Business Process Reengineering is a shift away from *tasks* to consideration of broad processes (see Figure 13-3). It was the same focus on *tasks* that left the classical methodologies and design approaches so short-handed when it came to high-level design.

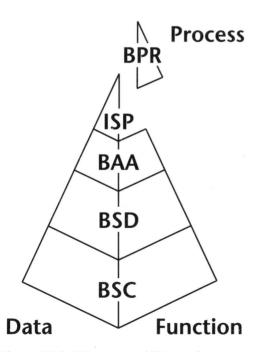

Figure 13-3: BPR means a shift toward processes.

One of the primary approaches used to consider the *functional* side of the application framework is called functional decomposition. *Functional decomposition*, well known by most application designers, is the exact equivalent of *dividing complex processes up into very small tasks.* It is the exact and total computer system equivalent of assembly-line division of labor. Functional decomposition starts with a description of a major process or task. Then the process or task is decomposed: it's cut up into smaller processes or tasks. This decomposition is then done again. And again. And before very long, the entire process or task has been sliced and diced into small mindless tasks that can then be programmed quickly and easily.

The fact that application design in the '60s, '70s, and '80s revolved so heavily around tasks is, of course, no accident. Computer professionals were just paralleling the organizational paradigm driving the rest of their organizations.

THE DESIGN CRISIS: SENIOR MANAGEMENT REVOLTS

In the early '90s something strange happened to the overall application design process. Computer people continued focusing primarily on the data model. Large-scale Information System Plans were dead, but data modeling on a smaller scale continued to be central to planning and design. Application function continued to be considered, but the approach, as before, was based on slicing and dicing into tasks. As a result, most active consideration of business rules and processes took place relatively late in the game. Downsizing experiments were being started up and later shut down. And, meanwhile, something strange was happening upstairs in the offices of senior management.

Just as MIS had their gurus, consultants, and helpers, senior management had theirs. And senior management's consultants were introducing them to Business Process Reengineering. While MIS was still trying to figure out ways to get senior management to understand data models, after all, as a tool for serious planning of future information systems, senior management was discovering a serious planning tool they could not only understand, but also work with, and even *like.* That tool, shown simply in Figure 13-4, is the process diagram.

In retrospect, the fact that nontechnical managers like process diagrams so much should have been obvious a long time ago. After all, everybody loves flowcharts (unlike data models) as soon as they see them. And the kinds of process diagrams at the heart of BPR are very similar to flowcharts. In any case, recognized early or not, while computer people continued doing things the normal way, senior management was actually designing the systems of the future.

As the pyramid in Figure 13-3 shows, even if the approach were different from how it was originally pictured, executives were building Information Systems Plans. In fact, to be more precise, executives *are* building information systems plans. They're doing it today and every day. As Michael Hammer and James Champy's book *Reengineering the Corporation* makes only too painfully clear, every large reengineering project invariably ends up revolving around new information systems, often quite different from the ones that came before. And as their book also makes clear, the people driving the reengineering process leading to those new information systems are not the information technology managers. It's the senior managers running the business who are doing it. Here's the rub; all too often they're not only doing it, but doing it in a way that deliberately leaves out the computer people altogether.

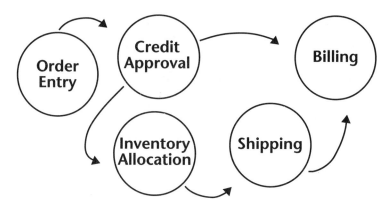

Figure 13-4: A typical process diagram.

COPERNICUS ALL OVER AGAIN: A NEW WORLD ORDER

At the time Copernicus suggested that the sun, not the earth, was at the center of the universe, that thought, that shift in model, was more than most people of the time could tolerate. In the same way, the shift to data-centered design, to a model in which the database, not the application, is at the center of the world, has been as much as most computer people can tolerate. Most organizations, frankly, are still dealing with the implications of databases, data-centered design, and data modeling. Twenty years hasn't been nearly enough for that single conceptual re-orientation to take place.

As it turned out, no sooner had the world become comfortable with the Copernican model than a new model emerged in which even the sun wasn't at the center of the world. In fact, in that model there was no center; the sun is just one more star, and perhaps not a very important one at that. A model in which the earth, the sun, and the solar system may be inconspicuous parts of a large, cold, anonymous universe is more than even most modern world citizens can easily be comfortable with. Fortunately, the second shift in the computer world order is much easier to both understand and live with.

The database is not the center of the world. After 20 years of increasing progress, understanding how to build entire application systems all centered around the almighty, all-present database, it turns out that that database is not the most important focus in this information-oriented, computer-based world. The database is still very important. It is, in fact, *one* of the centers of the new world order; it's just not the only center. And, in fact, if picking is required, it's the less important of the two centers. So what's the other center?

As should be obvious by now, that other center is the *process* (recall the pyramid in Figure 13-2). Fundamental, core business processes, the same kinds of process identified in Business Process Reengineering, are the true center of the new information world. Yes, database is there, right along with the process, but it is the process, in fact, that comes first and in many ways drives the overall design.

Recognizing the importance of process solves a huge problem in working with senior management. As long as computer people continue to view data models as the key first step in long-term Information System Planning, there will continue to be a huge credibility and understanding gap between computer people and business people. The moment that computer people, like business people, start their Information System Planning process by looking for and drawing high-level process diagrams, that moment the credibility gap starts to disappear. From that moment forward, the computer people can be viewed as friends, allies, and willing participants in the Business Process Reengineering endeavor.

But what about the all-important high-level data model, previously the centerpiece of the entire design process from top to bottom? Does it get thrown away? Does 20 years of progress at understanding databases and data models get thrown out the window? Of course not. The data model continues to be an important and central tool; it's just not one that necessarily figures heavily in discussions with nontechnical senior managers.

In designing a house, an architect may develop many complex technical models that are never shown to the client. Structural rigidity, soil loading, light and heat diagrams, and many others all play into his plans. Nontechnical clients, though, don't care about limitations on cantilevered beams, plumbing, building codes, or insulation requirements. The client wants to see floor plans, draw on them, and then move forward from there. The technical models, developed in parallel, are the designer's aides, not necessarily even relevant to the client.

In the same way, the data model continues to be important and even plays a huge role in influencing the developing process model. At times, it may be appropriate to bring up parts of the data model for discussion with senior management. For the most part, though, the process model provides a new set of diagrams and a hugely valuable tool for both thinking about and jointly working on the long-term Information System Plan and high-level application design. It is a tool that managers instinctively understand and love, just as house dwellers love floor plans. Best of all, it is the same tool and model driving BPR anyway, so that groundwork is already being laid, before the application design even gets started.

PROCESS BUILDING BLOCKS: COOPERATING COMPONENTS

What are the basic building blocks that process diagrams, and the processes themselves, are built out of? Cooperating components. When senior management is drawing their diagrams describing the order fulfillment process, those diagrams consist of circles connected by lines and arrows. The circles include "order entry," "credit authorization," "shipping," "manufacturing scheduling," "billing," and so on. Each such circle stands for a part of the overall process that encapsulates a set of business rules and all the underlying data required for implementation of those business rules. The data itself, of course, lives in a "lower layer," sitting in the database; however, the rules are clumped together into those things called *components*. And the essence of the diagram is that those components all work together to implement an overall business process — cooperating components.

If you think back to the application architecture, it becomes clear why it has been so hard to plan with senior management for the last 20 years. Systems professionals through most of those two decades have been focused either too high or too low in the abstraction hierarchy. On one hand, thinking about the database as being at the center pushes us down to too low a level of detail. Why? Because senior management itself does not understand data models. So instead, you try to translate your data model in order to talk about the functional requirements it implies: *transactions*. Transactions are directly derived from doing a complete job of functional decomposition; slicing and dicing the processes. Many methodologies, in fact, exactly prescribe that the functional decomposition process is complete exactly when it has broken things down into specific transactions. The problem is that these transactions are the "atomic" elements out of which cooperating components are built. This doesn't make the transactions bad; without them, the bigger components couldn't be built. It does, though, make the transactions far too detailed to be part of any discussion about organization-wide business processes. Senior management wants to talk about how credit authorization cooperates with order entry, and the system designers want to talk about the 432 different kinds of specific transactions required to deal with all the cases that arise throughout the credit authorization component's implementation. So focusing on data, or its functional counterpart, transactions, is too detailed.

Without cooperating components, the other alternative is to focus on the document layer — the applications that appear on the desktop. This is, in fact, a natural part of many planning discussions; for example, coming up with flowcharts showing all the documents in a system and how they relate to each other often helps bring the underlying process into clear focus. That is the point, though; documents with their focus on what the user sees point to the underlying processes, but the documents are still too specific to a particular user's view to make the processes come into clear focus.

Having that middle layer, with its intermediate level of abstraction, makes the entire planning and design process suddenly work. The business process layer, then, is the key to making system design really work, and cooperating components are the building blocks that give that layer meaning and around which all the design work in that layer is done. But what about getting to distributed systems?

DISTRIBUTED DATA — AT LAST

Recall the four tough questions introduced earlier:

+ What does a mainframe do?

+ How can servers replace part of a mainframe?

+ How are distributed databases designed?

+ Are distributed systems technically practical?

Finally, the groundwork has been laid for answering that third question. How are distributed databases designed? Is there a design strategy, a design model that makes it possible to decide how to distribute a database effectively? Classically, the exact reason this question has been so hard to deal with has been precisely because of the preoccupation with data-centered design and data models.

How deliciously ironic: exactly the preoccupation with database-centered design makes it so darn hard to design distributed databases. Unfortunately, it's true. What's true is that the following question essentially has no answer: *how do I convert a classical data model into a distributed data model?* I'll spend just another minute with the unanswerable form of the distributed database question.

Suppose that an organization has painstakingly developed a relatively detailed data model for either the complete organization or perhaps for a particular application. Now the move to self-managed teams, client/server, and distributed systems is under way. Questions start to arise about converting one or more applications to a distributed model. The design process begins. In a data-centered world, the first step is to be sure that the data model is correct; after all, everything else revolves around that data model. The problem is that the data model by definition is not correct; after all it's not distributed.

Nowhere in a classical data model diagram is the physical location of the data normally represented. Okay, that's easy to fix: mark the locations on the diagram. Now the next question comes up: how do you decide what data goes where? Is it better to locate all the customer data out in field offices on small servers? Or should all the data be kept centralized with personal computers pulling it down when needed? Perhaps regional servers are the answer: they can still be run by professional operators, but they can also be distributed to be closer to the users and to provide more computing power. What's the best way to decide which of these approaches, alone or in combination, is right?

What makes the question tricky is that, classically, it has to be answered *based on the data model alone.* Perhaps this seems strange: insisting that the answer come from the data model alone. It's not strange at all, though, to a computer professional deeply committed to a detailed methodology, defined and controlled by detailed design procedures, and supported by expensive CASE tools that are locked into the approach dictated by the methodology. That professional not only is committed to that methodology technically, but believes in it religiously too. And that methodology in the early stages of the design process focuses on the data model, virtually to the exclusion of all else. Yes, function creeps in in early decomposition steps. And, yes, interactions between function and data are considered in various ways. Nonetheless, all those approaches, procedures, and tools focus in on that data model and keep the design professional narrowly focused on the center of the world until the data model is pretty well done. To get to the distributed world, *done*, suddenly, means not only done in the old way, but distributed too. And so for quite a few years now, seasoned, experienced, pragmatic information system design professionals have struggled with the problem of determining how to transform a nondistributed (centralized) data model into a distributed one, based on that data model alone.

The problem can't be solved. Given only a data model, there is no basis, rational or otherwise, for choosing an effective distribution strategy. That is why for so long, so many people have considered distributed applications impossible to design. True, many examples of distributed applications exist, such as ATMs and department stores that confront us every day. Nonetheless, the belief that these systems can't be designed by normal human beings runs deep and wide. The problem, as it turns out, is both a fundamental technical problem and a design problem. That is, when it comes to distributed systems, thinking about them in terms of distributed databases *and* trying to find the underlying technology to build them that way is an unsolveable problem. Yet the answer to both of these problems is surprisingly simple: ask a different question.

RIGHT ANSWER; WRONG QUESTION

Since the mid '70s, researchers and developers around the world have been trying to build distributed databases. One approach has focused on making database systems themselves, the products sold by Oracle, IBM, Informix, and the like, intrinsically distributed. Ideally by adding the right features to the underlying database management system, a database distributed over many sites could be made to appear like one big database; the distinction between a local and distributed database would disappear. Another approach has focused on developing methodologies and design strategies for determining where data should be put. This approach would have allowed you to answer that question just described as "unanswerable": How do you convert a data model into a distributed model? And finally, a third approach, much more ad hoc in nature, has focused on building particular distributed systems, both to solve specific needs and to prove it can be done.

Of course, as has already been mentioned, a variety of working distributed systems *do* exist in the world. Interestingly enough, none of them (or at least none that I know of) was designed as *distributed database systems*. True, they all have data, and they all have databases. And since the systems are distributed, by definition their underlying databases are distributed, too. But in each case, the design center of the system was distributing the processing and then putting data where it was required to support the processing taking place at each location. So the third approach sometimes work, but only by shifting the focus away from the question of distributed database. And the reason for that shift, or at least one reason, is that distributed database per se doesn't work. The other two approaches prove that.

After more than 20 years of work, computer professionals are still not much closer to knowing how to build distributed database systems than they were two decades ago. Sure, a variety of specific techniques, strategies, and algorithms have been developed; enough has been written to fill a library. But put it altogether; try to build a true distributed database, of any real scale, and the pieces are just not all there. The pieces aren't there because distributing the database is the wrong approach to distributing the system. The answer is right: *the distributed system*. The question is wrong; don't ask *how do we distribute the database?*

Perhaps one day, distributed databases will be possible. What would that mean? Simply that you could assign to the database most of the responsibility for making distributed applications work. You would build your applications on top of the database, without worrying a great deal about the fact that the application might be distributed. Then the database, through the magic of sophisticated software, would make your distributed system effectively function as though it were all running at one location; you just wouldn't have to pay attention to the issues of distribution because the database would have taken care of all those issues for you. True, you might worry about the performance implications of where data was located, but largely, if this world ever came to pass, the database would make distribution work. Just as modern operating systems with virtual memory make our systems look bigger, and just like the World Wide Web makes many servers look like one big server, such distributed database software would make many separate databases appear like one big database. The only problem is that such software may never exist. Or if it will exist, nobody knows when. So if we want distributed systems, we better find another way to design and build them.

The fact that both the design framework for thinking about how to distribute data *and* the technical underpinnings to make that distribution of data possible have proven so stubbornly resistant should be a clue. It is a clue that we need to think about the whole problem of distributed systems in a different way. For years, inventors tried to build flying machines with flapping wings; in the end, a whole new way of thinking about the problem of flying was required. In the same way, a whole new way of thinking about the problem of distributed systems is required, too. And that way revolves around distributing the processing, not the data. Once the processing is distributed, in the form of cooperating components, it becomes relatively straightforward to decide what data goes with the processing, with the components, to make the system all work.

DISTRIBUTE THE PROCESSING: THE DATA WILL FOLLOW

The title says it all: distribute the processing, and the data will follow. When the focus of the entire application planning and design framework shifts from being data-centered to being process- *and* data-centered, the next step is quite straightforward. Best of all, it parallels the same steps that BPR will be insisting on anyway.

If business processes are going to be reengineered to revolve around self-regulating processes implemented by self-managed teams, it doesn't take very long before the question of supporting those self-managed teams comes up. Reengineering teams means looking for ways to consolidate tasks and shift responsibilities so that entire processes can be completed by either individuals or teams. That consolidation and shifting means moving tasks from the middle of the organization to the periphery of the organization. And as the tasks move, the information systems to support those tasks need to move as well.

So here it is. The BPR team draws those fancy (or not) process diagrams — the diagrams that look suspiciously similar to flowcharts and are built out of cooperating components. Then they start rearranging both bubbles (components) and ownership of the tasks represented by the bubbles. When they've finished, ownership of entire processes has drifted out to field offices, local warehouses, and plant-based self-managed teams. The processes owned by those teams *are distributed processes*. The business processes represented by the diagrams have been rearranged, from centralized to distributed. That's the opportunity for the computer people, hopefully either part of the BPR team or supporting it, to step right up and ask: *Would it help the self-managed team to have unlimited question-asking capability? Might that team benefit from the ability to customize the business procedures to meet local requirements? Can that team be better supported by having control over its own computer environment so that this kind of capability becomes possible?*

And finally, the trick. After the decision has been made to distribute particular processes, the steps required to determine how to distribute the data are almost trivial. It is precisely the data required by the distributed processes, the specific cooperating components, that in turn gets distributed out to the servers where the components run. Move credit authorization to local sales offices? When that decision is made, any competent computer professional, given the standard data model, can quickly determine what parts of the database have to be distributed too, to make that server run effectively. Give every salesperson a notebook computer equipped to process all orders? Fine, then obviously the parts of the database required to process an order better are located on that notebook computer. Local inventory management? Local inventory database. On and on. Distribute the process; the data will follow. It's distributed database design made simple.

DOESN'T THIS REQUIRE A WHOLE NEW METHODOLOGY?

At this point, answering one major question leads to another, potentially even larger, question. If the entire basis for designing distributed systems revolves around a fundamental shift in information engineering and other leading methodologies, doesn't that imply a pretty big change in the way applications are designed? Won't that in turn require new methodology manuals, new CASE tools, new training, and everything that goes with that? And what is the overall methodological (phew, long word) framework that defines this new approach? That's the question I get to in the next chapter.

14

A CLIENT/SERVER METHODOLOGY

Graphical, distributed, client/server applications. They're probably object-oriented, certainly easy to learn and use, and more than likely flexible, easy to maintain, and built from reusable, interoperable parts. Neat concepts. And although those things happen in new applications, don't forget the new focus shift required to support both distributed design and BPR, the shift that moves process front and center throughout our planning and design process. As Dagwood Bumstead says when confronted with the job of mowing the lawn, *it's enough to make you tired just thinking about it.*

After more than a decade of hard work, a number of methodologies have emerged that provide controlled approaches to the design and construction of applications. They work; managers and developers are already trained in them, many *computer-aided software engineering* (CASE) and other tools exist to support them, and when you're in doubt, armies of trainers, consultants, and systems integrators are standing by, ready to jump right in. All of this maturity and preparedness is based on the stability and maturity of *information engineering* (IE) and its family of methodologies. Yet the issues and requirements raised in the preceding paragraph imply (at least) that for all their virtues, the existing methodologies need to be at least modified, and at most replaced. Replaced with what? How extensive are the changes required?

Scary as the prospect of making major changes to existing methodologies is (and should be), there's a prospect that's even worse — a prospect that's downright terrifying. Many personal computer-based developers, particularly the ones who have never known any other type of computer through their entire professional lives, believe that today's methodologies are not only wrong, but actually unnecessary. "Just build it," they say. "Prototyping and rapid application development techniques, coupled with high-power tools like PowerBuilder and Visual Basic, make methodologies completely unnecessary." Can this be true? Should the methodologies that took so long to create be thrown away?

IS THERE A METHOD(OLOGY) TO THIS MADNESS?

The answer to all these questions depends on the scale of the application being built. Small applications, those that run completely on a single desktop, can be built in minutes or hours. Methodology would just get in the way. In recent years it has become possible to build medium-sized applications too, revolving around a single server and dozens of workstations almost as quickly as desktop applications are built. Access, PowerBuilder, and all the other tools *do* allow these applications to be built in days and weeks. Often such applications require some preliminary design; perhaps a data model and a simple process model help make the pieces of the system fit together when everything is done. Still, if the entire application can be built in several weeks, why bother with a complex methodology?

The amazing thing about the small- and medium-size applications is that their scope increases every year. Every 12 months, the size and complexity of the applications that can be built with modern tools takes a step forward. As a result, for the first time since the birth of the computer industry, many serious departmental, team, and workgroup applications *can* be built quickly and easily in a methodology-free environment. That's how those smaller applications should be built. What a relief. Nobody, this author included, is going to suggest that methodologies — past, present, or future — are going to get in the way of rapid, iterative development of small and medium applications. Self-managed teams can manage their own applications, build extensions, and even build complete new applications, and do it all without years of training, complicated processes, or hordes of professional helpers.

What about the bigger applications? Are they just slightly bigger versions of their smaller siblings? Is it just a question of waiting for today's power tools to grow up a little? Perhaps a few more of those big one-year steps will make it possible to build nationwide branch banking systems in days and weeks with no formal approach to the whole process? Absolutely not!

Big systems are *qualitatively* different from small ones. A truck is not just a larger, heavier car. It is designed totally differently, and it's built out of different components. It is a completely different kind of system. Similarly, the design process for a large office building is qualitatively different in approach and requirements from the ad hoc process that works for a cottage, garden shed, or small extension to a house. So in the first place, there is a complexity barrier. When that barrier is crossed, the approaches that worked before don't just work more poorly, *they stop working totally*. Imagine setting out to build a major bridge by simply assembling some work crews, providing them with tools, and pointing to a simple sketch pinned to a wall? Unimaginable? Well, the same is true when it comes to building substantial computer applications, whether the tools being used are modern or not.

Whenever a system, particularly one involving a database, expands to include more than one server (especially in more than one geographical location), complexity is *guaranteed* to go up. True, there are undoubtedly cases where even such systems can be kept simple. Overall, however, distributed systems, almost by definition, cross the complexity barrier.

All of this says three things:

✦ Methodologies are and will continue to be *required* for the construction of larger applications. In fact, the methodologies and the design strategies they contain *make the development of those larger systems possible in the first place.*

✦ Distributed systems in particular, precisely the kinds of client/server systems required to support self-managed teams, will need these methodologies most of all.

✦ Today's methodologies will have to change to meet the needs of a new generation of developers and users, to accommodate the design of distributed systems, and to yield friendly, maintainable systems.

DISCIPLINE CREATES FREEDOM

All of this talk about the need for methodologies sounds in some ways like a bitter pill to swallow. One of the key benefits of personal computers is the freedom they create to build applications on the fly, analyze information dynamically, and respond to new needs as they arise. The very introduction of high-powered development tools that can accommodate even simple client/server applications advances that freedom to a new dimension. Self-managed teams can finally imagine having self-built applications. Now, after reading this far into the book, do those ugly, cumbersome methodologies from the past turn out to be necessary after all? Does this mean that as soon as it comes time to talk about the serious applications, the ones that run the business, that personal computers will be turned back into inflexible mainframe equivalents? Yes and no. Mostly no.

At one level, self-managed teams can build applications today and have been able to for several years. All the tools — PowerBuilder, Paradox, Visual Basic, and the rest — are far from completely new. At the same time, self-managed teams are not building applications, and it's not because they aren't trying. The problem is that the applications these teams need to build don't run in a vacuum.

Providing customers with specialized customized order processing is exactly what self-managed teams want to do. But building the customized order-processing application and then finding out that it can't access central databases, determine inventory levels, or schedule shipments is an exercise in frustration. So when it comes to all the real operations required to meet customers' needs, self-managed teams can use any software they want as long as it's the software provided by the central MIS organization. This is a lose-lose proposition. The central development organization can never keep up with all the requirements of the increasingly autonomous self-managed teams, but those teams cannot build applications themselves because the applications must work with corporate-wide data.

The graph in Figure 14-1 illustrates both the answer to this problem and the focus of the new methodological framework needed for the client/server world. Sophisticated methodologies, even more sophisticated than those we use today, *are* required to build the overall structure, the framework that makes the distributed client/server systems run. The focus of those methodologies, however, must be increasingly framework — not self-contained — applications.

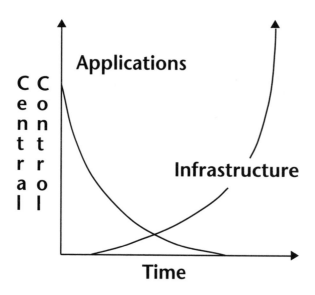

Figure 14-1: How more control yields more freedom over time.

Historically, the central development organization built complete applications. Users were confronted with a "take it or leave it" proposition. In the future, the central organization will build databases based on solid data models, core business rules processing modules, and fundamental toolkits for building desktop applications. All this will take the form of infrastructure. The central development group will provide the core common business rules processes, the fundamental database structures, the common user interface elements, and the overall system infrastructure, on top of which self-managed teams will be able to build their locally customized applications.

Eventually, when this process has come to its logical conclusion, teams will almost never see complete applications delivered to them by a central group. At the same time, those teams will never build applications completely from the ground up either. Instead, teams will find a rich design and construction environment provided to them as part of the organization in which they work. The high-powered development tools of today and tomorrow will then provide the facilities for customizing that environment to meet local needs. It is precisely the process of building that environment and the core applications at its center that the methodologies of the future will address. Through their increased discipline in the area of infrastructure, they will facilitate the real freedom for the team.

What is being described is, in fact, the world of cooperating components, but with a new twist. The job of the central organization is to build the core components that instantiate company-wide business rules and that are used, in turn, by teams throughout the rest of the organization. At the same time, the central team also builds prototypical components which it knows will always be modified by local teams to meet those needs. The system as a whole then consists of both the centrally built components and the ones built by the local team. Some of the local components will be built using tools like Excel and Visual Basic; otherwise, they will be built by modifying the prototypical components built internally. Put the whole thing together, and you have a complete business system. And the system gives a new meaning to the term *cooperating*. Not only is it the components themselves that are cooperating with each other, but also the teams that build all those components that are cooperating, too. The cooperating component framework provides a technical basis for the central development organization to cooperate with the developers and power users on all the local teams. Cooperation: technical and organizational — that's why cooperating components are so important. What is the methodological framework to make it all possible?

The rest of this chapter describes the framework within which those methodologies will fit. It describes a new class of methodologies that are at once built on today's approaches and at the same time contain substantial new perspectives of the world. Throw away what you've already got? No. Change it substantially? Yes. Retrain everybody completely from scratch? No. Facilitate a transition to new ways of working? Absolutely.

WHAT'S BROKEN AND WHAT NEEDS TO BE FIXED?

Classical methodologies suffer from several major problems, all of which are best described in terms of the kinds of applications these methodologies tend to produce:

♦ *Monolithic:* Difficult to break up into pieces and hard to maintain because changing any one part of the system unpredictably affects other parts. Reuse of code is particularly difficult to achieve, so each new application has to be written completely from scratch even though large parts of that application have already been written as parts of other applications. Monolithic applications are also often characterized as rigid, inflexible, and brittle — all side effects of being monolithic.

✦ *Centralized:* A side effect of being monolithic, applications historically have been very resistant to being distributed across several (let alone many) computers.

✦ *Hard to Use:* Terminal-oriented, non-graphical, and hard to learn and use.

Figure 14-2 (dare I call it a process model?) shows the heart — the core — of most current design methodologies. The process starts with careful documentation of the requirements the application is supposed to meet. Applied to a house, the architect would list the number of bedrooms, the need for a family room, degree of informality, overall square footage, cost, and so on.

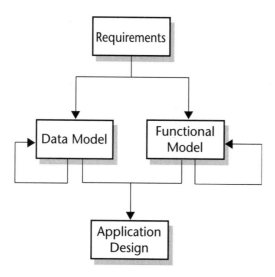

Figure 14-2: The core of most design methodologies.

The design process itself then focuses around the two classical models: data and function. As the arrows pointing from each model back into itself illustrates, the design process is *iterative:* designs are produced, reviewed, refined, reviewed, refined, and so on. It is in this part of the process that CASE tools are the most helpful for several reasons. First of all, they make it really easy to produce diagrams, print them, review them, and, most of all, change them quickly and easily. Second, because a team is likely to be involved, the CASE tools allow the entire team to see each other's work, and more importantly to keep track of the relationships between all the various diagrams being produced. Finally, as the work progresses, the CASE tools can constantly carry out consistency checks to ensure that decisions made in one part of the design don't contradict decisions made elsewhere.

Finally, after the iteration process is through, a complete application design is the result, ready for approval and implementation. Of course there is a lot more detail to the actual process. For example, the requirements stage includes preliminary sizing and phasing estimates, a technology assessment, and a first-cut budget. Similarly, data modeling itself has many detailed steps and techniques, as does functional modeling. Nonetheless, this process model captures the core of the classical design process. Revolving as it does around the two lonely models of data and function, this design process has several major problems:

1. When, where, and how do the issues associated with distributing processing and data get addressed?

2. Where in the process is the user interface and the graphical nature of the application designed?

3. How can this process be either managed or altered to yield less monolithic code; applications that are flexible and have lots of interoperable, reusable pieces? Sometimes, the more modern religious advocates state this question in terms of those mystical grails of today: *objects* and *object orientation*. Translating that into the terms relevant to this discussion: where in the process is the application (re)structured around cooperating components?

Keeping these three problems firmly in mind, this chapter lays out a broad methodological framework for developing graphical client/server applications.

A MODEL FOR MODELING

To develop a new framework for designing and building applications, we need to start with a model for the overall process. That model is based on, what else, the application architecture. It isn't really possible to overemphasize the importance of keeping that application architecture in mind at every stage of thinking about larger applications. It's come up again and again already, and before we're done it will come up a few more times again.

Figure 14-3 maps the three-layer application architecture on to a three-stage planning, design, and development process. The three-stage process is conceptually very similar to IE; the terms used for the stages are simply intended to be slightly more evocative. Look at the stages, one by one:

	Conceptual	Logical	Physical
Documents	Work flow	Form flow	Forms
Business rules	Process flow	Component model	Programs
Database	Data model	Database schema	Tables, indexes

Figure 14-3: Planning, designing, and developing applications.

✦ *Conceptual:* The first stage in any design is to review requirements and develop a broad first sketch of the overall design. Architecturally this is equivalent to the early floor plans, with huge variations from plan to plan, that an architect uses to zero in on a rough design. In the desktop area, this design considers broad work flow from office to office and person to person, without taking any detailed forms or interfaces into account. At the process level, the high-level bubbles and lines that senior managers and management consultants so love carry the day. And at the database level, this is the time for high-level, integrating framework, enterprise, and divisional models.

✦ *Logical:* This design takes detailed business rules into account and refines the design to show how those rules can be accommodated. At the process level, high-level bubbles are exploded into more detailed process interaction and request/action diagrams that show how the bigger bubbles work. On the desktop, detailed forms of sequences are mocked up, showing the exact sequences of steps required to complete specific tasks. And at the database level, the high-level model is transformed into a classical entity relationship diagram showing a potential database schema that takes into account fundamental issues about consistency and meaning.

✦ *Physical:* Finally, in the last column, the design is translated into an actual system. The primary input at this stage is performance considerations. As process flows are converted into specific pieces of code, algorithmic issues relating to speed or space may force redesign. At the desktop, programmers design individual forms, refine prototypes into detailed graphical interfaces, and write underlying behavioral code. The database design is refined, normalized if appropriate, and indexes are specified. With luck, the design tool automatically generates the database structure.

GETTING PHYSICAL

The process of moving from conceptual to logical to physical is important enough to spend a little more time on, particularly to understand where today's tools are in the client/server world (see Figure 14-4). Generally the easiest and most appealing thing for users and programmers to do is to "get physical" very quickly. Need a new system? Start throwing together screen prototypes right away. Database design? Mock it up, produce some reports and forms, and the design should fall right out. This tendency is supported by the fact that almost all the tools in the personal computer world today operate almost entirely at the physical level — building forms, generating code, and running databases and queries. Fortunately, senior management provides balance by thinking and talking in conceptual terms. It's the process of getting from one stage to the next that's important.

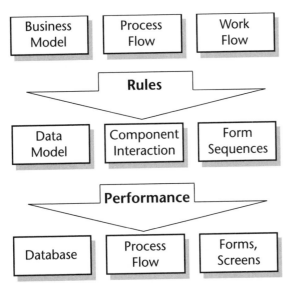

Figure 14-4: Moving from conceptual to logical to physical levels in application design.

The conceptual level deals with three related models. Senior management tends to focus the most on the process model: reengineering revolves around this model. Administrative managers and end users have a natural tendency to gravitate to the work flow model.

Workflow is currently a very popular concept in computer circles. The idea is that because forms are such a fixture in large organizations, if graphical facilities for automatically routing electronic forms around could be built, many applications could then be developed with no programming. Although attractive, in many ways this is the opposite of what Business Process Reengineering is about. Rather than eliminate the need for people to deal with forms, we get the forms to the people faster, with less programming. Nonetheless, forms and the user-visible portions of an application *are* important, and the workflow model, with its diagrams of forms flowing from place to place, provides a nice conceptual model for talking about applications conceptually.

Finally, of course, the computer professionals will continue to build their enterprise and other business data models, as well they should. In this new world, however, this process follows and supports the process modeling.

The fundamental difference between the conceptual and the logical model is the need to start paying attention to detailed business rules. Conceptually, it's easy to say "before scheduling shipment, wait for credit authorization; move that credit authorization out to the local offices." At the logical level, it's time to ask: "*what are all the rules that are used to determine whether credit will be authorized*" which in turn leads to the question: "*who knows enough to implement those rules and what steps are required before handling each rule in terms of other rules that should have been applied first.*" Thus, the logical level, while still removed from the technical necessities of detailed instructions, space, and speed, still provides a complete picture from a business perspective of how the previously conceptual system will really work.

A logical process diagram looks suspiciously similar to a flow chart, although with a more refined perspective, professionals talk about data flow diagrams, component interaction charts, and so on. In a reengineering context, each process flow diagram is worked on by the managers in the organization with the detailed knowledge of how the companies' processes really work. It is at this level that the tough questions get asked about whether reengineered processes, which look so neat at the conceptual level, can really work.

Another way of thinking about the logical level for processes is to ask "what are the *real* cooperating components after all?" It's easy for management to think in terms of "credit authorization," but in most companies, credit authorization is a relatively complex process that involves risk assessment, data collection, and a variety of other functions and departments. So where senior management thinks of a single large component, once the people doing the work start to map out the details of the process, that single large component becomes dozens of smaller components, all cooperating with each other. So cooperating components make sense at both a conceptual and a logical level. Both senior and middle management will find it a useful way of describing processes so they can be built.

The user interface equivalent of flow charts is the form sequence diagram. The fact that modern graphical tools have no concept of form sequence is just short of amazing. Most users designing even simple applications start out by cataloging the forms they will be using, diagramming how they fit together, and then sitting back and considering the flow. Conversely, when a system has to be maintained, the first thing that has to be done, at the UI level, is to develop a picture of how all the big pieces fit together: form sequence. The elegant thing about form sequence diagrams is that they show the big picture of the options available to the user without requiring detailed screens to be laid out; a big savings is in time and conceptual clarity.

In the database row, the concept of logical database models is well understood. Called entity relationship diagrams (ERDs), these models show all the key elements of the database while ignoring technical details related to normalization, indexes, storage formats, and so on.

The conceptual model, all three parts, answers these three questions:

✦ How will the new application look?

✦ How will it change the business?

✦ How will it map onto or require new business processes?

The logical model goes a step further and discusses this question:

✦ In some detail, what steps are required to make each of the larger conceptual processes actually happen?

The logical model proves that the new application can work. In other words, it demonstrates that even taking into account all the detailed business interactions required by the real world, the new overall application still holds up. The next two questions are

✦ Can it be implemented?

✦ Will it perform well?

The physical level, of course, answers that last question. The physical level in our process is where the application gets written. Databases are defined and constructed. Forms are designed, underlying code is written, and usability testing can take place. Business rule processes are translated into actual code by using a programming language or some other tool. The physical column has both a design and an implementation component. Process design involves specifying how the sets of business rules are implemented in terms of objects, processes, modules, and data structures. On the user interface side, the design involves extensive prototyping, the use of graphical tools, and the eventual convergence on a final actual interface. Finally on the database, the process involves detailed file and table design, development of an indexing strategy, and so on.

At one level that's the whole model for graphical client/server development. As I'll show right away, it already answers quite a few questions. The next issue is to define the appropriate models and techniques to use in working through each of the rows. Is classical data modeling still appropriate in the bottom row? How do object approaches fit in? How are processes modeled? Finally, what about the graphical, desktop part: what is the best model for that? I'm going to finish the high-level view and then dive down a level.

DIVIDE AND CONQUER

The last step before considering specific models is to look at how the classical design process gets rearranged to support the new model. The result is both a new framework and a new *organizational* approach.

The first and most obvious change in the new process diagram shown in Figure 14-5 is the presence of *four* parallel design streams instead of the previous two. Next, in looking at the names of the boxes, three are new. Actually, *Database, Components,* and *User Interface* speak for themselves: they correspond to the Database, Business Rules, and Documents layer of that omnipresent application architecture. The use of *Components* and *Behavior* to describe the business rules layer captures the design activities happening at the conceptual and later the more detailed stages, respectively. In other words, conceptually the design focuses on broad processes and the components of which they are built, but at the logical and particularly physical stages of the design, the focus shifts to the detailed behavior occurring inside each of the components. Similarly, on the desktop the conceptual focus is on work flow. Later it shifts to detailed user interfaces. But what about the fourth box — *Architecture?*

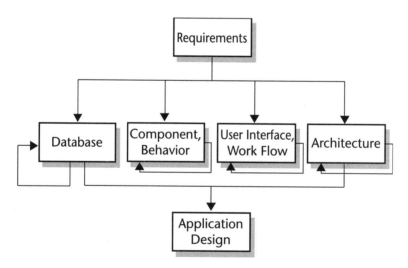

Figure 14-5: A new process diagram, with four parallel design streams instead of two.

While the application architecture itself has three layers, an implied fourth focus considers how the entire application fits together (see Figure 14-6). The architectural design process, in parallel to the other three, addresses the questions of overall structure and fit. The architectural design says finally what goes into which layer, how the application relates to other applications, and so on. Most important of all, the architectural design focuses on the cooperating components — how they fit together — and makes sure that they have been selected in a way that allows cooperation and reuse to really occur.

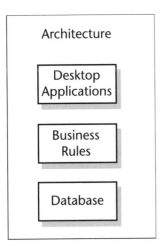

Figure 14-6: Architecture's role in application assembly.

JACK OF ALL TRADES, MASTER OF ANY?

Thinking of the design process in terms of four parallel activities solves an important feasibility problem that otherwise would prevent the construction of most large client/server applications. Consider the number of skills potentially required to design and build a graphical, distributed, database-oriented system. If all the members of the team needed to know everything, each individual would need both skill and experience with user interface design, graphical environments, wide- and local-area networking, distributed system design, business programming, personal computer programming, database design, database implementation, interprocess communication, workstation operating systems, server operating systems, network operating systems, and much more. Do such people even exist? Can they really be *good* at doing all these different activities? Can individuals be found who not only have all these skills but are strong at requirements analysis, business design, technical design, and finally actual programming, testing, and implementation? Can enough such people be found? At an affordable price? Finally, suppose that you find a group of supermen and superwomen with all the requisite skills, ready and waiting to be hired. Will they be truly eager to write mundane, everyday applications or will they want to be building only the core technical components on which everything else runs? And, even if they could be convinced to write the thousands of lines of necessary but routine general ledger code, is that even the best use of their talents?

Unfortunately, the answer to almost every question in the preceding paragraph is *no*. Fortunately, that doesn't matter. The process diagram and the application architecture it is based on are a model for both the design process *and* the organization best suited to implement it. In considering this, however, keep scale in mind.

On small projects, a single developer does it all. There is no formal separation between the parts of the process and of course no organization required to make it work.
On medium-size projects, work can be divided up according to needs and talents. The
big projects require some real organizational thinking.

In thinking about teams and organization, several underlying principles are critical:

✦ Small teams, generally not exceeding about a dozen individuals, are the most
   productive. Teams of 4 to 6 people can be even better. The design process
   proposed here helps move in that direction. Later in this chapter some other
   techniques that lead to small teams come to light.

✦ The skills and attitudes required by the four parallel design streams are
   intrinsically different. At times it is almost tempting to think that literally
   genetic differences are tied to the very different kinds of people required in
   each area:

   1. Database designers and database modelers are a distinct breed that
      generally keep to themselves, have very long time horizons, and think in
      terms of fundamental entities, consistency, and comparability. Database
      design teams are generally particularly small, but highly critical. A mistake
      in the basic database design, process notwithstanding, has greater long-
      term consequences than a mistake in any other area.

   2. Process and component designers come in several flavors. At the high
      level they focus on BPR. At the logical and physical level, these people
      love sets of rules, would be contract lawyers in a different life, and if they're
      good, lead to both flexible systems and beautifully structured code.

   3. User interface designers are a lot like artists. Working in a largely unstruc-
      tured fashion, they depend on breakthroughs and artistic insights more
      than do the designers in any other area.

   4. Architects are the rarest breed in this menagerie. Combining business
      understanding, technical depth, and more than solid judgment, they are
      worth their weight in precious metals.

✦ The four processes proceed in parallel and are quite different from each other.

✦ There must be both a great deal of interaction and regular checkpoints to
   keep the four streams synchronized with each other. Discoveries in the user
   interface area will influence the data model; the development of the data
   model will result in UI requirements, and both will interact heavily with the
   design of the components and their behavior.

At this point, you have a new approach for thinking about the design of systems, but I've ducked the question about whether any of the models driving the design process change. The following section looks at that question.

NEXT YEAR'S MODELS

Classical methodologies such as IE revolve around two fundamental models: a data model and a functional model. It should be clear by now that the data model is here to stay. It should also be clear that the functional model, although it doesn't exactly disappear, does get subsumed under some larger model related to processes, components, and behavior of components. What is the basis for that model? It turns out that question requires us to finally deal with the dreaded O-word — *objects*. When I first started developing the application architecture, the issue of scale and its impact on applications came up. At that time, two mechanisms for converting large, indecipherable systems into collections of smaller manageable systems were proposed: the application architecture itself and the principle of encapsulation. Objects provided the second principle, encapsulation. In order to position yourself to make use of *objects*, however, there is a lot of mystical imagery, vocabulary, and to be honest, fog to cut through. But doing so enables you to use objects to gain the advantages they can really confer. Best of all, as with all other computer-religious issues, after the technobabble is trimmed away, the resulting structure turns out to be approachable and understandable after all.

OBJECTS: AN OBJECTIVE VIEW

In the fall of 1991, no less an authority than *Business Week* used its cover to show a diaper-clad baby snapping toy blocks together to assemble a computer application. The blocks had labels such as *Accounts Payable, Order Entry,* and so on. The article on the inside reported an important technical advance that, like all other silver bullets, promised to simplify development, cut schedules by a factor of at least ten, and lead to better, more flexible, more maintainable applications. Objects promised even more, though: not only would they allow professional programmers to achieve these kinds of amazing results, but when objects were fully available, even *nonprogrammers* would be able to assemble major applications out of these building blocks. The cover implied that even infants who had not yet learned to talk could miraculously program; the article, while not threatening to break any child-labor laws, promised results hardly less amazing.

Several years have passed. Computer professionals continue to believe in and be excited about objects. Every new tool or operating system announcement contains claims about object support. Meanwhile, applications are still being produced in the same painful, step-by-step fashion. Major advances in development tool technology *are* occurring, but in general, they have very little to do in any direct fashion with objects. For example, spreadsheets genuinely allow nonprogrammers to build real applications. Visual Basic makes it possible for even amateur developers to build serious graphical programs in minutes and hours. Access and Paradox for Windows have made databases more approachable than ever. But, realistically, and more important, honestly, aside from some minor stylistic nuances, these advances have nothing to do with objects. So what's going on?

There are many ways of thinking about *objects*. The usual starting point is to look at the technical definition, talking about *encapsulating* code and data, packaging them in a fashion that allows standard operations and functions to be applied to a wide variety of different types of objects (*polymorphism*), and building all this in a development environment that allows new objects to be derived simply from old ones (*inheritance*). *Encapsulation*, *polymorphism*, and *inheritance*: real exciting, right? Perhaps the story lies in the benefits, the advantages that adopting *objects* provide. To understand those benefits, as usual, a little history is in order.

Since about 1959, programmers have been looking for ways to repackage pieces of code so that other programmers could use them. Every commercial application, for example, contains date routines: software to display dates, compute the number of days between two dates, compare dates, and so on. Obviously, it would be neat if these functions could be simply *packaged* so that each new application could simply use them over and over. Applications would get written more quickly with fewer bugs, and over time, any effort spent improving the common functions would be highly leveraged. *Packaging* and *reuse*: that's what programmers have been looking for. Like most visions of the early '60s, this one has proven stubbornly difficult to achieve.

Less than 5 percent of the programming in most large software systems consists of common, highly shared code. Individual programmers will write quite a lot of common code *for themselves*: pieces of specialized code used in several places throughout *their own work* that they write once and then use over and over. Developers sitting next to each other on a team will share a small amount of software too because it's so easy to just talk back and forth, providing support and trading requirements. Even here, programmers are much more likely to borrow some code *and then change it* than they are to use the shared code directly. Changed code *is not* shared code. After code is changed, almost all the leverage associated with common testing, common improvements, and so on disappears. So even on a small team, sharing is minimal, although borrowing is high.

Cross the team boundary and whatever small amount of sharing did exists drops in quantity and quality dramatically. Even within the confines of a single large project, achieving any significant amount of sharing requires real discipline, a clear architectural vision, and excellent design. Moving beyond projects, and looking across entire systems and organizations, sharing just doesn't happen; shared code doesn't exist.

Aside from the obvious technical problems arising from lack of sharing — lengthy development schedules, repetitive bugs, ever worsening maintenance costs — serious business problems come up over time too. Separate and different credit approval, shipment scheduling, billing, and address maintenance functions confuse customers, create extra work internally, and eventually lead to serious errors. The answers to all these problems and more is sharing and reuse. Technically, this is often also called *interoperability,* referring to the ability for a single common business module to interoperate with a wide variety of other modules through the system that calls on it for common functions.

THE MEDIUM IS THE MESSAGE

Historically the problems associated with sharing have been tied back to technical difficulties in the development environment: if only programmers had good enough packaging techniques, good enough facilities for producing packaged code for sharing, reuse would start to happen. As a result, about every ten years some major new advance in packaging technology comes along and promises to solve the reuse problem (see Table 14-1).

Table 14-1 Four Consecutive Decades and Their Packaging Promises

Year	Technology Advance
1959	Subroutines
1969	Processes
1979	Packages
1989	Objects

In 1959, FORTRAN was the first broadly popular language to introduce to the world the concept of *subroutines.* A *subroutine* allows a program to be packaged, with a set of *arguments,* and then called over and over. Each time the *arguments* allow the *parameters* of the problem to be specified so that the packaged code can be applied to this particular case; the answer is then returned to the *calling* program. By now, of course, FORTRAN is a very old language; some engineers have used it for over 30 years. Normally, a tool developed that long ago would be completely obsolete. However, FORTRAN's subroutines are such a powerful mechanism for extending the language that they have literally kept it alive to this day. Over the years, literally thousands of libraries of subroutines of all types have been developed, distributed, marketed, and sold. As a result, the value to programmers of those subroutine libraries was and is so high that any thought of replacing FORTRAN remains at best a mild daydream. Actually, problematic as the reuse problem is, the broad success of the subroutine paradigm, still at the center of every language since FORTRAN, is proof positive that reuse, at some level, is clearly possible and worthwhile.

A very attractive and lasting facet of subroutines is that they present the world with a very clean *interface.* The external structure of a subroutine consists of its name, its arguments, and the value it returns. By definition, at this level, a subroutine is self-describing: its interface, if written with a modicum of care, says quite a lot about how it is intended to be used. Even more important, though, the interface is the *only* visible part of the subroutine. The subroutine *encapsulates* its behavior. In fact, in many cases, over time, many parallel subroutines are written, all with the same interfaces, providing alternative implementations of the same functions (*polymorphism*). Thus, a date function may originally be written dealing with English dates. Later, another might deal with dates in foreign languages. At yet another time, the subroutine library is extended to handle other calendars (the Hebrew calendar, for example, has 13 months and every so often not leap days, but leap months). The beauty of encapsulation is that, because the user is shielded on purpose, from the underlying implementation, he or she is also positioned to switch implementations later, without changing the calling program at all. When several implementations of a subroutine share a common interface so one can be substituted for another, that is exactly what is meant by *polymorphism*. The interface plays a particularly important role because it provides the formal structure that separates the subroutine from its users, and because it describes the way in which the subroutine can be used.

In 1969, UNIX (yes! it's over 25 years old) first made *processes* broadly available in a simple-to-use form. Unlike subroutines, processes have two new characteristics. First, they are a higher level construct that can be used to build quite large pieces of reusable code, potentially in turn containing hundreds or thousands of subroutines. So, where subroutines provide reuse in the small, processes provide reuse in the large. Second, because a process is an independent running program, processes provide a mechanism for sharing *data* as well as code. What is a process? Simply put, it is a separate, independent program, kept separate by the operating system, which communicates with other processes and programs, through messages. If this sounds a lot like *client/server,* it is; the process concept is essentially the foundation, in software, for the entire client/server architecture.

A database can be put into a process. Sitting there, it can provide database services to other processes running on the same computer or on other computers. Another process can manage a series of print queues and provide print services to both the database process and to all other processes. Higher-level processes can manage credit authorization, shipment scheduling, or any other function that revolves around code and data and that be surrounded by a clean boundary line.

Just as subroutines provide the foundation for modern programming languages, processes provide the fundamental building blocks out of which virtually all modern operating systems, networks, and distributed environments are built. Powerful indeed.

Processes provide a convenient way of *encapsulating* complete running systems: wrapping them up into capsules that can be used by other processes. The only issue is that processes, by themselves, don't provide any mechanism for *describing* the mechanisms available for interacting with them (the *interfaces*). The developer can write documentation, and the user can read that documentation to figure out what messages the process will and won't accept, but if the documentation is missing or inadequate, the process can't be used. At first this might seem like a minor nuisance; all good software needs documentation anyway. With the arrival of sophisticated development tools, though, the lack of clear, computer-readable specifications describing the processes' *interfaces* became a serious limitation. Some mechanism is essential to allow development tools to ask about and understand those interfaces so that those tools can help developers use those processes. It is ironic in many ways, that while processes represented a step forward in the conceptual level of encapsulation they provided, they also represented a step backward, compared to subroutines, in terms of interface support.

Ten years later, in 1979, with the introduction of the ADA programming language, a first solution to the problem of describing the external structure of a process or other complex packaged component became available. ADA's *package* constructs included *interface definition* mechanisms that provided formal support for both building packaged reusable software and describing the interfaces to those packages to humans and the tools supporting them.

The story of ADA is both strange and sad. Developed at the behest of the U.S. Defense Department, carefully designed by an international committee, ADA was to become the Esperanto of computer programming languages. At one time, in the mid-'80s, many computer scientists even believed that, given the funding and influence of the Defense Department, ADA might become the dominant programming language worldwide. In retrospect, particularly given the complex nature of the ADA language, this was at best a fond dream. And because of the rather limited acceptance of ADA, *packages* are not a very well-known construct. Subroutines first, and processes later, marked major steps, broadly accepted and used, toward helping the reuse cause. *Packages*, tied as they were to ADA, never saw this kind of broad success. Nevertheless, packages, in the context of large defense-oriented systems, helped foster another major step forward in the development of reusable software. More important, *packages* laid the ground-work for today's *objects*.

AN OBJECT BY ANY OTHER NAME; IS IT STILL AN OBJECT?

So after all this, what are *objects*? The term has many meanings; too many, actually. One important use of the term picks up on the *subject-verb-object* distinction found in the English language. Following this definitive path, many modern designs, particularly designs focused on user interfaces, correctly recognize that humans think about the *object* they are working with before they think of the *verb* they want to apply to it. So typically a person thinks about the *nail* first and then about the *hammer* as the tool for pushing it into the wood. Similarly, object-oriented interfaces allow the user to think about memos, budgets, and presentations first, without necessarily even having to remember that these are built using word processors, spreadsheets, and graphics packages. Select the object, open it, and the appropriate verb/tool is invoked for you automatically. This *is* object-oriented, but it is *not* the kind of object-oriented that relates to code reuse or development methodologies.

Objects are also the latest in a series of ten-year steps producing ever better packaging techniques for developing and using reusable code. *They are not new and only marginally revolutionary*, although they are very important. What is an object then?

Technically, an object is a logical extension of the ADA package construct, which in turn is a logical extension of processes and subroutines. Packages provide the benefits of processes along with a formal structure for describing the interfaces that control those processes. Packages, though, are ADA specific. An object is essentially a more generalized package. In the best case, an object, supported by an *object operating environment,* is actually fully language neutral. If all this sounds terribly obscure and perhaps abstract, bear with it just a little longer.

WHAT OBJECTS ARE NOT

Along with all the technical definitions of objects are a series of prejudices and assumptions about the requirements associated with a *true* object-oriented system. Two languages always come up in conversation: SmallTalk and C++. Languages such as COBOL, FORTRAN, and BASIC, of course, can never be really object-oriented, so the prejudicial sayings go. Programmers all have to be completely retrained, all applications have to be redesigned from the ground up, and this will all cost a great deal and take a long time. True? Or religious hype?

Object-oriented systems do *not* require object-oriented languages like SmallTalk and C++. These are fine languages, but they are also tremendously complex languages that are quite difficult to learn. SmallTalk, in addition, can have major performance problems if not used in a very expert fashion. C++ can generate very efficient systems, but it is, face it, a *systems programming language.* Windows is written in C. OS/2 is written in C. C compilers are themselves written in C. So although C is a popular and powerful language, it is also one that is clearly not intended for developing everyday commercial software. Hard as C is to use, C++ is much harder. So if object-oriented development required every programmer in the commercial world to learn and use C++ effectively, object-oriented applications would virtually never appear. So if object-oriented is not about object-oriented programming or object-oriented programming languages, what, then, is it about?

One way to understand what object-oriented development is and is not, is to ask the question: *what will our objects be?* This leads to another question that is indirectly related to the first one: *if we were explaining object-oriented development to senior management, what would we say?* Let's look at the two questions in reverse order. Suppose, in considering the second question, that you have to justify spending $5 million to shift your development organization to an object-oriented footing. It's presentation time: what do you say?

Do you talk about encapsulation, inheritance, and polymorphism to the executive committee? Perhaps you show them some fragments of C++ or SmallTalk code, hoping that they immediately appreciate the intrinsic elegance of the new paradigms?

No? What then? Examples! That's it: you talk about benefits, giving them concrete examples of objects that, once implemented, obviously provide payback through organization-wide reuse. That's where that first question turns out to be so useful: *what are the objects?* If we knew that, we could tell senior management about those objects and have our budget approved. So what are they?

The first place to look for good examples is at the dozens of textbooks talking about object-oriented analysis, design, and programming. Looking at one leading book yields examples of temperature-control modules for sensors embedded in refrigerators or houses. That's not it. Other books, hoping to be more familiar, have lots of examples of objects that implement common slider bars for forms or standard calendar displays for personal information managers. This is a real problem: management will never approve $5 million dollars if the payback is embedded temperature controls or common slider bars.

The problem with these objects is they are all too *fine-grained*. That is, they are very small objects, which may well be used in thousands of places throughout larger systems, but they are far too small for management to even know they exist, let alone care how they are built. And, frankly, these small-grained objects can be reused just as effectively packaged in the form of subroutines, or perhaps processes, as they can be in the new fancy object form. No budget here.

Let's step back and approach the problem from the top. What would management themselves say they want if they were asked about reuse and interoperability? Put that way, the question is easy: common credit authorization, reusable shipment scheduling, interoperable order entry. Why not make those our objects? Why not indeed — they make great objects. In fact, much of this book has been built around the very idea that creating *components* around credit authorization and the like promises huge benefits; perhaps objects, in the form relevant here, really turn out to be no more and no less than cooperating components.

OBJECTS ARE COMPONENTS; COMPONENTS ARE OBJECTS

Figure 14-7 shows that the process flow of a simple application turns out to be an object diagram. In object-speak, each process becomes a component that cooperates with other components. The objects are very big, but they are also understandable and have high payback. Objects like these are easy to justify, explain, and gain funding for. Objects as components have two other huge advantages.

First, the process of discovering the fundamental high-level objects that drive the overall system design becomes very easy. The exact processes discovered anyway during BPR and the planning stages of the application design become the high-level objects in the system. As each of the bubbles above is exploded out into more detailed process diagrams, each of those process bubbles becomes an object too.

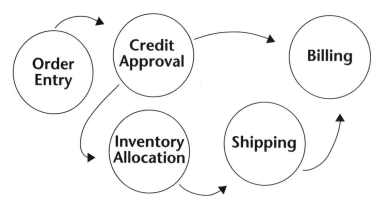

Figure 14-7: The process flow of a simple application.

Secondly, though, if objects are components, literally as well as conceptually, then the objects *are language independent.* The objects in our system can be written in CO-BOL, FORTRAN, or BASIC just as fully as they can be written in SmallTalk or C++. In fact, any combination of languages can be used: pick the best one for the job at hand.

But are these components really objects, or is this just a clever trick to say that objects have no meaning in the first place? They *are* really objects, or can be, and objects do have a meaning. One problem with deciding whether components are really objects is that you haven't yet learned about how *components* get implemented, so how do you know if they are objects or not? To help put this question aside, consider one implementation technique for components: processes. A component, as the term is used here, can be implemented as an operating system process; there are other implementations, but use this one to test how components do when considered as objects. First, they are absolutely objects because processes are fully capable of doing all the things we expect out of objects. Let's get technical for just a moment and see why:

✦ *Encapsulation:* Processes fully surround their code and data, often protecting them in a separate address space. The only way of communicating with a process is through its defined entry points, either in the form of procedure calls or messages.

✦ *Inheritance:* Accomplished by interposing a process that intercepts requests originally targeted at another process. By evaluating those requests, passing some on, and processing others, the new process literally *subclasses* the older one, as object people say.

✦ *Polymorphism:* Messages can be sent interchangeably to any number of processes, so common operations that apply to a wide variety of objects can be designed.

At a high level, components are objects, and objects are often components. Does this mean that object-oriented systems have really been around for a long time, but nobody recognized them? Not quite. Components by themselves provide the fundamental infrastructure to implement object-like systems, but there are some critical pieces missing to make the packaging really as convenient as object systems prescribe.

A MEANS TO AN END OR AN END TO A MEANS?

The trick to understanding objects is to separate between big benefits and small ones, and to also recognize what can be done *now* as opposed to what will only be possible *soon*. Recall the original reason for even exploring objects: finding a second technique to accompany the application architecture as a means of rendering big systems understandable. Along the way, we're also looking for some other benefits, like reusability, flexibility and interoperability. Objects, through encapsulation, are supposed to provide these benefits.

Object-oriented analysis	Yes
Object-oriented design	Yes
Object-oriented programming	Maybe

As both a technology and a philosophy, object-oriented development can be approached at three levels: analysis, design, and programming, corresponding roughly to the three levels in the conceptual/logical/physical model. And object-oriented approaches are possible at all three levels. However it is more than possible to be object-oriented at one level without necessarily having to be fully object-oriented at the level below. What does that mean?

To understand the different ways in which objects can be applied to the design, it helps to review the models available for thinking about the parts of our application architecture. Database design is easy: the data model provides a rich, deep, well-thought-out framework. On the user interface side, the issue of the role of models is a bit trickier; let's leave that aside just for now. What about the business rules layer, the place where the central Business Process Reengineering takes place? What is the model for thinking about that layer? This is where objects turn out to be darn useful, as long as we don't confuse the end with the means.

As the name implies, Business Process Reengineering revolves around processes. It revolves around processes in both the large and the small. In the large, it deals with entire processes that comprise core activities the organization engages in. In the small, each of these large processes consists of sets of smaller components that define the steps in the larger processes. So process plays a key role in the reengineering world. Similarly, approaching the discussion from the perspective of business rules, components and processes play a key role there too. Sets of business rules turn out to define processes built out of components. That is, the rules associated with credit authorization exist because there is a component called credit authorization that is defined by those rules. Ditto for shipment scheduling, invoicing, commission payment, and so on.

From a business perspective then, the critical middle layer in both the application architecture and the design framework revolves around the concept of processes and components. As it turns out, the entire framework that has been built up in the earlier part of this book, a framework that revolves around the concept of processes built out of components, basically sets the stage to embrace the object world, but to embrace it in a particularly focused and pragmatic fashion. Jump back into the object world by completing the consideration of object-oriented design versus object-oriented programming.

At one level, objects can be used purely as an analysis and design construct. That means that the developer is *doing* object-oriented analysis and design. What? Object-oriented analysis maps requirements into sets of objects, with formally defined interfaces. Diagrams are used to show how the objects communicate with each other. Object-oriented design takes the conceptual model coming out of the analysis phase, takes detailed business rules into account, and yields a more detailed set of objects cooperating with each other through formally defined interfaces (methods). What does it look like? Like the bubble diagrams you've been drawing all along. You've been doing object-oriented analysis and design without even knowing it; the only difference is that you've been calling the objects components. Now mind you, you haven't (yet anyway) insisted on throwing out all your standard tools, you haven't rejected all the existing design approaches like data modeling, and you haven't started out by insisting that all developers learn a new and difficult language. But still, what has been discussed is suspiciously similar to, if not identical to, object-oriented analysis and design.

All of this raises a critical question. Suppose that a technique or methodology can be implemented, gaining most of its benefits without causing everything that came before to be thrown out. Does that mean that the technique or methodology is somehow either inadequate or that its benefits are somehow less real? I, for one, hope not, because that is the issue in picking through the parts of the object-oriented movement searching for reality versus religion. And, that's exactly what is being proposed here. For sure, object-oriented analysis and design focused around cooperating components. And maybe, but only if there are other good reasons for it, fully embracing a complete, from the ground up, new world of tools, languages, and concepts.

Bottom line: for the purposes of designing distributed client/server systems, most of the benefits of object orientation can be gained without fully object-oriented programming. By thinking in terms of components, the result will be a fully object-oriented system, at the high level, with reuse, interoperability, flexibility, and best of all distributed operation, but without object-oriented programming.

If the goal is reuse, then object-oriented development with components is a fine means to the end. If the goal is object-oriented for its own sake, defined purely and narrowly and insisting that every last piece of the system be object-oriented, then object-oriented programming is the only way to go. The result is not necessarily a better system, though, and the cost in terms of risk of failure, increased training time, and so on is high.

If components are objects, why not just call them objects? One reason is to avoid the religious implications that go with the "o" word; but there's a more fundamental reason. The term *objects* means many things to many people. One of the things that it often stands for is carrying object-oriented approaches all the way through, thinking of every part of the application in object-oriented terms. This is certainly feasible. But consider some of the implications.

On the database front, for instance, standard data modeling techniques become replaced with object-oriented techniques. When it comes time to implement the system, an object-oriented database is probably called for. On the component front, not only the large components are objects; but when you look inside each component, you find the entire system, down to the level of lines of code, revolving around objects — many of them very fine grained. Of course there are benefits. While it might be hard to explain to management why common slider bars are important, they certainly aren't bad. More to the point, many sophisticated developers, once comfortable with an environment like C++ or SmallTalk, won't use anything else. They love the capability to build their own object frameworks as means to accelerate their own development process. All of this is a plus, but there are some minuses, too. First, notice that at this point in this paragraph, virtually the entire development and much of the operational environment has been replaced. This means a very steep learning curve. And in some cases, the trade-offs are more complex than they look on the surface. For example, object-oriented databases handle complex data structures well, but don't do nearly so well when it comes to handling large collections of records. Similarly, SmallTalk is great of experienced programmers, but others often find that it is hard to learn; and if not used well, it produces large, slow applications. Finally, while it's easy to say "let's go object-oriented all the way to the *n*th degree," actually finding all the tools and operational facilities to make this all work and work well is still not quite possible. And most importantly, from the perspective of changing fundamental breakthroughs in the way organizations by enabling the construction of distributed systems, cooperating components are more than enough; it's just not necessary to fully embrace the object religion. That *is* the point.

By talking about not just components but cooperating components, we gain the benefits of the object-oriented revolution. We get to see why object advocates are so excited. Yet, by keeping our focus on relatively large things called components, we can participate in the revolution while still hanging on to most of the tools and techniques we've worked so hard to pick up over the last 20 years. And by insisting that it is cooperating components we are interested in, we also get to participate in another revolution — a revolution that the object crusade is at best only indirectly interested in — the shift to distributed systems. Cooperating components, here we come.

PUTTING IT ALL TOGETHER: A NEW FRAMEWORK

Two fundamental perspectives drive the construction of our new framework. At the top level is the introduction of two fundamental abstraction mechanisms that together allow us to cut big systems down to size. And, based on that, secondly, there is a set of fundamental models used to drive the actual subsequent design. Looking at these in reverse order, the first step is to compare our new overall methodology with historical approaches.

Figure 14-8 compares the old and new ways of dealing with the four design streams driving the design of distributed systems.

	Past	Future
Architecture		• Component interaction model
Documents (desktop applications)		• Workflow (component interaction) model • Prototypes
Processes; behavior	Functional model	• Component interaction model • Functional model
Database	Data model	• Data model • Component interaction model

Figure 14-8: Old and new ways of using four design streams.

The component interaction model, which revolves around components/objects, is the common element across all four rows in our new model. Of course the architectural model revolves entirely around analyzing the large components and how they cooperate to create core business processes; the process row works in the same way but drills down a level in terms of detail. In the document layer, workflow is simply component interaction between documents. What about the database layer? There are two ways of thinking about the database layer in terms of components. The simplest way involves just thinking about the fact that the business rule components interact with the database tables whenever they invoke a transaction or run a query. Furthermore, the database tables interact with the business rule components whenever a trigger is raised. Taking a slightly more complex perspective, it is now fairly common to model databases in terms of "objects"; essentially, this means thinking about not only the fields or columns associated with a file or table, it means also thinking about the methods or operations that can be applied against the data. At this point, the table has become a component, and when we start diagramming who invokes those methods, we have a component interaction model. So cooperating components and component thinking runs all through our new model.

Figure 14-9 shows a small application that has been decomposed by using both abstraction mechanisms. First the entire system has been divided up architecturally into the three layers: desktop applications, business rules, and database. Before things even get going, this application architecture helps drive thinking in terms of work flow, process flow, and underlying business data model. Furthermore, by separating interface, behavior, and data, it helps ensure interoperable components before much design is ever done. Next, the components running in each layer are conceptualized and designed in terms of separate interacting components. The diagram shows the type of picture that can be drawn to show these components interacting with each other. In the UI layer, an *order entry* application sends a request to an *order processing* component in the *business rules* layer, which in turn passes it on to *credit authorization*. That component makes a request, expressed as a transaction to the underlying database, which decrements the customer's credit limit and responds affirmatively. Each component shows up as a bubble; each type of request is a line. Simple and straightforward, this is an *component interaction diagram.*

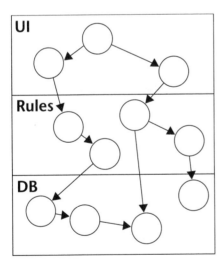

Figure 14-9: Decomposing a small application.

The point of this section is not to describe particular diagrams in detail; there are quite a few different ways to talk about and model objects and their interactions with each other from both a static and dynamic perspective. The point is to show how the two relatively simple mechanisms — layering and object encapsulation — lead to a complete approach to cut even very large systems down to an understandable size.

THE MODELS THEMSELVES

Looking at the table in more detail, there are basically three fundamental design processes in use:

♦ *Dynamic (component interaction) models:* The broad architecture, the high-level user work flow, the high-level process (rules) models, and the interactions with the database are all described best in terms of components and the way they interact with each other. The bubble charts shown in this book are more evocative than highly descriptive, but the basic idea is correct: capture the fundamental components and the interactions they have with each other.

♦ *Static structural models:* The data model in particular is best described by a model, like the boxes and arrows shown earlier, that captures the static structure of the individual components (entities and their attributes, objects and their interfaces) and the relationships between those components.

♦ *Prototyping:* Until now, every aspect of the design process we've discussed has been model driven. In the next chapter we'll talk more about the role of models in building applications. For now, suffice it to say that model design is the most central principle behind everything being laid out here. We have been talking not only about models, but pretty abstract ones too, based on diagrams and derived concepts. This approach works everywhere except for the user interface.

The design of the architectural, business rules, and database layers is very much a left-brain activity. The design of the top-level workflow in the document layer also is a left-brain activity. The left side of the brain, associated with the activities of the right hand in most of the population, controls the analytic, unemotional side of most people. It loves abstractions, formal approaches, and detailed analysis. Fine, except that good user interface design is not a left-brain, but rather a right-brain activity. The right side of the brain, in contrast to the left, is spontaneous, unstructured, and creative. So user interface design is not model driven. Rather it is a process of creation, prototyping, and artistic breakthrough.

There you have it, the models (or, in the case of the UI, lack thereof) that drive the design of graphical client/server applications.

ORGANIZING FOR SUCCESS

Given this broad methodology, how should a large development project be organized to maximize the opportunity of success? Several basic principles drive the overall organization. The first and most important is to build the entire organization around small teams.

Everybody by now knows that small teams are much more effective than large ones. What's not so obvious is how to arrange very large projects so that they can be carried out by small teams effectively. The two abstraction techniques at the core of our methodology provide the solution.

APPLICATION, APPLET, COMPONENT, SMALL TEAM

Historically, applications have been built by project teams. At best the application might be divided up into major subsystems, each in turn subdivided into modules. The problem is that these modules generally are highly interdependent on each other with large numbers of cross boundary code and data references. Therefore, while the modules might look separate, one team could hardly do anything without running into another. The result was to effectively force apparently many small teams to really act like one much bigger one.

Suppose instead, though, that in the process of designing our application in terms of components and objects, we start treating each such component as an application in its own right. For example, credit authorization becomes a little application with its own requirements, its own testing procedures, and even its own release schedule. If the bigger application is a word processor, the smaller application is the spell checker, the drawing program, or the mail-merge utility. Again, the smaller application, or *applet*, has its own requirements, testbed, and release schedule. By design each such applet is small enough that it can be built very competently by a team of 5 to 15 people. And, by design, setting the applets free in this way creates teams that can be highly self-motivated and that can build their own procedures to ensure quality, timeliness, and effective development.

What have we here? *Self-managed development teams!* Wait a minute: we're applying the very concepts behind effective TQM and BPR to software development! And why not. Sounds neat, but are there any more benefits besides teams that are in more control? Yes.

Think about the credit-authorization applet. Designed as such, it really is useable by a wide variety of other applications. In fact, the credit-authorization applet team now takes pride in ensuring that the interfaces and behavior of *their* applet are optimized to provide excellent service to as wide a variety of other applications as possible. Say again: applets lead to teams that prize and promote interoperability? Exactly. More. Say the company rules for credit authorization change. Because this is a separate applet, designed on purpose to insulate itself behind its interfaces from other applications, its internal behavior can be changed to reflect the new rules. And the other applications using it *don't have to be rereleased for the new rules to take effect.* Wow, the team is even motivated to promote flexible behavior. Any more? Yes, one more, but it's a big one.

Say a local team wants to customize the credit-authorization process for their region. First of all, because credit authorization is now an applet, it's easy to gain a handle on what is and is not handled by the component. Then writing a special front end, with the same interfaces, the local team traps certain special cases and handles them specially. Each time, though, whether or not special handling was done, the front end passes on the requests it has received to the normal credit-authorization applet to finish processing. Almost as easy to do as to say, and the reason is that the applet was appropriately packaged in a small enough piece in the first place, designed with specifically identified interfaces, all making it easy to subclass just the behavior that required customization without having to rewrite the entire application. Small teams, productivity, flexibility, interoperability, and even the ability to customize. All from applets, which are just the coarse-grained objects called cooperating components that seem to be so central to everything we touch and are wherever we look.

ARCHITECTURE AND TOOLS TEAMS

In addition to the normal development (now component applet) teams, two special teams are very important in larger development organizations. The architecture team, already described somewhat loosely several pages ago, provides the broad structure of both development in general and specific applications in particular. Finding individuals with the right mix of technical, business, and design skills is hard, but it's really worth it.

No matter how good the tools available are, there will always be specialized tools that must be built internally. Just as important, even when tools are purchased from the outside, a team is still required to evaluate those tools in the first place and then develop appropriate standards for their use once acquired.

How big should the architecture and tools teams be? It depends on the size of the overall development organization, but a rule of thumb might indicate that about 5 percent of the development staff be composed of an equal split between architects and tool engineers.

USER INTERFACE DESIGN

Although this topic has already been discussed, a few more words are still in order. Why is user interface design so hard? Here are some fundamental reasons, all related to the artistic nature of the process:

✦ Users know what they want, but only when they see it. That's why prototypes are so important. Even after years of experience, almost all the time, when you see the prototype that you so carefully asked for, it's *not what you want*. But, after some tuning, you will know it when the prototype is, after all, what you really do want, but only when you see it; it'll suddenly feel right. Verbalization doesn't work; only building and seeing does.

✦ Users often realize what they really want only after they see what they asked for. After they use it, most users realize that what they first wanted (and asked for) is not what is really needed. So iteration is even more important. Build that first prototype so that the users can figure out that much more quickly what they *really* should have asked for.

✦ Everyone considers himself or herself a designer (because they're alive). This is the trickiest rule of all. User interfaces are all around us. Everybody uses them, and everybody knows what they do and don't like. Not everybody can be a Picasso, a Hemingway, or even a good commercial artist. In the same way, most developers have very limited abilities when it comes to designing really effective user interfaces. Based on my own experience, about .5 percent to 1 percent of the development community really has good user interface taste: that's 1 in 100 or 1 in 200, depending on how lucky you are. Find those people, develop their skills, and put them at the center of your user interface design team because . . .

✦ The rules of GUI design are

   ✦ Still being discovered and invented

   ✦ Not written down anywhere

   It's an art, not a science, so get good (great?) artists on your team if happy users are important to the success of the project. Faster learning, more efficiency in use, lower error rates, fewer help calls, and best of all, happy users: it's worth it.

✦ Good GUIs change users' needs. This is the most important reason of all to have good or, if possible, great user interface designers. This year's great user interface design, the one with three new breakthroughs, becomes next year's baseline. The better you do, the more your users will expect. Who said the world is fair.

HIRE THE BEST

The United States of America, a world leader by most measures, was founded on the principle of equal opportunity for all. Many observers tend to interpret this somewhat loosely as *equality for all*, as though the country should or could somehow try to make all citizens either equivalent (shudder) or even in some other way equal. In fact, though, the real strength of the country lies in its ability to cater to a population with vast differences in talent, ability, and inclination, while coming close to really providing an equal opportunity to all.

In very few areas are the real differences between people with different talents as visible as in the area of software development. Good developers are up to ten times as productive as mediocre ones. And excellent developers in turn are ten times as productive as the good ones. Multiply it out: the great developers are *100 times as productive (or more) as the mediocre developers*. Notice the term: *developers*. The ratios apply to architects and designers just as much as to programmers. The stories about the fabled great developers really are true. They produce infinitely better software than their more normal colleagues.

Can one programmer, say, really write 100 times as much code every day as another? Well, first of all the answer sometimes really is yes, particularly when debugging, testing, and all the rest are taken into account. But the more important answer is more fundamental than that. The great developers generally don't crank out literally 100 times as many characters, words, or statements as the others. Rather than being more efficient, they are more effective (remember *that* distinction). They invent or discover the breakthrough algorithms. They turn the problem on its head and discover new ways of approaching it. They find ways to make one part of the code hundreds of times as fast so that the need for other parts of the code just goes away. How they do it is as varied as the number of individuals involved; the invariant part is the ability of great developers to produce results that are awesome qualitatively and quantitatively.

Do all of your developers have to be great, even if you could find and hire that many unusual individuals? Not at all, it wouldn't even be desirable. Effective teams consist of groups of individuals with complementary talents. The few great developers provide either the leadership or the core infrastructure for the rest of the team. Those few star performers, though, are what make the whole team look great.

What is the single biggest critical success factor determining the difference between projects that fail and those that don't? Not tools, not budget, not methodology, although those things do count a great deal. Rather it's the presence or absence of a few, usually one or two, central star performers with the right vision, leadership, and design talents to make the whole team do the right things at the right time.

FIND GREAT PEOPLE; KEEP GREAT PEOPLE

Whether we're talking about the very few great performers or the equally important larger numbers of good performers, finding them is tough. The first step is to be clear about looking for the best. The easiest way to attract good people is to start with good people.

After you've found them, it's equally important to keep them. Training, open communication, a pleasant work environment, all of these things contribute to making people want to stay. Small things count for a lot. Developers need quiet. A growing body of scientific evidence indicates that productivity is directly proportional to the amount of uninterrupted time once concentration is achieved; this is called flow time. Concentration takes most people about 20 minutes to achieve; so an interruption, no matter how minor, every 15 minutes, means flow time never happens. That's why offices with closed doors, rather than a status symbol, are a key profitability contributor when it comes to developers. It's not by accident that Microsoft, the leading software development organization in the world, from the beginning has given every developer his own office, his own door, and the ability to close that door at any time to help build that precious flow time.

Similarly, developers are one of the few classes of office workers today who use computers for directly productive tasks. The computers they use double in speed every two years, but only if they are upgraded. True, a new computer might cost $3,000 per developer *every other year*, but isn't that cheap at the price? More important, what kind of a statement does the programmer read into the willingness to upgrade that computer every 18 months, or the unwillingness to do so for five years because of the capital depreciation schedule? (Think about using a five-year-old computer today.)

GRAPHICAL CLIENT/SERVER DESIGN
A PROCESS-ORIENTED APPROACH

This chapter has laid out the methodological framework for designing a new class of applications that are friendly, distributed, flexible, and, most of all, support the shift to self-controlled computers for self-managed teams. The new approach builds on classical methodologies in many ways, but at the same time adds some critical new elements that provide the bridge into the future. Most of all, though, the new approach introduces a process orientation that both ties into BPR and provides a basis for distributed design. By thinking about and building applications out of cooperating components, we move into a new world in which distributed, locally customizable systems really are possible for the first time. Now the question is: what tools are needed to build these applications? That's the next chapter.

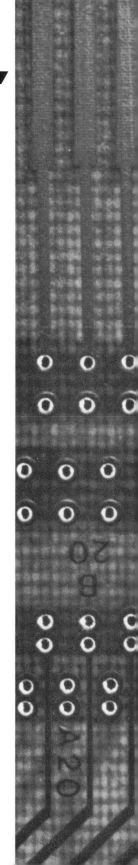

CHAPTER 15

TOOLS: IMPLEMENTS FOR BUILDING SYSTEMS

To everything there is a season and a time to every purpose under heaven.

Confronted with the task of building an application, many developers and even some users start out by thinking about what tool to use. Should I use Visual Basic, PowerBuilder, Paradox, or perhaps a programming language combined with a database? On larger projects the debate about which programming language is the best has been raging for at least 30 years. Today the choice, including COBOL, C, SmallTalk, BASIC, C++, Enfin, and more, is broader than ever. Yet another class of passionate advocates sees CASE tools as *the* answer to all the problems of building systems better and faster; buy the right CASE tool, take the right training, and the computer will do all your programming for you. This chapter puts a framework around the world of tools, putting each in its place, and describing the time in the development cycle to consider each class of helper.

There are two cardinal rules that help a great deal in evaluating tools:

✦ Development tools are for humans, not for computers. All too often it is tempting to think about languages, databases, and CASE tools as being *computer tools* somehow designed to help the computer. That's wrong. Every last one of these tools is designed with one purpose in mind: to help *people* develop programs.

✦ No tool, no matter how comprehensive or how good, can do the whole job for all applications. Applications vary greatly in size, complexity, and features. Development is a multifaceted activity. The development team and the individual developer need to have access to a toolkit with a variety of tools in it, each designed to do a particular job very well. There may be cases, particularly on smaller projects, where a single tool can do the whole job. In general, however, understanding and gaining experience with a variety of tools is the best way to ensure that you are building applications in the most efficient, most high-quality fashion. In the long run, and often even in the short run, trying to make a single tool do the whole job is a poor way to manage both training and production.

MAPPING THE MODEL ONTO THE TOOLS

Figure 15-1, carried over from Chapter 14, shows the stages in the development methodology for graphical client/server systems. In carrying the figure over, however, I replaced the individual entries with new ones describing the type of tool best designed to support the particular step in the process.

	Conceptual	Logical	Physical
Documents	Design Tool	Design Tool	Graphical Builder
Business rules	Design Tool	Design Tool	Programming Language
Database	Design Tool	Design Tool	Database Manager

Figure 15-1: The development methodology for graphical client/server systems.

The first two columns deal with the conceptual and logical phases of the process. Both columns are handled by the same class of tool, called a *design tool* in the table. More accurately, these two phases are handled by *planning, analysis, and design tools*. These are often referred to as *computer-aided software engineering* (CASE) tools in the computer world at large. This leads up to the big questions:

✦ What are CASE tools?

✦ Do they have any real value?

As usual, to answer those questions I have to answer some others first:

✦ How are applications really designed?

✦ What role do models play in that process?

MODEL-DRIVEN APPLICATION DEVELOPMENT

Where do great designs come from? What about the new car whose shape, performance, and style captures the public's imagination overnight? That lamp, like the Tizio, that is copied and photographed so often that it becomes the very symbol of style? Great buildings — whether homes, offices, or churches — combine the same elements used in other buildings for thousands of years, yet somehow they manage to stand out in the eyes of all beholders. How did the designer arrive at that one combination of elements that makes the structure widely recognized for its greatness?

Software can be great too, in many ways. Computer-based planning and budgeting was common all through the '70s. Yet it wasn't until VisiCalc introduced its spreadsheet metaphor that the idea suddenly took off. Dozens of competitors were developed over a period of years, on a variety of computers, including the IBM PC. Yet it wasn't until 1-2-3 was introduced that VisiCalc lost any market share. 1-2-3 was so successful that it propelled Lotus Development Corporation to $50 million in sales in just one year. Something about the combination of features, appearance, and function put the Lotus product on the top almost instantly. VisiCalc and 1-2-3, unlike the dozens of other spreadsheets and planning tools developed all around them, were *great* products — products with great design. The question is, how is great (or at least very good!) software designed?

By definition, all software is based on the same small set of elements. All programming languages offer the same essential constructs that are based on the underlying instruction set of the computer. User interfaces are limited to what the screen, the mouse, and the rest of the hardware environment make possible. All programmers work with basically the same operating systems, development tools, and design knowledge. Yet some developers produce great applications and some don't. The difference is in the design.

Great design comes from great designers. From that statement there is no escape, but even great designers need tools and processes to make their work possible. The concept of modeling lies at the center of almost all design activity.

The purpose of a model is to allow the designer to experiment with many possible designs without having to build a complete final system each time. Building an actual application is a slow and painstaking process. In this way, software is much like buildings, cars, and many other physical objects. An architect could demonstrate several potential floor plans by actually building each of the houses being considered. Certainly, considering the alternative designs in this way would provide the client with a thorough insight into the strengths and weaknesses of the various proposals. The problem, of course, is that building even one complete real house — let alone several — is far too expensive and time consuming to be practical as a design aide. Not only would each house take too long to build, but once built, the houses would be difficult to alter. Because design is always an iterative process involving successive refinement, alteration would be required to most of the houses as soon as they were complete. So building the real thing is not practical when it comes to houses — or even software — as a means to considering alternative final designs.

Yet designers need a way of visualizing designs both for themselves and for their clients. That's where the model comes in. Perhaps this sound like a very obvious idea, but, the critical role of model-driven design and development is far too rarely understood in the computer business.

The central role of a model is to function as a scaled-down representation that represents another larger object. Sometimes a model literally can be a smaller copy of the real thing; other times the model takes quite a different form. I would first like to consider the case of models that are miniatures of the final system.

Parts of most applications lend themselves to being modeled by smaller versions of the real thing. The parts we're talking about, as you've probably guessed, are the desktop components, the user interface. In fact, the single most powerful way of modeling the user interface is exactly to build a prototype of it. The prototype, which can be built with a variety of tools, including some designed just for the purpose of building prototypes, allows the designer in a matter of literally minutes or hours to develop a model of the user interface that looks for all practical intents and purposes exactly like the real thing, the final product.

Watching a skilled prototyper at work is quite an experience. Working with a tool like Visual Basic, Hypercard, or ToolBook, the modeler starts bringing up forms, radio buttons, menus, and other UI elements literally instantly. Within an hour or two, a complete representation of the application, with dialog boxes, help messages, transitions from one form to another, and function keys is running. In fact, one of the issues the developer must watch out for is not fooling the user. At one level it's important to be sure that the user knows that what he is seeing is not a working system; that's easy to watch out for. What's harder to prevent is the idea that if a prototype can be built this easily, then surely the entire application can only take a few hours, or at most days to build.

User interface prototypes, models, have value for everybody involved in the design process. The designer, no matter how much experience he has, finds the prototype invaluable as a tool for exploring what the system really looks like, and more important what it's really like to work with. The user often gets to understand the real operation of the proposed system for the first time; without a prototype, interfaces are amazingly difficult for most people to visualize. Best of all, prototypes are not only easy to build, but also just as easy to change. So once the first prototype or perhaps the first several alternative prototypes are built, the real design work begins: the careful refinement of the first crude ideas into a final design that will really work.

Unlike the document layer, the models used to describe the business rules and database layers are quite different from the final product, not a smaller version of the real thing. To see why this is so, think about the business rules and database management layers of a system. What does it even mean to model elements of the database or the business rules layers of the application architecture? In the case of these two layers, modeling makes more sense than ever, but the form of the model is different from that used for the user interface. In this case, the model is *not* based on a miniature image of the final product. In fact, in the case of a database file or an application built up out of business rules, there is no visual representation, no concrete image the model can be patterned after. Instead, the model for the business rules and database components is based on diagrams sometimes augmented with word-based descriptions.

MODELS, DIAGRAMS, AND CASE TOOLS: ART, SCIENCE, OR DISCIPLINE?

At some level, the idea of model-driven development has been around since programming was invented. Every programmer setting out to build a large system starts by planning his or her work, drawing some diagrams, writing down some preliminary specifications, and developing an outline of how the parts of the system will fit together. In the '60s, this process was first formalized through the introduction of flowcharts. IBM and others popularized the concept to the point where thousands of engineers, scientists, and other technical professionals who at one time learned to program, today remember fondly the green stencils originally introduced as an aide to drawing those flowcharts. In fact, Visio, a newly popular Windows-based drawing program, builds on this memory by literally building green templates into the product.

From the beginning, diagrams have held a strange fascination for many otherwise unemotional people. When flowcharting first took hold, many organizations decided that the same concepts and tools could be used to model not only their software-based applications, but, in fact, also all the business processes in the entire company. And so many companies, even if only briefly, launched efforts to develop comprehensive flowcharts showing every paper form, every bureaucratic flow, every communication, organization wide. Missing only the broader motivation to extend this effort higher and wider, these early flowcharting exercises, applied on this scale, were truly harbingers of today's Business Process Reengineering movement. In its most mechanical phases, BPR is in some ways no more than glorified flowcharting.

The early '80s, as was discussed at more length in the chapter on the computer crisis and the history leading up to it, was the decade in which a great deal of work was put into making mainframe-based development into far more of a predictable, controlled process. Model-based development and diagrammatic approaches in particular played a key role in that process.

So what is the best type of model for thinking about, say, a database? In fact, how can there even be a model for something as abstract as a database? Information stored on a disk, relationships between sets of records, structured collections of data; what does it mean to have a model of such objects? If you read Chapter 10, you've already seen the answer. Diagrams can be used to build very fine database models. In fact, in that chapter, we built several such diagrams, including the one reproduced in Figure 15-2.

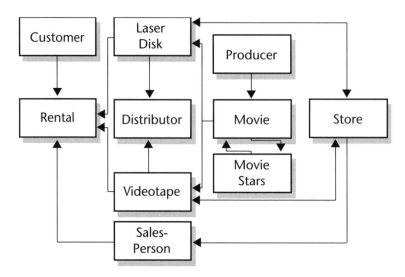

Figure 15-2: A data model diagram of the database.

Looking at the diagrammatic data model provides a sufficiently clear representation of the database, including the all-important relationships, that many nontechnical users can quickly learn to understand and work with that model. Being a simple diagram, it is easy to refine and change. Best of all, in the case of the data model, it is straightforward to move directly from a model like the one shown here to the definition and construction of the actual database. So, like the user interface prototype, the data model is not only a useful representation for the user, but also a strong platform for basing subsequent development.

If the user interface model is based on a prototype and the database model is based on a diagram, what is the business rule model based on? Putting it another way, how is all the code, all the language-based programmed software that makes up the bulk of many applications, modeled? The answer is: with more diagrams. A variety of diagrams can be used to represent the structure of the actual code making up the programs in the running system. These include functional decomposition diagrams, data flow and process dependency diagrams, object interaction and class hierarchy diagrams, and more. While the chapter on database technology developed some of the simpler diagrammatic techniques used to model databases, in the interest of not diving too deep into detail, this chapter does *not* show actual diagrams for modeling applications. Suffice it to say that, although many professionals would object to this simplification, most of the diagrams are based on elaborations of the simple concept of flowcharting.

The key point is that a combination of diagrams *can* be used to model all of the application except the user interface, and that can be modeled through prototypes. Obviously then, diagrams and diagrammatic techniques play a key role in supporting any model-driven design process. The problem that then arises is that diagrams are both easy and hard to work with.

Drawing a simple diagram in the first place is so natural and easy that people do it all the time. Every mythical inventor is supposed to have drawn pictures of early versions of her first products on the backs of envelopes. Once drawn though, diagrams are quite hard to modify, extend, and most of all, hard to share. Computers can help solve that problem, though. In fact, by the late '80s, just as diagrams were becoming popular, a whole class of products devoted to drawing diagrams were just starting to enjoy widespread commercial success.

CAD, CAM, AND CASE

Architects and engineers draw diagrams all day long. House plans, engineering drawings, and manufacturing specs all consist of diagrams. Historically, these diagrams were all drawn by draftsmen sitting at drafting tables working with T-squares. In the early '70s, though, special workstations designed to automate the process of producing diagrams started to appear. Perhaps *automate* is too strong a word to use; these workstations provided technical professionals with sophisticated drawing facilities for building, editing, extending, and even sharing diagrams and pictures. By the early '80s, this same software was just starting to become available on PCs, putting the facilities into an overall price range that every engineer and architect could finally afford.

In the late '70s, as a way of capturing the idea of controllable development, the phrase *software engineering* was coined. In theory, software engineering is a discipline based on well-understood approaches that allow complex software to be built in a predictable fashion, and with quality that can be measured and guaranteed. It's a great concept and one that many developers still consider worth pursuing today.

Just as software engineering was starting to capture the imaginations of development managers, diagrammatic techniques became popular at the same time. Index Technologies, one of the leading management consulting companies of the time, realized that if special software could help architects and engineers draw technical diagrams and that if software engineering was to depend heavily on diagrams, then perhaps the two went together. The resulting equation said, why not build software to help in the design of software? The *CASE (computer-aided software engineering)* industry was born.

Two diametrically opposed perspectives on the value of CASE tools best capture the state of this controversial product area today:

✦ CASE tools are just fancy drawing packages for constructing diagrams. At best, they automate the process of producing flowcharts that do very little to help in the real work of producing code. At worst, the tools burden the programmer with cumbersome methodologies, don't even function as well as more general drawing tools, cost a lot of money, and require expensive hardware to run.

✦ CASE tools provide a comprehensive environment for completely automated application development. They eliminate the need for programming alto-gether by generating high-quality, machine-independent code automatically from high-level design specifications. And by automatically supporting methodologies, they provide the benefits of predictable, controllable develop-ment while eliminating the tedious forms and paperwork normally associated with life-cycle-oriented processes.

The truth, of course, is somewhere in the middle.

At the time the first CASE tools were created, there was a common belief that eventu-ally the combination of complete methodologies, model-driven development, and tool support for the process could well lead to automated development. After all, in the manufacturing world, many engineering systems support not only CAD, computer-aided design, but also CAM, computer-aided manufacturing. Workstations produce complete sets of instructions that drive computerized manufacturing equipment, which literally builds parts directly from relatively high-level designs and drawings. Drawing on that experience, why shouldn't the same thing be possible for programs?

IF IT WALKS LIKE A DUCK AND LOOKS LIKE A DUCK...

After ten years of experience with CASE tools, two things have become painfully clear:

✦ At least in the foreseeable future, programming cannot be automated; pro-grammers cannot be replaced.

✦ In spite of overwhelming evidence to the contrary, many development man-agers continue to believe that CASE tools will, after all, replace programmers.

The challenge for everybody building software, then, is sorting out fact from fiction. And along the way, the next challenge is to recognize the true benefits that CASE tools *can* bring to bear even if they don't totally eliminate programmers.

CASE tools not only don't eliminate development, they don't even eliminate the need to write code, and relatively low-level code at that. Sure, tool vendors can demon-strate environments in which entire programs are specified in a purely diagrammatic fashion, starting with high-level designs, and then gradually adding in more detail, step by step, never dropping out of the diagrammatic environment. And, sure, at the end the tool will literally grind away and then produce code in C or COBOL that can even run on a variety of different computer systems. Very impressive, and potentially quite useful, but there's a catch. At the most detailed level of the system, where program logic is supposedly being specified diagrammatically, a tricky little transformation took place, a kind of sleight of hand, a shell game. Yes, everything is still happening diagrammatically, but the everything that is still happening is, in fact, *a kind of programming.*

Programming with and through diagrams is still as much "programming" as though typing words was involved. Programming can take a variety of forms. Commonly, programmers type words, phrases, and statements at a keyboard. However, program logic can be specified in other ways too. The computer can play a role in helping the programmer type in her program. After all, because the computer understands the structure of the programming language, it can literally anticipate the alternatives available to the programmer at each step, offer her alternatives, and thus eliminate a lot of editing. The resulting system is called a *syntax-directed editor.* CASE tools that supposedly automate the programming process simply substitute syntax-directed editors for classical text-oriented editors. At the finest level of detail, the developer is still programming and programming at the same level as if no CASE tool was involved. In the CASE environment, that developer is programming differently, but still programming, and doing just as much work as if he was programming any other way available today. American folk wisdom holds that *if it walks like a duck, looks like a duck, and quacks, it must be a duck, no matter what it's called.* By this logic, CASE environments eliminate no programming, and they replace no programmers.

There are some advantages to programming within the confines of the CASE environment. The CASE tool can keep track of all changes to the program and reflect them in the design model. The programming is done in an integrated environment, so references to variables, database elements, and forms are always guaranteed to be correct. And the CASE system can provide a limited amount of platform independence too. At the same time, let's be clear, this *is* programming in a closed, confined environment. By definition, the programmer is limited to a single programming language, a single set of development tools, and a single way of working.

So the first thing that is true about CASE tools is that they represent no silver bullet. They don't automate the development process, they don't eliminate the need for programming, and they don't make all our development problems go away.

The second thing that is true about CASE tools is that many development professionals refuse to believe that these limitations are really true. All too many MIS managers continue to cling to the belief that structured methodologies, model-driven development, and CASE tools offer a path that will lead, later if not sooner, to completely mechanical, totally predictable, wholly automated development. And it is those beliefs and some of the design models embodied in both the methodologies and the CASE tools that support them which stand in the way of both distributed development in particular and client/server development in general.

IS THE EMPEROR WEARING CLOTHES?

At this point a very natural question arises: do models, methodologies and CASE tools have any value at all? Perhaps that first perspective expressed earlier, the one that said CASE is just about fancy but useless diagrams, is correct after all.

Even if they don't lead directly to code, diagrams have a high intrinsic value. This is a good thing because both CASE tools and the models they support *are* very diagram-intensive. Yet these diagrams are not very rigorous. *Rigor* is a term mathematicians use to describe sets of rules and theorems that are logically complete, totally provable, and capable of being the basis for complex theories. Diagrammatic models are not like that. The first time many programmers see a set of diagrams describing the structure of an application, they are blown away, expecting that these diagrams will form the basis for completely provable code. In Chapter 10, the futility of trying to produce provably correct systems was discussed at some length. Diagrams are *not* just another attempt to achieve that goal. In fact, on purpose the diagrams describing an application are only loosely connected; they are not intended to form some theoretically perfect structure. Instead, they are designed to provide us with several loosely related perspectives for visualizing the design of an application before we spend the time and money to build it.

The fact that the diagrams and the CASE tools that support them are not very rigorous distresses many professionals almost as much as any suggestion that CASE tools don't eliminate programming. After all, if these expensive and complex tools just draw diagrams, they can't be much good, right? Diagrams, so the thought goes, are just pretty ways of artistically expressing things that ought to be expressed just as easily in words. If the diagrams were provably part of something scientific, or even better something that even eliminated programming, then obviously those diagrams and the tools that produced them would be worthwhile. But if they're *just diagrams,* isn't this just fancy artwork?

A popular children's story tells of the emperor who bought a complete set of fancy clothes that really did not exist. Because the clothes were so expensive and because the hucksters selling the clothes to the emperor appealed to his vanity, he was convinced to parade through the streets of the city wearing no clothes at all. He was convinced that after spending so much, his clothes were so fine that only refined people could even see them. Perhaps like the fabled emperor, purchasers of CASE tools are really just being fooled, and the invisible clothes, or in this case pretty diagrams, have no real value after all? And the answer to that dilemma revolves around the intrinsic value of diagrams in the design process.

THE POWER OF DIAGRAMS

Christopher Alexander is a practicing architect, a professor of architecture at the University of California, and the author of several books, including *Notes on the Synthesis of Form* and *The Timeless Way of Building.* These books have become widely read underground classics held in high esteem by designers around the world. Not just architects, but also software designers, car and furniture designers, and thoughtful professionals of all kinds have found Alexander's books invaluable in understanding the design process.

Architects, of course, use diagrams and drawings of many kinds to describe buildings. A small house or cottage will have dozens of diagrams associated with it detailing the floor plan, electrical wiring, plumbing, landscaping, structural specifications, roof design, and so on. The fact that these diagrams are only loosely coupled is not a problem; each provides a different perspective on the design of the house. Together they form a complete model of that house; complete not due to some mathematically rigorous theory, but because the diagrams provide enough information for a human to build a meaningful model in his or her head.

A model of a house can be built in many ways. Words and sentences, for instance, can obviously be used to do a very complete job. Pictures might be nice too, as would a tiny scale model. Yet diagrams play a uniquely central role; nothing else seems to work as well. In the preface to *Notes on the Synthesis of Form*, Alexander talks about the surprising power of diagrams.

Diagrams are not the convenient means to reach an end called *methodology*. Nor are diagrams something to be embarrassed about drawing. Instead, diagrammatic modeling is a fundamentally powerful approach, proven over hundreds of years, that helps produce and refine better designs.

Christopher Alexander ran into exactly the same problem with understanding the role of diagrams in designing buildings that computer people have run into with understanding the role of diagrams in designing software. When Alexander wrote the first edition of *Notes on the Synthesis of Form,* he talked extensively about the power of diagrams. In the same book, he also laid out some simple principles for approaching certain design problems. Unfortunately, many readers concluded that Alexander was proposing a formal methodology for designing buildings; a methodology which, when complete, would provide a step-by-step approach to the design art. The readers also assumed that diagrams drawn a particular way were a part of that methodology. Alexander was so upset by this misreading of his work that he devoted most of the foreword to subsequent editions of the book to explaining the true role of diagrams and methodologies. As Alexander points out, diagrams are useful in and of themselves as ways of sorting through all the tradeoffs inherent in any design. And just because he recommended some particular diagrams, in no way did he imply that they were the only good diagrams or that design had been converted from an art into a precise rote cookbook.

Ease of use, consistency, flexibility, efficiency, speed, space, and so on are all forces acting on us as designers and on the systems we produce. The application architecture and the concept of components and objects are precisely intended to create patterns and components with what Alexander would call force systems with very dense internal interaction. And diagrams are often the best way of describing and dealing with these forces systems — in software design as well as in building design. So not only is this advice relevant, it's highly targeted, too.

Diagrams are important in and of themselves. Just because diagrams don't do the whole job, just because producing neat diagrams does not by itself result in finished systems, in no way means that the diagrams are not important. And, similarly, just because the diagrams are not part of some mathematically complete, scientifically derived framework for automatically building programs doesn't mean that the diagrams aren't still very important. Tools that help us work with diagrams are therefore important, too. That's where CASE comes in.

CASE tools are critically important to the effective design of large systems. Yes, the design can be done without them, just as books can be written without word processors. But systems can be designed much more quickly and arguably more effectively by providing teams with appropriate tools to support the planning and design process for individuals and groups: that's CASE.

To put this situation in final perspective, consider the analogy with architectural and engineering design. Every project has three components, illustrated by the three circles in Figure 15-3. These three components overlap, but not very much, and different tools are appropriate for each area.

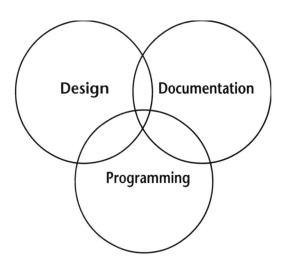

Figure 15-3: The three components of architectural and engineering design.

Architects, for example, use design tools to develop building and town plans. If you worked with an architect to design your dream home, you'd expect to see diagrams early, late, and often throughout the design process. Although those diagrams historically were produced by hand, today they are generally developed on workstations, often relatively high in price. So far, so good.

Now suppose that, once you had approved your house plan, the architect pressed a function key on her workstation, and the house was magically built by machines with no human intervention required. Pretty nice, right? But not imaginable today or even tomorrow. Yet would you expect your architect to therefore refuse to use a design workstation just because that workstation could not automatically build the whole house from the design? How about if the workstation couldn't build any part of the house at all; would you expect the architect *then* to refuse to use it? Pretty crazy, but then, if the workstation isn't building houses, isn't it *just* helping build diagrams? Of course, and valuable, or perhaps even invaluable, nonetheless.

As it goes in architecture so it goes in software design. Design, documentation, and programming are distinctly different parts of the development process. Overlap exists: CASE tools can generate database definitions, can generate *parts* of programs, and can help generate parts of the documentation. Nonetheless, for the most part CASE tools play a key role in the planning and design process; in fact, they even play an invaluable role in that process. Once done, having laid a solid foundation for the subsequent programming effort, they then clear the way to pick the best programming tools for the job and move into the next circle. So CASE tools are key; are the CASE tools we need available today?

CASE: YESTERDAY, TODAY, AND TOMORROW

The CASE industry is one of the great puzzles of the computer industry. On the one hand, a number of companies, including Texas Instruments, Knowledgeware, Bachman, Intersolv (nee Index), and more recently LBMS and Popkin, have developed nothing short of a billion-dollar-per year business selling sophisticated software tools. On the other hand, most programmers don't use CASE tools, many of the vendors are considered moribund, and nobody knows whether to think the category is on the way in or on the way out. Part of the problem is that, lacking a clear vision for CASE present and CASE future, it's hard to know what the fashionable view of this concept is. And unfortunately in an industry as prone to religions and fads as ours, lack of a fashion leader can often be debilitating. But beyond fashion, how *should* you think about CASE tools and vendors?

LEARNING FROM THE PAST

The CASE industry today is in about the same state as the word processing industry was in 1980. At that time, word processors came in two flavors. Large, self-contained, expensive systems running on expensive, proprietary hardware were sold by vendors like Wang, NBI, and IBM. Although law firms and large corporations could afford these systems in their word processing pools, they were far beyond the reach of ordinary writers in cost, complexity, and availability. In 1980, while the word processing industry was apparently grinding to a halt because these big systems appeared to have saturated their markets, a new generation of word processors was just appearing. The new generation, of course, consisted of products like WordStar, MultiMate, and The

Final Word. These new word processors were inexpensive and ran on garden-variety personal computers, but they were far too limited and hard to use to seriously challenge their big brothers.

In 1980 the vast majority of writers not only did not use word processors; most of them were also unfamiliar with the very concept. Even professional authors writing novels, self-help books, and technical reference volumes still viewed correcting typewriters as state of the art. Suggesting that tens of millions of writers, including everyday office residents mainly writing memos, would use word processors would have been viewed as fanciful indeed.

Today that fanciful vision is reality. Products such as Ami Pro, WordPerfect, and Word do more than even the most powerful high-end word processor could do in 1980. In fact these products today do more than not only word processors of the past, but also even more than sophisticated page-layout systems of only ten years ago. As a result, almost anyone can casually compose multicolumn newsletters with lots of fonts, embedded graphics, and sophisticated pagination. Most amazing of all, all of this can be done by naive users, with no training, on computers costing under $2,000, using a shrink-wrapped word processor that sells for under $500.

To learn from this history lesson, several observations are important:

✦ Sophisticated tools often appear first in complex, expensive form. There is often a point where the sales of the tool in that complex form stall while the industry figures out how to repackage the same functionality in a more usable form.

✦ At the point of stalling, only a very small percentage of the potential users are even aware of the tool category and many of those who are aware are firmly convinced that *they* would never use such a (complex) tool.

✦ Once the category picks up, it often segments into a high end and a low end. Long term, the low-end tools contain virtually all the features (and then some) originally found in the tools that once were high end. By then, of course, the real high-end products have become more sophisticated again.

If history repeats itself, then whither CASE? Virtually all professional programmers have a real need for design tools. Professional programmers include those working for large corporations, but the community also includes consultants, small system houses doing contract programming, system integrators, and many others, totaling, even today, from 5 to 10 million individuals worldwide. Besides the professionals who develop systems for a living, many other part-time, occasional, and amateur developers could use design tools, just as part-time, occasional, and amateur writers use word processors.

So over the next five years, the CASE industry is destined to split and then start growing again. On the one hand, a category of simple but incredibly powerful tools that facilitate visual planning and design will emerge. These tools will be shrink-wrapped products, priced under $1,000, that allow developers to construct data models, process models, and all the other forms of diagrams that help drive and inform the development process. The visual design tools will be directly linked to all the popular construction tools, described later in this chapter, so that as developers finish their design, a wide variety of tool choices are always available when the time to actually build systems comes. Best of all, the visual design tools will be agnostic, largely methodology free, and so well designed that most developers will learn how to use them with no training and probably without reading the manuals (what else is new?). As a result, the day will come when developers will no more build even moderately complex systems without first using a design tool than they would write the documentation without a word processor.

Reaching the point where most developers use design tools involves a huge cultural shift affecting millions of individuals. The world of widespread design tools usage is in stark contrast to the state of the present-day world. Today, many development organizations don't use design tools at all. Even those companies that do buy CASE tools often find them both so complex and so expensive that their use is limited to a small set of analysts and designers. So by far the vast majority of developers don't use CASE tools and may never have even seen one. Moreover, the tools have the reputation for being so complex and so tied to inflexible methodologies that most programmers seriously believe that using such a tool would be health-threatening.

Perhaps one reason these developers don't see the need to use CASE tools is that they don't do much designing? Walk into any developer's office. The first thing you will notice is the ubiquitous white board, the modern-day replacement for the chalkboard of the past. The next thing you'll notice is what's on the white board: diagrams. Not one diagram, or two, but many. Every developer draws diagrams all the time, both for her own use and to facilitate discussion with others. These diagrams capture the design being worked on. Here's the rub: guess what happens to those diagrams when the project ends? They get rubbed off. The next developer to work on the system has to deduce the design from scratch.

Software designers *need* design tools. Just as writers ten years ago hesitated to edit, modify, and polish their writing extensively because it was so painful to do with typewriters and pens, so developers today struggle when trying to share, edit, and preserve the design expressed in diagrams. Although the analogy is not exact, the point being made *is* exactly the same. Computer-based design tools stand to have as much of an impact on development as word processors and even electronic mail systems have had on writing and communication.

VISUAL DESIGN VERSUS FULL CASE

So a certainty of the next five years is the emergence of a new class of design tools that will play the same role for the CASE industry as personal computer word processors played for that industry. And an associated certainty is that as these tools mature, become both more sophisticated and much easier to use, millions of developers will discover them, buy them, and eventually take them for granted. Once that happens, what is today known as the CASE industry will have split sharply, but for the better.

Just as tens of millions of home hobbyists use lightweight power tools, millions of developers, both full time and part time, will use visual design tools. These tools, designed to be super approachable, will likely not even be thought of in terms of something as formal as *computer- aided software engineering*. Rather, they will be simply design tools built specifically to facilitate the development of a variety of models used to describe and analyze systems before they are built.

Where will the high-end CASE industry go? Some of the vendors, of course, will participate in the new low-end market, but probably not very many. The transition to a high-volume, low-priced, packaged product market, where all products are sold through indirect channels of distribution is a tough one, and history tells us that as complex products mature, quite often new players pick up where old ones left off. But what about the current players; will they all disappear?

Hand drills and table saws are great, but not enough to build skyscrapers or suspension bridges. In the same way, while visual design tools will facilitate many of the more straightforward planning and design activities, there will still be a need for more sophisticated tools and systems to support the development of really large applications. And that is where the CASE vendors of the future will continue to grow and flourish. In fact, if anything, the emergence of the new client/server systems required to support self-managed teams creates a huge opportunity for those CASE vendors who can see the future coming to position themselves to support tomorrow's methodologies early. After all, if most of today's big applications are going to be rewritten to support BPR and self-managed teams, there will be a huge need for high-end tools to support all that development.

CAN THE TOOLS DO THE JOB?

Given that design tools are here to stay, and given that they're quite necessary to support the graphical distributed systems design that needs to get done, where are those tools right now? That's a problem.

Today's CASE tools are either complex, expensive, and hard to use (the high end), or limited, inexpensive, and still too hard to use (the low end). Moreover, none of these tools fully supports the design methodology described in the previous chapters. For example, CASE vendors are only just starting to understand the importance of the three-layer application architecture. Furthermore, too many of the more powerful CASE tools are still oriented toward closed environments in which the choice of development tools to be used after design is complete is highly limited; an absolute killer in trying to build true client/server systems.

The news is not all bad, though. A wide variety of CASE tools is available. And the tools are evolving every year. At the high end, for example, Texas Instruments in particular, with its IEF Composer product, does seem to really understand where client/server is going and is working to adapt its tool to help support that direction. Seer, with their HPS product, also offers an intriguing tool set at the high end, particularly as they break away from their historical dependence on a highly IBM-centric environment. At the low end, tools like ERwin and Popkin's System Architect, although they are limited, do support PC-oriented and flexible development quite well. And in the middle a new generation of tools, best exemplified by LBMS, actually support some aspects of graphically oriented design today. The problem is that none of them does the whole job. So what to do?

The answer is to develop a clear picture of your needs, particularly based on the last few chapters. Then commit some people (remember architecture and tools teams?) to picking the best *combination* of tools that meet your needs. If your organization is too small to have internal architecture and tools teams, *use consultants*. Properly managed, consultants can provide a huge amount of value, particularly because they get to see not just your problems but also the problems of many other organizations too.

While sorting through a design tool strategy, don't wait, but continue to invest in designing software thoroughly. Writing was possible before word processors existed, although many authors would have a hard time believing that today. Architects developed and refined drawings before computers were invented. Good design can be done without computer-based tools to support the process. The first and most important thing is to be committed to design, models, and diagrams.

Experiment with design tools to learn what works and to keep up with the state of the art. As word processors and CAD systems developed, authors and architects started using them, at first haltingly and in limited ways, and eventually fully and naturally. In the same way as design tools evolve, it is not necessary to wait for the ultimate tool to start gaining value today. Perhaps sorting through a variety of tools, like ERwin, IEF, and others, seems too much like chewing gum and bailing wire; perhaps it even is. At the same time, even in the perfect tool environment of the future, no single tool will do the whole job every time. Cabinet makers, even the best, pick different tools for different jobs all the time. So, developing the habit of building a full toolkit, even if many of the tools are substandard today, is still a fine habit to have for the present and for the future.

So design is critical and possible, and there is even computer-based help to make it happen. What happens after the design is complete and it's time to start building the system?

THE DEVELOPMENT ENVIRONMENT

As Figure 15-4 shows, the development environment, at the highest level, consists of tools targeted at each of the three layers of the application architecture. In fact, the development environment is far more complex than this. It includes development tools, debuggers, testing tools. This book will not deal with the complete development environment for two reasons: it's too big a topic and hundreds of highly appropriate books already exist. So the focus here is particularly on the top two layers and on the aspects of those two layers that are unique.

	Conceptual	Logical	Physical
Documents	Design Tool	Design Tool	Graphical Builder
Business rules	Design Tool	Design Tool	Programming Language
Database	Design Tool	Design Tool	Database Manager

Figure 15-4: A data model diagram of the database.

HIGH LEVEL OR LOW LEVEL — WHICH GENERATION ARE YOU FROM?

Figure 15-4 approaches construction tools from the perspective of the application architecture and the type of tool best suited to each layer in that architecture. Tools can also be thought of, though, in terms of whether they are *high-level* or *low-level* tools. For example, programmers talk about *high-level programming languages* all the time, by comparison implying that these languages are not, in turn, *low-level programming languages*. The following discussion uses the *low-level, high-level* taxonomy for considering construction tools and which are best suited to particular jobs. So what is the difference between a high-level and a low-level tool?

Construction tools, including programming languages, have evolved through four generations, each at a higher level than the generation before. The first generation of tools, consisting almost entirely of programming languages alone, provided facilities for talking to computers directly in their own language. As I'll show in a minute, this approach is so detailed as to be literally painful. Later, a second generation of languages and other tools provided some amount of translation so that developers could deal with slightly less detail in building their applications. All of the languages and tools developed in the first two generations are best thought of as *low-level*; they force the programmer to dive deep into the computer's internals, operating at a level of detail barely removed from the computer's basic instruction set.

In the '60s the first modern programming languages led the third generation of tool development, providing development facilities that could be used by normal human beings without understanding and tracking all the details of the computer's step-by-step operation. Most of the next few pages deal with the relatively high-level languages that dominate third-generation development.

Finally, in the '80s and '90s a variety of fourth-generation tools have evolved that provide mechanisms for literally building applications without programming. The core concept of most of these tools is *nonprocedural* specification, an idea we'll explore in more detail after first looking at the third-generation programming languages that still dominate development today.

PROGRAMMING LANGUAGES

A low-level language is one that forces you to talk to the computer at a very low level of detail, to deal with every last aspect of the computer's activity. Computers are extremely literal machines. Saying *"please take a letter to Betty"* to an equally literal secretary would result in his picking a random letter and hand-carrying it to Betty. Computers are not only literal, but they also expect to receive instructions that are extremely detailed in nature. Telling your body how to walk at the same detailed level would require you to focus on breathing in, breathing out, lifting each foot a certain number of inches, and then moving it forward a different number of inches, and so on. All of this makes dealing with computers directly very tedious.

In the '50s, the direct and tedious approach was the only one; programs were written in *machine language. Machine language* consists of incredibly detailed instructions, all specified in terms of numbers (*bits*, or binary digits). Programs written in machine language are so detailed that building large programs becomes not just tedious and error prone, but literally impossible. Just as a person couldn't even walk if every breath, every physical movement, required conscious thought and direction, in the same way keeping track of all the detailed steps the computer takes makes it essentially impossible to build larger programs. The answer is the programming language.

Programming languages are designed for humans, not for computers. The languages can range in sophistication and complexity from low-level systems not far removed from the computer's own machine language to high-level languages almost resembling English. If these languages can be so different from the computer's own language, how does the computer get to know what to do? The mechanical components that make programming languages work are *compilers* and *interpreters*. Both compilers and interpreters are *translators*: they take a program written in a programming language and translate or convert it into an equivalent program consisting of machine language instructions. Sometimes such a translator is called a compiler and sometimes it is called an interpreter; for the purposes of this book the two are the same.

LANGUAGES FOR THE THOUSANDS

The first two popular languages were COBOL and FORTRAN. COBOL, which stands for Commercial Business-Oriented Language, was designed to make it easy to write business programs that could complete activities like order processing, general ledger, manufacturing scheduling, and so on. Programs written in COBOL are actually relatively English-like and quite verbose on the theory that such an approach makes it easier for even nontechnical readers to review and audit existing programs. COBOL is particularly good at dealing with applications that involve the manipulation of *records*. Thus, statements that read a record, move a field to another record, and perhaps add two fields together are simple and straightforward in the language.

FORTRAN, short for *Formula Translator*, was designed for engineers, mathematicians and scientists who deal mainly with formulas and computationally oriented problems. Although it is not particularly strong at working with records, it does make it very easy to express very complex computational expressions, manipulate arrays, and print output involving sets of numbers. And as was discussed earlier, FORTRAN broke important new ground by introducing a powerful and easy-to-use subroutine capability that resulted in the development of thousands of scientific, engineering, and math libraries still in widespread use to this very day.

COBOL and FORTRAN were the first two languages to really make programming accessible to normal human beings. Before the introduction of COBOL and FORTRAN, the population of programmers numbered perhaps in the low thousands. Machine language and even the early higher-level languages, called assembler languages, were just too hard to learn and too painstaking to use for any degree of broad acceptance. The true measure of the success of COBOL and FORTRAN was the degree to which they managed to substantially increase the size of the programming population. And succeed at that they did.

Tens of thousands of university students through the late '60s and early '70s received their first exposure to computers by learning to develop simple programs in FORTRAN. Whether this exposure came through an introductory computer science course or as part of an engineering or mathematics curriculum, by learning FORTRAN they became acquainted with the true meaning of the word *computer*. Later, many of these individuals found that, much as the computer world may have been changing, FORTRAN was still all they needed to know to write programs that would solve the problems confronting them in their continuing working lives. Even today, in the scientific and engineering community, FORTRAN may still be the dominant language worldwide.

Even more than FORTRAN though, COBOL rapidly became and still is the lingua franca in which large commercial applications are written. Many developers, particularly those fluent in C, consider COBOL to be ugly, limited, and essentially dead. Aesthetic considerations aside, today this could not be further from the truth. Literally millions of programmers over the years learned COBOL, often as their first and only language, and have written code happily ever since. Perhaps these programmers will never be able to develop an operating system, windowing environment, or compiler in COBOL, but then again nobody ever asks them to build such complex technical systems either. And for the purpose of building everyday commercial code, it works quite well, thank you very much. A modern-day problem facing COBOL programmers is that it is not particularly well suited to developing graphical applications either, but the three-layer application architecture represents a straightforward solution to that problem: use COBOL for the business rules and another language for the desktop applications.

So whatever limitations they may have, COBOL and FORTRAN actually succeeded beyond anybody's wildest dreams at making programming possible for thousands and even millions of programmers. In fact, today, COBOL is still by far the most heavily used *professional* programming language with over 2 million adherents worldwide.

PROGRAMMING FOR NONPROGRAMMERS

One problem that both COBOL and FORTRAN share is the requirement for a moderately technical understanding of computers on the part of the programmer. With the introduction of smaller and more approachable computers, this became an issue; could a language be built that would allow completely nontechnical individuals to learn to program? Since about 1970 several different approaches to this problem have been taken. The earliest, and most successful, originated at Dartmouth college, where the BASIC language was first developed. BASIC is a very simple language that most people, with any degree of motivation, can learn to use in a matter of hours. Historically, its main problem is that, because of its simplicity, it has not been possible to write very complex programs in BASIC; if a complex program was written, it was either slow or not maintainable. Over the years, though, the language has been extended and developed to the point where it is fully the equal of most other languages. Again, many programming professionals look down their noses at BASIC, but generally it is just because they haven't looked at the language or its implementations recently.

Going beyond BASIC, isn't it possible to have a programming language that requires no technical understanding of computers at all? Children and adults can certainly learn BASIC quickly, but in doing so they are still learning a conventional programming language. This means that once these students of programming move beyond simple programs, they will have to master all the intricacies of data structures, control logic, subroutines, and other complex constructs to solve larger problems. Couldn't there be a way to provide these same nonprofessionals with a programming language that somehow eliminated the need to learn so many nonintuitive conceptual constructs while still facilitating the solution of complex problems?

Two major languages have been developed over the past 20 years specifically designed to provide nonstandard approaches to programming for children and adult noncomputer professionals. The first was LOGO and the second was SmallTalk; neither truly succeeded in the fashion originally intended.

LOGO was designed by Seymour Pappert, one of the pioneers of artificial intelligence. Originally intended specifically for use in schools by children, it is most often thought of in connection with mechanical turtles sitting on the floor. Each turtle holds a pen or pencil, and as the LOGO program runs, the turtle moves around and draws geometrical patterns on paper taped to the floor. More recently the mechanical turtle has been replaced by sprites and turtles moving around on a screen, still drawing lines. By combining words like *right, left, up,* and *down* with other constructs that provide repetitive actions and conditional logic, the student can draw very complex figures. Despite the complexity of the figures, the resulting programs look very little like conventional software written in languages like BASIC or FORTRAN.

SmallTalk was invented more recently by Allan Kay while at the Palo Alto Research Center. More different, by far, than LOGO, SmallTalk's main goal was to see how quickly children could be taught to develop truly powerful programs without being dragged down by the minutiae of conventional languages. The degree to which Kay succeeded in making SmallTalk different can be seen from the fact that even today most programmers already fluent in another language take months to become comfortable in SmallTalk and many of them literally never make it. What about children, though; did SmallTalk make programming truly easy for them?

How well did LOGO and SmallTalk succeed at their original goals of enabling development of complex software by nonprogrammers? At one level they achieved some moderate degree of success, but at a more global level, the answer is that they did not succeed at all.

LOGO is still in use in thousands of schools all over the world. Implementations exist for IBM-compatible computers running both DOS and Windows, for the Mac, for the Apple II, and for many other computers as well. Children do learn how to program with LOGO and do get a kick out of causing turtles to draw interesting pictures. Yet once these children turn to serious programming, they invariably migrate to another language. And while LOGO is fun, it is hard to believe that, had it not been invented, the same children would not have learned how to program just as fast using, say, BASIC.

SmallTalk is more complex to evaluate, and the final verdict has a funny little twist. Is SmallTalk easy for children to learn? Yes, in fact, children have an easier time learning SmallTalk than adult professional programmers do. And unlike LOGO, SmallTalk is used to build very complex systems, so it is a language with a lot of depth. Here's the twist: its main use turns out to be the opposite of a language for beginners. *Au contraire,* SmallTalk is one of the most complex and difficult languages for even professional programmers to learn and use really well. Yes, these programmers can be extraordinarily productive using SmallTalk, but at the same time, many of their colleagues will have found it so challenging that they will literally give up in failure. So SmallTalk turns out to be a good language for building prototypes very quickly, if the prototype developer already knows the language, but it is too complex for normal use on everyday projects. What about our children — do they automatically become programming superstars through the wonder of SmallTalk? In fact, no. Children can learn SmallTalk, but they can learn BASIC too, and the kids become great programmers because they are great programmers, *not* because they learned one language or another. Children with innate programming talent do well with SmallTalk, but they do well with BASIC too. Children with limited talent do well with neither language. So SmallTalk, for all its advantages, is no silver bullet for children or nonprogrammers.

If COBOL is good for commercial programming, FORTRAN for scientific work, and BASIC for beginners and some professionals, and if SmallTalk is great for building complex prototypes quickly, what about all the other languages like C, C++, LISP, and so on? Which is the right one for any particular job and are they all necessary?

WHERE IS ESPERANTO?

Why have so many languages? Couldn't there be a single language that does it all? Particularly because all the languages are translated to machine language anyway, surely one super language ought to be possible that would meet everybody's needs. In a way the question of why there are so many programming languages is similar to the question of why there are so many spoken languages.

Early in the 20th century a language called *Esperanto* was invented. Based on Italian and Spanish, both easy-to-learn languages, Esperanto was designed to be particularly easy to learn. Following the deliberate development of the language, a movement got under way to somehow make Esperanto the universal language of the world. The goal was simple: over a period of years, convince every man, woman, and child in the world to speak Esperanto instead of the language they speak today. It was an ambitious goal and one that, if accomplished, would pay major dividends in terms of efficiency, good will, simplicity, and even peace on earth. Of course the end of the story, in retrospect, is obvious: Esperanto is nowhere and the thousands of individual languages and dialects spoken around the globe are everywhere. The question of why Esperanto did not succeed at becoming the universal language, though, is more complex than it seems. And it turns out, there are some distinct parallels in the computer industry to the Esperanto experience.

In the computer world at least two major attempts to develop and promote a universal language have failed. First, in the late '60s, IBM invented a language called PL/I (Public Language One). Based on a combination of COBOL, FORTRAN, and some ALGOL (the popular language in Europe) for good measure, PL/I was and is a complex but very powerful language. Most languages, like COBOL and FORTRAN, are designed either for the development of applications or, like C and C++, for the construction of operating systems, compilers, and other technical software. PL/I is one of the few languages that is suitable for both uses. On the one hand, thousands of companies have used PL/I as their mainline commercial programming language, and on the other hand, a huge, leading-edge operating system called MULTICS was written almost entirely in PL/I. So the language certainly is a strong contender for the title of *all-around champion*. More germane to this discussion, though, was the campaign, almost along the line of a military invasion, launched by IBM to make PL/I *the* programming language of the world, or at least the corporate world.

At the time, in the early '70s, IBM, much like Rome two thousand years ago, was the master of everything that could be seen in the world of computers. With market share exceeding 80 percent and account control that was legendary, the International Business Machines Corporation was in a position to virtually dictate the computing strategies of its customers. And making PL/I replace FORTRAN, COBOL, and ALGOL was declared a strategic imperative from the top of the company on down. For a time, there were reasons to believe that PL/I might even take over, but today it is little more than a footnote in history. The language is rarely used, never taught, and not even available on newer computers. The tremendous inertia, the huge historical base of existing code, and the reluctance of programmers to learn a new language proved too much even for IBM.

More recently, the U.S. Department of Defense set out to develop a language from the ground up, which it would then mandate as a standard. After chartering an international committee to develop the language called ADA, the government began awarding contracts requiring its use. As described earlier in the book, this effort was no more successful than IBM's effort to have PL/I replace the hundreds of programming languages in broad use worldwide.

Esperanto, PL/I, and ADA: is there some deeper reason that establishing a universal lingua franca is so darn difficult? Getting the majority of the people in the world or even in the computer community to agree on any one thing is incredibly difficult. Point made. However, beyond this difficulty the question arises: are there truly unique aspects of the various languages, both in the world and in the computer domain, that make it actually attractive to not have a single universal language?

WHAT YOU CAN SAY IS WHAT YOU CAN THINK

Benjamin Whorf was an insurance salesman who, in his spare time, also became one of the leading linguists of the 20th century. In studying the Hopi Indians, he made an amazing discovery. The Hopi language contains no words for dealing with the measurement of time. Talking about time intervals or appointments, comparing times, is literally impossible in that language. A Hopi child introduced into an English-speaking environment before the age of about eight to ten has no trouble learning English and acquiring time-related concepts. However, a Hopi child or adult not exposed to English until after about ten years of age *literally cannot acquire the concepts of time.* No amount of explanation, patient teaching, or illustration by example will equip such an adult to be able to make appointments, arrive at places at a particular time, or otherwise deal with the missing ideas. Not only the words to handle the concepts are missing, but also the words to explain the words and the words to define those other words too are all missing. These adults just can't deal with time. What we can think is limited by what we can say; that's what Whorf found. After studying the Hopi and completing some other research, together with another linguist, Edward Sapir, Whorf formulated the *Whorf Sapir Hypothesis.* This hypothesis states the belief that *our language, our vocabulary, shapes, controls, and limits the thoughts we are able to think.* Thus, Hopi Indians, lacking words for dealing with many aspects of time, eventually became simply unable to think about those aspects of time, even when exposed to another language containing the requisite words.

In mathematics too, what we can write limits what we can think. More recently, in developing the theory of relativity, Albert Einstein found himself required to invent new mathematical notations to describe more succinctly many of the abstract concepts being built up to support the new theory. Theoretically (pun intended), these notational constructs were not truly necessary to support the new theory; each construct is simply a shorthand or abbreviation for formulae that can be expressed equally well at greater length. In practice, though, Dr. Einstein ended up concluding that without the new constructs, the theory of relativity could have been neither invented nor explained and comprehended. Again, the language, in this case the notation, directly influenced the person's ability to think certain thoughts.

All of this leads back to the question of programming languages and how many of them are necessary. In theory one programming language should be enough. After all, no matter how many computer languages are invented, all of them are eventually translated to the same machine language (on any particular computer). Similarly, all mathematics is based on a small set of logical definitions and axioms, so notational abbreviations should not really be necessary, only convenient, for deriving major new theories. And, most globally of all, because all humans are built out of the same elements and think in much the same way, one spoken language ought to do the trick. What Whorf's work proves is that this apparently obvious chain of reasoning is actually not true.

The requirement that drives the need for multiple languages and notations comes back to the principle of layers of abstraction first discussed several chapters ago. *Humans cannot deal with complex systems directly.* They cannot keep track of lots of interconnected elements all at once. Layers of abstraction allow people to cut down complex systems, whether in the world, in mathematics, or in computers, to manageable size. And *the fundamental abstractions available to use when we approach a problem absolutely limit the types and sizes of problems we can solve.*

So Hopi Indians have abstractions that deal with horses, nature, and the other elements of their lives, but no abstractions for dealing with time. After these abstractions have become habitual, they become simply unable to deal with time; it's too much for them. Theoretical physicists lacking the abstractions defined by Einstein's new notations were literally unable to invent the theory of relativity. And absent those notations, a physicist today would still be unable to learn the theory, no matter how carefully explained. Each language is carefully designed to deal with a particular domain of discourse, a particular set of problems to be solved, a particular set of abstractions to be expressed and manipulated. And having multiple languages makes it possible for humans to deal with problems in a much wider variety of domains than any single language would make possible.

Speaking, thinking, modeling, programming: each can benefit from access to a rich set of languages. And Esperanto, surprisingly, although attractive in many ways, might actually limit human creativity in many other ways. And in the same way, a PL/I or an ADA, although superficially attractive in some ways, at least today, is far too limiting to be either practical or attractive.

FOR EVERY PURPOSE THERE IS A LANGUAGE

How many languages should the typical development organization use? It depends. The world certainly requires a wide variety of programming languages, but that doesn't mean that every development organization, let alone every programmer, needs to learn them all. So how many *is* the right number of languages, and which ones *are* the right ones?

Actually, there is no *right* answer, but some suggestions follow. The first step is to realize the overwhelming importance of the application architecture as a guide to structuring applications and picking the right languages and tools for particular components. Next, the size of the application makes a great deal of difference.

Small applications that will run entirely on the desktop generally should be built using a single language. Often the program written in that language, perhaps BASIC or xBase, will use components or subroutines written in a more technical language, like C or C++. Medium-sized applications, consisting of a graphical front end and a database back end, will likely be written in two languages: one for the graphical front end and one to handle database queries and transactions. Finally, the big applications, the ones with three layers, are the most likely to use two or even three languages, along with perhaps a major supporting role for a more technical language. In fact, in particularly large applications, a variety of languages is appropriate in each layer; the next section looks at the choices. The component and layered approach makes it easy for components written in several languages to all talk to each other without having to be aware of the language of implementation.

DESKTOP LANGUAGES

On the desktop, there are five broad languages frequently selected, each of which is available in a variety of dialects:

✦ *BASIC:* If amateur programmers are counted, BASIC is probably the single most widely used programming language in the world. A simple language, it has recently evolved to the point where it can be used to build even large, high-performance systems, with an expectation that the resulting code will run well and be maintainable. Although BASIC is simple and attractive, it does lack much of the formal structure that makes languages like C and C++ more appropriate for larger projects. For smaller projects or components, however, it is a great choice. BASIC is at the core of many of the higher-level development environments considered later in the chapter.

✦ *xBase:* Most programming language textbooks ignore one of the most popular programming language in use today: the one originally developed as part of dBASE. The dBASE language is now available in conjunction with dBASE for Windows, FoxPro, Clipper, and a variety of other products. Literally millions of small development organizations develop surprisingly sophisticated applications with it every day. xBase is particularly strong at manipulating dBASE style databases. Until recently, it was very weak at handling graphical interfaces, although the job could be done, and it is also pretty weak in dealing with relational databases.

The recent history of xBase is particularly interesting. Several years ago, Ashton Tate was acquired by Borland, and FoxPro was acquired by Microsoft.

Since then, FoxPro has become the leading xBase language, while dBASE has had a tough time as Borland struggles with its overall identity and with the conflict between Paradox and dBASE. In the meantime, to the surprise of many outside observers, Microsoft not only continued to promote FoxPro, but also decided to aggressively improve the product. As a result, the most recent release of FoxPro actually provides a very rich and powerful environment for developing "object-oriented," highly graphical applications. The underlying database engine remains fast and nonrelational, but Microsoft has also added facilities for accessing SQLserver and other ODBC-compliant databases from FoxPro. Now, the language is a first-class development environment.

Ironically, though, while FoxPro has continued to improve, the overall xBase market has lost its place of central importance in the PC database world. So, for small and medium applications, where there are good reasons to favor an xBase-style database, FoxPro (or dBASE for Windows, although the verdict is still out on that product) is a great choice in terms of productivity, development of efficient code, and even maintainability. In the context of larger applications, or if mainstream compatibility is important, it is an inappropriate choice.

◆ *C and C++:* What can be said about these two languages? For building operating systems, spreadsheet products, compilers, networks, windowing environments, and the like, they are virtually the only choice. Powerful and sophisticated languages that result in incredibly fast and efficient code, they are also supported by a rich variety of peripheral development tools. Without a doubt any part of a commercial application can be built in C or C++ too. The benefit is that the programmer will have complete control over the environment, and with appropriate skills can make the computer do almost anything imaginable. The problem? As is to be expected, these languages are, by far, too complex and low level for the average programmer. This is not a comment on such programmers. Understanding aeronautical engineering is not a requirement for either piloting a plane or being a passenger in one; programming in C is not the ultimate test of programming worthiness either.

A smaller development organization can get away with never programming in C. A larger shop, with a tools team, will need a few developers who can proficiently work, not just in C, but in the surrounding world of operating systems, windowing environments, and networks that goes right along with it. In either case, both the large and small development organizations can always contract with C gurus when particularly tricky supporting components or utilities need to be built.

◆ *SmallTalk:* In practice a relatively small fraction of the programming population works in SmallTalk, but that group is large and vocal enough to warrant some discussion here. SmallTalk is a highly specialized language. True, it is highly object-oriented, perhaps the most pure object-oriented environment commercially available. Object-oriented does not mean simple. Most programmers are even less likely to learn SmallTalk and learn it well than they are to learn C. In fact, the situation is worse than that. Given enough time, almost any programmer *can* become proficient in C; often it will be a waste of time making that happen, but at least the possibility is there. Many programmers, even given extensive training and time, will simply never become adequately competent in SmallTalk. They will write code and it will work after a fashion. However, once they are done, their teammates will just as soon throw their code away and rewrite it as use it. Although all of this sounds terrible, there is a good side to the picture too.

In the right hands, SmallTalk can be an incredibly proficient development environment. SmallTalk applications can often be modified and extended five to ten times as fast as programs written in conventional languages. This makes the language incredibly suitable, in the right hands, for prototyping projects. The flexibility comes at a high price. All these super-flexible programs are very big, often slow, and require a specialized self-contained environment to run in. So SmallTalk is worth thinking about, as long as its limitations are kept in mind.

✦ *Pascal:* Historically, Pascal was a major competitor to C. In the early '80s, many developers viewed Pascal as a more highly typed and more disciplined language, while C proponents pointed to its flexibility, parsimony of expression, and run-time efficiency. In the broad scheme of affairs, C won; it is the mainstream language for development of virtually all system software, and Pascal is most successful as a teaching language in computer science courses. However, before we complete Pascal's epitaph, one important exception needs to be considered. Borland — the same Borland that bought Ashton Tate — has been a proponent of Pascal for well over a decade. In fact, at the time that Phillipe Kahn was building his company, one of his earliest products was a small, inexpensive, and efficient Pascal compiler that found widespread acceptance all over the PC world. Normally, all of this would be just another interesting historical anecdote since even Borland, until recently, had far more success with its own C compiler than with its Pascal products. However, in an interesting gamble, Borland set out to develop a next generation client/server development tool called *Delphi* built around Pascal.

Delphi is an impressive tool. Like C, it generates compiled code that executes very efficiently. Like Visual Basic, though, it offers a highly interactive development environment that feels almost as though it was interpreted, in terms of responsiveness. In addition, Delphi provides a rich inheritance model that enables many classes of lightweight reuse, and some powerful client/server connectivity tools. Will Delphi succeed? It's very hard to tell at the time that this edition is being written. The fact that it is compiled is attractive, but not attractive enough to convert most C users; C still offers more control over the overall execution environment and an incredibly rich surrounding set of tools. So Delphi is really left to slug it out with PowerBuilder, Visual Basic, SmallTalk, and the rest. While Delphi's ultimate fate is uncertain, one thing is certain: as goes Delphi, so goes Pascal. If Delphi succeeds, then the next edition of this book will talk about Pascal again, and if not . . . .

BUSINESS RULE LANGUAGES

Business rules components can run on the desktop, on a database server, on a business rule server, or even on a mainframe. Typically, they are written in a language particularly suited to dealing with either extensive computation or manipulation of records:

+ *COBOL:* Latin may be dead, but COBOL isn't. It is still a highly appropriate language for writing business rules components. Particularly for organizations with hundreds of trained COBOL programmers and a huge installed base of existing COBOL code, writing business rules components in this way is nothing to be embarrassed about.

+ *BASIC:* Increasingly in the future, as construction of components becomes simple, BASIC may well turn to be a very appropriate language of choice for the development of business rules components that run in both workstations *and* servers. One advantage of this approach is that it makes it easy to have individual components run on big servers and also run on notebooks being carried around daily; that way, the same business rules live everywhere.

+ *FORTRAN:* For highly computational tasks, why not?

+ *C, C++:* Same discussion as before.

DATABASE LANGUAGES

There are four ways of thinking about database languages:

+ *xBase:* For small applications, xBase, as discussed before, was the high-volume language for some time but has now become more of a niche tool. It is a great choice for some small- and medium-size applications that have some reason to favor an xBase environment.

✦ *Access and Access Basic:* In the last three years, an interesting new player has emerged. Since introducing its Access desktop database, Microsoft has sold over five million copies. As a result, the product has taken on many of the aspects of a desktop standard. And along the way, a large community of developers has emerged who build database applications using Access' Access Basic language. In the long term, Access Basic will be separated out from Access, will merge fully with Visual Basic, and at that point, Access will become a desktop tool that happens to be linked to a particular external language.

✦ *Transaction specification:* In practice, in a three-layer application, much of the complex transaction logic will be expressed either in the business rule layer itself or in the same language used in the business rule layer.

✦ *SQL:* At some point queries and detailed database requests have to be expressed, and SQL (an acronym for *Structured Query Language,* pronounced *sequel*) is by far the dominant language for this purpose. Other languages specific to particular databases exist as well, and the choice depends on the application. Where SQL can be used, though, it offers significant advantages in terms of portability, broad acceptance, and so on.

The big question about SQL is: "Is it a programming language or just a query specification language?" The answer is "No and Yes." Today, a great deal of programming *is* done in SQL. It is the only language in which triggers and stored procedures can be written. In many applications, these triggers and stored procedures are the only mechanisms for easily causing code to run on the server. As a result, it is not unusual for literally half the code in a big application to be written in SQL. In the future, as has already been discussed, stored procedures and triggers will be replaced by standard components that can be written in any language at all. The components replacing the stored procedures will simply be invoked directly, whether from the desktop or from the server. The components replacing the triggers will be associated with database events that, in turn, cause certain methods to be invoked when the event arises.

So, at the point, the need to write programs in SQL because it is the only way to do certain things will have disappeared; much code that would now be written in SQL will be written in some other language in that new world. Even then, though, some code will still be written in SQL. Why? First, SQL is an industry standard, and writing code in this way provides a certain amount of portability, particularly across databases. Second, many packaged product developers will choose to develop some of their applications in SQL for a variety of reasons, including database portability; customers buying their products will be buying SQL code along the way. And third, SQL lends itself to writing certain kinds of set oriented, database focused code. Overall, in the new world, SQL becomes just one more programming language — one that is particularly suited to database functions. Looking at it in that way, there is no reason that some code won't be written in SQL forever.

GRAPHICAL DEVELOPMENT ENVIRONMENTS: TYING THE PIECES TOGETHER

Building an application with desktop, business rules, and database components, using three or more programming languages can be challenging, to say the least. In response to this problem, a variety of graphical development environments have become popular in the last few years. The environments take two major approaches to the problem.

Tools such as Visual Basic, PowerBuilder, Enfin, and Lotus Notes focus particularly on the desktop or graphical part of the applications. CASE tools, on the other hand, provide a broad architectural framework for thinking about the entire structure of a big application and then attempt to provide the stitching that will pull together all the various parts into an integrated whole. Each of these approaches has some major strengths and some major weaknesses.

EVENT-DRIVEN PROGRAMMING: ANOTHER COPERNICAN REVOLUTION

Moving beyond the choice of the programming language itself, the development of graphical applications really requires a new paradigm, approaching the problem as a whole at a higher level than the language itself. Building a graphical application is difficult and demanding at the best of times. One of the more challenging aspects of the problem is adapting to the fact that users must be provided with the freedom to use the various parts of the constructed application in the sequence that suits them best, not in some predetermined sequence built in by the programmer. Providing this degree of flexibility with conventional programming languages is next to impossible; the amount of code that must be written to deal with all the different ways in which users can get to different parts of the application is just overwhelming.

Apple's Hypercard for the Macintosh was the first tool to introduce a fundamental new paradigm for the construction of graphical applications. Rather than write programs that put forms and pictures up on the screen and then control the user's interaction with those graphical elements, why not turn the whole world around, inside out? Have the graphical elements control the program rather than have the program control the graphical elements. What say?

Imagine a picture and a form on the screen. The picture shows a floor plan for a room, and a number of forms linked to the parts of the room contain data about the furniture, paint scheme, and so on. Now imagine the user moving her mouse around on the screen, entering data in various forms, tabbing from field to field, moving the mouse some more, and generally interacting with the virtual world projected by the computer. Imagination in gear?

Okay, now imagine that each time the user takes an action, an event is generated; it's the same concept that came up way back in the chapter that began our investigation of the client/workstation technology behind the graphical user interface. Each click, each tab, each entry of data generates an event inside the computer. Now, here's the trick. Imagine that the programmer's job, instead of controlling the user, instead is to respond to all those events. Here's how that might work.

Suppose that the programmer is building the application in question. He starts out by drawing all the pictures, defining all the forms, putting together a complete graphical description of the appearance of the application. The entire definition involves no programming at all; rather the programmer is laying out graphical elements on the screen.

As the graphical elements are dragged, dropped, aligned, and generally embedded in the growing application, the computer is building a list of all the events each of those elements is capable of generating once the user is let loose. So, for example, whenever the programmer adds a field to a form, the computer automatically knows that this creates the possibility the user can generate an *enter field event*, an *exit field event*, a *validate field event*, and so on. Perhaps the *enter field event* is really two events, one occurring when the user enters the field by way of tabbing from a previous field and another that occurs when the user mouse-clicks her way into the field. By the time the complete application is defined, in terms of its appearance, hundreds, perhaps thousands, of these events waiting to happen have been generated along the way.

All these events are at the center of the paradigm that makes graphical applications easy to build. Who defined all those events, and who decides how to handle them all? The events are defined by the *programming environment* — Visual Basic, Enfin, PowerBuilder, or Notes. Each of these environments is a programming language or, more properly, *contains* a programming language, but each is also much more than just a programming language. Visual Basic and PowerBuilder are based on dialects of BASIC, Enfin on a dialect of SmallTalk, and Notes has its own formula-based programming language. Hypercard, the father of all such event-based programming environments, is based on HyperTalk, also its own unique language. However, in each case it is the overall framework, the graphical design environment, and more than anything else, the *event model* that really defines and distinguishes all these environments. In fact, in the future, particularly with the evolution of newer object-oriented development environments, it will be possible to build applications in this way while actually being free to choose any programming language at all for implementation. How does this all work?

Visual Basic, PowerBuilder, and all the rest of the graphical development environments (or GDEs) start out by providing a graphical designer that allows pictorial- and form-oriented elements to be placed on the screen. The GDE then automatically associates a set of *events* with each such screen element. So the answer to the first question — *who defined all the events* — is that the graphical development environment did. Visual Basic has one set of events, PowerBuilder another, and so on.

Associated with each event is a *default action*, the action the GDE will take when the user triggers that event, if no other action is specified by the programmer. So the default action for *exit field* is *proceed to next field*; as a result, once a form is defined, if the programmer writes no code, most GDEs will take the user from field to field as she tabs along or enters complete values into fields. These default actions are critical; otherwise, the programmer would have to specify actions for dozens, hundreds, or even thousands of events before any application could be even tested.

In addition to the *default action*, each event also provides an *event association mechanism*. A what? An *event association mechanism* allows the programmer to *specify his own action that is to occur when this event arises*. For example, when the user has entered a new customer number and leaves that field, complex edit checks can be performed, the customer number can be added to a database, or, in an extreme case, a security officer can be informed that a particularly delinquent customer is calling in again. Anything the programmer can write in a program can be made to happen when an event arises. The real power of event-driven programming is that the programmer gets to control the *results of the user's work while still allowing the user to control the order in which that work is done.*

Event-driven programming represents a true Copernican revolution in the development of graphical applications. By putting the user instead of the programmer in the center of the application world, the user gets increased flexibility and freedom while the programmer gets to put his carefully considered code into only those places where control or computation are really required. In fact, in an ironic twist of fate, the programmer in an event-driven world has more control over the user and the application, not less, while convincing the user that the opposite is true.

In a classical, terminal-oriented application, the programmer's application puts a form on the screen and then waits for the user to fill it in. In theory the programmer could keep track of every step the user takes along the way, but in practice the amount of code required to make this happen is so huge that no developer even thinks about it. So, in practice, the user fills the form in; the programmer then looks at the result.

The beauty of the event-driven model is that the GDE, watching every step, allows the programmer to step in at the time of the programmer's choice. In an event-driven world, once the form is defined, the GDE assumes responsibility for helping the user deal with the form: filling it in, moving around from place to place, or doing whatever makes sense at the time. Along the way, the GDE generates events the programmer can choose to *handle* or not. The default actions provided by the GDE make it very easy to choose not to handle most events; fortunately indeed for programmer sanity. However, should the programmer decide to do so, the rich set of events provided by the GDE makes it possible for him to *exercise a far higher degree of control over the user, with far less work, than was ever possible in the old application-driven world.*

The reason is that once the GDE starts generating events, particularly because each event has a very nice, well-thought-out default action, it's very easy to have events for every action or phase of an action the user ever does. Given all those actions, there are now hundreds or thousands of potential control points where the programmer can then look at the results of the user's work and decide what, if anything, to do.

Process customer numbers as soon as they're entered? Trap password fields, one keystroke at a time? Compute extended totals automatically as soon as unit price and quantity are entered? Alter the lighting in the room each time a piece of furniture is moved? All these and more represent situations where an event (furniture movement, password character entry, customer number field exit) creates an opportunity for the programmer to define his own processing rules, for that event only, without having to therefore control all the rest of the application as well. A rich model indeed.

IS THE DESKTOP ALL THERE IS?

GDEs are so attractive and so powerful that it is tempting to think that all application code should be written to run on the desktop. In an earlier chapter, I explored the consequences of thinking that the mainframe is just a database. It's not, and the importance of business rules defines the application architecture required for building large systems. In the same way, powerful as the event-driven model is, it is far from enough to facilitate the complete development of large applications. The problem is that many developers have become so enamoured of the power of the GDEs that they want to center all development around them.

Visual Basic provides limited facilities, particularly in version 3.0, for accessing databases. PowerBuilder provides richer facilities, and Enfin, in some ways, goes the farthest in terms of providing a good model for interacting with a database from a desktop application. These are not the only GDEs, and increasingly each GDE provides some infrastructure for defining queries, building reports, and accessing database-oriented data. All of these tools, though, are built with the idea of a simple two-layer application architecture in mind: front end/back end. Desktop application/ database server. And, as we've seen, although this model is fine for medium-size applications, it doesn't work at all for bigger systems. It also creates some real problems when it comes time to start designing interoperable components, particularly at the business rules level, where these components make the most sense.

What about Lotus Notes? Doesn't it actually contain a database? Yes, and as with all the other GDEs, this is both its strength and its weakness. For the kinds of document-oriented, two-layer applications that Notes handles well, it handles them very well. As soon as the application calls for either a real record-oriented, transactional database, or the design of a really large system, then Notes, particularly given its closed nature, becomes completely inappropriate.

In fact, in yet another ironic twist, the less complete a job of database access a GDE does, the better suited it is to building really big applications. Ideally, the GDE should provide a facility for designing a nice graphical interface and a rich, complete event model. However, at that point, the programmer should be free to associate components written in any language at all with the events that arise as the user moves around on the desktop. Not only should those components be language independent, but ideally, the programmer would also have complete control over where and in what layer components are triggered when events arise. Thus, an order-entry form, at the right time, could trigger an order-processing business rules component, even if that component is written in COBOL, running on a server.

If the GDE is not tying the parts of the application architecture together, what is?

THE DECLARATION OF INDEPENDENCE: TOOLS AS COOPERATING COMPONENTS, TOO

In Chapter 10, you discovered that to solve some otherwise impossible database problems, you had to rebuild the database itself as a set of cooperating components. Now, it turns out the same radical redesign is required to achieve the tool environment we need, too. It should start to be clear that the concept of cooperating components really does work its way all the way through everything we do, moving into the distributed world of the future. The problem is that there's no choice. Until now, the choices were to either build small applications, build big applications without enough help from the tools, or use a monolithic, closed CASE environment, accepting its strictures in return for the assistance it provides. In the future, we will need both the help of the tools in building big systems and the freedom to populate our toolkit as we see fit. That's where cooperating components comes in. And in a way, it's only right that the tools that will help us build cooperating component-based applications should be built out of cooperating components themselves.

The integration of the parts of a large application, at a logical level, is a design issue, not a construction issue. Ideally, a design tool would provide the facilities to specify the architectural diagrams showing the relationships between the pieces and then fill in the links to tie the whole system together. Isn't that just integrated CASE; the CASE tool builds the whole application? Absolutely not.

In a classical CASE environment, the CASE tool is the supreme emperor, in control of everything it can see. Programming is done in the CASE tool, the structure of the application is built in, and the programmer has zero degrees of freedom.

The CASE world brings three powerful strengths:

✦ The concept of design and design tools

✦ An integrating framework reaching from design through development

✦ A facility for storing a structured model of a complete application

Okay, we need design tools, and we need integration; why does that mean we need a single monolithic environment to accomplish it all? CASE tools offer one close environment, PowerBuilder another, and Visual Basic another — so how do we choose?

And why should we have to choose? Again, the solution to this problem lies in cooperating components. Specifically, what we need is an architectural framework for the development tools themselves. This framework should allow users to pick and choose the best combination of tools, languages, and engines for each particular project they need to complete.

Just as the Graphical Design Environment needs to become independent of any particular programming language and database, in the same way the design tools need to become independent of the other development tools, too. Figure 15-5 shows the architectural environment required to make this happen.

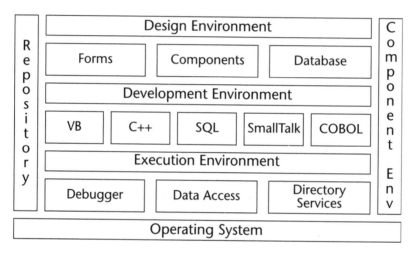

Figure 15-5: An architectural framework for development tools.

At the top is an open and extensible design environment. This environment will allow developers to pick from a wide range of "plug in" design tools. These will include today's standard database and application modeling tools. In addition, though, the design tools found in PowerBuilder, Visual Basic, Access, and Delphi will eventually find their way up into this tool independent layer. Why?

Take "forms" for example. Why should PowerBuilder have one forms model, Delphi another, Microfocus COBOL its own, and so on? Every commercial application uses forms or dialogs extensively; in fact, virtually every graphical application has multiple forms in it. Both the developer and the user would benefit from a single, powerful, cross tool forms package; in the future, this type of forms package will be standard.

Moving all the design tools up into a common layer provides an important integration benefit. Forms talk to components and databases. Components talk to each other, to components and databases, and so on. By dealing with all the design elements of an application in a single layer, the developer gains the ability to see all the relationships between *all* the pieces in one place.

When it comes time to write code, tomorrow's world will revolve around a common but integrated development environment. Instead of working one way when writing COBOL code, another with C++, and another with VB, the developer will have a familiar home from which he or she can work with all these languages. One reason that this is particularly important is that tomorrow, as today, most large applications will involve several languages. Desktop code may well be written in Visual Basic; perhaps business rules will be specified in COBOL; database queries in SQL; and particularly tricky algorithms may well be expressed in C++. The integrated development environment will make working with multiple languages in this way straightforward and elegant.

The key to making both the design and the development environment work in this way is *extensibility*. Simply put, these two environments must be built as independent components with published interfaces that are accessible to any developer building a tool. For example, Microsoft recently split the development environment associated with its VC++ (Visual C++) out in this way, published the interfaces, and several third-party tool vendors are now writing their own components that can "plug into" the common environment; we need the same thing, just on a broader scale.

Below the development environment will be several common services, sitting just above the operating system. One set of services will provide a common way of accessing database data. Another will connect in to the network through directory services. And quite important to building work code, debugging needs to become a language independent service, too. In fact, the debugger needs to work not only across several languages, but across multiple processes and machines, as well. How else will client/server applications ever get debugger otherwise?

At this point, we have a picture of a design and development environment that is the opposite of the monolithic *integrated CASE* while offering many of its benefits. However, in thinking about this kind of integrated environment, it is hard, so far, to see what makes it really integrated? Having a common set of interface services at the design and development level certainly ties things together in one way, but what keeps all the plug-in tools from looking completely separate from each other?

The two key integrators are the vertical boxes on the left and right of Figure 15-5: the repository and the component environment. At the simplest level, the component environment provides the basic plumbing to make it possible to build applications out of many pieces in the first place. For example, it's easy to talk about writing part of an application in COBOL and part in Visual Basic, but how do those two parts talk to each other? Through the common framework prescribed by the Component Environment. We will explore the whole notion of *components, component models,* and how they work more thoroughly in the next chapter. At this point, it is important to note that the kind of design and development environment just described simply can't be built without a common component model.

A component model makes it *possible* to build an application out of smaller pieces, but what keeps track of what all the pieces are in the first place? How does the designer find out which components are available to be built into a system? Or given a system that has already been built, how does a developer get to find out what pieces it has been built out of and how they fit together? The answer to all these questions is a thing called a *repository*.

A *THING* CALLED A REPOSITORY

Very few technical components are as poorly understood as repositories. Many people view a repository as a monstrous global store or database that stores everything to do with an application: its description, its code, the source underlying the system, the database, descriptions of the users — in short, the world. Others think of the repository as little more than the catalog or dictionary found at the center of most databases containing descriptions of the tables and columns found in that database. And many others view repositories as mystical constructs that can never be built. In fact, repositories, growing directly out of the CASE tool movement, are viewed by most observers in much the same way that CASE tools themselves are: repositories are viewed as either impossible or essential. It is for that reason that I have titled this section "A *Thing* Called a Repository" — because our first challenge is to understand what a repository really is.

We've already discussed the need for analysis and design tools at the beginning of this chapter; they're critical and can help tie big applications together. What we didn't get to discuss was the idea of storing all the information in the design model in a central database where it can be shared by tools of all kinds, whether design or construction. Such a database is called a repository, and in a model-driven world, the repository sits at the center of the developer's universe.

What is a repository? Sometimes also called an application *encyclopedia*, a *repository* is a database that contains the model describing all the applications in a system and the descriptions of the parts that are in the applications. In addition to the descriptions of the components of applications, the repository tracks the *relationships* between all those parts.

A repository allows developers to answer dozens of questions about how the parts of an application fit together. Suppose that the structure of the customer number field changes in a database. How many forms, business rules components, reports, and queries use that field? If a form is split in two, which pieces of code are affected? Suppose that a business rules component adds some new behavior: which other components might take advantage of the new behavior? A repository answers all these questions and more.

Repositories play three critical roles in application design and development:

✦ A repository is the database that stores a description of the structure of an application. The content of the application — the programs, databases, components, and forms — are stored somewhere else; the repository maintains the structure that explains how all those pieces fit together.

◆ Repositories allow many tools from a wide variety of vendors to all work together.

◆ Repositories help developers manage the complex configuration control and versioning problems associated with building and maintaining large applications.

REPOSITORY EQUALS APPLICATION STRUCTURE DATABASE

What is the *structure* of an application? The structure is the description that describes how the pieces of the application fit together. The operation of putting those pieces together is called *binding* (and sometimes *linking)*. For example when one module or component calls a subroutine or function located in another component or modules, the binding operation links the subroutine call to the called subroutine, ensuring that both pieces of code can find each other and that the call can execute successfully. Similarly, the operation of linking a database query to the underlying database tables and columns is also called binding. Binding is at the center of the repository construct; the repository is essentially a bindings database.

So to begin with, a repository is exactly a database. Historically, repositories have been built on custom data stores; increasingly in the future, they will be built on standard, off-the-shelf databases. At its core, the repository database stores information about the three major parts of every application: the documents, the business rule components, and the databases. Most often, the documents in question are forms; however, a document could also be a graph, a memo, or any other displayable object. The description of each of these objects — the forms, components, and database tables — centers around interfaces. The interface to a table is its columns; to a component, it is the methods and their arguments; and to a document or form, it is the data that is passed in and out of that document. In fact, the structural descriptions of all these objects is actually amazingly similar. This similarity is less surprising if we step back and think that the entire purpose of storing these descriptions is to enable binding operations; by definition, a binding must link together two similar things.

Besides the interfaces, which are the basis for binding, the repository also stores all the relationships between the interfaces — the bindings themselves. If a component has a query that is bound to a particular table in a database, that fact is stored in the repository database — similarly for a form being used by a component, a component talking to another component, or two tables being related to each other. Just these few pieces actually represent an almost complete picture of that supposedly mysterious system called a Repository. Interfaces that describe objects: documents, components and tables. Relationships or bindings that describe how all those objects are linked to each other through these interfaces. Only one thing is missing to make this picture complete: logical objects.

When designing a large application, it is very useful to work with logical objects that are comprised of the finer physical objects in the application itself. A logical object can be as big as "Accounts Payable," smaller like "Operating System Kernel," or just one level above the physical like "Customer Table." The repository not only stores the descriptions of these logical objects, it also stores the relationships that link these logical objects to the finer-grained objects they are built out of. (In some ways, the logical objects are special because they may live only in the repository; however, that fact makes no difference at all to our explanation.) Now we have a complete picture of a repository as a supporting structure for design tools. Of course, much more can be added to the central structure, but this is the core.

At this point, it is possible to see how the repository is the underlying engine and store that allows design tools to work. A design tool's purpose is to allow the designer to explore and manipulate the structure of an application. By focusing on the structure, the designer gets to think at a higher level and explore tradeoffs. The repository is the database that stores the description of that structure; the design tools work with and generate that information. In fact, given a repository, one way to think of CASE-like design tools is that those tools are just the administrative interface to the database defined by the repository. Perhaps such a tool set is the most powerful administrative interface ever built in history. At the same time, the need for a database to track the structure of large applications and sets of applications is so huge that even if administering that database were the only reasons to build the design tools, the cost would still be more than justified anyway. And the fact that the design tools are also critically important to build applications in the first place is the icing on the cake.

TOOLS OF THE WORLD: WORK TOGETHER

There are two basic models for arranging for tools to interoperate with each other. The first and simpler model is for pairs of tools to talk to each other. If Microfocus COBOL wants to use a form built in Visual Basic, then the COBOL system exchanges messages with the Visual Basic system to make the whole thing happen. What happens if COBOL wants to achieve the same effect with PowerBuilder? Another and probably different set of information exchange protocols must be defined. Given a small number of tools, this style of interoperation works; as soon as the toolset grows, it breaks down. For instance, when Microfocus calls on PowerBuilder, Microfocus finds that PowerBuilder already has a plan for talking to the outside world — a plan that Microfocus developed in response to a request from Borland. The only problem is that it's different from Microfocus' plan. Clearly as more tools talk to each other, there has to be a better idea than building dozens of specialized interchange protocols. That's where the repository comes in.

Recall the description of the application that drives all the design tools. That description is stored in a standard database — one that any tool can call just by writing database calls and defining SQL queries. The only thing that is missing is for the description of the structure of the application to be public; once that description becomes public, it becomes a standard way for any tool to find the information required for cooperation with any other tool. The description of that structure is often called a *meta-model*. That is, the description of the application itself, stored in the repository, is the *model*; the description of the model is called the *meta-model*.

Given a standard meta-model (also sometimes called a *tool information model*), it becomes possible to actually build the kind of tool architecture described in Figure 15-5. A developer can pick the tools of his or her choice; each developer can have a slightly different toolkit, and yet all the tools in each toolkit can still interoperate with each other on any application. The basis for all that interoperation is the common description of the application, its parts, and how they fit together — the meta-model — and a repository that implements it.

ALTERNATE UNIVERSES: CONFIGURATION MANAGEMENT

Suppose that you've just joined a development team and have been handed your first maintenance assignment: to improve the performance of a device driver. Where do you start? How does the piece you're working on relate to all the other pieces of the system? And how do you keep your work and errors along the way from making the whole system not work? The starting point, clearly, is to have a view of the structure of the entire application; the repository does that. But a little more is required.

By working with repository-driven design tools, you can quickly figure out where the device driver fits in, what other components it depends on, and which ones depend on it. When you are ready to really get going, the repository plays a new role; it constructs an alternate universe for you.

A large application can easily consist of thousands or tens of thousands of big and little pieces. The repository can keep track of the relationship between all those pieces. But what happens when many pieces are being changed by many people all at the same time? The repository plays a key role in keeping those many people out of each other's way. It accomplishes that through a technique called *versioning*.

As soon as you are ready to start making changes to the system, you ask the repository to create a *version branch* for you. The repository starts by analyzing the dependencies between the pieces you propose to work withand the rest of the system; this is called an *impact analysis*. The analysis is based on all those binding relationships the repository stores; those relationships allow it to quickly tell who might be affected by any changes you make. Next, the repository makes copies of all the components you've asked to work with *and all the components affected by them*. Once these copies are made, you have your alternate universe. From your perspective, you are working with the entire system. You are free to make changes, test things out, experiment at will; the only person affected by your changes is yourself.

Throughout the system, at any given point in time, the repository is tracking dozens or even hundreds of alternate universes of various sizes; each represents the work of an individual or team focused on a particular part of the overall system. As each team finishes their work, the repository also helps by merging various alternate universes into large alternate universes. As all of this is going on, the repository also ensures that older versions of the system, perhaps already released to customers and in production use, are never affected. Later, as various alternate universes become production releases in their own right, the repository keeps them intact too, both to protect users and to allow bugs to be tracked down in an unchanged version of the system.

TO DREAM THE IMPOSSIBLE DREAM

If such a repository is so critical, where will it come from? Isn't a real repository impossible to build anyway? The concept of an application structure database has been around since the early '80s. Several vendors, most notably Texas Instruments with its IEF product, have built very successful repositories that do work. More recently, Gupta, Intersolv, and others have built more modest but still successful repositories in relatively short periods of time. And then again, there's IBM.

In 1989, alarmed at the increasing mind share being focused by its largest accounts on the concept of CASE, IBM announced its CASE strategy. Rather than build its own design tools, IBM said, it would provide a framework that would allow tools from a variety of vendors to all work together. And to integrate all the pieces, IBM would provide one component: *an open repository*. In fact, in that announcement IBM introduced the world to the very word *repository* as the term to describe an application structure database.

The good news is that IBM got the concept almost exactly right. The problem with all repositories, called by any name whatsoever, before 1989, is that they were all closed and proprietary, designed to work with only the tools of the vendor selling the repository. In fact even today, virtually every repository shipping, strengths and all, is still closed and proprietary. So great concept, great timing. What about the execution?

As Shakespeare said, *aye, there's the rub*. And to quote another bard, Robert Burns in this case, *the best laid schemes o' mice and men gang aft a-gley*. In its desire to ensure the open nature of its repository, IBM set out to design the product by committee. Three years and many meetings later, even IBM, for all its perseverance, was forced to announce that the original repository, as announced in 1989, would never come to be. And as a direct result, many otherwise optimistic observers concluded that repositories, like artificial intelligences, pen-based computers, and other boldly projected grand projects, would never come to be.

Repositories can be built. They have been built, they will be built, and they are not even that hard to build. TI, Intersolv, Softlab, MSP, Platinum, Gupta, and others sell repositories every day, and thousands of customers are glad that they do. So the idea that repositories are science fiction is just so much fiction itself. If so, then what's missing?

What's missing is a repository that is open and extendible. Vendors are moving in this direction now, but getting there will undoubtedly take several more years. The benefits, though, are enormous. Design tools will be used to specify the structure of complex systems. A variety of construction tools will be used to build each part of the system in the exact best possible way. The repository will provide the coordination and tracking mechanism to tie it all together.

PROGRAMMING WITHOUT PROGRAMMING: THE FOURTH GENERATION

Although the picture presented so far in this chapter is already compelling, what about the fact that all the development, even if event-driven, still depends on conventional, line at a time, programming? Surely there's a way to start building big applications with no programming at all? In general, is there any hope that nonprogrammers — end users — will eventually be able to build real applications of any significant size? This question marks a watershed in this chapter. The first part of this chapter has focused on tools for professional developers; is there any hope for the nonprofessional? Perhaps. Two possible approaches offer real promise.

To be clear, I'm talking about approaches that might eliminate the need for programming altogether, at least for some apps. This is in distinct contrast to the more usual approach that focuses on building applications out of components. Recall the *Business Week* issue with the baby on the cover. The implication was that after enough components or objects become available, applications will be *assembled* (by children) in no time at all. In fact, over time this may well happen (except perhaps for the part about child labor). Taking it a step further, as we've already discussed, in the component world of the future, self-managed teams become able to customize applications quickly by accessing large libraries of components built by a central team. The point is that, although this approach offers tremendous power and flexibility, it doesn't eliminate programming per se. What it does is make the results of that programming *more useful*. Building components *instead of applications* creates a world of flexibility, choices, and customization by assembly of components. The key question is still *how do those components get built?* Granted, some components may be built from other components, but ultimately, some programming is required to build the core components everything else is then built from. And make no mistake, there are a great many of those core components, and many of them are complicated indeed. So can those components be built without programming?

Two possible approaches might play a real role in truly eliminating programming. In the business rules layer, rule-driven systems show some real promise, and on the desktop, the use of high-level personal productivity tools to build complete applications is known to work. Let's look deeper.

Large business rule components are composed of hundreds or thousands of business rules all expressed in *procedural code*. That is, a programmer working in, say, COBOL writes out code that in a prescribed sequence applies the rules to the situation and data at hand. The fact that the programmer specifies *both* the rules *and* the order in which they are applied makes the code *procedural*. Deciding the order in which these rules should be applied turns out to be surprisingly difficult, and accordingly is one of the more time-consuming aspects of programming. Moreover, once a program is written, finding the place in that program where a particular business rule is applied can be quite tricky, too.

What would happen if the programmer could just put the rules into the computer and *let the computer decide what order to apply them in?* Although trickier than it sounds, such a scenario is not completely impossible. For example, if one rule says *customers who pay on time receive early shipments,* and another rule defines *on-time payment,* the computer can analyze these rules and decide what order to apply them in. Programming time would be saved in the first place, and later, as new business rules are added, even more time would be saved because the new rules could be just dumped in and the computer would decide when and in what order to apply them. Add in some language facilities designed to make it particularly easy to define certain broad classes of business rules, and you have a *rule-driven system.*

Rule-driven systems are often called *nonprocedural* because the programmer does not decide what order the rules are processed in. And, in general, a characteristic of the so-called *fourth generation* of development tools is the elimination of the need for the programmer to think about the order in which things are done. So a fourth-generation database query language would decide on its own in what order to navigate through the database in order to find data instead of being told the order by the programmer. And, in the same way, a spreadsheet is nonprocedural because the user simply put formulas on the sheet without worrying about what order the recalculation is done in.

When they work, rule-driven systems can simplify programming a great deal. In fact, in some cases, once the basic rule base is established, it can be extended by business managers with little or no assistance from technical staff. Sounds great, right? Faster development and systems that can be extended by the users! The only problem is that these systems work in only a very limited domain. Besides problems with performance and understandability, the biggest problem with rule-based systems is that they are *brittle.* That is, they have a tendency to break unexpectedly as rules are added.

The brittleness of rule-based systems arises from the interactions between all the business rules. The reason that procedural programming is so that tricky is that the programmer has to think about *exactly* what order all the rules will be applied in so the whole system really works. Should credit-worthiness be taken into account when releasing the current shipment? Do payments get applied before or after the check clears the bank? The list of things to think about is literally endless. The problem with rule-based systems is that as the number of rules gets large, adding a single rule can have completely unexpected consequences. Why? Because nobody, other than the computer, is thinking about the relationship between all the rules and how they all fit together. So even though all the rules are applied correctly and literally, the result can still be wrong. Humans have known about this problem for centuries. Whenever new rules are introduced, there are always unexpected side effects. That's why building new organizations and processes, whether automated or not, takes a long time. The problem is that although we are familiar with this problem, we are not familiar enough with it to have computers make it go away. Yet.

So rule-based systems are tantalizing, promising, and even, in limited domains, practical, but for the foreseeable future most business rules components will still need to be expressed in conventional programming languages. On the desktop, though, there is more hope.

MACRO POWER

In 1984, with the introduction of 1-2-3, Lotus had a major impact on the programming world without even knowing it. 1-2-3 contained a *macro* language that allowed a user to take sequences of commands, normally entered from the keyboard, encapsulate them in a macro, and then use them over and over. More, though, the macro could also contain special keystrokes that caused looping, conditional logic that led to branches, and even keystrokes so that macro programs could change themselves.

One accounting customer, working with 1-2-3's macro language, wrote a complete auditing program, dealing with accounts in multiple currencies and time periods, that controlled an audit project from day one through to the end. The resulting program, written entirely in unreadable 1-2-3 macro keystrokes, filled 50 pages of program listing. Exciting and horrifying, both at the same time.

In 1986, with the introduction of Excel, Microsoft took the concept of macros a giant step forward in two ways:

✦ Macros could be recorded automatically with a kind of *tape recorder* that watched users' keystrokes as they completed normal activities, and put those keystrokes into a macro. Now any Excel user could be a macro programmer without ever actually writing a line of code.

✦ More importantly, rather than record actual keystrokes, the Excel macro recorder converted those keystrokes into equivalent statements in a dialect of *almost-BASIC*. Suddenly, the resulting programs were both readable and even maintainable.

Based on the sophistication and completeness of the resulting macro environment (which were by now a real programming environment), by 1990, several enterprising software developers even built complete accounting packages in Excel macro language. In 1990, with the introduction of Word for Windows, Microsoft advanced the macro state of the art once again.

Word for Windows, rather than having a macro language, contained a full-blown programming language called Word Basic. A complete dialect of BASIC, Word Basic responded to certain Word events — events raised by the word application as the user edited documents — and provided an environment in which a programmer could add his or her own commands at will to the already powerful word processing tool provided in the original package. To make the facility complete, Word Basic included facilities for controlling most aspects of a document; anything the user can do at the keyboard, a Word Basic program can do on his or her behalf.

What's this have to with eliminating programming? After all, Word Basic is just, returning full circle, a programming language itself. True. Here's the point: 1-2-3 for Windows, Excel, Word for Windows, WordPerfect for Windows, and a variety of other tools represent in themselves incredibly powerful nonprocedural environments for building certain classes of applications. By combining them with a classical programming language like Word Basic, it becomes possible to build many otherwise complex applications quickly and easily with almost no programming at all.

A bank built a loan officer's workstation around a spreadsheet. The formulas and rules to complete ratio calculations, margin calculations, and all the other mechanisms used to decide on particular loans were all built into the spreadsheet with no programming. Then the macro language was used to control some of the mechanical flow governing the loan-approval process. The complete application was built in a small fraction of the time that would have been required had a conventional language been used.

An insurance company used a combination of a spreadsheet, a database, and a word processor to build a marketing workstation for its agents. The workstation generates mass mailings, prints insurance projections, and tracks territory performance against plan. Some programming was required but less than 10 percent of the amount that would have been required had the high-level tools not been available.

THE CHANGING NATURE OF THE APPLICATION

By functioning as large-scale components, around which applications can be built, tomorrow's personal productivity tools will change the basic nature of application development as it is known today. Word processors, spreadsheets and desktop databases will not eliminate conventional programming tools — not now and not in the foreseeable future. These high-level packages will not be used to build the core applications required to run the business. However, an interesting shift is taking place that will change the nature of those core applications in a way that *will* make personal productivity tools important application development vehicles.

Ten years ago salesmen, customer service representatives, and other individuals responsible for dealing with customers directly had very little operating authority. When they received orders or complaints, they passed that information on to order entry and other specialists for *data entry* into the computer. The front-line workers did not process information themselves because they were not allowed to and also because they did not have the authority (or responsibility) to do anything with that data even if they could process it themselves. The result was rooms full of data-entry clerks entering orders, payments, complaints, and other information into terminals without really understanding any of the information flowing through their fingers. Meanwhile, the front-line sales reps and customer service agents who did have a use for that information had no real access to it.

Today those data-entry clerks are disappearing. Business Process Reengineering calls for the front-line employees to enter the information *themselves* into the computer as soon as they receive it. More important, though, as the jobs of those front-line employees expand, as self-managed teams are created, those employees now not only have access to the information, they also are dreaming up new ways to work with that information every day. And that's where the personal productivity tools come in.

Historically, building the core of a classical business application has always been simple. Order entry, shipping, accounts receivable: they're all a snap. The catch has been all the work that comes up after the *real* application is written. All the endless little reports, mass mailings, specialized queries that users are forever demanding. Those nuisance requests generally take far longer than the original application does. Then everybody's frustrated.

Order entry, shipping, accounts receivable: they still get written the same way. Excel does not make the need to build order forms disappear. WordPerfect does not automate shipment scheduling. What changes is what happens *after* the core part of the application is done. What changes is happiness and empowerment. The programmer finishes the core app and *is done*. All the little reports, queries, and mass mailings are built by the user himself, driven from the data in the core application. And that's what personal productivity tools make possible.

WILL IT RUN?

In this chapter, we've consider the tools required to build the distributed applications of the future. Not only will those applications be built out of cooperating components, but the tools used to build them will be cooperating components, too. The tools will take three broad forms. First will be design tools, which will allow us to specify and work with the broad structure of the application. Second will be lower-level construction tools, which will support the development of custom components from the ground up. And third will be today's personal productivity tools, which are both applications in their own right and large scale components that can be customized to fill in major parts of the larger systems we build with the bottom-up tools. So the tools are all there. And as you saw earlier, the databases, also recast as cooperating components, are there to provide us with performance, flexibility, and rich data structures. What about the rest of the infrastructure required to make it all run? Who keeps track of all the cooperating components? Who starts them up? Who shuttles requests from one component to another, guaranteeing that each such request arrives, arrives once, and arrives only once? That's what the next chapter is about.

CHAPTER 16

WHAT DISTRIBUTED SYSTEMS ARE MADE OF

C hapter 11 laid out four major questions as a road map to guide the journey through designing and building distributed systems:

+ What does a mainframe do?

+ How can servers replace part of a mainframe?

+ How are distributed databases designed?

+ Are distributed systems technically practical?

Of the four, one question still remains to be answered: *Are distributed systems technically practical?* In other words, can they be built? If they're built, will they run consistently? Finally, what are the components — the technical infrastructure — required to make them work?

To prevent you from skipping to the end of the chapter and missing all the best parts, the answer to this question is as follows:

+ Large distributed systems can't quite be built today without writing a great deal of complex systems code, which vendors normally write best.

+ The key to building these systems involves successfully making cooperating components possible. This process requires the move beyond the narrow concept of transactions and tasks to a broader concept of distributed processes.

◆ Although the technology isn't quite here, it is on the verge of being here. With careful design, it is possible to build systems today that will gracefully migrate and scale to more fully distributed systems tomorrow as new technology does become available and practical.

REFINING THE APPLICATION ARCHITECTURE

In Chapter 11, I developed a three-layer application architecture to facilitate the design of large business applications:

Three-Layer Application Architecture

Documents

Business rules

Database

To dig deeper, let's return to the application architecture and use it as a frame of reference. Each of the three layers has to be further subdivided into three more layers to fully describe distributed systems. The three sublayers of each layer are as follows:

1. *Navigation and control:* The top sublayer provides facilities for finding components, activating those components, and ensuring that they complete their tasks.

2. *Active components:* These are the actual objects in the layer: the applications, the business rules components, and the databases.

3. *Integration:* The final layer provides services that allow many independent components within the particular layer to work together as though they were one bigger component.

Table 16-1 shows the placement of these three sublayers into the architecture. I need, of course, to explain the details. By starting with the desktop, it becomes quickly possible to see how the whole model fits together. After exploring the desktop, I discuss databases and finally business rules.

Table 16-1   The Application Architecture and Its Sublayers

Application Layer	Navigation and Control	Active Components	Integration
Documents	Windows	Documents	OLE
Business rules	Component Coordinator	Business rules	Component Environment
Database	OLE DB, Query Processor	Database	Transaction Coordinator

DESKTOP NAVIGATION AND CONTROL

Recall that the top sublayer is responsible for navigation and control. In the case of a windowing environment like Microsoft Windows, it is the environment that allows the user to find and activate applications. Furthermore, if the application is not running at the time it is invoked, the windowing environment arranges for it to start up automatically. The function of the top layer is clear.

The middle layer, of course, is just the active components — window-based desktop applications. With desktop applications, the function of the bottom layer is really interesting. The bottom layer is supposed to provide *integration*. In other words, it's supposed to make many active components all look like a bigger one in the context of the overall layer. So what does that mean? To explain it, I need to describe a technology called *OLE*, short for *object linking and embedding*.

DESKTOP INTEGRATION: OLE

Early in your school years, you may have been taught that putting pictures and diagrams in projects and essays increases understandability and readability. Later, as you learned to use a word processor, it turned out that putting pictures and diagrams in your writing was not such a good idea after all. The word processor either didn't allow it at all or made it quite hard. OLE is designed to vindicate your grade school teachers and make integration easier.

Technically speaking, a document with pictures, diagrams, charts, numbers, and text is called a *compound document* — one that is composed of several parts coming from potentially several different sources. The computer industry has been trying to facilitate the creation of compound documents for over a dozen years.

Documents are created on a computer by using a variety of tools like word processors, spreadsheets, graphics packages, and so on. Generally, users may not even think of the objects created by their tools as being *documents*. The term is a convenient generalization that cuts across many uses. Although users don't see anything as common as a document, what they do see is *files*. Every software tool allows users to save their work files that can then be copied, duplicated, sent to other people, and reopened whenever necessary. The catch is that a file created by a particular tool can generally be opened only by that tool. A 1-2-3 spreadsheet cannot be opened, inspected, or changed by WordPerfect any more than a WordPerfect file can be worked on in the dBASE IV environment. Getting technical, each individual tool works with and saves information in its own proprietary format, and these formats have little in common.

Normally, the fact that you can't use a word processing tool to inspect spreadsheets is not a problem. After all, word processors process words, and spreadsheets crunch numbers. But when it comes time to create compound documents, you need to work on all the various types of information at the same time in the context of a single, larger document. The number of proprietary formats now becomes a problem. On the surface, it appears that all tool developers ought to adopt a common file format. Practically, this solution just doesn't work.

Tools are advancing in functionality and ease of use very rapidly. The difference between a spreadsheet or word processor today compared to five years ago is nothing less than startling. Each new advance creates the need to store more information and more sophisticated control structures as an intrinsic part of the file in which the user saves work. Adding multiple columns or embedded graphics to a word processor, for example, also means ensuring that the column and graphics information must be part of the saved file representing the document. As a result, tool developers are constantly tinkering with, modifying, and improving the structure of the file formats used to save work. Any attempt to create a common file format is therefore doomed from the start by the constant change and progress occurring in the software world. Does this fact suggest that compound documents are impossible?

Imagine a real estate sales proposal consisting of several pages of descriptive text, a picture of the property, a small spreadsheet containing the basic cost data, and a highly decorated graph projecting the potential cash flow associated with the investment. This proposal contains all the basic elements of a compound document: words, pictures, numbers, and graphs. When printed, the entire document looks like ink on a page. As ink on a page, it is passive and cannot be changed. On the screen, though, it is far from passive, so how should it behave in its electronic form?

COMPOUND DOCUMENT ARCHITECTURES

In the late 1970s, as the word processing industry was just taking off and the term *office automation* was becoming popular, the concept of compound documents was first invented. At that time, two basic approaches to facilitating the creation of these complex constructions were proposed: copying bitmaps and embedding objects. Linking, a term I'll define later, is a variation on embedding. As early as 1980, computer companies including Xerox, DEC, and IBM began proposing architectural approaches for facilitating compound documents. The big problem with most of these approaches was making them open enough to really be practical. With the increasing popularity of personal computers and the resulting proliferation in personal productivity tools, a compound document architecture has to encompass and be accepted by most of the tools a user might ever use.

Examining all the alternative compound document architectures is beyond the scope of this book. One architecture, though, appears to have achieved relatively broad acceptance: *object linking and embedding* (OLE), a technology first promulgated by Microsoft and several other vendors. Recently though, OLE has become a standard controlled and dominated by Microsoft. Because of its close association with Windows and the fact that it actually works, OLE appears to be well on its way to becoming at least one of the at most two or three compound document architectures that users will live with for the rest of this decade. For this reason, the rest of this discussion focuses on OLE alone. Although focusing solely on OLE simplifies the discussion, it also provides the conceptual foundation for understanding competitive approaches.

DON'T BE A COUCH POTATO

Copying bitmaps is the simplest and the most limited way to create compound documents. Every object manipulated by a computer has at least two representations:

✦ The *internal* representation, generally kept in the computer's memory, based on a model of the world, is active. That is, when working with this active representation, the user has complete freedom to make changes, add new information, and so on. Putting it another way, in the internal active world, a spreadsheet, is a spreadsheet and a word processor document is a word processor document. If this fact seems more than obvious, read on.

✦ The *external* representation, displayed on the screen and printed on pages, consisting of bits and pixels, is passive. In this context, a spreadsheet is merely a picture. This picture displays numbers in rows and columns, but numbers are simply letters on the screen or printed dots on a paper page. Computer people often speak of this passive, external representation as a *bitmap* — an image created from individual bits on the screen. In this external world, a spreadsheet is not a spreadsheet; a word processor document is not a document; a project plan is not a project plan. They are all dots, letters, and lines drawn on the screen or on the page for users to see.

The internal and external representation of objects are obviously related to each other. The external representation derives from the internal one. The external representation is in fact the projection of reality that makes the tool so useful to the user. When the user manipulates that projection with the mouse, keyboard, or other input device, the tool watches his or her action and changes the internal model to reflect the changes.

One way to think about compound documents is to examine the final, printed result. If the goal is to print a sales proposal containing a table of numbers, the external representation of that table of numbers must be somehow captured in the compound document. After all, all that really matters is printing or displaying the thing correctly in the first place. This strategy leads to the idea of copying.

Suppose that in a windowed environment, one window is the word processor document containing the text of the sales proposal; in another window is the spreadsheet with the cost figures. The computer, or more accurately the spreadsheet, displays the external representation of that spreadsheet in the spreadsheet window. The bits making up the bitmap are sitting there in the window, stored in the computer's memory so that the window can be displayed. That bitmap can easily be captured and *put into* the word processor document, and that new document will then contain the spreadsheet's table of numbers. It is this process of copying the external representa-tion that is called either *copying* or *cutting and pasting.* Mechanically, the way it works is simple.

While sitting in the spreadsheet, a user highlights a range of cells and specifies a *copy* operation. The user now switches to the word processor document and asks for the *paste* operation. Because the pasted information comes from a different document type, the result is that a bitmap — an external representation, not a range of cells or an internal representation — appears in the word processor document.

Copying and pasting in this way works as long as no changes are made to the under-lying data. It is a simple operation for tool vendors to implement and a simple mecha-nism for windowing environments to facilitate. For this reason, virtually every windowing environment built since 1980 has made this kind of compound document creation possible. Going back to the real estate agent example, by copying and past-ing a range of numbers, a picture, and a graph into the bigger word processor docu-ment, the agent generates a good-looking proposal, complete with words, pictures, numbers, and graphs. The process of creating this compound document is simple. The word processor has to accommodate only one broad new type of data: bitmaps. If the word processor, the spreadsheet, and the graphics package can support the re-quest to paste a bitmapped, external representation, then these tools can support the ability to create compound documents containing information generated by an arbi-trarily broad number of tools. This compound document isn't perfect, though. What's wrong with the picture is that the process of copying the bitmap broke the connection between the internal and external representation of the copied data.

Suppose that the real estate agent has just finished putting together the proposal and suddenly the phone rings. The photograph in the document was taken from an angle that neglected to show some damage that requires attention by any prospective pur-chaser. The damage may affect the sale price of the property, the cost estimates, and the resulting cash flow projections. A new photograph is on the server, and estimates of the required repairs are available in a database, too. Thinking quickly, the agent, who was about to meet a prospective purchaser, realizes that in less than 20 minutes, he can update the spreadsheet and the graph. The photograph could also be simply replaced, but because the new picture is less attractive than the old one, the agent decides to incorporate *both* pictures in the proposal. This change is simple enough to contemplate, but there's a catch.

After updating the spreadsheet and its accompanying graph, the agent gets ready to put together a new proposal. Ideally, the word processor document would be auto-matically updated too. Unfortunately, the word processor document has no reason to know anything about pictures, spreadsheets, or graphs. What's contained in that document is just a series of bitmaps — external representations. Those external repre-sentations are totally passive. When it comes to changes, those bitmaps are couch potatoes: they never budge or change no matter what happens around them.

Getting close to appointment time, the agent realizes that the only way to get the updated pictures, numbers, and graphs into the document is to copy and paste them in all over again — a great deal of tedious work, especially because he has already done the work once (or twice or three times). It gets worse. After recopying the numbers and the graph, the agent gets ready to add the new picture. Because both pictures need to be included, the document is now longer, and all the elements in the document start moving around on the page. The spreadsheet and the graph, both of which looked quite elegant in their old locations, now don't fit very well. By working in the spreadsheet or the graphics package, the agent can change the formatting of both objects, but each time the agent changes the formatting, he must recopy the bitmaps from one tool to the other. The whole process is tedious, slow, and error prone. Running out of time, the frustrated agent gives up on his nice-looking compound document, grabs a quick spreadsheet printout on a separate page, forgets about the graph, and rushes off to the appointment.

BODY AND SOUL: EMBEDDING OBJECTS, NOT BITMAPS

Why was the agent frustrated? Even though the numbers in the document *looked like* a spreadsheet, it wasn't a spreadsheet at all. The compound document, created from bitmaps, contained a *picture* of a spreadsheet, and like all pictures, this one portrayed the body but not the soul of the spreadsheet. How should the process work?

Ideally, the agent would see the proposal with its words, numbers, and pictures. When it came time to change the numbers, instead of having to go back to the spreadsheet, the agent would change the numbers *inside* the word processor document. To perform this task, what is embedded in the compound document somehow has to be the spreadsheet itself, not a picture of it. That's what OLE makes possible.

If a word processor document can contain a picture of a spreadsheet, why can't it contain the spreadsheet itself? A picture of a spreadsheet consists of just computer data that causes a picture to be printed on a page or displayed on a screen. Similarly, a file containing the stored representation of the spreadsheet also consists of computer data. That file can be copied, backed up, and generally handled by many different tools. All tools treat the file as just a bunch of computer data. Of course, to make the file come alive, to turn it into a spreadsheet, the spreadsheet tool is required. Typically, it's not just any spreadsheet tool that is needed, but the same one that created it: 1-2-3, Excel, SuperCalc, or whatever. If a spreadsheet can be saved in a file, why can't the same information be encapsulated somehow so that it can be saved as part of a larger word processor document?

It can, and embedding is the first part of object linking and embedding. OLE provides a mechanism whereby entire documents created by one tool can literally be stored and embedded as part of bigger documents created by other tools. Just storing a spreadsheet in this way is not enough, though. When stored, the bigger document and the tool that maintains it has to remember how the embedded object was created. Why?

Suppose that the agent decides to change the numbers. If they are in a bitmap, the agent has to remember where the spreadsheet was, start it up, make the changes, and then copy them back. If the numbers are in the spreadsheet itself, then the word processor has to remember that the changes are in a spreadsheet, start the spreadsheet tool, and get it to work with the user to make changes. At its core then, OLE is a mechanism to get many applications to *work together* as though they were one big application.

UNITED WE STAND

The very reason for talking about OLE is that it is an example of the *integration* sublayer for desktop applications: a mechanism for getting many desktop applications to work together as though they were one. That integration requires both a supporting infrastructure — that's OLE — *and* the cooperation of each of the applications themselves. Here's how that process works.

Application Architecture Sublayers

Navigation and control

Active components

Integration

In the new world of OLE, the real estate agent creates some financial projections, charts, and photographs in preparation for the presentation of a proposal. In the spreadsheet, he selects a range of cells, highlights them, and specifies a *copy* operation, just as before. The spreadsheet and the word processor now both support OLE. So when the agent switches to the word processor and specifies a *paste* operation, rather than embed a picture of the spreadsheet, the word processor embeds part of the spreadsheet itself. How did it know what to embed? The spreadsheet software sent a copy of its internal representation for that range of cells. So far, so good. The same process happens for the graph and the picture, so the word processor document now contains part of a spreadsheet, a graph, and a picture.

Next, the agent receives that infamous phone call and goes to change the spreadsheet. In Windows, the standard operation for activating a document is the *double click*. Looking at the table of numbers, the agent moves the mouse there and double-clicks it. The word processor remembers that what the agent is looking at is not a picture but an actual spreadsheet, so the double click causes the word processor to wake up the spreadsheet. The spreadsheet then takes over until the agent is done with his changes. Later, the agent uses the same mechanism to access and update the chart and the picture, resulting in a completely updated document — with no repeated copies and pastes.

Historically, the process of shifting from the word processor document to, for example, the spreadsheet has been somewhat awkward. True, the user can double-click on the table of numbers, but then the spreadsheet takes over the screen, and the user has to remember the context within which the table existed. As this book goes to press, however, even this awkwardness is being eliminated. In the world of OLE version 2.0, users can shift from words to numbers and back without ever leaving the image and window representing the overall document. What's so great about this feature? Well, picture the process that occurs when the real estate agent pastes the second photograph, causing everything else to be rearranged on the pages. Without ever leaving the word processor and the convenient page-layout environment, the agent can also pop into the spreadsheet or graphing program at will to rearrange the formats of those elements and poke and prod at the enclosing document until everything looks perfect.

Numerous elements make OLE happen. All at one time, the real estate agent works with the word processor, the spreadsheet, the graphing tool, and the photograph editor all together as one large application. That's integration in action. However, it's more than that. It's a complete example of real components cooperating: cooperating components, in real life, on the desktop, every day — today.

LIVING DOCUMENTS

Calling OLE a compound document architecture raises the image of sophisticated systems for laying out printed pages. OLE enables this type of scenario, but in an environment of self-managed teams, the possibilities raised by this kind of integration reach much further. In the first place, the integration enabled by OLE includes the possibility of combining information *dynamically* as well as statically. In addition, it also makes it possible to include much more than printable data.

Accessing information dynamically requires *linking* instead of *embedding*. An *embedded* object is one that's literally encapsulated and stored right in the surrounding document. So the real estate agent's proposal literally contains a complete little spreadsheet, a complete little graph, and two complete photographs. Linking to an object allows the contained object to be shared by other people while still being integrated into the containing document.

Suppose that several people are now working on the real estate proposal. A financial analyst is generating the cost table and wants to keep that table in a separate spreadsheet that can be shared by everybody on the team. If the real estate agent, the point man for the team, copies the spreadsheet into the proposal, even if it's embedded as a spreadsheet, then that spreadsheet when it's copied will no longer reflect changes made by the financial analyst. So instead, the agent *links* the spreadsheet. Now the proposal contains a *link* or *reference* to the spreadsheet instead of a complete copy of the spreadsheet.

On the screen, linked objects look just like embedded ones. The linked object can be accessed and changed, just like an embedded one, just by double-clicking. However, the result of double clicking is to access and activate the linked object *wherever* it is stored. There's more, though. Whenever the document is opened, the word processor, through OLE, will automatically check whether any linked objects it contains have changed. If so, the user can decide to incorporate the changed version. The members of the team can move ahead at their own pace. When the agent gets ready to make a new presentation, he can open up the proposal, automatically see changes made by other members of the team, and quickly make any required formatting changes.

Link-enabled, dynamic integration allows some types of documents to even be created automatically. For example, in a monthly report containing a graph and a table that are both derived from a database-driven report, linking makes it possible for the report document to automatically include the most recent copy of the sales data contained in the graph and the table.

Because both linked and embedded objects automatically activate the tool that created the contained object, why not have objects that themselves are active? For example, an embedded object could contain sound recordings or full-motion video. Of course, playing the sound or the video requires that the object somehow be activated — that's just a double click.

The beauty of all this active integration is that the desktop layer appears almost alive. Picture the real estate salesman in the not-too-distant future. A new property is ready for presentation to several prospects. The entire team that he's part of has worked for several days to support the proposals he's about to make. Using the database, he selects several clients to alert to the opportunity. Pulling together numbers, pictures, and graphs into a nice textual presentation, he sends electronic mail to each client. The mail also includes embedded video clips providing a short property tour, complete with narration, which the client activates after receiving the mail. When a client responds with a question, the agent takes a pre-canned tax-analysis illustration, makes a few changes causing the entire analysis to recompute and reformat itself, sends the reply, and closes the sale. To prepare for closing, the agent works with a custom-built program written in SmallTalk that drives a word processor. The custom program selects contract clauses from a desktop database and passes them to the word processor, which then formats and prepares the 45-page contract for delivery to the buyer and seller. All automatic and all enabled by desktop integration.

Cooperating components make compound documents possible, but they also do more than that. Compound documents are about passive, essentially visual representations created by a variety of tools combined into a larger document. In a compound document world, most of the tools that create the visual elements are built by professional tool builders: Microsoft, Lotus, IBM, and so on. Cooperating components can include any component written by anybody. Self-managed teams might create components by using a spreadsheet, Visual Basic, or Paradox to offer special services to customers. The beauty of the cooperating component world is that all the components really can and do work together, regardless of who wrote them. They cooperate computationally to arrive at answers, they cooperate visually to produce compound documents, and they cooperate systematically to yield an integrated application. So on the desktop, cooperating components are real today. What about the other two layers?

IN THE DATABASE

With the desktop layer as a reference model to keep in mind, how do the same three sublayers apply to the database environment? The active components are, of course, the databases themselves, or more correctly, the database files or tables under the control of a database manager. But what are the navigation and control and integration layers? To understand these layers, think about the fundamental function of a database: making data available for queries and managing changes to the data (transactions) to ensure consistency. Clearly, then, navigation and control has to do with finding data more effectively, and integration has to do with making many databases all look like one (see Table 16-2).

Table 16-2   Another Look at the Application Architecture and Its Sublayers

Application Layer	Navigation and Control	Active Components	Integration
Document	Windows	Documents	OLE
Business rules	Component Coordinator	Business Rule Components	COM
Database	OLE DB, Query Processor	Database	Transaction Coordinator

NAVIGATION AND CONTROL

The navigation and control layer for databases is based on the concept of *componentized databases* that were introduced at the end of Chapter 10. At that time, after considering all the stresses and strains that databases are subject to today, a solution was proposed that involved re-architecting databases into sets of cooperating components. Many of these components will take the form of *physical table containers*, containing the actual records and data users that drive applications. The advantage of componentizing the database, at this level, is that now a wide variety of such containers become possible; users can choose to store data in a spreadsheet, a project manager, or a true industrial strength database manager. Then, to make queries possible, another kind of container was introduced, one that was based on *logical records* — records derived from the other containers holding the physical records. The prototypical logical record container is the *query processor,* and it is that query processor, built right, that becomes the navigation and control layer for the database as a whole.

Figure 16-1 shows how the whole thing fits together. Suppose that you have a database environment with a number of different databases and database files or tables.

These are shown in the diagram as DB_1 through DB_n. Each of these represents a container of records. Most of the time, they will be physical record containers; however, logical record containers (like the profitability calculator or the geographical query processor of Chapter 10) are quite likely to be in this set of containers, too. In fact, the whole point of this generalized structure is that all the various containers of records throughout the entire system can be included in the architecture.

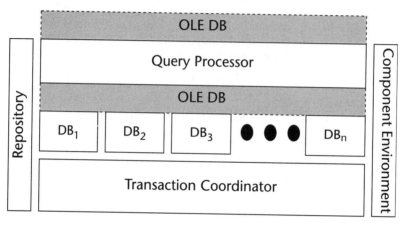

Figure 16-1: A revised database model.

The role of the query processor is to find records, retrieve them, and, where appropriate, combine them with other records. In this role, it is playing two core functions: navigation *and* integration. However, because the navigation function is so critical and unique, I've chosen to place the query processor in that top layer of the diagram. So given a query processor designed as a separate and separable cooperating component, you can now start to picture how the database layer is built. In order for the query processor to function in this way, the OLE DB interface, described in Chapter 10, is also critical; it is the architectural glue that allows a wide variety of record containers to offer their records for the query processor to find and work with.

How does the query processor know where to find records? There are two answers to this question with slightly different names and the same overall meaning. Historically, query processors are driven by a *database catalog*. The catalog, sometimes also called a *data dictionary*, contains the descriptions of all the tables in a database, their columns, indexes, and so on. A query processor, like the one being discussed, requires a *global catalog* — a catalog that contains information about all the tables in all the record containers throughout the system. Thinking back to Chapter 15, clearly the same function could also be played by a *repository*; and in the long term, a repository is *exactly* the right place to store these global descriptions.

The preceding solution works for both local and distributed databases. In fact, in a distributed database environment, separating the query processor, normally an integral part of the database, so that it becomes its own component is the *only* way to combine data from multiple locations and make the distribution work. It is the job of the query processor to take the query and figure out the best way to pull all the data together. Of course, to make this work, that query processor will need help from the other sites, too. In fact, what happens is that each site — each server — has at least one query processor, and it is the query processors that talk to each other to ship records back and forth in the most efficient way possible.

Drawing a diagram like Figure 16-1 is relatively simple; building the system is, of course, harder. Today a variety of products — EDA/SQL, Sybase's OmniServer, MicroDecisionWare's gateway products, for example — offer the kind of distributed query capability described earlier. They are all limited to retrieving data only from large scale databases like Oracle, DB2, and SQLserver. The idea of using an interface like OLE DB to provide this kind of unification across data stores of all types is a new idea that will become available in products only in the next few years.

With the advent of the Internet and as pressure for ubiquitous servers and heterogeneous data stores continues to grow, the demand for exactly this kind of broad unification will only increase. Cooperating components is the only way to get there. The one problem with this picture is that so far, we have only talked about ways to *retrieve* data across many databases. What about updating data when that data lives in several places?

TRANSACTION COORDINATION

The function of the *transaction coordinator* is to allow updates to be made to multiple databases and record containers all at the same time. Historically, this has been viewed as one of the hardest functions to perform in a database environment. While there is a variety of products that promise to provide query processing across several databases, finding products that offer the same integration function for updates is much harder. In fact, much of the drive and market demand for replication services is driven precisely by a desire to avoid having to deal with distributed updates. On one hand, replication is a wonderful service for a database to provide; in fact, replicated data often provides performance advantages for queries as well as updates. At the same time, there are many cases where, replication or not, you just can't avoid the necessity to deal with distributed updates.

Why are distributed transactions so hard? Supporting distributed transactions is the core operational problem that must be solved in order to bring about the client/server world. The whole point of providing self-managed teams with their own self-managed computing environment is to allow them to customize processes to meet local needs. This means that the team must have its own local database and must be in a position to change the data in that database. Simply put, self-managed teams must be able to create local transactions.

No matter how carefully data is distributed, there will be cases in which the self-managed team needs to make changes to data that is not local: someone will need inventory from another location; a funds transfer will cross office boundaries; a large customer will need shipments coordinated across the country. In each case, the team will need to initiate a transaction that changes local *and* remote data as part of the same transaction. That's a distributed transaction.

Suppose that a large customer places a local order. Because the customer deals with the company on a national scale, the credit authorization for that customer takes place at company headquarters. So here's how the transaction must occur in order to process the order:

✦ A sales rep enters the order in New York and computes the total.

✦ The sales rep also makes a request for credit authorization to the national computer located in Memphis.

✦ The national computer confirms that the customer has enough credit and *provisionally* reduces the credit limit by the amount of the order.

✦ The New York computer, upon receiving provisional confirmation, checks whether all the products requested are in stock.

✦ After the products are found and reserved, the transaction is completed. The products are allocated to the customer, the credit limit is reduced, and the order moves ahead.

If everything proceeds smoothly, the preceding transaction is straightforward. But things can go wrong:

✦ If credit is not approved, the order needs to be backed out.

✦ If the order cannot be fulfilled because of missing inventory, the order needs to be backed out, and the customer's credit limit should not be decreased.

✦ If the credit authorization computer fails in the middle of the transaction, what happens? Can the company afford to risk reducing the customer's credit limit if the order didn't ship? Can the company afford to *not* decrease the credit limit if the order *does* ship? Because the credit authorization computer is down, how do the local reps know what to do so that the right thing happens?

✦ If the order processing computer fails in the middle of the transaction, what does the credit authorization computer do?

✦ What if the network fails and neither computer can tell what state the other one is in?

Although this simple example is already complex enough, it can easily get worse. Suppose that the order requires reserving parts that are located in Chicago and Rochester. Before the transaction can be completed, four different computers in four different cities all need to be coordinated around this single transaction, all at one time.

The answer to dealing with distributed transactions like the one just described is called *two-phase commit*. Two-phase commit is a *protocol* that allows any number of databases to coordinate with each other so that transactions distributed across many locations all work. A protocol is an agreed-on set of procedures and communications that allows several parties to all work together in a coordinated fashion. In this case the parties are databases. And *work together* means that the parties ensure that any given transaction either completes at all site or completes at none of the sites, period.

So the credit limit is decreased *if and only if* the order is processed. Otherwise, the two-phase commit protocol ensures that all the databases go back to the state they were in before the transaction was ever started. Straightforward, to say the least.

Two-phase commit is not just a theory; it is a known protocol that has been implemented successfully in a number of shipping products. Oracle, IBM, Tandem, DEC, and others have been shipping products that provide two-phase commit coordination for several years so that transactions can be distributed across several databases and geographical sites. One problem with the implementations these vendors provide is that they are all database specific: IBM coordinates transactions that naturally involve *only* IBM databases; Oracle supports its own databases, and so on. One way to solve this problem is to have an infrastructural component whose primary job is to manage transactions that are independent of the underlying databases that hold the data. Such a component is called a *transaction coordinator*.

Several higher-level *transaction coordinators* — Tuxedo, Top End, Encina, and others — provide two-phase commit that works with databases from *different* vendors. Microsoft also recently announced its plans to make transaction coordination a part of its overall OLE infrastructure based on a set of interfaces called *OLE Transactions*. A variety of products offering transaction coordination facilities may be available now or will be soon.

One problem with this approach has been getting all the different database vendors to provide the correct fundamental database facilities to make this external coordination possible. In 1990, a standards body called *X/Open* defined a standard called *XA* that specifies the protocol that a third-party transaction coordinator talking to any database can use so that two-phase commit becomes possible. If all this sounds like gobbledygook, it is. The net result is that because of recent evolving standards like XA and OLE Transactions, it is possible to buy transaction coordinators — shipping products that really work — that make it possible to distribute transactions across many databases from different vendors.

Does the technology really work today? The answer is, "Yes, as long as you proceed in a step-by-step fashion." This technology does exist and does work. The wrinkles are still being worked out, but there are several sources to choose from. So if an application is being built today, by the time it rolls out, there is an excellent chance that it will easily perform distributed transactions.

Why isn't everybody implementing distributed systems? In increasing order of severity, there are three reasons:

1. The technology is new, and most organizations are only barely aware that it exists. Furthermore, some of the critical links and supporting facilities are still on the verge of being available as opposed to being available. Not all databases support XA today, but they all will soon (or, as computer people say with a look of pain on their faces: *real soon now*).

2. The technology is far too complex. Learning to use existing transaction managers requires a significant investment, and when everything is said and done, only a few expert programmers will really understand them. In the next section of this chapter, I look at the long-term solution to this problem.

3. Having both two-phase commit and distributed transactions is not enough to really implement distributed databases. That's the killer. Most knowledgeable computer professionals express the following sentiments about two-phase commit and distributed transactions:

   • Two-phase commit isn't really available, it's too hard to use, and I don't trust it.

   • Even if I did trust it, the protocol requires that every part of the network involved in a transaction be up all the time. As soon as any part of my network goes down, everything grinds to a halt. So even if I could implement two-phase commit, why would I do it?

This appears to be an impossible dilemma. Distributed systems are really necessary. As the point-of-sale systems and other examples illustrate, they are really possible too. On the one hand, if two-phase commit is critically necessary to building distributed systems, users can't live without it. On the other hand, if two-phase commit really depends on the whole network being up all the time, users can't live with it either. Can't live without it and can't live with it. What's a person to do?

The more we look at the dilemma of two-phase commit, the more puzzling it actually becomes. This seems most clear when we look at the picture of a distributed network as a whole. Superficially, a distributed network should be *more* robust than a centralized system. After all, in a centralized system, when the main computer goes down, everything stops. Yet the implications of the two-phase commit dilemma are that in a distributed system, if any server or network link goes down, if there are many distributed transactions, the whole network also goes down. So there are *more*, not fewer, points of failure. The central system, given a backup computer at the central site, actually appears to be more reliable. Yet *something* must be wrong with this picture; we all know that there has to be a way to make that distributed system be the robust choice, the one that keeps working even when the central site, or any other remote site, is down. But how do we get there? The answer revolves around the rest of the cooperating component infrastructure described in the next section — specifically around something called a *component coordinator.*

DATABASES AS COOPERATING COMPONENTS

At this point, you have a complete picture of how to build the database layer around cooperating components. And as you have discovered with the document layer, not only can it be done, it can even be done today with off-the-shelf products. Some of the products, particularly those that depend on newer approaches like OLE DB and OLE Transactions, are still one or two years old. At the same time, other alternatives exist, and certainly at the very least, both the direction and the structure of the applications of the future is clear. Therefore, given this picture of the database layer, consider the last layer, the critical business rules layer.

BUSINESS RULES: COOPERATING COMPONENTS IN ACTION

It's time to look at the last major layer — the business rules layer — and see how its sublayers come into play (see Table 16-3). The active components in this layer are the business rules process written in COBOL, FORTRAN, BASIC, or some other language. This discussion begins with integration, the last sublayer. What does integration mean for these languages?

Table 16-3 **Focusing on the Business Rules Layer and Its Sublayers**

Application Layer	Navigation and Control	Active Components	Integration
Documents	Windows	Documents	OLE
Business rules	Component Coordinator	Business rules	Component Environment
Database	OLE DB, Query Processor	Database	Transaction Coordinator

INTEGRATION

In this layer, more than in the other two, it is critical to keep the central function of the whole layer in mind. After all, both the desktop and database layers are somewhat familiar creatures, but the business rules layer is a new beast. The justification for this beast is the management and operation of the fundamental business processes that keep an organization running. These processes consist of business rule components that implement particular collections of rules. Each component receives requests, carries out activities triggered by the request, and generally returns some form of response.

Integration means providing a mechanism so that several business rule components can work together as though there were one bigger collection of business rules. If each business rule component receives and responds to requests, what would it mean for several components to look like one bigger one? Essentially, it would mean that the apparently bigger component would respond to all the same requests the individual components responded to alone.

Another way to think of this concept is to consider the difference between a single organization and the departments in it. Imagine dealing with the order department, the accounting department, and the shipping department of a large organization. Each might have its own phone line, its own procedures, and its own ways of dealing with problems. As long as each department does things its own way, it is obvious that the customer has to be painfully aware of the departments and the boundaries between them.

Now, suppose that the departments all instituted standard ways of interacting with customers. Internally, all departments are still free to work any way they want, but when it comes to processing orders, notifying customers about shipments, and re-sponding to complaints, all the departments now use standard forms, protocols, and communication procedures. Now take it a step farther. Imagine that the organization as a whole sets up a standard phone number, mailing address, and delivery point so that all requests, no matter what type, can be handled in the same way. Even though the departments may all still operate according to totally different internal principles, the entire organization looks like one big department from a customer perspective. The customer can't tell how the organization is set up internally because all requests are routed and handled in the same way regardless of where they go internally.

This type of homogeneity may look like just a luxury or a convenience, but it has deep-seated consequences. Suppose that the customer has a complex order to schedule. Credit authorization is an issue because of the size of the order; shipments have to be scheduled in a way that matches the rate at which the customer can pay; and the order is further complicated because of some currency-related considerations. In an old-style organization, the customer has to deal individually with each of the various departments, going back and forth until the whole deal is put together. In the new organization, the departments sort the whole thing out on the customer's behalf. Frequently, this task requires that one department initiate requests to be processed by other departments. But because of the way things are organized, departments can't distinguish between internal requests and external ones. The end result, which builds on the very interoperability I discussed in Chapter 12, benefits customers as well as developers of systems. This is what integration means in the business rules layer.

When we talk about integrating business rule components, we're talking about exactly the same mechanisms required to integrate components in general. Considering that business rule components are just particular components whose code happens to implement business rules, this is hardly surprising — but it is a key observation, nonetheless. So the question is, what is the glue, the mechanism that allows any number of otherwise separate components to interoperate together as though they were one big component?

At this point, we are talking about the heart of components themselves, and as a result, it is the *component environment* itself that is responsible for providing this glue. There are three or four such component environments available today, including IBM's SOM, Microsoft's COM, and Next's NextStep. In addition, many of the functions I associate with the component environment are also provided through the kind of object brokers promoted by the Object Management Group. It is hard to be certain which of these will be long-term survivors. Because of its close relationship to Windows, COM will certainly be one of the winners, but the question is whether there will also be any others and who they will be.

The fundamental job of the component environment is *make interfaces work*. Components are defined in terms of their interfaces. Cooperation between components is based on one component being able to make a request of another through an interface. At some point, requesters and requestees have to be matched up; that is the key, hard job that the component environment is responsible for. Consider requests and interfaces in more detail.

Business rule components receive requests. A request can be either a *message* or a *procedure call*. In object speak, procedure calls are also known as *method invocations* — they're the same thing. A credit authorization component, for example, may offer to receive requests that

✦ Ask for a response that says how much credit a customer has left

✦ Check whether a customer has a certain amount of credit available

✦ Reduce a customer's credit limit by a fixed amount, responding whether or not the request succeeds

✦ Increase a customer's credit limit by a specified amount

✦ Put a customer on credit hold

The collection of all such requests a component responds to is called its interface. If a programmer knows which business rule components are available, where they are located, and what their interfaces are, making requests and building programs is relatively easy. If he or she doesn't know this information, though, things get tricky. Furthermore, the distributed nature of the system also can make things tricky. How does a request get from one server or computer to another? What happens if a business rule component moves from one place to another? Does the requester have to know the exact name of a rule component or can the requester ask for a component that supplies a class of service — for example, shipping services?

The job of the component environment is to make all these problems go away. This is accomplished by providing services at two different levels. At the lowest level are basic interface services that deal with both local and remote requests and that take care of making those requests happen. Then, wrapped on top of that, making the component environment complete are services that allow components to find each other in the first place so the low-level services can be brought into play.

COMPONENT REQUEST SERVICES: REQUESTS VERSUS MESSAGES

Two fundamental low-level request mechanisms are in broad use today: *message passing (messages)* and *remote procedure calls (RPCs)*. There are huge, almost religious differences between these two approaches. In terms of what these two request mechanisms do, though, they are completely equivalent. In fact, it is even possible to mechanically convert messages into procedure calls and vice versa, but no existing system does this.

At first, there does appear to be one fundamental difference between messages and procedure calls in general. Procedure calls historically have been based on the notion of real-time or immediate interaction. That is, one program calls another, the resulting code is executed, and a result is returned as soon as the "callee" is done. Message passing, on the other hand, historically has been based on a notion of queues. The role of the queue is to buffer messages until the receiver has time to get around to processing the message. In a local system, immediate execution is normally preferable. In a distributed environment, on the other hand, queues appear to offer a lot of flexibility and resilience. If real time is the modus operandi, what happens if the component being invoked is on a remote machine and the connecting network link is down? In a messaging environment, the answer is clear; the message is just queued until the link comes back up. Given this framework, it's easy to see why, in a distributed world, message passing might appear to be the wave of the future. As it turns out, though, the choice is not nearly as clear cut as the preceding discussion would seem to indicate. Why? Simply because procedure calls can be made to operate in a queued environment, too. If a message can be queued, why can't a procedure call be queued in the same way? Once the procedure call is on the queue, it can stay there until the conditions are right for it to be activated. All of a sudden, the choice is not clear cut, after all. And that is the point; there is a choice.

How is all this likely to turn out? I happen to believe that distributed systems built around components and interfaces are the ones that will turn out to be most dominant. It's true that message passing has many attractions, but so does the interface approach. And there's one piece of data that happens to be really compelling in this context. Suppose that we look at applications built in message-passing environments. Here's the case where message passing has *won;* what do we find? We find, most of the time, that the programmers who work with message-passing mechanisms ultimately end up building a layer of procedure call code on top of each message-passing interface in their components. How much more natural then to just provide support for procedure calls directly.

So, what we are talking about is building components. Each component has interfaces through which it may be called, and it in turn calls on the services of other components using their interfaces. The question is how does this all work? As discussed earlier, there are two levels. The bottom level answers the question: "How do we handle an interface invocation that happens to call on a remote component?"

When we get to the "chewy center," an interface is just a packaged set of subroutine calls. In object speak, the interface is a collection of methods. Each method is exactly as has been defined: a subroutine entry point complete with a name and arguments. In a local machine, making components work is relatively straightforward. But what happens when the subroutine (method) call crosses machine (or even process) boundaries? That's where remote procedure calls come in. Here's how remote procedure calls work.

A remote procedure call is, as its name suggests, just a subroutine call — a reference to some code that lives in another procedure. Procedure call references are *resolved* at the time the program actually executes by *binding* the calling program to the subroutine that was invoked (although some systems resolve and bind earlier). Without a remote procedure call, that binding involves putting the memory address of the subroutine into that point in the program where the subroutine was referenced. Then the program can execute and the subroutine will be executed each time it is invoked. A remote procedure call mechanism augments this process by adding a new binding option. Instead of binding to a local subroutine in the same computer, the calling program is bound instead to a subroutine running in another computer. How can that happen? How can a memory reference for something existing in another computer be created locally?

A remote procedure call or RPC mechanism works by intercepting the subroutine calls, converting them to messages, sending the messages to the computer where the subroutine really is, and then arranging to invoke the subroutine in that computer. The response from that subroutine is then intercepted, converted into a message, and sent back. That's it. The key part is that the interception process is totally invisible to both the calling and the called program.

The beauty of this mechanism is that every programmer knows how to call subroutines. With procedure calls, they continue to call subroutines exactly as before. In fact, in a distributed program, it is literally impossible to tell a remote procedure call apart from a local one; they are exactly the same. Going further, the same procedure call may even be local one time and remote the next — there's still no difference.

Remote procedure calls (and yes, message-passing systems) have been around for several years and work well. Unlike two-phase commit technology, there's no reason to even think twice before using them. There are still some issues about cross-system compatibility, but by picking the right RPC or message passing vendor, even these problems can be made to disappear. In fact, one strategy for building systems with distributed components is to simply stay at the RPC level. Don't pick up a complete component environment like COM; just use RPCs. This is a strategy that works; but it does leave some key questions unanswered.

COMPONENTS: WHY GO ALL THE WAY?

Going back to Chapter 13, recall that subroutines, objects, and components are all part of the same progression — a progression whose goal is to make it possible to re-use code more effectively. Each step in the progression essentially adds to the sophistication of the *packaging* mechanisms we use to build and publish our applications. Subroutines were the first and earliest form of publishing mechanism; RPCs extend that mechanism to distributed systems without adding any new packaging functionality per se.

A component environment goes beyond RPCs and message passing to provide a complete set of services that make components work. This includes mechanisms for packaging sets of related methods into interfaces, services that allow those interfaces to be both described and inquired about, conventions for managing memory, and much more. In fact, neither procedure calls nor remote procedure calls are adequate mechanisms for building our desired future world of cooperating components; there is just too much missing. A complete component environment, like SOM or COM, on the other hand, with the addition of the component coordinator described later in this chapter, is enough. Why make this point?

Component models are becoming understood very gradually. There is still far too much religion around them for clear focus to be easy. In addition, most of the leading implementations are incomplete in one major way or another. Remote procedure calls, on the other hand, are now a mature technology that is easy to understand. So given a quick choice, it's easy to see why RPCs are so popular. The good news is that one does not come at the complete expense of the other. COM, in its distributed flavor for instance, is literally built on top of RPC. While this construction is transparent to the developer and user, it has major implications in terms of robustness and performance — all good. So the question is what to do starting now?

RPC is certainly a fine technology to use. As this book is being written in 1995, it is the only choice actually available that can be used across a wide variety of platforms. Even in a pure Microsoft environment when it comes to truly distributed applications, since the distributed flavor of COM is not a 1995 product, RPC is still the best choice. Carefully written applications based on it should be convertible to COM applications with minimal effort. At the same time, I believe that when building applications for the future, the first choice should be a component environment, and only when good reasons intervene should other choices be made.

NAVIGATION AND CONTROL: MANAGING BUSINESS PROCESSES

Finally, it's time to discuss the last piece in the technical infrastructure. Table 16-4 shows that the *component coordinator,* the first sublayer, is responsible for controlling business rule components, activating them, and managing the processes they are part of. In many ways, it's the most important piece of the technical infrastructure, but it is also the most missing piece today. To understand component coordinators, consider a few scenarios:

Table 16-4   **Focusing Again on the Business Rules Layer and Its Sublayers**

Application Layer	*Navigation and Control*	*Active Components*	*Integration*
Business rules	Component Coordinator	Business rules	Component Environment

✦ An order for 7,000 units of a product is processed in New York in January. Credit authorization takes place in realtime, and before that first transaction is completed, the credit limit is decreased and the order is queued up for further processing. The order calls for product to be shipped in stages over an 11-month period.

✦ The first part of the order is scheduled for immediate shipment in Cincinnati, but the remote computer is down. Who assumes responsibility for queuing the shipment request and ensuring that it is processed once and only once, particularly considering that it's on a remote computer?

✦ The order includes the shipment of spare parts every month for a year from six locations around the world. How do these shipments get scheduled so that they automatically take place at the right time?

✦ After four months, when it comes time to ship 65 units in Sacramento, those units are out of stock. What happens?

✦ After six months, while processing a shipment of 140 units in Spain, the warehouse computer suffers a power failure in the middle of processing the order. When the database comes back up, it backs out all the incomplete transactions, including the entire shipment. Who restarts the task so that the shipment happens after all?

✦ In November, the last month of shipments, the company is experiencing an exceptionally busy month. When it comes time to queue up all the remaining shipments, several of the warehouse computers are so busy that some requests are being delayed for several days even though other computers in the same warehouses are running under capacity. Who rearranges the workload so that shipments are not delayed unnecessarily?

These scenarios relate to a core question: who manages all the tasks and activities that collectively make up the business processes? There is a popular and simple answer to this question today, and there's also the real answer waiting in the future.

THE MAGICAL ATTRACTION OF WORKFLOW

Right behind object-oriented programming is another silver bullet in the process of being cast and hardened: workflow. The concept of workflow is that business procedures are essentially all based on forms, so if it were possible to design a class of intelligent forms, most large-scale business processes could be easily automated by drawing a flowchart showing how all the forms flow from place to place in an organization.

Much of the original motivation for workflow products stems from the popularity of electronic mail. When electronic mail becomes popular in an organization, most users check their mail first thing in the day, last thing before they leave, and regularly throughout the day. The In box quickly becomes the place to find out about new meetings, schedule changes, quick requests, and answers to questions. In short, the In box becomes a kind of realtime tickler, reminder, and control panel system. Sending and receiving mail is fast and convenient; most office procedures are slow and clumsy. Most office procedures are, however, based on forms in one way or another. Therein lies the idea.

Why can't an electronic mail system transport forms just as easily as it transports text messages? It can, of course. Supplies forms can be filled out on the screen and sent directly to the right person. Expense reports can be handled the same way. Taking this process a step further, why send forms to the right person? Why can't forms just know where to go?

In a workflow system, how does the form know where to go? It knows because at the same time the form was designed, the designer also drew a flowchart showing where the form should travel after being filled out. The flow chart deals in names, places, and roles. For example, an expense report can be told to always go first to the supervisor of the person filling it out and then to the accounting department. Similarly, a supplies form can go to directly to the purchasing department for small orders, or it can go first to the appropriate manager or supervisor for larger orders. The concept is simple and appealing.

Even more than the diagrams, the thing that really makes workflow work is the use of mail. The whole point of workflow is that forms are flowing from one person to another. By putting all incoming requests into the In box, each user — a manager, a clerk, or anybody else — has only one place to check to see everything on his or her plate. Because mail is so ubiquitous, delays are minimized because people check their mail regularly. In fact, the more that requests and communications flow through the mail system, the better it works.

For small, lightweight procedures — expense reporting, ordering supplies, travel requests, and so on — workflow can work very well. But even in these cases, many tricky questions surface when the system grows. Will work ever be lost? How can progress be monitored? However, the real issue with workflow is that it is an inappropriate concept for handling the larger-scale business processes that organizations are built around.

PROCESS FLOW, NOT WORK FLOW — INTRODUCING THE COMPONENT COORDINATOR

The central idea behind workflow is the automatic movement of task requests in the shape of forms from person to person. Mail is such an appropriate mechanism because it works well as a person-to-person communication vehicle. The problem is that the whole point of Business Process Reengineering is to not expedite processing of tasks but to eliminate those tasks altogether. Instead of quickly hustling forms from queue to queue, most users want to get rid of the forms and have the computer system handle the entire process automatically. Rather than workflow, users need *process flow*.

The component coordinator (see Table 16-4) is the component of the technical infrastructure that runs all the sequences of tasks that make up a business process. Imagine the complex logistics and scheduling of a large military operation: hundreds of thousands of soldiers, tanks, airplanes, tents, field hospitals, food, fuel, and so on. Before launching an operation, someone at a high level must have put together a complete plan. As the operation unfolds, a staff organization keeps the whole thing running smoothly. As problems arise, they are solved; other problems are logged to be resolved later. Through it all, scheduling, materials, men, and equipment are kept on the move all the time. The component coordinator is the computer equivalent of that central staff organization. Just as the staff organization coordinates activities across many locations by dealing with its local counterparts in each place, the component coordinator, running in every server in the system, provides the same distributed coordination to the system as a whole.

How does it work? There's a component called the component coordinator in each server in the system. It is tied directly into the component execution environment, and this connection allows it to know what is going on. By tracking requests, the component coordinator is able to track activity, take special action when requests can't be dealt with immediately, replay requests after power failure, and perform other such maintenance tasks. To see this in more detail, reconsider the questions I raised in the preceding section:

✦ *The situation:* An order for 7,000 units of a product is processed in New York in January. Credit authorization takes place in realtime, and before that first transaction is completed, the credit limit is decreased and the order is queued up for further processing. The order calls for product to be shipped in stages over an 11-month period.

The solution: First, the component coordinator just watches and waits. The transaction coordinator in the database layer took care of the distributed transaction because of its realtime requirements. After credit is authorized, the order processing component queues a long series of component coordinator requests for all the orders that are to be shipped on a scheduled basis over a period of time. By making requests of the appropriate shipping components through the component environment, the component coordinator directly processes other orders that are specified for immediate shipment.

✦ *The situation:* The first part of the order is scheduled for immediate shipment in Cincinnati, but the remote computer is down. Who assumes responsibility for queuing the shipment request and ensuring that it is processed once and only once, particularly considering that it's on a remote computer?

The solution: The component coordinator accepts the request at the New York computer and logs it until the Cincinnati computer comes back on-line. At that time, it relays the request, ensuring that the component coordinator receives it at the other end, which in turn ensures that the shipment is processed by the local shipping component.

✦ *The situation:* The order includes the shipment of spare parts every month for a year from six locations around the world. How do these shipments get scheduled so that they automatically take place at the right time?

The solution: At the time the order was placed, the component coordinator was asked to schedule a series of requests, one per month for a year, at each of six locations. When queued, the order processing component forgets about the requests because the component coordinator will ensure that they are automatically activated at the right times and places. The New York component coordinator immediately passes each request to its local counterparts in the six locations, who in turn schedule them for future monthly execution.

✦ *The situation:* After four months, when it comes time to ship 65 units in Sacramento, those units are out of stock. What happens?

The solution: The component coordinator can't solve *all* problems. After four months, the component coordinator activates a request in Sacramento for shipment of the 65 units. The business rule component, recognizing that the units are out of stock, takes the appropriate action as specified in either the base business rules or the order. In this case, it simultaneously sets up a back order and sends a notice to the customer.

✦ *The situation:* At the six-month point, while processing a shipment of 140 units in Spain, the warehouse computer suffers a power failure in the middle of processing the order. When the database comes back up, it backs out all the incomplete transactions, including the entire shipment. Who restarts the task so that the shipment happens after all?

   The solution: After it queues a request, the component coordinator does not discard it until the request is complete. If the request for some reason is not completed successfully, then the component coordinator will first back out the associated transactions so that nothing is done twice. It then resubmits the request. In this case, the database has already backed out the transaction, so the component coordinator restarts the business rule component (if that's necessary) and then resubmits the request.

✦ *The situation:* In November, the last month of shipments, the company is experiencing an exceptionally busy month. When it comes time to queue up all the remaining shipments, several of the warehouse computers are so busy that some requests are being delayed for several days even though other computers in the same warehouses are running under capacity. Who rear-ranges the workload so that shipments are not delayed unnecessarily?

   The solution: Because the component coordinator is wired into the compo-nent environment, it can track all requests as they come and go. Part of its responsibility is to monitor the amount of time taken to process requests. When that processing time becomes excessive, the component coordinator will look around, talk to its colleagues on other computers, and see whether there is a machine that can help balance the workload. This balancing is transparent and automatic.

That's a component coordinator in action. Let's look at how the coordinator works, at a more technical level now. In doing so, we will see how to deal with the limitations of two-phase commit that came up earlier in this chapter; this will provide a clear view of how distributed updates really can be practical.

REALTIME? OR REAL *ENOUGH* TIME?

If this book has one theme, it is that focusing on tasks results in large systems that don't work well, so to reengineer those systems, the focus has to shift away from tasks and toward processes built out of cooperating components. The same theme, the same Copernican shift, surfaces again.

Transactions are the database equivalents of tasks. They are relatively small units of work that must complete all at once or not complete at all. A transaction may be spread across several databases and cities, but it is associated with a discrete task, nonetheless. Just as focusing too much on databases made distributed system design impossible, focusing too much on transactions makes running distributed systems impossible, too.

Imagine the business discussion that leads to a decision to use two-phase commit. This is a business discussion, not a technical discussion. A designer is meeting with a general manager of a division discussing how the order-processing system is to be implemented. The conversation goes something like this:

> *Designer:* Okay, so the orders are processed in local offices around the country. And you want to keep credit authorization centralized, running on a single computer here in Memphis. Now how important is it to you, from a business perspective, to always authorize credit at the exact same time the order is entered? For example, if that single credit authorization computer goes down, are you willing to stop processing orders until it comes back up?

> *Manager:* Yes, if I tell a customer that an order is accepted, I always want to know that his or her credit is okay. I'm willing to shut down order processing at all of my field offices whenever the credit authorization computer is un-available or the network connecting the credit authorization computer to the field is unavailable.

Fine, now the designer knows just what to do. Two-phase commit and distributed transactions are the technical answers. The decision to stop transactions whenever the network goes down is a business decision having nothing to do with two-phase com-mit. The key to this decision is the *realtime* nature of the transaction. To better see this, consider another example of realtime processing.

Besides interacting with people, computers are used to run many other kinds of op-erations in which no human interaction is involved. For example, nuclear power plants are always run by a computer or series of computers. These computers are connected to sensors distributed throughout the plant that provide constant information about the status of every valve, every piece of equipment, every fuel element, and so on. The computer monitors all these sensors and then adjusts valves and other controls throughout the plant to keep everything running smoothly. Whenever a change occurs, the computer is said to react in *realtime,* which means that the computer's response to a situation happens *while* the situation is occurring. To see this clearly, consider the alternative to *realtime* reaction. Suppose that the computer monitored the sensors and printed reports. Periodically, a person would read the reports and decide after the fact what to do — not a realtime response.

In the same way, distributed transactions can be viewed as *realtime transactions.* The general manager is willing to shut down order entry when the credit authorization computer is unavailable precisely because he wants credit authorization decisions to be made in realtime. Two-phase commit derives both its strengths and weaknesses from being a realtime protocol. The only reason to ever implement two-phase commit is that the many parts of a distributed transaction have to be coordinated across multiple databases in realtime. But, you may ask, is there an alternative to realtime?

Imagine that the designer is continuing to question the general manager, and now the conversation turns to shipment scheduling:

Designer: We've agreed that orders get processed only if the credit is okay. Now, what about when we have to schedule shipment dates? The inventory control and shipment scheduling computers are located in warehouses that are generally in different locations from the offices where customers place orders. What if the warehouse computer goes down? Do you want to refuse to process orders if we can't tell customers exactly when we will ship their orders?

Manager: Well, this case is different. If you can tell customers when their orders will be shipped, then of course I'd like to do that. But if you can't, book the order anyway. Now, I do want to know that after the order is accepted it will be scheduled for shipment as soon as possible. If the warehouse computer is down when the order comes in, book it and then schedule delivery later.

Why would the manager expect two-phase commit in this case? The two parts of the transaction — order entry and shipment scheduling — need to be coordinated, but *not* in realtime. In fact, should the two parts of this process even be considered to be part of the same transaction? No! That's the point. Because the two parts of the process are parts of two different transactions, two-phase commit is neither necessary nor even appropriate.

Distributed systems implement *business processes*. These processes are not themselves *transactions*. Even the tasks those processes are built out of are not transactions. They are instead long-running *sequences* of transactions. What a distributed system needs is both facilities for managing distributed transactions and also higher-level facilities for managing long-running sequences of transactions. The difference between a transaction and a sequence of transactions is the difference between realtime and *real enough time*. When the general manager says "Schedule that shipment as soon as you can, but it doesn't have to be done right away," he's also saying "As soon as possible is real enough time for me."

Here's an example from later in the conversation:

Designer: After the order is shipped, what about billing? How soon does that have to happen?

Manager: Make sure that the customer gets billed, but any time within 15 days is soon enough, so don't worry at all if the billing computer isn't up when shipment happens.

In this situation, real-enough time is not even close to realtime — it's any time within 15 days.

COORDINATING COMPONENTS: HANDLING SEQUENCES OF TRANSACTIONS

Now, we're ready to talk about the component coordinator in pretty complete detail. The component coordinator is the technical component that manages *sequences of transactions and requests*. Individual requests are handled by the component environment. Individual transactions are handled by the database. If those transactions span several servers or several stores, then the transactions are managed by the transaction coordinator so that changes happen in all the stores at once or in none of them; that guarantees consistency. All of this is fine as long as only single transactions and requests are involved. When it comes to sequences of transactions and requests, that's where the component coordinator comes in.

How are systems like this built today? The answer involves cobbling together a nasty combination of services. Non transactional requests are handled by the component environment; transactions are handled by the database. If more than one server is involved, a transaction monitor often enters the picture. While the transaction monitor provides scaling by allowing transactions to span several computers and databases, it introduces a completely new programming model into the picture. The other problem is that all these components deal only with the real time case. To deal with the real enough time case a message queuing system is required. And, guess what; it has yet another programming model too. Finally, to handle tasks that are scheduled for deferred execution, a batch scheduling system is required.

All these pieces are certainly available today. COM is a fine component model. Many database management systems are available; all offer transactions. CICS, Tuxedo, Encina, Top End, and other products are all proven transaction monitors. And queuing systems like Peerlogic's Pipes, IBM's MSGq, and others have been available for some time. It is the challenge of using them all in one system that makes the whole thing unimaginable. Even ignoring the cost of acquiring and running all these products, the technical challenge of dealing with all the programming models within a single application is overwhelming. And then there's the issue of potential incompatibilities that arise when so many complex products are intermingled.

The solution to this problem arises from the observation that what we have here is a scenario that lies right at the core of the whole concept of components in the first place. So if we can solve the problem by adding infrastructure to the center of the component environment, then maybe a simple solution might be possible after all.

SNAPPING APPLICATIONS TOGETHER OUT OF COMPONENTS

Let's think back to that most favorite scenario that comes up in every conversation about components and objects: building an application by just snapping off the shelf pieces together. Suppose it were possible. Imagine any two large components. For example, order entry, credit authorization, shipping, etc. Suppose we are using two components and they were built by two different teams, maybe in two different companies. Still, we want to use them together; you know just snap them to each other. How do we answer these basic questions about how the components work together:

✦ Does one component know what database the other one is using? If not, how do transactions get coordinated across the two components? If, the answer is yes, "who" does the coordination?

✦ When one component makes a request of another component, "who" ensures that that request is acted on, acted on once, and acted on only once? "Who" assumes this responsibility when the components are on two widely separated machines?

✦ If a component providing a fundamental service is running on a really busy server; "who" notices and starts another copy of that component on a less busy server?

If we think about these questions in the context of transactions or distributed applications, they seem like pretty important questions. When we think about them in terms of components themselves, though, their importance becomes magnified substantially. If we are ever to get to a world where applications can be assembled from components, then we better figure out who that "who" is. The answer, of course, is that that "who" is central, and it is the component coordinator. Let's see how it actually works.

MAGICALLY TRAPPING INTERFACE REQUESTS

At the center of any component environment is the interface. Most of the magic of the component environment itself derives from the fact that the component environment literally *traps* all interface interactions. Thus, there is code written as part of the component environment itself that is able to see every method invocation, every argument passed in, every result passed back. Since that component kernel sees all this interaction going back and forth, it can process those interactions, queue them, modify them, make decisions about them, basically do anything it wants with them. Also, since there is this intelligent agent that can filter and process all interface interactions, the possibility becomes available for the application to talk to that agent itself, to give it hints and instructions about how requests should be handled.

For example, an application can now tell the component kernel whenever a transaction begins or ends. The kernel can then ensure that, no matter how many databases and no matter how many servers are involved, the transaction coordinator is invoked to coordinate the transactions across all the databases and all the machines. And once it has been told about the transaction, all of that invocation can happen transparently. This is more magic than it might appear on the surface. For instance, suppose our application calls a database on a remote server, in the middle of a transaction. How does the remote database even know that a transaction is in progress? The local database knows. But that local database doesn't necessarily know about the remote database, and vice versa. Aside from the application itself, the only agent in a position to keep track of all the communication — to local machines and remote ones — is that component kernel.

In a similar way, the application can tell the kernel that a series of method invocations are to be classified as real enough-time. Now, the application makes the calls normally. (Calls of this kind can have input only, no output arguments.) The kernel picks up the call and sends it to the remote machine if possible; however, if the machine or the communication link is down, the kernel queues the call and sends it later, even if the calling program has disappeared by the time the call can finally be sent. And most important of all, at the other end, the local kernel guarantees that the call happens exactly once.

Exactly-once execution has tricky, magic implications, too. For example, say a series of calls is part of a transaction. If the power goes out in the middle of the series, the transaction must be rolled back. But just as important, the entire series of calls must all be replayed, even though the original calling program may have long disappeared.

The preceding paragraphs referred quite frequently to the component *kernel*. In fact, that kernel does play a role in the whole interaction, but that role is primarily to trap all those interface interactions and then pass them on. Pass them on? Yes, to a new component called the component coordinator. The point of emphasizing the role of the kernel is simple; by stepping in and examining interface interactions for us, the kernel allows the operation of the component coordinator to be *nearly invisible*. And that is a huge point.

For over 25 years, transaction monitors have offered great advantages in terms of scalability and manageability. Yet, except on the mainframe and a few other special cases like the Tandem, transaction monitors have not been very widely used. Why? Because they called for a different (and generally more difficult) programming model than was used for building smaller applications. The gain was not worth the pain. Adding the requirements of distributed systems and real enough time only makes the situation worse. Now we have a solution.

By building a component coordinator into the heart of the component execution environment, we get all the advantages of a TP Monitor without having to adopt a new programming model at all. And on top of that, we get real enough time and distributed transaction support at the same time. The only question is when will component coordinators become available?

At the time that this edition of the book is being written in 1995, Microsoft has announced a component coordinator tied to COM and OLE; no other vendor has announced such plans. I believe that every major component execution environment will eventually have a component coordinator for the reasons described earlier. After all, if cooperating components is the major wave driving the '90s and the '00s, then this is the critical piece of infrastructure most missing to make it happen.

PUTTING IT ALL TOGETHER: CAN DISTRIBUTED SYSTEMS BE BUILT?

Table 16-5 shows how all the pieces of the technical infrastructure described in this chapter fit together to form a complete system. Naturally, the table has three rows, one for each layer in the application architecture. The second column shows the nature of communication occurring within each row. For example, in the document layer, communication is person to person. Finally, the third column shows the type of activity happening in the respective layers: transactions in the database layer, sequences of tasks in the business rules layer, and discrete tasks in the document layer.

Table 16-5   A Complete System Formed by the Pieces of the Technical Infrastructure

Layer	Type of Communication	Type of Activity
Document	Person to person	Discrete tasks
Business rules	Process to process	Task sequences
Database	Database to database	Realtime transactions

The center of the system is the business rules layer, which deals with process-to-process communication. It is in this layer that the extended sequences of tasks that make up business processes are managed and implemented.

Underneath the business processes, the database records every transaction as it occurs, responds to queries, and ensures the integrity of the data. Communication at this level is database to database. The trickiest service provided by this layer is the automatic coordination of distributed transactions so that the requester doesn't have to know that transactions are distributed. The requester can rely on the transaction either finishing cleanly or arranging the database as it was before the transaction started.

From the user's perspective, the desktop applications provide the user with the mechanism to complete discrete tasks. Taken together, these tasks can be viewed as workflow. Workflow is directly related to process flow in two ways. First, any step in the workflow can initiate a long running process consisting of a sequence of tasks extended over time. Entering an order can therefore result in the shipment of orders all around the world over the course of a year. When initiated, the process flow also periodically initiates workflows. For example, when a product is out of stock in Sacramento, the automatic process started by the component coordinator may initiate an alert or perhaps a request for action and then wait for a response. So workflow and process flow, although quite different, are also directly linked.

Putting it all together, we have a very nice technical infrastructure for supporting distributed self-managed teams who are all working as part of a large cooperating organization.

MAY YOU LIVE IN INTERESTING TIMES

The Chinese have a curse: *May you live in interesting times.* As the computer world continues to change at an accelerating rate, it is often hard to keep track of where things are really heading. Stepping back often simplifies this task.

The report card in Table 16-6 shows how the client/server alternative has compared to mainframes over a ten-year period starting in 1985 and stretching slightly into the future. Like most report cards, there are subjects and grades: A+ is a star performance and D represents abject failure. A quick glance shows that I compare the improving client/server world to a supposedly static mainframe technology. That comparison is slightly unfair but also necessary for the purpose of simplicity. To compensate, the report card goes out of its way to be generous to the mainframe.

Table 16-6   An Information Systems Report Card

Subject	Mainframe	Client/server In '85	In '90	In '95
Personal productivity	D	C	A	A+
Office automation	B	D	B	A
DBMS	A	D	B	A
Development tools	B	D	B	A
Development management.	B	D	C	A
Transaction processing	A	D	C	B
User interface	C	C	B+	A
Operational management	A	D	C	B
Reliability	B	B	B	A
Aggregate throughput	B-	C+	B	A

In 1985, the first year in which computer professionals took personal computers and LANs seriously, that report card looked pretty terrible. By any objective measure relevant to the development of applications for running organizations, client/server systems were nowhere. Development tools, serious databases, and transaction-processing facilities were all virtually nonexistent. Even the user interface was hardly any better than the cryptic displays found on either mainframes or UNIX systems. The only reason to even consider a personal computer was the combination of reliability and personal productivity tools. Office automation? Without networks and electronic mail, it just wasn't possible. In terms of reliability, personal computers don't break very often, but backup and other protective facilities weren't available, so when a failure did occur, the results were likely to be pretty terrible. What about the C for personal productivity tools? Although quite powerful, the leading applications of the time — Multimate, WordStar, dBASE II, and 1-2-3 — were still too limited and hard to use to really rate an A or B. The conclusion in 1985 was clear: networked personal computers were great personal appliances, but the technology wasn't available to even think about building serious applications around them, much less distributed systems.

By 1990, the situation had changed, and the result was tantalizing and frustrating at the same time. Personal computer productivity tools had become first-class by then, and as a result, tens of millions now use them daily. Anything that a high-end word processor or engineering workstation could do in 1980, an inexpensive personal computer with shrink-wrapped applications could do by 1990. With the introduction of sophisticated network operating software and electronic mail, client/server office automation was a daily reality in thousands of companies worldwide. Server-based database managers were just becoming available with impressive throughput capabilities and even moderately competent transaction-processing facilities. Development tools that acknowledged the needs of programmers were starting to appear, and some of the operational management facilities required to run production networks were, if not available, at least being talked about. Although serious distributed systems could not be built, it was possible to imagine that they would one day become practical.

What is the state of things as we pass through 1995? Client/server tools such as PowerBuilder and Visual Basic now define in many ways the state of the art in their categories. Databases such as Oracle and SQLserver offer real reliability, distributed system support, and significant transaction throughput. Even tools for managing distributed networks are starting to ship. In areas such as replication, the client/server environment leads the world. Client/server is coming of age.

If you are building a system to be shipped today, don't plan on building a distributed system, but do start taking advantage of client/server technology. If, however, the system you are building doesn't ship for 18 to 36 months, then you'd better start thinking about what the target is. When you're done, do you want to ship software written for the state of the art that exists today or the one that will exist when your system ships? When answering that question, be sure to keep in mind the hugely powerful nature of the Business Process Reengineering cultural transformation. Like it or not, self-managed teams are literally waiting for the systems you will be building in the next five years; they want those systems and they want them sooner rather than later.

PART IV

CONCLUSION:
THE GLOBAL VILLAGE

There is only one chapter left in this book. With a little luck, by now you have a clear view of a new business and organizational world revolving around computers. Computers in this world become tools for much more than just efficiently processing administrative data or quickly crunching numbers. Instead, the computer becomes a tool, a fundamental enabler that provides empowerment. That empowerment means that organizations can operate more efficiently: get more work done, be more effective, and do it in less time. More importantly, by relying on their computers, organizations can offer their customers better products and services. Finally, by enabling employees and teams to do the right things in the right way, the computer plays a fundamental role in making our jobs more interesting and exciting.

The computer systems that will make all of this possible are distributed systems. They will be distributed not so much in a technical sense, but more importantly in the sense that the computers will shift from being servants of central bureaucracy to agents of local teams and departments.

This will not happen without pain and turmoil, and the resulting systems may be more complex than the centralized systems many of us depend on today. That complexity, however, will bring with it the power and freedom so characteristic of decentralization. Yes, trying to understand how dozens, hundreds, or thousands of distributed servers all interact with each other is hard. Understanding all the elements of a decentralized economy is hard, too. Yet by focusing on providing freedom to local teams and organizations, the net result is vastly increased creativity and productivity. That is the future. All of that is pretty exciting in itself, but does it apply only to the business environment?

Is there a role for client/server, and servers in particular, in homes and personal lives? If businesses can offer homes to tens of millions of servers, how many servers will there be if every home has one, too? That is what Chapter 17 is about. It explores how client/server will reach past the office and into the home.

CHAPTER 7

OUT OF THE OFFICE AND INTO THE HOME

To see a world in a grain of sand
And a heaven in a wild flower,
Hold infinity in the palm of your hand
And eternity in an hour.

— William Blake

As this century approaches its close, the world is changing so quickly that few can keep up with it. The technological advances of this century would probably be unimaginable for someone living 100 years ago. The automobile, the telephone, the airplane, the television, mass production, and all the rest of the technology we now take for granted have totally changed civilization. This observation reveals two key points:

✦ Technology really can change society in larger and faster ways than any person, even a farsighted one, can imagine.

✦ The true scope of such changes ultimately has its biggest effect in the homes and lives of ordinary individuals everywhere.

The telephone, the airplane, and the automobile are all good examples of technologies that created huge industries and changed the face of the corporate landscape. But these technologies had their biggest effect on the lives of billions of individuals.

TELEPHONES: CAN THEY BE COST JUSTIFIED?

In many third-world countries today, telephone use is carefully rationed and controlled to save costs. It's not unusual in these situations to find telephones limited to one per department or one per floor — a distribution similar to that of copiers in the rest of the world. Imagine how hard it would be to economically justify putting a telephone on every desk if it was not an accepted necessity. It is more than likely that if telephones were not viewed as virtual entitlements, companies would think twice before giving them to most employees. How did the corporate environment change to the point where virtually every individual in developed countries has at least one telephone both at the office and at home?

The answer to this question lies in realizing the power of the individual and the deep-seated personal need for freedom and control. Individual consumers expressed this need, and this need made the telephone an absolute fact of life in less than half a century. Were it up to corporations alone, telephones would still be expensive, limited, and rare.

Much of the growth of the telephone industry is fueled by individual consumer demand. Cellular telephones are a prime example of a technology whose spread was caused almost entirely by personal purchase decisions. True, the capital investment required to build the infrastructure of cellular networks came from large organizations. However, after the service became available, individuals, valuing their personal productivity more than the initially high cost of the service, created the demand that justifies the original investment and the continued growth of the industry.

In the case of the airplane industry, even with large corporate customers, the real growth of the industry is ultimately fueled by individual travel. The presence of major airports in every city, the availability of frequent flights, and the development of the reservation systems were all driven by the growth of personal demand for convenient and fast long-distance transportation.

It's easy to see how the concept of individual/consumer-driven industrial growth applies to personal computers, but what about client and server? Isn't the client/server concept uniquely suited to corporate and organizational arenas? Not so. Servers will ultimately continue to grow, change, and mature because of both corporate *and* personal consumer demand.

THE HOME SERVER

What could a server possibly do in the home? The server plays three roles in a client/server environment, all appropriate to offices as well as homes:

✦ Manager of shared resources, including communication lines, printers, and databases

✦ Guardian and administrator of rules

✦ Manager of rule-based automated processes that must run all the time

Given these roles, imagine what a server will be doing in the home of the not-too-distant future.

Plugged into the WAN, the server receives at 5:30 a.m. a weather bulletin indicating that enough snow is on the roads to slow traffic. Realizing that the family will have to get up earlier than normal in order to be on time, the computer wakes each family member up a little earlier than usual. For their alarm, the parents get to hear the morning news; the teenagers wake up to gradually increased volume of their favorite radio station; the younger children hear musical chimes over the intercom.

As the family begins to wake up, the server automatically alters the temperature of each room, balancing conservation with comfort and personal preferences. Just as the house temperature stabilizes, the market wakes up. What market? The stock market, of course. Joan, in addition to her responsibilities as wife, mother, and creative housing architect at a nearby firm, manages the family's investments. Acting on her behalf, the household server constantly monitors both the news wire and the stock market feed. Acting on a complex set of rules derived from all the experience Joan has painfully accumulated over the years, the server is always on the lookout for stocks meeting certain criteria. In addition, the server acts on a variety of preset buy and sell rules to keep the stocks in the portfolio under control all the time. On this particular day, by the time Joan reaches the kitchen, the server has completed two trades on her behalf.

All through the night, the server has been interacting with other servers worldwide. Planning ahead, the family has already invited some friends to join them for a week-long celebration of Frank's 40th birthday. Frank's brother, who lives in the UK, can make it for only part of the week and wanted to know if the big dinner planned for the third night could be moved to later in the week. How did the dinner even end up being planned for that third night? Knowing how complex it can be juggling the schedules of many people, Joan and Frank provided the server with a set of about 20 straightforward rules constraining various aspects of the overall week's events: The big dinner can't be on the first or last night; Frank's closest relatives should be at that dinner, and so on. The server has deduced that quite a few other rules apply, including some which are standing rules in the family. For example, the family is never comfortable scheduling any early-morning events after a late-evening event; the family assumes that guests arriving from out of town will be late, and so on. Armed with all these rules, the server tentatively rearranged the night of the dinner, responded to the request from Frank's brother, and posted a notification for Frank and Joan to see first thing in the morning. Not only could Frank's brother receive an immediate answer, but also the server handled the problem without Frank or Joan having to take any action.

Later in the night, after handling the party schedule change, the server noticed that the family's new car was consuming too much gas. The car of course has a server too. Even today, most modern cars have several computers. The digital radio is computer driven; the antilock brakes have a computer, as do the fuel injection and climate control systems. Computers are all around us when we drive. In the interest of safety and engineering simplicity, rather than control everything through one computer, a car typically has several. Because these computers all have memories, mechanics even today can attach a probe and interrogate the computers in cars to see how they are doing. For example, a car's computer may reveal that the car misfires when it's cold and only between 2,500 and 3,000 rpm. A mechanic, after connecting his or her computer to the car's computers, can determine how many times the car has misfired, when the car has misfired, and what caused the problem. Looking into the future, the idea that the household server might talk to the car's computer regularly is not only likely, but a certainty even without significant advances in the state of the art.

Returning to my story, the household server tracks the health of all the family cars. Credit card bills, which arrive directly from the bank's computer, are automatically reconciled, and when a gas charge shows up, the household computer already knows about it from the car. In this case, noticing the problem with the mileage, the server has done some research on its own, checking first with the car manufacturer's network-accessible public database and then with the local public library. A note in the public library describes the particular problem for the make and model of the family car. The server, acting on the family's behalf, schedules an appointment at the car dealer and puts it on the schedule, all done subject to approval.

Finally, around four in the morning, another household's server sends a birthday party invitation to Cathy, the six-year-old daughter. The server places the invitation (which includes a cute, animated graphic) into the mailboxes of both Cathy and her parents. Knowing that Cathy is best friends with the girl inviting her to the party, the server sends a positive reply on her behalf. The only problem is that Cathy was scheduled for a dentist appointment at the same time. By talking to the dentist's office computer, the server moves the appointment to another time, being careful not to upset any other arrangements in the process. It then lets Joan know what it has done.

By the time the family finally straggles into the kitchen, they discover that their server has really been quite busy on their behalf while they slept. Reaching out to local servers and distant databases, coordinating with a server in another country, buying and selling stocks, checking the weather, arranging and rearranging appointments, researching car problems, and generally acting as an intelligent intermediary, the server turns out to be a very useful servant, to say the least. Much more than just an arcane computing device, the server is a virtual extension of the family itself.

THE MORE THINGS CHANGE, THE MORE THEY *DON'T* STAY THE SAME

The problem with seeing into the future is that we humans are all pretty poor at forecasting true change. It's easy to forecast different ways of doing the same things. When it comes to forecasting different ways of doing *different* things, it's quite hard. That's why the French saying, *the more things change, the more they stay the same,* makes so much sense.

At the beginning of this century, Henry Ford predicted that automobiles would make it possible for city dwellers to visit the country. The automobile actually extended the city into the country, creating suburbia and converting large parts of the countryside into housing developments. Ford's view of the future was an *extrapolation* of the present. Mathematically, extrapolation means extending the line of a graph into an unknown interval based on data from a known interval. In the case of Ford's erroneous extrapolation of cars and cities, people lived in cities, and cars allowed them to travel farther and faster; therefore, people would visit the country more often.

Looking into the future, most people love to extrapolate because they are so uncomfortable with true change. The entire century, though, has been one of *discontinuous change* rather than extrapolation. Referring back to mathematics, a discontinuity appears on a graph in the form of a completely new line starting from a completely new place and replacing the old one. Cars didn't take city dwellers into the country; they replaced the country with suburbs.

As the first *integrated circuits* — chips with hundreds of transistors on them — were becoming common in the late 1960s, a new generation of typewriters was just catching the imaginations of office workers around the world. The typewriter, after all, was a fixture in every office — an appliance that could never disappear. Everybody with any sense could see that. Electronic technology, though, *could* make typewriters better, so the *mag card correcting typewriter* was introduced. Capable of storing up to a page of text on a flexible magnetic card made out of plastic, this new typewriter could type and retype text and handle simple corrections. At the same time, technologists were starting to talk about newfangled *word processors*, but given the tens of millions of typewriters and trained typists, such talk was clearly wishful thinking at best. Today, both the typewriter and many of the people who used them are gone. Word processing is a standard operation that's intrinsic to virtually every personal computer application. The more things change, the more they *don't* stay the same. Typewriters don't become fancier; city dwellers don't just visit the country more frequently. The landscape changes.

A SERVER IN EVERY OFFICE

Several times in this book, I've discussed the idea of having a server in every office. Every office means every location at which people work: every church, movie theater, retail store, restaurant, school, warehouse, dentist's office, public park, community swimming pool, sales office, hotel, art gallery, veterinarian's office — need I say more? What are these servers, these tens of millions of computers that will be everywhere in the future? At one level, they are appliances. Wherever there's a front door with a lock on it, a telephone line, and electricity, there will be one of these appliances. If you are thinking of setting up a store, an office, or a warehouse, plan on having a server sitting in the corner minding the business.

"Minding the business" refers to the material this book covers: business rules and databases. I hope that by now, the details of managing these two concepts are anything but magical. With a handle on how to mind the business, how will things change in the future?

At one level, the sheer ubiquitousness of servers results in change. As they become cheap and the software they use becomes available, businesses of all sizes will take advantage of the technology. In very large companies, small offices are a real problem today. Huge companies typically have sales and service organizations in very small places. The computer solutions that work extremely well in skyscrapers or offices of 50 don't work at all in 2- or 3-person field locations. With a server costing a few thousand dollars or less, every location will finally have one.

Cost isn't the only factor in making servers ubiquitous. Hardware and its software need to become totally self-installing. Complex interrupt conflicts, arcane batch files, and obscure installation procedures have no place in a world with tens of millions of servers. Will cheap computers, self-installing software, and omnipresent installation and support be enough? Will these factors lead to a significantly changed world? One more element ties it all together.

CONNECTIONS: IT'S NOT WHAT YOU KNOW BUT WHOM YOU KNOW

Just having servers, no matter how powerful, cheap, and easy to use, isn't quite enough. These servers need to be connected together in a global network. The fact that it is the servers that are connected and not the people who use them is a subtle but critical point. As it turns out, those servers become our servers and agents, both in the office and at home, and it is the very fact that those servers can work together instead of alone that makes them so useful.

Make no mistake: just providing access to servers and their databases worldwide will be incredibly useful, but that service will not be quite enough in the future. In any event, I will explore that first step and imagine out loud some of the various things that will be possible:

✦ You will review your bank statements, credit card status, and other financial information on-line. You will pay your bills by arranging for the automatic transfer of money from one account to another.

✦ From your personal computer in the office or at home, you will make flight reservations, compare fares, and sort through various routing alternatives.

✦ You will search for names and phone numbers at your computer screen, not just in your local calling area, but across the entire country. Searching for particular stores or services by subject will be much simpler because the electronic yellow pages, instead of listing each phone number under the one heading judged most common, will list all numbers under as many headings as possible. Combining the low cost of phone books with the up-to-date nature of directory assistance, the computer will always have the most current number.

✦ Shopping in electronic supermarkets, you will price goods and services at hundreds of stores across the country. Specialized goods will be tracked using electronic indexing systems. When ordered, products will typically arrive the next morning, even if ordered as late as midnight the day before.

✦ Electronic mail will allow you to carry on conversations with friends and colleagues around the world at literally light speed.

✦ Electronic bulletin boards will provide discussion forums on thousands of topics, so you will be able to either research current issues quickly or participate in areas of interest over long periods of time.

✦ Specialized databases will cover company histories for investors, legal precedents for lawyers, technical and scientific papers in hundreds of disciplines, and medical research findings. All of this will allow professionals to explore sophisticated issues without leaving their desks.

The surprising thing is that all these possibilities are available today. Every one of them is used by communities numbering in the millions, but the vast majority of the billions of people alive today have no idea that these services are even available. Today's electronic databases and servers point to the future, but they hardly demonstrate what it will really be like. Why? Is it price? Availability? Complexity? The answer involves all of these issues, but there's more to consider.

First, consider price and availability. Today's electronic services require access to a terminal or personal computer. In addition, they require that the customer be willing to pay significant monthly fees. Worse, the fees are open-ended so that the more you use, the more you pay. These factors alone are a very real barrier.

Over a decade ago in France, the government decided to make phone books extinct. To make this change possible, inexpensive terminals were distributed, at no cost, to every telephone subscriber. These terminals provided access to a computerized telephone directory system, which was also available at no charge. In a stroke of genius, the government then offered third parties the opportunity to sell additional services to its subscribers by using the terminals and network already in place. The result is a huge and prosperous aftermarket used by tens of millions for a variety of purposes. Products are advertised and sold. Theaters, cinemas, and other places of entertainment buy listings. Electronic mail flourishes. In an interesting twist, both romance and pornography have turned out to be key parts of the system. Because the communication system is so widespread, hundreds of thousands of subscribers use their terminals to arrange liaisons and carry on romantic relationships over the ether. The French experiment demonstrates conclusively that computer-based communication can catch on in a big way and even change the culture in at least a small way. Yet, even in France, the system has had only a limited impact on the way people live and work. Why?

HAVE MY SERVER CALL YOUR SERVER

Reconciling a checkbook is truly one of life's small hardships. Despite the growing popularity of home accounting software, most people still balance their accounts by hand. Why? This particular question has another equally puzzling side. Many banks have invested heavily in the development of home banking systems that allow customers, corporate and personal, to do their banking from a personal computer. In spite of heavy marketing, most of these services never saw widespread use. One more time: why?

The answer to all these questions lies in one answer: repetitive tasks and duplicated information. For example, home accounting software works well only if the user painstakingly enters the details of every expenditure into the computer. Home banking, for all its superficial appeal, also requires the user to enter the details of all payments, and when all is said and done, all of the reconciliation of the information displayed by the bank computer must still be done by hand. What if the two systems could be connected together?

If the bank computer could automatically post to the home accounting software the details of credit card transactions, cashed checks, and deposits, then wouldn't both systems suddenly become useful? Suppose that as stocks are bought and sold, the brokerage computer is updating the home accounting system too. How about the store's computer? It's Saturday night and you suddenly want to know how much a saddle might cost for your daughter's next birthday. The tack store you normally buy from is closed, but its server is on duty. You check on the price, order the saddle, and request that it be held until you can pick it up. The store's computer charges your credit card account, and your home computer tracks the expenditure and makes ready to reconcile it against the credit card statement when it arrives from the bank's computer at the end of the month.

What about purchases made away from the home? In the not-too-distant future, your credit card will become a wallet-sized computer too. Every night when you return home, the credit card will update the home server so that you can have a running total of how badly your account is hurting. In theory, the wallet computer can be thought of as a personal computer. In practice, there is virtually no interaction between the user and this kind of computer. That computer riding around in your pocket will be a portable pocket server. The thing that makes that portable server so valuable is precisely the fact that it can talk to other servers on your behalf. In fact, it is only after talking to other servers, particularly the one in your home, that the information in your pocket server even becomes available to you. After your credit card brings your home server up-to-date, your home server will update your home accounting system. Sitting at your personal computer, you will then review your expenses. This convenience will exist because the servers talk to each other.

In the home and in the office, the server becomes a tireless servant, an autonomous agent dealing on its owner's behalf with other servers distributed around the world. It is precisely the fact that these servers are all connected that makes it all work.

THE GLOBAL VILLAGE

In the town or village of the 19th century, everybody knew everybody else. Life was much more informal, and most things could be arranged by traveling a short distance on foot or horseback. Goods and services from other cities and towns, let alone other countries, were hard to come by, so nobody expected to have access to these goods and services anyway. Life was simpler.

Today, the supermarket or shopping center exposes us to dizzying variety; the world is literally within earshot; life is far richer and also far more complex. The problem is to determine how to keep up with it all. Acting as servant, the computer, in the form of a server, offers the potential for returning us to the slower-paced life of the 19th century village while retaining the richness of the 20th century.

For organizations of all sizes, this change will mean understanding the true implications of server-based and server-supported processes. As a first step, the server, the client, the LAN, and the WAN offer an important architecture that makes many of the benefits offered by Business Process Reengineering possible. A direct consequence of that first step is the facilitation of self-managed-teams. As these teams grow used to depending on their ever-present server, a new world of information will open up to them. This information will allow these teams to understand their products, their customers, and their processes in ways that have never been possible before. Sophisticated information analysis will no longer be the exclusive domain of senior management and the MBAs that support them. Moving beyond asking questions, self-managed teams will quickly customize and develop their own applications to meet the local needs of themselves and their customers. All of this is revolutionary, but it is only the beginning.

One direct consequence of Business Process Reengineering will be the increasing automation of many processes handled manually today. A core tenet of reengineering is the elimination of queues. Each eliminated queue represents either the removal of a step or the automatic handling of a step by a computer. Each mechanical task handled automatically by a computer is a task that no longer need be handled by a person, freeing that person to design products, make sales, handle complaints, and interact with team members. Of course, the tasks referred to so far are internal tasks, within organizations. If tasks can be eliminated within organizations, why not eliminate them externally as well?

Many companies worldwide are already implementing a technology called *electronic data interchange* (*EDI*) which allows trading partners to deal commercially through computers. What? EDI allows a manufacturing computer to order parts from a warehouse computer even if the computers are owned by different companies. After the parts are shipped, the two companies exchange invoices and payment automatically by having one computer talk to another with no humans involved. More queues are eliminated; more processes automated; and servers, talking to servers. This communication is critical. The server is serving its team in the foreground and in the background too.

Eventually, almost every server in the world will wear three faces. One face will be the one it presents to its interactive users — the people who talk to it directly. Some servers may never wear this face in the world of the future because so much of their work will be automatic. The second face each server will wear will be the one it presents to other servers within its own organization. Organizations will run around the clock as these servers tirelessly talk to each other to keep things going all the time. In homes, the scheduling and information server will talk to the security server, the environmental server, the servers in the cars, and the servers riding in each resident's pockets.

Finally, the third and most important face each server will wear will be the one it presents to other servers in the outside world. Need some product from your local store after hours? No problem: your server talks to its server. Change the doctor's appointment? The office server is always available. Need information from the local library? The library may be closed, but its server never is. Suppose that your library doesn't have the information you need. Still not a problem because the library's server knows how to find that information for you. Suppose that the search might take a few days? How about having the library server return information as it finds it to your home or office server over the course of the next week? You can check the status of the search at any time by looking in the relevant folder.

All of this raises some interesting questions about life in the future. Every person, professionally and personally, has trouble keeping up with the rate at which events, decisions, and information are rushing at us. A personal computer may help users deal with the events, decisions, and information more productively, but beneath the surface, the real truth is that users just don't want to deal with most of that data at all.

Users want somebody else to do it for them. The server is that personal secretary, servant, agent, or whatever — an always turned on, always up-to-date decision maker that helps to slow life down just a little. That's the client/server world of the future.

At one level, every organization and every provider of goods or services needs to think about how it will arrange for its computer-based service provider to come into existence. After customers and partner organizations get used to the idea that their server will talk to your server, suddenly nothing else will be acceptable. Not having access to information will be unacceptable. Although servers that are servants don't exist today, they will tomorrow. And when they do, they will quickly become not just convenient, but also necessary.

This discussion leads to one last question: What is the role of an office, a warehouse, a factory, or even a store when servers are talking to servers? Meeting people face to face, inspecting and trying out products in person, traveling to a clinic for medical care — these interactions will still be necessary. At the same time, many of the aspects of today's society may not be necessary or acceptable anymore when the new server/servants come to exist. The car did make it easier to reach the country. The computer does make it easier to complete many of today's tasks and processes. Within a relatively short period of time, however, the car also changed the city and the country by creating the suburbs. What will be the impact of the computer on the city, the country, and the people who live in them?

It's hard to really tell, but the hope is that by potentially extending the ability of every person to reach out into the world, communicate more effectively with others, and gain more control over our work and our lives, the computer will not only speed things up, but also slow them down. Someday, perhaps we really will "see a world in a grain of sand/And a heaven in a wild flower."

INDEX

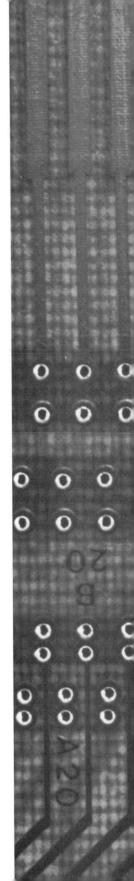

B

C

D

(continued)

The Fun & Easy Way™ to learn about computers and more!

9/19/95

Windows® 3.11 For Dummies® 3rd Edition
by Andy Rathbone

ISBN: 1-56884-370-4
$16.95 USA/
$22.95 Canada

SUPER STAR

Mutual Funds For Dummies™
by Eric Tyson

ISBN: 1-56884-226-0
$16.99 USA/
$22.99 Canada

SUPER STAR

DOS For Dummies® 2nd Edition
by Dan Gookin

ISBN: 1-878058-75-4
$16.95 USA/
$22.95 Canada

SUPER STAR

The Internet For Dummies® 2nd Edition
by John Levine & Carol Baroudi

ISBN: 1-56884-222-8
$19.99 USA/
$26.99 Canada

Personal Finance For Dummies™
by Eric Tyson

ISBN: 1-56884-150-7
$16.95 USA/
$22.95 Canada

PCs For Dummies® 3rd Edition
by Dan Gookin & Andy Rathbone

ISBN: 1-56884-904-4
$16.95 USA/
$22.99 Canada

Macs® For Dummies® 3rd Edition
by David Pogue

ISBN: 1-56884-239-2
$19.99 USA/
$26.99 Canada

SUPER STAR

The SAT® I For Dummies™
by Suzee Vlk

ISBN: 1-56884-213-9
$14.99 USA/
$20.99 Canada

SUPER STAR

Here's a complete listing of IDG Books' ...For Dummies® titles

Title	Author	ISBN	Price
DATABASE			
Access 2 For Dummies®	by Scott Palmer	ISBN: 1-56884-090-X	$19.95 USA/$26.95 Canada
Access Programming For Dummies®	by Rob Krumm	ISBN: 1-56884-091-8	$19.95 USA/$26.95 Canada
Approach 3 For Windows® For Dummies®	by Doug Lowe	ISBN: 1-56884-233-3	$19.99 USA/$26.99 Canada
dBASE For DOS For Dummies®	by Scott Palmer & Michael Stabler	ISBN: 1-56884-188-4	$19.95 USA/$26.95 Canada
dBASE For Windows® For Dummies®	by Scott Palmer	ISBN: 1-56884-179-5	$19.95 USA/$26.95 Canada
dBASE 5 For Windows® Programming For Dummies®	by Ted Coombs & Jason Coombs	ISBN: 1-56884-215-5	$19.99 USA/$26.99 Canada
FoxPro 2.6 For Windows® For Dummies®	by John Kaufeld	ISBN: 1-56884-187-6	$19.95 USA/$26.95 Canada
Paradox 5 For Windows® For Dummies®	by John Kaufeld	ISBN: 1-56884-185-X	$19.95 USA/$26.95 Canada
DESKTOP PUBLISHING/ILLUSTRATION/GRAPHICS			
CorelDRAW! 5 For Dummies®	by Deke McClelland	ISBN: 1-56884-157-4	$19.95 USA/$26.95 Canada
CorelDRAW! For Dummies®	by Deke McClelland	ISBN: 1-56884-042-X	$19.95 USA/$26.95 Canada
Desktop Publishing & Design For Dummies®	by Roger C. Parker	ISBN: 1-56884-234-1	$19.99 USA/$26.99 Canada
Harvard Graphics 2 For Windows® For Dummies®	by Roger C. Parker	ISBN: 1-56884-092-6	$19.95 USA/$26.95 Canada
PageMaker 5 For Macs® For Dummies®	by Galen Gruman & Deke McClelland	ISBN: 1-56884-178-7	$19.95 USA/$26.95 Canada
PageMaker 5 For Windows® For Dummies®	by Deke McClelland & Galen Gruman	ISBN: 1-56884-160-4	$19.95 USA/$26.95 Canada
Photoshop 3 For Macs® For Dummies®	by Deke McClelland	ISBN: 1-56884-208-2	$19.99 USA/$26.99 Canada
QuarkXPress 3.3 For Dummies®	by Galen Gruman & Barbara Assadi	ISBN: 1-56884-217-1	$19.99 USA/$26.99 Canada
FINANCE/PERSONAL FINANCE/TEST TAKING REFERENCE			
Everyday Math For Dummies™	by Charles Seiter	ISBN: 1-56884-248-1	$14.99 USA/$22.99 Canada
Personal Finance For Dummies™ For Canadians	by Eric Tyson & Tony Martin	ISBN: 1-56884-378-X	$18.99 USA/$24.99 Canada
QuickBooks 3 For Dummies®	by Stephen L. Nelson	ISBN: 1-56884-227-9	$19.99 USA/$26.99 Canada
Quicken 8 For DOS For Dummies® 2nd Edition	by Stephen L. Nelson	ISBN: 1-56884-210-4	$19.95 USA/$26.95 Canada
Quicken 5 For Macs® For Dummies®	by Stephen L. Nelson	ISBN: 1-56884-211-2	$19.95 USA/$26.95 Canada
Quicken 4 For Windows® For Dummies® 2nd Edition	by Stephen L. Nelson	ISBN: 1-56884-209-0	$19.95 USA/$26.95 Canada
Taxes For Dummies™ 1995 Edition	by Eric Tyson & David J. Silverman	ISBN: 1-56884-220-1	$14.99 USA/$20.99 Canada
The GMAT® For Dummies™	by Suzee Vlk, Series Editor	ISBN: 1-56884-376-3	$14.99 USA/$20.99 Canada
The GRE® For Dummies™	by Suzee Vlk, Series Editor	ISBN: 1-56884-375-5	$14.99 USA/$20.99 Canada
Time Management For Dummies™	by Jeffrey J. Mayer	ISBN: 1-56884-360-7	$16.99 USA/$22.99 Canada
TurboTax For Windows® For Dummies®	by Gail A. Helsel, CPA	ISBN: 1-56884-228-7	$19.99 USA/$26.99 Canada
GROUPWARE/INTEGRATED			
ClarisWorks For Macs® For Dummies®	by Frank Higgins	ISBN: 1-56884-363-1	$19.99 USA/$26.99 Canada
Lotus Notes For Dummies®	by Pat Freeland & Stephen Londergan	ISBN: 1-56884-212-0	$19.95 USA/$26.95 Canada
Microsoft® Office 4 For Windows® For Dummies®	by Roger C. Parker	ISBN: 1-56884-183-3	$19.95 USA/$26.95 Canada
Microsoft® Works 3 For Windows® For Dummies®	by David C. Kay	ISBN: 1-56884-214-7	$19.99 USA/$26.99 Canada
SmartSuite 3 For Dummies®	by Jan Weingarten & John Weingarten	ISBN: 1-56884-367-4	$19.99 USA/$26.99 Canada
INTERNET/COMMUNICATIONS/NETWORKING			
America Online® For Dummies® 2nd Edition	by John Kaufeld	ISBN: 1-56884-933-8	$19.99 USA/$26.99 Canada
CompuServe For Dummies® 2nd Edition	by Wallace Wang	ISBN: 1-56884-937-0	$19.99 USA/$26.99 Canada
Modems For Dummies® 2nd Edition	by Tina Rathbone	ISBN: 1-56884-223-6	$19.99 USA/$26.99 Canada
MORE Internet For Dummies®	by John R. Levine & Margaret Levine Young	ISBN: 1-56884-164-7	$19.95 USA/$26.95 Canada
MORE Modems & On-line Services For Dummies®	by Tina Rathbone	ISBN: 1-56884-365-8	$19.99 USA/$26.99 Canada
Mosaic For Dummies® Windows Edition	by David Angell & Brent Heslop	ISBN: 1-56884-242-2	$19.99 USA/$26.99 Canada
NetWare For Dummies® 2nd Edition	by Ed Tittel, Deni Connor & Earl Follis	ISBN: 1-56884-369-0	$19.99 USA/$26.99 Canada
Networking For Dummies®	by Doug Lowe	ISBN: 1-56884-079-9	$19.95 USA/$26.95 Canada
PROCOMM PLUS 2 For Windows® For Dummies®	by Wallace Wang	ISBN: 1-56884-219-3	$19.99 USA/$26.99 Canada
TCP/IP For Dummies®	by Marshall Wilensky & Candace Leiden	ISBN: 1-56884-241-4	$19.99 USA/$26.99 Canada

Microsoft and Windows are registered trademarks of Microsoft Corporation. Mac is a registered trademark of Apple Computer. SAT is a registered trademark of the College Entrance Examination Board. GMAT is a registered trademark of the Graduate Management Admission Council. GRE is a registered trademark of the Educational Testing Service. America Online is a registered trademark of America Online, Inc. The "...For Dummies Book Series" logo, the IDG Books Worldwide logos, Dummies Press, and The Fun & Easy Way are trademarks, and ---- For Dummies and ... For Dummies are registered trademarks under exclusive license to IDG Books Worldwide, Inc., from International Data Group, Inc.

r scholastic requests & educational orders please
l Educational Sales at 1. 800. 434. 2086

FOR MORE INFO OR TO ORDER, PLEASE CALL ▶ 800. 762. 2974

For volume discounts & special orders please call
Tony Real, Special Sales, at 415. 655. 3048

Title	Author	ISBN	Price
The Internet For Macs® For Dummies,® 2nd Edition	by Charles Seiter	ISBN: 1-56884-371-2	$19.99 USA/$26.99 Canada
The Internet For Macs® For Dummies® Starter Kit	by Charles Seiter	ISBN: 1-56884-244-9	$29.99 USA/$39.99 Canada
The Internet For Macs® For Dummies® Starter Kit Bestseller Edition	by Charles Seiter	ISBN: 1-56884-245-7	$39.99 USA/$54.99 Canada
The Internet For Windows® For Dummies® Starter Kit	by John R. Levine & Margaret Levine Young	ISBN: 1-56884-237-6	$34.99 USA/$44.99 Canada
The Internet For Windows® For Dummies® Starter Kit, Bestseller Edition	by John R. Levine & Margaret Levine Young	ISBN: 1-56884-246-5	$39.99 USA/$54.99 Canada

MACINTOSH

Title	Author	ISBN	Price
Mac® Programming For Dummies®	by Dan Parks Sydow	ISBN: 1-56884-173-6	$19.95 USA/$26.95 Canada
Macintosh® System 7.5 For Dummies®	by Bob LeVitus	ISBN: 1-56884-197-3	$19.95 USA/$26.95 Canada
MORE Macs® For Dummies®	by David Pogue	ISBN: 1-56884-087-X	$19.95 USA/$26.95 Canada
PageMaker 5 For Macs® For Dummies®	by Galen Gruman & Deke McClelland	ISBN: 1-56884-178-7	$19.95 USA/$26.95 Canada
QuarkXPress 3.3 For Dummies®	by Galen Gruman & Barbara Assadi	ISBN: 1-56884-217-1	$19.95 USA/$26.95 Canada
Upgrading and Fixing Macs® For Dummies®	by Kearney Rietmann & Frank Higgins	ISBN: 1-56884-189-2	$19.99 USA/$26.99 Canada

MULTIMEDIA

Title	Author	ISBN	Price
Multimedia & CD-ROMs For Dummies,® 2nd Edition	by Andy Rathbone	ISBN: 1-56884-907-9	$19.99 USA/$26.99 Canada
Multimedia & CD-ROMs For Dummies Interactive Multimedia Value Pack, 2nd Edition	by Andy Rathbone	ISBN: 1-56884-909-5	$29.99 USA/$39.99 Canada

OPERATING SYSTEMS:

DOS

Title	Author	ISBN	Price
MORE DOS For Dummies®	by Dan Gookin	ISBN: 1-56884-046-2	$19.95 USA/$26.95 Canada
OS/2® Warp For Dummies,® 2nd Edition	by Andy Rathbone	ISBN: 1-56884-205-8	$19.99 USA/$26.99 Canada

UNIX

Title	Author	ISBN	Price
MORE UNIX® For Dummies®	by John R. Levine & Margaret Levine Young	ISBN: 1-56884-361-5	$19.99 USA/$26.99 Canada
UNIX® For Dummies®	by John R. Levine & Margaret Levine Young	ISBN: 1-878058-58-4	$19.95 USA/$26.95 Canada

WINDOWS

Title	Author	ISBN	Price
MORE Windows® For Dummies,® 2nd Edition	by Andy Rathbone	ISBN: 1-56884-048-9	$19.95 USA/$26.95 Canada
Windows® 95 For Dummies®	by Andy Rathbone	ISBN: 1-56884-240-6	$19.99 USA/$26.99 Canada

PCS/HARDWARE

Title	Author	ISBN	Price
Illustrated Computer Dictionary For Dummies,® 2nd Edition	by Dan Gookin & Wallace Wang	ISBN: 1-56884-218-X	$12.95 USA/$16.95 Canada
Upgrading and Fixing PCs For Dummies,® 2nd Edition	by Andy Rathbone	ISBN: 1-56884-903-6	$19.99 USA/$26.99 Canada

PRESENTATION/AUTOCAD

Title	Author	ISBN	Price
AutoCAD For Dummies®	by Bud Smith	ISBN: 1-56884-191-4	$19.95 USA/$26.95 Canada
PowerPoint 4 For Windows® For Dummies®	by Doug Lowe	ISBN: 1-56884-161-2	$16.99 USA/$22.99 Canada

PROGRAMMING

Title	Author	ISBN	Price
Borland C++ For Dummies®	by Michael Hyman	ISBN: 1-56884-162-0	$19.95 USA/$26.95 Canada
C For Dummies,® Volume 1	by Dan Gookin	ISBN: 1-878058-78-9	$19.95 USA/$26.95 Canada
C++ For Dummies®	by Stephen R. Davis	ISBN: 1-56884-163-9	$19.95 USA/$26.95 Canada
Delphi Programming For Dummies®	by Neil Rubenking	ISBN: 1-56884-200-7	$19.99 USA/$26.99 Canada
Mac® Programming For Dummies®	by Dan Parks Sydow	ISBN: 1-56884-173-6	$19.95 USA/$26.95 Canada
PowerBuilder 4 Programming For Dummies®	by Ted Coombs & Jason Coombs	ISBN: 1-56884-325-9	$19.99 USA/$26.99 Canada
QBasic Programming For Dummies®	by Douglas Hergert	ISBN: 1-56884-093-4	$19.95 USA/$26.95 Canada
Visual Basic 3 For Dummies®	by Wallace Wang	ISBN: 1-56884-076-4	$19.95 USA/$26.95 Canada
Visual Basic "X" For Dummies®	by Wallace Wang	ISBN: 1-56884-230-9	$19.99 USA/$26.99 Canada
Visual C++ 2 For Dummies®	by Michael Hyman & Bob Arnson	ISBN: 1-56884-328-3	$19.99 USA/$26.99 Canada
Windows® 95 Programming For Dummies®	by S. Randy Davis	ISBN: 1-56884-327-5	$19.99 USA/$26.99 Canada

SPREADSHEET

Title	Author	ISBN	Price
1-2-3 For Dummies®	by Greg Harvey	ISBN: 1-878058-60-6	$16.95 USA/$22.95 Canada
1-2-3 For Windows® 5 For Dummies,® 2nd Edition	by John Walkenbach	ISBN: 1-56884-216-3	$16.95 USA/$22.95 Canada
Excel 5 For Macs® For Dummies®	by Greg Harvey	ISBN: 1-56884-186-8	$19.95 USA/$26.95 Canada
Excel For Dummies,® 2nd Edition	by Greg Harvey	ISBN: 1-56884-050-0	$16.95 USA/$22.95 Canada
MORE 1-2-3 For DOS For Dummies®	by John Weingarten	ISBN: 1-56884-224-4	$19.99 USA/$26.99 Canada
MORE Excel 5 For Windows® For Dummies®	by Greg Harvey	ISBN: 1-56884-207-4	$19.95 USA/$26.95 Canada
Quattro Pro 6 For Windows® For Dummies®	by John Walkenbach	ISBN: 1-56884-174-4	$19.95 USA/$26.95 Canada
Quattro Pro For DOS For Dummies®	by John Walkenbach	ISBN: 1-56884-023-3	$16.95 USA/$22.95 Canada

UTILITIES

Title	Author	ISBN	Price
Norton Utilities 8 For Dummies®	by Beth Slick	ISBN: 1-56884-166-3	$19.95 USA/$26.95 Canada

VCRS/CAMCORDERS

Title	Author	ISBN	Price
VCRs & Camcorders For Dummies™	by Gordon McComb & Andy Rathbone	ISBN: 1-56884-229-5	$14.99 USA/$20.99 Canada

WORD PROCESSING

Title	Author	ISBN	Price
Ami Pro For Dummies®	by Jim Meade	ISBN: 1-56884-049-7	$19.95 USA/$26.95 Canada
MORE Word For Windows® 6 For Dummies®	by Doug Lowe	ISBN: 1-56884-165-5	$19.95 USA/$26.95 Canada
MORE WordPerfect® 6 For Windows® For Dummies®	by Margaret Levine Young & David C. Kay	ISBN: 1-56884-206-6	$19.95 USA/$26.95 Canada
MORE WordPerfect® 6 For DOS For Dummies®	by Wallace Wang, edited by Dan Gookin	ISBN: 1-56884-047-0	$19.95 USA/$26.95 Canada
Word 6 For Macs® For Dummies®	by Dan Gookin	ISBN: 1-56884-190-6	$19.95 USA/$26.95 Canada
Word For Windows® 6 For Dummies®	by Dan Gookin	ISBN: 1-56884-075-6	$16.95 USA/$22.95 Canada
Word For Windows® For Dummies®	by Dan Gookin & Ray Werner	ISBN: 1-878058-86-X	$16.95 USA/$22.95 Canada
WordPerfect® 6 For DOS For Dummies®	by Dan Gookin	ISBN: 1-878058-77-0	$16.95 USA/$22.95 Canada
WordPerfect® 6.1 For Windows® For Dummies,® 2nd Edition	by Margaret Levine Young & David Kay	ISBN: 1-56884-243-0	$16.95 USA/$22.95 Canada
WordPerfect® For Dummies®	by Dan Gookin	ISBN: 1-878058-52-5	$16.95 USA/$22.95 Canada

Windows is a registered trademark of Microsoft Corporation. Mac is a registered trademark of Apple Computer. OS/2 is a registered trademark of IBM. UNIX is a registered trademark of AT&T. WordPerfect is a registered trademark of Novell. The "...For Dummies Book Series" logo, the IDG Books Worldwide logos, Dummies Press, and The Fun & Easy Way are trademarks, and ---- For Dummies and ... For Dummies are registered trademarks under exclusive license to IDG Books Worldwide, Inc., from International Data Group, Inc.

For scholastic requests & educational orders please call Educational Sales at 1. 800. 434. 2086

FOR MORE INFO OR TO ORDER, PLEASE CALL ▸ 800. 762. 2974

For volume discounts & special orders please call Tony Real, Special Sales, at 415. 655. 3048

NEW!

The Internet For Macs® For Dummies® Quick Reference
by Charles Seiter

ISBN:1-56884-967-2
$9.99 USA/$12.99 Canada

NEW!

Windows® 95 For Dummies® Quick Reference
by Greg Harvey

ISBN: 1-56884-964-8
$9.99 USA/$12.99 Canada

SUPER STAR

Photoshop 3 For Macs® For Dummies® Quick Reference
by Deke McClelland

ISBN: 1-56884-968-0
$9.99 USA/$12.99 Canada

SUPER STAR

WordPerfect® For DOS For Dummies® Quick Reference
by Greg Harvey

ISBN: 1-56884-009-8
$8.95 USA/$12.95 Canada

Title	Author	ISBN	Price
DATABASE			
Access 2 For Dummies® Quick Reference	by Stuart J. Stuple	ISBN: 1-56884-167-1	$8.95 USA/$11.95 Canada
dBASE 5 For DOS For Dummies® Quick Reference	by Barrie Sosinsky	ISBN: 1-56884-954-0	$9.99 USA/$12.99 Canada
dBASE 5 For Windows® For Dummies® Quick Reference	by Stuart J. Stuple	ISBN: 1-56884-953-2	$9.99 USA/$12.99 Canada
Paradox 5 For Windows® For Dummies® Quick Reference	by Scott Palmer	ISBN: 1-56884-960-5	$9.99 USA/$12.99 Canada
DESKTOP PUBLISHING/ILLUSTRATION/GRAPHICS			
CorelDRAW! 5 For Dummies® Quick Reference	by Raymond E. Werner	ISBN: 1-56884-952-4	$9.99 USA/$12.99 Canada
Harvard Graphics For Windows® For Dummies® Quick Reference	by Raymond E. Werner	ISBN: 1-56884-962-1	$9.99 USA/$12.99 Canada
Photoshop 3 For Macs® For Dummies® Quick Reference	by Deke McClelland	ISBN: 1-56884-968-0	$9.99 USA/$12.99 Canada
FINANCE/PERSONAL FINANCE			
Quicken 4 For Windows® For Dummies® Quick Reference	by Stephen L. Nelson	ISBN: 1-56884-950-8	$9.95 USA/$12.95 Canada
GROUPWARE/INTEGRATED			
Microsoft® Office 4 For Windows® For Dummies® Quick Reference	by Doug Lowe	ISBN: 1-56884-958-3	$9.99 USA/$12.99 Canada
Microsoft® Works 3 For Windows® For Dummies® Quick Reference	by Michael Partington	ISBN: 1-56884-959-1	$9.99 USA/$12.99 Canada
INTERNET/COMMUNICATIONS/NETWORKING			
The Internet For Dummies® Quick Reference	by John R. Levine & Margaret Levine Young	ISBN: 1-56884-168-X	$8.95 USA/$11.95 Canada
MACINTOSH			
Macintosh® System 7.5 For Dummies® Quick Reference	by Stuart J. Stuple	ISBN: 1-56884-956-7	$9.99 USA/$12.99 Canada
OPERATING SYSTEMS:			
DOS			
DOS For Dummies® Quick Reference	by Greg Harvey	ISBN: 1-56884-007-1	$8.95 USA/$11.95 Canada
UNIX			
UNIX® For Dummies® Quick Reference	by John R. Levine & Margaret Levine Young	ISBN: 1-56884-094-2	$8.95 USA/$11.95 Canada
WINDOWS			
Windows® 3.1 For Dummies® Quick Reference, 2nd Edition	by Greg Harvey	ISBN: 1-56884-951-6	$8.95 USA/$11.95 Canada
PCs/HARDWARE			
Memory Management For Dummies® Quick Reference	by Doug Lowe	ISBN: 1-56884-362-3	$9.99 USA/$12.99 Canada
PRESENTATION/AUTOCAD			
AutoCAD For Dummies® Quick Reference	by Ellen Finkelstein	ISBN: 1-56884-198-1	$9.95 USA/$12.95 Canada
SPREADSHEET			
1-2-3 For Dummies® Quick Reference	by John Walkenbach	ISBN: 1-56884-027-6	$8.95 USA/$11.95 Canada
1-2-3 For Windows® 5 For Dummies® Quick Reference	by John Walkenbach	ISBN: 1-56884-957-5	$9.99 USA/$12.95 Canada
Excel For Windows® For Dummies® Quick Reference, 2nd Edition	by John Walkenbach	ISBN: 1-56884-096-9	$8.95 USA/$11.95 Canada
Quattro Pro 6 For Windows® For Dummies® Quick Reference	by Stuart J. Stuple	ISBN: 1-56884-172-8	$9.95 USA/$12.95 Canada
WORD PROCESSING			
Word For Windows® 6 For Dummies® Quick Reference	by George Lynch	ISBN: 1-56884-095-0	$8.95 USA/$11.95 Canada
Word For Windows® For Dummies® Quick Reference	by George Lynch	ISBN: 1-56884-029-2	$8.95 USA/$11.95 Canada
WordPerfect® 6.1 For Windows® For Dummies® Quick Reference, 2nd Edition	by Greg Harvey	ISBN: 1-56884-966-4	$9.99 USA/$12.99/Canada

Microsoft and Windows are registered trademarks of Microsoft Corporation. Mac and Macintosh are registered trademarks of Apple Computer. UNIX is a registered trademark of AT&T. WordPerfect is a registered trademark of Novell. The "...For Dummies Book Series" logo, the IDG Books Worldwide logos, Dummies Press, The Fun & Easy Way, and Fun, Fast, & Cheap! are trademarks, and ---- For Dummies and ... For Dummies are registered trademarks under exclusive license to IDG Books Worldwide, Inc., from International Data Group, Inc.

or scholastic requests & educational orders please
ll Educational Sales at 1. 800. 434. 2086

FOR MORE INFO OR TO ORDER, PLEASE CALL ▶ 800. 762. 2974

For volume discounts & special orders please call
Tony Real, Special Sales, at 415. 655. 3048

Windows® 3.1 SECRETS™
by Brian Livingston

ISBN: 1-878058-43-6
$39.95 USA/$52.95 Canada
Includes software.

MORE Windows® 3.1 SECRETS™
by Brian Livingston

ISBN: 1-56884-019-5
$39.95 USA/$52.95 Canada
Includes software.

Windows® GIZMOS™
by Brian Livingston & Margie Livingston

ISBN: 1-878058-66-5
$39.95 USA/$52.95 Canada
Includes software.

Windows® 3.1 Connectivity SECRETS™
by Runnoe Connally, David Rorabaugh, & Sheldon Hall

ISBN: 1-56884-030-6
$49.95 USA/$64.95 Canada
Includes software.

Windows® 3.1 Configuration SECRETS™
by Valda Hilley & James Blakely

ISBN: 1-56884-026-8
$49.95 USA/$64.95 Canada
Includes software.

Internet SECRETS™
by John Levine & Carol Baroudi

ISBN: 1-56884-452-2
$39.99 USA/$54.99 Canada
Includes software.

Internet GIZMOS™ For Windows®
by Joel Diamond, Howard Sobel, & Valda Hilley

ISBN: 1-56884-451-4
$39.99 USA/$54.99 Canada
Includes software.

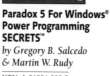

Network Security SECRETS™
by David Stang & Sylvia Moon

ISBN: 1-56884-021-7
Int'l. ISBN: 1-56884-151-5
$49.95 USA/$64.95 Canada
Includes software.

PC SECRETS™
by Caroline M. Halliday

ISBN: 1-878058-49-5
$39.95 USA/$52.95 Canada
Includes software.

WordPerfect® 6 SECRETS™
by Roger C. Parker & David A. Holzgang

ISBN: 1-56884-040-3
$39.95 USA/$52.95 Canada
Includes software.

DOS 6 SECRETS™
by Robert D. Ainsbury

ISBN: 1-878058-70-3
$39.95 USA/$52.95 Canada
Includes software.

Paradox 4 Power Programming SECRETS,™ 2nd Edition
by Gregory B. Salcedo & Martin W. Rudy

ISBN: 1-878058-54-1
$44.95 USA/$59.95 Canada
Includes software.

Paradox 5 For Windows® Power Programming SECRETS™
by Gregory B. Salcedo & Martin W. Rudy

ISBN: 1-56884-085-3
$44.95 USA/$59.95 Canada
Includes software.

Hard Disk SECRETS™
by John M. Goodman, Ph.D.

ISBN: 1-878058-64-9
$39.95 USA/$52.95 Canada
Includes software.

WordPerfect® 6 For Windows® Tips & Techniques Revealed
by David A. Holzgang & Roger C. Parker

ISBN: 1-56884-202-3
$39.95 USA/$52.95 Canada
Includes software.

Excel 5 For Windows® Power Programming Techniques
by John Walkenbach

ISBN: 1-56884-303-8
$39.95 USA/$52.95 Canada
Includes software.

Windows is a registered trademark of Microsoft Corporation. WordPerfect is a registered trademark of Novell. ----SECRETS, ----GIZMOS, and the IDG Books Worldwide logos are trademarks, and ...SECRETS is a registered trademark under exclusive license to IDG Books Worldwide, Inc., from International Data Group, Inc.

For scholastic requests & educational orders please call Educational Sales, at 1. 800. 434. 2086

FOR MORE INFO OR TO ORDER, PLEASE CALL ▶ 800. 762. 2974

For volume discounts & special orders please call Tony Real, Special Sales, at 415. 655. 3048

PC PRESS

IDG BOOKS WORLDWIDE

9/19/95

"A lot easier to use than the book Excel gives you!"

Lisa Schmeckpeper, New Berlin, WI, on PC World Excel 5 For Windows Handbook

Official Hayes Modem Communications Companion
by Caroline M. Halliday

ISBN: 1-56884-072-1
$29.95 USA/$39.95 Canada
Includes software.

1,001 Komputer Answers from Kim Komando
by Kim Komando

ISBN: 1-56884-460-3
$29.99 USA/$39.99 Canada
Includes software.

BESTSELLER!

PC World DOS 6 Handbook, 2nd Edition
by John Socha, Clint Hicks, & Devra Hall

ISBN: 1-878058-79-7
$34.95 USA/$44.95 Canada
Includes software.

PC World Word For Windows 6 Handbook
by Brent Heslop & David Angell

ISBN: 1-56884-054-3
$34.95 USA/$44.95 Canada
Includes software.

BESTSELLER!

PC World Microsoft Access 2 Bible, 2nd Edition
by Cary N. Prague & Michael R. Irwin

ISBN: 1-56884-086-1
$39.95 USA/$52.95 Canada
Includes software.

PC World Excel 5 For Windows Handbook, 2nd Edition
by John Walkenbach & Dave Maguiness

ISBN: 1-56884-056-X
$34.95 USA/$44.95 Canada
Includes software.

PC World WordPerfect 6 Handbook
by Greg Harvey

ISBN: 1-878058-80-0
$34.95 USA/$44.95 Canada
Includes software.

QuarkXPress For Windows Designer Handbook
by Barbara Assadi & Galen Gruman

ISBN: 1-878058-45-2
$29.95 USA/$39.95 Canada

NATIONAL BESTSELLER!

Official XTree Companion, 3rd Edition
by Beth Slick

ISBN: 1-878058-57-6
$19.95 USA/$26.95 Canada

NATIONAL BESTSELLER!

PC World DOS 6 Command Reference and Problem Solver
by John Socha & Devra Hall

ISBN: 1-56884-055-1
$24.95 USA/$32.95 Canada

SUPER STAR

Client/Server Strategies™: A Survival Guide for Corporate Reengineers
by David Vaskevitch

ISBN: 1-56884-064-0
$29.95 USA/$39.95 Canada

"PC World Word For Windows 6 Handbook is very easy to follow with lots of 'hands on' examples. The 'Task at a Glance' is very helpful!"

Jacqueline Martens, Tacoma, WA

"Thanks for publishing this book! It's the best money I've spent this year!"

Robert D. Templeton, Ft. Worth, TX, on MORE Windows 3.1 SECRETS

Microsoft and Windows are registered trademarks of Microsoft Corporation. WordPerfect is a registered trademark of Novell. ----STRATEGIES and the IDG Books Worldwide logos are trademarks under exclusive license to IDG Books Worldwide, Inc., from International Data Group, Inc.

or scholastic requests & educational orders please ll Educational Sales, at 1. 800. 434. 2086

FOR MORE INFO OR TO ORDER, PLEASE CALL ▶ 800. 762. 2974

For volume discounts & special orders please call Tony Real, Special Sales, at 415. 655. 3048

IDG BOOKS WORLDWIDE

Order Center: **(800) 762-2974** *(8 a.m.–6 p.m., EST, weekdays)*

Quantity	ISBN	Title	Price	Total

Shipping & Handling Charges

	Description	First book	Each additional book	Total
Domestic	Normal	$4.50	$1.50	$
	Two Day Air	$8.50	$2.50	$
	Overnight	$18.00	$3.00	$
International	Surface	$8.00	$8.00	$
	Airmail	$16.00	$16.00	$
	DHL Air	$17.00	$17.00	$

*For large quantities call for shipping & handling charges.
**Prices are subject to change without notice.

Ship to:

Name _____

Company _____

Address _____

City/State/Zip _____

Daytime Phone _____

Payment: ☐ Check to IDG Books Worldwide (US Funds Only)

☐ VISA ☐ MasterCard ☐ American Express

Card # _____ Expires _____

Signature _____

Subtotal _____

CA residents add
applicable sales tax _____

IN, MA, and MD
residents add
5% sales tax _____

IL residents add
6.25% sales tax _____

RI residents add
7% sales tax _____

TX residents add
8.25% sales tax _____

Shipping _____

Total _____

Please send this order form to:

IDG Books Worldwide, Inc.
7260 Shadeland Station, Suite 100
Indianapolis, IN 46256

*Allow up to 3 weeks for delivery.
Thank you!*

IDG BOOKS WORLDWIDE REGISTRATION CARD

RETURN THIS REGISTRATION CARD FOR FREE CATALOG

Title of this book: Client Server Strategies, 2E

My overall rating of this book: ❏ Very good [1] ❏ Good [2] ❏ Satisfactory [3] ❏ Fair [4] ❏ Poor [5]

How I first heard about this book:

❏ Found in bookstore; name: [6]

❏ Advertisement: [8]

❏ Word of mouth; heard about book from friend, co-worker, etc.: [10]

❏ Book review: [7]

❏ Catalog: [9]

❏ Other: [11]

What I liked most about this book:

What I would change, add, delete, etc., in future editions of this book:

Other comments:

Number of computer books I purchase in a year: ❏ 1 [12] ❏ 2-5 [13] ❏ 6-10 [14] ❏ More than 10 [15]

I would characterize my computer skills as: ❏ Beginner [16] ❏ Intermediate [17] ❏ Advanced [18] ❏ Professional [19]

I use ❏ DOS [20] ❏ Windows [21] ❏ OS/2 [22] ❏ Unix [23] ❏ Macintosh [24] ❏ Other: [25]_____
(please specify)

I would be interested in new books on the following subjects:
(please check all that apply, and use the spaces provided to identify specific software)

❏ Word processing: [26]

❏ Data bases: [28]

❏ File Utilities: [30]

❏ Networking: [32]

❏ Other: [34]

❏ Spreadsheets: [27]

❏ Desktop publishing: [29]

❏ Money management: [31]

❏ Programming languages: [33]

I use a PC at (please check all that apply): ❏ home [35] ❏ work [36] ❏ school [37] ❏ other: [38] _____

The disks I prefer to use are ❏ 5.25 [39] ❏ 3.5 [40] ❏ other: [41]_____

I have a CD ROM: ❏ yes [42] ❏ no [43]

I plan to buy or upgrade computer hardware this year: ❏ yes [44] ❏ no [45]

I plan to buy or upgrade computer software this year: ❏ yes [46] ❏ no [47]

Name: _____ Business title: [48] _____ Type of Business: [49] _____

Address (❏ home [50] ❏ work [51] /Company name: _____)

Street/Suite#

City [52]/State [53]/Zipcode [54]: _____ Country [55] _____

❏ **I liked this book!** You may quote me by name in future
IDG Books Worldwide promotional materials.

My daytime phone number is _____

IDG BOOKS

THE WORLD OF
COMPUTER
KNOWLEDGE

☐ **YES!**

Please keep me informed about IDG's World of Computer Knowledge.
Send me the latest IDG Books catalog.

COMPUTER
BOOK SERIES
FROM IDG

NO POSTAGE
NECESSARY
IF MAILED
IN THE
UNITED STATES

BUSINESS REPLY MAIL
FIRST CLASS MAIL   PERMIT NO. 2605   FOSTER CITY, CALIFORNIA

IDG Books Worldwide
919 E Hillsdale Blvd, STE 400
Foster City, CA 94404-9691